Survival Communications in Oregon: Western Region

John E. Parnell, KK4HWX

13 ISBN 978-1-62512-000-7

Cover design by:
Lynda Colón
FREELANCE GRAPHIC DESIGN &
MARKETING COMMUNICATIONS
www.hirelynda.webs.com

I do wish to acknowledge the hard work of **Angie Shirley** in putting together the database
required for this book. Without her efforts, this book could not have been done.

Titles available in this series:

Survival Communications in Alabama
Survival Communications in Alaska
Survival Communications in Arizona
Survival Communications in Arkansas
Survival Communications in California
Survival Communications in Colorado
Survival Communications in Connecticut
Survival Communications in Delaware
Survival Communications in Florida
Survival Communications in Georgia
Survival Communications in Hawaii
Survival Communications in Idaho
Survival Communications in Illinois
Survival Communications in Indiana
Survival Communications in Iowa
Survival Communications in Kansas
Survival Communications in Kentucky
Survival Communications in Louisiana
Survival Communications in Maine
Survival Communications in Maryland
Survival Communications in Massachusetts
Survival Communications in Michigan
Survival Communications in Minnesota
Survival Communications in Mississippi
Survival Communications in Missouri

Survival Communications in Montana
Survival Communications in Nebraska
Survival Communications in Nevada
Survival Communications in New Hampshire
Survival Communications in New Jersey
Survival Communications in New Mexico
Survival Communications in New York
Survival Communications in North Carolina
Survival Communications in North Dakota
Survival Communications in Ohio
Survival Communications in Oklahoma
Survival Communications in Oregon
Survival Communications in Pennsylvania
Survival Communications in Rhode Island
Survival Communications in South Carolina
Survival Communications in South Dakota
Survival Communications in Tennessee
Survival Communications in Texas
Survival Communications in Utah
Survival Communications in Vermont
Survival Communications in Virginia
Survival Communications in Washington
Survival Communications in West Virginia
Survival Communications in Wisconsin
Survival Communications in Wyoming

The above titles are available from your favorite online or brick-and-mortar bookstore or directly from the publisher at Tutor Turtle Press LLC, 1027 S. Pendleton St. – Suite B-10, Easley, SC 29642.

TABLE OF CONTENTS

Appendix A – Oregon Ham Radio Clubs

ARRL Affiliated Amateur and Ham Radio Clubs – By City

Appendix B – Oregon: Western Region Ham Licensees by City

Survival Communications in Oregon

Perhaps you have prepared for WTSHTF or TEOTWAWKI with respect to food, water, self-defense and shelter. But what about communication?

Whenever there is a disaster (hurricane, earthquake, economic collapse, nuclear war, EMF, solar eruption, etc.), the normal means of communication that we're all reliant upon (cell phone, land line phone, the Internet, etc.) will probably be, at best, sporadic and at worst, non-existent.

As this author sees it, short of smoke signals and mirrors, there are three options for communication in "trying times": (1) GMRS or FRS radios; (2) CB radios; and (3) ham or amateur radio. Let's consider each of these options to come up with the most acceptable one.

GMRS (General Mobile Radio Service) / FRS (Family Radio Service)

GMRS (General Mobile Radio Service) / FRS (Family Radio Service) radios work optimally over short distances where there is minimal interference. Originally designed to be used as pagers, particularly inside a building or other such confined area, these radios are low-cost and convenient to carry. Unfortunately their small size and light weight comes with a trade-off – short range and short battery life. These radios are supposed to be able to communicate for up to 25-30 miles. Right. That's on level terrain, without buildings or trees getting in the way. While battery life technology is constantly improving, you will need spare batteries to keep communicating or someway of recharging the ones in the radio. In this author's opinion, GMRS/FRS radios are not first choice when concerned with medium or long range communication.

CB (Citizens Band)

CB (Citizens Band) radios operate in a frequency range originally reserved for ham or amateur radio operation. Because of the overwhelming number of people wishing quick, low-cost, regulation-free communication, the FCC (Federal Communication Commission) split off a portion of the frequency spectrum and allowed anyone to purchase a CB radio and start communicating. No test. No license. Just personal/business communication. Today, CB radios are readily available in such outlets as eBay and Craigslist. This author has seen them at yard/garage/tag sales and at flea markets.

CB radios come in a variety of "flavors." Fixed units, sometimes referred to as base units are intended for home use. For the most part, they derive their power from the utility company. In the event of loss of electricity, most base units can also be connected to a 12-volt battery, like that in your car/truck. If you choose to obtain a fixed unit, make sure you know how to connect the unit to the battery – ahead of time. Trying to figure this out when you're under extra stress is not a good situation.

A second type of CB radio is designed to be mobile, that is, installed in your car/truck. It gets its power from the vehicle's battery. You can either attach an antenna permanently to the vehicle or have a removable, magnetic type antenna.

The third type of CB radio is designed for handheld use. They are small and light. Most weigh less than a pound and operate on batteries. Yes, using batteries in a CB poses the same limitations as those by the GMRS/FRS radios, but have the added advantage that most handheld units come with a cigarette lighter adapter. Comes in handy when you are on the move and wish to be able to communicate both from a vehicle and also when you have to abandon it.

While they have a greater range than GMRS/FRS radios, CB radios are, legally, limited to operate on 40 channels, with a power rating of four (4) watts or less. Yes, it is possible to alter CB radios to get around these limitations, but not legally,

Ham/Amateur Radio

Ham/Amateur radio is very appealing. With a ham radio, you are not limited to less than 50 miles, but can communicate with anyone in the world (who also has access to a ham radio, of course).

Standardized Amateur Radio Prepper Communications Plan

In the event of a nationwide catastrophic disaster, the nationwide network of Amateur Radio licensed preppers will need a set of standardized meeting frequencies to share information and coordinate activities between various prepper groups. This Standardized Amateur Radio Communications Plan establishes a set of frequencies on the 80 meter, 40 meter, 20 meter, and 2 meter Amateur Radio bands for use during these types of catastrophic disasters.

Routine nets will not be held on all of these frequencies, but preppers are encouraged to use them when coordinating with other preppers on a routine basis. Routine nets may be conducted by The American Preparedness Radio Net (TAPRN) on these or other frequencies as they see fit. However, TAPRN will promote the use of these standardized frequencies by all Amateur Radio licensed preppers during times of catastrophic disaster. The promotion of this Standardized Amateur Radio Communications Plan is encouraged by all means within the prepper community, including via Amateur Radio, Twitter, Facebook, and various blogs.

Standardized Frequencies and Modes
80 Meters – 3.818 MHz LSB (TAPRN Net: Sundays at 9 PM ET)
40 Meters – 7.242 MHz LSB
40 Meters Morse Code / Digital – 7.073 MHz USB (TAPRN: Sundays at 7:30 PM ET on CONTESTIA 4/250)
20 Meters – 14.242 MHz USB
2 Meters – 146.420 MHz FM

Nets and Network Etiquette

In times of nationwide catastrophic disaster, the ability of any one prepper to initiate and sustain themselves as a net control may be limited by the availability of power and other resource shortages. However, all licensed preppers are encouraged to maintain a listening watch on these frequencies as often as possible during a catastrophic disaster. Preppers may routinely announce themselves in the following manner:

• This is [Your Callsign Phonetically] in [Your State], maintaining a listening watch on [Standard Frequency] for any preppers on frequency seeking information or looking to provide information. Please call [Your Callsign Phonetically]. Preppers exchanging information that may require follow up should agree upon a designated time to return to the frequency and provide further information. If other stations are utilizing the frequency at the designated time you return, maintain watch and proceed with your communications when those stations are finished. If your communications are urgent and the stations on frequency are not passing information of a critical nature, interrupt with the word "Break" and request use of the frequency.

For More Information

Catastrophe Network: http://www.catastrophenetwork.org or @CatastropheNet on Twitter The American Preparedness Radio Network: http://www.taprn.com or @TAPRN on Twitter

In order to use a ham radio, legally, one must be licensed to do so by the FCC (other countries have analogous governmental bodies to regulate ham radio). To obtain a license is quite easy – take a test and pay your license fee. There are currently three classes of license – Technician, General, and Amateur Extra. With each of these licenses come specific abilities.

Technician class is the beginning level. The exam consists of 35 multiple choice questions randomly drawn from a pool of 395 questions. The question pool is readily available online for free downloading (http://www.ncvec.org/downloads/Revised%20Element%202.Pdf) or in such publications at *Ham Radio License Manual Revised 2nd Edition* (ISBN 978-0-87259-097-7). The current Technician pool of questions is to be used from July 1, 2010 to June 30, 2014. Be sure the question pool you are studying from is current. You will need to score at least 26 correct to pass. (Do not worry, Morse Code is no longer on the test, although many ham operators use it anyway.) You do not need to take a formal class in order to qualify to take the exam. You can learn the material on your own. Most people spend 10-15 hours studying and then successfully take the exam. The cost of taking the exam is under $20. The exam is given in MANY locations throughout the US. Usually the exam is given by area ham clubs. You do not have to belong to the club to take the exam. Check Appendix A for a listing of clubs in Oregon.

Topics for the Technician License in Amateur Radio

The Technician license exam covers such topics as basic regulations, operating practices, and electronic theory, with a focus on VHF and UHF applications. Below is the syllabus for the Technician Class.

Subelement T1 – FCC Rules, descriptions and definitions for the amateur radio service, operator and station license responsibilities

[6 Exam Questions – 6 Groups]

T1A – Amateur Radio services; purpose of the amateur service, amateur-satellite service, operator/primary station license grant, where FCC rules are codified, basis and purpose of FCC rules, meanings of basic terms used in FCC rules

T1B – Authorized frequencies; frequency allocations, ITU regions, emission type, restricted sub-bands, spectrum sharing, transmissions near band edges

T1C – Operator classes and station call signs; operator classes, sequential, special event, and vanity call sign systems, international communications, reciprocal operation, station license licensee, places where the amateur service is regulated by the FCC, name and address on ULS, license term, renewal, grace period

T1D – Authorized and prohibited transmissions

T1E – Control operator and control types; control operator required, eligibility, designation of control operator, privileges and duties, control point, local, automatic and remote control, location of control operator

T1F – Station identification and operation standards; special operations for repeaters and auxiliary stations, third party communications, club stations, station security, FCC inspection

Subelement T2 – Operating Procedures

[3 Exam Questions – 3 Groups]

T2A – Station operation; choosing an operating frequency, calling another station, test transmissions, use of minimum power, frequency use, band plans

T2B – VHF/UHF operating practices; SSB phone, FM repeater, simplex, frequency offsets, splits and shifts, CTCSS, DTMF, tone squelch, carrier squelch, phonetics

T2C – Public service; emergency and non-emergency operations, message traffic handling

Subelement T3 – Radio wave characteristics, radio and electromagnetic properties, propagation modes

[3 Exam Questions – 3 Groups]

T3A – Radio wave characteristics; how a radio signal travels; distinctions of HF, VHF and UHF; fading, multipath; wavelength vs. penetration; antenna orientation

T3B – Radio and electromagnetic wave properties; the electromagnetic spectrum, wavelength vs. frequency, velocity of electromagnetic waves

T3C – Propagation modes; line of sight, sporadic E, meteor, aurora scatter, tropospheric ducting, F layer skip, radio horizon

Subelement T4 - Amateur radio practices and station setup

[2 Exam Questions – 2 Groups]

T4A – Station setup; microphone, speaker, headphones, filters, power source, connecting a computer, RF grounding

T4B – Operating controls; tuning, use of filters, squelch, AGC, repeater offset, memory channels

Subelement T5 – Electrical principles, math for electronics, electronic principles, Ohm's Law

[4 Exam Questions – 4 Groups]

T5A – Electrical principles; current and voltage, conductors and insulators, alternating and direct current

T5B – Math for electronics; decibels, electronic units and the metric system

T5C – Electronic principles; capacitance, inductance, current flow in circuits, alternating current, definition of RF, power calculations

T5D – Ohm's Law

Subelement T6 – Electrical components, semiconductors, circuit diagrams, component functions

[4 Exam Groups – 4 Questions]

T6A – Electrical components; fixed and variable resistors, capacitors, and inductors; fuses, switches, batteries

T6B – Semiconductors; basic principles of diodes and transistors

T6C – Circuit diagrams; schematic symbols

T6D – Component functions

Subelement T7 – Station equipment, common transmitter and receiver problems, antenna measurements and troubleshooting, basic repair and testing

[4 Exam Questions – 4 Groups]

T7A – Station radios; receivers, transmitters, transceivers

T7B – Common transmitter and receiver problems; symptoms of overload and overdrive, distortion, interference, over and under modulation, RF feedback, off frequency signals; fading and noise; problems with digital communications interfaces

T7C – Antenna measurements and troubleshooting; measuring SWR, dummy loads, feedline failure modes

T7D – Basic repair and testing; soldering, use of a voltmeter, ammeter, and ohmmeter

Subelement T8 – Modulation modes, amateur satellite operation, operating activities, non-voice communications

[4 Exam Questions – 4 Groups]

T8A – Modulation modes; bandwidth of various signals

T8B – Amateur satellite operation; Doppler shift, basic orbits, operating protocols

T8C – Operating activities; radio direction finding, radio control, contests, special event stations, basic linking over Internet

T8D – Non-voice communications; image data, digital modes, CW, packet, PSK31

Subelement T9 – Antennas, feedlines

[2 Exam Groups – 2 Questions]

T9A – Antennas; vertical and horizontal, concept of gain, common portable and mobile antennas, relationships between antenna length and frequency

T9B – Feedlines; types, losses vs. frequency, SWR concepts, matching, weather protection, connectors

Subelement T0 – AC power circuits, antenna installation, RF hazards

[3 Exam Questions – 3 Groups]

T0A – AC power circuits; hazardous voltages, fuses and circuit breakers, grounding, lightning protection, battery safety, electrical code compliance

T0B – Antenna installation; tower safety, overhead power lines

T0C – RF hazards; radiation exposure, proximity to antennas, recognized safe power levels, exposure to others

Once your name and call sign are available in the FCC database, you have the privilege of operating on all VHF (2 m) and UHF (70 cm) frequencies above 30 megahertz (MHz) and HF frequencies 80, 40, and 15 meter, and on the 10 meter band using Morse code (CW), voice, and digital mode. For a Technician license in Oregon, your call sign will consist of a two-letter prefix beginning with K or W, the number seven (7), and a three-letter suffix. The single digit number in the call sign is determined according to which area of the US you obtain your first license. Even though you may move to another state, you keep this number in your call sign. This is also true should you upgrade to a higher license and get a new call sign. The numeral portion of your call sign stays the same.

Call Sign Numbers

Below is a chart showing the various numbers and the state(s) in which you would obtain the number.

Call Sign Number	State(s)
0	CO, IA, KS, MN, MO, NE, ND, SD
1	CT, ME, MA, NH, RI, VT
2	NJ, NY
3	DE, DC, MD, PA
4	AL, FL, GA, KY, NC, SC, TN, VA
5	AR, LA, MS, NM, OK, TX
6	CA
7	AZ, ID, MT, NV, OR, WA, UT, WY
8	MI, OH, WV
9	IL, IN, WI

Residents of Alaska may have any of the following call sign prefixes assigned to them: AL0-7, KL0-7, NL0-7, or WL0-7. Likewise, residents of Hawaii may have the prefix AH6-7, KH6-7, NH6-7, or WH6-7 assigned.

Once you obtain your Technician license, do not stop there. Go and get your General license.

General is the second of three ham license classes. Like the Technician license, to get a General license, you merely have to take a 35-question multiple choice exam and pay your license fee. Passing is still at least 26 correct answers and the fee is the same (less than $20). Again the question pool is available for free online (http://www.ncvec.org/page.php?id=358). It is also available in such print publications as *The ARRL General Class License Manual 7th Edition* (ISBN 978-0-87259-811-9). The current General pool of questions is to be used from July 1, 2011 to June 30, 2015. Be sure the question pool you are using is current. Being a bit more comprehensive than the Technician license, the General license usually requires 15-20 hours of study to learn the material. Check Appendix A for a listing of clubs in Oregon where you might take your exam. Once your name and NEW call sign is listed in the FCC database, you're good to go. For a General license in Oregon, your call sign will consist of a one-letter prefix beginning with K, N or W, the number seven (7), and a three-letter suffix.

Topics for the General License in Amateur Radio

The General license exam covers regulations, operating practices and electronic theory. Below is the syllabus for the General Class.

Subelement G1 – Commission's Rules
(5 Exam Questions – 5 Groups)
G1A – General Class control operator frequency privileges; primary and secondary allocations
G1B – Antenna structure limitations; good engineering and good amateur practice, beacon operation; restricted operation; retransmitting radio signals
G1C – Transmitter power regulations; data emission standards
G1D – Volunteer Examiners and Volunteer Examiner Coordinators; temporary identification
G1E – Control categories; repeater regulations; harmful interference; third party rules; ITU regions

Subelement G2 – Operating procedures
(5 Exam Questions – 5 Groups)
G2A – Phone operating procedures; USB/LSB utilization conventions; procedural signals; breaking into a OSO in progress; VOX operation
G2B – Operating courtesy; band plans, emergencies, including drills and emergency communications
G2C – CW operating procedures and procedural signals; Q signals and common abbreviations; full break in
G2D – Amateur Auxiliary; minimizing interference; HF operations

G2E – Digital operating; procedures, procedural signals and common abbreviations

Subelement G3 – Radio wave propagation

(3 Exam Questions – 3 Groups)

G3A – Sunspots and solar radiation; ionospheric disturbances; propagation forecasting and indices

G3B – Maximum Usable Frequency; Lowest Usable Frequency; propagation

G3C – Ionospheric layers; critical angle and frequency; HF scatter; Near Vertical Incidence Sky waves

Subelement G4 – Amateur radio practices

(5 Exam Questions – 5 Groups)

G4A – Station Operation and setup

G4B – Test and monitoring equipment; two-tone test

G4C – Interference with consumer electronics; grounding; DSP

G4D – Speech processors; S meters; sideband operation near band edges

G4E – HF mobile radio installations; emergency and battery powered operation

Subelement G5 – Electrical principles

(3 Exam Questions – 3 Groups)

G5A – Reactance; inductance; capacitance; impedance; impedance matching

G5B – The Decibel; current and voltage dividers; electrical power calculations; sine wave root-mean-square (RMS) values; PEP calculations

G5C – Resistors; capacitors and inductors in series and parallel; transformers

Subelement G6 – Circuit components

(3 Exam Questions – 3 Groups)

G6A – Resistors; capacitors; inductors

G6B – Rectifiers; solid state diodes and transistors; vacuum tubes; batteries

G6C – Analog and digital integrated circuits (ICs); microprocessors; memory; I/O devices; microwave ICs (MMICs); display devices

Subelement G7 – Practical circuits

(3 Exam Questions – 3 Groups)

G7A – Power supplies; schematic symbols

G7B – Digital circuits; amplifiers and oscillators

G7C – Receivers and transmitters; filters, oscillators

Subelement G8 – Signals and emissions

(2 Exam Questions – 2 Groups)

G8A – Carriers and modulation; AM; FM; single and double sideband; modulation envelope; overmodulation
G8B – Frequency mixing; multiplication; HF data communications; bandwidths of various modes; deviation

Subelement G9 – Antennas and feed lines
(4 Exam Questions – 4 Groups)
G9A – Antenna feed lines; characteristic impedance and attenuation; SWR calculation, measurement and effects; matching networks
G9B – Basic antennas
G9C – Directional antennas
G9D – Specialized antennas

Subelement G0 – Electrical and RF safety
(2 Exam Questions – 2 Groups)
G0A – RF safety principles, rules and guidelines; routine station elevation
G0B – Safety in the ham shack; electrical shock and treatment, safety grounding, fusing, interlocks, wiring, antenna and tower safety

With a General license, you can use all VHF and UHF frequencies and most of the HF frequencies. You would have access to the 160, 30, 17, 12, and 10 meter bands and access to major parts of the 80, 40, 20, and 15 meter bands. Of course, this is in addition to all bands available to Technician license holders.

Amateur Extra is the third of three ham license classes. Like the Technician and General classes, you merely have to pass a test and pay your fee to get your Amateur Extra license. This class of license is more comprehensive than the lower license classes. The exam is longer – 50 questions – and the minimum passing score is higher – 37. However, once you get your Amateur Extra license, all ham frequencies, VHF, UHF and HF are available for your enjoyment. The Extra exam covers regulations, specialized operating practices, advanced electronics theory, and radio equipment design.

Like for the other license classes, the question pool for the Amateur Extra license is available online for downloading (http://www.ncvec.org/downloads/REVISED%202012-2016%20Extra%20Class%20Pool.doc). It is also available in print form in such publications as *The ARRL Extra Class License Manual Revised 9th Edition* (ISBN 978-0-87259-887-4).

Topics for the Extra License in Amateur Radio

Below is the syllabus for the Amateur Extra Class for July 1, 2012 to June 30, 2016.

Subelement E1 – Commission's Rules
[6 Exam Questions – 6 Groups]
E1A – Operating Standards: frequency privileges; emission standards; automatic message forwarding; frequency sharing; stations aboard ships or aircraft

E1B – Station restrictions and special operations: restrictions on station location; general operating restrictions, spurious emissions, control operator reimbursement; antenna structure restrictions; RACES operations

E1C – Station control: definitions and restrictions pertaining to local, automatic and remote control operation; control operator responsibilities for remote and automatically controlled stations

E1D – Amateur Satellite service: definitions and purpose; license requirements for space stations; available frequencies and bands; telecommand and telemetry operations; restrictions, and special provisions; notification requirements

E1E – Volunteer examiner program: definitions, qualifications, preparation and administration of exams; accreditation; question pools; documentation requirements

E1F – Miscellaneous rules: external RF power amplifiers; national quiet zone; business communications; compensated communications; spread spectrum; auxiliary stations; reciprocal operating privileges; IARP and CEPT licenses; third party communications with foreign countries; special temporary authority

Subelement E2 – Operating procedures

[5 Exam Questions – 5 Groups]

E2A – Amateur radio in space: amateur satellites; orbital mechanics; frequencies and modes; satellite hardware; satellite operations

E2B – Television practices: fast scan television standards and techniques; slow scan television standards and techniques

E2C – Operating methods: contest and DX operating; spread-spectrum transmissions; selecting an operating frequency

E2D – Operating methods: VHF and UHF digital modes; APRS

E2E – Operating methods: operating HF digital modes; error correction

Subelement E3 – Radio wave propagation

[3 Exam Questions – 3 Groups]

E3A – Propagation and technique, Earth-Moon-Earth communications; meteor scatter

E3B – Propagation and technique, trans-equatorial; long path; gray-line; multi-path propagation

E3C – Propagation and technique, Aurora propagation; selective fading; radio-path horizon; take-off angle over flat or sloping terrain; effects of ground on propagation; less common propagation modes

Subelement E4 – Amateur practices

[5 Exam Questions – 5 Groups]

E4A – Test equipment: analog and digital instruments; spectrum and network analyzers, antenna analyzers; oscilloscopes; testing transistors; RF measurements

E4B – Measurement technique and limitations: instrument accuracy and performance limitations; probes; techniques to minimize errors; measurement of "Q"; instrument calibration

E4C – Receiver performance characteristics, phase noise, capture effect, noise floor, image rejection, MDS, signal-to-noise-ratio; selectivity

E4D – Receiver performance characteristics, blocking dynamic range, intermodulation and cross-modulation interference; 3rd order intercept; desensitization; preselection

E4E – Noise suppression: system noise; electrical appliance noise; line noise; locating noise sources; DSP noise reduction; noise blankers

Subelement E5 – Electrical principles

[4 Exam Questions – 4 Groups]

E5A – Resonance and Q: characteristics of resonant circuits: series and parallel resonance; Q; half-power bandwidth; phase relationships in reactive circuits

E5B – Time constants and phase relationships: RLC time constants: definition; time constants in RL and RC circuits; phase angle between voltage and current; phase angles of series and parallel circuits

E5C – Impedance plots and coordinate systems: plotting impedances in polar coordinates; rectangular coordinates

E5D – AC and RF energy in real circuits: skin effect; electrostatic and electromagnetic fields; reactive power; power factor; coordinate systems

Subelement E6 – Circuit components

[6 Exam Questions – 6 Groups]

E6A – Semiconductor materials and devices: semiconductor materials germanium, silicon, P-type, N-type; transistor types: NPN, PNP, junction, field-effect transistors: enhancement mode; depletion mode; MOS; CMOS; N-channel; P-channel

E6B – Semiconductor diodes

E6C – Integrated circuits: TTL digital integrated circuits; CMOS digital integrated circuits; gates

E6D – Optical devices and toroids: cathode-ray tube devices; charge-coupled devices (CCDs); liquid crystal displays (LCDs); toroids: permeability, core material, selecting, winding

E6E – Piezoelectric crystals and MMICs: quartz crystals; crystal oscillators and filters; monolithic amplifiers

E6F – Optical components and power systems: photoconductive principles and effects, photovoltaic systems, optical couplers, optical sensors, and optoisolators

Subelement E7 – Practical circuits

[8 Exam Questions – 8 Groups]

E7A – Digital circuits: digital circuit principles and logic circuits: classes of logic elements; positive and negative logic; frequency dividers; truth tables

E7B – Amplifiers: Class of operation; vacuum tube and solid-state circuits; distortion and intermodulation; spurious and parasitic suppression; microwave amplifiers

E7C – Filters and matching networks: filters and impedance matching networks: types of networks; types of filters; filter applications; filter characteristics; impedance matching; DSP filtering

E7D – Power supplies and voltage regulators

E7E – Modulation and demodulation: reactance, phase and balanced modulators; detectors; mixer stages; DSP modulation and demodulation; software defined radio systems

E7F – Frequency markers and counters: frequency divider circuits; frequency marker generators; frequency counters

E7G – Active filters and op-amps: active audio filters; characteristics; basic circuit design; operational amplifiers

E7H – Oscillators and signal sources: types of oscillators; synthesizers and phase-locked loops; direct digital synthesizers

Subelement E8 – Signals and emissions

[4 Exam Questions – 4 Groups]

E8A – AC waveforms: sine, square, sawtooth and irregular waveforms; AC measurements; average and PEP of RF signals; pulse and digital signal waveforms

E8B – Modulation and demodulation: modulation methods; modulation index and deviation ratio; pulse modulation; frequency and time division multiplexing

E8C – Digital signals: digital communications modes; CW; information rate vs. bandwidth; spread-spectrum communications; modulation methods

E8D – Waves, measurements, and RF grounding: peak-to-peak values, polarization; RF grounding

Subelement E9 – Antennas and transmission lines

[8 Exam Questions – 8 Groups]

E9A – Isotropic and gain antennas: definition; used as a standard for comparison; radiation pattern; basic antenna parameters: radiation resistance and reactance, gain, beamwidth, efficiency

E9B – Antenna patterns: E and H plane patterns; gain as a function of pattern; antenna design; Yagi antennas

E9C – Wire and phased vertical antennas: beverage antennas; terminated and resonant rhombic antennas; elevation above real ground; ground effects as related to polarization; take-off angles

E9D – Directional antennas: gain; satellite antennas; antenna beamwidth; losses; SWR bandwidth; antenna efficiency; shortened and mobile antennas; grounding

E9E – Matching: matching antennas to feed lines; power dividers

E9F – Transmission lines: characteristics of open and shorted feed lines: 1/8 wavelength; 1/4 wavelength; 1/2 wavelength; feed lines: coax versus open-wire; velocity factor; electrical length; transformation characteristics of line terminated in impedance not equal to characteristic impedance

E9G – The Smith chart

E9H – Effective radiated power; system gains and losses; radio direction finding antennas

Subelement E0 – Safety

[1 exam question – 1 group]

E0A – Safety: amateur radio safety practices; RF radiation hazards; hazardous materials

Once your new call sign is listed in the FCC database, you are good to go. For an Amateur Extra license in Oregon, your call sign will consist of a prefix of K, N or W, the number seven (7), and a two-letter suffix, or a two-letter prefix beginning with A, N, K or W, the number seven (7), and a one-letter suffix, or a two-letter prefix beginning with A, the number seven (7), and a two-letter suffix.

Ham radio equipment can be expensive or you can do it "on the cheap." The cost will run from a couple hundred dollars to well in the thousands, depending on what you have available. eBay, and Craigslist are good places to start looking. Most ham clubs do some sort of hamfest annually wherein club members or others are willing to part with older equipment. See Appendix A for a list of clubs in Oregon.

Another excellent source of equipment, as well as advice on setting the equipment up and how to use it properly, is current ham operators. In Appendix B, the author has listed all the FCC licensed ham operators in Oregon, listed by city, and then sorted by street and house number on the street. Who knows, maybe someone who lives close to you is a ham operator. Be a good neighbor, stop by and have a chat with him/her.

Like CB radios, ham radios come in three formats – base, mobile, and handheld. They can use the electric company for power, or operate off a car battery. In the opinion of this author, in spite of the slightly higher cost of the equipment and having to take a test to legally use the equipment, ham radio is the way to go when concerned about communication during times of crisis.

Canadian Call Sign Prefixes

Because of our proximity to Canada, many times ham contact is made with our northern neighbors. Below is a chart showing the origin of Canadian call sign prefixes.

Call Sign Prefix	Provence or Territory
CY0	Sable Island
CY9	St. Paul Island
VA1, VE1	New Brunswick, Nova Scotia
VA2, VE2	Quebec
VA3, VE3	Ontario
VA4, VE4	Manitoba
VA5, VE5	Saskatchewan
VA6, VE6	Alberta
VA7, VE7	British Columbia
VE8	North West Territories
VE9	New Brunswick
VO1	Newfoundland
VO2	Labrador
VY0	Nunavut
VY1	Yukon
VY2	Prince Edward Island

Common Radio Bands in the United States

Certain radio bands are more popular with ham radio enthusiasts than others. Below is a chart showing these bands and when they are most popular.

	Band (meter)	Frequency (MHz)	Use
HF	160	1.8 – 2.0	Night
	80	3.5 – 4.0	Night and Local Day
	40	7.0 – 7.3	Night and Local Day
	30	10.1 – 10.15	CW and Digital
	20	14.0 – 14.350	World Wide Day and Night
	17	18.068 – 18.168	World Wide Day and Night
	15	21.0 – 21.450	Primarily Daytime
	12	24.890 – 24.990	Primarily Daytime
	10	28.0 – 29.70	Daytime during Sunspot highs
VHF	6	50 – 54	Local to World Wide
	2	144 – 148	Local to Medium Distance
UHF	70 cm	430 – 440	Local

Common Amateur Radio Bands in Canada

160 Meter Band - Maximum bandwidth 6 kHz
1.800 - 1.820 MHz - CW
1.820 - 1.830 MHz - Digital Modes
1 830 - 1.840 MHz - DX Window
1.840 - 2.000 MHz - SSB and other wide band modes

80 Meter Band - Maximum bandwidth 6 kHz
3.500 - 3.580 MHz - CW
3.580 - 3.620 MHz - Digital Modes
3.620 - 3.635 MHz - Packet/Digital Secondary
3.635 - 3.725 MHz   CW
3.725 - 3.790 MHz - SSB and other side band modes*
3.790 - 3.800 MHz - SSB DX Window
3.800 - 4.000 MHz - SSB and other wide band modes

40 Meter Band - Maximum bandwidth 6 kHz
7.000 - 7.035 MHz - CW
7.035 - 7.050 MHz - Digital Modes
7.040 - 7.050 MHz - International packet
7.050 - 7.100 MHz - SSB
7.100 - 7.120 MHz - Packet within Region 2
7.120 - 7.150 MHz - CW
7.150 - 7.300 MHz - SSB and other wide band modes

30 Meter Band - Maximum bandwidth 1 kHz

10.100 - 10.130 MHz - CW only
10.130 - 10.140 MHz - Digital Modes
10.140 - 10.150 MHz - Packet

20 Meter Band - Maximum bandwidth 6 kHz

14.000 - 14.070 MHz - CW only
14.070 - 14.095 MHz - Digital Mode
14.095 - 14.099 MHz - Packet
14.100 MHz - Beacons
14.101 - 14.112 MHz - CW, SSB, packet shared
14.112 - 14.350 MHz - SSB
14.225 - 14.235 MHz - SSTV

17 Meter Band - Maximum bandwidth 6 kHz

18.068 - 18.100 MHz - CW
18.100 - 18.105 MHz - Digital Modes
18.105 - 18.110 MHz - Packet
18.110 - 18.168 MHz - SSB and other wide band modes

15 Meter Band - maximum bandwidth 6 kHz

21.000 - 21.070 MHz - CW
21.070 - 21.090 MHz - Digital Modes
21.090 - 21.125 MHz - Packet
21.100 - 21.150 MHz - CW and SSB
21.150 - 21.335 MHz - SSB and other wide band modes
21.335 - 21.345 MHz - SSTV
21.345 - 21.450 MHz - SSB and other wide band modes

12 Meter Band - Maximum bandwidth 6 kHz

24.890 - 24.930 MHz - CW
24.920 - 24.925 MHz - Digital Modes
24.925 - 24.930 MHz - Packet
24.930 - 24.990 MHz - SSB and other wide band modes

10 Meter Band - Maximum band width 20 kHz

28.000 - 28.200 MHz - CW
28.070 - 28.120 MHz - Digital Modes
28.120 - 28.190 MHz - Packet
28.190 - 28.200 MHz - Beacons
28.200 - 29.300 MHz - SSB and other wide band modes
29.300 - 29.510 MHz - Satellite
29.510 - 29.700 MHz - SSB, FM and repeaters

160 Meters (1.8-2.0 MHz)

1.800 - 2.000 CW
1.800 - 1.810 Digital Modes
1.810 CW QRP
1.843-2.000 SSB, SSTV and other wideband modes
1.910 SSB QRP
1.995 - 2.000 Experimental
1.999 - 2.000 Beacons

80 Meters (3.5-4.0 MHz)

3.590 RTTY/Data DX
3.570-3.600 RTTY/Data
3.790-3.800 DX window
3.845 SSTV
3.885 AM calling frequency

40 Meters (7.0-7.3 MHz)

7.040 RTTY/Data DX
7.080-7.125 RTTY/Data
7.171 SSTV
7.290 AM calling frequency

30 Meters (10.1-10.15 MHz)

10.130-10.140 RTTY
10.140-10.150 Packet

20 Meters (14.0-14.35 MHz)

14.070-14.095 RTTY
14.095-14.0995 Packet
14.100 NCDXF Beacons
14.1005-14.112 Packet
14.230 SSTV
14.286 AM calling frequency

17 Meters (18.068-18.168 MHz)

18.100-18.105 RTTY
18.105-18.110 Packet

15 Meters (21.0-21.45 MHz)

21.070-21.110 RTTY/Data
21.340 SSTV

12 Meters (24.89-24.99 MHz)

24.920-24.925 RTTY
24.925-24.930 Packet

10 Meters (28-29.7 MHz)

28.000-28.070 CW
28.070-28.150 RTTY
28.150-28.190 CW
28.200-28.300 Beacons
28.300-29.300 Phone
28.680 SSTV
29.000-29.200 AM
29.300-29.510 Satellite Downlinks
29.520-29.590 Repeater Inputs
29.600 FM Simplex
29.610-29.700 Repeater Outputs

6 Meters (50-54 MHz)

50.0-50.1 CW, beacons
50.060-50.080 beacon subband
50.1-50.3 SSB, CW
50.10-50.125 DX window
50.125 SSB calling
50.3-50.6 All modes
50.6-50.8 Nonvoice communications
50.62 Digital (packet) calling
50.8-51.0 Radio remote control (20-kHz channels)
51.0-51.1 Pacific DX window
51.12-51.48 Repeater inputs (19 channels)
51.12-51.18 Digital repeater inputs
51.5-51.6 Simplex (six channels)
51.62-51.98 Repeater outputs (19 channels)
51.62-51.68 Digital repeater outputs
52.0-52.48 Repeater inputs (except as noted; 23 channels)
52.02, 52.04 FM simplex
52.2 TEST PAIR (input)
52.5-52.98 Repeater output (except as noted; 23 channels)
52.525 Primary FM simplex
52.54 Secondary FM simplex
52.7 TEST PAIR (output)
53.0-53.48 Repeater inputs (except as noted; 19 channels)
53.0 Remote base FM simplex
53.02 Simplex
53.1, 53.2, 53.3, 53.4 Radio remote control
53.5-53.98 Repeater outputs (except as noted; 19 channels)
53.5, 53.6, 53.7, 53.8 Radio remote control
53.52, 53.9 Simplex

2 Meters (144-148 MHz)

144.00-144.05 EME (CW)
144.05-144.10 General CW and weak signals
144.10-144.20 EME and weak-signal SSB
144.200 National calling frequency
144.200-144.275 General SSB operation
144.275-144.300 Propagation beacons
144.30-144.50 New OSCAR subband
144.50-144.60 Linear translator inputs
144.60-144.90 FM repeater inputs
144.90-145.10 Weak signal and FM simplex (145.01,03,05,07,09 are widely used for packet)
145.10-145.20 Linear translator outputs
145.20-145.50 FM repeater outputs
145.50-145.80 Miscellaneous and experimental modes
145.80-146.00 OSCAR subband
146.01-146.37 Repeater inputs
146.40-146.58 Simplex
146.52 National Simplex Calling Frequency
146.61-146.97 Repeater outputs
147.00-147.39 Repeater outputs
147.42-147.57 Simplex
147.60-147.99 Repeater inputs

1.25 Meters (222-225 MHz)

222.0-222.150 Weak-signal modes
222.0-222.025 EME
222.05-222.06 Propagation beacons
222.1 SSB & CW calling frequency
222.10-222.15 Weak-signal CW & SSB
222.15-222.25 Local coordinator's option; weak signal, ACSB, repeater inputs, control
222.25-223.38 FM repeater inputs only
223.40-223.52 FM simplex
223.52-223.64 Digital, packet
223.64-223.70 Links, control
223.71-223.85 Local coordinator's option; FM simplex, packet, repeater outputs
223.85-224.98 Repeater outputs only

70 Centimeters (420-450 MHz)

420.00-426.00 ATV repeater or simplex with 421.25 MHz video carrier control links and experimental
426.00-432.00 ATV simplex with 427.250-MHz video carrier frequency
432.00-432.07 EME (Earth-Moon-Earth)
432.07-432.10 Weak-signal CW
432.10 70-cm calling frequency

432.10-432.30 Mixed-mode and weak-signal work
432.30-432.40 Propagation beacons
432.40-433.00 Mixed-mode and weak-signal work
433.00-435.00 Auxiliary/repeater links
435.00-438.00 Satellite only (internationally)
438.00-444.00 ATV repeater input with 439.250-MHz video carrier frequency and re-
    peater links
442.00-445.00 Repeater inputs and outputs (local option)
445.00-447.00 Shared by auxiliary and control links, repeaters and simplex (local option)
446.00 National simplex frequency
447.00-450.00 Repeater inputs and outputs (local option)

33 Centimeters (902-928 MHz)

902.0-903.0 Narrow-bandwidth, weak-signal communications
902.0-902.8 SSTV, FAX, ACSSB, experimental
902.1 Weak-signal calling frequency
902.8-903.0 Reserved for EME, CW expansion
903.1 Alternate calling frequency
903.0-906.0 Digital communications
906-909 FM repeater inputs
909-915 ATV
915-918 Digital communications
918-921 FM repeater outputs
921-927 ATV
927-928 FM simplex and links

23 Centimeters (1240-1300 MHz)

1240-1246 ATV #1
1246-1248 Narrow-bandwidth FM point-to-point links and digital, duplex with 1258-
    1260.
1248-1258 Digital Communications
1252-1258 ATV #2
1258-1260 Narrow-bandwidth FM point-to-point links digital, duplexed with 1246-1252
1260-1270 Satellite uplinks, reference WARC '79
1260-1270 Wide-bandwidth experimental, simplex ATV
1270-1276 Repeater inputs, FM and linear, paired with 1282-1288, 239 pairs every 25
    kHz, e.g. 1270.025, .050, etc.
1271-1283 Non-coordinated test pair
1276-1282 ATV #3
1282-1288 Repeater outputs, paired with 1270-1276
1288-1294 Wide-bandwidth experimental, simplex ATV
1294-1295 Narrow-bandwidth FM simplex services, 25-kHz channels
1294.5 National FM simplex calling frequency
1295-1297 Narrow bandwidth weak-signal communications (no FM)
1295.0-1295.8 SSTV, FAX, ACSSB, experimental
1295.8-1296.0 Reserved for EME, CW expansion

1296.00-1296.05 EME-exclusive
1296.07-1296.08 CW beacons
1296.1 CW, SSB calling frequency
1296.4-1296.6 Crossband linear translator input
1296.6-1296.8 Crossband linear translator output
1296.8-1297.0 Experimental beacons (exclusive)
1297-1300 Digital Communications

2300-2310 and 2390-2450 MHz

2300.0-2303.0 High-rate data
2303.0-2303.5 Packet
2303.5-2303.8 TTY packet
2303.9-2303.9 Packet, TTY, CW, EME
2303.9-2304.1 CW, EME
2304.1 Calling frequency
2304.1-2304.2 CW, EME, SSB
2304.2-2304.3 SSB, SSTV, FAX, Packet AM, Amtor
2304.30-2304.32 Propagation beacon network
2304.32-2304.40 General propagation beacons
2304.4-2304.5 SSB, SSTV, ACSSB, FAX, Packet AM, Amtor experimental
2304.5-2304.7 Crossband linear translator input
2304.7-2304.9 Crossband linear translator output
2304.9-2305.0 Experimental beacons
2305.0-2305.2 FM simplex (25 kHz spacing)
2305.20 FM simplex calling frequency
2305.2-2306.0 FM simplex (25 kHz spacing)
2306.0-2309.0 FM Repeaters (25 kHz) input
2309.0-2310.0 Control and auxiliary links
2390.0-2396.0 Fast-scan TV
2396.0-2399.0 High-rate data
2399.0-2399.5 Packet
2399.5-2400.0 Control and auxiliary links
2400.0-2403.0 Satellite
2403.0-2408.0 Satellite high-rate data
2408.0-2410.0 Satellite
2410.0-2413.0 FM repeaters (25 kHz) output
2413.0-2418.0 High-rate data
2418.0-2430.0 Fast-scan TV
2430.0-2433.0 Satellite
2433.0-2438.0 Satellite high-rate data
2438.0-2450.0 WB FM, FSTV, FMTV, SS experimental

3300-3500 MHz

3456.3-3456.4 Propagation beacons

5650-5925 MHz
5760.3-5760.4 Propagation beacons

10.00-10.50 GHz
10.368 Narrow band calling frequency 10.3683-10.3684 Propagation beacons 10.3640 Calling frequency

Now that you have your license (you do, don't you?), and your equipment, you are ready to go live. Below is a suggested start.

1) Assuming you have the HT set up to the appropriate frequency, and offset, press the mic button on the HT and say, "KK4HWX listening." Replace the KK4HWX with your own call sign, the one assigned to you by the FCC (it's the law). If no one responds to your call, you may wish to try again. Hopefully someone will respond to your call.

2) Once you get a response, it will be in the form of something like, "KK4HWX this is ??1??? in Eastport returning. My name is Florence. Back to you. ??1???" then a tone. Let us examine the response more closely. She first acknowledged your call sign (KK4HWX), then identified hers (??1???). From the 1 in her call sign, you know that she first got her license in Region 1, meaning she got it while a resident of CT, ME, MA, NH, RI, or VT. She then told you where she's transmitting from (Eastport). The term "returning" means that she is returning your call. Her name is Florence. The phrase, "Back to you" indicates that she is turning over the conversation to you. She then repeats her call sign. The tone indicates to you that it is okay to proceed with your response. BTW if she had used the term "Over" instead of "Back to you," it would mean the same thing, just fewer words.

3) At this point, press the mic button and continue with the conversation. You should restate your call sign often during the conversation (perhaps every 10 minutes or less and whenever you begin transmitting). Don't forget to say, "Over" or "Back to you" whenever you are giving Florence control of the conversation again.

4) When you are ready to stop the conversation, you should say goodbye or use the phrase "73", meaning "best wishes." Your conversation would end something like, "??1??? 73, this is KK4HWX clear and monitoring." The "clear and monitoring" indicates that you are going to continue to monitor the frequency. If you are not going to continue monitoring, you may wish to end the conversation with Florence with, "clear and QRT" instead. The QRT means that you are stopping transmissions.

Call Sign Phonics

Because of different accents of various people, sometimes it is difficult to understand call sign letters when spoken. For this reason, most ham operators verbalize their call sign using phonics. Below is a table listing the accepted phonics for letters and numbers.

A = ALFA		S = SIERRA	
B = BRAVO		T = TANGO	
C = CHARLIE		U = UNIFORM	
D = DELTA		V = VICTOR	
E = ECHO		W = WHISKEY	
F = FOXTROT		X = X-RAY	
G = GOLF		Y = YANKEE	
H = HOTEL		Z = ZULU (ZED)	
I = INDIA		1 = ONE	
J = JULIETT		2 = TWO	
K = KILO		3 = THREE (TREE)	
L = LIMA		4 = FOUR	
M = MIKE		5 = FIVE (FIFE)	
N = NOVEMBER		6 = SIX	
O = OSCAR		7 = SEVEN	
P = PAPA (PA-PA')		8 = EIGHT	
Q = QUEBEC (KAY-BEK')		9 = NINE (NINER)	
R = ROMEO		0 = ZERO	

The words in parentheses are the pronunciation or the alternate pronunciations for the words or numbers, but you will hear both used. With the letter Z, (ZED) is by far the most commonly used. With the number 9, NINER is the most common and easiest to understand ON THE AIR.

If you wish to use Morse code (CW) instead of voice communication, the "conversation" would follow the same steps, with a few modifications. To type out each word would require a lot of typing and translating. If you are like this author, more means more, i.e., more typing means more typos are likely. To help with this situation, CW enthusiasts have developed a language all their own – they use abbreviations for common phrases. Below is a chart showing some of these abbreviations.

Abbreviation	Use
AR	Over
de	From or "this is"
ES	And
GM	Good Morning
K	Go
KN	Go only
NM	Name
QTH	Location
RPT	Report
R	Roger
SK	Clear
tnx	Thanks
UR	Your, you are
73	Best Wishes

Morse Code and Amateur Radio

If you wish to use CW, but are concerned about accuracy, you might consider purchasing a Morse code translator. This is an electronic device that you place in front of your speakers. It takes the CW sounds and translates them into English and displays the transmission on an LCD display. For the reverse, you can pick up a CW keyboard. With the keyboard, you type in your message and it converts the text to Morse code. The translator does not need to be attached to your ham equipment, whereas the keyboard would.

For your convenience, below is a table showing the Morse code signals and their meaning.

Character	Code
A	· —
B	— · · ·
C	— · — ·
D	— · ·
E	·
F	· · — ·
G	— — ·
H	· · · ·
I	· ·
J	· — — —
K	— · —
L	· — · ·
M	— —
N	— ·
O	— — —
P	· — — ·
Q	— — · —
R	· — ·
S	· · ·
T	—
U	· · —
V	· · · —
W	· — —
X	— · · —
Y	— · — —
Z	— — · ·
0	— — — — —
1	· — — — —
2	· · — — —
3	· · · — —
4	· · · · —
5	· · · · ·

6	— · · · ·
7	— — · · ·
8	— — — · ·
9	— — — — ·
Ampersand [&], Wait	· — · · ·
Apostrophe [']	· — — — — ·
At sign [@]	· — — · — ·
Colon [:]	— — — · · ·
Comma [,]	— — · · — —
Dollar sign [$]	· · · — · · —
Double dash [=]	— · · · —
Exclamation mark [!]	— · — · — —
Hyphen, Minus [-]	— · · · · —
Parenthesis closed [)]	— · — — · —
Parenthesis open [(]	— · — — ·
Period [.]	· — · — · —
Plus [+]	· — · — ·
Question mark [?]	· · — — · ·
Quotation mark ["]	· — · · — ·
Semicolon [;]	— · — · — ·
Slash [/], Fraction bar	— · · — ·
Underscore [_]	· · — — · —

An advantage of using Morse Code is that when broadcasting CW, you are using reduced power, thereby saving your battery. Your battery is used only while actually transmitting or receiving.

International Call Sign Prefixes

As was stated earlier, all ham radio call signs begin with letters (or numbers) taken from blocks assigned to each country of the world by the *ITU - International Telecommunications Union,* a body controlled by the United Nations. The following chart indicates which call sign series are allocated to which countries.

Call Sign Series	Allocated to
AAA-ALZ	**United States of America**
AMA-AOZ	Spain
APA-ASZ	Pakistan (Islamic Republic of)
ATA-AWZ	India (Republic of)
AXA-AXZ	Australia
AYA-AZZ	Argentine Republic
A2A-A2Z	Botswana (Republic of)
A3A-A3Z	Tonga (Kingdom of)
A4A-A4Z	Oman (Sultanate of)
A5A-A5Z	Bhutan (Kingdom of)

A6A-A6Z	United Arab Emirates
A7A-A7Z	Qatar (State of)
A8A-A8Z	Liberia (Republic of)
A9A-A9Z	Bahrain (State of)
BAA-BZZ	China (People's Republic of)
CAA-CEZ	Chile
CFA-CKZ	Canada
CLA-CMZ	Cuba
CNA-CNZ	Morocco (Kingdom of)
COA-COZ	Cuba
CPA-CPZ	Bolivia (Republic of)
CQA-CUZ	Portugal
CVA-CXZ	Uruguay (Eastern Republic of)
CYA-CZZ	Canada
C2A-C2Z	Nauru (Republic of)
C3A-C3Z	Andorra (Principality of)
C4A-C4Z	Cyprus (Republic of)
C5A-C5Z	Gambia (Republic of the)
C6A-C6Z	Bahamas (Commonwealth of the)
C7A-C7Z	World Meteorological Organization
C8A-C9Z	Mozambique (Republic of)
DAA-DRZ	Germany (Federal Republic of)
DSA-DTZ	Korea (Republic of)
DUA-DZZ	Philippines (Republic of the)
D2A-D3Z	Angola (Republic of)
D4A-D4Z	Cape Verde (Republic of)
D5A-D5Z	Liberia (Republic of)
D6A-D6Z	Comoros (Islamic Federal Republic of the)
D7A-D9Z	Korea (Republic of)
EAA-EHZ	Spain
EIA-EJZ	Ireland
EKA-EKZ	Armenia (Republic of)
ELA-ELZ	Liberia (Republic of)
EMA-EOZ	Ukraine
EPA-EQZ	Iran (Islamic Republic of)
ERA-ERZ	Moldova (Republic of)
ESA-ESZ	Estonia (Republic of)
ETA-ETZ	Ethiopia (Federal Democratic Republic of)
EUA-EWZ	Belarus (Republic of)
EXA-EXZ	Kyrgyz Republic
EYA-EYZ	Tajikistan (Republic of)
EZA-EZZ	Turkmenistan
E2A-E2Z	Thailand
E3A-E3Z	Eritrea
E4A-E4Z	Palestinian Authority

E5A-E5Z	New Zealand - Cook Islands (WRC-07)
E7A-E7Z	Bosnia and Herzegovina (Republic of) (WRC-07)
FAA-FZZ	France
GAA-GZZ	United Kingdom of Great Britain and Northern Ireland
HAA-HAZ	Hungary (Republic of)
HBA-HBZ	Switzerland (Confederation of)
HCA-HDZ	Ecuador
HEA-HEZ	Switzerland (Confederation of)
HFA-HFZ	Poland (Republic of)
HGA-HGZ	Hungary (Republic of)
HHA-HHZ	Haiti (Republic of)
HIA-HIZ	Dominican Republic
HJA-HKZ	Colombia (Republic of)
HLA-HLZ	Korea (Republic of)
HMA-HMZ	Democratic People's Republic of Korea
HNA-HNZ	Iraq (Republic of)
HOA-HPZ	Panama (Republic of)
HQA-HRZ	Honduras (Republic of)
HSA-HSZ	Thailand
HTA-HTZ	Nicaragua
HUA-HUZ	El Salvador (Republic of)
HVA-HVZ	Vatican City State
HWA-HYZ	France
HZA-HZZ	Saudi Arabia (Kingdom of)
H2A-H2Z	Cyprus (Republic of)
H3A-H3Z	Panama (Republic of)
H4A-H4Z	Solomon Islands
H6A-H7Z	Nicaragua
H8A-H9Z	Panama (Republic of)
IAA-IZZ	Italy
JAA-JSZ	Japan
JTA-JVZ	Mongolia
JWA-JXZ	Norway
JYA-JYZ	Jordan (Hashemite Kingdom of)
JZA-JZZ	Indonesia (Republic of)
J2A-J2Z	Djibouti (Republic of)
J3A-J3Z	Grenada
J4A-J4Z	Greece
J5A-J5Z	Guinea-Bissau (Republic of)
J6A-J6Z	Saint Lucia
J7A-J7Z	Dominica (Commonwealth of)
J8A-J8Z	Saint Vincent and the Grenadines
KAA-KZZ	**United States of America**
LAA-LNZ	Norway
LOA-LWZ	Argentine Republic

LXA-LXZ	Luxembourg
LYA-LYZ	Lithuania (Republic of)
LZA-LZZ	Bulgaria (Republic of)
L2A-L9Z	Argentine Republic
MAA-MZZ	United Kingdom of Great Britain and Northern Ireland
NAA-NZZ	**United States of America**
OAA-OCZ	Peru
ODA-ODZ	Lebanon
OEA-OEZ	Austria
OFA-OJZ	Finland
OKA-OLZ	Czech Republic
OMA-OMZ	Slovak Republic
ONA-OTZ	Belgium
OUA-OZZ	Denmark
PAA-PIZ	Netherlands (Kingdom of the)
PJA-PJZ	Netherlands (Kingdom of the) - Netherlands Antilles
PKA-POZ	Indonesia (Republic of)
PPA-PYZ	Brazil (Federative Republic of)
PZA-PZZ	Suriname (Republic of)
P2A-P2Z	Papua New Guinea
P3A-P3Z	Cyprus (Republic of)
P4A-P4Z	Netherlands (Kingdom of the) - Aruba
P5A-P9Z	Democratic People's Republic of Korea
RAA-RZZ	Russian Federation
SAA-SMZ	Sweden
SNA-SRZ	Poland (Republic of)
SSA-SSM	Egypt (Arab Republic of)
SSN-STZ	Sudan (Republic of the)
SUA-SUZ	Egypt (Arab Republic of)
SVA-SZZ	Greece
S2A-S3Z	Bangladesh (People's Republic of)
S5A-S5Z	Slovenia (Republic of)
S6A-S6Z	Singapore (Republic of)
S7A-S7Z	Seychelles (Republic of)
S8A-S8Z	South Africa (Republic of)
S9A-S9Z	Sao Tome and Principe (Democratic Republic of)
TAA-TCZ	Turkey
TDA-TDZ	Guatemala (Republic of)
TEA-TEZ	Costa Rica
TFA-TFZ	Iceland
TGA-TGZ	Guatemala (Republic of)
THA-THZ	France
TIA-TIZ	Costa Rica
TJA-TJZ	Cameroon (Republic of)
TKA-TKZ	France

TLA-TLZ	Central African Republic
TMA-TMZ	France
TNA-TNZ	Congo (Republic of the)
TOA-TQZ	France
TRA-TRZ	Gabonese Republic
TSA-TSZ	Tunisia
TTA-TTZ	Chad (Republic of)
TUA-TUZ	Côte d'Ivoire (Republic of)
TVA-TXZ	France
TYA-TYZ	Benin (Republic of)
TZA-TZZ	Mali (Republic of)
T2A-T2Z	Tuvalu
T3A-T3Z	Kiribati (Republic of)
T4A-T4Z	Cuba
T5A-T5Z	Somali Democratic Republic
T6A-T6Z	Afghanistan (Islamic State of)
T7A-T7Z	San Marino (Republic of)
T8A-T8Z	Palau (Republic of)
UAA-UIZ	Russian Federation
UJA-UMZ	Uzbekistan (Republic of)
UNA-UQZ	Kazakhstan (Republic of)
URA-UZZ	Ukraine
VAA-VGZ	Canada
VHA-VNZ	Australia
VOA-VOZ	Canada
VPA-VQZ	United Kingdom of Great Britain and Northern Ireland
VRA-VRZ	China (People's Republic of) - Hong Kong
VSA-VSZ	United Kingdom of Great Britain and Northern Ireland
VTA-VWZ	India (Republic of)
VXA-VYZ	Canada
VZA-VZZ	Australia
V2A-V2Z	Antigua and Barbuda
V3A-V3Z	Belize
V4A-V4Z	Saint Kitts and Nevis
V5A-V5Z	Namibia (Republic of)
V6A-V6Z	Micronesia (Federated States of)
V7A-V7Z	Marshall Islands (Republic of the)
V8A-V8Z	Brunei Darussalam
WAA-WZZ	**United States of America**
XAA-XIZ	Mexico
XJA-XOZ	Canada
XPA-XPZ	Denmark
XQA-XRZ	Chile
XSA-XSZ	China (People's Republic of)
XTA-XTZ	Burkina Faso

XUA-XUZ	Cambodia (Kingdom of)
XVA-XVZ	Viet Nam (Socialist Republic of)
XWA-XWZ	Lao People's Democratic Republic
XXA-XXZ	China (People's Republic of) - Macao (WRC-07)
XYA-XZZ	Myanmar (Union of)
YAA-YAZ	Afghanistan (Islamic State of)
YBA-YHZ	Indonesia (Republic of)
YIA-YIZ	Iraq (Republic of)
YJA-YJZ	Vanuatu (Republic of)
YKA-YKZ	Syrian Arab Republic
YLA-YLZ	Latvia (Republic of)
YMA-YMZ	Turkey
YNA-YNZ	Nicaragua
YOA-YRZ	Romania
YSA-YSZ	El Salvador (Republic of)
YTA-YUZ	Serbia (Republic of) (WRC-07)
YVA-YYZ	Venezuela (Republic of)
Y2A-Y9Z	Germany (Federal Republic of)
ZAA-ZAZ	Albania (Republic of)
ZBA-ZJZ	United Kingdom of Great Britain and Northern Ireland
ZKA-ZMZ	New Zealand
ZNA-ZOZ	United Kingdom of Great Britain and Northern Ireland
ZPA-ZPZ	Paraguay (Republic of)
ZQA-ZQZ	United Kingdom of Great Britain and Northern Ireland
ZRA-ZUZ	South Africa (Republic of)
ZVA-ZZZ	Brazil (Federative Republic of)
Z2A-Z2Z	Zimbabwe (Republic of)
Z3A-Z3Z	The Former Yugoslav Republic of Macedonia
2AA-2ZZ	United Kingdom of Great Britain and Northern Ireland
3AA-3AZ	Monaco (Principality of)
3BA-3BZ	Mauritius (Republic of)
3CA-3CZ	Equatorial Guinea (Republic of)
3DA-3DM	Swaziland (Kingdom of)
3DN-3DZ	Fiji (Republic of)
3EA-3FZ	Panama (Republic of)
3GA-3GZ	Chile
3HA-3UZ	China (People's Republic of)
3VA-3VZ	Tunisia
3WA-3WZ	Viet Nam (Socialist Republic of)
3XA-3XZ	Guinea (Republic of)
3YA-3YZ	Norway
3ZA-3ZZ	Poland (Republic of)
4AA-4CZ	Mexico
4DA-4IZ	Philippines (Republic of the)
4JA-4KZ	Azerbaijani Republic

4LA-4LZ	Georgia (Republic of)
4MA-4MZ	Venezuela (Republic of)
4OA-4OZ	Montenegro (Republic of) (WRC-07)
4PA-4SZ	Sri Lanka (Democratic Socialist Republic of)
4TA-4TZ	Peru
4UA-4UZ	United Nations
4VA-4VZ	Haiti (Republic of)
4WA-4WZ	Democratic Republic of Timor-Leste (WRC-03)
4XA-4XZ	Israel (State of)
4YA-4YZ	International Civil Aviation Organization
4ZA-4ZZ	Israel (State of)
5AA-5AZ	Libya (Socialist People's Libyan Arab Jamahiriya)
5BA-5BZ	Cyprus (Republic of)
5CA-5GZ	Morocco (Kingdom of)
5HA-5IZ	Tanzania (United Republic of)
5JA-5KZ	Colombia (Republic of)
5LA-5MZ	Liberia (Republic of)
5NA-5OZ	Nigeria (Federal Republic of)
5PA-5QZ	Denmark
5RA-5SZ	Madagascar (Republic of)
5TA-5TZ	Mauritania (Islamic Republic of)
5UA-5UZ	Niger (Republic of the)
5VA-5VZ	Togolese Republic
5WA-5WZ	Samoa (Independent State of)
5XA-5XZ	Uganda (Republic of)
5YA-5ZZ	Kenya (Republic of)
6AA-6BZ	Egypt (Arab Republic of)
6CA-6CZ	Syrian Arab Republic
6DA-6JZ	Mexico
6KA-6NZ	Korea (Republic of)
6OA-6OZ	Somali Democratic Republic
6PA-6SZ	Pakistan (Islamic Republic of)
6TA-6UZ	Sudan (Republic of the)
6VA-6WZ	Senegal (Republic of)
6XA-6XZ	Madagascar (Republic of)
6YA-6YZ	Jamaica
6ZA-6ZZ	Liberia (Republic of)
7AA-7IZ	Indonesia (Republic of)
7JA-7NZ	Japan
7OA-7OZ	Yemen (Republic of)
7PA-7PZ	Lesotho (Kingdom of)
7QA-7QZ	Malawi
7RA-7RZ	Algeria (People's Democratic Republic of)
7SA-7SZ	Sweden
7TA-7YZ	Algeria (People's Democratic Republic of)

7ZA-7ZZ	Saudi Arabia (Kingdom of)
8AA-8IZ	Indonesia (Republic of)
8JA-8NZ	Japan
8OA-8OZ	Botswana (Republic of)
8PA-8PZ	Barbados
8QA-8QZ	Maldives (Republic of)
8RA-8RZ	Guyana
8SA-8SZ	Sweden
8TA-8YZ	India (Republic of)
8ZA-8ZZ	Saudi Arabia (Kingdom of)
9AA-9AZ	Croatia (Republic of)
9BA-9DZ	Iran (Islamic Republic of)
9EA-9FZ	Ethiopia (Federal Democratic Republic of)
9GA-9GZ	Ghana
9HA-9HZ	Malta
9IA-9JZ	Zambia (Republic of)
9KA-9KZ	Kuwait (State of)
9LA-9LZ	Sierra Leone
9MA-9MZ	Malaysia
9NA-9NZ	Nepal
9OA-9TZ	Democratic Republic of the Congo
9UA-9UZ	Burundi (Republic of)
9VA-9VZ	Singapore (Republic of)
9WA-9WZ	Malaysia
9XA-9XZ	Rwandese Republic
9YA-9ZZ	Trinidad and Tobago

Third-Party Communications and Amateur Radio

If all of this information about ham radios is somewhat intimidating, do not despair. "You" can still use ham radios for communications without being a licensed operator. Yes, you do have to have a ham license in order to legally transmit by ham equipment (or be under the direct supervision of someone else who is licensed), but there is an alternative – third-party communication.

Third-party communications occur when a licensed operator sends either written or verbal messages on behalf of unlicensed persons or organizations. There are two "controls" on third-party communication.

First, the communication must be noncommercial and of a personal nature. Asking a ham operator to contact another ham operator located in an area just hit by tornados and, because of being without power, phones do not work in Grandma Sally's city so you can check up on her, is okay. Asking a ham to send a message out that you have an old Chevy for sale would not be okay.

Second, the message must be going to a permitted area. Transmitting from a US location to another US location is okay, but transmitting from the US to another country may not. Because third-party communications bypass a country's normal telephone and postal systems, many foreign governments forbid such communications. In order to transmit from one country to another, the other country must have signed a third-party agreement with the US. What follows is a list of those countries that do have third-party a communications agreement with the US.

V2	Antigua / Barbuda
LU	Argentina
VK	Australia
V3	Belize
CP	Bolivia
T9	Bosnia-Herzegovina
PY	Brazil
VE	Canada
CE	Chile
HK	Colombia
D6	Comoros (Federal Islamic Republic of)
TI	Costa Rica
CO	Cuba
HI	Dominican Republic
J7	Dominica
HC	Ecuador
YS	El Salvador
C5	Gambia, The
9G	Ghana
J3	Grenada
TG	Guatemala
8R	Guyana
HH	Haiti
HR	Honduras
4X	Israel
6Y	Jamaica
JY	Jordan
EL	Liberia
V7	Marshall Islands
XE	Mexico
V6	Micronesia, Federated States of
YN	Nicaragua
HP	Panama
ZP	Paraguay
OA	Peru
DU	Philippines
VR6	Pitcairn Island

V4	St. Christopher / Nevis
J6	St. Lucia
J8	St. Vincent and the Grenadines
9L	Sierra Leone
ZS	South Africa
3DA	Swaziland
9Y	Trinidad / Tobago
TA	Turkey
GB	United Kingdom
CX	Uruguay
YV	Venezuela
4U1ITUITU	Geneva
4U1VICVIC	Vienna

Remember, before TSHTF, keep your pantry well stocked, your powder dry, and your batteries fully charged. 73

APPENDIX A

American Radio Relay League

Affiliated Amateur Radio Clubs in

Oregon

ARRL Affiliated Club	Terac Inc.
City:	Aloha, OR
Call Sign:	K7AUO
Section:	OR
Links:	www.terac.org
ARRL Affiliated Club	Sunset Empire Amateur Radio Club
City:	Astoria, OR
Call Sign:	W7BU
Section:	OR
Links:	www.w7bu.org, www.sunset-empire-arc.org
ARRL Affiliated Club	Western Oregon Radio Club Inc.
City:	Beaverton, OR
Call Sign:	WB7DZG
Section:	OR
Links:	www.worc.info
ARRL Affiliated Club	Hospital Emergency Amateur Radio Team
City:	Beaverton, OR
Call Sign:	K0HSU
Section:	OR
ARRL Affiliated Club	High Desert Amateur Radio Group
City:	Bend, OR
Call Sign:	W7JVO
Section:	OR
Links:	www.hidarg.org
ARRL Affiliated Club	Central Oregon DX Club
City:	Bend, OR
Call Sign:	N7LE
Section:	OR
Links:	codxc.org
ARRL Affiliated Club	Coos County Radio Club
City:	Coos Bay, OR
Call Sign:	K7CCH
Section:	OR
Links:	www.coosradioclub.net
ARRL Affiliated Club	Oregon State Univ. Amateur Radio Club
City:	Corvallis, OR
Call Sign:	W7OSU
Section:	OR

ARRL Affiliated Club	Radio Operators Assn. 0f Dallas (ROADS)
City:	Dallas, OR
Call Sign:	W7ORE
Section:	OR
Links:	www.w7ore.com

ARRL Affiliated Club	Lane County Sheriffs Amateur Radio Operators, Inc.
City:	Eugene, OR
Call Sign:	W7EUG
Section:	OR
Links:	www.lcsaro.org

ARRL Affiliated Club	Valley Radio Club of Oregon
City:	Eugene, OR
Call Sign:	W7PXL
Section:	OR
Links:	www.valleyradioclub.org

ARRL Affiliated Club	Emerald Amateur Radio Society (EARS)
City:	Eugene, OR
Call Sign:	WA7FQD
Section:	OR
Links:	emerald-ars.us/

ARRL Affiliated Club	Southern Oregon A.R.C.
City:	Grants Pass, OR
Call Sign:	K7LIX
Section:	OR
Links:	www.SOARC.org, www.qsl.net/soar/SOARC/index.html

ARRL Affiliated Club	Hoodview Amateur Radio Club
City:	Gresham, OR
Call Sign:	WB7QIW
Section:	OR
Links:	www.wb7qiw.org

ARRL Affiliated Club	Hermiston Amateur Radio Club
City:	Hermiston, OR
Call Sign:	KC7KUG
Section:	OR
Links:	www.kc7kug.org

ARRL Affiliated Club	Oregon Tualatin Valley Amateur Radio Club
City:	Hillsboro, OR
Call Sign:	W7OTV
Section:	OR
Links:	www.otvarc.org/

ARRL Affiliated Club	Tualatin Valley Contesters
City:	Hillsboro, OR
Call Sign:	W7TVC
Section:	OR

ARRL Affiliated Club	Harney County Radio Association
City:	Hines, OR
Call Sign:	KE7YLC
Section:	OR

ARRL Affiliated Club	Radio Amateurs of The Gorge
City:	Hood River, OR
Call Sign:	W7RAG
Section:	OR
Links:	www.W7RAG.com

ARRL Affiliated Club	OIT Amateur Radio Club
City:	Klamath Falls, OR
Call Sign:	W7MHS
Section:	OR
Links:	www.w7mhs.blogspot.com

ARRL Affiliated Club	Klamath Basin Amateur Radio Association
City:	Klamath Falls, OR
Call Sign:	W7VW
Section:	OR
Links:	kbara.net

ARRL Affiliated Club	Grande Ronde Radio Amateurs Association
City:	La Grande, OR
Call Sign:	W7GRA
Section:	OR
Links:	www.grraa.org

ARRL Affiliated Club	McMinnville Amateur Radio Club
City:	McMinnville, OR
Call Sign:	W7RXJ
Section:	OR
Links:	wwww.marcwireless.org

ARRL Affiliated Club	Rogue Valley Amateur Radio Club
City:	Medford, OR
Call Sign:	W7DTA
Section:	OR
Links:	www.qsl.net/w7oek, www.qsl.net/w7dta

ARRL Affiliated Club	Lincoln County Amateur Radio Club
City:	Newport, OR
Call Sign:	N7OY
Section:	OR
Links:	N7OY.blogspot.com, www.lcarc.net, www.larc.net

ARRL Affiliated Club	Cascade Amateur Radio Society
City:	Oregon City, OR
Call Sign:	KE7AWR
Section:	OR
Links:	www.cascadeamateurradio.net, www.carsradio.org

ARRL Affiliated Club	Pendleton Amateur Radio Club
City:	Pendleton, OR
Call Sign:	W7PL
Section:	OR
Links:	www.w7pl..com

ARRL Affiliated Club	Oregon Amateur Television Association
City:	Portland, OR
Call Sign:	W7AMQ
Section:	OR
Links:	www.oregonatv.org

ARRL Affiliated Club	Providence Portland Med Ctr. Dis Comm. Tea
City:	Portland, OR
Call Sign:	W7PMC
Section:	OR

ARRL Affiliated Club	Beaverton Certified Radio Team
City:	Portland, OR
Call Sign:	WB7CRT
Section:	OR
Links:	beavertoncertradio.org

ARRL Affiliated Club	Amateur Radio Relay Group, Inc.
City:	Portland, OR
Call Sign:	K7RPT
Section:	OR
Links:	www.arrg.org

ARRL Affiliated Club	Willamette Valley DX Inc. Club
City:	Portland, OR
Call Sign:	W7AC
Section:	OR
Links:	www.wvdxc.org

ARRL Affiliated Club	Salem Amateur Radio Club Inc.
City:	Salem, OR
Call Sign:	W7SAA
Section:	OR
Links:	www.w7saa.com, www.w7saa.net

ARRL Affiliated Club	Coast to Range Amateur Radio Club
City:	Salem, OR
Section:	OR
Links:	www.qsl.net/w7nat

ARRL Affiliated Club	Seaside Tsunami Amateur Radio Society
City:	Seaside, OR
Call Sign:	WA7VE
Section:	OR
Links:	www.freewebs.com/wa7ve_stars

ARRL Affiliated Club	Ham Operators Group
City:	The Dalles, OR
Call Sign:	K7HOG
Section:	OR

ARRL Affiliated Club	Gorge East Amateur Radio
City:	The Dalles, OR
Call Sign:	KE7EEM
Section:	OR

APPENDIX B

Amateur Radio License Holders

in

Oregon: Western Region
(by City)

FCC Amateur Radio Licenses in Adams

Call Sign: K7KRF
Clarence A Gross
1015 N Watts St
Adams OR 97810

Call Sign: WD7E
Richard D Johnson Sr
140 S Rogers St
Adams OR 97810

Call Sign: KC7OOJ
Douglas L Walker
Adams OR 97810

FCC Amateur Radio Licenses in Adrian

Call Sign: N7HZN
Charles J Witty
3900 Bridgeport
Adrian OR 97901

Call Sign: KD7BEI
Brett O Sipes
2336 NE 23rd
Adrian OR 99701

FCC Amateur Radio Licenses in Agness

Call Sign: KE7FPO
Anthony R Perez
1860 Sunset Ln
Agness OR 97406

FCC Amateur Radio Licenses in Allegany

Call Sign: W7ZXS
Tamara C Allender
Allegany OR 97407

FCC Amateur Radio Licenses in Alvadore

Call Sign: KE7UOF
Tony Trigg
Alvadore OR 97409

Call Sign: AD7VQ
Tony Trigg
Alvadore OR 97409

Call Sign: NJ7N
Tony Trigg
Alvadore OR 97409

Call Sign: W7TM
Tony Trigg
Alvadore OR 97409

FCC Amateur Radio Licenses in Antelope

Call Sign: W7EUH
Ronald H Pomeroy
Union And Wallace St
Antelope OR 97001

Call Sign: N7ZTL
Cody R Chapman
Antelope OR 97001

FCC Amateur Radio Licenses in Applegate

Call Sign: WB6HTP
Carmen V Mercadante Jr
36299 Hwy 58
Applegate OR 97530

Call Sign: W7THV
John R Warmington
1772 Iron Horse Rd
Applegate OR 97530

Call Sign: KD7MLQ
Sue V George
13370 Thompson Rd
Applegate OR 97530

Call Sign: WB7OPC
Michael B Hines
Applegate OR 97530

Call Sign: KE7NPR
Patricia A Breidenthal
Applegate OR 97530

FCC Amateur Radio Licenses in Arlington

Call Sign: KC7VNC
Inabelle K Brown
Arlington OR 97812

Call Sign: N7ASM
Leon F Hughes
Arlington OR 978120204

FCC Amateur Radio Licenses in Ashland

Call Sign: KE7MVS
Katherine T Burtis
100 Angela Ct
Ashland OR 97520

Call Sign: KI6OQA
Gregory J Babush
1594 Angelcrest Dr
Ashland OR 97520

Call Sign: KE7KZV
Gary D Powell
7860 Atlantic Ave
Ashland OR 97520

Call Sign: KF6WPJ
Vincent E Moscaritolo
1215 Auburn Ave

Ashland OR 97520

Ashland OR 97520

Ashland OR 975203677

Call Sign: K7BJA
Jack Eagleson
22052 Banff Dr
Ashland OR 97520

Call Sign: KE7CIJ
Daniel A Ragen
8183 Blackwell Rd
Ashland OR 97520

Call Sign: KB8UXI
Bruce P Comstock
1371 Brookdale
Ashland OR 975201459

Call Sign: KE7SZQ
Timothy R Learmont
5185 Barger Dr
Ashland OR 97520

Call Sign: KF7UMJ
Marc J Loring
1489 Board Shanty Rd
Ashland OR 97520

Call Sign: KD7HAY
Nate J Monosoff
19208 Carpenterville Rd
Ashland OR 97520

Call Sign: KG6GNX
James Cossolias
479 Berrydale Ave
Ashland OR 97520

Call Sign: AB7ZD
Mildred I Narum
Rt 2 Box 2215
Ashland OR 97520

Call Sign: WB7NKR
William C Webb
1540 Central Ave
Ashland OR 97520

Call Sign: KE7ERK
Peter K Wu
9 Berwick Ct
Ashland OR 97520

Call Sign: W7LIV
Richard O Burnham
Rt 2 Box 2307
Ashland OR 97520

Call Sign: W7NWH
John S Webb
86520 Central Rd
Ashland OR 97520

Call Sign: WB7SZL
Norbert C Krause
530 Bessie St
Ashland OR 97520

Call Sign: KG6DJG
Emily C Dean
Rt 2 Box 239 48
Ashland OR 97520

Call Sign: KL1XI
David A Hoffmann
633 Cessna St
Ashland OR 97520

Call Sign: KE7KBW
Terry N Otto
1648 Best Ln
Ashland OR 97520

Call Sign: KG6DKN
Peter E Warren
Rt 2 Box 241
Ashland OR 97520

Call Sign: W7PNY
Vernon G Ludwig
20135 Crystal Mountain Ln
Ashland OR 97520

Call Sign: KJ6S
James Brady
1648 Best Ln
Ashland OR 97520

Call Sign: KR2DAK
Dakota T Otto
Hc 84 Box Op13
Ashland OR 97520

Call Sign: KF7IG
Gregory A Skoog
6660 Doncaster Dr
Ashland OR 97520

Call Sign: K7GFE
George R Burrell
1648 Best Ln
Ashland OR 97520

Call Sign: W7CUS
Anthony J Kanclier
9180 Boxwood Ln
Ashland OR 97520

Call Sign: W7ZPE
Robert V Vestal
2 Doral Ln
Ashland OR 97520

Call Sign: KE7LAE
Sean Gordon
2058 Best Ln

Call Sign: W7IXE
Raymond E Hines
66724 Brook Rd

Call Sign: KC7BIQ
R Michael Henry
2242 Doral St

Ashland OR 97520

Ashland OR 97520

Ashland OR 97520

Call Sign: KF7AI
Alvin R Jenkins
255 Douglas Rd
Ashland OR 97520

Call Sign: KD7VZS
Erica M Benoit
1044 Hall
Ashland OR 97520

Call Sign: N6VIM
Richard M Barth
1923 High St SE
Ashland OR 97520

Call Sign: KB7FMO
Aaron W Brown
30811 Ehlen Dr SW
Ashland OR 97520

Call Sign: KA7SQC
William H Marschall
755 Harvard Ave
Ashland OR 97520

Call Sign: KD6MYU
Phillip E King
560 Hillcrest Rd
Ashland OR 97520

Call Sign: KB7YFP
Robert J Ensley
10307 Emily Dr
Ashland OR 97520

Call Sign: KI6MIA
Douglas J Aiken
820 Hass Ln
Ashland OR 97520

Call Sign: KD7LOP
David M Kelly
450 Hunter Ct
Ashland OR 97520

Call Sign: KE7CCP
John R Reynolds
3580 Eola Dr NW
Ashland OR 97520

Call Sign: N8MIA
Douglas J Aiken
2676 Hasting St
Ashland OR 97520

Call Sign: AC7LY
David M Kelly
17324 Hunter Ct
Ashland OR 97520

Call Sign: N7VTM
Joshua S Moulin
1065 Fenwick St
Ashland OR 97520

Call Sign: N3SPY
Douglas J Aiken
3450 Hathaway Ave
Ashland OR 97520

Call Sign: KD7MLP
Ann L Kelly
184 Hunter Hill Ln
Ashland OR 97520

Call Sign: W7MMZ
Michael M Zanoni
92837 Garden Ln
Ashland OR 97520

Call Sign: AE7EQ
James P Kennedy
8360 Helmick Rd
Ashland OR 97520

Call Sign: K7ALK
Ann L Kelly
25117 Hunter Rd
Ashland OR 97520

Call Sign: KE7LAB
Clark Custodio Jr
2104 Gettle St
Ashland OR 97520

Call Sign: KB7CPB
James P Kennedy
11650 Helmick Rd
Ashland OR 97520

Call Sign: W6JFG
Edwin H Russell Jr
16265 Hwy 101 S
Ashland OR 97520

Call Sign: KF7YW
Richard L Trout
69300 Hackamore
Ashland OR 97520

Call Sign: WA1ADK
Stephen C Coffin
3780 Hemlock Pl SE
Ashland OR 97520

Call Sign: AA6NP
Gene C Davies
90071 Hwy 202
Ashland OR 97520

Call Sign: N6HLD
Heidi P Grossman
1582 Hackamore Way

Call Sign: KB7LHM
Charles R Meek
555 Henley Way

Call Sign: KD7DVU
Timothy Rutter
13350 Hwy 66

Ashland OR 97520

Call Sign: N7THT
Gerald L Green
401 Jefferson Scio Dr 14
Ashland OR 97520

Call Sign: KC7CNU
Duane J Ogren
401 Jefferson Scio Dr 65
Ashland OR 97520

Call Sign: KE7CCN
Deborah S Evans
401 Jefferson Scio Rd 17
Ashland OR 97520

Call Sign: KE7KZZ
Justin M Skillman
69 Jefferson St
Ashland OR 97520

Call Sign: KE7KZY
Mark D Skillman
201 Jefferson St
Ashland OR 97520

Call Sign: KE7WTD
Aaron J Maffatt
552 Jefferson St
Ashland OR 97520

Call Sign: KE7CCO
Ronald C Schaaf
5342 Jeffrey Ct N
Ashland OR 97520

Call Sign: KE7CCM
Adam W Hanor
88323 Jenica Way
Ashland OR 97520

Call Sign: KE7CCL
Jennifer R Hanor
22875 Jennie Rd

Ashland OR 97520

Call Sign: NL7UY
Cathleen N Mclaughlin
1558 Jerome Ave
Ashland OR 97520

Call Sign: WA7USX
Michael S Mclaughlin
1786 Jerome Ave Apt B
Ashland OR 97520

Call Sign: KE7CII
Donald A Politis
6901 Jessica Dr
Ashland OR 97520

Call Sign: KE7DAP
Donald A Politis
980 Jev Ct NW
Ashland OR 97520

Call Sign: KD7VTR
Jackson County Health Dept
5275 Joan Dr N
Ashland OR 97520

Call Sign: KD7VTS
Jackson County ARES
Providence Med Ctr
1307 Jodelle Ct N
Ashland OR 97520

Call Sign: KD7VTT
Jackson County ARES
Rogue Val Med Ctr
3798 Joe Ave
Ashland OR 97520

Call Sign: KD7VTU
Jackson County ARES
Ashland Comm Hosp
29790 Joe Day Way
Ashland OR 97520

Call Sign: KD7VTV
Jackson County ARES
Ashland
1660 Joe Wright Rd
Ashland OR 97520

Call Sign: KD7VTW
Jackson County ARES
Medford
1660 Joe Wright Rd
Ashland OR 97520

Call Sign: KD7VTX
Jackson County ARES
Jackson Cnty
1660 Joe Wright Rd
Ashland OR 97520

Call Sign: KD7VTY
Jackson County Back Up
281 Joelson Rd
Ashland OR 97520

Call Sign: K7JAX
Jackson County ARES
1113 John Adams
Ashland OR 97520

Call Sign: KF7KCW
Jackson County ARES
142 John Day St
Ashland OR 97520

Call Sign: KA1PEG
Elena Hynes
1745 John St S
Ashland OR 97520

Call Sign: W7CGO
Charles A Parlier III
656 Juntura Way SE
Ashland OR 97520

Call Sign: KF7UMU
Anne Marie R Smith

28562 Lakeside Dr
Ashland OR 97520

Call Sign: KC7PMR
Herbert E Vasconcelles
87211 Louvring Ln
Ashland OR 97520

Call Sign: KA7VOK
Nathan C Holtey
811 Main St
Ashland OR 97520

Call Sign: KA7VOJ
Jud A Holtey
2114 Main St SE
Ashland OR 97520

Call Sign: N7XPH
Terry J Pettinger
12124 Mallory Dr
Ashland OR 97520

Call Sign: KG6MOB
Ken A Berg
32048 Mally Rd
Ashland OR 97520

Call Sign: KA7COS
Robert T Deuel
2291 Manchester Dr
Ashland OR 97520

Call Sign: K2GLO
Robert T Deuel
1271 Mandarin St NE
Ashland OR 97520

Call Sign: K7RPM
Randy P Miltier
1321 Mandrin St
Ashland OR 97520

Call Sign: N6QHP
Sally Miltier

4060 Mandy Ave SE
Ashland OR 97520

Call Sign: W7MLM
William J Williams Jr
2475 Mangan St
Ashland OR 97520

Call Sign: KF7JWC
John L Griffin
1675 Morgan Ln
Ashland OR 97520

Call Sign: KC7ARV
Darrell E Metcalf
151 N 19th
Ashland OR 97520

Call Sign: KD7SE
Peter D Ingalls
2967 N Bay Dr
Ashland OR 97520

Call Sign: KB7WKV
Jay T Ferguson
65935 N Bay Rd
Ashland OR 97520

Call Sign: KC7FLK
Oren R Edwards
230 NE 100th Ave 10
Ashland OR 97520

Call Sign: KF7QNE
Victoria M Bones
2227 NE 102 Ave
Ashland OR 97520

Call Sign: KB7ONF
Jim A Chamberlain
2227 NE 102 Ave
Ashland OR 97520

Call Sign: KA7PQD
Garrett P Edmands

2833 NE 47th Ave
Ashland OR 97520

Call Sign: KB7IGC
Douglas Hoxmeier
1719 Nut Tree Dr NW
Ashland OR 97520

Call Sign: KE7FNV
Darrell A Barker
1837 NW 156th Ave
Ashland OR 97520

Call Sign: WA7MUY
Gary R Pederson
3755 Old Military Rd
Ashland OR 97520

Call Sign: N7GK
Gary R Pederson
32940 Old Mill Rd
Ashland OR 97520

Call Sign: KF7UMO
Heidi Thomas III
91238 Old Mill Town Rd
Ashland OR 97520

Call Sign: KC7IBE
Oren R Edwards III
4535 Old Stage Rd
Ashland OR 97520

Call Sign: WA6LQL
Fred E Muller
543 Oxyoke Rd
Ashland OR 97520

Call Sign: KF6ZCB
James L Mau
1895 Parkdale Dr
Ashland OR 97520

Call Sign: K6CPM
John W Ames

58708 Pebble Creek Rd
Ashland OR 97520

Call Sign: KF6SUE
Janet Boggia
4628 Peck Dr
Ashland OR 97520

Call Sign: KD7VZP
Richard G Walters
4000 Pheasant Dr
Ashland OR 97520

Call Sign: KA7LYO
Henriette J Picaud
9192 Phey Ln
Ashland OR 97520

Call Sign: K7VM
Charles M Armstrong III
2250 Phillips Rd
Ashland OR 97520

Call Sign: KF7UMZ
Terry S Bateman
1851 Pinedale St
Ashland OR 975209130

Call Sign: W1AYJ
Walter P Hoffman
25712 Powerline Rd
Ashland OR 97520

Call Sign: KD7JQN
Daniel L Champion
34621 Ranch Dr
Ashland OR 97520

Call Sign: KD7EYB
James H Meidl Jr
700 Rayner Ave
Ashland OR 97520

Call Sign: KB6HIZ
Lisa A Bach

4420 Ridge Dr NE
Ashland OR 975203645

Call Sign: K7NNQ
Roger G Christianson
5305 River Rd N 12
Ashland OR 97520

Call Sign: KF7JWB
Katherine L Lehman
5355 River Rd N 17
Ashland OR 97520

Call Sign: KB7KIS
Daniel J Shulters
876 S Comstock
Ashland OR 97520

Call Sign: W6UPG
John C Smith
11125 S Norway Ct
Ashland OR 97520

Call Sign: W7LZG
Robert B Reinholdt
31861 S Shady Dell Rd
Ashland OR 975201643

Call Sign: N6XH
David D Hanna
4301 SE 117th St
Ashland OR 97520

Call Sign: KD7AUC
Donald R Montgomery
1415 Shortridge SE
Ashland OR 97520

Call Sign: WB7Q
Donald R Montgomery
1415 Shortridge SE
Ashland OR 97520

Call Sign: WA7SKM
John D Weisinger

1050 Slate Creek Rd
Ashland OR 97520

Call Sign: W5BGP
John D Weisinger
8600 Sleepy Hollow Rd
Ashland OR 97520

Call Sign: N6BLO
Roy J Levy
3522 Small Ct
Ashland OR 97520

Call Sign: N4YMQ
Bryan S Constable
61228 Small Graffi Rd
Ashland OR 97520

Call Sign: KD7ZYH
Nigel A Knapton
13 Smith Dr
Ashland OR 97520

Call Sign: KB7EEF
Sherita P Weisinger
32932 Smith Rd
Ashland OR 97520

Call Sign: KF6LWA
Seth J Ceteras
14758 Smith Spring Ct
Ashland OR 97520

Call Sign: WL7CTB
Janet L Vidmar
91488 Stallings Ln
Ashland OR 97520

Call Sign: WL7CTC
David J Vidmar
42165 Stanciu Rd
Ashland OR 95720

Call Sign: KD7MLL
Steven R Sutfin

1517 Terrace Dr
Ashland OR 97520

2464 Tynel Ct NE
Ashland OR 97520

460 Wilson Rd
Ashland OR 97520

Call Sign: N7BWG
John F Spiegel
20435 Timberline Ct
Ashland OR 97520

Call Sign: KB7NOB
Dale A Van Cleave
644 Valleywood Dr SE
Ashland OR 97520

Call Sign: AA7HA
Robert A Krevitz
1370 Wilson Rd
Ashland OR 97520

Call Sign: KE7LAA
Lucy J Edwards
920 Tolman Creek Rd
Ashland OR 97520

Call Sign: KB7WIU
Cynthia L Mc Collum
257 W Nevada
Ashland OR 97520

Call Sign: KC7UQG
Launa K Hulse
416 Wimer St
Ashland OR 97520

Call Sign: KE7CIK
Martin A Haas
1257 Tolman Creek Rd
Ashland OR 97520

Call Sign: KD7CNY
Dawn K Varney
108 W Nevada St
Ashland OR 97520

Call Sign: KC7WQM
Lisa K Hulse
416 Wimer St
Ashland OR 97520

Call Sign: KF7DNY
Nathan S Ostovar
1940 Tolman Creek Rd
Ashland OR 97520

Call Sign: W7MBK
L Austin Hegarty
151 W Nevada St
Ashland OR 97520

Call Sign: N7NQQ
Linda R Hulse
416 Wimer St
Ashland OR 97520

Call Sign: KE7WTE
Paul A Collins
1940 Tolman Creek Rd
Ashland OR 97520

Call Sign: KE7SZP
Shannon M Hickman
183 W Nevada St
Ashland OR 97520

Call Sign: WA7YLX
James L Hulse
416 Wimer St
Ashland OR 97520

Call Sign: KD7VZR
James P Lemay
30085 Tolomei Ln
Ashland OR 97520

Call Sign: KJ6SZN
Dallas T Jamme
745 W Pebble Beach Dr
Ashland OR 97520

Call Sign: KF7JWH
Laura N Glasscock
15 Winburn Way 8
Ashland OR 97520

Call Sign: N7NSE
James P Lemay
94409 Tom Cat Hill Rd
Ashland OR 97520

Call Sign: KE7CIG
Diane B Kirkendall
990 Walker Ave
Ashland OR 97520

Call Sign: KF7HGB
Stephen E Parks III
1455 Woodland Dr
Ashland OR 97520

Call Sign: KA7DRH
Charles A White
2030 Tudor Way SE
Ashland OR 97520

Call Sign: KD7TTN
Charles M Dungan
132 Wightman St 1
Ashland OR 97520

Call Sign: KA7KZN
Virgil M Hulse
869 Wrights Cr Dr
Ashland OR 97520

Call Sign: KK7FP
Dennis A Adams

Call Sign: KD7TTO
Daniel A Milan

Call Sign: KB7FMK
Betty Jane Hulse

869 Wrights Cr Dr
Ashland OR 97520

Call Sign: KB7A
David A Rose
Ashland OR 97520

Call Sign: KA7ETV
Karen L Perez
Ashland OR 97520

Call Sign: KC7LMK
Lis D Adams
Ashland OR 97520

Call Sign: KD7CKX
Mary J Ferguson
Ashland OR 97520

Call Sign: KE6MGZ
Geralyn S Winters
Ashland OR 97520

Call Sign: N6LTG
Arnold G Rubenstein
Ashland OR 97520

Call Sign: N7AGX
William M Ostrander
Ashland OR 97520

Call Sign: N7BCR
Richard A Perez
Ashland OR 97520

Call Sign: N7GLG
Douglas P Steinmetz
Ashland OR 97520

Call Sign: W2RYI
David E Seybold
Ashland OR 97520

Call Sign: KD7HMS
John L Johnston

Ashland OR 97520

Call Sign: KD7IBH
Jackie M Johnston
Ashland OR 97520

Call Sign: KF7ARH
Anita R White
Ashland OR 97520

Call Sign: KE7CIH
Charles N Stewart
Ashland OR 97520

Call Sign: KD7VZQ
Daniel E Shaw
Ashland OR 97520

Call Sign: K6KSI
Gerald H Fulstone
Ashland OR 97520

Call Sign: AD7VI
John M Greer
Ashland OR 97520

Call Sign: KD7SPH
Michael M Zanoni
Ashland OR 97520

Call Sign: N6WVX
Sally Fulstone
Ashland OR 975200024

FCC Amateur Radio Licenses in Athena

Call Sign: KA7RSQ
Walter E Veatch
2064 Elmwood Dr S
Athena OR 97813

Call Sign: KF7I
Roland E Wright Sr
1230 Fairview Ave

Athena OR 978130034

Call Sign: N7KMJ
Mike L Bergman
4867 Harlan Dr
Athena OR 97813

Call Sign: K7LW
Lynn Wilson
Athena OR 97813

Call Sign: KB7OMX
Renee S Daniel
Athena OR 97813

Call Sign: N7EG
Alton L Alderman
Athena OR 97813

Call Sign: KA7ZQJ
Elizabeth Wilson
Athena OR 97813

Call Sign: KE7NWB
Roy A Mcgill Sr
Athena OR 97813

Call Sign: KC7YGL
Carl F King
Athena OR 978130743

FCC Amateur Radio Licenses in Azalea

Call Sign: KF6HBL
Robert T Rupp
16067 Blackfeather Ln
Azalea OR 97410

Call Sign: KE7WVC
Anthony R Giegler
1154 Grandview Ave
Azalea OR 97410

Call Sign: KF7QKM

Jasson L Brown
2677 Upper Dr
Azalea OR 97410

Call Sign: KA7AAR
La Don L Snyder
18610 Upper Highland Rd
Azalea OR 97410

Call Sign: N6AHR
Robert L Van Housen
932 Yeust Rd
Azalea OR 97410

Call Sign: N7YS
James R Warren
Azalea OR 97410

Call Sign: W7DZB
James R Warren
Azalea OR 97410

**FCC Amateur Radio
Licenses in Baker City**

Call Sign: N7VYV
Fred E Gray
263 5th St
Baker City OR 97814

Call Sign: KC7PEK
Richard L Hanson
156 5th St Apt 3
Baker City OR 97814

Call Sign: N7TAH
W Glenn Daniel
2655 5th St NE
Baker City OR 97814

Call Sign: K7OID
Gordon E Allen
1445 6th St
Baker City OR 97814

Call Sign: KD7AEH
Andrew M Ballard
649 7th St
Baker City OR 97814

Call Sign: WA6KGY
Rand H Chmara
1715 7th St
Baker City OR 97814

Call Sign: N7JEC
Gary D Higgins
5138 8th Ave NE
Baker City OR 97814

Call Sign: KB6QED
Michael A Hall
2209 8th St
Baker City OR 97814

Call Sign: KE7DUL
Mercy J Ballard
1811 9th St
Baker City OR 97814

Call Sign: KE7DUS
Jason Mc Kinnon
525 A St
Baker City OR 97814

Call Sign: KE7DUQ
Katherine L Kincaid
57551 Alder Creek Rd
Baker City OR 97814

Call Sign: KE7DUT
Michael J Rudi
1860 Alder St Apt 11
Baker City OR 97814

Call Sign: K7MJR
Michael J Rudi
25198 Alderbark St
Baker City OR 97814

Call Sign: KD7CXP
Penny W Rienks
91895 Alderwood Ln
Baker City OR 97814

Call Sign: KE7DUN
Philip A Wilson
918 Archer Ave
Baker City OR 97814

Call Sign: KC7BPQ
Pam L Smith
358 Archie St
Baker City OR 97814

Call Sign: K7DLK
Larry G Lambeth
2623 Arroyo Ridge Dr NW
Baker City OR 97814

Call Sign: NR6X
Leonard R Reitz
1975 Ash St
Baker City OR 97814

Call Sign: KD7IDP
Lana M Chambers
29144 Berlin Rd
Baker City OR 97814

Call Sign: KE7DU
Ernest R Metcalf
767 Berntzen Rd
Baker City OR 97814

Call Sign: KE7FG
Donna Gay Metcalf
14190 Berry Creek Rd
Baker City OR 97814

Call Sign: KB7SSK
Ronald J Stoaks
14190 Berry Creek Rd
Baker City OR 97814

Call Sign: KB7ING
Linda C Tate
181 Beverly Dr
Baker City OR 97814

Call Sign: KB7SRT
Jack A Mc Crain
2575 Campus Dr 442
Baker City OR 97814

Call Sign: KC5DJB
Johnny L Waggoner Sr
1284 Courtney Pl
Baker City OR 97814

Call Sign: N7IJG
Victor L Tate
2670 Beverly Dr
Baker City OR 97814

Call Sign: KC7UL
Harold C Webb
32810 Canaan Rd
Baker City OR 97814

Call Sign: KD7BBW
Jonathan G Hamlin
1659 Danebo Ave
Baker City OR 97814

Call Sign: KB7HQA
Arlyn W Davis
Rt 1 Box 3195
Baker City OR 97814

Call Sign: KC7VDL
Xeno W Cain
6206 Canary Rd
Baker City OR 97814

Call Sign: KC7YGK
Andrew L Marlette
1740 Derby St
Baker City OR 97814

Call Sign: KC7JKS
Mike D Fors
276 Boyer Rd
Baker City OR 97814

Call Sign: KC7PEH
Athena M Street
26482 Cannon
Baker City OR 97814

Call Sign: K7SAS
Robert W Schurman Sr
2251 Dry Creek Rd
Baker City OR 97814

Call Sign: N7ONB
Jack Fors
276 Boyer Rd
Baker City OR 97814

Call Sign: KC7VDK
Gilbert W Carpenter
1236 College Green Dr
Baker City OR 97814

Call Sign: N7HSO
Terry J Robinson
4132 Dry Creek Rd
Baker City OR 97814

Call Sign: KC7PEI
Keri M Myers
1814 Bristol Dr
Baker City OR 97814

Call Sign: KC7AM
Richard E Wilson
3885 Colony Oaks Dr
Baker City OR 97814

Call Sign: KA7MXN
Deloris L Palmer
509 E 7th St
Baker City OR 978147785

Call Sign: N7ONC
Jack Q Myers
2095 Broadview Ave
Baker City OR 97814

Call Sign: KC7FM
Karen J Wilson
1950 Colorado Ln
Baker City OR 97814

Call Sign: KB7SG
William D Palmer
607 E 7th St
Baker City OR 978147785

Call Sign: KB7SSH
Pamela J Tritt
758 Cabana Ln
Baker City OR 97814

Call Sign: W7EIV
Richard W Grove
1950 Colorado Ln
Baker City OR 97814

Call Sign: KE7DUU
Christopher M Galiszewski
31533 Fern Rd
Baker City OR 97814

Call Sign: KB7OKZ
William R Martin
1630 Camino Dr
Baker City OR 97814

Call Sign: KI7XE
Garwood R Allen
204 Court St
Baker City OR 97814

Call Sign: K7NBC
Christopher M Galiszewski
31533 Fern Rd
Baker City OR 97814

Call Sign: W7IXZ
Larry R Wilson
1380 Forestview Dr
Baker City OR 97814

Call Sign: KB7OCP
Diane M Hartman
8650 Hill Rd
Baker City OR 97814

Call Sign: N7DUF
Lester J Hall
84687 Hwy 339
Baker City OR 97814

Call Sign: W7IYA
Nancy E Wilson
42200 Fort Hill Rd
Baker City OR 97814

Call Sign: KB7YTQ
Gregory S Berglund
8650 Hill Rd
Baker City OR 97814

Call Sign: KD7LXY
Shannon L Flores
17782 Hwy 36
Baker City OR 97814

Call Sign: KB7RGX
Camber L Bybee
555 Freeman Rd 171
Baker City OR 97814

Call Sign: KD7EXP
Ronald J Davis
9321 Hill Rd
Baker City OR 97814

Call Sign: KB7TXK
Ronald E Lehman
69084 Hwy 47
Baker City OR 97814

Call Sign: KE7DUP
Gary A Timm
410 Glendening
Baker City OR 97814

Call Sign: KD7EXQ
Anthony Chee
11447 Hill Rd
Baker City OR 97814

Call Sign: KC7JKR
Matthew W Lehr
2847 Indigo Way
Baker City OR 97814

Call Sign: N0ZKB
Allen R D Long
1173 Glengrove Ave
Baker City OR 97814

Call Sign: KD7EXR
Jennie Chee
900 Hill Rd Apt 325
Baker City OR 97814

Call Sign: W6ECX
John A Driscoll
1125 Ingersoll
Baker City OR 97814

Call Sign: KD7MEC
William L Hanley
945 Heather Turn
Baker City OR 97814

Call Sign: KD7IYP
Jonathan S Porach
1655 Hill St SE
Baker City OR 97814

Call Sign: K7BCC
Baker County Office Of
Emergency Management
ARC
101 Irving Rd
Baker City OR 97814

Call Sign: KC7BTI
Cheryl J Webb
888 Highland NE
Baker City OR 97814

Call Sign: KC7JKQ
Charles G Jones
6281 Hwy 20 Sp24
Baker City OR 97814

Call Sign: K7OEM
Baker County Office Of
Emergency Management
ARC
777 Irvington Dr
Baker City OR 97814

Call Sign: KC7IYY
Kirk D Webb
630 Highline Rd
Baker City OR 97814

Call Sign: KA7KBW
Wilma W Hall
61209 Hwy 207
Baker City OR 97814

Call Sign: KE7QWO
Wingville Township ARC
822 Isherwood Dr
Baker City OR 97814

Call Sign: KD7EXS
Jesse S Webb
630 Highline Rd
Baker City OR 97814

Call Sign: KC7YAG
James H Culbertson
22001 Hwy 229
Baker City OR 97814

Call Sign: WT7RC

Wingville Township ARC
923 Island Dr S
Baker City OR 97814

Call Sign: N6UI
Cops Contest Club
43085 Island Inn Dr
Baker City OR 97814

Call Sign: NK6U
Baker County 911
Communications Center A
264 Island Pointe Dr
Baker City OR 97814

Call Sign: KW7J
Gerald W Boyd
264 Island Pointe Dr
Baker City OR 97814

Call Sign: N7WR
Gerald W Boyd
62803 Isthmus Heights Rd
Baker City OR 97814

Call Sign: N7WRJ
Jay Boyd
62803 Isthmus Heights Rd
Baker City OR 97814

Call Sign: KJ7AY
Jay Boyd
63250 Isthmus Heights Rd
Baker City OR 97814

Call Sign: KD7UWQ
Ruth M Boyd
1850 Isthmus Hts Rd
Baker City OR 97814

Call Sign: KR7UTH
Ruth M Boyd
62833 Isthmus Hts Rd
Baker City OR 97814

Call Sign: N7AQH
Ruth M Boyd
4659 Ivory Ct NE
Baker City OR 97814

Call Sign: KB7ZJG
Gary R Vernholm
1846 Johnson Ave
Baker City OR 978141623

Call Sign: KC7AWD
Peggy L Vernholm
1846 Johnson Ave
Baker City OR 978141623

Call Sign: KC7AWC
Charalene V Fennimore
1723 Lytle St
Baker City OR 97814

Call Sign: KC7VDJ
Carl H Dedrick
85610 McDaniels Rd
Baker City OR 97814

Call Sign: K0TZ
Edward H D Kotz
3000 Mossy Ln
Baker City OR 97814

Call Sign: AD7GR
Edward H D Kotz
3010 Mossy Ln
Baker City OR 97814

Call Sign: KC7IZE
Dub Cates
4746 NE 78th Pl
Baker City OR 97814

Call Sign: KD7BBV
Michael S Martin
10336 NE Russell Ct
Baker City OR 97814

Call Sign: KC7EVS
Steven E Feiling
1200 Pacific Ter
Baker City OR 97814

Call Sign: WA7JRH
Robert L Bennett
7298 Park Ter Dr NE
Baker City OR 97814

Call Sign: KC7EGU
Timothy C Rutter
4086 Pfeifer Ct
Baker City OR 97814

Call Sign: KC7QXX
Terry K Fosback
1731 Pheasant Ct
Baker City OR 97814

Call Sign: KE7QC
D Blaine Kenney
93703 Pope Rd
Baker City OR 97814

Call Sign: N7IHH
Faith M Kenney
3553 Poplar
Baker City OR 97814

Call Sign: KD7GXF
Seth M Davis
7592 Pudding Cr Dr SE
Baker City OR 97814

Call Sign: N7VYA
Richard B Tritt
7732 Pudding Creek Dr SE
Baker City OR 97814

Call Sign: W7ABP
James C Longwell
4882 Scenic Dr
Baker City OR 978148118

Call Sign: WB7SOH
Hans P Brunner
3345 SE Wake St
Baker City OR 97814

Call Sign: KE7DUO
Corinna K Jacobs
7336 Snow Peak Way SE
Baker City OR 97814

Call Sign: WA7EZY
Harold R Badger Jr
1309 Springbrook Rd
Baker City OR 97814

Call Sign: KC7SRM
Edra A Dangerfield
2340 Springbrook Rd
Baker City OR 97814

Call Sign: KB7HDQ
Keith E Dangerfield
3112 Springbrook Rd
Baker City OR 97814

Call Sign: KC7TYQ
Gary G Williams
3204 Springbrook Rd
Baker City OR 97814

Call Sign: KC7PEG
Joe D Street
280 St Helens St
Baker City OR 97814

Call Sign: N7JDV
Jerry D Nickell
92748 Sunrise Dr
Baker City OR 97814

Call Sign: N7IMT
Del Terry
21273 Thomas Creek Rd
Baker City OR 97814

Call Sign: KD7EXM
Calvin M Henshaw
2460 Valley Ave
Baker City OR 97814

Call Sign: KD7EXO
Deborah L Henshaw
2460 Valley Ave
Baker City OR 97814

Call Sign: N7DLH
Deborah L Henshaw
2460 Valley Ave
Baker City OR 97814

Call Sign: KD7IDO
Robert M Henshaw
3343 Valley Crest Way
Baker City OR 97814

Call Sign: N7CMH
Calvin M Henshaw
2140 Valley Ct
Baker City OR 97814

Call Sign: KC7ZVY
Wanda G Ballard
18850 W Campbell Loop
Baker City OR 97814

Call Sign: KC7ZVZ
De Forest M Ballard
18850 W Campbell Loop
Baker City OR 97814

Call Sign: KE7ZSG
Jason C Bybee
3065 Walnut
Baker City OR 97814

Call Sign: KC7PEJ
Eris S Merritt
1100 Washington
Baker City OR 97814

Call Sign: KD7DYT
Justin D Merritt
1100 Washington
Baker City OR 97814

Call Sign: KK7OF
Donald R Merritt
1100 Washington
Baker City OR 97814

Call Sign: KE7WZF
Toni B Myers
46996 Wirth Rd
Baker City OR 97814

Call Sign: W7SMF
Toni B Myers
46996 Wirth Rd
Baker City OR 97814

Call Sign: NK7J
Jack Q Myers
46996 Wirth Rd
Baker City OR 97814

Call Sign: KC7BPP
Kathy A Moudy
Baker City OR 97814

Call Sign: KB7VFU
Dorothy A Ferguson
Baker City OR 97814

Call Sign: K7JR
Snake River Contest Club
Baker City OR 97814

Call Sign: KA7LTO
Kim W Lethlean
Baker City OR 97814

Call Sign: KB7SRV
Steve L Moudy
Baker City OR 97814

Call Sign: KC7IZA
Kenneth P Spence
Baker City OR 97814

Call Sign: KC7IZD
Daniel P Marshall
Baker City OR 97814

Call Sign: N7PAV
Sharon A Rudi
Baker City OR 97814

Call Sign: N7VVH
Marilee J Wellersdick
Baker City OR 97814

Call Sign: NK7U
Joseph O Rudi
Baker City OR 97814

Call Sign: W7NYW
Eastern Oregon Amateur
Radio Soc
Baker City OR 97814

Call Sign: KD7HUP
Kazue R Marlette
Baker City OR 97814

Call Sign: KD7MEE
Brandon C Marshall
Baker City OR 97814

Call Sign: KF7UPB
Tony J Yost
Baker City OR 97814

Call Sign: KE7NWC
William D Quigley
Baker City OR 978140845

**FCC Amateur Radio
Licenses in Bandon**

Call Sign: N7ERV

Jerry L Davinroy
2265 12th St
Bandon OR 97411

Call Sign: KD7EZO
Thomas A Ryan
1930 29th St
Bandon OR 97411

Call Sign: KD7JLC
Matt D Eadie
1015 54th St
Bandon OR 97411

Call Sign: WA6TUY
Joseph W Layfield
238 5th St
Bandon OR 97411

Call Sign: K6MMQ
Clifford A Lint
2655 5th St NE
Bandon OR 97411

Call Sign: KF6TLP
Anita Straus
204 6th St
Bandon OR 97411

Call Sign: N6AEN
Joseph E Mc Kay
777 Agee Dr
Bandon OR 97411

Call Sign: WB7OVF
Robert P Gerken
91895 Alderwood Ln
Bandon OR 97411

Call Sign: KE7HOA
David C Nazer
1594 Angelcrest Dr
Bandon OR 97411

Call Sign: K7NNJ

William K Emmons
16060 Antioch Rd
Bandon OR 97411

Call Sign: KF7HWT
Herbert C Karlebach
20750 Antioch Rd
Bandon OR 97411

Call Sign: W7FNZ
Leo W Marsh
20750 Antioch Rd
Bandon OR 97411

Call Sign: KC7PVS
Jeffrey H Stitt
2305 C Ashland St 203
Bandon OR 97411

Call Sign: W7UHN
John L Gamble
2130 Boes Ave
Bandon OR 974119616

Call Sign: N7JGL
David A Weston
1565 Bogart Ln
Bandon OR 97411

Call Sign: KB2VIY
Phillip R Callison
Rt 1 Box 234
Bandon OR 97411

Call Sign: KC6YLB
Grant A Prescott
Rt 2 Box 2357
Bandon OR 97411

Call Sign: KD6WDF
Charles F Wales
63389 Brightwater Dr
Bandon OR 97411

Call Sign: W3VHE

Charles H Norman
61135 Cabin Ln
Bandon OR 974119220

Call Sign: KB6PCC
Terry L Kozak
2010 Calderwood Dr
Bandon OR 97411

Call Sign: KC7JNO
Curtis J Mc Kinney
277 Calico St NE
Bandon OR 97411

Call Sign: N7NYY
John W Van Natter
4121 Camellia St
Bandon OR 97411

Call Sign: N6PUO
Gregory H Sparacino
86664 Croft Lake Ln
Bandon OR 974119333

Call Sign: KE7SAF
John C Lee Thiem
3783 Dorchester
Bandon OR 97411

Call Sign: KB0VAX
Dallas G Nicholson
25 E Cedar St
Bandon OR 97411

Call Sign: KE7RZX
Eugene N Fitch Jr
610 E Sunset Dr
Bandon OR 97411

Call Sign: KD7KTS
Robert B Sturtevant
2290 Gibson Woods Ct NW
Bandon OR 97411

Call Sign: N7YYG

Jeri L Bissell
3464 Grand Ave
Bandon OR 97411

Call Sign: W7WVF
Glenn D Bissell
3204 Grand Ave
Bandon OR 97411

Call Sign: KA7AGV
Lawrence F Baker
605 Grant St
Bandon OR 97411

Call Sign: K7LFB
Lawrence F Baker
2433 Grant St
Bandon OR 97411

Call Sign: KE7HDS
Dan B Long
14452 Hunt Mountain Ln
Bandon OR 97411

Call Sign: KE7HKD
Jacqueline G Haggerty
5640 Imai Rd
Bandon OR 97411

Call Sign: KF7GVN
Dorothy J Tharsing
15994 Keasey Rd
Bandon OR 97411

Call Sign: KF7GVO
Phileta E Riley
41320 Keel Mountain Dr
Bandon OR 97411

Call Sign: W6SQN
Leon H Crouch Sr
6626 McLeod Ln NE
Bandon OR 97411

Call Sign: KE7ZIJ

Coos Curry Contest Club
768 N Baker Dr
Bandon OR 97411

Call Sign: KO7OS
Coos Curry Contest Club
768 N Baker Dr
Bandon OR 97411

Call Sign: K7MI
Larry E Gillespie Jr
2525 N Baker Dr
Bandon OR 97411

Call Sign: N7GAP
Grant A Prescott
1685 NW 130th
Bandon OR 97411

Call Sign: N7ZAQ
Carlene Scorby
930 NW 161st Ter
Bandon OR 97411

Call Sign: N7ZAR
Gary D Scorby
6035 NW 163rd Pl
Bandon OR 97411

Call Sign: W7MXQ
Rodney W Junge
6704 Pierce Ct N
Bandon OR 97411

Call Sign: KC7YRU
Ann F Sandstrom
6865 Pierce Dr N
Bandon OR 97411

Call Sign: KD7WPH
Peter L Larsen
403A Red Blanket Rd
Bandon OR 97411

Call Sign: K7BAA

Peter L Larsen
3687 Red Cedar Way
Bandon OR 97411

Call Sign: WA6OWT
John D Kight
59 S 6th St
Bandon OR 97411

Call Sign: KC6BSU
Todd J Adelman
24165 S Brockway Rd
Bandon OR 97411

Call Sign: KD6DEV
Nancy I Adelman
24165 S Brockway Rd
Bandon OR 97411

Call Sign: KD7QPO
Randall L Caccamise
9254 Shaw Square Rd SE
Bandon OR 97411

Call Sign: N7OJJ
Lisa J De Salvio
7180 Shawn Ct
Bandon OR 97411

Call Sign: W7ALN
Alan A Cooper
7180 Shawn Ct
Bandon OR 974117373

Call Sign: KA7KAJ
Jacquie Cooper
3546 Shawna Dr
Bandon OR 974117373

Call Sign: KB7IDA
Michael S Fitzgerald
38386 Shelburn Dr
Bandon OR 97411

Call Sign: W7MIK

Michael S Fitzgerald
34 Sheldon Ave
Bandon OR 97411

Call Sign: KC6VLQ
Sharon L Killough
2012 Stringer Gap Rd
Bandon OR 97411

Call Sign: N6YRP
Ronald E Killough
2310 Stringer Gap Rd
Bandon OR 974117222

Call Sign: KC7ZRC
Ira J Chase
450 Stringer Rd
Bandon OR 97411

Call Sign: KF6TIH
Catherine C Schneider
1130 Tolman Creek
Bandon OR 97411

Call Sign: KE7ADB
David B Fedukowski
3272 Top View Ct
Bandon OR 97411

Call Sign: N2LR
Leonard Rosen
4664 Tragen Ct SE
Bandon OR 97411

Call Sign: N0FB
Jeffrey W Cook
513 Tryon Ave NE
Bandon OR 97411

Call Sign: N6ADK
David R Allen
2640 Whale Watch Way
Bandon OR 97411

Call Sign: KO7W

Jon K Schmit
88836 Whiskey Run Ln
Bandon OR 97411

Call Sign: K7CES
Caroline E Schmit
88836 Whiskey Run Ln
Bandon OR 97411

Call Sign: KB7DNM
Robert W Davison
Bandon OR 97411

Call Sign: W7HZU
Allan B Evans
Bandon OR 97411

Call Sign: AK7A
Guy D Lalic
Bandon OR 97411

Call Sign: W7OKM
William O Ellis
Bandon OR 97411

Call Sign: KB7BYU
John H Kidby
Bandon OR 97411

Call Sign: KB7NIS
James A Meler Sr
Bandon OR 97411

Call Sign: KC7FZJ
Allene J Kidby
Bandon OR 97411

Call Sign: KC7UWS
Michael S Nelson
Bandon OR 97411

Call Sign: KE6LNT
Kathleen R Mac Donald
Bandon OR 97411

Call Sign: N7FDK
Gerald E Sullivan
Bandon OR 97411

Call Sign: N7OKM
Hugh G Mac Donald
Bandon OR 97411

Call Sign: W7CN
Carl L Sandstrom Jr
Bandon OR 97411

Call Sign: KD7JQF
Gary C Matlock
Bandon OR 97411

Call Sign: AC7XF
Hugh G Mac Donald
Bandon OR 97411

Call Sign: KE7SAB
James Giambrone Jr
Bandon OR 97411

Call Sign: KF7RSF
Thomas W Noel
Bandon OR 97411

Call Sign: WB7EZI
Fairylee Dedrickson
Bandon OR 974110115

Call Sign: KC6JXJ
Kathleen J Mc Dowell
Bandon OR 974110273

Call Sign: KK6WF
James A Mc Dowell
Bandon OR 974110273

FCC Amateur Radio Licenses in Beatty

Call Sign: K6RIO
Todd C Secoy

804 Jacquelyn St
Beatty OR 97621

Call Sign: K6OBA
Ann E Secoy
19705 Jade Ct
Beatty OR 97621

Call Sign: KF7KBV
Beverly S Mallams
Beatty OR 97621

FCC Amateur Radio Licenses in Bend

Call Sign: KF7BW
Gregory H Miller
1714 12th Ave SE
Bend OR 977013854

Call Sign: KD7EQR
Jacqueline A Rex
1179 3rd St NW
Bend OR 97701

Call Sign: N7RGD
Mary A Winter
331 40th St
Bend OR 97701

Call Sign: N6KPZ
Edwin J Spalinger
1422 47th Ave
Bend OR 97702

Call Sign: KD7WPM
Anita Jaquat Bryant
3386 48th Ave NE
Bend OR 97702

Call Sign: KE7TPQ
Arleigh D Mooney
1107 4th St
Bend OR 97701

Call Sign: KD7PQU
Scott D Parsons
5345 Addison Dr S
Bend OR 97701

Call Sign: N7CLD
Scott D Parsons
61475 Admiral Way
Bend OR 97701

Call Sign: KD7FXL
Jennifer S Banning
5025 Alder Dr
Bend OR 97701

Call Sign: KB7ZDO
Keith W Banning
84326 Alder Dr
Bend OR 97701

Call Sign: KE7GYB
John P Cherry
92595 Applegate Trl
Bend OR 97701

Call Sign: K7VSC
Robert E Starkie
501 Aqua Vista Dr
Bend OR 977018948

Call Sign: KE6GIZ
Marilyn G Schreiner
2110 Aries Ln
Bend OR 97701

Call Sign: KF7TFB
Pilae Davami
1500 Ash St
Bend OR 97701

Call Sign: N7VMB
Edward F Caulfield
462 Azalea Glen Rd
Bend OR 97702

Call Sign: KD7AUW
Joseph D Beery
21093 Azalia Ave
Bend OR 97702

Call Sign: N7QMM
Michael D Stenkamp
955 Bennett Creek Rd
Bend OR 97702

Call Sign: N7VMC
Judith M Leach
13542 Bonney Rd NE
Bend OR 97702

Call Sign: KF7TGC
Taylor L Shoupe
214 B St
Bend OR 97702

Call Sign: W6AYO
Grover P Fike
446 Blackfoot Ave
Bend OR 97702

Call Sign: KF7TGD
Jonathan L Dodge
724 Border St
Bend OR 97701

Call Sign: N6GC
Bruce R Wesley
855 B St
Bend OR 977027919

Call Sign: N7IFC
Bill L Peterson
35633 Blakesley Creek Rd
Bend OR 97701

Call Sign: N7VYU
Kevin D Creech
Rt 1 Box 319
Bend OR 97701

Call Sign: N7RFP
Albert F Debons
590 Baltimore
Bend OR 97701

Call Sign: N7FIN
Rodney G Engeman
1700 Blankenship Rd
Bend OR 97701

Call Sign: KJ7XZ
Victor G Hallin
Rt 1 Box 378
Bend OR 977018109

Call Sign: KD7LVL
Ed Van Hatten
91346 Barklow Ln
Bend OR 97701

Call Sign: KE7OHF
Christine K Teicheira
7716 Blinkhorn Way
Bend OR 97702

Call Sign: KB7LNR
Gerald L Kenyon
Rt 2 Box 378B
Bend OR 97701

Call Sign: N9LPZ
Dwayne R Sohn
32255 Baxter Rd
Bend OR 97702

Call Sign: KE7OHH
Todd B Teicheira
185 Blodgett Rd
Bend OR 97702

Call Sign: KC7UJD
Cindy J Kenyon
Rt 3 Box 379
Bend OR 97701

Call Sign: KD7PDC
David J Neys
32614 Baxter Rd
Bend OR 97702

Call Sign: KD7BHY
Hector R Guevara
14718 Bluegrass Lp
Bend OR 97702

Call Sign: KD7AKM
Brian C Banker
Rt 2 Box 396
Bend OR 97701

Call Sign: KC7FTR
Shirley J Livingston
20070 Beaver Ln
Bend OR 97702

Call Sign: KB7SID
Kenneth D Paplinski
2911 Bluegrass Way
Bend OR 97702

Call Sign: KF6CSE
Justin D Kenney
390 Boyer Rd
Bend OR 977022652

Call Sign: KC7FYV
John W Livingston
20079 Beaver Ln
Bend OR 97702

Call Sign: KB7W
Michael V Bond
1565 Bogart Ln
Bend OR 977029644

Call Sign: W0GLT
Gerald L Thye
20572 Brightenwood Ln
Bend OR 977072560

Call Sign: K7BH
Bruce D Hoisington
417 Brimstone Rd
Bend OR 97702

Call Sign: KE7NHC
Lyman H Potts
5718 Casa Way
Bend OR 97702

Call Sign: KB7SHY
Robin R Bugge
1325 Center St SE
Bend OR 97702

Call Sign: N7UAF
Lee Ann Hoisington
4220 Bristol Ave
Bend OR 97702

Call Sign: KE7NGZ
Teresa G Potts
5718 Casa Way
Bend OR 97702

Call Sign: KE7LDH
Karen L Poulsen
9635 Chance Rd
Bend OR 97701

Call Sign: K7RQZ
Alice M Mc Cullough
444 Browning Ave SE
Bend OR 97702

Call Sign: KE7BHU
Rebecca M Hoshi
750 Cascade Ave 311
Bend OR 97701

Call Sign: KE7LDI
Ole D Poulsen
9635 Chance Rd
Bend OR 97701

Call Sign: KF6JMQ
Donald L Trask
61089 Buckshot Pl
Bend OR 977022990

Call Sign: KE7BHK
Vanessa D Julian
8475 Cason Ln
Bend OR 97701

Call Sign: KC7RQM
Nelvin H Vinluan
19409 Cherokee Rd
Bend OR 97701

Call Sign: KA6JPQ
Martee Avalier
11660 Butte Falls Hwy
Bend OR 97701

Call Sign: K7JPI
Betty L Swanzy
2646 Cedar Flat Rd
Bend OR 97702

Call Sign: KC7EPQ
Ralph M Mabee III
1131 Chestnut Ave A
Bend OR 97702

Call Sign: KC7YRL
Ian Crowe
16826 Butteville Rd
Bend OR 97701

Call Sign: KB7WTU
David R Williams
3600 Cedar Flat Rd
Bend OR 97702

Call Sign: K7TWR
Ralph M Mabee III
1080 Chestnut St NW
Bend OR 97702

Call Sign: KC7AMX
Frederick J Crowe
16826 Butteville Rd NE
Bend OR 97701

Call Sign: KC7RIB
Derek B Slinchak
23471 Cedar Grove Rd
Bend OR 97702

Call Sign: KF7FPA
Christopher M Swofford
33470 Chinook Pl 115
Bend OR 97702

Call Sign: K6DSX
Aubrey F Blake
31200 Canter Ln
Bend OR 97701

Call Sign: N7RUS
Lee K Halout
23471 Cedar Grove Rd
Bend OR 97702

Call Sign: N7QKR
Philip J Hodapp
925 Clark St
Bend OR 97702

Call Sign: KD7FUG
Norma E Dannenbring
31200 Canter Ln
Bend OR 977018215

Call Sign: KC7PYY
Charles F Ksenzulak
4155 Center St NE
Bend OR 97702

Call Sign: KD7HXK
Donald R Shaffer
84420 Cloverdale Rd
Bend OR 97701

Call Sign: W7DRS
Donald R Shaffer
2351 Cloverlawn Dr
Bend OR 97701

Call Sign: WB7PWB
Carolyn K Miller
2233 Country Club Terr
Bend OR 97702

Call Sign: K7VRK
Richard M Baird
90228 Deadwood Creek Rd
Bend OR 97701

Call Sign: K7DBW
Albert D Dunham
4291 Colver Rd
Bend OR 97701

Call Sign: KC7PYK
Christopher M Bowe
873 Country Commons
Bend OR 97702

Call Sign: WA7ND
Richard Conners
89346 Dellmoore Lp
Bend OR 97701

Call Sign: KB7JCL
Charles L Chamberlain
29901 Colvin St
Bend OR 97701

Call Sign: KD7ZWW
Robert E Starkie
21655 Crateer Lake Hwy
Bend OR 97702

Call Sign: W7UND
R Richard Conners IV
2426 Dellwood Ave
Bend OR 97701

Call Sign: KE7NRN
Charles W Stahn
29901 Colvin St
Bend OR 97701

Call Sign: KE6GOQ
Bonnie J Fevergeon
2630 Cresta De Ruta
Bend OR 97702

Call Sign: KF7TGE
James H Powell
400 Detrick Dr
Bend OR 97702

Call Sign: KD7AUV
Dennis J Lusby
1001 Cornutt St
Bend OR 97702

Call Sign: KD6WWK
Darrell A Fevergeon
2630 Cresta De Ruta
Bend OR 97702

Call Sign: NB7E
Grant R Heise
33470 Dever Conner Rd
Bend OR 97702

Call Sign: KE7BHO
Kathleen I Alexander
1001 Cornutt St
Bend OR 97702

Call Sign: KC7PYX
Randle A Le Roy
3554 Crooker Finger Rd
Bend OR 977019054

Call Sign: KD7EQN
James P Hutchison
2019 Doral
Bend OR 97701

Call Sign: KC7RID
James L Mc Neil
148 Country Club Ln
Bend OR 97702

Call Sign: WB6CSV
Jeffrey C Barlow
5098 Cultus Ave SE
Bend OR 97701

Call Sign: KD7VKH
Peter C O Reilly
19098 Double Eagle Rd
Bend OR 97701

Call Sign: W6HSY
James P Allan
1590 Country Club Rd
Bend OR 97702

Call Sign: WB6WWF
John R Rudolph
60475 Dakota Trl
Bend OR 97701

Call Sign: KB7BNP
George M Mc Neil
3190 Douglas Cir
Bend OR 97702

Call Sign: KE7ACY
Jeffery H Moore
2230 Country Club Rd
Bend OR 97702

Call Sign: KE7MYE
Lori L Osburn
712 Deadly Crossing Rd
Bend OR 97701

Call Sign: KA9LWO
Jess W Sager
4115 Dove Ln
Bend OR 97702

Call Sign: N7DDA
Duane D Anderson
1786 Duke Ct
Bend OR 977017747

Call Sign: KE7TMU
Andrew W Johnson
5027 Dumore Dr SE
Bend OR 97702

Call Sign: KE7TMV
Laura L Johnson
5577 Dumore Dr SE
Bend OR 97702

Call Sign: NW7E
Michael E Kroh
3435 Duncan Ave NE
Bend OR 97701

Call Sign: KE7KRZ
Howard M Day Jr
1109 E 31st
Bend OR 97701

Call Sign: WB0DVS
Donald O Shurtleff Jr
1109 E 31st
Bend OR 97701

Call Sign: WB6EVQ
Ronnie W Schlitzkus
405 E 4th St
Bend OR 97701

Call Sign: KD7OIK
Terry J Bird
633 E Archwood 98
Bend OR 97701

Call Sign: KI7PW
O Ed Folland
565 E Fairfield St
Bend OR 97701

Call Sign: KC7RIF
Arnold F Powelson
805 E Gerone St
Bend OR 97702

Call Sign: N7RGB
William M Johnson
54120 E Marmot Rd
Bend OR 97702

Call Sign: KF7BFM
Christopher R Kronberg
305 E St 4
Bend OR 97701

Call Sign: KD7DQA
Ricky J Land
2924 Elysium Ave
Bend OR 977029641

Call Sign: KC7RIE
Kenneth J Hanson
2456 Essex Ln
Bend OR 97701

Call Sign: KC6ZHM
Francis E Wissler
850 Fairview Ave SE Apt 1
Bend OR 97701

Call Sign: KD7ILS
Matthew A Swanson
3926 Fairview Dr
Bend OR 97701

Call Sign: KD7ILX
John S Swanson
54672 Fairview Rd
Bend OR 97701

Call Sign: KC7LPW
Susan H Robertson
15016 Fern Ridge Rd SE
Bend OR 97701

Call Sign: KF7NGA
James M Kessel
29374 Ferncrest Rd
Bend OR 97701

Call Sign: N7XCT
Michael A Grigsby
4703 Fir Dell Dr SE
Bend OR 97707

Call Sign: WD6FXR
Lawrence M Sutter
16880 Fir Dr
Bend OR 97707

Call Sign: KE7DDD
Angelo C Micheletti
752 Florence Ave
Bend OR 97702

Call Sign: N7PTC
Angelo C Micheletti
161 Florentine Ave
Bend OR 97702

Call Sign: K7ZSS
Angelo C Micheletti
177 Florentine Ave
Bend OR 97702

Call Sign: WA7OR
Angelo C Micheletti
877 Florida St
Bend OR 97702

Call Sign: KA7EMG
Fred G Heise
320 Forest Ct
Bend OR 97701

Call Sign: KA7ENX
Maxine D Heise
3258 Forest Gale Dr
Bend OR 97701

Call Sign: KB7SHX
Richard S Wyman III
4531 Franklin Blvd Sp 46
Bend OR 97701

Call Sign: KF4VFM
Isaac W Testerman
1755 Garfield St
Bend OR 99702

Call Sign: N7LE
Central Oregon Dx Club
7917 Gearhart St
Bend OR 97702

Call Sign: KE7KKF
Central Oregon Dx Club
3624 Geary St
Bend OR 97702

Call Sign: NE6LE
Central Oregon Dx Club
1960 Geary St SE
Bend OR 97702

Call Sign: N7XU
Bend Cw Contesters
3713 Geary St SE
Bend OR 97702

Call Sign: K4XU
Richard B Frey
3713 Geary St SE
Bend OR 97702

Call Sign: KD7JOE
Bend Cw Contesters
3812 Geary St SE
Bend OR 97702

Call Sign: W7ESU
Bend Cw Contesters
2186 Geary St SE 4
Bend OR 97702

Call Sign: N6GAN
Stephan A White
871 Glengary Loop
Bend OR 97701

Call Sign: N6ZZX
David W Peters
39716 Grove Ln
Bend OR 97702

Call Sign: KD7JXF
Steven D Westberg
248 Gunnell Rd
Bend OR 97701

Call Sign: N7YDK
Charles E Rhodes
79400 Hamlet Rd
Bend OR 97707

Call Sign: N0JWC
Charles R Anderson
2133 Harrison Ave
Bend OR 97701

Call Sign: KC7ANA
Elva M Watson
1755 Hart St
Bend OR 97701

Call Sign: WA3YXW
Stephanie K Morton
945 Helen Ln
Bend OR 97702

Call Sign: KD7AKH
Timothy A Beuschlein
1501 Hess Creek Ct
Bend OR 97702

Call Sign: WB9JOY
Pamela J Beyer
6761 Hess Rd
Bend OR 97702

Call Sign: WB9UTZ
Russell J Sykes
6761 Hess Rd
Bend OR 977022856

Call Sign: N6OMQ
Mike A Lichter
24155 Hewett Rd
Bend OR 97702

Call Sign: KF6DLI
Phyllis D Van Etten
104 High St
Bend OR 977019705

Call Sign: KF6BPV
David A Van Etten
204 High St
Bend OR 97701

Call Sign: KE7JXD
Kris W Hakkila
30301 Hillside Ter
Bend OR 97702

Call Sign: KC7MBA
Steve Hehn
90947 Hollywood Ln
Bend OR 97701

Call Sign: KC7MBB
Mary Sue Hehn
90947 Hollywood Ln
Bend OR 97701

Call Sign: KF6NR
Eugene G Lauziere
90947 Hollywood Ln
Bend OR 97701

Call Sign: KF6HDO
Steve T Smith
90947 Hollywood Ln
Bend OR 97701

Call Sign: N7LXT
Leroy A Daniels
2426 Hwy 101 N
Bend OR 97707

Call Sign: W7RMM
Donald A Svinth
22640 Ilafern Ln
Bend OR 97701

Call Sign: WX7DS
Donald A Svinth
1617 Iler St S
Bend OR 97701

Call Sign: KE7DRO
Joan L Wheeler
704 J St
Bend OR 97707

Call Sign: KE7CLU
William A Wheeler
1917 J St
Bend OR 97707

Call Sign: KD7RMP
Eric Kozowski
19725 Jade Ct
Bend OR 97701

Call Sign: K7LLC
William C Hall
19725 Jade Ct
Bend OR 97701

Call Sign: KF7PPN
David W Boyd
305 Jade St
Bend OR 977019121

Call Sign: N7RFN
Laurence R Beach
67866 Jones Rd
Bend OR 97702

Call Sign: KA7QQA
Stanley C Patrick
13080 Keasey Rd
Bend OR 97707

Call Sign: N7RDN
James J Sellers
1986 Kelly Way
Bend OR 97702

Call Sign: K7TEM
James N Weaver
17790 Kelok Rd
Bend OR 97702

Call Sign: W7AAL
James N Weaver
17790 Kelok Rd
Bend OR 97702

Call Sign: KA6EZL
Robert L Rhodes Jr
17790 Kelok Rd
Bend OR 97702

Call Sign: K7PSA
Robert L Rhodes Jr
770 Kelowna St
Bend OR 97702

Call Sign: KV7H
Bernard W Schnippert
576 Kent Cr Rd
Bend OR 97701

Call Sign: KE7LLN
James A Givens
5521 King Arthur Ct
Bend OR 97701

Call Sign: AD7MM
James A Givens
16035 King Charles Ave
Bend OR 97701

Call Sign: KJ7F
James A Givens
20922 King David Ave
Bend OR 97701

Call Sign: KF7KBR
Evan E Elbek
1229 Kokanee Ln
Bend OR 97701

Call Sign: KE7BHR
Kate C Beardsley
1332 Kokanee Ln
Bend OR 97701

Call Sign: WA7IUF
Kefton O Black
408 L Ave
Bend OR 977019177

Call Sign: KF7NKK
Joseph W Black
1814 L St Apt 6
Bend OR 97701

Call Sign: KB7WTQ
Raymond G Hildenbrand
4689 Lariat Ct NE
Bend OR 97701

Call Sign: KE7JST
Gary Dolezal
2634 Laurel Hill Dr
Bend OR 97702

Call Sign: K7WTT
Gary Dolezal
916 Laurel Ln
Bend OR 97702

Call Sign: KE7BHL
Susan M Dolezal
758 Laurel Pl
Bend OR 97702

Call Sign: KK7SMD
Susan M Dolezal
758 Laurel Pl
Bend OR 97702

Call Sign: K7PDL
Susan M Dolezal
1861 Laurel Rd
Bend OR 97702

Call Sign: N7ZTE
Lyle F Newman
890 Leigh St
Bend OR 97702

Call Sign: W6ABC
Robert J Lewalski
612 Lexington Ave
Bend OR 97702

Call Sign: WA6ESO
Jack D Martin
1515 Liberty St NE
Bend OR 97702

Call Sign: N7ASO
Clarence H Gilpin
441 Logus St
Bend OR 97701

Call Sign: KE7NRP
Shelly K Smith
9081 Lower River Rd
Bend OR 97701

Call Sign: WA8TRZ
Robert L Hamilton
4638 Maplewood Ct
Bend OR 97701

Call Sign: K7OUP
Robert L Hamilton
2878 Maranta St
Bend OR 97701

Call Sign: WB7TYM
Robert E Hall
1742 Marigold St NE
Bend OR 97702

Call Sign: KD7SMC
Donald W Mercer
200 Market St Sp 274
Bend OR 977072707

Call Sign: WA7ITJ
Richard B Hoffmann
5420 Maryland St
Bend OR 97701

Call Sign: KF7ELX
Brian M Vaughan
44990 McKenzie Hwy
Bend OR 97701

Call Sign: KF7MAX
Brian M Vaughan
52667 McKenzie Hwy
Bend OR 97701

Call Sign: AA5TL
Richard Maxey Jr
605 Meadow Ave
Bend OR 97702

Call Sign: KA5ZLQ
Jacqueline J Maxey
605 Meadow Ave
Bend OR 97702

Call Sign: KE7JXB
Raymond P Mcgrath
33408 Medlik Dr
Bend OR 97701

Call Sign: KA7EQR
Eva L Anderson
207 Melrose Ter Ln
Bend OR 97701

Call Sign: KA7EQS
Del R Anderson
155 Melvin Ave
Bend OR 97701

Call Sign: WB7PAD
Joseph K Sheldon
39125 Military Rd
Bend OR 97701

Call Sign: WB7PBS
Virginia R Sheldon
7853 Mill Creek Ct SE
Bend OR 97701

Call Sign: KE7JXC
Sally Deitchler
2480 Mill Creek Dr
Bend OR 97701

Call Sign: KB7QCF
Keith W Harless
909 Millview St
Bend OR 97701

Call Sign: W8KED
Glenn R Hayes
830 Mimosa St S
Bend OR 97701

Call Sign: KJ7LY
Wolfgang C Geihe
18418 Mineral Springs Rd
NE
Bend OR 97701

Call Sign: W6JY
Wolfgang C Geihe
215 Miners Way
Bend OR 97701

Call Sign: WA7IGB
Robert C Foote
986 Moneda Ave N
Bend OR 97701

Call Sign: KB5ZVR
Christopher D Rankin
16500 Mt Angel Scotts
Mills Rd NE
Bend OR 97707

Call Sign: KD7ZUU
Scott B Robbins
724 Mt Pitt St
Bend OR 97702

Call Sign: K9FTR
Scott B Robbins
33901 Mt Tom Dr
Bend OR 97702

Call Sign: KE7BHS
Gary W Winter
5085 Mtn Crest Way
Bend OR 97702

Call Sign: KE7CQO
Lisa C Robbins
5085 Mtn Crest Way S
Bend OR 97702

Call Sign: KC7IOU
Raye M Johnson
315 Mtn View Blvd
Bend OR 977029004

Call Sign: KE5CC
Jack L Johnson
2200 Mtn View Ct
Bend OR 97702

Call Sign: KC7PYN
Don R Gamble
1078 N 20th
Bend OR 97702

Call Sign: N7KHV
Roy D Johnson
424 N 3rd St

Bend OR 97702

Call Sign: KE7AB
Roy D Cook
228 N 7th St
Bend OR 977019537

Call Sign: KD7WRT
David D Terreri
90811 N Bank Ln
Bend OR 97701

Call Sign: KB7HAH
Eric D Freed
6225 N Coast Hwy 101
Bend OR 97701

Call Sign: N7NJI
Tim C Bass
2115 N Danebo Ave
Bend OR 97701

Call Sign: KB7JEM
Michael J Leno
3355 N Delta Hwy 52
Bend OR 97702

Call Sign: KC7LPV
John E Green
1900 N Interstate Ave Bldg
355
Bend OR 97701

Call Sign: KC7OTK
Emma Nadine Green
11642 N Island Cove
Bend OR 97701

Call Sign: N1TCB
Tim C Bass
230 N Lotus Isle Dr
Bend OR 97701

Call Sign: K7RTB
Scott K Kearsley

207 N Maple
Bend OR 97701

Call Sign: KC7ANO
Don E Franks
6935 N Richmond Ave
Bend OR 97701

Call Sign: W7KUO
Darrel W Shafer
43176 N River Dr
Bend OR 97701

Call Sign: KA7QZA
Charles C Brown
1015 N Watts St
Bend OR 97701

Call Sign: W8ABF
Richard Layne
7089 N Wellesley
Bend OR 97701

Call Sign: KE7RUF
Deschutes County ARES
8517 N Weyerhauser Ave
Bend OR 97701

Call Sign: W7HLP
Deschutes County ARES
6136 N Wilbur
Bend OR 97701

Call Sign: KE7RGY
Deschutes County ARES
6335 N Wilbur
Bend OR 97701

Call Sign: KE7RUE
Deschutes County ARES
7071 N Wilbur
Bend OR 97701

Call Sign: W7HWY
Deschutes County ARES

5927 N Wilbur Ave
Bend OR 97701

6600 NE 78th Ct A3 10839
Bend OR 97701

36375 NE Chamberlain Rd
Bend OR 97701

Call Sign: W7DCO
Deschutes County ARES
5927 N Wilbur Ave
Bend OR 97701

Call Sign: KD7OIH
James F Sloter Jr
6600 NE 78th Ct A3 12802
Bend OR 977014046

Call Sign: KD7OIE
Darrin Isaak
5525 NE Couch St
Bend OR 97701

Call Sign: KG6UIQ
Cynthia A Blacketor
3101 NE 158th Ave
Bend OR 97701

Call Sign: KB7JMP
Richard B Gribble
3115 NE 87th Pl
Bend OR 97701

Call Sign: KF7TFX
Sherry L Burke
23900 NE Dillon Rd
Bend OR 97701

Call Sign: KD7AUZ
Brad M Ruder
360 NE 1st St
Bend OR 97701

Call Sign: KF7TFA
Daniel E Beougher
805 NE Baldwin Dr
Bend OR 97701

Call Sign: N6DDS
Jack E Ulstad Sr
1293 NE Estelle Ct
Bend OR 97701

Call Sign: KB7WTS
Gary S Kontich
1552 NE 21st St
Bend OR 97701

Call Sign: KB7NBO
George W Marshall
882 NE Baldwin Dr
Bend OR 97701

Call Sign: KF7RPR
David W Adams
2833 NE Everett St
Bend OR 97701

Call Sign: KB7JDR
John P Cannon
1145 NE 24th
Bend OR 97702

Call Sign: KB6NTO
Jacqueline C Yake
1324 NE Barnes Ct
Bend OR 97701

Call Sign: KD7AVA
Brian P Ruder
17650 NE Flanders
Bend OR 97701

Call Sign: W7GPV
Robert M Hulst
2121 NE 27th St
Bend OR 97701

Call Sign: W6JDB
Jay A Yake
2326 NE Baron Ct
Bend OR 97701

Call Sign: KD7AVB
Paul C Ruder
18241 NE Flanders
Bend OR 97701

Call Sign: KC7CKF
Glen L Taylor
6600 NE 78th Ct A3 10827
Bend OR 97701

Call Sign: KC7RIG
John C Copley
4525 NE Campaign St
Bend OR 97701

Call Sign: KC7HJA
Jerry W Rozelle
18241 NE Flanders
Bend OR 97701

Call Sign: KE6VMZ
Randy J Black
6600 NE 78th Ct A3 10834
Bend OR 977013854

Call Sign: WB2QND
Eugene W Gulbrandsen
36375 NE Chamberlain Rd
Bend OR 97701

Call Sign: KF7TGB
Joel T Brown
566 NE Franklin
Bend OR 97701

Call Sign: AA7ZC
Barry Landson

Call Sign: WB2RDD
Virginia Gulbrandsen

Call Sign: W7ALE
Steven L Bennett

1546 NE Greensword Dr
Bend OR 97701

Call Sign: KC7WPE
Randolph H Butler Jr
4005 NE Hazelfern Pl
Bend OR 97701

Call Sign: WA6BNO
Stanley R Schliep
2041 NE Josephine Dr
Bend OR 97701

Call Sign: W7AJT
Arthur Tarin
2041 NE Josephine Dr
Bend OR 97701

Call Sign: KD7VKF
Arthur J Tarin
2041 NE Josephine Dr
Bend OR 97701

Call Sign: KL0VZ
Steven C Jensen
991 NE Josephine St
Bend OR 97701

Call Sign: KF6JWX
Ronald D Beery
2388 NE Lindsey Dr
Bend OR 97701

Call Sign: KB7WQR
Rodney L Little
1324 NE Malheur St
Bend OR 97701

Call Sign: W7CTC
Rodney L Little
5723 NE Mallory Ave
Bend OR 97701

Call Sign: WA0UNU
Perry A Johnson

3520 NE Manchester
Bend OR 977016487

Call Sign: KE7UCE
Michael A Cofer
4756 NE Mason
Bend OR 97701

Call Sign: KF7BFJ
Sarah L Cofer
5105 NE Mason Ct
Bend OR 97701

Call Sign: KB7OGK
Fred B Durgin Jr
5600 NE Mlk Blvd 162
Bend OR 97701

Call Sign: WB7FGF
Jack A Stickel
2130 NE Multnomah St
Bend OR 97701

Call Sign: KF7OMM
Jacob A Cappel
29215 NE Putnam Rd
Bend OR 97701

Call Sign: KJ7NJ
Donald L Adams
29601 NE Putnam Rd
Bend OR 97701

Call Sign: KI7FK
Gregory D Chilcote
570 NE Rawhide Ln
Bend OR 977017604

Call Sign: KD7OIC
Fredrick K Gerke
24062 NE Riverside Dr
Bend OR 97701

Call Sign: K2RL
Robert H Lauzon

1602 NE Riverside Dr 38
Bend OR 97701

Call Sign: KC7NKP
Adam P N Leask
1602 NE Riverside Dr 38
Bend OR 97701

Call Sign: K1WDW
Adam P N Leask
1602 NE Riverside Dr 80
Bend OR 97701

Call Sign: W7PJ
Roy Hanson
2015 NE Roberts Ave
Bend OR 97701

Call Sign: KE7NK
Joseph J Winter
609 NE Robin Pl
Bend OR 97701

Call Sign: WB7OVQ
Oral S King
75 NE Robin Way
Bend OR 97701

Call Sign: KE7RPM
Raymond P Mcgrath
1504 NE Rosa Parks Way
Bend OR 97701

Call Sign: N7CSH
Roger A Kryzanek
1733 NE Rosewood Dr
Bend OR 97701

Call Sign: KE7TMS
Timothy M Mcginnis
547 NE Royal Ct
Bend OR 97701

Call Sign: KB7QCC
Richard W Vincent

8715 NE Russell St
Bend OR 97701

Call Sign: N7YCK
Matthew T Chastain
7331 NE Sacramento St
Bend OR 977018260

Call Sign: N7HR
George H Morton
1292 NE Setting Sun Dr
Bend OR 97701

Call Sign: N7VIY
Richard E Lovin
1725 NE Shepard Rd
Bend OR 97701

Call Sign: K4HT
Irving R Groves
1810 NE Stanton St
Bend OR 97701

Call Sign: KC7CKD
Scott M Mc Coy
3403 NE Stanton St
Bend OR 97701

Call Sign: KF7HIJ
Kenneth P Mcclain
2408 NE Stephanie Ct
Bend OR 97701

Call Sign: KF7OMN
Joel E Lisson
499 NE Sterling Dr C4
Bend OR 97701

Call Sign: KF7LM
William R Elliott
8 NE Tandem Way Apt 220
Bend OR 97701

Call Sign: KF6APO
Erin C Brooker

1715 NE Taurus Ct
Bend OR 97701

Call Sign: W7JVO
Donald L Peters
657 NE Terry Cir
Bend OR 97701

Call Sign: KM7RC
Rudy V Catania
657 NE Terry Cir
Bend OR 97701

Call Sign: W7PMS
Lisa D Jeffcott
15846 NE Thompson Ct
Bend OR 97701

Call Sign: W7MED
Lisa D Jeffcott
15846 NE Thompson Ct
Bend OR 97701

Call Sign: WA7AJ
Addison J Parry
8701 NE Tillamook
Bend OR 977014027

Call Sign: KD7WRV
Carolyn M Laird
1224 NE Walnut St 207
Bend OR 97701

Call Sign: KD7VZN
Jesse S Laird
1224 NE Walnut St Pmb
294
Bend OR 97701

Call Sign: K7YAF
David R Cronk
1273 NE Westview Dr
Bend OR 97701

Call Sign: KC7RHY

John W Barton
54582 Nehalem Hwy
Bend OR 97701

Call Sign: K7HRY
John W Barton
63664 Nehalem Hwy N
Bend OR 97701

Call Sign: KC7HIZ
Billy D Sansom
3020 New Hope Rd
Bend OR 977018232

Call Sign: K7HIZ
Billy D Sansom
4160 New Hope Rd
Bend OR 977018232

Call Sign: WI7L
Randall C Craig
890 Newport Ave
Bend OR 97701

Call Sign: KD7SYG
Linda W Reinthal
41149 Nichol Dr
Bend OR 97701

Call Sign: KB7JFF
Michael S Leitner
2528 Noah St
Bend OR 97701

Call Sign: KJ6FU
Gerald L Inman
202 NW 11th St
Bend OR 97702

Call Sign: N6NSK
Betty J Inman
245 NW 11th St Apt A2
Bend OR 97702

Call Sign: KE7OHG

Ken M Rose
354 NW 25th
Bend OR 97701

Call Sign: KE7KFD
Kent A Vander Kamp
6741 NW 69th Pl
Bend OR 97701

Call Sign: KC7RQL
Michael D Ennis
655 NW 7th K
Bend OR 97701

Call Sign: KD7QWP
Cynthia H Engel
12572 NW Amethyst Ct
Bend OR 97701

Call Sign: KE7CQM
Thomas J Rose
14830 NW Baker Creek Rd
Bend OR 97701

Call Sign: K7MEK
Mary E Kelly
4215 NW Boxwood Dr
Bend OR 97701

Call Sign: K7JRY
Joseph Ray
4066 NW Boxwood Dr
Bend OR 97701

Call Sign: KD7OCX
John R Fox
1107 NW Carden Ave
Bend OR 97701

Call Sign: KF7BFP
David M Bassett
6944 NW Cardinal Dr
Bend OR 97701

Call Sign: K7KEG

David M Bassett
6944 NW Cardinal Dr
Bend OR 97701

Call Sign: KA7JJJ
Kenyon B Courts
970 NW Dale Ave
Bend OR 97701

Call Sign: W7KUF
Richard S Nelson
47665 NW Deer Ct
Bend OR 97701

Call Sign: KD7OIN
Carl H Hellis
330 NW Elks Dr Ste A
Bend OR 977015651

Call Sign: KD7IYE
Clarence E Carnahan
4175 NW Elmwood Dr
Bend OR 97701

Call Sign: KE7MOG
Fred J Tanis
4534 NW Elmwood Dr
Bend OR 97701

Call Sign: KD7VKE
Michael T Donohue
4534 NW Elmwood Dr
Bend OR 97701

Call Sign: KC7HUU
Ragnar R Hartman
466 NW Flagline Dr
Bend OR 97709

Call Sign: W7KYO
Harold E Eckes
1957 NW Florence Ave
Unit 309
Bend OR 97701

Call Sign: KC7UZI
Arthur L Eytchison
18582 NW Holly St 204
Bend OR 97701

Call Sign: KC7PYI
Altamay M Rowe
3485 NW Honeywood Dr
Bend OR 97701

Call Sign: W7TGR
Harley D Nimmo
3108 NW Horizon Dr
Bend OR 97701

Call Sign: KF7OTJ
David W Hice
22115 NW Imbrie Dr 258
Bend OR 97701

Call Sign: WA6TNQ
Donald A Turnage
3120 NW John Olsen Ave
24301
Bend OR 97701

Call Sign: KC7WMB
Bruce M Campbell
1675 NW Lakeway Ln
Bend OR 97701

Call Sign: WB7BRT
Toivo J Hirn Sr
1961 NW Larch Ave
Bend OR 97701

Call Sign: KD7WRU
John F Klein
17864 NW Lone Rock Dr
Bend OR 97701

Call Sign: KF7BFL
Noah C Pugsley
12877 NW Lorraine Dr
Bend OR 97701

Call Sign: N2LPB
Lewis J Colby Jr
9145 NW Lovejoy
Bend OR 97701

Call Sign: KA7ZQS
Mark W Thomas
425 NW Marshall St
Bend OR 97701

Call Sign: N7UAB
Sandra S Thompson
13330 NW Marshall St
Bend OR 97701

Call Sign: KC7SOM
Jonathan G Ash
2575 NW Marshall St 11
Bend OR 97701

Call Sign: KC7GBV
Kris L Pitman
2188 NW Maser Pl
Bend OR 97701

Call Sign: NU7N
Leland S Williams
572 NW Mawrcrest Pl
Bend OR 97701

Call Sign: KD7WRY
Erik A Johnson
2620 NW Neptune
Bend OR 97701

Call Sign: KE7NOF
Martin R Huber
527 NW Oak Ave
Bend OR 97701

Call Sign: KC7YVV
Carolyn J Swisher
927 NW Oak Ave
Bend OR 97701

Call Sign: KD7OIO
Roger S C Wolcott Jr
5665 NW Oak Creek Dr 3
Bend OR 97701

Call Sign: KE7BHT
Judith A Barton
14525 NW Perimiter Dr
Bend OR 97701

Call Sign: KG6DRI
Stephen R Bott
47633 NW Pongratz Rd
Bend OR 97701

Call Sign: AE7DI
Curtis R Ciszek
47633 NW Pongratz Rd
Bend OR 97701

Call Sign: KA7ZDP
Richard L Williams
11100 NW Reeves St
Bend OR 97701

Call Sign: N2GJG
Kenneth C Hollemon
2719 NW Romancier Dr
Bend OR 97701

Call Sign: KG6RCR
Michael J Elliott
5837 NW Skyline Blvd
Bend OR 97701

Call Sign: KG6UIR
Robert J Blacketor
5837 NW Skyline Blvd
Bend OR 97701

Call Sign: KE7BHM
Dennis C Rilling
7360 NW Soda Springs Rd
Bend OR 97701

Call Sign: N0LWI
Peter C Mayer Jr
10115 NW St Helens Rd
Bend OR 977087004

Call Sign: KE7CSL
Donna J Pfeiffer
1649 NW Summit Dr
Bend OR 97701

Call Sign: N7RFR
Douglas M Williams
2650 NW Upshur 29
Bend OR 97701

Call Sign: KB7RFC
Paul A Schroeder
3260 NW Westside Rd
Bend OR 97701

Call Sign: KC7EXW
Tina A Pavelic
39655 NW Wilksboro Rd
Bend OR 977012165

Call Sign: N6SBH
Richard C Warner
191 NW Willamina Dr
Bend OR 97701

Call Sign: K7CHH
Carl H Hellis
15800 NW Windhill Dr
Bend OR 977013652

Call Sign: KD7OIB
Steven Mcburnett
3930 NW Witham Hill Dr
Apt 245
Bend OR 97701

Call Sign: K7STV
Steven Mc Burnett
1805 NW Woodland Dr

Bend OR 97701

Call Sign: K7TJD
Thomas W Adams
3826 Oak Meadows Loop
Bend OR 97701

Call Sign: KD7ILN
Thomas J Muller
4953 Oak Park Dr NE
Bend OR 97701

Call Sign: KF7TGG
James W Mahoney
1015 Oak St Lot 20
Bend OR 97701

Call Sign: KB7MTF
Russell Hulet
18748 Oaktree Ave
Bend OR 97701

Call Sign: KE7SZM
Herbert L Tucker Jr
18748 Oaktree Ave
Bend OR 97701

Call Sign: KC7OTL
Jeffrey L Huey
35643 Oakview Dr
Bend OR 97701

Call Sign: KB2RLD
Roy K Erberich
33983 Oakville Rd SW
Bend OR 977011936

Call Sign: KF6ZSI
Stoddard B Reid
21655 Obsidian Ave
Bend OR 97701

Call Sign: KD7WRX
Thomas A Dean
937 Odom Ln

Bend OR 97701

Call Sign: KF7TGF
Rex S Wolf
133 Omni Cir Apt 1
Bend OR 97702

Call Sign: WF7REX
Rex S Wolf
501 Onion Ave
Bend OR 97702

Call Sign: KC7LPU
Richard A Mc Clanahan II
501 Onion Ave
Bend OR 97702

Call Sign: N7YBN
Kathy L Mc Clanahan
3529 Onyx Ave
Bend OR 97702

Call Sign: KF7KEX
Samuel C Corliss
4731 Onyx Ave
Bend OR 97702

Call Sign: KE7BSU
Kenneth P Scholz
4786 Onyx Dr
Bend OR 97702

Call Sign: KC7GBU
Richard A Mc Clanahan
3092 Onyx Pl
Bend OR 97702

Call Sign: AB7UN
Harold S Worcester
2352 Onyx St
Bend OR 97702

Call Sign: KD7TGG
Stig A Tuck
1405 Oregon St

Bend OR 97701

Call Sign: KB7SIG
Karen L Easlon
2011 Oregon St Hwy 101
Bend OR 97701

Call Sign: N7IOO
Robert F Main Jr
3084 Oxford St
Bend OR 97702

Call Sign: KB7RDX
James R Stephan
57943 Parkersburg Rd
Bend OR 97702

Call Sign: KB7REC
Sarah J Tripp
56902 Parkersburg Rd
Bend OR 97702

Call Sign: W7EYM
Robert J Martin
7238 Parkplace Ct NE
Bend OR 97702

Call Sign: KE7BEK
Randy F Potter
327 Parkrose Chateau 3141
NE 148th Ave
Bend OR 97702

Call Sign: KF7TFC
Richard W Coffman
7158 Parkview Dr
Bend OR 97707

Call Sign: KE7TMO
Andy L Tresness
58702 Parkwood Dr
Bend OR 97702

Call Sign: KD6NEC
Aleta W Warren

1364 Parnell Dr
Bend OR 97701

Call Sign: KD7YPF
Thomas L Houck
4450 Pearl St
Bend OR 97701

Call Sign: WB7VRF
Thomas L Houck
4450 Pearl St
Bend OR 97701

Call Sign: KB7OL
Robert F Smith
811 Pine Grove Rd
Bend OR 977022604

Call Sign: WB7AFO
Noma V Smith
811 Pine Grove Rd
Bend OR 977022604

Call Sign: N7DUX
Paul K Findley
2810 Pine Grove Rd
Bend OR 97702

Call Sign: KF7CCY
Donovan L Smith
86161 Pine Grove Rd
Bend OR 97702

Call Sign: KE6SF
Oren W Winton
2430 Pine Ln SE
Bend OR 97702

Call Sign: WA7TBY
Walter E Bouche
392 Pintail Ct SE
Bend OR 97701

Call Sign: KD7VKC
Lisa D Jeffcott

32831 Pittsburg Rd
Bend OR 97701

Call Sign: KF7UOI
Byron C Cotton
2190 Poplar Dr Apt 3
Bend OR 97702

Call Sign: WA7T
Scott T Powell
1666 Powell Creek Rd
Bend OR 97702

Call Sign: KE7BSV
Kim Woolaway
594 Poysky Ave
Bend OR 97701

Call Sign: WB6CJJ
Steven A Engquist
230 Prairie Landing Dr
Bend OR 97701

Call Sign: K7IMO
Kim Woolaway
269 Prairie Landing Dr
Bend OR 97701

Call Sign: KA7NAA
Allan R Chambers
901 J Q Adams St
Bend OR 97701

Call Sign: N7QQH
Bonnie L Turnbull
638800 Quail Haven
Bend OR 97701

Call Sign: KD7AGV
Vicky J Hughes
63820 Quail Haven Dr E
Bend OR 97701

Call Sign: KD7AGW
Alan J Hughes

115 Quail Ln
Bend OR 97701

Call Sign: KD7SMD
Edmond A Perregaux III
3200 Quail Pl
Bend OR 97701

Call Sign: K7ZMZ
Vicki D Sawders
2131 Quail Point Cir
Bend OR 97702

Call Sign: K7ZZZ
Central Oregon Dx Club
2131 Quail Point Cir
Bend OR 97702

Call Sign: WB7PSE
Clifford R Vaniman
657 Quarry Rd
Bend OR 97707

Call Sign: KB8LGE
Lee R Mc Murrin
1755 Queenborough SE
Bend OR 97702

Call Sign: KB7SHU
Nancy K Gill
1755 Queenborough SE
Bend OR 97702

Call Sign: KB7SIE
David G Gill
269 Queens Branch Rd
Bend OR 97702

Call Sign: KF7GTN
Mark L Kanko
770 Queens Branch Rd
Bend OR 97702

Call Sign: KE7JII
Jody A Mills

1054 Queens Branch Rd
Bend OR 97702

Call Sign: K7HIQ
Jody A Mills
1420 Queens Branch Rd
Bend OR 97702

Call Sign: KD7VAQ
Deschutes Cw Contest Club
2649 Rabun Way
Bend OR 97702

Call Sign: AH8K
Michele J Young
332 Rancho Vista Dr
Bend OR 97702

Call Sign: KC7HMY
Ed Straka
24037 Redwood Hwy
Bend OR 97701

Call Sign: N7RLX
Richard H Ettinger
24949 Redwood Hwy
Bend OR 97701

Call Sign: WA7AIM
Kim S Waterhouse
210 Rice Creek Rd
Bend OR 97702

Call Sign: KB7QKY
Dayton H Herron
14168 Ridge Pl
Bend OR 97701

Call Sign: KD6NED
Ryan C Root
1810 Rifle Range Rd
Bend OR 97702

Call Sign: KE6ABL
Lora A Root

27450 Riggs Hill Rd
Bend OR 97702

Call Sign: KF7OUF
Karen S MARCotte
34560 Riverside Dr SW
Bend OR 97702

Call Sign: KF7OUE
Robert A MARCotte
34626 Riverside Dr SW
Bend OR 97702

Call Sign: KB6MPJ
Erik P Lonnquist
3251 Roberts Cr Rd
Bend OR 97702

Call Sign: KF7TFD
Alan P Sandner
60584 Robinette Rd
Bend OR 97701

Call Sign: KE7IDE
Oscar Allen
56515 Robinson Dr
Bend OR 97702

Call Sign: K6KYN
Robert I Naidis
1264 Rockinghorse Ln
Bend OR 97702

Call Sign: KC6PYH
John J Aklonis
211 Rockridge Loop
Bend OR 97702

Call Sign: KB7OJR
Charla J Sargent
666 Rockwood St SE
Bend OR 97702

Call Sign: KC7RHX
Frances O Nichols

2524 Rockydale Rd
Bend OR 97702

Call Sign: KC7QPP
Donald L Swisher
584 Romie Howard Rd
Bend OR 97702

Call Sign: KD7OXA
Le J Jones
1130 Rose Valley Dr
Bend OR 977072710

Call Sign: K7PAW
Le J Jones
1778 Rosebank Way
Bend OR 977072710

Call Sign: KF7TGH
John M Graves III
5200 Royal Ave
Bend OR 97702

Call Sign: KC7LUC
Michael A Skeels
28738 Royal Ave
Bend OR 97702

Call Sign: KD6PXC
Kenneth E Fayal Jr
1418 Russet Dr
Bend OR 97702

Call Sign: N7JZS
Kenneth E Fayal Jr
1664 Russet Dr
Bend OR 97702

Call Sign: KO6HA
Thomas D Mc Glinn Jr
165 Ryland Dr
Bend OR 977019498

Call Sign: NB6GC
Uss Hornet ARC

681 S 10th
Bend OR 97701

610 S 4th St
Bend OR 977085815

561 Savage Creek Rd
Bend OR 977018566

Call Sign: WH6OL
David C Abell
319 S 13th St
Bend OR 97702

Call Sign: W7VS
Walter S Knodle
610 S 4th St
Bend OR 977085815

Call Sign: KA8M
Duncan A Ross
613 Savage Creek Rd
Bend OR 977018568

Call Sign: AC7WF
David C Abell
319 S 13th St
Bend OR 97702

Call Sign: KE7ZSN
Eric V Arbak
819 S 7th St
Bend OR 97707

Call Sign: KF7TFW
Gina T Smith
522 SE 10th
Bend OR 97702

Call Sign: K7ES
David C Abell
622 S 15th St
Bend OR 97702

Call Sign: KB7QCD
Gene B Cota
16070 S Carus Rd
Bend OR 97702

Call Sign: KC7UZH
Kenneth R Reiswig Sr
3026 SE 112th Ave
Bend OR 97702

Call Sign: WB9SAT
William L Logan
240 S 1st Ave
Bend OR 97702

Call Sign: KE7DDE
Joy A Newhart
314 S Columbia Dr
Bend OR 977022321

Call Sign: KF7TSA
John W Cox
14928 SE 122nd Ave
Bend OR 97701

Call Sign: KF7HIK
James R Doggett
240 S 1st Ave
Bend OR 97702

Call Sign: K7NHB
Paul W Chance
83415 S Cove Dr
Bend OR 977022321

Call Sign: N7TQE
Duane D Anderson
2706 SE 131st
Bend OR 977019819

Call Sign: W7CCZ
James R Doggett
240 S 1st Ave
Bend OR 97702

Call Sign: KE7QLW
Joey J Shaw
377 S E 5th
Bend OR 97702

Call Sign: KE7NOG
Cornelius J Peeples
14734 SE 131st Dr
Bend OR 97701

Call Sign: N7NPD
Ames D Hendrickson
240 S 1st Ave
Bend OR 97702

Call Sign: KD7WPN
Leonard C Bryant
30775 S Oswalt
Bend OR 97702

Call Sign: KB7ZCQ
Daniel N Driskill
206 SE 132nd Ave
Bend OR 97701

Call Sign: KB7VKU
Donald G Peters
1730 S 21 St
Bend OR 97708

Call Sign: K7ARM
Robert D Watkins
1111 Sandy Ln
Bend OR 977022358

Call Sign: N7VMH
Charles W Strawn Sr
1019 SE 37th Ave
Bend OR 97702

Call Sign: W7TTE
Walter S Knodle

Call Sign: W6VKG
Theodore B Wood

Call Sign: KD7EQL
Ronald A West

910 SE 37th Ave 104
Bend OR 97702

5191 SE Coot Way
Bend OR 97702

13141 SE Ramona
Bend OR 97702

Call Sign: N7ZMS
Bradley E Hoover
5406 SE 39th Ave
Bend OR 97702

Call Sign: KC7ZEF
Richard R Kilby
9999 SE Frenchacres Dr
Bend OR 97702

Call Sign: KS6U
Leonard Premselaar
515 SE Rene Sp 3
Bend OR 97702

Call Sign: KD7RZA
David G Lenhart
4916 SE 80th
Bend OR 97702

Call Sign: KB7HVJ
Sabrina J Mattioda
450 SE La Creole Dr 2
Bend OR 97702

Call Sign: KS6U
Dorothy J Premselaar
17509 SE Reserve Loop
Bend OR 97702

Call Sign: KD7KYH
Rick P Christen
6478 SE Austin Ct
Bend OR 97702

Call Sign: KF7TFZ
Douglas B Kiepert
1934 SE Lambert St
Bend OR 97702

Call Sign: KF7LFY
Bradley J Ward
15644 SE River Rd
Bend OR 97702

Call Sign: KE7ECA
Michael R Kelley
5032 SE Belmont Ct
Bend OR 977022368

Call Sign: KF7TGA
Kassidy J Kiepert
1934 SE Lambert St
Bend OR 97702

Call Sign: KC7NOR
Dennis E Walker
13505 SE River Rd 110
Bend OR 97702

Call Sign: N7MFR
David D Stucky III
5087 SE Belmont Ct
Bend OR 97702

Call Sign: KE7JXA
Bonnie L Dickman
7719 SE Lambert St
Bend OR 97702

Call Sign: KF7RQE
Donald B Stuart
7822 SE Stephanie Ct
Bend OR 97702

Call Sign: KI7MM
Harrison Townsend
5945 SE Blossom St
Bend OR 97702

Call Sign: KE7JWY
Paul F Dickman
8240 SE Lambert St
Bend OR 97702

Call Sign: K7DBS
Donald B Stuart
7998 SE Stephanie Ct
Bend OR 97702

Call Sign: N7NYJ
Laura L Townsend
9150 SE Blue Jay Ln
Bend OR 97702

Call Sign: KD7EPD
Christine B Baker
15100 SE Monner Rd
Bend OR 97702

Call Sign: N0ABO
Donald J Taylor
2400 SE Stratus Ave 22
Bend OR 97702

Call Sign: KD7SKY
Jody A Mills
14430 SE Center St
Bend OR 97702

Call Sign: KK1U
Donald E Nevin
4296 SE Oak St
Bend OR 97702

Call Sign: KE7AZA
David G Anderson
38925 SE Trubel Rd
Bend OR 97702

Call Sign: KB7WTR
Robin M Ritter

Call Sign: K7HSJ
Charles D Krug

Call Sign: K7OTK
Emma N Green

44200 SE Tuckridge Rd
Bend OR 97702

Call Sign: K7LPV
John E Green
13324 SE Tumbleweed Ct
Bend OR 97702

Call Sign: AA7WN
Randy S Sargent
16683 SE Vanzyl Dr
Bend OR 97702

Call Sign: KD7EQJ
Carol A Bruno
18615 SE Wilmot St
Bend OR 97702

Call Sign: N7VMD
Phoebe T Larsen
35 Seagrove Pl
Bend OR 97702

Call Sign: KD7AUX
Gerald D Evans
4869 Seapine Dr
Bend OR 97702

Call Sign: N7RGE
Norman D Aller
2865 Seckel Ct
Bend OR 97702

Call Sign: KE7BJC
Barbara J Blaine
1175 Shady Ln NE
Bend OR 97701

Call Sign: KF7IQY
Richard A Olson
583 Shangrila
Bend OR 97702

Call Sign: KD7OIJ
Gary W Zimmerman

7011 Solarian Dr SE
Bend OR 97701

Call Sign: N7ZIM
Gary W Zimmerman
275 Soldier Creek D
Bend OR 97701

Call Sign: KF7TK
Donald L Kelley
551 Stanton Blvd
Bend OR 97702

Call Sign: KD7JFV
Benjamin W Bruegeman
1919 State St
Bend OR 977018512

Call Sign: KD7RTB
Glenna M Larsen
900 State St E222
Bend OR 97707

Call Sign: N7IHQ
James G Larsen
900 State St F254
Bend OR 97707

Call Sign: KF7PLP
Ronald J Corso
1963 Stonecrest Dr
Bend OR 97702

Call Sign: KA7FUY
Marvin L Walters
650 Stonehill St
Bend OR 97707

Call Sign: KC7LPX
Karen S Walters
110 Stoneway Dr NW
Bend OR 97707

Call Sign: KE7CSM
Sarah E Swaney

2095 Stortz Ave NE
Bend OR 97701

Call Sign: K1GA
Stanley C Lipin
2095 Stortz Ave NE
Bend OR 97701

Call Sign: WS7N
Robert D Swaney
2095 Stortz Ave NE
Bend OR 97701

Call Sign: KE7JEY
Stephen L Gates
428 Sugarpine Ct SE
Bend OR 97702

Call Sign: K7KWP
Jack L Pierson
96314 Sunlake Ln
Bend OR 97702

Call Sign: KF6KNH
Louis M Warren
3221 Sunshine Pl
Bend OR 977022096

Call Sign: N7YBS
Karen D Martin
16110 SW 103rd Ave
Bend OR 97701

Call Sign: K7AGB
John R Martin
16110 SW 103rd Ave
Bend OR 97701

Call Sign: W9CZ
John E Ogden
11390 SW 108th Ave
Bend OR 977029271

Call Sign: KC7PYF
David R Gassaway

8033 SW 166th Pl
Bend OR 97702

Call Sign: KE6UOD
Jason M Durham
445 SW 167th Dr
Bend OR 97702

Call Sign: WA7JCU
Alvin R Corson
445 SW 167th Dr
Bend OR 97702

Call Sign: KC7GOE
Glenn Parker
10085 SW Century Oak Dr
Bend OR 97702

Call Sign: KE7EFT
Stephanie G Gonser
10195 SW Century Oak Dr
Bend OR 97702

Call Sign: KD7ZYU
Thomas H Gonser
3021 SW Champlain Dr
Bend OR 97702

Call Sign: KI6Y
Charles M Southall
5175 SW Elm Ave
Bend OR 97702

Call Sign: KC7HIU
Mark A Davis
1495 SW Foundry St
Bend OR 97702

Call Sign: KC7HIY
Joan C Docter
6987 SW Foxfield Ct
Bend OR 97702

Call Sign: N7VOR
Edward P O Neill

12885 SW Glacier Lily Cir
Bend OR 97701

Call Sign: WA7PFN
Neil W Coulter
9035 SW Reiling St
Bend OR 97702

Call Sign: W7DUG
Douglas D Reinthal
28142 SW Sioux Ter
Bend OR 97709

Call Sign: KD7EQQ
Michael J Nichols
55659 Swan Rd
Bend OR 97701

Call Sign: K7JDC
Jeffrey D Collins
34696 Swank Dr
Bend OR 97707

Call Sign: W7MJC
Michele J Collins
124 Swarthout Cir
Bend OR 97707

Call Sign: W7ESI
Jack B Thornton
64575 Sylvan Loop
Bend OR 97701

Call Sign: W7YOW
Ronald E Remsen
4100 Sylvia St SE
Bend OR 977019375

Call Sign: KE7KEL
Margene A Smith
60548 Tall Pine Ave
Bend OR 97702

Call Sign: KD7ZFR
Michael L Smith

3348 Talon St
Bend OR 977029739

Call Sign: AD7GC
Michael L Smith
3348 Talon St
Bend OR 977029739

Call Sign: KC7UVS
Merle H Edwards
2504 Taylor Ave
Bend OR 97702

Call Sign: KE7CQN
Kim B Rich
959 Terry St
Bend OR 97701

Call Sign: KB7SHV
Jack M Ipock
475 Thomas Rd
Bend OR 97702

Call Sign: KC7TJA
Robert A Harrison
1222 Timberline Dr
Bend OR 97702

Call Sign: KE7JXH
Robert C Henry
2060 Timberline Dr
Bend OR 97702

Call Sign: KF7BFQ
Brian A Wetter
76 Touchstone
Bend OR 97701

Call Sign: K7BBQ
Brian A Wetter
4 Touchstone 121
Bend OR 97701

Call Sign: KD7YGA
David F Meyers

20622 Tumalo Rd
Bend OR 97702

Call Sign: WA7EMT
David F Meyers
20622 Tumalo Rd
Bend OR 97702

Call Sign: KC7HJE
Nathan S Danielson
20894 Tumalo Rd
Bend OR 97701

Call Sign: N7RFM
Bruce G Danielson
22840 Tumbleweed Ct
Bend OR 97701

Call Sign: N7YBK
Frederic E Ruder
22865 Tumbleweed Ct
Bend OR 97701

Call Sign: WA7ZBL
Mahlon R Hale
15761 Tumbleweed Turn
Bend OR 977019729

Call Sign: KD7AUY
Michael K Watson
6985 Tunnel Loop Rd
Bend OR 97701

Call Sign: KA7MDG
Ted A Keener
888 Twin Creeks Xing Apt
102
Bend OR 97701

Call Sign: KA7MDH
Larkelyn Keener
7521 Twin Fir Ln S
Bend OR 97701

Call Sign: WA6WMO

Jeff J Morrison
2175 Valhalla St
Bend OR 97701

Call Sign: KC7TR
Jeff J Morrison
3924 Valinda Way
Bend OR 97701

Call Sign: KC7WOU
Lester D Brush
2210 Varney Creek Rd
Bend OR 97701

Call Sign: KD7QVN
Evelyn A Brush
22716 Varney Creek Rd
Bend OR 97701

Call Sign: KF7GTM
John E Rhetts
63945 W Quail Haven Dr
Bend OR 97701

Call Sign: N9AUD
Vernon D Carmichael
20869 W View Dr
Bend OR 97702

Call Sign: WA7OYY
Richard A Adair
20937 W View Dr
Bend OR 97702

Call Sign: AB7GS
Robert M Walker
20957 W View Dr
Bend OR 97702

Call Sign: KC7LPR
Ruth E Walker
20957 W View Dr
Bend OR 97702

Call Sign: K7RNB

Larry R Hiatt
25345 Walker Rd
Bend OR 97701

Call Sign: WB7BZT
Roger L Freed
61329 Wecoma
Bend OR 97702

Call Sign: WB7CBC
Carol A Freed
61329 Wecoma Ct
Bend OR 977022748

Call Sign: KC6NTX
Robert L Speik
61334 Wecoma Ct
Bend OR 97702

Call Sign: KC6NTY
Margaret T Speik
61334 Wecoma Ct
Bend OR 97702

Call Sign: KJ7GO
Paul J Mc Clellan
61453 Westridge Ave
Bend OR 977023132

Call Sign: KC7SMB
Ronald I Ruby
22280 White Peaks Dr
Bend OR 97702

Call Sign: KF7JEZ
Matthew R Hornback
22360 White Peaks Dr
Bend OR 97702

Call Sign: W7DEL
Del S Van Camp
21040 Wilderness Way
Bend OR 977021783

Call Sign: KE7BMD

Douglas A Wells
21155 Wilderness Way
Bend OR 97702

Call Sign: KD7VKG
Thomas L Wells
21155 Wilderness Way
Bend OR 97702

Call Sign: W7PIG
Thomas L Wells
21155 Wilderness Way
Bend OR 97702

Call Sign: W7JEP
Thomas L Wells
21155 Wilderness Way
Bend OR 97702

Call Sign: N5JRA
John J Wolcott
60749 Willow Creek Loop
Bend OR 97702

Call Sign: KB0CBT
Oscar J Sorlie Jr
3343 Windwood Way NW
Bend OR 97701

Call Sign: KD7WRW
Chris K Williams
20101 Winston Loop
Bend OR 97701

Call Sign: KC7SLG
Ernest J Lemos
63200 Wishing Well Ln
Bend OR 97701

Call Sign: KF6ABW
Judith E Neville
55906 Wood Duck Dr
Bend OR 97707

Call Sign: N6VOR

Stephen C Neville
55906 Wood Duck Dr
Bend OR 97707

Call Sign: KC7PYG
John R Bramall
21024 Wood Haven Ave
Bend OR 977022404

Call Sign: KD7EQU
Debra R Rufener
21067 Woodhaven Ave
Bend OR 97702

Call Sign: KE7BHJ
David D Mark
60310 Woodside Loop
Bend OR 97702

Call Sign: KC7TAG
Brent W Nichols
60747 Woodside Rd
Bend OR 97702

Call Sign: KA7BHY
Robert H Goodale
42 Xerxes Ave
Bend OR 97701

Call Sign: KC7LPS
Randolph H Butler Sr
15134 Yellow Pine Loop
Bend OR 97707

Call Sign: KC7PYQ
Carmen I Butler
15134 Yellow Pine Loop
Bend OR 97707

Call Sign: WA7TUE
Karl E Dykstra
22915 Yucca Ct
Bend OR 97701

Call Sign: K7SQ

Joseph D Barry
60886 Zircon Dr
Bend OR 97702

Call Sign: KC7LPK
Christine L Barry
60886 Zircon Dr
Bend OR 97702

Call Sign: W6RA
Randolph E Tomer
60933 Zircon Dr
Bend OR 97702

Call Sign: N7RFQ
James C Fleming Sr
Bend OR 97702

Call Sign: KB7SHZ
Mark L Glass
Bend OR 97708

Call Sign: KC6AAN
Belinda J Beck
Bend OR 97709

Call Sign: N6UZJ
Gary A Meyer
Bend OR 977091396

Call Sign: KA7NTE
Carl E Browning
Bend OR 97708

Call Sign: KB7SHA
Christy J Knowles
Bend OR 97708

Call Sign: KC6SFR
Stefan B Barton
Bend OR 97708

Call Sign: KC7ITZ
Peter W Knowles
Bend OR 97708

Call Sign: KC7OOD
Timothy L Nielson
Bend OR 97708

Call Sign: KC7PYO
Gary L Powell
Bend OR 97708

Call Sign: KD7AVC
William P Moore
Bend OR 97708

Call Sign: KD7QB
Terry A Cowan
Bend OR 97708

Call Sign: KE6RJN
Gary L Curry
Bend OR 97708

Call Sign: KE6RJO
Lisa F Curry
Bend OR 97708

Call Sign: KL7IOW
Marvin G Wright
Bend OR 97708

Call Sign: N7FRE
Karen M Cowan
Bend OR 97708

Call Sign: W7VEE
Terry H Thorne
Bend OR 97708

Call Sign: WA7TPD
Central Oregon Radio
Amateurs
Bend OR 97708

Call Sign: KD7GQG
Martha M Moore
Bend OR 97708

Call Sign: KD7JQG
Dennis K Griffin
Bend OR 97708

Call Sign: KD7OJI
Molly A Mccallum
Bend OR 97708

Call Sign: KD7QVO
Randall C Roberson
Bend OR 97708

Call Sign: N0DOS
Archturiat C Baumann
Bend OR 97708

Call Sign: KF7TRY
David L Reich
Bend OR 97708

Call Sign: KE7JXE
Jill D Simmons
Bend OR 97708

Call Sign: KF7OMO
Katherine L Knapp
Bend OR 97708

Call Sign: AE7IK
Martin A Held
Bend OR 97708

Call Sign: KG6YKM
Simon S Kramedjian
Bend OR 97708

Call Sign: KE7BLQ
Susan L Marriott
Bend OR 97708

Call Sign: KF7TRZ
Teri J Reich
Bend OR 97708

Call Sign: AE7PP
Gert Carlsson
Bend OR 97708

Call Sign: W7JVO
High Desert Amateur Radio
Group
Bend OR 97709

Call Sign: KF7IKX
High Desert Amateur Radio
Group
Bend OR 97709

Call Sign: KF7IKY
High Desert Amateur Radio
Group
Bend OR 97709

Call Sign: KC7JMJ
Robert W Rodgers
Bend OR 97709

Call Sign: KC7LPL
William F Hanlon
Bend OR 97709

Call Sign: KC7LPM
William W Hanlon
Bend OR 97709

Call Sign: N7ZTH
Sterling D Williver
Bend OR 97709

Call Sign: WB7WRB
Wayne R Brown
Bend OR 97709

Call Sign: KD7QHO
Jack W Thomas
Bend OR 97709

Call Sign: KD7TDQ
Lonny L Tittle

Bend OR 97709

Call Sign: WN7K
Sterling D Williver
Bend OR 97709

Call Sign: KD7ZPT
Terry A Bingham
Bend OR 97709

Call Sign: N6YOW
Thomas E Bahrman
Bend OR 97709

Call Sign: KD7NBS
Randall C Wiggins
Bend OR 97709

Call Sign: KC7RQN
Robert F Carr
Bend OR 977085033

Call Sign: N7EGN
Alvin P Cluster
Bend OR 977085397

Call Sign: KC7QU
Donald G Mc Mahon
Bend OR 977086226

Call Sign: KD7EQH
Donald R Childs III
Bend OR 977086267

Call Sign: KE0PJ
Charles E Cavanaugh
Bend OR 977087135

Call Sign: N7SOX
Steve E Mc Neil
Bend OR 977088457

Call Sign: KD7VKD
Larry J Swenson
Bend OR 977091263

Call Sign: WL7AFN
William F Harris
38434 Hwy 20 E
Blachly OR 97412

Call Sign: N7NXW
David A Rapp
39378 Jasper Lowell Rd
Blachly OR 97412

Call Sign: KB7IGG
James E Larsen
24431 Queen Anne Dr
Blachly OR 97412

Call Sign: KA7DPH
Barbara C Newtown
983 Scepter Way NE
Blachly OR 97412

Call Sign: N7LYA
Waldo M Claflin
19658 Schaefer Dr
Blachly OR 97412

Call Sign: WZ7D
Priscilla G Claflin
908 Schaefers Ln
Blachly OR 97412

Call Sign: KD7WYV
Ronald M Earle
Blachly OR 97412

Call Sign: KE7EXE
Daniel W Gilloaley
Black Butte Rfpd
Hawksbeard
Black Butte Ranch OR 97759

Call Sign: KE7EXF
Kelly E Shelton
39622 Howard Rd
Black Butte Ranch OR 97759

Call Sign: KC7TYE
Sean J Hartley
82671 Howe Ln
Black Butte Ranch OR 97759

Call Sign: KE7EXD
Cody C Smith
Black Butte Ranch OR 97759

Call Sign: KD7KOI
Rosalind M Leve
3730 Buccaneer Ln Apt D
Blue River OR 97413

Call Sign: KD4WZ
Timothy Palange
34579 E Columbia Ave
Blue River OR 97413

Call Sign: WA7UUP
Robert A Magne
1231 Laurel St
Blue River OR 97413

Call Sign: W7JJH
Geraldine E Sinsel
364 Monica Dr
Blue River OR 97413

Call Sign: KD6WUW
Linda L Laskowski
471 Monmouth Ave S Apt 1
Blue River OR 97413

Call Sign: KD6WUZ
Wolfgang F Laskowski
15505 Monmouth Hwy
Blue River OR 97413

Call Sign: KD7TYG
Patrick L O Rasmussen
2685 Montello Ave
Blue River OR 97413

Call Sign: K7MPC
Patrick L O Rasmussen
2735 Montello Ave
Blue River OR 97413

Call Sign: KD7KOJ
William L Leve
Blue River OR 97413

Call Sign: KF7CRG
Debra L Bell
Blue River OR 97413

Call Sign: KF7CRI
James A Nuttall
Blue River OR 97413

**FCC Amateur Radio
Licenses in Bly**

Call Sign: N7WVN
Mitsuo Oshiro
1055 Mayfair Ln
Bly OR 97622

Call Sign: AB7IU
Alfred L Buell
2498 Russell Rd
Bly OR 97622

Call Sign: KB7LOD
Steven R Kolu
Bly OR 97622

Call Sign: KB7HIY
Fred L Schenk
Bly OR 97622

Call Sign: KF7UKF
Joshua J Meadowcroft
Bly OR 97622

Call Sign: KF7UKH
Michael Holmes
Bly OR 97622

**FCC Amateur Radio
Licenses in Boardman**

Call Sign: K7DSW
Gunnar A Skoubo
7528 Buckhorn Rd
Boardman OR 978180015

Call Sign: N5QEN
Bobbi R Scogin
4072 Del Rio Rd
Boardman OR 97818

Call Sign: KD7EQB
Fred J Walters
201 Fern Valley Rd
Boardman OR 97818

Call Sign: KJ7MI
Jeff L Sak
14452 Hunt Mountain Ln
Boardman OR 97818

Call Sign: KE7DKM
Tod R Files
749 Leeper Rd
Boardman OR 97818

Call Sign: KD5KAF

Timothy P Curtis Jr
15450 SW Koll Pkwy
Boardman OR 97818

Call Sign: KF7MUI
Larry E Braden
11230 SW Muirwood Dr
Boardman OR 97818

Call Sign: N7RES
Irvin L Peterson
2232 SW Willowbrook
Boardman OR 97818

Call Sign: KD7MQT
Lavern E Gertlar
403 Willowfork Dr
Boardman OR 97818

Call Sign: KC7DNT
Albino J Quarisa
Boardman OR 97818

Call Sign: KC7PIY
Carolyn J Skoubo
Boardman OR 97818

Call Sign: KL7HKS
Cecil W Greer Jr
Boardman OR 97818

Call Sign: KD7GMT
Barbara E Reed
Boardman OR 97818

Call Sign: KF7MUJ
Donald F Drayton
Boardman OR 97818

Call Sign: KE7UOP
Dustin R Harper
Boardman OR 97818

Call Sign: KF7NPI
Mark C Pratt

Boardman OR 97818

FCC Amateur Radio Licenses in Bonanza

Call Sign: N7WVP
Vodas N Fleetwood
1912 25th St
Bonanza OR 97623

Call Sign: W7OXS
Glen R Fleetwood
1912 25th St
Bonanza OR 97623

Call Sign: AB0SY
John A Hamilton
7528 Buckhorn Rd
Bonanza OR 97623

Call Sign: KC7NQB
Shelby R Asbill
7528 Buckhorn Rd
Bonanza OR 97623

Call Sign: N4CUJ
Jack L Stewart
6560 Canary Rd
Bonanza OR 97623

Call Sign: WB7WSL
Roger D Reid
4121 Chapman Way
Bonanza OR 97623

Call Sign: KD7NGL
Shawn C Earp
555 Freeman Rd 52
Bonanza OR 97623

Call Sign: KE7PTQ
Cindy K Ducette
7443 Harley Way SE
Bonanza OR 97623

Call Sign: KE7PNU
Donald E Ducette
7443 Harley Way SE
Bonanza OR 97623

Call Sign: KC7YNV
Norman L Stalbird
1990 Hawkins Ln
Bonanza OR 976237786

Call Sign: KD6VBA
Ed R Gailey
4335 Hilsinger Rd
Bonanza OR 97623

Call Sign: KD6VBB
Alisa M Gailey
4335 Hilsingor Rd
Bonanza OR 97623

Call Sign: KC7IXB
Marilyn E Gingerich
1232 Hilton Dr
Bonanza OR 97623

Call Sign: WB6IYP
William F Gingerich
4487 Hilton Dr
Bonanza OR 97623

Call Sign: KD7CNX
Sidney R Dyer Sr
2056 Hollywood Dr NE
Bonanza OR 97623

Call Sign: WA7VTB
Francis F Farnworth
3205 Hollywood Dr NE
Bonanza OR 97623

Call Sign: WA6QFO
Geraldine A Cooper
94416 Langlois Mt Rd
Bonanza OR 97623

Call Sign: KA7OPX
Helen C Jones
455 Lantana Ave
Bonanza OR 976239730

Call Sign: WB7VMA
Robert E Jones
69572 Lantz Ln
Bonanza OR 97623

Call Sign: K7ADW
Noel D Williams
2078 Lemuria St
Bonanza OR 97623

Call Sign: KF7KBU
Lawrence N Payne
250 Tech Way
Bonanza OR 97623

Call Sign: KC7KWR
John F King
250 Tech Way
Bonanza OR 97623

Call Sign: KA7QBZ
Shirley L Chapman
Bonanza OR 97623

Call Sign: WA6QFN
Albert H Cooper
Bonanza OR 97623

Call Sign: KC7FEY
Ross L Tomlin
Bonanza OR 97623

Call Sign: N7WVL
Raymond L Crisman
Bonanza OR 97623

Call Sign: WV6K
Richard R Risley
Bonanza OR 97623

FCC Amateur Radio Licenses in Broadbent

Call Sign: NZ7F
David C Grimes
7543 N Edgewater St
Broadbent OR 97414

Call Sign: KD7WPG
Billi J Ludington
3755 NE Sumner St
Broadbent OR 97414

FCC Amateur Radio Licenses in Brookings

Call Sign: N7XWF
Dennis J Barbee
511 36th Ave NW
Brookings OR 97415

Call Sign: WB8YPO
Chris M Teague
451 3rd Ave
Brookings OR 97415

Call Sign: KD7ITG
Kathleen M Teague
764 3rd Ave
Brookings OR 97415

Call Sign: KD6AZI
Henry L Strattan
18125 3rd Ave
Brookings OR 97415

Call Sign: KD7FVN
David D Pettigrew
1210 Arcadia Dr
Brookings OR 97415

Call Sign: WA6KCU
Kirby L Anderson
57596 Becky Ln
Brookings OR 97415

Call Sign: KE6NCU
Stuart W Anthony
533 Buckhorn Rd
Brookings OR 97415

Call Sign: KE7BBK
Jeremy M Warner
2503 Canterbury St
Brookings OR 97415

Call Sign: KA6AOQ
Ladner Cameron
6115 Carfield St
Brookings OR 97415

Call Sign: KE7OMK
Robert J Fitton
18811 Cathy Adams Dr
Brookings OR 97415

Call Sign: KE6NVU
Paul B Carlin
1970 Chambers St
Brookings OR 97415

Call Sign: NX1P
Paula D Keezer
8965 Chance Rd
Brookings OR 97415

Call Sign: NM7W
Arlon Helms
32305 Church Rd
Brookings OR 974159249

Call Sign: N6JDS
Glenn A Woodfin
1145 Clayton Way
Brookings OR 97415

Call Sign: KC7WHF
James A Harrell
7515 Clear Creek
Brookings OR 97415

Call Sign: KF7DQT
Albert L Harrell
7356 Clear Creek Rd
Brookings OR 97415

Call Sign: KE7LBJ
Daisy L Carr
60291 Cleveland Rd
Brookings OR 97415

Call Sign: KE7LBI
Don D Carr
60291 Cleveland Rd
Brookings OR 97415

Call Sign: KE7TFR
Holly Carr
60291 Cleveland Rd
Brookings OR 97415

Call Sign: KE7KAP
Karen D Carr
130 Cleveland St
Brookings OR 97415

Call Sign: KF7KVQ
Loren Giffith
4630 Clinton Ave
Brookings OR 97415

Call Sign: KE7YUI
Larry E Mostachetti
1764 Derby St
Brookings OR 97415

Call Sign: N7CEI
Albert R Walker
600 Devils Knob Rd
Brookings OR 97415

Call Sign: W7KSE
Luther A Page
6610 Doncaster Dr
Brookings OR 97415

Call Sign: K6JFC
George K Sievers
2070 Doral Ct
Brookings OR 97415

Call Sign: KC7YCO
Clinton W Patterson
2530 Drift Creek Rd NE
Brookings OR 97415

Call Sign: N7XWC
Betty C Grant
431 E 34th Ave
Brookings OR 97415

Call Sign: KD7CXA
Laurie H Calef
343 E St Helens St
Brookings OR 97415

Call Sign: N6SGM
Warren N Glaze
1306 Elm St
Brookings OR 974159484

Call Sign: KH7RD
Michael J Mcqueen
200 Ferndale Dr
Brookings OR 97415

Call Sign: KB6HLW
Patricia A Land
260 Ferndale Dr
Brookings OR 974159738

Call Sign: N6ASA
Herbert D Sanders
27373 Fernridge Rd
Brookings OR 97415

Call Sign: KC7YCQ
Larry L Carter
3361 Franklin Ave
Brookings OR 97415

Call Sign: KD7QXZ
Mindy Hamilton
60750 Gensman Rd
Brookings OR 97415

Call Sign: W7ZAP
Mindy G Hamilton
35725 Gentry St
Brookings OR 97415

Call Sign: WL7QU
Dorice L Gustafson
35725 Gentry St
Brookings OR 97415

Call Sign: AL7PE
Douglas M Gustafson
437 Gentry Way
Brookings OR 97415

Call Sign: W7SPY
Douglas M Gustafson
437 Gentry Way
Brookings OR 97415

Call Sign: KT3V
Douglas M Gustafson
437 Gentry Way
Brookings OR 97415

Call Sign: W6JGD
Lloyd R Shipman Jr
2825 Heather Way
Brookings OR 974159264

Call Sign: N7GIP
Evelyn B Helms
710 Holbrook Ln
Brookings OR 974159249

Call Sign: W7FEF
Vernon R Keays
475 Holcomb Springs Rd
Brookings OR 97415

Call Sign: KC7EEV
Janet I Biagini
365 Humphrey Addition Rd
Brookings OR 97415

Call Sign: KJ7RG
Ray A Biagini Jr
38764 Hungry Hill Dr
Brookings OR 97415

Call Sign: KF7UBJ
Linda M Hunter
201 Hunsaker Ln
Brookings OR 97415

Call Sign: WA7LBN
Linda M Hunter
201 Hunsaker Ln
Brookings OR 97415

Call Sign: W6ZU
Wesley H Wiley
600 Hunsaker Ln
Brookings OR 974159698

Call Sign: KB7YPK
Thomas K Eaton
5640 Imai Rd
Brookings OR 97415

Call Sign: KE7WJR
Dale B Stimson
2832 Indigo Way
Brookings OR 97415

Call Sign: KC7WHI
William M Smith
789 Jackson St E
Brookings OR 974158138

Call Sign: K6AZE
Richard W Steele
122 Knight
Brookings OR 97415

Call Sign: N6FKM
Marjorie E Steele
5392 Knightwood Dr
Brookings OR 97415

Call Sign: K6CKL
Eugene W Lieb
1651 McBee Rd
Brookings OR 97415

Call Sign: KE7JFY
Douglas R Merrell
85240 McBeth Rd
Brookings OR 97415

Call Sign: KE7PNB
Patricia J Kelsoe
21965 McBurney
Brookings OR 97415

Call Sign: KD7QAZ
Lara Shing
260 McClure Ave
Brookings OR 97415

Call Sign: KE6GPD
Alecia Buonocore Elvstad
28033 Meridian Heights
Loop
Brookings OR 974159686

Call Sign: N6LGS
William H Graham
2743 Merriman Rd
Brookings OR 97415

Call Sign: K7VPL
Richard W Keusink
2946 Merriman Rd
Brookings OR 97415

Call Sign: KE6CDE
Reginald W Dewar
913 Merryman Dr

Brookings OR 97415

Call Sign: KC7ENY
John D Siebenborn
10256 Mourning Dove Dr
Brookings OR 97415

Call Sign: K7JCS
James C Speas
411 Mtn View Ct
Brookings OR 97415

Call Sign: WB7ESA
Matthew W Mjelde
49425 Mtn View Rd
Brookings OR 97415

Call Sign: KE7EFS
James C Speas
49425 Mtn View Rd
Brookings OR 97415

Call Sign: KC7QZV
Lee Tinner
5017 N Amherst
Brookings OR 97415

Call Sign: KD7DA
Lewis A Sapp
413 N Brown Cpo Box 10D
Brookings OR 97415

Call Sign: K6LKK
Oscar R Marks
31919 N Lake Creek Dr 33
Brookings OR 97415

Call Sign: KB7JGF
Jim Lindley
701 N Lincoln St
Brookings OR 97415

Call Sign: KC7VUU
Judith M Rupert
4635 N Lombard

Brookings OR 97415

Call Sign: AA7QW
Joseph B Bogner
2542 Orchard Hill Ln
Brookings OR 974159328

Call Sign: W6SEA
Neil C Gardenheir
2626 Orchard Hill Pl
Brookings OR 97415

Call Sign: WB7VOP
C Walter Baty
1908 Orchard Hts Ct NW
Brookings OR 97415

Call Sign: W6KYV
David F Homes
1953 Orchard Hts Ct NW
Brookings OR 974159327

Call Sign: KB6VKM
William J Lennartz
780 Paloma Ave
Brookings OR 97415

Call Sign: K7UF
William A Roberts
6444 Palomino Way
Brookings OR 97415

Call Sign: N7SJJ
Joann S Bates
4763 Patricia St NE
Brookings OR 97415

Call Sign: KC6POW
John E Pohl
1716 Pilgrim St SE
Brookings OR 97415

Call Sign: K6ZZB
Frank L Towne
1526 Pine Ave

Brookings OR 97415

Call Sign: WA7GJC
Hank B Shields
19248 Pine Ave
Brookings OR 97415

Call Sign: K3BIV
David G White Jr
310 Pitney Ln 100
Brookings OR 97415

Call Sign: W7BNG
Clarence M Sorvaag
310 Pitney Ln Sp 50
Brookings OR 974150107

Call Sign: K6RSC
Raymond L Smock
56039 Prosper Jct Rd
Brookings OR 97415

Call Sign: KC7WHG
Virgil E Cox
1601 608 Rhododendron Dr
Brookings OR 97415

Call Sign: KE7ALF
Wendy J Cox
1600 Rhododendron Dr 47
Brookings OR 97415

Call Sign: KC7RAB
Randal L GARCia
41720 Ridge Dr
Brookings OR 97415

Call Sign: K7DRY
Roger W Haag
484 Scotts Glenn Dr
Brookings OR 97415

Call Sign: K6ECL
Daniel W Walters Jr
253 SE 126th Dr

Brookings OR 97415

Call Sign: WA6KXK
Richard E Morse
6140 SE 128 Ave
Brookings OR 97415

Call Sign: KF6JWJ
Darlene J Walters
3245 SE 129 Ave
Brookings OR 97415

Call Sign: KI7CR
Almond J Bates
6125 SE Division St Apt
322
Brookings OR 97415

Call Sign: N7YGY
Shirley M Bates
36725 SE Double Creek Dr
Brookings OR 97415

Call Sign: NX7M
Stephen A Mathis
409 SE Nursery St
Brookings OR 97415

Call Sign: KK6XT
John K Gauger
80798 Sfk Wwr
Brookings OR 97415

Call Sign: W6AUH
Dalton J Bergstedt
3150 Siskiyou
Brookings OR 97415

Call Sign: KE7TFQ
Sean W Armstrong
2937 Stark St
Brookings OR 97415

Call Sign: WB7RGW
Keith P Brooks

32227 Tangent Dr
Brookings OR 97415

Call Sign: KG6FHR
Fred W Johnson
300 Thornberry Dr
Brookings OR 97415

Call Sign: W6DWY
Brian T Pacchetti
1400 Tucker Rd
Brookings OR 97415

Call Sign: KK7GY
John M Gibbs
7130 Ventura Dr
Brookings OR 97415

Call Sign: AA7XQ
Howard C Ayer
97940 W Benham Ln 16
Brookings OR 97415

Call Sign: KB7PAD
Marion L Ayer
97940 W Benham Ln 16
Brookings OR 97415

Call Sign: AC7CL
Marion L Ayer
97940 W Benham Ln 16
Brookings OR 97415

Call Sign: KC7OEI
Mike V Elia
16944 Westwood Ln
Brookings OR 97415

Call Sign: KA6DFM
Calvin E Murphy Jr
200 Winchuck River Rd
Brookings OR 97415

Call Sign: KD7TAW
Alissa K Ajimine

1011 Winchuck River Rd
Brookings OR 97415

Call Sign: KD7TAX
Amy M Ajimine
1011 Winchuck River Rd
Brookings OR 97415

Call Sign: KD7VOP
Conny L Ajimine
1011 Winchuck River Rd
Brookings OR 97415

Call Sign: KD7TAV
Edwin Ajimine
1011 Winchuck River Rd
Brookings OR 97415

Call Sign: KE7OOF
Richard Arledge
1521 Winchuck River Rd
Brookings OR 97415

Call Sign: KE7ALG
Alfred Mikkelsen
99353 Winchuck River Rd
Brookings OR 97415

Call Sign: KC7QZW
Thomas L Taylor
15524 Winriver Dr
Brookings OR 97415

Call Sign: KB7EYY
Edward E Cobb
15563 Winriver Rd
Brookings OR 97415

Call Sign: KB7HSR
Perrie L Cobb
15563 Winriver Rd
Brookings OR 97415

Call Sign: KE7ORJ
Gary R Lowden

14626 Wollam Rd
Brookings OR 97415

Call Sign: KF7ALR
Curry County ARES Station
Club
19048 Woodton Ln
Brookings OR 97415

Call Sign: K7URY
Curry County ARES Station
Club
19048 Woodton Ln
Brookings OR 97415

Call Sign: N6MD
Robert E Wilkinson
19048 Woodton Ln
Brookings OR 974159796

Call Sign: WA6RFC
Lorraine H Wilkinson
19048 Woodton Ln
Brookings OR 974159796

Call Sign: W7RFC
Lorraine H Wilkinson
19048 Woodton Ln
Brookings OR 974159796

Call Sign: W7VN
Robert E Wilkinson
19048 Woodton Ln
Brookings OR 974159796

Call Sign: KB7HIA
Roy E Miller
Brookings OR 97415

Call Sign: N7KPY
Willard A Groff
Brookings OR 97415

Call Sign: N7OFN
Elizabeth J Groff

Brookings OR 97415

Call Sign: N7TEA
Paul A Harman
Brookings OR 97415

Call Sign: N7XWA
Melvin L Fox
Brookings OR 97415

Call Sign: N7XWB
Margaret E Fox
Brookings OR 97415

Call Sign: WB6JKL
Elmer Hitchcock
Brookings OR 97415

Call Sign: N7NEG
John A Eckert
Brookings OR 97415

Call Sign: KB7BIB
Samuel A Hall Sr
Brookings OR 97415

Call Sign: KC7EKO
Shayne C Musser
Brookings OR 97415

Call Sign: KC7VUT
Michael M Rupert
Brookings OR 97415

Call Sign: KC7WAA
Kalina F Parker
Brookings OR 97415

Call Sign: KE6YLM
Francis A Meccia III
Brookings OR 97415

Call Sign: KF6CTM
Mike G Henry
Brookings OR 97415

Call Sign: KI7HN
Charles D De Salvo
Brookings OR 97415

Call Sign: N1EQG
Bruce Warren
Brookings OR 97415

Call Sign: N7SJH
Polly W Keusink
Brookings OR 97415

Call Sign: N7XWE
Ray P Sundblad
Brookings OR 97415

Call Sign: WA6VIB
Mary A Coggins
Brookings OR 97415

Call Sign: WB6GUM
Andrew M Tullis
Brookings OR 97415

Call Sign: KE7UOR
Bart O Ickes
Brookings OR 97415

Call Sign: KE7VHU
Colette I Ickes
Brookings OR 97415

Call Sign: KE7NTF
Donny S Dotson
Brookings OR 97415

Call Sign: KF7JCA
Gary W Burton
Brookings OR 97415

Call Sign: KF7KVP
James P Fournier
Brookings OR 97415

Call Sign: KF7GPF
Janet J Norman
Brookings OR 97415

Call Sign: KE7ERM
Martin Palmer
Brookings OR 97415

Call Sign: KE7YUH
Mei Tang
Brookings OR 97415

Call Sign: KF7UIH
Norman E Alander
Brookings OR 97415

Call Sign: KF7UII
Richard M Tylock
Brookings OR 97415

Call Sign: KF7HNO
Rita Dotson
Brookings OR 97415

Call Sign: KE7NTG
Robert J Lake
Brookings OR 97415

Call Sign: KF7HNP
Samuel W Dotson
Brookings OR 97415

Call Sign: KD7YCD
Von Williams
Brookings OR 97415

Call Sign: KE7ERL
Michi C Deremiah Palmer
Brookings OR 97415

Call Sign: WA6QOX
Jimmy N Conger
Brookings OR 974150282

Call Sign: KC7RLP

Teri J Johnston Dougan
Brookings OR 974150369

Call Sign: W6TTU
Jerry V Lahtinen
Brookings OR 974150377

Call Sign: W7CLS
R Wayne Fields
Brookings OR 974150378

Call Sign: N7ENN
R Wayne Fields
Brookings OR 974150378

FCC Amateur Radio Licenses in Burns

Call Sign: KD7AKL
Don F Hall
1980 25th St
Burns OR 97720

Call Sign: KF7JDT
Jeff D Dorroh
2251 Dick George Rd
Burns OR 97720

Call Sign: KF7JDO
Mary T Dorroh
2251 Dick George Rd
Burns OR 97720

Call Sign: WL7AIV
Edna Dunaway
2251 Dick George Rd
Burns OR 97720

Call Sign: KA7GQH
Richard L Fly
1523 E Ave
Burns OR 97720

Call Sign: WB7BCH
Richard L Fly

504 E B St
Burns OR 97720

3927 N Massachusetts Ave
Burns OR 97720

61 S Court Ave
Burns OR 97720

Call Sign: WB7BCG
Dorothy M Fly
66642 E Bay Dr Sp 50
Burns OR 97720

Call Sign: WB7UHP
Christine M Rider
4227 N Massachusetts Ave
Burns OR 97720

Call Sign: KD7IYC
Jonathan R Angell
620 S Ivy St
Burns OR 97720

Call Sign: KF7JDR
Lynda Q Ward
1525 Essex St
Burns OR 97720

Call Sign: KJ7JC
Arthur L Knowles
4227 N Massachusetts Ave
Burns OR 97720

Call Sign: KB7USG
David J Tindle Jr
1535 S Ivy St
Burns OR 97720

Call Sign: WB7NRI
Robert E Fulton
1307 F St
Burns OR 97720

Call Sign: KE7KIB
Hoyt L Johnson
555 N River Rd 32
Burns OR 97720

Call Sign: KF6QPD
William B Douglas III
1630 Samuel Dr
Burns OR 97720

Call Sign: W0OT
Richard D Schwieren
14640 Ferns Corner Rd
Burns OR 97720

Call Sign: KB7NMF
William R Rines
418 N Ross Ln
Burns OR 97720

Call Sign: W7NQA
Arthur L Runnels
287 W B St
Burns OR 97720

Call Sign: KF7EOF
Jess B Tate
4928 Jennifer Ave S
Burns OR 97720

Call Sign: KE7SEA
Eric C Guthrie
4035 N Vancouver Ave
Burns OR 97720

Call Sign: KF7EOE
John Stinnett
184 W D St
Burns OR 97720

Call Sign: KF7EOG
Jess W Tate
711 Jenny Ln
Burns OR 97720

Call Sign: KA7NFA
Pamela L Keller
1202 NE 193
Burns OR 97720

Call Sign: KC7COV
Raymond F Angell
388 W D St
Burns OR 97720

Call Sign: WB7SFC
James C Fulton
2351 N Irvine St
Burns OR 97720

Call Sign: K7COW
Thomas J Sharp Sr
1438 Rainier Rd
Burns OR 97720

Call Sign: WB7SJK
Carl H Voegtly
30414 Windmill Ln
Burns OR 97720

Call Sign: KC7HUV
James W Gibson
1441 N Marine Dr
Burns OR 97720

Call Sign: KF7JDN
James R Ward
1600 221 Rhododendron Dr
Burns OR 97720

Call Sign: WB7RHC
Harold W PeARCe Jr
Burns OR 97720

Call Sign: KA7MEI
Mark P Keller

Call Sign: KF7GRK
Donald W Williams

Call Sign: K7BMH
Harney County ARES
Burns OR 97720

Call Sign: KF7CIS
Linda K Watts
Burns OR 97720

Call Sign: KF7EOH
Marjorie E Thelen
Burns OR 97720

Call Sign: KF7CIO
Robert J Thelen
Burns OR 97720

Call Sign: KF7JDM
Thresa M Geisler
Burns OR 97720

Call Sign: W7HRN
Harney County ARES
Burns OR 97720

Call Sign: W7HDH
Harney County ARES
Burns OR 97720

FCC Amateur Radio Licenses in Butte Falls

Call Sign: N6WJK
Linda R Stockton
378 Lori Ave SE
Butte Falls OR 97522

Call Sign: N7YHZ
Blanche O Campbell
Butte Falls OR 97522

Call Sign: K6AGD
James E Arnold
Butte Falls OR 97522

Call Sign: KB7TXH
Robert L Moberly
Butte Falls OR 97522

Call Sign: KE7HFB
Hugh F Simpson
Butte Falls OR 97522

FCC Amateur Radio Licenses in Camas Valley

Call Sign: K6GUE
Clifford E Clinton
1464 Wildcat Rd
Camas Valley OR 97416

Call Sign: N6UK
John V Walsh
Camas Valley OR 97416

Call Sign: KD7CCP
Lloyd T Nelson
Camas Valley OR 97416

Call Sign: KE7LDX
Stephen C Beardsley
Camas Valley OR 97416

Call Sign: KF7DFY
Wanda K Chapman
Camas Valley OR 97416

FCC Amateur Radio Licenses in Camp Sherman

Call Sign: KA1TZO
Sayward J Ayre
Camp Sherman OR 97730

Call Sign: KE7DF
Kim Lundgren
Camp Sherman OR 97730

Call Sign: KD7LBF
Jarett H Hancock
Camp Sherman OR 97730

FCC Amateur Radio Licenses in Canyon City

Call Sign: N7YB
John W Nydam
2806 3rd St
Canyon City OR 97820

Call Sign: K7GLD
Garald L Davidson
2769 Ave A
Canyon City OR 97820

Call Sign: KC5LN
Lynn E Nicholson
2829 Ave A
Canyon City OR 97820

Call Sign: KC7LN
Lynn E Nicholson
3686 Ave A
Canyon City OR 97820

Call Sign: KB6OWX
William S Rose
445 C Ave
Canyon City OR 97820

Call Sign: W7TDJ
John W Nydam
6206 Canary Rd
Canyon City OR 97820

Call Sign: WA7TDJ
John W Nydam
Izee Rt
Canyon City OR 97820

Call Sign: WR7X
Rex A Kamstra
316 NE 19th Ave
Canyon City OR 97820

Call Sign: KA7ELJ
J Leroy Jolley

Canyon City OR 97820

Call Sign: N7ZMT
Joan C Tayles
Canyon City OR 97820

Call Sign: N7ZMU
Joel T Tayles
Canyon City OR 97820

Call Sign: KF7MOY
Rebecca E Jarnes
Canyon City OR 97820

FCC Amateur Radio Licenses in Canyonville

Call Sign: KL7GKY
Jack R Bone
275 Azalea Dr
Canyonville OR 97417

Call Sign: WB7TFW
Roy M Yokoyama
18100 Hillside Ct
Canyonville OR 97417

Call Sign: KD7AOR
Marion E Faulkner
536 Madison St
Canyonville OR 97417

Call Sign: KC6VHP
Charles L Fransen
94924 Mystery Ln
Canyonville OR 97417

Call Sign: W7CBH
Meryle R Hansen
23966 S Rondevic
Canyonville OR 974171194

Call Sign: KA6IXY
Frederick W Finke
254 Wild Creek Way

Canyonville OR 97417

Call Sign: N7IXY
Frederick W Finke
254 Wild Creek Way
Canyonville OR 97417

Call Sign: KG7UY
Dennis G Deaton
Canyonville OR 97417

Call Sign: N7CRU
Richard V Williams
Canyonville OR 97417

Call Sign: WB4GTV
David H Mc Neese
Canyonville OR 97417

Call Sign: AB5BF
Charles G Spindel
Canyonville OR 97417

Call Sign: AB7NC
James E Hargraves
Canyonville OR 97417

Call Sign: KB6WF
Eric J Neill
Canyonville OR 97417

Call Sign: KB7KAC
Catherine E Deaton
Canyonville OR 97417

Call Sign: KD7AXR
Leonard J Faulkner
Canyonville OR 97417

Call Sign: KK7OJ
Vivian M Hargraves
Canyonville OR 97417

Call Sign: KD7YNW
Carleon J Kekacs

Canyonville OR 97417

Call Sign: AD7EI
Carleon J Kekacs
Canyonville OR 97417

Call Sign: AD7FK
Carleon J Kekacs
Canyonville OR 97417

Call Sign: AE7FK
Charles G Spindel
Canyonville OR 97417

FCC Amateur Radio Licenses in Cascade Locks

Call Sign: KD7AV
Del S Van Camp
4308 Madrona Way SE
Cascade Locks OR
970140579

Call Sign: N7OFV
Frank L Corbin
24165 S Brockway Rd
Cascade Locks OR 97014

Call Sign: KB7QXL
Randy L Markwell
Cascade Locks OR 97014

FCC Amateur Radio Licenses in Cave Junction

Call Sign: KE7LY
Warren C Goines
4562 Chaparral Dr SE
Cave Junction OR 97523

Call Sign: K7OVW
Michael T Sloan
4392 Cloudview Dr S
Cave Junction OR 97523

Call Sign: KE7IKU
Cathleen S Von Breithaupt
5494 Coleman Ck Rd
Cave Junction OR
975239761

Call Sign: KC7EWL
Joshua A Robinson
625B E Jackson St
Cave Junction OR 97523

Call Sign: KD7EJK
Russell W Dyer
3410 Pacific Blvd SW 17
Cave Junction OR 97523

Call Sign: W7GQU
Nelson L Eshelman
6086 Coleman Creek Rd
Cave Junction OR 97523

Call Sign: KC7WEV
Matthew L Robinson
334 E Jefferson
Cave Junction OR 97523

Call Sign: N5WBC
Carl V Mustol
702 Palm St
Cave Junction OR 97523

Call Sign: N7NAJ
David E Marsh
963 Colinwood Ln
Cave Junction OR 97523

Call Sign: KC7CNY
Bethany R Robinson
396 E Jennie Ave
Cave Junction OR 97523

Call Sign: WA6GLX
Francis P Fox
707 Palmer Ave
Cave Junction OR 97523

Call Sign: N7SUN
Sally K Borth
50015 Collar Dr
Cave Junction OR 97523

Call Sign: KC7COD
Nedd L Wyant
23882 Hall Rd
Cave Junction OR 97523

Call Sign: KC7CJC
George H Doersch
90196 Prairie Rd
Cave Junction OR 97523

Call Sign: KF4LMI
Elizabeth A Hale
50015 Collar Dr
Cave Junction OR 97523

Call Sign: WB6RPD
Erwin F Sawall Jr
7909 Hwy 66
Cave Junction OR 97523

Call Sign: N7YUR
James R Price
1600 445 Rhody Dr
Cave Junction OR 97523

Call Sign: AB7FT
Noah E Robinson
825 E Jackson St
Cave Junction OR 97523

Call Sign: W7LEV
Robert G Braden
6248 Lost Creek Rd
Cave Junction OR 97523

Call Sign: KE7GTM
Michael A Davis
60677 River Bend Dr
Cave Junction OR 97523

Call Sign: KC7CNX
Arynne L Robinson
920 E Jackson St
Cave Junction OR 97523

Call Sign: KA6JLC
Meg Kelsey
5634 Munsel Ln
Cave Junction OR 97523

Call Sign: N2LOF
George A Branigan
538 River Bend Rd
Cave Junction OR 97523

Call Sign: KC7CNZ
Zachary W Robinson
2130 E Jackson St
Cave Junction OR 97523

Call Sign: KB7EKC
William G Reid
2690 N 3rd St
Cave Junction OR 97523

Call Sign: N7LOF
George A Branigan
784 River Bend Rd
Cave Junction OR 97523

Call Sign: KC7CSH
Arthur B Robinson
2136 E Jackson St
Cave Junction OR 97523

Call Sign: WA7ISX
William P Pence
404 Pacific
Cave Junction OR 97523

Call Sign: N7LOH
George A Branigan
784 River Bend Rd
Cave Junction OR 97523

Call Sign: KA7CZF
Jerry L Lamb
740 S 15th St
Cave Junction OR 97523

Call Sign: KA7WEE
Russell L House
480 S 17th
Cave Junction OR 97523

Call Sign: KE7ATM
Donna J Lapierre Brown
1470 S 17th
Cave Junction OR 97523

Call Sign: N7KVA
Betty L Rupe
141 S 17th 27
Cave Junction OR 97523

Call Sign: KF7IBO
Joseph J Latva
16675 S Pam Dr
Cave Junction OR 97523

Call Sign: N6JDY
George H Savord
7514 Skyline Rd S
Cave Junction OR 97523

Call Sign: N6JDX
Melanie J Savord
17450 Skyliners Rd
Cave Junction OR 97523

Call Sign: K7JK
Jonathan D Klein
208 Talemena Dr
Cave Junction OR 97523

Call Sign: WB6SHV
Melvin C Benson
202 W River St
Cave Junction OR 97523

Call Sign: KA7CKI
Laurence M Zetzman
210 W River St
Cave Junction OR 97523

Call Sign: KC7CAF
Charles R Parks
6722 Westside Rd
Cave Junction OR 97523

Call Sign: KB7TST
Clyde J Highbarger
Cave Junction OR 95723

Call Sign: AA7GH
Lee M Sundstrom
Cave Junction OR 97523

Call Sign: KB7EKE
William T Atkins
Cave Junction OR 97523

Call Sign: N7NLS
Reuel W Schlarb
Cave Junction OR 97523

Call Sign: N6AXB
Lee Eschen
Cave Junction OR
975230978

Call Sign: KD7BAQ
Scott E Bauer
Cave Junction OR 97523

Call Sign: KE6LAU
Mauri L Hammersmith
Cave Junction OR 97523

Call Sign: KF6CBK
William J Rafael Jr
Cave Junction OR 97523

Call Sign: KK6NC

Mary C Sears
Cave Junction OR 97523

Call Sign: KG4EJH
Vincent D Monti
Cave Junction OR 97523

Call Sign: KD7QIU
Peter A Davies
Cave Junction OR 97523

Call Sign: KD7RTH
David W Prebble
Cave Junction OR 97523

Call Sign: KE7ATL
Christopher J Highbarger
Cave Junction OR 97523

Call Sign: KE7IZY
John A Brown
Cave Junction OR 97523

Call Sign: KE7ATK
Laurel F Highbarger
Cave Junction OR 97523

Call Sign: KE7JAA
Samuel J Williams
Cave Junction OR 97523

Call Sign: KE7IZZ
Valerie K Brown
Cave Junction OR 97523

Call Sign: KE7NPO
Ronald W Thorp
Cave Junction OR 97532

Call Sign: KG6HBX
Peter Block
Cave Junction OR
975230793

FCC Amateur Radio Licenses in Central Point

Call Sign: KF7LVS
Richard G Samuelson Jr
5410 Bartlett
Central Point OR 97502

Call Sign: KF7UMN
Rich L Bartlett
31728 Berlin Rd
Central Point OR 97502

Call Sign: N7WWN
Robert L Aaronson
Rt 3 Box 272F
Central Point OR 97502

Call Sign: KC7ARW
Guy R Stults
Rt 1 Box 30B
Central Point OR 97501

Call Sign: KF7LTA
Jordan M Mingus
Hc 84 Box 512
Central Point OR 97502

Call Sign: KA7AJK
Lawrence E Headley
38295 Brooten Rd
Central Point OR 97501

Call Sign: N7XBI
Richard D Baker
121 Brosi Orchard Rd
Central Point OR 97502

Call Sign: N7YIC
Robert T Baker
121 Brosi Orchard Rd
Central Point OR 97502

Call Sign: KA7DWE
Bonnie D King
61000 Broster House Sp
544
Central Point OR 97502

Call Sign: KA7DWF
Eugene King
61355 Brosterhaus Rd
Central Point OR 97502

Call Sign: KB7QMT
Joseph F Gunderson
61416 5 Brosterhous Rd
Central Point OR 97502

Call Sign: KA7WRU
Ivy B Taylor
61000 Brosterhous Rd 545
Central Point OR 97502

Call Sign: WA7RFY
Jeffrey A Sherman
61000 Brosterhous Rd Unit
5
Central Point OR 97502

Call Sign: KB7RGO
Paul M Vickland
17405 Brown Rd
Central Point OR 97502

Call Sign: KE7YLG
Jennifer A Graham
901 Brutscher St Ste D Pmb
357
Central Point OR 97502

Call Sign: K7YLG
Jennifer A Graham
1100 Bryan St
Central Point OR 97502

Call Sign: KE7LKP
Michael S Graham
4314 Bryan St S
Central Point OR 97502

Call Sign: K7LKP
Michael S Graham
1705 Bryant Ct
Central Point OR 97502

Call Sign: KB7IIE
Mitchell D Anstine
421 Buena Vista Loop
Central Point OR 97502

Call Sign: K7MOI
Charles N Fletcher
12555 Buena Vista Rd
Central Point OR
975029482

Call Sign: KF7JWF
Patricia M Bishop
96471 Cape Ferrelo Rd
Central Point OR 97502

Call Sign: KD7EHF
Stephen S Brown
2600 Cape Meares Loop
NW
Central Point OR 97502

Call Sign: W7CQF
Franklin A Knox
1561 Chemeketa NE
Central Point OR
975022937

Call Sign: W7OJA
Berry J Albright Jr
18160 Cottonwood Rd Apt
756
Central Point OR 97502

Call Sign: WB7BJW
V R T ARC
522 Cummings Ln
Central Point OR 97502

Call Sign: KF7UMS
Elaine B Wheeler
832 Cummings Ln N
Central Point OR 97502

Call Sign: KL7VK
Kirby R Wheeler
15101 Cunningham Ln NE
Central Point OR 97502

Call Sign: W7WJY
James H Lulay
236 Dan Ave
Central Point OR 97502

Call Sign: KB8AP
Joseph D Planisky
2472 Dan Ave NW
Central Point OR 97502

Call Sign: KF7JWD
Alitia L Monasmith
5353 Dark Hollow Rd
Central Point OR 97502

Call Sign: KF7JVX
Brian C Monasmith
5353 Dark Hollow Rd
Central Point OR 97502

Call Sign: KA7DWZ
Eugene J Strong
6066 Deer Creek Rd
Central Point OR 97502

Call Sign: N7IWZ
Eric S Mellgren
4336 Duane Dr S
Central Point OR
975023743

Call Sign: KA7BGR
Russell G Jump
1040 E 13th St
Central Point OR 97502

Call Sign: KQ7P
Gary L Blank
25183 E Bolton Rd
Central Point OR 97502

Call Sign: KA7SPZ
Martha M Olson
39226 Eagles Rest Rd
Central Point OR 97502

Call Sign: N7WWK
O Elmer Olson
39226 Eagles Rest Rd
Central Point OR 97502

Call Sign: KE7RZR
Mark W Bowen
91634 Earl Barnett Ln
Central Point OR 97502

Call Sign: KC7OOY
Matt A Stagg
3950 Goodpasture Loop
W222
Central Point OR 97502

Call Sign: KC7APC
Ja Nae C Jackson
1640 Goucher St
Central Point OR 97502

Call Sign: N4MTD
Frank R Spencer
352 Greenfield Ave
Central Point OR 97502

Call Sign: KD7HIY
Gayle J Williams
522 Greenhill Dr
Central Point OR 97502

Call Sign: KA7DWX
Robert W Hale
5304 Greenlea Way SE

Central Point OR 97502

Call Sign: W7BTG
James R Thanos
20852 Greenmont
Central Point OR 97502

Call Sign: W6VSM
Robert P Brown
20890 Greenmont Dr
Central Point OR 97502

Call Sign: KD7LTZ
Calvin L Zurowski
20894 Greenmont Dr
Central Point OR 97502

Call Sign: W6NPX
Fred N Souleles
20979 Greenmont Dr
Central Point OR 97502

Call Sign: K6YSL
Martha M Souleles
60 Greenmoor Dr
Central Point OR 97502

Call Sign: W7OFY
Paul A White Sr
565 Harlow Rd 1
Central Point OR 97502

Call Sign: KA7KWB
Fred D Ketcham
3655 Harmony Ln
Central Point OR 97502

Call Sign: KD7AUB
Robert D Madore
240 Harrison St
Central Point OR 97502

Call Sign: W7NER
Robert D Madore
710 Harrison St

Central Point OR 97502

Call Sign: KA7NOX
Robert L Schmidt
14570 Hart Rd 239
Central Point OR 97502

Call Sign: KD7HSD
Carrie L Clifford Bishop
2016 Harvard Way
Central Point OR 97502

Call Sign: KB7SKB
James T Stadtfeld
1931 Harvey Rd
Central Point OR 97502

Call Sign: KC7GMB
Cathy E Stadtfeld
1631 Harvey St SE
Central Point OR 97502

Call Sign: KC7TCQ
Rick S Speziale
1294 Heritage Loop
Central Point OR 97502

Call Sign: KF7IBK
Michael A Hemingway
911 Huron Ct SE
Central Point OR 97502

Call Sign: N6PZ
David C Rozzana
2722 Kalmia St
Central Point OR
975023623

Call Sign: N7CET
Wayne Revelle
3585 Kinsrow Ave 407
Central Point OR
975021311

Call Sign: KC7YNY

Gordon D Marx
42017 Knappa Ter Ln
Central Point OR 97502

Call Sign: K7HWX
Allen W Hill
973 La Loma Dr
Central Point OR 97502

Call Sign: N7UPR
Hilda E Hill
123 La Mar St
Central Point OR 97502

Call Sign: K7GRT
Glenda R Taylor
6120 Lake Labish Rd NE
Central Point OR 97502

Call Sign: K7GT
Allan G Taylor
6312 Lake Labish Rd NE
Central Point OR 97502

Call Sign: N7LWP
John R Campbell
48750 Little Nestucca River
Rd
Central Point OR 97502

Call Sign: N7TLW
Pamela J Haynes
19142 Little Plains Pkwy
Central Point OR 97502

Call Sign: KB7WIR
Matthew D Mc Collum
602 Manning Rd
Central Point OR 97502

Call Sign: KD6LUB
Paul R Stang
10109 Marquam Cr
Central Point OR
975024803

Call Sign: KA7WRW
James M Long
2514 Melrose Loop
Central Point OR 97502

Call Sign: W6EZO
M Kathy Crawford
533 Memory Ln
Central Point OR 97502

Call Sign: KE7KBV
M Kathy Crawford
536 Memory Ln
Central Point OR 97502

Call Sign: N7ZHB
Michael T Collins
921 Mendolia Way
Central Point OR 97502

Call Sign: KF7JWA
David J Grotting
12 Monticello Dr
Central Point OR 97502

Call Sign: KF7JWE
Marjorie L Grotting
6217 Monument Dr
Central Point OR 97502

Call Sign: KC7LYV
Jana K Harvey
1014 Morse Ln SW
Central Point OR 97502

Call Sign: WA6NBH
George G Fletcher
40401 Mowhawk River Rd
Central Point OR
975023913

Call Sign: KA7LGA
Martha J Hanks
736 N Gould St

Central Point OR 97502

Call Sign: K7DZJ
William W Cox
85164 N Hideaway Hills Rd
Central Point OR 97502

Call Sign: N7KVS
Donald F Mang
1125 N Holladay
Central Point OR
975072323

Call Sign: N6QZU
Richard D Pruitt
177 Olivia Ln
Central Point OR 97502

Call Sign: KB7QMV
Joseph M Frodsham
1190 Osprey Dr
Central Point OR 97502

Call Sign: KC7PZC
Julianne E Frodsham
1840 Ostman Rd
Central Point OR 97502

Call Sign: KB7QMW
Aaron E Frodsham
36 Oswego Summit
Central Point OR 97502

Call Sign: KB7REN
Spencer E Frodsham
122 Oswego Summit
Central Point OR 97502

Call Sign: KB7ZMZ
Jodianne Frodsham
20432 Outback Ct
Central Point OR 97502

Call Sign: KG7YT
Gene M Frodsham

41920 Outpost Rd
Central Point OR 97502

Call Sign: KF6EWN
Terry Purcell
17720 Overlook Cir
Central Point OR 97502

Call Sign: N7RVM
James A De Koekkoek
1281 Overlook Dr
Central Point OR 97502

Call Sign: N7AVD
Marcia R Connolly
1281 Overlook Dr
Central Point OR 97502

Call Sign: KD6RCC
Michael A Simpson
856 Pacific
Central Point OR 97502

Call Sign: KC7OOZ
Paul H Rutter
3839 Pacific 111
Central Point OR 97502

Call Sign: N7UOF
Marc G Jackson
576 Pacific Ave
Central Point OR
975029713

Call Sign: N6PKG
Ed W Cutler
1060 Pacific Ave
Central Point OR 97502

Call Sign: KC7OOX
Raymond G Suiter
4204 Pacific Ave 30
Central Point OR 97502

Call Sign: N7YIH

Martin L Sherman
3839 Pacific Ave Sp 1
Central Point OR 97502

Call Sign: KE7FVC
Russell O Brown
3839 Pacific Ave Unit 163
Central Point OR 97502

Call Sign: W7ADF
Arthur R Melvin
6500 Pacific Blvd SW
Central Point OR 97502

Call Sign: N7DYN
Harvey E Varner
6500 Pacific Blvd SW
Central Point OR
975029783

Call Sign: KD7AUD
Lelan E Starks
5001 Pacific Blvd SW 104
Central Point OR 97502

Call Sign: N1GEO
George H Doersch II
1898 Pacific Crest Dr
Central Point OR 97502

Call Sign: K7YLO
J Edward Vaughn
424 Pacific Dr
Central Point OR 97502

Call Sign: KA7BJZ
Nancy N Vaughn
94177 Pacific Ln
Central Point OR 97502

Call Sign: N6HYD
Carl F Metzger
94177 Pacific Ln
Central Point OR
975029794

Call Sign: KA7VBN
Steve H Patterson
14449 Pole Ct
Central Point OR 97502

Call Sign: KE7F
Michael J Barlow
312 Poling Hall
Central Point OR 97502

Call Sign: K6RLB
Renee L Lambert
1114 Polk St
Central Point OR 97502

Call Sign: WA7ADV
Elizabeth A Weber
1298 Princeton Rd
Central Point OR
975022900

Call Sign: KE7RUB
Richard H Wooton
240 Princeton St
Central Point OR 97502

Call Sign: KJ6I
Gerald W Smith
66567 Quail Rd
Central Point OR 97502

Call Sign: KC7VZY
Kathleen J Bramblet
635 Reuben Boise
Central Point OR 97502

Call Sign: W7FPS
Timothy L Bramblet
1460 Reuben Boise Rd
Central Point OR 97502

Call Sign: KC7USD
Gregory L Arnold
1601 673 Rhododendron Dr

Central Point OR 97502

Call Sign: WB6RIS
Michael P Herbst
1325 Ridge Way
Central Point OR 97502

Call Sign: K7OSP
Oregon State Police
Amateur Radio Group
810 S 5th St
Central Point OR 97502

Call Sign: KF7NAE
Kelly Carsten
2150 S 5th St
Central Point OR 97502

Call Sign: KF7UMT
Kathryn J Anderson
824 S 70th St
Central Point OR 97502

Call Sign: W6GER
Alfred D Tipsword
17900 S Anderson Rd
Central Point OR 97502

Call Sign: K7BFK
Bud F Kilbury II
1425 S Ivy St
Central Point OR 97502

Call Sign: K7TEK
Teresa E Kilbury
14950 S Leland Rd
Central Point OR 97502

Call Sign: KC7TLC
Steven J Yungen
291 Salem Heights Ave
Central Point OR 97502

Call Sign: N7OL
Neil M Olsen

493 Skookum Ct
Central Point OR
975021901

Call Sign: NO7L
Pamela L Olsen
518 Skookum Ct
Central Point OR
975021901

Call Sign: KE7ZRA
Esther K Olsen
564 Skookum Ct
Central Point OR 97502

Call Sign: KF7CPG
Zachary E Olsen
564 Skookum Ct
Central Point OR 97502

Call Sign: KE7DNB
Emily L Olsen
215 Sky Crest Dr
Central Point OR
975021901

Call Sign: N6RYW
Michael F Oliver
676 Sunset Way
Central Point OR 97502

Call Sign: KC7QBC
Kenneth R Pariseau
2669 Tahitian Ave
Central Point OR 97502

Call Sign: KC7GDZ
Lawrence D Edwards Jr
1300 Tamarisk Dr
Central Point OR 97502

Call Sign: W7UXM
William B Dyer
880 Taylor St
Central Point OR 97502

Call Sign: N7QDB
Larry E Winebrenner
830 Tivoli
Central Point OR 97502

Call Sign: KG7KG
Robert E Land
7521 Twin Fir Ln S
Central Point OR
975025500

Call Sign: KF7KLM
Kevin S Wheeler
2 Valley Heights Rd
Central Point OR 97502

Call Sign: KE7FCZ
Kline H Charles
380 W Gregorys Pl
Central Point OR 97502

Call Sign: KB7IGD
Fred K Harrison
204 Wells Rd
Central Point OR 97502

Call Sign: KA7JYT
Don O Grandfield
885 Westrop Dr
Central Point OR
975024819

Call Sign: N7FHR
Del C Rasmussen
972 Westrop Dr
Central Point OR 97502

Call Sign: N7ORZ
Joan Rasmussen
972 Westrop Dr
Central Point OR 97502

Call Sign: N8BKJ
Thomas H Hartkop

4070 Willow Springs
Central Point OR 97502

Call Sign: KE7SZO
David J Fosdal
578 Wilson Rd
Central Point OR 97502

Call Sign: KB7KGY
Ken J Mc Garvey
Central Point OR 97502

Call Sign: KC7ARX
Claire B Martin
Central Point OR 97502

Call Sign: KC7ZML
Nicholas W Beeson
Central Point OR 97502

Call Sign: KE6ADJ
Charles R Herndon
Central Point OR 97502

Call Sign: N7EU
William B Martin
Central Point OR 97502

Call Sign: KF7JWI
Lynn L Davis
Central Point OR 97502

**FCC Amateur Radio
Licenses in Charleston**

Call Sign: KE7ADG
Leon Kramer
1027 Laurel St
Charleston OR 97420

Call Sign: KB7SBE
William Baxter
Charleston OR 97420

Call Sign: W7WAT

Glynn P Mc Cready Sr
Charleston OR 97420

Call Sign: WA7MIC
Larry L Overman
Charleston OR 97420

Call Sign: WB6UHW
Aleta M Carte
Charleston OR 97420

Call Sign: KG6AZD
David L Leader
Charleston OR 97420

Call Sign: KE7ADF
Andrew L Durfey
Charleston OR 97420

Call Sign: KD7VCR
Carolyn T Unruh
Charleston OR 97420

Call Sign: KD7VMP
Jeffrey L Dardozzi
Charleston OR 97420

Call Sign: W7HRZ
Loretta K Hafen
Charleston OR 97420

Call Sign: N7HIZ
Merlyn J Hafen Sr
Charleston OR 97420

**FCC Amateur Radio
Licenses in Chemult**

Call Sign: KC7LVE
Peter M Petros
3330 Cannon Ave
Chemult OR 97731

**FCC Amateur Radio
Licenses in Cheshire**

Call Sign: WA6LXF
Robert F Gage
1855 5th St
Cheshire OR 97419

Call Sign: W7CCX
Robert F Gage
1145 6th St
Cheshire OR 97419

Call Sign: KC6APV
Spencer L Jayne
3305 Hillcrest Way
Cheshire OR 97419

Call Sign: KG6MCR
Stephen P Burton
1234 Hillendale Dr SE
Cheshire OR 97419

Call Sign: N7CLU
Gerald L Nickolaus
1378 Hillendale Dr SE
Cheshire OR 97419

Call Sign: KE7PGS
Tonya M Johnson
39721 Jasper Lowell Rd
Cheshire OR 97419

Call Sign: KA7MWW
David E Salveson
40041 Jasper Lowell Rd
Cheshire OR 97419

Call Sign: KC7ZLK
Nancy C Doornink
38513 Jasper Lowell Rd
Cheshire OR 97419

Call Sign: KC7ZAL
Charles R Woods
85309 Jasper Park Rd
Cheshire OR 97419

Call Sign: K7CRW
Charles R Woods
85414 Jasper Park Rd
Cheshire OR 97419

Call Sign: W7MWW
David E Salveson
85414 Jasper Park Rd
Cheshire OR 97419

Call Sign: N7XAL
Mary D Dean
4163 Jasper Rd
Cheshire OR 97419

Call Sign: AA7GG
Laurie P Algeo
1517 Jasper St
Cheshire OR 97419

Call Sign: KF7IMB
Carl D Shepherd
2781 Jaunipero
Cheshire OR 97419

Call Sign: KF7IMA
Gabriel S Shepherd
1047 Jayne St
Cheshire OR 97419

Call Sign: KD7GES
Christopher M Manghelli
9081 Lower River Rd
Cheshire OR 97419

Call Sign: KD7VKN
Natalie S Lillie
442 Sherwood Loop
Cheshire OR 97419

Call Sign: KF7DTU
Gisele D Garrity
644 Valleywood Dr SE
Cheshire OR 97419

Call Sign: AC7UN
Karen D Crisp
Cheshire OR 97419

**FCC Amateur Radio
Licenses in Chiloquin**

Call Sign: N6DZI
Robert A Durgin Sr
5682 1st Ct
Chiloquin OR 976248657

Call Sign: N7JXG
Adeline I Stephens
849 1st St
Chiloquin OR 976248656

Call Sign: KD7LKD
Diana Z Durgin
2303 1st St
Chiloquin OR 976248657

Call Sign: KD6UYD
Dennis Jefcoat
5325 B St
Chiloquin OR 97624

Call Sign: N7NEQ
Phillip Tillson
1606 Best Ln 4
Chiloquin OR 97624

Call Sign: KC7IXA
Kevin L Crowder
2077 Cooper Dr
Chiloquin OR 97624

Call Sign: KH6CTQ
Peter L Demmer
64654 E Bay Rd
Chiloquin OR 97624

Call Sign: WA6TYJ
David W Martin

5825 E St
Chiloquin OR 97624

Call Sign: KD6LUD
Gay E Jarvinen
1 Jefferson Pkwy Apt 97
Chiloquin OR 976247750

Call Sign: W1VDE
Roger M Jarvinen
2 Jefferson Pkwy B11
Chiloquin OR 976247750

Call Sign: KC7ARS
Richard W Coryell
321 N 3rd St
Chiloquin OR 97624

Call Sign: KE7PNW
Joseph R Robideau
1865 Parliament
Chiloquin OR 97624

Call Sign: KB7OKE
Ronald K Miller
22182 S Ferguson Rd
Chiloquin OR 97624

Call Sign: K6TPF
Michael L Brown
33227 Squaw Vly Rd
Chiloquin OR 97624

Call Sign: KH6KS
Edward F Atkin
14390 St 222 Dr
Chiloquin OR 97624

Call Sign: K7ENX
Howard R Paine
14785 SW 104th Ave
Chiloquin OR 976248711

Call Sign: KF6MUZ
Barbara Turner

5144 Trevon St
Chiloquin OR 97624

Call Sign: KB7ZLA
Ronald J Hogan
Chiloquin OR 97624

Call Sign: N7EDE
Sara L Sanchez
Chiloquin OR 97624

Call Sign: N7ORG
Robert M Tillson
Chiloquin OR 97624

Call Sign: N7ORH
Janet L Tillson
Chiloquin OR 97624

Call Sign: N7ORI
D Arcy M Tillson
Chiloquin OR 97624

Call Sign: N7PRH
Philicia J King
Chiloquin OR 97624

Call Sign: N7RPH
James R Spangler
Chiloquin OR 97624

Call Sign: N7SAR
Claudette M Beare
Chiloquin OR 97624

Call Sign: N7LLY
Patricia Coryell
Chiloquin OR 97624

Call Sign: KD7GPQ
Paul P Tillson
Chiloquin OR 97624

Call Sign: KD7POL
Gerald L Day

Chiloquin OR 97624

Call Sign: N0BUL
Dana A Nelson Jr
Chiloquin OR 97624

Call Sign: KE7DDO
Linda R Nelson
Chiloquin OR 97624

Call Sign: KD7VMM
Dana A Nelson Jr
Chiloquin OR 97624

FCC Amateur Radio Licenses in Christmas Valley

Call Sign: N7UMG
Glenda M Reynolds
1881 Country Club Rd
Christmas Valley OR 97641

Call Sign: KA7GNO
Harold K Offel
Christmas Valley OR 97641

Call Sign: W7ELX
Lyle E Walther
Christmas Valley OR 97641

Call Sign: KA6KWD
Clinton R Johnson
Christmas Valley OR 97641

Call Sign: KB7NJW
Earl J Reynolds Jr
Christmas Valley OR 97641

Call Sign: KC7WZC
Christina J Johnson
Christmas Valley OR 97641

Call Sign: KC7WZD
Linda F Neuschwanger

Christmas Valley OR 97641

Call Sign: KD7AKJ
James R Brookins
Christmas Valley OR 97641

Call Sign: KR7Z
Daniel L Dobson Jr
Christmas Valley OR 97641

Call Sign: KD7HAO
Keith R Bumpass
Christmas Valley OR 97641

Call Sign: KD7HAP
Olga C Bumpass
Christmas Valley OR 97641

Call Sign: KB7YFL
Linda M Tsatskowski
Christmas Valley OR
976410865

Call Sign: KB7YFM
Paul F Tsatskowski
Christmas Valley OR
976410865

**FCC Amateur Radio
Licenses in Coburg**

Call Sign: KD7LOO
Drew M Prociw
5906 NW 181st Ave
Coburg OR 97408

Call Sign: KC7YMG
Benton L Ulm
7360 S West Rd
Coburg OR 97408

Call Sign: KB7NJF
Marion F Davis
33022 Van Duyn Rd
Coburg OR 97408

Call Sign: KD7LDN
Suzie B Davis
348 Van Duyn St
Coburg OR 97408

Call Sign: KA7PGA
Hubert J Lockard
Coburg OR 97401

Call Sign: KC7EAD
Darrell L Ulm
Coburg OR 97401

Call Sign: KA7WZE
Charles R Solin
Coburg OR 97408

Call Sign: KD7ZOP
James H Stenklyft
Coburg OR 97408

Call Sign: K7JHS
James H Stenklyft
Coburg OR 97408

Call Sign: W7FV
James H Stenklyft
Coburg OR 97408

**FCC Amateur Radio
Licenses in Condon**

Call Sign: N7GSU
Robin L Faulkner
Condon OR 978230134

Call Sign: KD7OTY
Kathleen E D Faulkner
Condon OR 978230134

**FCC Amateur Radio
Licenses in Coos Bay**

Call Sign: KB7JVT

Lloyd E Pedro
2245 23rd St
Coos Bay OR 97420

Call Sign: KC7PMH
George E Millen
645 35th SE
Coos Bay OR 97420

Call Sign: KB7PXM
William C Anger
2943 44th Ave
Coos Bay OR 97420

Call Sign: KE7DWE
J Lee Byer
465 48th St
Coos Bay OR 97420

Call Sign: KE7DSZ
James Lee Byer
465 48th St
Coos Bay OR 97420

Call Sign: KA7MYM
Lizette A Marr
875 57th St
Coos Bay OR 974200416

Call Sign: W7EUS
Louis C Sperling
3105 7th Pl NE 103
Coos Bay OR 97420

Call Sign: KE7FXK
Clarence C Covely Jr
26751 Adam Rd
Coos Bay OR 97420

Call Sign: N5QOS
Doyle C Payne
92987 Airport Rd
Coos Bay OR 97420

Call Sign: KC7DVY

John P Maguire
5630 Alder Ct
Coos Bay OR 97420

Richard J Kelley
505 Ballad Way
Coos Bay OR 97420

Allen M Solomon
2391 Claxter Rd NE
Coos Bay OR 97420

Call Sign: KE7ADH
Forrest E Rogoschka
2004 Arizona St
Coos Bay OR 97420

Call Sign: KG4PWC
Leo Kusuda
505 Ballad Way
Coos Bay OR 97420

Call Sign: WD4GYH
Jean M Adamson
1833 Claxter Rd NE 39
Coos Bay OR 97420

Call Sign: W7ETC
Forrest E Rogoschka
42555 Arizona St
Coos Bay OR 97420

Call Sign: WA7UR
Leo Kusuda
26015 Ballston Rd
Coos Bay OR 97420

Call Sign: KD7VCM
James R Moore
2640 Clay Ct SE
Coos Bay OR 97420

Call Sign: N7WSA
Arthur B Pescod
750 Arleta Pl NE
Coos Bay OR 97420

Call Sign: KE7EUM
William R Fordham Jr
3621 Bayonne Dr SE
Coos Bay OR 97420

Call Sign: AD7CR
James R Moore
25988 Clay Dr
Coos Bay OR 97420

Call Sign: KC7ACD
Connie J Thorhaven
4448 Avalon Pl
Coos Bay OR 97420

Call Sign: WA6JOW
Carl Siminow
1702 Big Bend Rd
Coos Bay OR 97420

Call Sign: N7JRM
James R Moore
25964 Clay Dr
Coos Bay OR 97420

Call Sign: KI7PA
John C Thorhaven
4024 Avalon St
Coos Bay OR 97420

Call Sign: KE7CMY
Loren L Fleming Jr
33306 Bonneville Dr
Coos Bay OR 97420

Call Sign: KC7OQU
Kaleb I Mc Kinnis
4158 Clay Pl SE
Coos Bay OR 97420

Call Sign: KF7QPE
Donald W Proffitt
623 Azalea Dr
Coos Bay OR 97420

Call Sign: K7CMY
Loren L Fleming Jr
33493 Bonneville Dr
Coos Bay OR 97420

Call Sign: KC7UWU
Jeffery N Woodcock
27619 Clear Lake Rd
Coos Bay OR 97420

Call Sign: KE6SMW
Walter L Cox III
4100 Azalea Dr
Coos Bay OR 97420

Call Sign: KC7JJI
Richard F Bryan
2210 Canal
Coos Bay OR 97420

Call Sign: KD7CMM
Dan S Hongell
1574 Coburg Rd 503
Coos Bay OR 97420

Call Sign: W7BAH
Coos County ARES
599 Ball Rd
Coos Bay OR 97420

Call Sign: KF3ER
Allen M Solomon
31911 Clatsop Ln
Coos Bay OR 97420

Call Sign: K7AIA
Paul A Andersen
18160 Cottonwood Rd 552
Coos Bay OR 974200401

Call Sign: KC7WTS

Call Sign: KK7YS

Call Sign: KF6KRM

Kirby L B Gee
910 Cowl St 49
Coos Bay OR 974207230

Call Sign: KB7IHJ
Richard A Kimker
1020 Cunningham Ln S Apt
39
Coos Bay OR 97420

Call Sign: KF7EIO
Mark A Juelke
39875 Davis St
Coos Bay OR 97420

Call Sign: KE7CNB
Terry R Benjamin
2144 Debra Dr
Coos Bay OR 97420

Call Sign: N7IJD
Forest D Nicoson
5555 Deer Creek Rd
Coos Bay OR 97420

Call Sign: KD7KGF
Matthew N Schmidt
2126 Del Rio Rd
Coos Bay OR 97420

Call Sign: KD7NKR
Matthew N Schmidt
3950 Del Rio Rd
Coos Bay OR 97420

Call Sign: KE7CNC
George A Tinker
3950 Del Rio Rd
Coos Bay OR 97420

Call Sign: WB3FJQ
Oreste F Bertozzi
480 Douglas Ave SW
Coos Bay OR 97420

Call Sign: W6KAG
Marion A Mason
61875 E Cottonwood Rd
Coos Bay OR 97420

Call Sign: KD7ZRS
Edward L Jackson
91634 Earls Ln
Coos Bay OR 974208722

Call Sign: KB7PXP
Fred P Simonson
61255 Ferguson Rd
Coos Bay OR 97420

Call Sign: KE7FXG
Don Whereat
3300 Forest Gale Dr
Coos Bay OR 97420

Call Sign: WB7UMW
Fred F Burdick
30035 Fox Hollow Rd
Coos Bay OR 974202891

Call Sign: KF7FJW
Karin P Kenney
317 Fox St
Coos Bay OR 97420

Call Sign: N7ILP
Myron W Rencehausen
4036 Frieda Ave
Coos Bay OR 974207832

Call Sign: KC7WRF
Bruce R Latta
71443 Gateway Ln
Coos Bay OR 97420

Call Sign: W7ICO
George F Hartley Sr
3033 Gateway St Apt 49
Coos Bay OR 97420

Call Sign: KE7FCJ
Ralph R Barnes III
5541 Gatewood Dr
Coos Bay OR 97420

Call Sign: N7ODD
Louis W Lindberg Sr
3585 Griffin Creek Rd
Coos Bay OR 97420

Call Sign: K7GRL
Barbara J Jackson
218 H St
Coos Bay OR 97420

Call Sign: KE7ADC
Brett R Jackson
3100 H St
Coos Bay OR 97420

Call Sign: K7BAY
Brett R Jackson
3100 H St
Coos Bay OR 97420

Call Sign: KD7ZDR
Gordon W Gates
3100 H St
Coos Bay OR 97420

Call Sign: KE7DTA
Brandon R Jackson
3100 H St
Coos Bay OR 97426

Call Sign: KE7CJA
Matthew D Fields
1044 Hall
Coos Bay OR 97420

Call Sign: KA7PWL
Darrell D Saxton
14452 Hunt Mountain Ln
Coos Bay OR 97420

Call Sign: KF7PJC
James A Pallo
81007 Hwy 103
Coos Bay OR 97420

Call Sign: KE7FXI
William J Paxton
82316 Hwy 103
Coos Bay OR 97420

Call Sign: KB7URW
Julie M Brown
26880 Hwy 140 E
Coos Bay OR 97420

Call Sign: WA6TAK
Jack D Baley
93126 Hwy 42 S
Coos Bay OR 97420

Call Sign: N0BCD
Bernhard M Amdahl
66568 Hwy 78
Coos Bay OR 97420

Call Sign: KD7LPR
Wayne D Burklund
85123 Hwy 82
Coos Bay OR 97420

Call Sign: KD7MXA
Deborah Burklund
68625 Hwy 82
Coos Bay OR 97420

Call Sign: K7MXA
Deborah Burklund
68625 Hwy 82
Coos Bay OR 97420

Call Sign: K7OOS
Harold C Mardock
37986 Hwy 86
Coos Bay OR 97420

Call Sign: KF6NJB
Marc D Rohlfes
1999 Jansen Way 40
Coos Bay OR 97420

Call Sign: KE7JSI
Vasil Naumov
11919 Jantzen Ave N Ste
169
Coos Bay OR 97420

Call Sign: WA7NLT
Sherwood L Davis
1353 Jones Rd
Coos Bay OR 97420

Call Sign: N7SBU
Anthony J Purdom
4555 Jubilee Ln NE
Coos Bay OR 97420

Call Sign: N1PYO
Athan R Kramer
5559 Kane Creek Rd
Coos Bay OR 97420

Call Sign: N7JKC
Dorwin Lovell
385 Kaneeta Ln
Coos Bay OR 97420

Call Sign: N1RAG
Nancy L Kramer
19081 Kantara Ct
Coos Bay OR 97420

Call Sign: KD7DQU
Jesse A Wood
1911 Kapteyns St
Coos Bay OR 97420

Call Sign: KD7DAK
Levi B Wood
3596 Karen Ave S
Coos Bay OR 97420

Call Sign: KC7UWT
Stephanie M Sherman
327 Kees St
Coos Bay OR 97420

Call Sign: N7CIR
Elise Ciraolo
39780 Lacomb Dr
Coos Bay OR 974207381

Call Sign: K7CIR
Jerry M Ciraolo
815 Lacresta Ct SE
Coos Bay OR 974207381

Call Sign: KE7GA
Joe W Johnson
6140 Lakeshore Ct N
Coos Bay OR 97420

Call Sign: KJ7O
Joe W Johnson
6140 Lakeshore Ct N
Coos Bay OR 97420

Call Sign: KG7VX
Ken B Bonsall
1957 Lawrence St
Coos Bay OR 97420

Call Sign: KD7HOT
Michael J Fisher
6840 Lemongrass Loop SE
Coos Bay OR 974207544

Call Sign: WB7DZM
John W Long
155 Lexington Pl
Coos Bay OR 97420

Call Sign: KF7QKL
Donald C Havens
5612 Lipscomb St SE
Coos Bay OR 97420

Call Sign: KE7EIA
Mary J Graham
19708 Mahogany St
Coos Bay OR 97420

Call Sign: KE7EIE
Thomas S Graham
2513 Maia Loop
Coos Bay OR 97420

Call Sign: KG6OAU
Chris D Hutcheson
210 Main St
Coos Bay OR 97420

Call Sign: KJ7LB
Paul T Kearns
504 Main St Ste A
Coos Bay OR 97420

Call Sign: N7ZWX
Evelyn R Collins
92499 Maki Rd
Coos Bay OR 97420

Call Sign: WH6RU
Bj L Moniz
405 Mansfield St
Coos Bay OR 97420

Call Sign: WH6QD
Sahoni Redbird E English
405 Mansfield St
Coos Bay OR 97420

Call Sign: KC7FZI
Donald E Marr
25400 McClun Rd
Coos Bay OR 97420

Call Sign: KB7NTJ
John J Pedro
909 Millview St
Coos Bay OR 97420

Call Sign: N7DID
Julie K Stivers
231 Mt Echo Dr
Coos Bay OR 97420

Call Sign: W7QOF
William C Whitaker
925 N 9th St
Coos Bay OR 97420

Call Sign: W7SYG
Jean V Whitaker
925 N 9th St
Coos Bay OR 974203161

Call Sign: KE7EIC
Jason J Goodson
116 N Elm St
Coos Bay OR 97420

Call Sign: KB7UCP
Jay D Farr
695 N Fairmont
Coos Bay OR 97420

Call Sign: KB7UCQ
Will M Farr
1250 N Farragut St
Coos Bay OR 97420

Call Sign: KE7BDQ
Philip J Keizer Jr
3135 N Farragut St
Coos Bay OR 97420

Call Sign: W7EUV
Irwin R Doty
7014 N Fenwick
Coos Bay OR 97420

Call Sign: WA6VUP
James W Cheadle
7225 N Fowler Ave
Coos Bay OR 97420

Call Sign: KD7IHZ
Janet R Sears Cheadle
7225 N Fowler Ave
Coos Bay OR 97420

Call Sign: KD7MXC
Gary L Goodson
406 N Holladay
Coos Bay OR 97420

Call Sign: WA7QOM
Patricia E Brooks
3220 N Michigan Ave
Coos Bay OR 97420

Call Sign: KB6OTJ
Duane Davidson
6437 N Willamette Blvd
Coos Bay OR 97420

Call Sign: W7EHW
Charles K Griffin
1188 Nautical Dr
Coos Bay OR 974203466

Call Sign: KF7QPF
Marvin R Mccleary
1500 NE 10th 26
Coos Bay OR 97420

Call Sign: K7QPF
Marvin R Mccleary
718 NE 10th Ave
Coos Bay OR 97420

Call Sign: KC7WHS
Mark S Smith
721 NE 167 Pl
Coos Bay OR 97420

Call Sign: WA7HNG
Thomas W Rolen
2531 NE 16th Ave
Coos Bay OR 97420

Call Sign: KA7QCA
Emily P Howard
1462 NW 15 St
Coos Bay OR 97420

Call Sign: KA7WDS
Anthony G Pasqualetti
1777 NW 173rd Ave 612
Coos Bay OR 97420

Call Sign: K7AGP
Anthony G Pasqualetti
4692 NW 173rd Pl
Coos Bay OR 97420

Call Sign: KE7ADE
Barbara J Jackson
18380 H NW Cornell Rd
Coos Bay OR 97420

Call Sign: WT7O
Edwin R Kiaser
3510 Onyx St 6
Coos Bay OR 97420

Call Sign: K0LPN
James H Meidl Jr
6735 Opaca Ct
Coos Bay OR 97420

Call Sign: KB7RNL
Christopher R Jantzen
33678 Ophir Rd
Coos Bay OR 97420

Call Sign: KD7SLV
Judy K Jantzen
34944 Ophir Rd
Coos Bay OR 97420

Call Sign: AC7UI
Richard J Kelley
367 Oxyoke Rd
Coos Bay OR 97420

Call Sign: W7TZO
Raymond A Schall
4495 Pacifica Way Apt 101
Coos Bay OR 97420

Call Sign: KF7OAJ
Brad D Veldstra
1455 Pacwood Ct SE
Coos Bay OR 97420

Call Sign: KF7OAI
Susan M Veldstra
6005 Paddock Ln
Coos Bay OR 97420

Call Sign: N7PXJ
Clare V Stadden
663 Paiute Plr
Coos Bay OR 97420

Call Sign: KE7FXO
William D Autry Jr
607 Park St 6
Coos Bay OR 97420

Call Sign: KK7JQ
James A Cason
20850 Parry Rd
Coos Bay OR 97420

Call Sign: KI0S
Harvey A Willis
4954 Parsons Ave
Coos Bay OR 97420

Call Sign: KD7VMO
Harold C Mardock
4954 Parsons Ave
Coos Bay OR 97420

Call Sign: KC7OTF
Rex C Zeebuyth
56725 Plantation Dr
Coos Bay OR 97420

Call Sign: KA7OKW
H Cranson Fosburg
60860 Raintree Dr
Coos Bay OR 97420

Call Sign: WD6CUE
Byron J Hudson
635 Ralston Dr
Coos Bay OR 974206801

Call Sign: N6OQ
Kenneth L Rich
3931 Redondo Way
Coos Bay OR 97420

Call Sign: KA7PGX
Jon K Schmit
525 Reuben Boise Rd
Coos Bay OR 97420

Call Sign: KD7MWV
Caroline E Schmit
2750 Reuben Boise Rd
Coos Bay OR 97420

Call Sign: KC7FLO
Joseph L Thomas
240 S 1st Ave
Coos Bay OR 97420

Call Sign: AB7VC
Rudolph Litte
1556 S Adams Dr
Coos Bay OR 97420

Call Sign: KB7QJT
William F Hudson
6723 S Anderson Rd
Coos Bay OR 97420

Call Sign: WA7WLY
Dorious J Smith
6723 S Anderson Rd
Coos Bay OR 97420

Coos Bay OR 974201008

Coos Bay OR 97420

Call Sign: KE7NXV
Peggy J Morris
4240 S Beaver Creek Rd
Coos Bay OR 97420

Call Sign: KF6YPH
Thomas J Marshall
2176 S Downing St
Coos Bay OR 97420

Call Sign: KC7OZX
Stephen P Wood
38250 Sandy Heights St
Coos Bay OR 97420

Call Sign: K7PIG
Peggy J Morris
20110 S Beavercreek Rd
Coos Bay OR 97420

Call Sign: KE7ADJ
Robert H Christensen
1401 S Elder Ct
Coos Bay OR 97420

Call Sign: KE7HTC
Morrie L Ghattas
6512 Scottsbluff Rd
Coos Bay OR 97420

Call Sign: W7PHM
Richard W Putney
23348 S Central Pt Rd
Coos Bay OR 97420

Call Sign: NI0N
Paul A Andersen
331 S Eldorado
Coos Bay OR 974204512

Call Sign: N7TAS
Lawrence M Wood
21000 Scottsdale Dr
Coos Bay OR 97420

Call Sign: KC7KVJ
Yolanda H Ferguson
23348 S Central Pt Rd
Coos Bay OR 97420

Call Sign: KF7ALM
Andrew J Knight
949 S Ivy
Coos Bay OR 97420

Call Sign: KD7IOP
Russell J Billmeyer
8603 SE 133rd Pl
Coos Bay OR 97420

Call Sign: KA7QAS
Timothy J Hershiser
35891 S Chiloquin Rd
Coos Bay OR 97420

Call Sign: KC7WHT
Emery D Barnett
3860 S Santiam
Coos Bay OR 97420

Call Sign: N7SBF
Robert J Lyon
2175 SE 55th Ave
Coos Bay OR 97420

Call Sign: K7KZT
Louis M Mc Carthy
128 S Church St
Coos Bay OR 97420

Call Sign: KD7JFB
Edward H Makaruk
3660 S Santiam Hwy
Coos Bay OR 97420

Call Sign: N7VRT
Patricia D Lyon
1743 SE 60th Ave
Coos Bay OR 97420

Call Sign: KA7NZL
Donald M Long Sr
15047 S Clackamas River
Dr
Coos Bay OR 97420

Call Sign: KF7ALN
Charles M Sprague
4212 S Shore Blvd
Coos Bay OR 97420

Call Sign: W7IJK
Wayne E Milburn
42882 SE Phelps Rd
Coos Bay OR 97420

Call Sign: W7WHY
Thomas K Osborne
13360 S Cliffside Dr
Coos Bay OR 97420

Call Sign: KA7FHA
Mark B Grigsby
2123 Salem Ave SE
Coos Bay OR 97420

Call Sign: WG7D
Albert C Whitney
59175 Sevendevils Rd
Coos Bay OR 97420

Call Sign: KE7RZZ
Keith G Coates
602 S Columbus Ave

Call Sign: K7IDB
Robert W Scott
105 Samuel Ln

Call Sign: KB7JXL
Joseph A Borsky
9243 Shaw Square Rd SE

Coos Bay OR 97420	Coos Bay OR 97420	Coos Bay OR 97420

Call Sign: WA2KKT
Joseph R Doman Sr
4490 Silverton Rd NE
Coos Bay OR 97420

Call Sign: KC7OTE
Joseph J Thomas
89135 Spindrift Way
Coos Bay OR 97420

Call Sign: K7RG
Joe A Pedro
2810 Strong Rd SE
Coos Bay OR 97420

Call Sign: KD7OUG
Joseph R Doman
5043 Silverton Rd NE
Coos Bay OR 97420

Call Sign: KB6PPY
Ronald A Baker
15908 Sprague River Rd
Coos Bay OR 974201199

Call Sign: KD7FZH
Gary S Ustica
22360 SW 108th
Coos Bay OR 97420

Call Sign: KD7PMJ
Joseph R Doman
5155 Silverton Rd NE
Coos Bay OR 97420

Call Sign: KD7YPG
Bill J Bartels
1122 Spring St Unit 224
Coos Bay OR 97420

Call Sign: KC7RUB
Mark R Magill
1910 SW 195th Ave
Coos Bay OR 974204516

Call Sign: WA2KKT
Joseph R Doman
4490 Silverton Rd NE 51
Coos Bay OR 97420

Call Sign: N6SFE
Judith E Baker
2695 Spring Valley Ln
Coos Bay OR 974201199

Call Sign: KC7PMG
Dennis P La Praim
2180 SW 208th Ave
Coos Bay OR 97420

Call Sign: N8SAR
Joseph R Doman
4490 Silverton Rd NE Sp 46
Coos Bay OR 97420

Call Sign: KC7FZL
Ted Smiley
61042 Springcrest Dr
Coos Bay OR 97420

Call Sign: KD7VCP
Kyle G Stubblefield
562 SW 257th
Coos Bay OR 97420

Call Sign: KF7KYQ
Michael C Tribble
3150 Siskiyou
Coos Bay OR 97420

Call Sign: KA7YZO
Ruth C Whaley
286 Stadium Dr N Apt 5
Coos Bay OR 97420

Call Sign: KD7IS
Jack W Fuller
431 SW Tichenor
Coos Bay OR 97420

Call Sign: KE6IBC
Ralph J Crawford
514 Siskiyou Bl
Coos Bay OR 97420

Call Sign: WA7NQQ
Claud D Whaley
13670 Stag Hollow Rd
Coos Bay OR 97420

Call Sign: KE7CMZ
Colette M Souza
21273 Thomas Creek Rd
Coos Bay OR 97420

Call Sign: KD7VCN
Gary C Cameron
2249 Siskiyou Blvd
Coos Bay OR 97420

Call Sign: KC7CZC
Ralph H Richmond III
359 Stoneway Dr NW
Coos Bay OR 97420

Call Sign: KC7WRC
Albert Kramer
16008 Timberline Ln
Coos Bay OR 97420

Call Sign: KE7RZY
Una P Scott
30219 Sparta Ln

Call Sign: KF7GTW
Joe A Pedro
96883 Strome Ln

Call Sign: KD7MXB
Marie Sweet
35485 Upper Loop Rd

Coos Bay OR 97420

Coos Bay OR 97420

Call Sign: KE6ADY
Kenneth D Braden
Coos Bay OR 97420

Call Sign: K7WCA
Marie Sweet
93701 Upper Loop Rd
Coos Bay OR 97420

Call Sign: KA6OBR
Lawrence B Crabtree
93642 W Mill Ln
Coos Bay OR 97420

Call Sign: W7EUU
Patricia H Garner
Coos Bay OR 97420

Call Sign: N7WCA
Ralph L Thomas
1225 Upper Powell Creek
Coos Bay OR 97420

Call Sign: N7YYH
Fredrick G Ashby
4076 Wallace Ave
Coos Bay OR 97420

Call Sign: W7GQL
Philip Ryan
Coos Bay OR 97420

Call Sign: KJ6VR
Byron C Richards Sr
5922 Village View
Coos Bay OR 97420

Call Sign: KC7FLN
Tom E Hainline
1816 Welcix
Coos Bay OR 97420

Call Sign: WB7OZN
Stacy K Rossman
Coos Bay OR 97420

Call Sign: KB7TC
Carroll J Klein
5922 Village View Ct
Coos Bay OR 97420

Call Sign: WA6APV
Arnold H Henderson
4886 Wildahl Ave
Coos Bay OR 97420

Call Sign: K7IQX
Gless T Connoy
Coos Bay OR 97420

Call Sign: N7MXJ
Nathan A Parker
4182 Vitae Springs Rd S
Coos Bay OR 97420

Call Sign: K7ARB
Clinton C Crawford
172 Wildwood Ln
Coos Bay OR 97420

Call Sign: KA6PIN
Warren E Booth Jr
Coos Bay OR 97420

Call Sign: KA7CTG
Gerald D Pratt
Coos Bay OR 97420

Call Sign: W6RAT
Bruce R Jackson
62899 W Catching Rd
Coos Bay OR 97420

Call Sign: KF7SGB
Mary A Moore
1575 Woodland Dr
Coos Bay OR 97420

Call Sign: KF6DXP
Peter C Brandt
Coos Bay OR 97420

Call Sign: KG6HSM
Marsha S Jackson
62899 W Catching Rd
Coos Bay OR 97420

Call Sign: KD7GET
Dennis E Schad
811 Woodruff Rd
Coos Bay OR 974208242

Call Sign: WA7FFE
Charles J Porter
Coos Bay OR 97420

Call Sign: KE7JSH
Jacob T Waggoner
62899 W Catching Rd
Coos Bay OR 97420

Call Sign: KA6DMG
Gordon R Waldron
831 Woodruff Rd
Coos Bay OR 97420

Call Sign: K7MNS
Matthew N Schmidt
Coos Bay OR 97420

Call Sign: KF7PJB
Allen G Mathias
Coos Bay OR 97420

Call Sign: K7BJG
Roger M Flanagan
620 W Commercial

Call Sign: KB7JXN
Ted C Smith
Coos Bay OR 97420

Call Sign: KF7FJY
Connie A Bunnell
Coos Bay OR 97420

Call Sign: KD7VCO
Jean A Mccurdy
Coos Bay OR 97420

Call Sign: KD7WDO
Kenneth D Braden
Coos Bay OR 97420

Call Sign: KE7OAO
Kenneth D Braden
Coos Bay OR 97420

Call Sign: N7NSA
Kenneth D Braden
Coos Bay OR 97420

Call Sign: KF7FJX
Will C Bunnell
Coos Bay OR 97420

Call Sign: K7OWR
Will C Bunnell
Coos Bay OR 97420

FCC Amateur Radio Licenses in Coquille

Call Sign: WB6WAF
Donald T Baker
2274 37th St
Coquille OR 97423

Call Sign: W7WAF
Donald T Baker
1006 38th Ave SE
Coquille OR 97423

Call Sign: KE7FND
Kathy E Baker
1006 38th Ave SE
Coquille OR 97423

Call Sign: KA7NKY
Lloyd E Fowler
1060 Callaway Dr
Coquille OR 97423

Call Sign: KB7LGW
William G Noyce
180 Calvert Dr
Coquille OR 97423

Call Sign: KB7BMM
Michael L Barnett
1993 Camellia Ave
Coquille OR 97423

Call Sign: KE7VQQ
Jens R Jorgensen Sr
470 Doran Rd
Coquille OR 97423

Call Sign: K7MNB
Benjamin E Miller
1155 E Main St
Coquille OR 97423

Call Sign: K7TDM
Cleola Miller
11829 E Mapleton Rd
Coquille OR 97423

Call Sign: KC7CI
Gene C Neumann
88504 E Of Eden Rd
Coquille OR 974231528

Call Sign: KE7PLI
Dan G Childs
35116 Ede Rd
Coquille OR 97423

Call Sign: N7XEJ
George E Shinn
124 F St
Coquille OR 974231402

Call Sign: W7VPF
George E Eckholm
2721 Fallon Ct W
Coquille OR 97423

Call Sign: KE7JHW
Kimberly O Smith
4507 Garden Ct SE
Coquille OR 97423

Call Sign: KE7IHU
Lorraine F Smith
1773 Garden Dr
Coquille OR 97423

Call Sign: N6SQ
Cary A Norman
92837 Garden Ln
Coquille OR 97423

Call Sign: KE7JSF
Samuel A Wilson
2485 Greenwood Rd S
Coquille OR 97423

Call Sign: KE7IHV
William C Brohm
3100 H St
Coquille OR 97423

Call Sign: W7WCB
William C Brohm
69300 Hackamore
Coquille OR 97423

Call Sign: N7VRQ
William P Jonsson
3555 Harrison Dr
Coquille OR 97423

Call Sign: KD7LXG
Don R Swenson
146 N 8th St
Coquille OR 97423

Call Sign: KD7MWW
Kathleen M Swenson
435 N Alameda
Coquille OR 97423

Call Sign: WB6SPI
Edward Padgett
4625 N Montana Ave
Coquille OR 97423

Call Sign: W7DDO
Danny G Upton
80590 N Turkey Run Rd
Coquille OR 97423

Call Sign: KE7ADD
Don L Delyria III
1520 N Hwy 97 Ste 192
Coquille OR 97423

Call Sign: W7UIH
Alden D Clymer
10136 N Osego Ave
Coquille OR 974231355

Call Sign: WA7JAW
Carl T Burkleo
5206 N Willis Blvd
Coquille OR 97423

Call Sign: KE7CXG
Don L Delyria Jr
8045 N Hwy 97 Unit 24
Coquille OR 97423

Call Sign: WB6JJS
William W Moody
145 N Roanoke Box 237
Coquille OR 97423

Call Sign: NH6DQ
Virginia Gilliard
1202 NE 193
Coquille OR 97423

Call Sign: KF7EIP
Joel A Sullivan
1660 N Mist Dr
Coquille OR 97423

Call Sign: KA6CVQ
Margaret M Moody
145 N Roanoke St
Coquille OR 97423

Call Sign: N7PNR
Ingeborg T Amdahl
3765 NW 163rd Ter
Coquille OR 97423

Call Sign: KF7FJZ
Joel A Sullivan
7051 N Mobile Ave
Coquille OR 97423

Call Sign: KD7NN
George S Zeigler
2215 N Skidmore Terr
Coquille OR 97423

Call Sign: KB7TVB
Walter R Esterlein
5112 NW 167 Pl
Coquille OR 97423

Call Sign: W7WBC
Joel A Sullivan
7114 N Mohawk Ave
Coquille OR 97423

Call Sign: WB7SON
Steven R Myers
1401 N Springbrook Rd 125
Coquille OR 97423

Call Sign: KC7CNT
Wilma I Turley
744 NW 16th St
Coquille OR 97423

Call Sign: WA7OXM
Zane C Albertson
317 N Molalla Ave
Coquille OR 97423

Call Sign: KE7SAC
Bunny A Upton
500 N Tomahawk Island Dr
Coquille OR 97423

Call Sign: N7VSG
Kurt D Erichsen
744 NW 16th St
Coquille OR 97423

Call Sign: N7DCD
Robert B Mason
345 N Monmouth Ave
Coquille OR 97423

Call Sign: KE7OAN
Danny G Upton
24 N Troutlane
Coquille OR 97423

Call Sign: W6RAD
Jim K Beard
3768 NW Devoto Ln
Coquille OR 97423

Call Sign: WA6RPM
Carolee Padgett
345 N Monmouth Ave
Coquille OR 97423

Call Sign: KF7Q
Danny G Upton
80590 N Turkey Run Rd
Coquille OR 97423

Call Sign: KC7ZCV
Cory A Judd
4835 NW Elmwood Dr
Coquille OR 97423

Call Sign: KF7ALL
Betty W Bassett
5035 Prospect St
Coquille OR 97423

Call Sign: KE7ORM
Rhett Bassett
56039 Prosper Jct Rd
Coquille OR 97423

Call Sign: K7TDH
Jane Williams
2133 Rickard Rd
Coquille OR 97423

Call Sign: KC7PIJ
Dean E Eisteld
3235 SE 7th St
Coquille OR 97423

Call Sign: KD7VPH
North West Military Radio
Enthusiasts
538 Shan Cr Rd
Coquille OR 97423

Call Sign: WA7OBB
Frederick A Sell
538 Shan Cr Rd
Coquille OR 97423

Call Sign: KE6IVR
Michael R Mc Cullough
595 Shore Pines Pl
Coquille OR 97423

Call Sign: KG6AKW
Alice L Mccullough
595 Shore Pines Pl
Coquille OR 97423

Call Sign: AI0M
Loren F Chase
595 Shore Pines Pl

Coquille OR 97423

Call Sign: AI7M
Loren F Chase
131 Shoreline Dr
Coquille OR 97423

Call Sign: KA7VWL
John T Reichlein
3410 Videra Dr
Coquille OR 97423

Call Sign: K7AXF
Robert N Crawford
917 W 11th St
Coquille OR 97423

Call Sign: KF7QPC
Reggie V Boles
55 W 6th St
Coquille OR 97423

Call Sign: KC7IXW
Donald E Brown
1055 W 9th St
Coquille OR 97423

Call Sign: KD7IIA
Gerald F Lueger
2367 Western Dr
Coquille OR 97423

Call Sign: KE7ZO
Clifford C Cottam Sr
Coquille OR 97423

Call Sign: N7ZAS
John W Brazer
Coquille OR 97423

Call Sign: KC7JJJ
Kori L Frasier
Coquille OR 97423

Call Sign: KC7MAG

Ben C Frasier
Coquille OR 97423

Call Sign: N7HBF
Guy J Ralph
Coquille OR 97423

Call Sign: KD7QBV
Allyne J Schneider
Coquille OR 97423

Call Sign: KD7QPN
Edward J Serdziak
Coquille OR 97423

Call Sign: W7VMU
Guy J Ralph
Coquille OR 97423

Call Sign: KF7JFW
Warren S Stafford Jr
Coquille OR 97423

Call Sign: KC0UOU
William R Fordham Jr
Coquille OR 97423

FCC Amateur Radio Licenses in Cottage Grove

Call Sign: K6ZGH
Francis L Cobb
619 38th Pl
Cottage Grove OR 97424

Call Sign: W7UN
Rick L Bailor
3185 Ave G
Cottage Grove OR 97424

Call Sign: KF7BBA
James D Yourdon
1099 Barbra Ave NE
Cottage Grove OR 97424

Call Sign: W7BBA
James D Yourdon
823 Barclay Meadows Rd
Cottage Grove OR 97424

Call Sign: KF7MRG
Myra B Yourdon
5171 Barger Dr
Cottage Grove OR 97424

Call Sign: AL7HY
Henry Walters
5185 Barger Dr
Cottage Grove OR 97424

Call Sign: KB7OWG
Dorothy A Johnson
2870 Bear Ridge Dr
Cottage Grove OR 97424

Call Sign: N7XRH
Curtis H Johnson
31889 Beave Homes Rd
Cottage Grove OR 97424

Call Sign: N7BFP
Richard H Nelson
26825 Berg Dr
Cottage Grove OR 97424

Call Sign: AE7N
Larry D Doggett
18880 Boynton St
Cottage Grove OR 97424

Call Sign: N6TRR
Brice W Vineyard
17590 Braden Ct
Cottage Grove OR 97424

Call Sign: N7VTC
Linda S Velasquez
2350 Bradley Ct
Cottage Grove OR 97424

Call Sign: KD7HRD
Daniel G Kuebler
231 Bradley Dr
Cottage Grove OR 97424

Call Sign: KD7HRE
Kristine M Kuebler
231 Bradley Dr
Cottage Grove OR 97424

Call Sign: N7ZTI
Scott O Thayer
2360 Brush College Rd NW
Cottage Grove OR 97424

Call Sign: W7BAD
Wade R Lehman
35960 Bryant Dr
Cottage Grove OR 97424

Call Sign: W6PHK
Edward Krafchow
1826 Cedar St
Cottage Grove OR 97424

Call Sign: W7DQQ
George D Drury
61170 Chuckanut Dr
Cottage Grove OR 97424

Call Sign: N7SXA
Gary D Nichols
5560 Collins Rd
Cottage Grove OR 97424

Call Sign: K7SLA
South Lane Amateur Radio
Association
5560 Collins Rd
Cottage Grove OR 97424

Call Sign: KD7CGF
South Lane Amateur Radio
Association
8890 Collins Rd

Cottage Grove OR 97424

Call Sign: W7SLA
South Lane Amateur Radio
Assn
64485 Collins Rd
Cottage Grove OR 97424

Call Sign: W7ZQD
Joe D Brown
4352 Coloma Dr SE
Cottage Grove OR 97424

Call Sign: W7ZQE
South Lane Amateur Radio
Association
4352 Coloma Dr SE
Cottage Grove OR 97424

Call Sign: KE7RRT
Leeann S Brown
4472 Coloma Dr SE
Cottage Grove OR 97424

Call Sign: N7AAB
Gary R Kofoid
2831 Columbia Blvd
Cottage Grove OR 97424

Call Sign: KB6RAS
Norman E Bender
301 Columbia Dr 30
Cottage Grove OR 97424

Call Sign: KF7PTH
Jonathan R D Caldwell
607 Cottonwood
Cottage Grove OR 97424

Call Sign: KC6ZGI
Robert E Madden
19330 Dayton Rd
Cottage Grove OR 97424

Call Sign: KD7QQT

Robert E Madden
19411 Dayton Rd
Cottage Grove OR 97424

Call Sign: KE6OTK
Brook E Taylor
32917 Diamond Hill Dr Sp
B
Cottage Grove OR 97424

Call Sign: KF6NJR
Marian Tennison
32917 Diamond Hill Dr Sp
B
Cottage Grove OR 97424

Call Sign: W6RZY
Marian Tennison
615 Diamond St
Cottage Grove OR 97424

Call Sign: N7PKW
Daniel N Anseth
1720 Drake St
Cottage Grove OR 97424

Call Sign: N7TTM
Sharon W Anseth
19557 Drakes Rd SE
Cottage Grove OR 97424

Call Sign: KL7ISB
Andrew G Watkins
187 Draper St NE
Cottage Grove OR
974240032

Call Sign: AD7WD
Andrew G Watkins
228 Draper St NE
Cottage Grove OR
974240032

Call Sign: W7EQ
Andrew G Watkins

249 Draper St NE
Cottage Grove OR
974240032

Call Sign: K7OHW
Olga H Watkins
185 Dreamhill Dr
Cottage Grove OR
974240032

Call Sign: KE7RCA
Leslie W Villa
185 Elizabeth Dr
Cottage Grove OR 97424

Call Sign: KE7OWH
Sarah A Villa
37566 Elizabeth Dr
Cottage Grove OR 97424

Call Sign: KD7ZYZ
Lynn P Osburn
706 F Ave
Cottage Grove OR 97424

Call Sign: W7REG
Robert E Groff Sr
15016 Fern Ridge Rd SE
Cottage Grove OR 97424

Call Sign: WB6FXA
William W Noah
3551 Harrison Cir
Cottage Grove OR 97424

Call Sign: KF4VHA
Howard P Krutzler
1590 Hondeleau Ln
Cottage Grove OR 97424

Call Sign: AB0KT
John L Cummings
91160 Hwy 101
Cottage Grove OR 97424

Call Sign: K7LM
John L Cummings
3760 Hwy 101 13
Cottage Grove OR 97424

Call Sign: ND7R
Charles M Deaton
8221 Hwy 66
Cottage Grove OR 97424

Call Sign: KF7KDC
William A Hemphill
9043 Hwy 66
Cottage Grove OR 97424

Call Sign: KA7WKS
Ethel M Saunders
39040 Jerger St
Cottage Grove OR 97424

Call Sign: K7VCT
Blaine D Ogle
410 Jerome Ave
Cottage Grove OR 97424

Call Sign: KE7KJS
Bernie C Gay Jr
5322 Knoll Way
Cottage Grove OR 97424

Call Sign: KF7BUD
John G Royer
145574 Lanewood Dr
Cottage Grove OR 97424

Call Sign: W7JGR
John G Royer
18660 Langensand Rd
Cottage Grove OR 97424

Call Sign: N7NDV
Corrie L Taylor
Lorane Rt Box 609
Cottage Grove OR 97424

Call Sign: N7NDW
Seth T Taylor
Lorane Rt Box 609
Cottage Grove OR 97424

Call Sign: WB0QMD
Thomas B Taylor Jr
Lorane Rt Box 609
Cottage Grove OR 97424

Call Sign: KC7SVM
Jerry H Eckstine
2217 Marion St
Cottage Grove OR 97424

Call Sign: KK7IT
Joseph H Rawlings
3074 Marion St SE
Cottage Grove OR 97424

Call Sign: WD6AJN
Jack Miller
3623 Marion St SE
Cottage Grove OR 97424

Call Sign: KC7SVL
Doris M Rawlings
2350 Marion St SE
Cottage Grove OR 97424

Call Sign: KD7KOA
Ryan K Ward
3022 Marion St SE
Cottage Grove OR 97424

Call Sign: KD7AJB
James M Stohler
1093 Montgomery Ave
Cottage Grove OR 97424

Call Sign: W2MEE
Kenneth R Almberg
1037 Murray Dr
Cottage Grove OR 97424

Call Sign: KD7EVJ
Eston F Wicks
643 N Berkeley Way
Cottage Grove OR 97424

Call Sign: W7WIX
Eston F Wicks
285 N Bertelsen Rd
Cottage Grove OR 97424

Call Sign: KA7NAY
David L Clark
116 N Elm St
Cottage Grove OR 97424

Call Sign: KB7DTI
James C Shepard
1532 N Holman St
Cottage Grove OR 97424

Call Sign: KB7JLV
Cecil Rivers
10215 N Hudson St
Cottage Grove OR 97424

Call Sign: KD7ZOM
Billy G Jones
2138 NE 112th Ave
Cottage Grove OR 97424

Call Sign: KA8TOK
Bradford A Kellison
826 NE 127th Ave
Cottage Grove OR
974241358

Call Sign: K6TFK
Bruce C Dutcher
2140 NW 135th Ave
Cottage Grove OR 97424

Call Sign: KF7CRF
Sam L Mccullough
20509 Pine Vista Dr
Cottage Grove OR 97424

Call Sign: KF7IYF
Mona L Meyer
1322 S Cherry
Cottage Grove OR 97424

Call Sign: K7SIS
Mona L Meyer
2661 S Cherry St
Cottage Grove OR 97424

Call Sign: KD7TU
James M Rachetto
17700 S Dick Dr
Cottage Grove OR 97424

Call Sign: KE7WSW
Earle C Quinlan
200 S Longview Way 41
Cottage Grove OR 97424

Call Sign: KH6OV
Earle C Quinlan
891 S Marple St
Cottage Grove OR 97424

Call Sign: WB6ORC
Steve D Lawson
20895 Sawyer Rd
Cottage Grove OR 97424

Call Sign: W7SMK
Steve D Lawson
4740 Sayler St
Cottage Grove OR 97424

Call Sign: KF7KTV
Matthew B Devore
908 Schaefers Ln
Cottage Grove OR 97424

Call Sign: W7MBD
Matthew B Devore
775 Schaeffer Rd
Cottage Grove OR 97424

Call Sign: KG6DBQ
Jerry T Kerns
280 Seward Ave
Cottage Grove OR 97424

Call Sign: KC7CIP
Katherine W Walker
3295 Spearmint St
Cottage Grove OR 97424

Call Sign: N7NBH
Stanley D Walker
97 Speedwell
Cottage Grove OR 97424

Call Sign: KD7WSQ
Isaac B Mingus
724 Spencer Ave
Cottage Grove OR 97424

Call Sign: KD7SQN
Louis J Ralston
1451 Spruce St Apt 115
Cottage Grove OR
974249464

Call Sign: KE7SLW
Richard K Firth
1124 T St
Cottage Grove OR 97424

Call Sign: K7OMT
David J Thompson
1109 Talent Ave
Cottage Grove OR 97424

Call Sign: W6OVH
Jerry W Crabtree
232 Talent Ave 36
Cottage Grove OR 97424

Call Sign: W7JRT
Warren E Luse
7760 Village Green Cir
Cottage Grove OR 97424

Call Sign: KC7PYA
E Laverne Edwards
12849 Village Loop Rd
Cottage Grove OR 97424

Call Sign: KF7KFB
Leo N Swain
1505 W Harrison Ave
Cottage Grove OR 97424

Call Sign: WA3OCW
Robert L Onaitis
2224 W Harrison Ave
Cottage Grove OR 97424

Call Sign: WA7OIG
Jerry M Abbott
1149 W Main
Cottage Grove OR 97424

Call Sign: WP2ACY
Kristian R Kallaway
1853 W Main
Cottage Grove OR 97424

Call Sign: KC7OUA
Geoffrey D Jones
Cottage Grove OR 97424

Call Sign: N7QZV
David P Edmondson
Cottage Grove OR 97424

Call Sign: KC7FFT
Vicky R Hill
Cottage Grove OR 97424

Call Sign: KE6PDZ
Michael E Budris Cudak
Cottage Grove OR 97424

Call Sign: N6LF
Rudolf P Severns

Call Sign: N7KAK
Tanya Stone
Cottage Grove OR 97424

Call Sign: N7TLF
Robert D Quigley
Cottage Grove OR 97424

Call Sign: WB7BMY
Michael L Hendrick
Cottage Grove OR 97424

Call Sign: KD7IDX
Thomas G Pearson
Cottage Grove OR 97424

Call Sign: KE7OUS
Clinton J Petit
Cottage Grove OR 97424

Call Sign: AD7SG
Clinton J Petit
Cottage Grove OR 97424

Call Sign: AB7N
Clinton J Petit
Cottage Grove OR 97424

Call Sign: KF7FYA
Ida J Weathers Pearson
Cottage Grove OR 97424

Call Sign: W7KPI
Ida J Weathers Pearson
Cottage Grove OR 97424

Call Sign: KE7LDK
Michael L Dempsey
Cottage Grove OR 97424

Call Sign: K7MLD
Michael L Dempsey
Cottage Grove OR 97424

Call Sign: W7MLD
Michael L Dempsey
Cottage Grove OR 97424

Call Sign: W7XJ
Michael L Dempsey
Cottage Grove OR 97424

Call Sign: W7RDQ
Robert D Quigley
Cottage Grove OR 97424

Call Sign: AE7DQ
Thomas G Pearson
Cottage Grove OR 97424

Call Sign: W7KP
Thomas G Pearson
Cottage Grove OR 97424

Call Sign: KE7DPT
Jacquie Cooper
Cottage Grove OR
974240326

Call Sign: KC7MBV
Carl A Parker
82083 Bay Rd
Cove OR 97824

Call Sign: N7BCW
Charles R Rich
2705 Cedar St
Cove OR 97824

Call Sign: KD7KAO
Byron K Morris
75718 London Rd
Cove OR 97824

Call Sign: KE7ZRY

Robert D Nelson
5022 Mazama Dr
Cove OR 97824

Call Sign: KF7KHI
Charles W Campbell Sr
415 State St
Cove OR 97824

Call Sign: WA7TJ
John D Shoemaker
1209 State St
Cove OR 97824

Call Sign: KC7FLP
Steven D Baer
Cove OR 97824

Call Sign: KE7UFC
David F Jensen
Cove OR 97824

Call Sign: W7DFJ
David F Jensen
Cove OR 97824

Call Sign: KE7ZSK
Teddi Montes Botham
Cove OR 97824

Call Sign: KF7HPT
Joseph W Dimatteo
Crane OR 97732

Call Sign: KD7JPT
Daniel F Zurfluh
Crane OR 97732

Call Sign: KF7JDP
Carolyn R Dimatteo
Crane OR 97732

Call Sign: KF7CIM
Tammy J Valentine
Crane OR 97732

Call Sign: KA7KFF
Alan R Lane
Riddle Rd
Crescent OR 97733

Call Sign: WA7JNR
Catherine M Lane
Riddle Rd
Crescent OR 97733

Call Sign: WB7DIP
Milo F Davidson Sr
3519 Dogwood Dr S
Crescent Lake OR 97733

Call Sign: KD7NXW
Camp Makualla Staff Assn
Crescent Lake OR 97425

Call Sign: N7WBX
Gordon D Jenness
Crescent Lake OR 97425

Call Sign: N7WYA
Debra Diane Jenness
Crescent Lake OR 97425

Call Sign: KE7GHN
Nicholas L Goevelinger
Crescent Lake OR 97425

Call Sign: W7NLG
Nickolas L Goevelinger
Crescent Lake OR 97425

Call Sign: N7MOM
Richard H Allison
751 Azalea Dr
Creswell OR 97426

Call Sign: KF7EFQ
John Koza
3759 Berkshire St
Creswell OR 97426

Call Sign: N7NO
Francis W Rogers
Rt 3 Box 3140C
Creswell OR 97426

Call Sign: KC7ZFO
Monty C Howard
1240 College Green Dr
Creswell OR 97426

Call Sign: N7DGE
Theodore L Schneider
559 Crystal Srpings Ln N
Creswell OR 97426

Call Sign: N7EYV
Frank K Brown
3240 Duncan Ave 91 E
Creswell OR 97426

Call Sign: N7CGS
Charlene G Smith
572 E 1st St
Creswell OR 974269391

Call Sign: NO7RM
Norman A Smith
704 E 21 Pl
Creswell OR 974269391

Call Sign: W7DGF
Kenneth L Sears

838 Erie Ave
Creswell OR 974260873

Call Sign: KD7MUN
Lorna K Young
61255 Ferguson Rd
Creswell OR 97426

Call Sign: K9CZI
J C Thorpe
565 Howard St SE
Creswell OR 97426

Call Sign: K0OWF
Horace H Hansen
12790 Hwy 39
Creswell OR 97426

Call Sign: KA0IZT
Gerald F Hansen
822 Hwy 395 S Pmb 131
Creswell OR 97426

Call Sign: N7IGY
Donilea K Shelder Ives
38909 Hwy 58 Sp Q
Creswell OR 97426

Call Sign: KF7VJ
Lewis M Rankin
4330 Imperial Dr
Creswell OR 97426

Call Sign: KC7DMH
Lawrence R Faught
262 Latigo Ranch Rd
Creswell OR 97426

Call Sign: W7ADL
Lawrence R Faught
1937 Laura St
Creswell OR 97426

Call Sign: K7DML
Robert L Conley

41886 McKenzie Hwy
Creswell OR 97426

Call Sign: KD7OU
Stanley D Sloan
41993 McKenzie Hwy
Creswell OR 97426

Call Sign: KD7KLO
Martin M Klos
7217 N Wall Ave
Creswell OR 97426

Call Sign: AA7KJ
Chris Bichsel
8011 N Washburne
Creswell OR 97426

Call Sign: KD7MTR
Daniel K Nakooka
835 Nandy Dr
Creswell OR 97426

Call Sign: KD7BDW
Thomas J Macauley
1915 NE 148th Ave
Creswell OR 97426

Call Sign: N7APB
William T Macauley
3141 NE 148th Ave 209
Creswell OR 97426

Call Sign: KC7VWQ
Kristopher R Arens
1320 Oregon Ave
Creswell OR 97426

Call Sign: N7LLP
Charles A Hawks
40823 Rodgers Mtn Lp
Creswell OR 97426

Call Sign: KA7NXO
Jack A Day

8552 Rodlum Rd
Creswell OR 97426

Call Sign: KA7IXH
Robert C Franklin
695 W F St
Creswell OR 97426

Call Sign: KF7NAN
Gary J Mcmahan
750 W F St
Creswell OR 97426

Call Sign: N7GVH
Melvin U Grote
Creswell OR 97426

Call Sign: KC7VWR
Robert M Cooley
Creswell OR 97426

Call Sign: W7ISV
Richard Ives
Creswell OR 97426

Call Sign: KE7UOC
Dq Johnson
Creswell OR 97426

Call Sign: KE7VXK
Dq Johnson
Creswell OR 97426

Call Sign: KE7JFM
Laurel A Cooley
Creswell OR 97426

Call Sign: WB7ROB
Robert M Cooley
Creswell OR 97426

Call Sign: KC7GTR
Myron B Cooley
Creswell OR 974260190

Call Sign: AC7WU
Myron B Cooley
Creswell OR 974260190

Call Sign: KG6TCS
William E Hall
Creswell OR 974260970

FCC Amateur Radio Licenses in Crooked River Ranch

Call Sign: N7MQL
Jack C Peasley
6353 SW Childs Rd
Crooked River Ranch OR 97760

Call Sign: KK7XA
Dwight F Small
13410 SW Cresmer Dr
Crooked River Ranch OR 977609320

Call Sign: W1LGR
Dwight F Small
13595 SW Cresmer Dr
Crooked River Ranch OR 977609320

Call Sign: K7TYE
Sean J Hartley
65 SW Crestview Ln
Crooked River Ranch OR 97760

Call Sign: KD7HB
Paul C Drahn
1533 SW Nancy Dr
Crooked River Ranch OR 97760

Call Sign: N7FMM
Edward C Mattive
10 SW Porter Apt 107

Crooked River Ranch OR 97760

Call Sign: W7OMN
Walter J Harrington
7160 SW Shady Ct
Crooked River Ranch OR 97760

Call Sign: KB7RUF
Karen F Duke
8714 SW Waterhole Pl
Crooked River Ranch OR 97760

Call Sign: K6WOW
Karen F Duke
4675 SW Watson
Crooked River Ranch OR 97760

Call Sign: W7WHO
Dennis P Duke
16036 SW Waxwing Way
Crooked River Ranch OR 97760

FCC Amateur Radio Licenses in Culp Creek

Call Sign: KD7SKZ
William P Braaten
Culp Creek OR 97427

FCC Amateur Radio Licenses in Culver

Call Sign: W7GVM
Garold V Morey
4124 Orchard Way
Culver OR 97734

Call Sign: KD7MGN
Haystack Repeater Group
4124 Orchard Way

Culver OR 97734

Call Sign: KC7CKG
Phillip M Sledge
140 SE Olvera Ave
Culver OR 97734

Call Sign: KB7WJM
George A Sanborn Sr
7450 SW Alden St
Culver OR 97734

Call Sign: K7TFD
George A Sanborn Sr
7575 SW Alden St
Culver OR 97734

Call Sign: KC7UZM
James L Peterson
10130 SW Cynthia St
Culver OR 97734

Call Sign: KE7ASB
Dean D Monson
43060 SW Dudney Ave
Culver OR 97734

Call Sign: K7UAJ
Robert C Paterno
22851 SW Hosler Way
Culver OR 97734

Call Sign: WB7PQD
Danny L Freeman
20033 SW Joann Ct
Culver OR 97734

Call Sign: KE7HKC
April L Stream
10410 SW Johnson Ct
Culver OR 97734

Call Sign: K7TJR
Lee R Strahan
15315 SW Lark Ln

Culver OR 97734

Call Sign: KE7HKE
Blaine T Buckle
1933 SW Laura Ct
Culver OR 97734

Call Sign: KE7HJW
Bronwen J Buckle
1959 SW Laura Ct
Culver OR 97734

Call Sign: KE7EXG
Bruce T Turney
6501 SW Macadam Ave
Culver OR 97734

Call Sign: N2WEW
Laverna R Wruble
5005 SW Meadows Rd 100
Culver OR 97734

Call Sign: W7GG
Robert S Wruble
10450 SW Meier Dr
Culver OR 97734

Call Sign: KC7JLV
David M Sledge
1797 SW Songbird St
Culver OR 97734

Call Sign: KD7THC
Harvey R Plunkett
30950 SW Willamette Way
W
Culver OR 97734

Call Sign: WB7OYY
Gene P King
Culver OR 97734

Call Sign: KC7PZB
William E Mc Cheshey
Culver OR 97741

FCC Amateur Radio Licenses in Dairy

Call Sign: KD7SHW
William P Basil
7528 Buckhorn Rd
Dairy OR 97625

Call Sign: WB7WUC
John A Bodnar
2890 Fir Ct
Dairy OR 976258718

Call Sign: KC7LZW
Mellody S Asbill
Dairy OR 97625

FCC Amateur Radio Licenses in Days Creek

Call Sign: KE6VDI
Marilyn J Dyer
470 Colonial Ct
Days Creek OR 974299729

Call Sign: W7INI
James E Dyer
470 Colonial Ct
Days Creek OR 974299729

Call Sign: KD7LOQ
James E Donavan
64700 Deer Island Heights
Dr
Days Creek OR 97429

Call Sign: WB7QCD
James E Donavan
64700 Deer Island Heights
Dr
Days Creek OR 97429

Call Sign: WB7EQC
Jerry D Goodrich

1509 E 2nd St
Days Creek OR 97429

Call Sign: ND7U
Donald L Bovee
94323 Gauntlett St
Days Creek OR 97429

Call Sign: WD6ENW
Bobby E Atwood
95773 Timber Hill
Days Creek OR 97429

Call Sign: KF6MSV
H Eugene Miller
6010 View Loop
Days Creek OR 97429

Call Sign: N7SHH
Randall S Bovee
Days Creek OR 97429

FCC Amateur Radio Licenses in Dayville

Call Sign: KA7DWV
Daron M Dierks
1561 Franklin St
Dayville OR 978250303

Call Sign: KB7WFG
Monty G L Smith
Dayville OR 97825

FCC Amateur Radio Licenses in Deadwood

Call Sign: KC7IMY
James Sliwinski
243 Delmar Dr N
Deadwood OR 97430

Call Sign: KD7UCR
Daniel C Yates
225 E 39th Ave

Deadwood OR 974309702

Call Sign: N7AXV
Ann M Benscoter
87814 Limpit Ln
Deadwood OR 974300037

Call Sign: AG7X
Leslie M Benscoter
87891 Limpit Ln
Deadwood OR 97430

Call Sign: KD7WXW
James M Parmenter
745 NW 107th Ave
Deadwood OR 97403

FCC Amateur Radio Licenses in Dexter

Call Sign: KF6MND
Patricia E Fulbright
94200 3rd St Apt 3
Dexter OR 97431

Call Sign: KF7UBK
James M Logajan
4044 Cedar Oak Dr
Dexter OR 97431

Call Sign: KB7RBI
Todd C Gruener
122 E Holley Rd
Dexter OR 97431

Call Sign: N7NDM
Helen G Ballard
488 Fairway Ct
Dexter OR 97431

Call Sign: WQ7K
Ward E Ballard
922 Fairway Dr
Dexter OR 97431

Call Sign: KF7FGU
Gary A Burke
12484 Mascher Rd NE
Dexter OR 97431

Call Sign: KF7FGV
Penny L Burke
12314 Mascher Rd NE
Dexter OR 97431

Call Sign: KF7QKC
Kevin C Kovarik
94050 Mather Ln
Dexter OR 97431

Call Sign: KF7BUB
Richard L Kovarik
20140 Mathers Dr
Dexter OR 97431

Call Sign: K7POC
Richard L Kovarik
95367 Mattson Ln
Dexter OR 97431

Call Sign: KD7AHU
Kevin D King
23083 Maverick Ln
Dexter OR 97431

Call Sign: WB7EDT
George W Atkinson
2494 Ridgeway Dr
Dexter OR 97431

Call Sign: N1OPA
Daniel J Orleck
34400 Squaw Valley Rd
Dexter OR 97431

Call Sign: W7GGL
Alfred M Land Jr
38216 Wheeler Rd
Dexter OR 97431

Call Sign: W7JEC
Barbara E Land
38216 Wheeler Rd
Dexter OR 97431

Call Sign: W7EKK
Dottie J Folz
Dexter OR 97431

FCC Amateur Radio Licenses in Diamond Lake

Call Sign: KB7FYL
Jan J Mornarich
Diamond Lake Rv Park
Diamond Lake OR 97731

FCC Amateur Radio Licenses in Dillard

Call Sign: KC7JNN
Arnold H Ryder
Dillard OR 97432

Call Sign: KD7SPI
Charles W Pifher
Dillard OR 97432

Call Sign: KF7FIC
Karl H Tanner
Dillard OR 97432

FCC Amateur Radio Licenses in Dorena

Call Sign: KD7LON
Ian S Lounsbury
35121 Burt Rd
Dorena OR 97434

Call Sign: KC6CSP
Donald R Lounsbury
220 Burton Dr
Dorena OR 97434

Call Sign: AC7KW
Donald R Lounsbury
32633 Bush Garden Dr
Dorena OR 97434

Call Sign: N7KKS
Erik E Land
67180 Harrington Loop
Dorena OR 97434

Call Sign: KE7CRB
Ian C Gwalthey
1355 S Bay Rd
Dorena OR 97434

Call Sign: WA7ZCE
Douglas L Farley
96900 Sitkum Ln
Dorena OR 97434

FCC Amateur Radio Licenses in Drain

Call Sign: WB7OOU
Robert S Miller
6560 Canary Rd
Drain OR 97435

Call Sign: KD7HAC
Frank I Gilpin
1551 Center Str NE Apt 323
Drain OR 974358717

Call Sign: KF7GPP
Donald P Mcintyre Jr
61697 Fargo Ln
Drain OR 97435

Call Sign: KB7VIZ
Richie W Harris
3934 Hwy 101 N
Drain OR 97435

Call Sign: N6NQF
Phillip R Intravia Jr

63589 Jd Estates Dr
Drain OR 97435

Call Sign: KB7TWO
Frank C Swain
Drain OR 97435

Call Sign: N7QNC
David W Abercrombie
Drain OR 97435

Call Sign: KE7YZP
Michael Dunn
Drain OR 97435

Call Sign: W7ORX
Michael Dunn
Drain OR 97435

FCC Amateur Radio Licenses in Dufur

Call Sign: KA7NEO
Hilary F Welp
150 Eagle View Dr
Dufur OR 97021

Call Sign: KC7TI
Paul A Killeen
222 Echo Way
Dufur OR 97021

Call Sign: W7PAK
Paul A Killeen
100 Eckloff Rd
Dufur OR 97021

Call Sign: N7FIU
James H Lash
3760 Market St NE 187
Dufur OR 97021

Call Sign: KA7KXM
Claude A Robertson
1339 NE Jackson School Rd

Dufur OR 97021

Call Sign: WA7CKS
Robert A Crosby
1649 NW Bonney Dr
Dufur OR 97021

Call Sign: KA7WNP
Berton A Clark
Dufur OR 97021

Call Sign: KB7IOM
L Jane West
Dufur OR 97021

Call Sign: KF7MYP
Marsha A Highfield
Dufur OR 97021

FCC Amateur Radio Licenses in Durkee

Call Sign: W7QEN
Donald E Schwartz
Durkee OR 97905

FCC Amateur Radio Licenses in Eagle Point

Call Sign: KF7ICJ
Brian A Horton
225 41st St 27
Eagle Point OR 97524

Call Sign: KE7WTI
Kyle G Macwilliams
35385 Bayside Gardens Rd
Eagle Point OR 97524

Call Sign: N7WNU
Melvin L Russell Jr
Box 8005 Black Butte
Ranch
Eagle Point OR 975246528

Call Sign: N7PCV
Sally W Marsh
3125 Boardman 1
Eagle Point OR 97524

Call Sign: N7JSF
Raymond J Angel
40039 Booth Kelly Rd
Eagle Point OR 97524

Call Sign: K7UCB
Arthur J Machovec Sr
Butte Falls Hwy Box 8965
Eagle Point OR 97524

Call Sign: KF6BNZ
Julia L Blackwell
95629 Cape Ferrelo Rd
Eagle Point OR 97524

Call Sign: WA7DCG
Donald W Brown
115 Cedar St
Eagle Point OR 97524

Call Sign: KA6AHO
Judith A West
5228 Cherry Heights Rd
Eagle Point OR 97524

Call Sign: KC6YRL
Terry W Boughamer
4251 Cherry Ln
Eagle Point OR 97524

Call Sign: N7ZHA
Garry L Wilson
2251 Dick George Rd
Eagle Point OR 97524

Call Sign: N7JNN
Robert L Beyer
1316 Dogwood Dr
Eagle Point OR 97524

Call Sign: KC0MKY
Steven W Kelsay
3940 Dove Ln
Eagle Point OR 97524

Call Sign: KC7ZCE
Michael S Porter
62860 Eagle Rd
Eagle Point OR 97524

Call Sign: KB6QVI
Joel P Caulkins
18765 Effinger Way
Eagle Point OR 975249755

Call Sign: KD6AGR
Nancy E Caulkins
9700 Egert Rd
Eagle Point OR 975249481

Call Sign: KE7BNX
Rick J Steelman
17483 Egret Dr
Eagle Point OR 97524

Call Sign: N6GPL
Daniel C Evison
60450 Elkai Woods Dr
Eagle Point OR 97524

Call Sign: NL7DB
Michael K Evans
243 F St 25
Eagle Point OR 975247876

Call Sign: NL7DH
Carolyn L Evans
1111 F St 4
Eagle Point OR 975247876

Call Sign: N3AL
Neal P Jones
6309 Fairway Ave SE
Eagle Point OR 97524

Call Sign: KB7NUC
Victor E Gardener
2586 Haig
Eagle Point OR 97524

Call Sign: WB6ZAO
La Vaine V Eastman
484 Limnell
Eagle Point OR 97524

Call Sign: KD7GVH
George C Reed
333 Mt View Rd 17
Eagle Point OR 97524

Call Sign: N8KZE
James W Leffingwell
3450 Hathaway Ave
Eagle Point OR 975248596

Call Sign: KB7YNC
Lori J Grigsby
16142 Lost Ln
Eagle Point OR 97524

Call Sign: KC7BVP
Mark E Hamilton
13938 Pompei Dr
Eagle Point OR 97524

Call Sign: KE7ALI
James W Leffingwell
3450 Hathaway Ave
Eagle Point OR 975248596

Call Sign: N7ZZF
Barry M Grigsby
16164 Lost Ln
Eagle Point OR 97524

Call Sign: KF7ICK
Gerald S Shute
6970 Rainbow Dr SE
Eagle Point OR 97524

Call Sign: AD7ON
James W Leffingwell
378 Hatton Ave
Eagle Point OR 975248596

Call Sign: KD6MBR
Mary Russell
463 Lynnbrook Dr
Eagle Point OR 97524

Call Sign: K8PFY
Joseph A Vande Kieft
6970 Rainbow Dr SE
Eagle Point OR 97524

Call Sign: KB0YUL
Michael T Stavish
439 Heywood Ave
Eagle Point OR 97524

Call Sign: KF7LAF
Carl S Van Orden
3760 Market St NE Pmb420
Eagle Point OR 97524

Call Sign: KF7ICL
Richard A Wickham
1307 S Water St Sp 84
Eagle Point OR 97524

Call Sign: N7WLX
George F Matusich
36310 Hillside Ln
Eagle Point OR 97524

Call Sign: KA0CZW
William C Wright III
81942 Mattson Rd
Eagle Point OR 97524

Call Sign: K7JBU
Robert W Householder
16472 S Wayne Dr
Eagle Point OR 97524

Call Sign: WS7G
Eston Jones
11791 Jefferson Hwy 99 SE
Eagle Point OR 97524

Call Sign: KA0TXX
Rebecca W Wright
23051 Maverick Ln
Eagle Point OR 97524

Call Sign: KF7LAE
Rick I Haptonstall
2827 SE 109
Eagle Point OR 97524

Call Sign: KB7QVX
Jennie E Jones
401 Jefferson Scio Dr 73
Eagle Point OR 97524

Call Sign: N7AIE
James R Powers
2128 Mayfield Dr
Eagle Point OR 975249590

Call Sign: KF7MMV
Shannon L Wheeler
1427 SE 109th Ave
Eagle Point OR 97524

Call Sign: KD7DYV
Hal R Reichart Jr
3285 Lakemont Dr
Eagle Point OR 97524

Call Sign: KD7AUA
Jessee D Reed
33721 Mt Tom Dr
Eagle Point OR 97524

Call Sign: KE7VPN
Tracy L Van Hee
6740 Shepherd Ct N
Eagle Point OR 97524

Call Sign: KB6HWZ
Gregory K Green
6740 Shepherd Ct N
Eagle Point OR 97524

Call Sign: K7LZW
Wesley E Householder
15985 Sparks Dr
Eagle Point OR 97524

Call Sign: KD6ON
George A Kardoos
53872 State Line Rd
Eagle Point OR 97524

Call Sign: N6KKN
Richard T Babcock
2651 Stratford St
Eagle Point OR 97524

Call Sign: KD7FZQ
Ture Henry Carlstrom
2651 Stratford St
Eagle Point OR 97524

Call Sign: WB6FFC
Michael W Bach
3294 Strathmore Pl
Eagle Point OR 97524

Call Sign: KD7YYY
Mary A Shostrom
60 Wedgewood Dr
Eagle Point OR 97524

Call Sign: KA7PVR
William E Payne
419 Westwind Cir
Eagle Point OR 975249766

Call Sign: K5CMZ
Jimmie A Roberts
500 Winston Ct
Eagle Point OR 97524

Call Sign: KE7PMP
Josiah B Salcido
148 Wren Ridge Dr
Eagle Point OR 97524

Call Sign: KF7YY
Scott L Salcido
148 Wren Ridge Dr
Eagle Point OR 97524

Call Sign: N7UHO
Anna D Salcido
148 Wren Ridge Dr
Eagle Point OR 97524

Call Sign: KI6WXM
Lynn A Wise
103 Wren Ridge Dr
Eagle Point OR 97524

Call Sign: KB7FML
John F Heilbronner
Eagle Point OR 97524

Call Sign: KB7MMN
Patricia M Wilson
Eagle Point OR 97524

Call Sign: N5FNC
Carla L Williams
Eagle Point OR 97524

Call Sign: N7JL
John D Luthy
Eagle Point OR 97524

Call Sign: W7EGM
Edward S Gilkey
Eagle Point OR 97524

Call Sign: W7IRZ
Clayton W Simmons
Eagle Point OR 97524

Call Sign: WA7BMJ

Glenn D Clymer
Eagle Point OR 97524

Call Sign: KC7FET
Sheldon R Gilliam
Eagle Point OR 97524

Call Sign: KA6UAM
William K Bibbins
Eagle Point OR 97524

Call Sign: KA7JBE
Eugene W Lauener
Eagle Point OR 97524

Call Sign: KA7WBF
Joyce L Richardson
Eagle Point OR 97524

Call Sign: KA7ZQI
Barry D Phelps
Eagle Point OR 97524

Call Sign: KB6MHL
Bruce A Rawles
Eagle Point OR 97524

Call Sign: W7WJD
Robert L Temple
Eagle Point OR 97524

Call Sign: KF7LVQ
Dave A Roche
Eagle Point OR 97524

Call Sign: KA7HWS
Connie S Dunham
Eagle Point OR 975240699

Call Sign: N6YGX
Jacqueline L Wilson
Eagle Point OR 975241082

FCC Amateur Radio
Licenses in Echo

Call Sign: KA7ROX
Delwyn M Hendrickson
1617 Dragon Tail Pl
Echo OR 97826

Call Sign: N7PJZ
Chester E Dowell
1950 Elm
Echo OR 97826

Call Sign: KD7DPV
Jason S Smith
8239 Salmon River Hwy
Echo OR 97826

Call Sign: N7YIW
Terry L Schultz
61867 Somerset Dr
Echo OR 97826

Call Sign: KC7JFF
Phyllis A Shovelski
2690 Sorrel Way
Echo OR 97826

Call Sign: N7JMW
Joseph M Willis
100 W Bridge St
Echo OR 97826

Call Sign: KB7LEI
Mary A Dowell
Echo OR 97826

Call Sign: AA7SL
Michael E Duffy
Echo OR 97826

Call Sign: KA7PTZ
David W Morris
Echo OR 97826

Call Sign: KD7TFJ
Joseph M Willis

Echo OR 97826

FCC Amateur Radio Licenses in Elgin

Call Sign: W7ZO
Keith W Dodd
28501 Bodenhamer Rd
Elgin OR 97827

Call Sign: KA7SKA
Sidney W Ratzlaff
1022 E 12th
Elgin OR 97827

Call Sign: KA7SKB
Billee T Ratzlaff
2009 E 12th St
Elgin OR 97827

Call Sign: AA7U
Stephen W Ratzlaff
514 E 13th
Elgin OR 978278201

Call Sign: KE7LXY
Brent A Linville
1125 N Holladay
Elgin OR 97827

Call Sign: KB7DUI
Hazel F Ficken
13937 S Cleveland
Elgin OR 97827

Call Sign: N7FBL
Annie L Follett
465 S Dogwood St
Elgin OR 97827

Call Sign: K7LKG
Warren K Follett
1515 S Downing Apt A
Elgin OR 97827

Call Sign: KA7EJB
Derrill D Chandler
Elgin OR 97827

Call Sign: N7DXD
Audrie L Chandler
Elgin OR 97827

Call Sign: KA7YWY
John A Johnson
Elgin OR 97827

Call Sign: KB7VSX
Ty J Russell
Elgin OR 97827

Call Sign: N7SOY
Kevin M Lynch
Elgin OR 97827

Call Sign: WA7DZB
Donald S Ficken
Elgin OR 97827

Call Sign: KE7RVJ
John F Davis
Elgin OR 97827

Call Sign: AE7JD
John F Davis
Elgin OR 97827

FCC Amateur Radio Licenses in Elkton

Call Sign: WB6IZT
Paul R Ellis
752 Florence Ave
Elkton OR 97436

Call Sign: WB7CYB
Francis W Albro
63589 Jd Estates Dr
Elkton OR 97436

Call Sign: N7COZ
Howard F Carnes
2950 Wells Rd
Elkton OR 97436

Call Sign: KC7AGS
Donna D Semas
Elkton OR 97436

Call Sign: KC7AGT
Albert A Smith
Elkton OR 97436

Call Sign: KC7NKY
Laura L Caig
Elkton OR 97436

Call Sign: KD6OJW
Dennis E Borlek
Elkton OR 97436

FCC Amateur Radio
Licenses in Elmira

Call Sign: N0SHA
Jamie D Porter
244 Benjamin St
Elmira OR 97437

Call Sign: N7DOA
Donald A Weaver Jr
355 E Colver Rd 39
Elmira OR 97437

Call Sign: KC7YMY
Wesley C Weaver
355 E Colver Rd 39
Elmira OR 974379617

Call Sign: N7IXB
Joseph A Wanores
61875 E Cottonwood Rd
Elmira OR 97437

Call Sign: N7MPH

Harold L Weston
2164 Gettle St
Elmira OR 97437

Call Sign: AA7LE
Bary F Foster
4625 Gettle St
Elmira OR 97437

Call Sign: KC7IMI
Will F Foster
34809 Gibbon Ln
Elmira OR 97437

Call Sign: KC7VWU
Lydia J Foster
34809 Gibbon Ln
Elmira OR 97437

Call Sign: KD7TSJ
Boy Scouts Of America
Venture Crew 185
6241 Juniper Way
Elmira OR 97437

Call Sign: K7JRA
Dennis R Clark
20747 Livengood Way
Elmira OR 974379753

Call Sign: KD7AJF
Robert F Hermann
2838 Shirley St
Elmira OR 974379771

Call Sign: K6SQG
Flavius J Williams
87845 Territorial Rd
Elmira OR 97437

Call Sign: N7YYI
June C Bonsall
63120 Terry Dr
Elmira OR 97437

Call Sign: N7PKO
Josephine R Germaine
24615 W Demming Rd
Elmira OR 97437

Call Sign: N7NFS
Frank J Germaine
24615 W Demming Rd
Elmira OR 974379620

Call Sign: N7IZU
Thorne E Peterson
24439 Warthen Rd
Elmira OR 97437

Call Sign: KB7TNA
Harold A Stanley
Elmira OR 97437

Call Sign: N7CKB
Melvin D Evers
Elmira OR 97437

Call Sign: KB7CSJ
Miles A Paul Sr
Elmira OR 97437

Call Sign: K7AJB
Hannah M Koch
Elmira OR 97437

Call Sign: K7MSY
Arthur E Koch
Elmira OR 97437

Call Sign: N7WJG
Douglas L Damerval
Elmira OR 97437

Call Sign: NS7P
Phillip W Shepard
Elmira OR 97437

Call Sign: W7SX
Robert J Zavrel Jr

Elmira OR 97437

Call Sign: KD7ZOQ
Benjamen J Smith
Elmira OR 97437

FCC Amateur Radio Licenses in Enterprise

Call Sign: W7HYJ
Vincent M Nitzke
1945 Cal Young Rd
Enterprise OR 97828

Call Sign: KA7WGW
Matthew D Cross
1825 Derding St
Enterprise OR 97828

Call Sign: W7JRB
Marie A Eden
701 Elm Ave
Enterprise OR 97828

Call Sign: KB7ZNP
Louis C Dougherty
22018 Erica Dr NE
Enterprise OR 97828

Call Sign: KB7ZNQ
Andy N Dougherty
22120 Erickson Rd
Enterprise OR 97828

Call Sign: KE7ZRX
Lee D Perkins
2508 Hawkins Ln
Enterprise OR 97828

Call Sign: KD7RMO
Michael C Hansen
1074 Hemlock
Enterprise OR 97828

Call Sign: N7NEM

Deborah L Hayes
19747 Hermo Rd
Enterprise OR 97828

Call Sign: KD7QVZ
Gary L Parr
8448 Hwy 140 E 2D
Enterprise OR 97828

Call Sign: K7ZNP
Gary L Parr
56361 Hwy 197
Enterprise OR 97828

Call Sign: KD7SYO
Wesley M Olsen
15706 Miniview Ct
Enterprise OR 97828

Call Sign: KE7JEZ
Darci M Calhoun
3428 NE 128 Ave
Enterprise OR 97828

Call Sign: KF7NCE
David M Mcconathy
54 SE 73 Rd
Enterprise OR 97828

Call Sign: KC7CLQ
Malvin F Clary
5541 SE Gill St
Enterprise OR 97828

Call Sign: KC7PTW
Robert D Graffi
53780 Sombrio Ct
Enterprise OR 97828

Call Sign: KE7RVI
Lorna G Cook
75334 Valley Ln
Enterprise OR 97828

Call Sign: KD7RMR

Glenn A Mc Donald
75334 Valley Ln
Enterprise OR 97828

Call Sign: K7CWV
William E Parks
104 W Alder St
Enterprise OR 97828

Call Sign: KE7RVL
Tim Perales
65487 Williamson Rd
Enterprise OR 97828

Call Sign: K7BUY
Lawrence R Smith
66698 Williamson Rd
Enterprise OR 97828

Call Sign: N7UNF
Efrain T Suarez Jr
Enterprise OR 97828

Call Sign: KD7MGX
Roy A Morrison
Enterprise OR 97828

FCC Amateur Radio Licenses in Eugene

Call Sign: KD7JGN
Margie R Melton
1420 10th St
Eugene OR 97408

Call Sign: KD7KPA
Walter P Freihube
3354 12th St SE
Eugene OR 97402

Call Sign: KF7BBB
Brent D Jernberg
661 14th St
Eugene OR 97405

Call Sign: KC7KOV
Gregory A Stewart
2190 20th St
Eugene OR 97402

Call Sign: KC7SVQ
James I Carroll
740 23rd St
Eugene OR 97402

Call Sign: W7SME
Philip D Smith
618 46 Pl SE
Eugene OR 97405

Call Sign: KC6PLS
Scott H Fratcher
1410 4th St
Eugene OR 97440

Call Sign: WB7PRJ
Norman L Hill
5736 A St
Eugene OR 974051396

Call Sign: KA7EOX
Raymond G Roberts
1005 Augustine St
Eugene OR 974027618

Call Sign: N7AKS
Alden S Cole
2769 Ave A
Eugene OR 97402

Call Sign: KA0RFU
Patrick D Mc Ilrath
3095 Ave G
Eugene OR 97405

Call Sign: KD7LYH
Tervani Valerie D Riggs
1664 Axtell Ave
Eugene OR 97405

Call Sign: KB9MLT
Peter L Wood
751 Azalea Dr
Eugene OR 97404

Call Sign: AB0MI
Everett W Hogue
3360 Azalea Dr S
Eugene OR 97401

Call Sign: KB9VAV
Lorie L Parker
300 B Ave
Eugene OR 97402

Call Sign: KD7FNW
Ken G Cox
24830 Bachelor Ln
Eugene OR 974029523

Call Sign: KA7PQC
Philip G Dylina
287 Bailey Rd
Eugene OR 97402

Call Sign: KD7ZLJ
Darren D Reynolds
23200 Bald Peak Rd
Eugene OR 97401

Call Sign: KB7CPW
William H Haines
23200 Bald Peak Rd
Eugene OR 97405

Call Sign: KF7NXZ
Greg E Aitken
23200 Bald Peak Rd
Eugene OR 97405

Call Sign: KB7KNW
Fredrick J Scherette
4425 Battle Creek Rd SE
Eugene OR 97404

Call Sign: KC7YRV
Clarence H Bull III
7089 Battle Creek Rd SE
Eugene OR 97404

Call Sign: KC7MSK
Killian D Corwin
3702 Bayonne Dr SE
Eugene OR 97404

Call Sign: KC7NHR
James J Sturman
35215 Bayside Gardens Rd
Eugene OR 974041375

Call Sign: KE7UYA
Adam J Burns
39871 Bear Gulch Rd
Eugene OR 97401

Call Sign: AB7RF
Leland W Nebeker
3760 Bell St
Eugene OR 97402

Call Sign: KA7GTP
Arthur Galvez
211 Bellevue Dr SE
Eugene OR 97402

Call Sign: WA7AG
Arthur Galvez
8774 Bellflower St
Eugene OR 97402

Call Sign: KB7FLW
Stephan G Horejs
30894 Bellfountain Rd
Eugene OR 97404

Call Sign: KE7YYH
T Ardel Wicks
1042 Belmont Ave SW Apt
B24
Eugene OR 97408

Call Sign: WB7PAM
Jesse L Smoot
61148 Benham Rd
Eugene OR 97402

Call Sign: WB7UPQ
Helen M Smoot
2310 Bennett Creek Rd
Eugene OR 974029723

Call Sign: N6VHO
Shelly L Schmidt
42344 Bennett Ln
Eugene OR 97404

Call Sign: KN1X
James T Perkins
480 Benton View Dr
Eugene OR 97405

Call Sign: N7KEM
Peter H Ffolliott Jr
2824 Biehn St
Eugene OR 97404

Call Sign: KA7TRZ
Peter H Ffolliott Jr
1022 Big Bend Rd
Eugene OR 97404

Call Sign: KB7IEE
Harold G Wolfe Sr
515 Birch St
Eugene OR 97402

Call Sign: KF7MRE
Jason S Forcier
1205 Birch St
Eugene OR 97402

Call Sign: KD7HQX
W Logan Dhonau
4412 Blackberry Ct
Eugene OR 97404

Call Sign: N7NTJ
Samuel G Boice
31823 Blair Rd
Eugene OR 97401

Call Sign: N7YUK
Ralph S Kuehl
31823 Blair Rd
Eugene OR 97401

Call Sign: N7WPB
David G Freeman
75501 Blue Mtn Ln
Eugene OR 97402

Call Sign: KD7KOF
David L Ordway
4000 Blue Ox Dr SE 1
Eugene OR 97401

Call Sign: KB7CHO
Stanley F Hruby
4000 Blue Ox Dr SE Sp 40
Eugene OR 97405

Call Sign: AK7L
Edward E Cooper
12275 Blue Ridge Dr
Eugene OR 97401

Call Sign: KD7KQM
Christopher M Ordway
51605 Blue River Dr
Eugene OR 97401

Call Sign: KD7VYN
Katheryn G Ordway
4555 Blue Sky Ct SE
Eugene OR 97401

Call Sign: KC7UWZ
Marc Daniel A Huntley
4555 Blue Sky Ct SE
Eugene OR 974016926

Call Sign: KK7IW
John C Huntley
4912 Bluebelle Way
Eugene OR 974016926

Call Sign: W7EXH
Carl J Di Paolo
6963 Bluebelle Way
Eugene OR 97401

Call Sign: WB7UJJ
Rebecca L Di Paolo
230 Bluebird Ln
Eugene OR 97401

Call Sign: N7GFM
Oral R Robbins
24846 Bolin Dr
Eugene OR 97401

Call Sign: KF7EFR
Richard H Mar
2 Bolivar St
Eugene OR 97402

Call Sign: KD7ESB
Barger RC
2 Bolivar St
Eugene OR 97402

Call Sign: N7CNH
Douglas D Cooper
200 Bolz Rd
Eugene OR 97402

Call Sign: N7JRB
Sharlotte K Cooper
194 Bond
Eugene OR 97402

Call Sign: KA6MZN
Thomas C Liempeck
33880 Bond Butte Dr
Eugene OR 97402

Call Sign: KC7NKZ
Gene H Gosda Sr
33583 Bond Butte Rd
Eugene OR 97402

Call Sign: KD7SVZ
Melissa A Phillips
11254 Branch Ln SE
Eugene OR 97408

Call Sign: KC7RVN
Anatoli Polevik
276 Bridge
Eugene OR 974018221

Call Sign: KB7RDT
Richard Tyler
33698 Bond Rd
Eugene OR 97402

Call Sign: N6VIL
James E Emerson
1016 Brandon Way
Eugene OR 97401

Call Sign: KC7MHV
Lisa M Dillon
2625 Broadview Ave
Eugene OR 97401

Call Sign: WB7BNA
John K Pratt
190 Boone Rd SE 56
Eugene OR 97401

Call Sign: KA7RTF
Eugene E Johnson
1301 Braunda Dr
Eugene OR 97402

Call Sign: KE7SAL
Rick C Osgood
2672 Broadview Ave
Eugene OR 97401

Call Sign: K7QCJ
Raymond W Richart Sr
Rt 1 Box 248K
Eugene OR 97404

Call Sign: KC7UUV
Tabitha R Carson
1635 Brewer
Eugene OR 97401

Call Sign: KD7VIY
Andy Mc Auliffe
930 Brookdale Ave
Eugene OR 97405

Call Sign: KF7KTZ
Kirt E Stockwell
Hc32 Box 40
Eugene OR 97404

Call Sign: KB7VIR
Ronald M Cluster
4077 Briar Knob Loop NE
Eugene OR 974018258

Call Sign: KC7OTV
Brian M Hoyland
861 Brookhaven Dr
Eugene OR 97405

Call Sign: KC7YDE
James H Stewart III
Rt 5 Box 50
Eugene OR 974042953

Call Sign: KC7GTQ
Bob D Cluster
4782 Briars St
Eugene OR 974018258

Call Sign: W7BMH
Brian M Hoyland
1785 Brookhurst Way
Eugene OR 97405

Call Sign: W7NKY
Norton Minster
Rt 3 Box 6
Eugene OR 97402

Call Sign: AC7TK
Ronald M Cluster
4782 Briars St
Eugene OR 974018258

Call Sign: WB7OVH
Peter W Thurston
26555 Brooks Ln
Eugene OR 97404

Call Sign: WE7X
Arden C Hawn
18876 Boynton St
Eugene OR 97404

Call Sign: KC7HNI
Phillip W Carson
5180 Brickyard Rd
Eugene OR 97401

Call Sign: KA7GSE
James D Hoffstot
26555 Brooks Ln
Eugene OR 97404

Call Sign: KD7SVY
Edward M Phillips
11254 Branch Ln SE
Eugene OR 97408

Call Sign: KC7RVM
Mikhail Klokov
5235 Brickyard Rd
Eugene OR 974018221

Call Sign: WA5KBZ
Larry J Ormsby
1143 Brookside Dr
Eugene OR 97405

Call Sign: N7VTB
Andrew J Mc Farland
374 Brown St
Eugene OR 97402

Call Sign: W7BJA
Allen B Laing
3525 Brownsboro Hwy
Eugene OR 974044204

Call Sign: KA5ZJM
Lin Bowman
476 Buckhorn Springs Rd
Eugene OR 974041590

Call Sign: KC7RJK
Ross V Johnson
6750 Buckingham Ct
Eugene OR 97404

Call Sign: KA7NFK
Louise M Hamilton
101 Buena Ct
Eugene OR 97402

Call Sign: WB7RVX
Arlo A Hamilton
16172 Buena Vista Dr
Eugene OR 97402

Call Sign: WB6BRM
Kevin R Gowen
12555 Buena Vista Rd
Eugene OR 97401

Call Sign: W7BRM
Kevin R Gowen
747 Buena Vista St
Eugene OR 97401

Call Sign: KD7ZUV
David D Brown
4731 Burlwood Lp
Eugene OR 97405

Call Sign: N7JTH
Vivian R Hyman
90410 Cape Arago Hwy
Eugene OR 97405

Call Sign: N7HLK
Michael B Miles
90410 Cape Arago Hwy
Eugene OR 97405

Call Sign: N7HKA
Anne Y Rumfelt
22046 Carissa Ave NE
Eugene OR 974055534

Call Sign: KD7AHS
Gloria A Varner
92424 Carnegie Rd
Eugene OR 97404

Call Sign: KD7BKU
Richard D Varner
3676 Carnes Rd
Eugene OR 97404

Call Sign: KD7TIL
Ann M Varner
3676 Carnes Rd
Eugene OR 974043806

Call Sign: KE7AMH
Robyn L Varner
4359 Carnes Rd
Eugene OR 97404

Call Sign: KD7AJD
Ann M Varner
4359 Carnes Rd
Eugene OR 974043806

Call Sign: KD7ZUT
Gerald G Wright
287 Carol Ct
Eugene OR 97401

Call Sign: K7PYS
William C Biser
4044 Carolina Ave NE
Eugene OR 97404

Call Sign: WA7ZUK
Sharon L Biser
912 Caroline Way E
Eugene OR 97404

Call Sign: KE7PGP
Alan J Buck
820 Cascade Dr
Eugene OR 97405

Call Sign: W1AJB
Alan J Buck
2315 Cascade Dr
Eugene OR 97405

Call Sign: KC7HI
Kenneth A Springate
18025 Cascade Estates Dr
Eugene OR 97405

Call Sign: N7DDM
Scott T Springate
18025 Cascade Estates Dr
Eugene OR 97405

Call Sign: N7YUZ
Donald F Woodman
46957 Cason Rd
Eugene OR 97405

Call Sign: KF7IMD
Cheryl A Easterwood
2750 Caves Hwy
Eugene OR 97405

Call Sign: KE7JAO
Paul M Thompson
10931C Caves Hwy
Eugene OR 97405

Call Sign: W8IEB
Paul M Thompson
2122 Cedar
Eugene OR 97405

Call Sign: KC7DMG
Anita L Harrington
4950 Center Way
Eugene OR 974023139

Call Sign: KD7RWZ
Robert L Watson
4998 Center Way
Eugene OR 97402

Call Sign: KC7FFW
Ralph E Johnston
1837 Charnelton St
Eugene OR 97405

Call Sign: KB7ZRE
Holly C Hartmann
4909 Chenowith Rd
Eugene OR 97404

Call Sign: WB7QJT
James F Lamb Jr
482 Cheri Pl NW
Eugene OR 97404

Call Sign: NS7M
Robert R Sappington
19285 Cherokee Rd
Eugene OR 97404

Call Sign: W7ELM
Eldon L Mc Clellan
3289 Cheyenne Ct NW
Eugene OR 974017655

Call Sign: KD7QNZ
Wendy L Mcclellan
85391 Chezem Rd
Eugene OR 974017655

Call Sign: K7MCC
Wendy L Mc Clellan
2622 Chicago St
Eugene OR 974017655

Call Sign: KC7BIH
Barbara A Mitchell
3507 Chicago St SE
Eugene OR 97401

Call Sign: KF7BUF
J Priscilla Sokolowski
2301 Chickadee Ct
Eugene OR 97401

Call Sign: W7BUF
J Priscilla Sokolowski
852 Chickadee Ct NE
Eugene OR 97401

Call Sign: W7DWL
David W Lange
18037 Chickaree Dr
Eugene OR 97401

Call Sign: WB7RVY
Lester E Morin
87296 Chinquapin Loop
Eugene OR 97404

Call Sign: KE7QXW
Rick L Bailor
87298 Chinquapin Loop
Eugene OR 97404

Call Sign: W7BBQ
Rick L Bailor
13311 Chippendale Ln
Eugene OR 97404

Call Sign: KA7AMH
Virgel L Clark Sr
18924 Choctaw Rd
Eugene OR 97404

Call Sign: KB7WUV
Sandra J Kite
81752 Christmas Tree Rd
Eugene OR 974043300

Call Sign: W7QBT
William F Reynolds
61091 Chuckanut Dr
Eugene OR 97401

Call Sign: WB7WNK
Eldon L Mc Clellan
61123 Chuckanut Dr
Eugene OR 97401

Call Sign: N7MWL
Bill Louis
61167 Chuckanut Dr
Eugene OR 97402

Call Sign: KD7RLF
Leonard M Stolfo
2635 City View St
Eugene OR 97402

Call Sign: KD7WKW
James P Rova
1247 Clark Mill Rd
Eugene OR 97404

Call Sign: W9PJT
James P Rova
41744 Clark Smith Dr
Eugene OR 97404

Call Sign: K7VJO
Joan R Hunt
925 Clark St
Eugene OR 97404

Call Sign: KB7IGZ
Chris D Roberson
2769 Clarks Branch Rd
Eugene OR 97404

Call Sign: N7KYI
Pauline L Austin
4707 Cloudcrest Dr
Eugene OR 974041082

Call Sign: W7SB
Donald C Austin
4707 Cloudcrest Dr
Eugene OR 974041082

Call Sign: WA7RWJ
Andrew Yaniw Sr
580 Clover Ln
Eugene OR 97402

Call Sign: KD7ZYY
Doug R Brown
5050 Columbus St SE 117
Eugene OR 97402

Call Sign: KD7WIO
Brent W Hottle
5050 Columbus St SE Sp 17
Eugene OR 97405

Call Sign: KC7EEH
James K Sanislo
5050 Columbus St SE Sp 17
Eugene OR 97405

Call Sign: KD7KOD
Timothy W Winder
7059 Combest Ln SE
Eugene OR 97402

Call Sign: W7YUY
William L Hendrick
4676 Commercial St SE 3
Eugene OR 97401

Call Sign: KA7WCJ
Marc R Higgins
3482 Concomly Rd S
Eugene OR 97405

Call Sign: KD6RFC
Tyrone T Teal
3752 Concomly Rd S
Eugene OR 97405

Call Sign: KF7ECK
Mark Kruger
2691 Concomly Rs
Eugene OR 97405

Call Sign: W7RDT
Richard Tyler
2761 Concord Ct SE
Eugene OR 97405

Call Sign: KD7ZHS
Don A Keller
18774 Conifer Dr
Eugene OR 97403

Call Sign: KF7BUE
Brad T Jeske
8665 Cooper Spur Rd
Eugene OR 97401

Call Sign: WA7UUE
Peter A Powers
3170 Cottonwood Ct
Eugene OR 97401

Call Sign: KE7FXB
Zachary A Narkin
18160 Cottonwood Rd 446
Eugene OR 97405

Call Sign: KE7FOT
Douglas C Doty
81471 Country Garden Rd
19
Eugene OR 97403

Call Sign: N7WJJ
Randall R Beiderwell
50350 Cowens Rd 8

Eugene OR 974051088

Call Sign: K7BFA
James A Mitchelmore
5258 Coyote Creek Rd
Eugene OR 97404

Call Sign: N7TQG
William J Mc Cowen
882 Coyote Ct SE
Eugene OR 97404

Call Sign: AC7DX
Ron G Lago
33391 Craig Loop
Eugene OR 97402

Call Sign: N7PGM
Victoria H G Santoro
1181 Craiglea Dr
Eugene OR 97405

Call Sign: AA7NS
Richard F Santoro
1366 Cramner St
Eugene OR 97405

Call Sign: KD7JRN
Tye M Lewin
70839 Crane Buchanan Rd
Eugene OR 97405

Call Sign: KD7HUJ
Guy R Ivy
68488 Crane Buchanan Rd
Eugene OR 97404

Call Sign: KE7ICY
Joseph H Hunter
8495 Crater Lake Hwy Sec
6
Eugene OR 97402

Call Sign: N7OX
Joseph H Hunter

8495 Crater Lake Hwy Sect
4
Eugene OR 97402

Call Sign: KF7LKO
Uss Turner Joy ARC
21950 Cresent Lake Hwy
Eugene OR 97402

Call Sign: NS7DD
Uss Turner Joy ARC
340 Crest 64
Eugene OR 97402

Call Sign: KE7CQY
Dixie A Lillie
1962 Crest Ct
Eugene OR 97402

Call Sign: WA7AIP
Dixie A Lillie
1962 Crest Ct
Eugene OR 97402

Call Sign: KB7OHW
Barbara J Niles
1331 Crest Dr
Eugene OR 97402

Call Sign: KB7OHX
Patrick H Niles
381 Crest Dr
Eugene OR 97402

Call Sign: KE7MEB
Ross A Overton
2630 Cresta De Ruta
Eugene OR 97402

Call Sign: WA7AIP
Gerald L Lillie
183 Crestdale Way
Eugene OR 97402

Call Sign: AD7EG

Gerald L Lillie
1438 Cresthill Ave NW
Eugene OR 97402

Call Sign: W7JY
Gerald L Lillie
97826 Crestline Loop
Eugene OR 97402

Call Sign: KA7AOR
Gwendolyne L Butler
201 Crestview Dr
Eugene OR 97405

Call Sign: WB7TAT
Roger E Rix
165 Crestview Loop
Eugene OR 97405

Call Sign: KC7PIL
Michael R Sutton
165 Crestview Loop
Eugene OR 97405

Call Sign: WB7TRL
Richard E Butler
162 Crocker St
Eugene OR 97405

Call Sign: KF7AHU
Mara Solano
55241 Crockett Rd
Eugene OR 97405

Call Sign: KE7CWI
David L Keck
14557 Crossroads Loop
Eugene OR 97401

Call Sign: N7MQ
Mark W Perrin
5005 Cumberland Ct SE
Eugene OR 97405

Call Sign: KB7AIG

Kathryn L Miles
14830 Currleaf
Eugene OR 97401

Call Sign: KB7ZXF
Theodore J Flug
78536 Currin Blvd
Eugene OR 97401

Call Sign: WB7QFZ
Dayne A Smoot
78536 Currin Blvd
Eugene OR 97408

Call Sign: KE6UCA
John R Heer
163 Curtin Hill Ln
Eugene OR 97401

Call Sign: KD7RQR
Jeanie K Hendricks
163 Curtin Hill Ln
Eugene OR 97401

Call Sign: KD7TLW
Rex G Hendricks
163 Curtin Hill Ln
Eugene OR 97401

Call Sign: KD7ZOO
Justin P Lewis
163 Curtin Hill Ln
Eugene OR 97401

Call Sign: KE7CWH
Del D Shuck
1786 Curtis Ave
Eugene OR 97402

Call Sign: KE7UGY
Dee Helm
2472 Dan Ave NW
Eugene OR 97405

Call Sign: N6OMZ

Benjamin D Cartledge
2196 Davis Rd S
Eugene OR 97402

Call Sign: KD7UYE
Dwain W Kemrer
53272 Day Rd
Eugene OR 97402

Call Sign: WB7WVE
Velma V Stocking
531 Dayton Ave
Eugene OR 97402

Call Sign: AC7IQ
Phillip T Winters
22975 Dayton Ave NE
Eugene OR 97402

Call Sign: N4ATC
Carl E Sundberg
4668 Deepwood Pl NE
Eugene OR 974026455

Call Sign: KB9VDV
Reid B Ligon
39261 Deer Creek Rd
Eugene OR 97405

Call Sign: KD7PQO
Reid B Ligon
59689 Deer Haven Ln
Eugene OR 97405

Call Sign: K7TEX
Reid B Ligon
59689 Deer Haven Ln
Eugene OR 97405

Call Sign: KB7BKG
Richard R Earl
18406 Deer Oak Ave
Eugene OR 97404

Call Sign: KD7LCB

Christopher R Bernard
34324 Deerwood Dr
Eugene OR 97404

Call Sign: W7MUK
Einar E Ingebretsen
19637 Derby Ct
Eugene OR 97401

Call Sign: KE7QXV
Jason L Wilson
1015 Derby Ct SE
Eugene OR 97408

Call Sign: AE7HM
Julian Floether
7652 Derksen Hill Rd SE
Eugene OR 97405

Call Sign: K7DKV
Eugene W Ellis
6710 Devon Ave SE
Eugene OR 97401

Call Sign: KA7NWP
Megan Ellis
6710 Devon Ave SE
Eugene OR 97401

Call Sign: KB7ONX
Robert S Benson
60631 Devon Cir
Eugene OR 97401

Call Sign: KC7PRQ
Karen D Benson
160 Devon Dr
Eugene OR 97401

Call Sign: KA7OCR
James R Young
50856 Doe Loop
Eugene OR 97408

Call Sign: KA7OTF

Joyce A Young
188 Dog Creek Rd
Eugene OR 97408

Call Sign: KD7TPT
Linda F Krueger
188 Dog Creek Rd
Eugene OR 97408

Call Sign: AB7QI
Harry N Leuallen
930 Dogwood St
Eugene OR 97405

Call Sign: NH0T
Koji Yoshida
10880 Doll Rd
Eugene OR 974031849

Call Sign: AA9WV
Kunihiko Nakano
10880 Doll Rd
Eugene OR 974031849

Call Sign: KH0HX
Tatsuya Sasaki
1340 Dollar St
Eugene OR 974031849

Call Sign: AB2GH
Shigeo Hatanaka
5150 Dome Rock Ct SE
Eugene OR 974031849

Call Sign: WA7EU
Shigeo Hatanaka
924 Donald St
Eugene OR 974031849

Call Sign: N6TGZ
Peter J Mc Closky
6468 Doral Dr SE
Eugene OR 97404

Call Sign: K7EXA

Carmen M Brambora
7 Doral Ln Po Box 3248
Eugene OR 97404

Call Sign: N7HIA
R Joseph Newton
737 Doty
Eugene OR 97402

Call Sign: KB7YJA
Kenneth R Dless
53223 Double O Rd
Eugene OR 97402

Call Sign: KF7MMT
Laura Seymour
20735 Double Peaks Dr
Eugene OR 97402

Call Sign: N7LUX
James L Harris
4632 Douglas
Eugene OR 97402

Call Sign: KF7DTT
Charles A Bergfeld
2142 Dowell Rd
Eugene OR 97402

Call Sign: KC7PYJ
Travis L Ayriss
2142 Dowell Rd
Eugene OR 97402

Call Sign: K7YQN
Travis L Ayriss
2305 Dowell Rd
Eugene OR 97402

Call Sign: KB7FPX
Mary E Green
185 Dreamhill Dr
Eugene OR 97401

Call Sign: N7LUT

William L Green
2530 Drift Creek Rd NE
Eugene OR 97401

Call Sign: K7AXE
John W Brambora
37390 Dubarko Rd
Eugene OR 97404

Call Sign: KB7FWV
Eric M Rice
11916 Dupee Valley Rd
Eugene OR 97404

Call Sign: KF7PEN
Michael A Shubert
4388 Durbin Ave SE
Eugene OR 97404

Call Sign: KE7CWM
Jeffrey J Laramee
3813 Dustin Ct NE
Eugene OR 97404

Call Sign: KA7COD
Loyd W George
36981 Dusty Ln
Eugene OR 974042392

Call Sign: KF7SZ
Jeffery L Hite
1044 Dutcher Creek Rd
Eugene OR 97402

Call Sign: W7NVA
Lawrence L Edmunson
315 Dutchman View Rd
Eugene OR 97402

Call Sign: KD7SWY
Kimberly K Mcclellan
16029 Dykes Rd
Eugene OR 97402

Call Sign: AI7W

Steven R Jepsen
416 E 10th St Apt 13
Eugene OR 97401

Call Sign: N7KTY
Loretta L Jepsen
523 E 11th
Eugene OR 97401

Call Sign: N7WJF
Brent M Combs
2540 E 12 St
Eugene OR 97401

Call Sign: KE7YYI
Bruce N Ward
642 E 13th St
Eugene OR 97404

Call Sign: KE7YYJ
Daniel J Ward
1708 E 13th St
Eugene OR 97404

Call Sign: KE7EWM
Michael D South
3850 E Antelope Rd
Eugene OR 97404

Call Sign: W7MDS
Michael D South
3850 E Antelope Rd
Eugene OR 97404

Call Sign: WA7LHM
Donald D Wiltse
5300 E Baseline 351
Eugene OR 974044007

Call Sign: WA7ELV
Leslie P Hardie
21955 E Beaver Creek Rd
Eugene OR 97405

Call Sign: KA7GGQ

James A Mc Han
22055 E Beaver Creek Rd
Eugene OR 97405

Call Sign: N7MBZ
Randal E Wood
681 E Bridge St
Eugene OR 97405

Call Sign: AD5QI
Karmin D Peterson
681 E Bridge St
Eugene OR 97405

Call Sign: KD5ZAH
Rose C Peterson
25267 E Bright Ave
Eugene OR 97405

Call Sign: WB7OKL
Mac G Allison
205 E Clarendon St
Eugene OR 97405

Call Sign: KB7YGJ
Gray M Goodman
149 E Grove Ave
Eugene OR 97405

Call Sign: KC7BXX
Irwin L Goodman
870 E Harding Ave
Eugene OR 97405

Call Sign: KB7LDR
Tonja L Phillippe
675 E Hereford St
Eugene OR 97402

Call Sign: KF7CRH
Jennifer A Phillippe
33421 E Hishway 224 Unit
P
Eugene OR 97402

Call Sign: KB7NWI
Carl G Arvidson
61550 E Lake Dr
Eugene OR 97405

Call Sign: NK7Z
David C Cole
708 E Lincoln St
Eugene OR 97405

Call Sign: KG4RXZ
Kevin J Bourgault
89605 E Little Trl
Eugene OR 97405

Call Sign: WB7UOO
Hazel J Carson
3072 E Mcandrews Rd
Eugene OR 97408

Call Sign: K6VDV
Howard F Downing
304 E Myrtlewood Ct
Eugene OR 97402

Call Sign: N7EWS
Gordon L Brandt
301 E North St
Eugene OR 97402

Call Sign: KD7UYF
Jason D Peterson
301 E North St
Eugene OR 97402

Call Sign: WD9IWM
Richard D Bronson
350 E Powell St Apt 8
Eugene OR 97405

Call Sign: KD7SYH
Oscar Johnson
2895 E Powell Valley Rd
Rm 206
Eugene OR 97405

Call Sign: K7RAA
Richard A Andrews
729 E Scenic Dr
Eugene OR 97401

Call Sign: KC7RAA
John I Fields
6545 E St
Eugene OR 97404

Call Sign: N7MOX
Lois E Downing
865 E St
Eugene OR 97402

Call Sign: KB7ZDN
Jon A Ericson
65443 E Timberline Dr
Eugene OR 97440

Call Sign: WA7HZS
Edward J Schultz
444 E Vine St
Eugene OR 97402

Call Sign: KA7PAH
Lorraine M PARCe
1122 E Washington Ave
Eugene OR 97401

Call Sign: K7LCR
Eugene L Carson
23307 E Wildwood
Eugene OR 97401

Call Sign: KB7DME
Roberta M Mohr
45678 Eagle Creek Rd
Eugene OR 974043812

Call Sign: N7KUQ
Gerald Mohr
47 Eagle Crest Dr 57
Eugene OR 974043812

Call Sign: AE6PG
Nicholas J Randal
702 Earls Ct
Eugene OR 97401

Call Sign: KF7IMJ
Craig Thornley
3717 Edgewood Dr
Eugene OR 97405

Call Sign: WB7ELM
Marilyn J Nelson
11696 Falcon Ct NE
Eugene OR 97405

Call Sign: KE7UUO
Michael F Beardsworth
63177 Eastview Dr Apt 12
Eugene OR 97403

Call Sign: KF7SOA
Laurie P Thornley
3717 Edgewood Dr
Eugene OR 97405

Call Sign: KD7TAG
Scott E Alexander
674 Fall Creek Dr N
Eugene OR 97405

Call Sign: N0GTH
M G Laubach
17105 Eastwood Ln
Eugene OR 97405

Call Sign: K7OLN
Stanton J Nelson
3765 Edgewood Dr
Eugene OR 97405

Call Sign: WB7LCS
David W Kemp
2721 Fallon
Eugene OR 97401

Call Sign: KD7TIN
Christian L Beck
228 Easy St
Eugene OR 97403

Call Sign: K7BOB
Robert A Melcher
460 Edgewood Dr
Eugene OR 97405

Call Sign: KB7JC
Loyd S Sims
580 Fenster St
Eugene OR 97404

Call Sign: KD7MTO
Russel J Edmonds
460 Edgecliff Dr
Eugene OR 97405

Call Sign: K7YHI
Michael D Criswell
130 Elm St
Eugene OR 97402

Call Sign: KF7SOD
Thomas A Warberg
89246 Fields Rd
Eugene OR 97404

Call Sign: AC7NH
Russel J Edmonds
718 Edgemont Way
Eugene OR 97405

Call Sign: W7TRW
Thomas R Williams
935 Elm St
Eugene OR 974042610

Call Sign: KA7NFT
Marvin L Sparks
2498 Fillmore St
Eugene OR 97404

Call Sign: WB7WQD
James M Elias
1644 Edgevale Ave
Eugene OR 974053762

Call Sign: KC7RYH
John W Smith
1715 Elm St
Eugene OR 97402

Call Sign: KF7RFS
Marian M Sparks
2498 Fillmore St
Eugene OR 97404

Call Sign: N7QBK
Daniel L Shankle
3330 Edgewater Dr
Eugene OR 97405

Call Sign: KA7YHI
Michael D Criswell
1806 Elm St
Eugene OR 97402

Call Sign: K7MRS
Marian M Sparks
753 Finch Ct NE
Eugene OR 97404

Call Sign: KI7XI
Tanis Sales
1302 Edgewood Dr
Eugene OR 97405

Call Sign: W7FHM
James W Fletcher
2622 Falcon 62
Eugene OR 97403

Call Sign: AI7MS
Marian M Sparks
13480 Finlay Rd NE
Eugene OR 97404

Call Sign: KV7P
Marian M Sparks
610 Fir Ave
Eugene OR 97404

Call Sign: KE7U
Marvin L Sparks
1058 Fir Ave
Eugene OR 97404

Call Sign: W7MLS
Marvin L Sparks
392 Fir Ave Ste 102
Eugene OR 97404

Call Sign: KC7NHQ
James F Lovely
29665 Fir St
Eugene OR 97405

Call Sign: N7QNX
Cindy J Fent
47329 Fire Station Allery
Ln
Eugene OR 97401

Call Sign: W7IL
Charles E Agol
2953 Firwood Way
Eugene OR 97405

Call Sign: N7MLH
Robert J Wood
515 Fisher St
Eugene OR 97402

Call Sign: AB7ZL
George M Kennedy
887 Florida St
Eugene OR 97404

Call Sign: N7IY
Peter J Mc Closky
1802 Flournoy Valley Rd

Eugene OR 97404

Call Sign: KB1PSP
Elizabeth A Liljengren
4430 Flournoy Valley Rd
Eugene OR 97404

Call Sign: N7QU
George M Kennedy
4622 Flournoy Valley Rd
Eugene OR 97404

Call Sign: N7CQU
Elizabeth A Liljengren
1384 Flower Ln
Eugene OR 97404

Call Sign: KD7QYX
Steve D Williamson
365 Fountain St
Eugene OR 97402

Call Sign: KB7KRD
Paul T Ortman
4545 Fox Hollow Rd
Eugene OR 97401

Call Sign: KC7LZE
Nanette G Forney
4545 Fox Hollow Rd
Eugene OR 974018257

Call Sign: KE7QXU
John K Miller
4789 Fox Hollow Rd
Eugene OR 97401

Call Sign: N7LID
John K Miller
30035 Fox Hollow Rd
Eugene OR 97401

Call Sign: W7GKB
Ray B Carnay
2645 Foxhaven Dr SE

Eugene OR 97404

Call Sign: KD7BKS
Alice K Burch
301 Frankham Rd
Eugene OR 974053564

Call Sign: AB7TV
Janet M Peterson
18310 Franklin Way
Eugene OR 97404

Call Sign: KB7OKI
Michael E Peterson
18310 Franklin Way
Eugene OR 97404

Call Sign: KF7PEM
Jordi Humphreys
12 Freedom Dr
Eugene OR 97403

Call Sign: KD7SY
James E Trodglen Jr
2690 Gable Rd Apt B
Eugene OR 97402

Call Sign: KB7JQC
George A Mc Cully
1624 Gaffney Way
Eugene OR 97403

Call Sign: K7BW
George A Mc Cully
1000 Gale St SW
Eugene OR 97403

Call Sign: WA7KMT
Isabelle J Fuller
58812 Garden Valley Rd
Eugene OR 97404

Call Sign: K7CJB
Ramon H Fuller
830 Garden Way

Eugene OR 974043010

Eugene OR 97401

Eugene OR 97402

Call Sign: K7DBV
Gene A Williamson
923 Garden Way
Eugene OR 97401

Call Sign: N7YW
Gene A Williamson
1257 Gardendale Ave
Eugene OR 97401

Call Sign: KB7VIT
Chris M Taylor
1562 Gary St
Eugene OR 97401

Call Sign: N7FPA
Glenn J Taylor
931 Gatch St
Eugene OR 97401

Call Sign: K7USA
Chris M Taylor
55635 Gatehouse Ln
Eugene OR 97401

Call Sign: W7JM
Emory W Readen
24465 Gellatly Way
Eugene OR 97404

Call Sign: W7VTV
Charles R Readen
24465 Gellatly Way
Eugene OR 97404

Call Sign: KA7QHS
Walter J Taubenkrau
24465 Gellatly Way
Eugene OR 97404

Call Sign: KC7UDT
Steven E Van Devender
990 Genie St SE

Call Sign: K7YFU
Helene A Kaplan
437 Gentry Way
Eugene OR 97405

Call Sign: K7SW
Stephen M Weersing
437 Gentry Way
Eugene OR 97405

Call Sign: KE7OUR
Jeffery A Newton
437 Gentry Way
Eugene OR 974023364

Call Sign: KA7CJB
Jeanette I Steele
2380 Gibsonwoods Ct NW
Eugene OR 97402

Call Sign: KC7DMD
Brian L Steele
3370 Gienger Rd 3
Eugene OR 97402

Call Sign: KS7Y
Larry E Steele
610 Gilbert
Eugene OR 97402

Call Sign: KD7SDB
John P Roberts
3721 Gilham Rd
Eugene OR 974051825

Call Sign: WJ7P
John P Roberts
36826 Gilkey Rd
Eugene OR 974051825

Call Sign: K7JJX
Philip B Grenon
2220 Gilman Dr 310

Call Sign: N7TQI
Wayne L Harrison
19985 Glen Vista
Eugene OR 97403

Call Sign: WA7WJX
Marvin O Schwaegler
5531 Glenridge Way
Eugene OR 97401

Call Sign: N7SKP
Henry Lr Perkins
215 Glenview Dr
Eugene OR 974022252

Call Sign: KB7GBO
Paul H Moore
2050 Goodpasture Loop Apt
135
Eugene OR 97402

Call Sign: WA7UIR
Robert J Larson
1905 Grandview Ave
Eugene OR 97405

Call Sign: KF7IMF
Steve G Thorpe
3120 Grandview Dr
Eugene OR 97405

Call Sign: KE7DFS
Geoffrey S Simmons
6775 Grandview Dr
Eugene OR 97405

Call Sign: KF7TFL
Vance N Thompson
99145 Grandview Dr
Eugene OR 97405

Call Sign: K7VNZ
Vance N Thompson

657 Grandview Hts
Eugene OR 97405

Call Sign: KD7YKH
Tim D Dallas
657 Grandview Hts
Eugene OR 97405

Call Sign: KA7BVU
Arloa A Simonis
657 Grandview Nts
Eugene OR 97405

Call Sign: KA7P
Roger A Simonis
5195 Grange Rd
Eugene OR 97405

Call Sign: KE7UUP
Yona Appletree
330 Granite Hill Rd
Eugene OR 97405

Call Sign: AE7CY
Yona Appletree
1499 Granite Hill Rd
Eugene OR 97405

Call Sign: K7ARL
Karl L Fuller
1060 Grays Creek Rd
Eugene OR 97403

Call Sign: W7LGA
Virgil V Hall
1491 Grays Creek Rd
Eugene OR 97403

Call Sign: W7OPG
Dean E Northup
1491 Grays Creek Rd
Eugene OR 97405

Call Sign: N6DVI
Neil H Rosenberg

584 Great Oaks Dr
Eugene OR 97403

Call Sign: KA6EPP
Phillip B Giberson
1020 Green Acres Rd 4
1188
Eugene OR 97403

Call Sign: KA6EPU
Ethel I Giberson
1020 Green Acres Rd 4
1188
Eugene OR 97403

Call Sign: KD7IR
William D Dickinson
1475 Green Acres Rd Sp 14
Eugene OR 974032444

Call Sign: N7FBU
Nancy A Dickinson
1475 Green Acres Rd Sp 31
Eugene OR 974032444

Call Sign: KD7GNK
Brian C Miller
69450 Greenridge Loop
Eugene OR 97404

Call Sign: KD7QYY
Sandra J Miller
511 Greens Creek Rd
Eugene OR 97404

Call Sign: KB7HHR
Patricia G Delong
1200 Greens Crk Rd
Eugene OR 97404

Call Sign: KD7AJD
Bert O Bowman
1473 Greentree Cir
Eugene OR 974042155

Call Sign: KD7BKV
Jo Ann R Bowman
2445 Greentree Dr NE
Eugene OR 97404

Call Sign: WB7PRK
Annette C Pershern
2445 Greentree Dr NE
Eugene OR 97405

Call Sign: KA7HEP
Monica I Millican
2007 Griffin Creek Rd
Eugene OR 97402

Call Sign: K7BFD
Jon J Haterius
25631 Hall Rd
Eugene OR 97402

Call Sign: W7CQ
Jimmy L Oldaker
3345 Harlow Rd
Eugene OR 974059708

Call Sign: KE7CWE
Walter A Biddle
7770 Harmony Rd
Eugene OR 97408

Call Sign: KC7UDS
Richard D Born
7823 Harmony Rd
Eugene OR 97402

Call Sign: K7ORU
Walter A Biddle
69219 Harness
Eugene OR 97408

Call Sign: KC7VWL
C W Biddle
69219 Harness
Eugene OR 97408

Call Sign: KC7CAE
Thomas S Wood
467 Harris Ln
Eugene OR 97404

Call Sign: WB2LXU
Harry Genet
555 Henley Way
Eugene OR 97401

Call Sign: KK7WR
Jeffery L Hite
204 High St
Eugene OR 97405

Call Sign: KC7ESI
Betty L Wood
124 Harrison Ave
Eugene OR 97404

Call Sign: W7OQL
Joseph R Young
555 Henley Way
Eugene OR 97401

Call Sign: KD7YNQ
Barbara A Dill
283 High St
Eugene OR 97404

Call Sign: W7WLF
William L Fletcher
6250 Haverhill Ct
Eugene OR 97404

Call Sign: K7XJ
Gerald E Messinger Jr
296 Heritage Ave
Eugene OR 97404

Call Sign: KD7YNP
Peter C Dill
1146 High St
Eugene OR 97404

Call Sign: KO6RR
Brian J Perry
2045 Haviland Dr
Eugene OR 97478

Call Sign: K7JOS
James O Sindt
67997 Heritage Hills Rd
Eugene OR 974029427

Call Sign: KA7WGZ
J Lee Lashway
1292 High St 151
Eugene OR 97405

Call Sign: KE7FCI
Isabel Leonor
90329 Hawkins Rd
Eugene OR 97401

Call Sign: K1ELK
James O Sindt
1294 Heritage Loop
Eugene OR 974029427

Call Sign: WA7ORS
James M Holst
28450 Hillaire
Eugene OR 97401

Call Sign: KC7PAL
Richard C Anderson
13511 Hawks Beard
Eugene OR 97401

Call Sign: KE7CWK
Aaron D Williams
4816 Herrin Rd NE
Eugene OR 97404

Call Sign: KB7FLH
Clyde H Mc Ardle
95983 Hillcrest Ln
Eugene OR 97402

Call Sign: KD7RLG
Tucker A Teague
83686 Hawks Way
Eugene OR 97401

Call Sign: KE7DFB
Mark Mantuani
540 Hidden Valley Rd
Eugene OR 97405

Call Sign: KD7ZFN
Dan R Boyer
301 Hillside Loop
Eugene OR 97401

Call Sign: KD7CUT
Thomas R Germaine
13511 Hawksbeard
Eugene OR 97401

Call Sign: KE7DFC
Mary A Mantuani
610 Hidden Valley Rd
Eugene OR 974051225

Call Sign: W7AAB
Dan R Boyer
301 Hillside Loop
Eugene OR 97401

Call Sign: WA7YYO
Jerry C Nairns Sr
65839 Hay Canyon Rd
Eugene OR 97404

Call Sign: KB7HCW
Ernest E Kries
32421 Hidden Valley Rd
Eugene OR 97404

Call Sign: KD7IZZ
Charles W Hunt
85 Hillview Dr
Eugene OR 97404

Call Sign: KB7CJA
Curtis C Crabtree
154 Hillview Dr
Eugene OR 97404

Call Sign: KD7LCC
Katharine E Hunt
840 Hillview Dr
Eugene OR 97404

Call Sign: WA7KJV
Kenneth J Martin Jr
8405 Holden Rd
Eugene OR 97404

Call Sign: KD7DWH
Garth D Reiber
3351 Holland Loop Rd
Eugene OR 97401

Call Sign: KF7KTY
John S Moomey
573 Homewood Rd
Eugene OR 97405

Call Sign: K3DUW
Alan Goodman
3624 Honolulu St
Eugene OR 97404

Call Sign: KF7LQD
George A Poling
2742 Honor Dr
Eugene OR 97401

Call Sign: K7SGT
George A Poling
657 Hood Ave
Eugene OR 97401

Call Sign: KF7EFW
Glenda L Poling
657 Hood Ave
Eugene OR 97401

Call Sign: W6OPF
Glenda L Poling
930 Hood View Ct
Eugene OR 97401

Call Sign: N7ISN
Michael R Obie
20225 Hoodview Ave
Eugene OR 97404

Call Sign: KE7RRS
Roland L Jillings
64629 Horseman Ln
Eugene OR 97405

Call Sign: AD7UG
Roland L Jillings
370 Horseshoe Dr
Eugene OR 97405

Call Sign: W7LU
Roland L Jillings
30606 Horseshoe Dr SW
Eugene OR 97405

Call Sign: AE7GF
Andrew J Stern
6 Hotspur
Eugene OR 97405

Call Sign: N7UL
Andrew J Stern
16 Hotspur St
Eugene OR 974051203

Call Sign: KD7DZI
Gerald A Barker
95612 House Rock Rd
Eugene OR 97405

Call Sign: N4NMJ
Marjorie S Barker
88542 Houston Ln
Eugene OR 97405

Call Sign: W7AHX
George D Heitzman II
1085 Hoyt St SE
Eugene OR 97402

Call Sign: KF7FYC
Leland M Holst
181 Hrubetz Rd SE
Eugene OR 97402

Call Sign: KE7AMG
Randy D Morris
14452 Hunt Mountain Ln
Eugene OR 97403

Call Sign: W7RAN
Randy D Morris
1452 Hunter Ave
Eugene OR 97403

Call Sign: KF7IMG
Judy A Kinworthy
62788 Hunter Rd
Eugene OR 97404

Call Sign: WB7AVU
Scot C Mc Math
67826 Hunter Rd
Eugene OR 97404

Call Sign: WB7BYL
Richard D Bigelow
54300 Huntington Rd
Eugene OR 97404

Call Sign: KJ7FU
Arnold R Dillon
84983 Hwy 101
Eugene OR 974041968

Call Sign: W7PXL
Valley RC Of Oregon
87667 Hwy 101
Eugene OR 97404

Call Sign: W7ARD
Arnold R Dillon
88530 Hwy 101
Eugene OR 974041968

Call Sign: KF7IJQ
Peter R Knox
3760 Hwy 101 N Sp 13
Eugene OR 97401

Call Sign: KE7HVC
Ethan Emeson
15549 Hwy 101 S
Eugene OR 97401

Call Sign: KF7BAZ
Nancy L Hammer
15549 Hwy 101 S
Eugene OR 97405

Call Sign: KC7RYW
Larry R Bingham
43481 Hwy 226
Eugene OR 97402

Call Sign: W7IEB
Larry R Bingham
37750 Hwy 228
Eugene OR 97402

Call Sign: W7UI
Larry R Bingham
38959 Hwy 228
Eugene OR 97402

Call Sign: KC7ENC
Kenneth H Schmidt
20479 Hwy 42
Eugene OR 97402

Call Sign: KD7MHT
Judah M Mcauley
20479 Hwy 42
Eugene OR 97405

Call Sign: KE7SLU
Mark A Gorham
27301 Hwy 62
Eugene OR 97404

Call Sign: K7ERN
Mark A Gorham
6499 Hwy 66
Eugene OR 97404

Call Sign: KD7ABM
Steven O Olson
9687 Hwy 66
Eugene OR 97408

Call Sign: WA7SDI
Paul R Yaniw
295 Idaho St
Eugene OR 97404

Call Sign: KF7HB
Andrew C Meier
295 Idaho St
Eugene OR 974087530

Call Sign: KE7ZLP
Dorothy I Carter
611 Immonen Rd
Eugene OR 97404

Call Sign: KC7OTG
Brett T Howard
3821 Independance Hwy
Eugene OR 97404

Call Sign: N7MG
Brett T Howard
3821 Independance Hwy
Eugene OR 97404

Call Sign: KE7GMJ
Brianne E Howard
262 Independence Dr
Eugene OR 97404

Call Sign: KE7OFG
Mindy C Beaver
1395 Inglewood
Eugene OR 97402

Call Sign: K7MCB
Mindy C Beaver
470 Inglewood Ln
Eugene OR 97402

Call Sign: KE7LDL
Robert R Beaver
1033 Ingrid St
Eugene OR 97402

Call Sign: AD7OP
Robert R Beaver
19341 Inishbride Ct
Eugene OR 97402

Call Sign: KB7OZG
Orrin K Johnson
3650 Inland Ct 2
Eugene OR 97402

Call Sign: K7QXI
Kathleen M Knights
2351 Ironwood St
Eugene OR 97404

Call Sign: K7ZYD
Richard J Knights
1240 Irvine
Eugene OR 97404

Call Sign: KD6YRA
Raymond M Ludlam
1234 Irving Ave
Eugene OR 974042419

Call Sign: KC7PIH
Jason L Sutton
525 Judson SE
Eugene OR 97402

Call Sign: KF7KTX
Jeffery S Ryals
2003 Jupiter Way
Eugene OR 97402

Call Sign: N7BSX
Jerry O Truhill
2140 Justice Way Ct S
Eugene OR 97440

Call Sign: KA0OLN
Howard C Ownbey
2140 Justice Way Ct S
Eugene OR 97440

Call Sign: KT7S
Cleve D Le Clair
54408 Kalberer Rd
Eugene OR 974042092

Call Sign: W7EGT
Herbert G Fortner
5372 Kali St SE
Eugene OR 974041066

Call Sign: WA7NUZ
Harold E Lee
7750 Keller Ln NE
Eugene OR 97402

Call Sign: W6KPH
Philip H Diehl
2161 Kincaid Rd
Eugene OR 97404

Call Sign: AC7OF
Michael W Ferguson
20922 King David Ave
Eugene OR 97402

Call Sign: KB7HID
Terrence P La Mora
20922 King David Ave
Eugene OR 97402

Call Sign: KC7CAS
Robert R Purkey
630 Kingwood Dr NW
Eugene OR 97401

Call Sign: KD7NWC
Jay A Fox
865 Kingwood Dr NW
Eugene OR 97401

Call Sign: KE7HTB
William H Condron
2644 Kristin Ct NE
Eugene OR 97402

Call Sign: KC7TKV
Daryl F Judd
945 Kumler St SE
Eugene OR 97402

Call Sign: KC7RYI
Glenn E Jones
1347 Kyle St
Eugene OR 97402

Call Sign: W7OTM
Robert J Fisher
5228 Lacey Ct N
Eugene OR 97402

Call Sign: W7TZR
Darwin T Lajoie
17543 Lake Haven Dr
Eugene OR 974041854

Call Sign: N7IWX
Barbara J Stinson
70215 Lakewood Rd
Eugene OR 97404

Call Sign: W7BJS
Barbara J Stinson
430 Laksonen Loop
Eugene OR 97404

Call Sign: WB7ALW
James M Stinson
507 Laksonen Loop
Eugene OR 97404

Call Sign: WA7JS
James M Stinson
155 Lamar
Eugene OR 97404

Call Sign: W7JLB
Andrew G Hood
1118 Lancaster Dr NE 314
Eugene OR 97404

Call Sign: KE7MEC
Thomas A Woods Jr
2150 Lansing Ave NE
Eugene OR 97401

Call Sign: KE7ZY
John N Beebe
1590 Larch St
Eugene OR 97401

Call Sign: KB7IAO
Roscoe W Jolliff
2373 Laurel Ave
Eugene OR 97405

Call Sign: N5ZUX
Daniel C Berry
2355 Laurel Ave NE
Eugene OR 97405

Call Sign: KB7MYG
Jeffrey G Hubbard
1905 Laurel Dr
Eugene OR 97402

Call Sign: KD7WS
John V Hedtke
2334 Laurelhurst Dr
Eugene OR 974011913

Call Sign: AB7PN
Clarence H Story
20985 Lava Flow Ln
Eugene OR 97404

Call Sign: KC7PWD
Carolyn J Story
93050 Lavender Ln
Eugene OR 97404

Call Sign: WX7E
Clarence H Story
3328 Lavina Dr
Eugene OR 97404

Call Sign: KA7NVB
Douglas S Wade
3328 Lavina Dr
Eugene OR 97404

Call Sign: KE7MTB
Robert E Groff Sr
54008 Lefore Rd
Eugene OR 97401

Call Sign: KE7ZKB
Julie A Donohue
30016 Leghorn Rd
Eugene OR 97401

Call Sign: WA6UDT
David J Wright
1315 Lehigh Wy SE
Eugene OR 97401

Call Sign: AD7OQ
David J Wright
1380 Leigh Ct
Eugene OR 97401

Call Sign: KB7KKL
Betty A Kirsch
5756 Leland Dr
Eugene OR 97404

Call Sign: WA7ZZF
Ray D Young
71666 Lentz Rd
Eugene OR 97404

Call Sign: WB7UHA
Dorothy F Young
1716 Leon Dr
Eugene OR 97404

Call Sign: KC7VWS
Matthew E Snyder
2915 Lewellyn
Eugene OR 97404

Call Sign: KB7ZDM
Brandon K Hunt
7441 Liberty Rd S
Eugene OR 97402

Call Sign: KB7ZKN
Daniel A Conklin
1466 Liberty St NE Apt 1
Eugene OR 97404

Call Sign: WA7GGD
Charles B Kilen
906 Lillie Circle Ct
Eugene OR 974085940

Call Sign: AG4BP
H Walter Anderson
1611 Lincoln St
Eugene OR 97408

Call Sign: AC7MB
H Walter Anderson
105 Lincoln St Apt B
Eugene OR 97408

Call Sign: N7MBW
Wallace G Anderson
2411 Lindley Way
Eugene OR 97408

Call Sign: WB7PRS
John H Quiner II
2411 Lindley Way
Eugene OR 974085935

Call Sign: KA7WAL
Sharon L Mc Ghehey
39431 Little Fall Creek Rd
Eugene OR 97408

Call Sign: W7FBA
Henry L Kearney
71836 London Rd
Eugene OR 97404

Call Sign: N7PUN
Alan S Corbeth
3111 Long St
Eugene OR 97404

Call Sign: KD7LIH
Nancy L Parkhill
81742 Lost Creek Rd
Eugene OR 97403

Call Sign: KF7FGT
James E Hazen
2010 Lowen NW
Eugene OR 97402

Call Sign: K7RTC
Carl A Wuorinen
39547 Luckiamute Rd
Eugene OR 97401

Call Sign: W7JD
William R Mickey
69250 Lucky Lady
Eugene OR 97401

Call Sign: KE7JFK
Aubrey E Anderson
300 Luman Rd 40
Eugene OR 97405

Call Sign: K7CIY
William E Patterson
78061 Lupine Ln
Eugene OR 97401

Call Sign: KB7RBF
Mary J Hornig
78061 Lupine Ln
Eugene OR 97405

Call Sign: KF6CYE
Saul Wold
628 Luscombe St
Eugene OR 97405

Call Sign: W7CYE
Saul Wold
638 Luscombe St
Eugene OR 97405

Call Sign: N6ERR
Robert H Mc Clelland
768 Luscombe St
Eugene OR 974041711

Call Sign: KF7BBD
Jonathan B Seagoe
2536 Lyman Ave
Eugene OR 97404

Call Sign: KB7IYI
Wayne R Hafdahl
51442 Mac Ct
Eugene OR 97401

Call Sign: KC7VM
Eugene W Reck
51442 Mac Ct
Eugene OR 97402

Call Sign: KB7RVP
Theresa A Hafdahl
6472 Macleay Rd SE
Eugene OR 97401

Call Sign: KD7BF
Truman D Wiles
7732 Macleay Rd SE
Eugene OR 97401

Call Sign: K7RRD
Gregory A Nance
195 Madison St
Eugene OR 97402

Call Sign: KC7DME
Beverly M Nobel
1204 Madison St
Eugene OR 97402

Call Sign: KB7ZXC
Danny J Venis
1505 Madison St Sp 43
Eugene OR 97402

Call Sign: KF7SOE
Duncan J Rhodes
1806 Madrona St
Eugene OR 97402

Call Sign: W7BG
Kermit W Raaen
8475 Magnolia Dr
Eugene OR 97403

Call Sign: KD7OCW
Daniel R Gusset
32048 Mally Rd
Eugene OR 974013914

Call Sign: KC7OJG
Donald E Buckley
5299 Mango Ave SE
Eugene OR 97401

Call Sign: WL7CSL
Michael T Miller
1125 Marigold Dr
Eugene OR 97404

Call Sign: W0PAI
Gary L Ludeke
23 Mariner Ln
Eugene OR 97405

Call Sign: KD7KLN
Michael P Thieme
20155 Marsh Rd
Eugene OR 97405

Call Sign: KB7CPZ
George C D Kjaer
731 Marshall
Eugene OR 97405

Call Sign: WB2ZAU
George C Towe
3895 Marshall
Eugene OR 97405

Call Sign: KA7LSP
Angela T Janz
4683 Marshall
Eugene OR 97405

Call Sign: KC7RYF
Eric Engelstad
3630 Marshall Ave
Eugene OR 97405

Call Sign: KD7KLK
George S Ralph
3630 Marshall Ave
Eugene OR 97405

Call Sign: K6SIP
George S Ralph
3980 Marshall Ave
Eugene OR 97405

Call Sign: W7GSR
George S Ralph
2080 Martin Dr
Eugene OR 97405

Call Sign: KA7VXP
David H Beaver
2112 Martin Dr
Eugene OR 97401

Call Sign: K6BSU
Floyd E Carter
1360 Mayview Dr NE
Eugene OR 97402

Call Sign: KD7ABI
Darrin M Lajoie
16435 McDonald Rd
Eugene OR 974025030

Call Sign: KK7VX
Darrin M Lajoie
55371 McDonald Rd
Eugene OR 974025030

Call Sign: KB7HUF
Wayne L Fetters
64620 McGrath Rd
Eugene OR 97404

Call Sign: W7AAN
Leonard K Galer
41886 McKenzie Hwy
Eugene OR 97404

Call Sign: KC7IJY
Susan L Cutsogeorge
3160 McNaught St
Eugene OR 97405

Call Sign: KE7QLZ
Bradley G Black
3160 McNaught St
Eugene OR 97405

Call Sign: K7EUG
Bradley G Black
3425 McQuire Way
Eugene OR 97405

Call Sign: KC7FYW
Tony C Willett
605 Meadow Ave
Eugene OR 97402

Call Sign: KB7DTL
Alan L Beebe
1375 Meinecke Rd
Eugene OR 97402

Call Sign: KC7QYN
Karen L Beebe
225 Meissinger Pl
Eugene OR 97402

Call Sign: WA9DQM
Robert H Welfel
65881 Meissner Rd
Eugene OR 97402

Call Sign: WB9UST
Grace C Welfel
65931 Meissner Rd
Eugene OR 97402

Call Sign: KE7FCK
Carl W Jenkins
174 Melissa
Eugene OR 97404

Call Sign: KD7QLC
Melvin W Louis
4909 Memorie Ln
Eugene OR 97404

Call Sign: KD7UGZ
Oregon Amateur Radio
Emergency
Communications Service
513 Memory Ln
Eugene OR 97404

Call Sign: W7OEC
Oregon Emergency
Communications

536 Memory Ln
Eugene OR 97404

Call Sign: W7FPK
John B Schaerer
37253 Meredith Dr
Eugene OR 97404

Call Sign: N7NDR
Gary A Jacobs
633 Mill St
Eugene OR 97402

Call Sign: KD7JTT
Phillip T Winters
650 Mill St 7
Eugene OR 97402

Call Sign: KE7KJT
Jamie M Hammersley
5437 Miller Ave
Eugene OR 97402

Call Sign: KE7PGR
Sharon K Hammersley
33890 Miller Ln
Eugene OR 97402

Call Sign: KD7LCD
Donald W Hildebrand
33890 Miller Ln
Eugene OR 97402

Call Sign: KD7MTL
Bradley D Lewis
6305 Miller Rd
Eugene OR 97401

Call Sign: KF7LQC
Richard B Bremer
29365 Miller View Ln
Eugene OR 97405

Call Sign: KB7FLI
Nita A Agol

20399 Mission Ridge
Eugene OR 97405

6 Mtn View Ln
Eugene OR 97402

1050 N 5th St
Eugene OR 974052443

Call Sign: W7DKG
Vernon W Anibal
2635 Montana St
Eugene OR 97402

Call Sign: W7KUT
John T Cuff III
6 Mtn View Ln
Eugene OR 97402

Call Sign: WA7WGL
Richard L Johnson
925 N 9th St
Eugene OR 97401

Call Sign: KE7HVD
John G Schaad
6217 Monument Dr
Eugene OR 97405

Call Sign: KD7LSA
Jonathan B Shrope
6 Mtn View Ln
Eugene OR 97402

Call Sign: N7WJI
James M Steele
7312 N Applegate Rd
Eugene OR 97402

Call Sign: K7JU
John G Schaad
7150 Monument Dr
Eugene OR 97405

Call Sign: KF7FYB
Charles M Whitmore Jr
34565 Mtn View Pl NE
Eugene OR 97402

Call Sign: KC7ZFQ
Henry Lr Perkins
8833 N Applegate Rd
Eugene OR 974022252

Call Sign: KE7NWM
Dylan W Wiggins
31880 Moon Ridge Ct
Eugene OR 97405

Call Sign: WB7ULK
Danny E Schumacher
225 Munsel Creek Loop
Eugene OR 97404

Call Sign: NL7OP
Gerald H Clark
6678 N Astor
Eugene OR 97405

Call Sign: W2ALI
Donald H Gudehus
1441 Morrow Rd Apt 712
Eugene OR 97408

Call Sign: KC7DPJ
Albert G Pelfrey
225 Munsel Creek Loop
Eugene OR 97404

Call Sign: NL7RO
Joanne C Clark
7153 N Atlantic Ave
Eugene OR 97405

Call Sign: KF7EFU
Michael A Whitney
6 Mtn View Ln
Eugene OR 97402

Call Sign: K7YGB
Ernest L Rankin
1928 N 18th St
Eugene OR 97402

Call Sign: KD7AHQ
Tsuyoshi Okita
14557 N Blue Grass
Eugene OR 97403

Call Sign: K7ELI
Michael A Whitney
6 Mtn View Ln
Eugene OR 97402

Call Sign: W7IAS
George C Amrhein
445 N 36th
Eugene OR 97402

Call Sign: KD7DUP
Richard A Andrews
915 N Holland St
Eugene OR 97477

Call Sign: KF7POP
Rebecca S Horton
6 Mtn View Ln
Eugene OR 97402

Call Sign: WB7AEV
Richard D Kraft
101 N 5th St
Eugene OR 97402

Call Sign: KB7GSL
Marcus C Lynch
2657 N Hwy 101 Apt 27
Eugene OR 97402

Call Sign: N7FSU
Rebecca S Horton

Call Sign: KA7ETY
William H Allen Sr

Call Sign: KD7WKV
Jacob V Shaw

6310 N Hwy 101 Sp 31
Eugene OR 97402

Call Sign: WA7IXU
Thomas C Murry
1013 N Madison St
Eugene OR 97402

Call Sign: KC7OZA
Alan C Wiggins
3477 N Myrtle Rd
Eugene OR 97408

Call Sign: KD7VKM
Richard E Shrope
6506 N Omaha Ave
Eugene OR 974021129

Call Sign: KC7QAG
Elmer W Mc Clellan
6526 N Omaha Ave
Eugene OR 974021183

Call Sign: W7EWM
Elmer W Mc Clellan
19 N Orange St
Eugene OR 974021183

Call Sign: KB7GYN
O Murray Olson
311 N Peach St
Eugene OR 974085900

Call Sign: KT7T
Byron G Rainwater
1467 N Pine
Eugene OR 97401

Call Sign: WB6ESG
William O Roberts
1467 N Pine
Eugene OR 97408

Call Sign: K7ZIE
Harold E Bender

382 N Pleasure Dr
Eugene OR 97401

Call Sign: N7KKT
Edgar R Craiger
440 N Pleasure Dr
Eugene OR 97401

Call Sign: KD7NWD
Martin M Gaffer
1699 N Terry St Sp 7
Eugene OR 97402

Call Sign: KD7UYD
Ryan J Fling
1537 NE 141 Ave
Eugene OR 97402

Call Sign: KC7ZFP
Mike L Abrams
440 NE 143rd
Eugene OR 97402

Call Sign: KC7KYV
Arthur E Alpers
440 NE 143rd Ave
Eugene OR 97402

Call Sign: W7AEA
A Edward Alpers
440 NE 143rd Ave
Eugene OR 97402

Call Sign: W7BCN
Lawrence L Jack
2045 NE 144th Ave
Eugene OR 97402

Call Sign: KE7ZKC
John A Holechek
2045 NE 144th Ave
Eugene OR 97402

Call Sign: WA7UKF
Clifford S Rylands

2430 NE 144th Ave
Eugene OR 97402

Call Sign: KE7JNE
Timothy E Durkin
235 NE 146 Ave
Eugene OR 97402

Call Sign: W7WTQ
Ralph R Cook
235 NE 146th
Eugene OR 97402

Call Sign: K9ZMT
Douglas A Scheuerell
671 NE 21st Ave
Eugene OR 97401

Call Sign: KE7ZKD
Kathy D Farrier
1514 NE 22nd St
Eugene OR 97404

Call Sign: KF7EON
Nelson J Farrier
380 NE 23
Eugene OR 97404

Call Sign: KD7RLE
Donald S Robertson
317 NW 12th St
Eugene OR 97404

Call Sign: W7ORE
Donald S Robertson
2082 NW 12th St
Eugene OR 97404

Call Sign: KF7SNZ
Felicia A Kenney
355A NW 12th St
Eugene OR 97402

Call Sign: AC7VX
Donald S Robertson

27 NW 12th St 10
Eugene OR 97404

Call Sign: KA7EFE
William E Mc Intyre
1628 NW 143
Eugene OR 97402

Call Sign: KD7IES
Michael J Callahan
3734 NW 144th Pl
Eugene OR 974029787

Call Sign: K7LCC
John A Bredesen
2075 NW 14th
Eugene OR 974054234

Call Sign: KA7BLW
Keith W Peterson
4185 NW 178th Pl
Eugene OR 97402

Call Sign: N7IDD
Carol A Petersen
2058 NW 17th St
Eugene OR 97402

Call Sign: WB7TBF
Charles W Petersen
1045 NW 180th Ave
Eugene OR 97402

Call Sign: W7CWP
Charles W Petersen
4070 NW 180th Ct
Eugene OR 97402

Call Sign: KE7WMG
Melford T Strong
4920 NW 180th Ter
Eugene OR 97402

Call Sign: KE6BGO
Robert D Robertson

3300 NW 185th Ave 203
Eugene OR 97405

Call Sign: KB7GBG
Clarence A Jessee
1900 NW Laura Vista Dr
Eugene OR 97405

Call Sign: WB7BXX
John W Wagner
2703 Old Hwy 99 S Trl 9
Eugene OR 974053480

Call Sign: W7JWW
John W Wagner
2703 Old Hwy 99 S Trl 9
Eugene OR 974053480

Call Sign: KD7OJZ
Tim J Chapek
21715 Old Red Rd
Eugene OR 97402

Call Sign: W7EUD
S Riley Mc Lean
98045 Olsen Ln 4
Eugene OR 974015412

Call Sign: W7RIL
S Riley Mc Lean
19183 Olson Ave
Eugene OR 974015412

Call Sign: KF7BUG
Nicholas B Johnson
4248 Omaha Ave
Eugene OR 97402

Call Sign: KD7BKX
Arnold L Taylor
17684 Paladin Dr
Eugene OR 97405

Call Sign: KD7ZOL
Timothy R Riley

1125 Panther Gulch Rd
Eugene OR 97403

Call Sign: NB7J
Robert C Benafel
1125 Panther Gulch Rd
Eugene OR 97403

Call Sign: W7DAU
James L Brock
1125 Panther Gulch Rd
Eugene OR 97405

Call Sign: KB7ZXG
Kenneth R Cook
83430 Papenfus Rd
Eugene OR 97405

Call Sign: KB3MSI
Richard M Nelson
212 Park St
Eugene OR 974032177

Call Sign: N7MBU
Gail L Ragsdale
2002 Parkside Ct
Eugene OR 97405

Call Sign: N7MBV
David E Atkin
1415 Parkside Ct NE
Eugene OR 97405

Call Sign: KC7VXC
Martin L Greig
20308 Parr Ln
Eugene OR 97404

Call Sign: KC7VJY
Mark J Greig
20308 Parr Ln
Eugene OR 97404

Call Sign: K7JMB
James M Boyle

61310 Parrell Rd 28
Eugene OR 974042684

Call Sign: N7RWC
Rory A Funke
27639 Pelican Rd
Eugene OR 97402

Call Sign: KD7ABH
Janet S Kieser
556 Pelton Ln
Eugene OR 97401

Call Sign: KD7AHT
Stanley J Cox
556 Pelton Ln
Eugene OR 97405

Call Sign: K7TWD
Frances L Dillman
1983 Perry Grove Ct NE
Eugene OR 974043029

Call Sign: K7TWE
William H Dillman
3373 Perrydale Ct
Eugene OR 97404

Call Sign: WB7QBX
Foster R Anderson
15088 Persimmon Way
Eugene OR 974055515

Call Sign: K7DIP
Floyd D Stead
17212 Pine Dr
Eugene OR 97404

Call Sign: KC7DMI
Sherman A Dillon
17212 Pine Dr
Eugene OR 97405

Call Sign: KF7EFV
Ananda J Burke

19472 Pine Dr
Eugene OR 97404

Call Sign: KF7DWM
Kahli R Burke
52165 Pine Forest Dr
Eugene OR 97404

Call Sign: AE7CZ
Kahli R Burke
52254 Pine Forest Dr
Eugene OR 97404

Call Sign: KF7FGS
Rebecca C Fisher
1666 Pine Gate Way
Eugene OR 97404

Call Sign: KE7MEA
Greg S Anson Sr
529 Pine St
Eugene OR 97402

Call Sign: N7EUU
Greg S Anson Sr
1300 Pine St
Eugene OR 97402

Call Sign: K7ZU
Gordon R Larson Jr
3660 Pine St
Eugene OR 974041199

Call Sign: N9VNK
John H Koschwanez
4497 Pinecrest Dr
Eugene OR 97405

Call Sign: KA7DFT
Wanda K Dawdy Wirths
392 Pintail Ct SE
Eugene OR 97405

Call Sign: N7RVW
John D Bowman

392 Pintail Ct SE
Eugene OR 974053466

Call Sign: KT7T
John D Bowman
215 Pioneer Dr
Eugene OR 974053466

Call Sign: KD7ZNV
City Of Eugene ARES
3403 Pioneer Dr SE
Eugene OR 97401

Call Sign: W7COE
City Of Eugene ARES
3448 Pioneer Dr SE
Eugene OR 97401

Call Sign: KF7KFA
Jeanette Saul
2540 Pioneer Pike
Eugene OR 97401

Call Sign: KB7SXW
Catherine M Halverson
39700 Pleasant Ave
Eugene OR 97402

Call Sign: KD7PAX
Matthew M Bryant
6374 Ponderosa St
Eugene OR 97405

Call Sign: W7ADT
Matthew M Bryant
2552 Pony Creek Rd
Eugene OR 97405

Call Sign: KE7SJL
Erik A Thompson
21660 Pope Rd
Eugene OR 97405

Call Sign: KB7DIB
Howard R Kershner

20073 Porter Pl 2
Eugene OR 97402

1107 R St
Eugene OR 97405

3500 Redwood Rd
Eugene OR 97404

Call Sign: KE7LDG
Dell R Mcdiarmid
199 Powell Crk Rd
Eugene OR 97405

Call Sign: KF7HE
Donald L Marr
690 Radar Rd
Eugene OR 97405

Call Sign: KD7DTM
Mark A Harpham
375 Reiter Dr
Eugene OR 97401

Call Sign: AA7G
Dell R Mcdiarmid
41510 Powell Ln
Eugene OR 97405

Call Sign: KD7SQL
Susan E Lunas
333 Ragan Rd
Eugene OR 97405

Call Sign: K6EGR
Edward J Tye
35123 Reith Larson Ln
Eugene OR 974018525

Call Sign: W7JL
Dell R Mcdiarmid
41510 Powell Ln
Eugene OR 97405

Call Sign: WD6DFH
Jon T Goss
83428 Raghorn Rd
Eugene OR 97408

Call Sign: KD7TIM
Marilyn J Miller
2665 Renaissance Ct
Eugene OR 97404

Call Sign: W7BE
Dell R Mcdiarmid
2925 Powell St
Eugene OR 97405

Call Sign: KC7VGV
William K Boyanton
6971 Rainbow Dr SE
Eugene OR 97402

Call Sign: KD7TKX
Staci M Miller
91 Renault Ave
Eugene OR 974042084

Call Sign: N7XIN
Jack T Duncan
805 Prefontaine Dr
Eugene OR 97401

Call Sign: W7XWW
Paul M Mc Kay Sr
18079 Rainbow Rock Rd
Eugene OR 97402

Call Sign: AA7GM
Edgar E Soults
1325 Ridge Way
Eugene OR 97401

Call Sign: W6AGD
Jodi R Lugo
2666 Purisima Ct NE
Eugene OR 97405

Call Sign: KC7WGQ
Paul M Mc Kay Sr
18079 Rainbow Rock Rd
Eugene OR 974029654

Call Sign: N7MQV
George F Turbyne
1507 Ridge Way
Eugene OR 97401

Call Sign: KA7BOY
Vadette C Deisner
24431 Queen Anne Dr
Eugene OR 97404

Call Sign: KB7LGL
Bradley S Michelson
332 Rancho Vista Dr
Eugene OR 97405

Call Sign: KF7AHR
Thomas P Herrmann
6574 Rim Rock Ct NE
Eugene OR 97405

Call Sign: N7AIB
Howard E Deisner
24431 Queen Anne Dr
Eugene OR 97404

Call Sign: KA7TPN
Wallace J Donnelly
20165 Red Sky Ln
Eugene OR 97401

Call Sign: KC4WBE
Richard J Burton
2006 River Loop 1
Eugene OR 97401

Call Sign: W7KPZ
Jerry B Eagle

Call Sign: W6CFB
Robert C Parina

Call Sign: KD7IVB
Eric A Burton

530 River Rd
Eugene OR 97401

48446 Rogers Ln
Eugene OR 97404

255 S 6th Ave
Eugene OR 97402

Call Sign: KB7NKN
George K Bowling
94015 River Rd
Eugene OR 97402

Call Sign: KE7OAY
James S Showker
48446 Rogers Ln
Eugene OR 97404

Call Sign: KE7PGN
David L Stone
345 S 6th Ave
Eugene OR 97402

Call Sign: KB7IVT
Michael R Jacque
61020 Riverbluff
Eugene OR 97402

Call Sign: AB7WL
John D Craig
2011 Rogue River Hwy
Eugene OR 974042633

Call Sign: KF7DFZ
Thomas G Amabisca
287 S 7th St
Eugene OR 97402

Call Sign: K7ULA
Ula C Weight
5146 Roberts Cr Rd
Eugene OR 974016559

Call Sign: W1LLA
Willa K Campbell
2510 Rosebay St
Eugene OR 97401

Call Sign: KD5IRS
John M Hayward
671 S 9th St
Eugene OR 97401

Call Sign: KC7GTO
Gary J Oakes
66925 Rock Island Ln
Eugene OR 97404

Call Sign: K7ZRJ
Milon G Whittier
700 Royal Ave Apt 20
Eugene OR 97402

Call Sign: KD7JWR
Shane S Gillespie
671 S 9th St
Eugene OR 97404

Call Sign: KC7UBJ
Mary J Weiland
1400 Rockford Rd
Eugene OR 97404

Call Sign: KE7PXV
Allen D Faigin
1225 S 10th St
Eugene OR 974054845

Call Sign: KB7VIQ
Paul I Allen
25150 S Beavercreek Rd
Eugene OR 97402

Call Sign: N7WXL
Joseph W Weiland
1400 Rockford Rd
Eugene OR 97404

Call Sign: KB7KHF
Randy M Higley
415 S 12th
Eugene OR 97401

Call Sign: KB7ZXH
Cecil R Allen
28465 S Beavercreek Rd
Eugene OR 97402

Call Sign: AC7AP
Robert C Lo Grasso
1626 Rodlun Ct
Eugene OR 97404

Call Sign: KD7KF
William A Mc Ginnis
240 S 1st Ave
Eugene OR 97401

Call Sign: KD7PJW
Kathleen S Allen
19093 S Beavercreek Rd
354
Eugene OR 97402

Call Sign: K6ICW
Blaine H Carruth
574 Roesepark Ln NE
Eugene OR 97404

Call Sign: KA7MXM
Herman J Daily
331 S 43rd St
Eugene OR 97404

Call Sign: K7VIQ
Paul I Allen
19093 S Beavercreek Rd
Pmb 327
Eugene OR 97402

Call Sign: KA7CWU
Roger M Mortensen

Call Sign: KB5NCG
Leo W Marsh

Call Sign: N7EVK
Kenneth S Wyman
19093 S Beavercreek Rd
Pmb 351
Eugene OR 97402

Call Sign: AC7UG
William P Dart
28322 S Bittner Mill Rd
Eugene OR 97402

Call Sign: KE7JNC
Susan L Guyant
7360 S Bluebird Dr
Eugene OR 97402

Call Sign: KB7VIY
Jeffrey R Johnson
26926 S Bolland Rd
Eugene OR 97402

Call Sign: KC7JNM
Hanne R Halladay
15784 S Boulder Dr
Eugene OR 97402

Call Sign: W7RWK
Marvin C Quick
15092 S Bradley Rd
Eugene OR 97402

Call Sign: WA7LXO
James R Degge
501 S Broad St
Eugene OR 97404

Call Sign: KF7DTW
Bonny D Thomas
30450 S Candlelight Ct
Eugene OR 97401

Call Sign: KF7DTV
Steven F Thomas
57221 S Candy Ln
Eugene OR 97401

Call Sign: KD7FLS
Mark J Koss
12190 S Carus Rd
Eugene OR 97401

Call Sign: KC7MGV
Robert D Allen
532 S Cascade Dr
Eugene OR 97404

Call Sign: N7KYP
Mary L Lange
510 S Center St
Eugene OR 97404

Call Sign: WJ7S
Larry M Lange
510 S Center St
Eugene OR 97404

Call Sign: KC7LWB
Kevin S Cramer
1569 S Franklin St
Eugene OR 97403

Call Sign: W7BH
Robert R Bennett
4053 Sabrena Ave
Eugene OR 97405

Call Sign: KS4JH
Robert K Wright Jr
95691 Saunders Cr Rd Sp
21
Eugene OR 97404

Call Sign: N7UXQ
William E Lewis Jr
69310 Scabbard
Eugene OR 97408

Call Sign: KA7TAM
Thomas A Johnson
1560 Scandia St

Eugene OR 974087380

Call Sign: KA7ZQA
Joanne Johnson
1604 Scandia St
Eugene OR 97408

Call Sign: KD7VYP
Dorothy Blackmarr
8715 Scholfield Rd
Eugene OR 97404

Call Sign: KE7VXI
Michael E Blackmarr
7799 Scholls Fry Rd
Eugene OR 97404

Call Sign: KD7GNM
Carl A Gross
6512 Scottsbluff Rd
Eugene OR 97402

Call Sign: KA7VAH
Jonathan M Ward
12460 SE 110th Ct
Eugene OR 97405

Call Sign: KD7SKV
Joseph P Schiefelbein
2529 SE 111
Eugene OR 97405

Call Sign: AE7QM
Joseph P Schiefelbein
3441 SE 111 Ave Sp 1
Eugene OR 97405

Call Sign: KD7SKW
Robert L Schiefelbein
3306 SE 111th
Eugene OR 97405

Call Sign: KI7WT
George B Lewis
1917 SE 112th Ave

Eugene OR 97405

Eugene OR 974041160

Eugene OR 97405

Call Sign: KD7IRT
Sheri L Ivy
2620 SE 112th Ave Apt 25
Eugene OR 97401

Call Sign: W7LK
Dale R Hayes
201 SE 11th
Eugene OR 97404

Call Sign: K7VYE
Carol L Silke
10664 Silver Falls Hwy
Eugene OR 97405

Call Sign: KA7C
Sidney A Strong
5327 SE 115th
Eugene OR 97402

Call Sign: KD7ZHR
Stacey R Hayes
4207 SE 11th
Eugene OR 97404

Call Sign: KF7NRM
Suzanne C Mason
1626 Silver Water Ln
Eugene OR 97404

Call Sign: KB7SYB
Ryan M Whitlock
3131 SE 115th Ave
Eugene OR 97402

Call Sign: W7AAB
Marvin C Wines
26343 Shady Oak Dr
Eugene OR 974043309

Call Sign: W7SWR
Suzanne C Mason
4830 Silversands St W
Eugene OR 97404

Call Sign: KE7LEB
Lester L Ellis
4301 SE 117th Ave
Eugene OR 97404

Call Sign: W7KV
Marvin C Wines
26360 Shady Oak Dr
Eugene OR 974043309

Call Sign: KD7UFT
North Eugene Radio
Amateurs
796 Skyhawk Dr
Eugene OR 97404

Call Sign: KA7LES
Lester L Ellis
12450 SE 117th Ave
Eugene OR 97404

Call Sign: W7AE
Marvin C Wines
29703 Shady Oak Dr
Eugene OR 974043309

Call Sign: W7NHS
North Eugene Radio
Amateurs
624 Skylane Dr
Eugene OR 97404

Call Sign: W7CM
Stephen D Snyder
7319 SE 118th Dr
Eugene OR 97404

Call Sign: W7UTC
Up The Crick RC
300 Shafer Ln G3
Eugene OR 974043309

Call Sign: KA7MYL
Helen M Clark
97 Skyline Ave
Eugene OR 97402

Call Sign: KF7BUA
Mark L Cook
7429 SE 118th Dr
Eugene OR 97404

Call Sign: N7KXW
Rodney L Workman
364 Shan Creek Rd
Eugene OR 97402

Call Sign: KK7WN
Robert A Olsen
2013 Smithoak
Eugene OR 97405

Call Sign: KD7LYN
Dale R Hayes
2827 SE 119th Ave
Eugene OR 97404

Call Sign: KA6IXG
Sue E Mc Clelland
3317 Shasta Way
Eugene OR 974043881

Call Sign: W7LVN
James C Walsh
599 Snow White Way SE
Eugene OR 97404

Call Sign: KD7RLC
Bethe B Hayes
7707 SE 119th Ct

Call Sign: K7TBL
James D Silke
9358 Silver Falls Hwy

Call Sign: KC7LGB

William S Mc Lean
4319 Snowberry St NE
Eugene OR 97404

Call Sign: KB7NJA
John M Pilafian Sr
1785 Snowbird Dr NW
Eugene OR 97404

Call Sign: KB7ACV
Jefferson R Griffin
61182 Snowbrush Dr
Eugene OR 97404

Call Sign: KD7QHJ
John E Greig
61182 Snowbush Dr
Eugene OR 97404

Call Sign: KB7YPI
Robert J Ewing
7790 Spring Valley Rd NW
Eugene OR 97402

Call Sign: KD7NWA
Jennifer L Ewing
7790 Spring Valley Rd NW
Eugene OR 97402

Call Sign: KD7YDJ
Curtis R Ewing
953 Spring Way
Eugene OR 97402

Call Sign: KB7RVN
April L Morris
85715 Springfield Creswell
Hwy
Eugene OR 97404

Call Sign: KC7YFH
Helen C Miller
920 St Andrews Way
Eugene OR 97405

Call Sign: KD7FCW
Loyd H Kruse
7012 St Hazel
Eugene OR 97405

Call Sign: K7TMB
Roy R Mc Caul
60916 Stackland Rd
Eugene OR 97404

Call Sign: KA7VSP
Charles G Martin
611 Startouch Dr
Eugene OR 97402

Call Sign: KC7DMC
Crosby Stone
1875 State Rd
Eugene OR 97402

Call Sign: KF6OUP
David A Foust
900 State St E143
Eugene OR 97402

Call Sign: WB7AAJ
Neil C Lyda
900 State St F332
Eugene OR 97408

Call Sign: KK7NJ
Ross H Hart
40040 Stayton Scio Lp
Eugene OR 94708

Call Sign: KF7RHS
Ken W Smith
38939 Stayton Scio Rd
Eugene OR 97404

Call Sign: W7KSW
Ken W Smith
20454 Steamboat Ct
Eugene OR 97404

Call Sign: WA7KS
Ken W Smith
874 Stearman St
Eugene OR 97404

Call Sign: WB7NJP
Robert N Minster
56151 Stellar Dr
Eugene OR 97404

Call Sign: W7RNM
Robert N Minster
56151 Stellar Dr
Eugene OR 97404

Call Sign: N7FCO
Graydon A Lewis
340 Stellers Eagle St NW
Eugene OR 97404

Call Sign: KA7NSI
Kevin N Sparks
30400 Stellmacher Dr SW
Eugene OR 97404

Call Sign: KA7NSJ
Cynthia A Sparks
100 Stemmerman Way
Eugene OR 97404

Call Sign: KF7RWA
Shelia A Smith
62515 Stenkamp Rd
Eugene OR 97404

Call Sign: K7SAS
Shelia A Smith
62515 Stenkamp Rd
Eugene OR 97404

Call Sign: W7HIT
Gilbert J Johnson
1950 Sterlng Pl 209
Eugene OR 97405

Call Sign: N7FFO
Monte B Olsen
2095 Stortz Ave NE
Eugene OR 97408

Call Sign: KB7NVJ
Dan J Cohn
22920 Superior Ct
Eugene OR 97404

Call Sign: WB7VXW
Wallace S Sherman
585 Sweetwater Ln
Eugene OR 97401

Call Sign: AD7AQ
Dwight N West
428 Sugarpine Ct SE
Eugene OR 97401

Call Sign: KA7ZQH
Gordon C Tibbitts III
32890 Surfside Dr
Eugene OR 97404

Call Sign: KA7BQK
Donald J Sherry
4732 Swegle Rd NE
Eugene OR 97404

Call Sign: K7TAK
Timothy A Keller
24861 Summit Ln
Eugene OR 974041991

Call Sign: K7TER
Clifford E Smith
143 Surrey Dr
Eugene OR 97404

Call Sign: KE7DPU
Cale G Bruckner
951 T Ct
Eugene OR 97403

Call Sign: KD7OJX
Adam J Keller
630 Summit Loop
Eugene OR 974041991

Call Sign: KC5HJI
Benjamin A Bayma Jr
89308 Sutton Lakes Dr
Eugene OR 97440

Call Sign: KF7EFS
Stanley A Petroff IV
1265 Tamara Ave S
Eugene OR 97408

Call Sign: K7AJK
Adam J Keller
1190 Summit Loop Rd
Eugene OR 974041991

Call Sign: KB7VO
Robert A Bauer
14230 SW 103rd
Eugene OR 97403

Call Sign: AB7NH
Stanley A Petroff IV
1265 Tamara Ave S
Eugene OR 97408

Call Sign: KC7MHX
Dwight D Brimley
10473 Summit Loop SE
Eugene OR 97405

Call Sign: KD7KOE
Theresa L Freihube
14785 SW 104th Ave
Eugene OR 97403

Call Sign: KF7CR
Dean E Hale
32210 Tangent Dr
Eugene OR 97401

Call Sign: N7IXA
Kenton E Sturdevant
63869 Sunset Dr
Eugene OR 97405

Call Sign: KC7DMJ
Robert D Cluster
16674 SW 108th
Eugene OR 97404

Call Sign: KB7DHZ
Luther J Brower
68015 Taylor Ln
Eugene OR 97404

Call Sign: K7BQ
Kenton E Sturdevant
34140 Sunset Dr NE
Eugene OR 97405

Call Sign: N7YUM
Michael R Reed
1217 SW 11 Ave 407
Eugene OR 97405

Call Sign: KD7GNL
Theodore R Jones
2504 Taylor St
Eugene OR 97405

Call Sign: WB6WFB
Ronald T Gietter
34140 Sunset Dr NE
Eugene OR 97405

Call Sign: KA7DSW
Linda L Satterfield
2211 Swan Hill Rd
Eugene OR 97404

Call Sign: W7TRJ
Theodore R Jones
91712 Taylorville Rd
Eugene OR 974051845

Call Sign: KE7INX
Zachary A Hussey
7126 Teal Dr
Eugene OR 97404

Call Sign: KF7SYA
Lorenzo Cavicchi
2545 Terwilliger Blvd Apt
446
Eugene OR 97401

Call Sign: K7EQI
Lorenzo Cavicchi
2992 Tess Ave NE
Eugene OR 97401

Call Sign: W7WPM
Charles L Mc Lean
1516 Thompson Rd
Eugene OR 97404

Call Sign: KE7FLC
Randy Birzer
1335 Tiburon Ct SE
Eugene OR 97405

Call Sign: KD7FNV
Edward J Buzalsky
16008 Timberline Ln
Eugene OR 974052981

Call Sign: KA7TWC
Kerry E Watkins
2335 Todd St
Eugene OR 97404

Call Sign: KD7CYQ
Pearl M Young Anderson
2335 Todd St
Eugene OR 97405

Call Sign: KD7VYO
Amanda M Brambora
2335 Todd St
Eugene OR 974055507

Call Sign: W7TGX
Carmen M Brambora
2335 Todd St
Eugene OR 974055507

Call Sign: W7GX
John W Brambora
35185 Tohl Ave
Eugene OR 974055507

Call Sign: KD7WBY
Johnnie D Brambora
35325 Tohl Ave
Eugene OR 974055507

Call Sign: KF7BBC
Sergio A Chinchilla
5195 Trevon St
Eugene OR 97402

Call Sign: N7BBC
Sergio A Chinchilla
5144 Trevon St
Eugene OR 97402

Call Sign: KD7WSK
Brandon S Nichols
510 Triller Ln
Eugene OR 97402

Call Sign: KB7YIZ
Sergio A Chinchilla
510 Triller Ln
Eugene OR 97402

Call Sign: KB7FNP
Martin J Bennett
1305 U Ave
Eugene OR 97402

Call Sign: KE7UUQ
Alex Edward Roberts
Weeks
1960 University St

Eugene OR 97403

Call Sign: W9WLB
Alex Edward Roberts
Weeks
3315 University St
Eugene OR 97403

Call Sign: KE7UUN
Jackson C Roberts
3715 University St
Eugene OR 97403

Call Sign: KI7OA
Arthur H Kane
3715 University St
Eugene OR 97405

Call Sign: W7EUG
Lane County Sheriff
Amateur Radio Operators
1651 Upas St
Eugene OR 97405

Call Sign: WJ7R
Ronald E Vincent
323 Upham
Eugene OR 974054347

Call Sign: W0MQJ
Sharon R Mastin
5455 Val View Dr SE
Eugene OR 97401

Call Sign: W0MQJ
Benjamin F Mastin
4148 Valinda Way
Eugene OR 97401

Call Sign: KB7CHP
Robert E Jackson
33022 Van Duyn Rd
Eugene OR 97405

Call Sign: KB3SCJ

Keith D Fritzinger
33022 Van Duyn Rd 52
Eugene OR 97408

Call Sign: N7FAP
Nancy A Cheffings
111 Vancouver Ave
Eugene OR 97408

Call Sign: KD7KOG
Duane L Hatch
1330 Vanderbeck Ln
Eugene OR 97401

Call Sign: N6HJI
Thomas Parker
4856 Ventura Lp N
Eugene OR 97405

Call Sign: WA7JTX
Marvin M Jeffcoat
6908 Verda Vista Pl
Eugene OR 97404

Call Sign: W1CAP
Steven A Senderling
2595 Victory Ln
Eugene OR 974044079

Call Sign: AE7PL
Steven J Webster
2115 View Ct
Eugene OR 97405

Call Sign: W7AAR
Steven J Webster
19515 View Dr
Eugene OR 97405

Call Sign: WA7YNN
Ray R Berkey
1783 View St
Eugene OR 97405

Call Sign: N7GLO

Michael V Hoffman
2075 Villard St
Eugene OR 97403

Call Sign: KC7END
Patricia S Roach
10855 Vincent Dr
Eugene OR 97403

Call Sign: NG7E
Buford I Roach
1633 Vincent Ln
Eugene OR 97403

Call Sign: N7JI
Scott R Rosenfeld
306 Vine St
Eugene OR 97405

Call Sign: KB7YZD
Eugene L Nichols Jr
2021 Violet Ave NE
Eugene OR 97408

Call Sign: KC7DPZ
Fernandita T Nichols
5600 Violet Dr
Eugene OR 97408

Call Sign: KB7LOK
Johannes P Marquardt
1997 Virginia Ln
Eugene OR 97404

Call Sign: KD7PR
James C Thurmond
1034 W 10th Ave
Eugene OR 97402

Call Sign: KD4FWG
Tyler S Stewart
388 W 10th Ave
Eugene OR 97401

Call Sign: KE7MDZ

Brandon T Davidson
658 W 11th Alley
Eugene OR 97402

Call Sign: KD7QPC
Andrew W Wilson
1445 5 W 11th Ave
Eugene OR 97402

Call Sign: KB7YPG
Marcela D Leal
2104 W 12th St
Eugene OR 97402

Call Sign: WA7QJC
Jerry C Mohler
1208 W 13th
Eugene OR 97402

Call Sign: W7PGB
Frazier F Davidson Jr
1875 5 W 14th St
Eugene OR 97402

Call Sign: K7YNB
Harris L Lipsit
3079 W 15th Ave
Eugene OR 97401

Call Sign: WB5YMS
Michael W Steene
3295 W 15th Ave
Eugene OR 97402

Call Sign: KF7EFP
Perry L Mcgill
3088 W 15th Ave 32
Eugene OR 97402

Call Sign: KC7PZG
Sheryl A Hart
1160 W 15th L4
Eugene OR 97402

Call Sign: KB7RBG

Paul J Wold
77 W 16th Ave
Eugene OR 97402

Call Sign: KD7CHM
Dean J Hill
3377 W 16th Ave
Eugene OR 97402

Call Sign: KD7NFE
D Stephen Pickering
1325 5 W 16th Ave
Eugene OR 97402

Call Sign: AB9AK
Jonathan W Day
618 W 17th
Eugene OR 97401

Call Sign: KB7OPI
Rachel E Kidd
2040 W 17th Ave
Eugene OR 97402

Call Sign: N7WJH
Joseph A Kidd
3782 W 18 Ave
Eugene OR 97402

Call Sign: KB7LWE
Michael A Bagaason
3324 W 18th
Eugene OR 97402

Call Sign: W6CKH
C Kent Helwig
3620 W 18th Apt 4
Eugene OR 97402

Call Sign: W7CSB
C Kent Helwig
3620 W 18th Apt 4
Eugene OR 97402

Call Sign: W7OSS

Edwin W Mc Ardle
1945 W 18th Ave
Eugene OR 97402

Call Sign: AA7CC
James C Fleck
880 W 19th
Eugene OR 97402

Call Sign: N7XIX
Howard E Snortland
965 W 19th
Eugene OR 97402

Call Sign: AA7Y
Donald A Moser
695 W 21st Ave
Eugene OR 97405

Call Sign: KA7FZF
Carla S Moser
695 W 21st Ave
Eugene OR 97405

Call Sign: KC7FWV
Melanie R Moser
695 W 21st Ave
Eugene OR 97405

Call Sign: KF7MHJ
John M Shorack
695 W 21st Ave
Eugene OR 97405

Call Sign: N7RWB
Craig D Cherry
835 W 22nd Ave
Eugene OR 97405

Call Sign: KE7GMI
Steven N Shegedin
1955 W 22nd Ave
Eugene OR 97405

Call Sign: N7STS

Steven N Shegedin
1955 W 22nd Ave
Eugene OR 97405

Call Sign: KD7DYP
Stephanie A Barker
483 W 23rd Ave
Eugene OR 97405

Call Sign: KE6DJ
Russell Olsen
848 W 23rd Ave
Eugene OR 97405

Call Sign: KE7SLX
Lester N Garwood
2525 W 23rd Ave
Eugene OR 97405

Call Sign: KE7SLT
Sylvia Sycamore
68 W 25th Ave
Eugene OR 97405

Call Sign: KA7VCG
Lewis R Johnson
2015 W 25th Ave
Eugene OR 97405

Call Sign: N7IOW
James S Hance
730 W 25th Ave
Eugene OR 97405

Call Sign: AE7IY
Russell J Mitchell
2227 W 25th Pl
Eugene OR 97405

Call Sign: KD7ABF
Alan B Mc Neill
2210 W 27th Ave
Eugene OR 97405

Call Sign: N7ICK

Steven L Myers
2240 W 27th Ave
Eugene OR 97405

Frederick A Leser Jr
60 W 35th Ave
Eugene OR 97405

Larry L Kirkpatrick
4030 W Amazon
Eugene OR 97405

Call Sign: KB7ZXE
Karen D Myers
2240 W 27th Ave
Eugene OR 97405

Call Sign: WA7QPC
Michael R Piper
205 W 36th Ave
Eugene OR 974055108

Call Sign: KD7OON
Stephen D Reinken
4730 W Amazon Dr
Eugene OR 97405

Call Sign: WB7SEO
Charles E Hallin
1105 W 28th Ave
Eugene OR 97405

Call Sign: W7EXB
William R Riley
863 W 38th Ave
Eugene OR 97405

Call Sign: KC7HZA
Randall B Phillips
669 W Broadway
Eugene OR 97402

Call Sign: WB7SEP
Ethel J Hallin
1105 W 28th Ave
Eugene OR 97405

Call Sign: W7SBS
Amy L Riley
863 W 38th Ave
Eugene OR 97405

Call Sign: KE7IGU
Paul D Shegedin
251 W Broadway Apt 231
Eugene OR 97401

Call Sign: K7QKD
Alfred R Strassmaier
2290 W 28th Ave
Eugene OR 97405

Call Sign: KF7PEO
Wesley T Mccomb
1392 W 5th Ave
Eugene OR 97402

Call Sign: N5WLW
Stuart G Spurgeon
377 W Eighth Ave Apt 312
Eugene OR 974018337

Call Sign: KF7FGE
Wade T Cline
2030 W 29th Ave
Eugene OR 97405

Call Sign: KD7YDI
Gailord D Hamit
871 W 5th Ave 2
Eugene OR 97402

Call Sign: WB7OLW
Philip S Summers
129 W Hilliard Ln
Eugene OR 974043058

Call Sign: W7UVU
William W Kingsley
74 W 29th Ave Apt 1206
Eugene OR 974053292

Call Sign: KA3LLX
Cyndi Marsico
1117A W 6th Ave
Eugene OR 97402

Call Sign: K7OLW
Philip S Summers
129 W Hilliard Ln
Eugene OR 974043058

Call Sign: KF4DQR
Frederick A Leser Jr
60 W 35th Ave
Eugene OR 97405

Call Sign: KB7PSR
Robert A Clark
1105 W 6th Ave Apt B
Eugene OR 97402

Call Sign: KD7WKZ
Heechun Kang
4175 Wagner St 431
Eugene OR 97402

Call Sign: KE7POW
Frederick A Leser Jr
60 W 35th Ave
Eugene OR 97405

Call Sign: W7YMS
Michael W Steene
265 W 8th Ave Apt 411
Eugene OR 97401

Call Sign: KF6LWV
William H Condron
5494 Wales Dr
Eugene OR 97402

Call Sign: K7FAL

Call Sign: KA7DQG

Call Sign: N7NU

Lee P Hallin
3413 Walton Ln
Eugene OR 974084673

Call Sign: KD6LRV
Sean P Donovan
2771 Warren St
Eugene OR 97405

Call Sign: N2UFD
Seth Cohn
39 Washington St
Eugene OR 97401

Call Sign: KD7GTN
Patrick A Thies
875 Washington St 29
Eugene OR 97401

Call Sign: KD7NCA
Mi-Cree-Ni Quash Mah
3835 Watkins Ln
Eugene OR 97405

Call Sign: K7YDI
George E Warner
4795 Wendover
Eugene OR 97404

Call Sign: KC7DYA
Cheryl M Meeker
3584 Westleigh St
Eugene OR 97405

Call Sign: WA7SVU
James E Howells
3575 Westward Ho
Eugene OR 97401

Call Sign: WA7SVV
Carolyn L Howells
3575 Westward Ho
Eugene OR 974015882

Call Sign: KF7ZN

Ronald C Wilcox
3593 Westward Ho
Eugene OR 97401

Call Sign: KD7JGM
Gordon D Melton
10391 Wheatland Rd
Eugene OR 97408

Call Sign: WB7AOC
Glenn L Gwinn
40 Wilkes Dr
Eugene OR 97404

Call Sign: KE7ICX
Thomas E Musselwhite
419 Wilkie St
Eugene OR 97402

Call Sign: KC5JJP
Mark W Dau
1232 Willagillespie Rd
Eugene OR 974011824

Call Sign: AC5DN
Cheryl L Dau
1232 Willagillespie Rd
Eugene OR 97401

Call Sign: K0ECA
Wilburn P Hampton
2440 Willakenzie Rd Apt
127
Eugene OR 97401

Call Sign: KB7DHJ
Jan A Gibbens
2936 Willamette 14
Eugene OR 97405

Call Sign: KE7HND
Jonathan M Feldman
1430 Willamette 306
Eugene OR 97401

Call Sign: KD7KVL
Jana I Bartell
2852 Willamette Ave 265
Eugene OR 97405

Call Sign: N7WEZ
Renee L Sweatt
1430 Willamette St 2
Eugene OR 97401

Call Sign: N7WFA
Dale R Myers
1430 Willamette St 2
Eugene OR 974014073

Call Sign: AA7CU
Allan R Hills
1430 Willamette St 419
Eugene OR 97401

Call Sign: KF7IMC
Dale Offet
1430 Willamette St Ste 127
Eugene OR 97401

Call Sign: KC7RDP
Suzanne M Robbins
4389 Willhi St
Eugene OR 97402

Call Sign: N7QGZ
William J Robbins
4389 Willhi St
Eugene OR 97402

Call Sign: K7DKV
Suzanne M Robbins
4389 Willhi St
Eugene OR 97402

Call Sign: KE7ISU
Rodney M Lewis
958 Williams St
Eugene OR 97402

Call Sign: K7XPS
Rodney M Lewis
958 Williams St
Eugene OR 97402

Call Sign: KB7ZWA
Kenneth M Smith
4120 Willki St
Eugene OR 97402

Call Sign: KE6YM
James J Mackin Jr
2317 Willona Park
Eugene OR 97408

Call Sign: N7ISZ
Stephen R Darby
820 Willow Ave
Eugene OR 97404

Call Sign: KC7OM
Roy Earhart
2655 Wilshire Dr
Eugene OR 97405

Call Sign: KE7TIO
Larry L Canpbell
2435 Wilson Dr
Eugene OR 97405

Call Sign: KF7KUA
Charlie V Fernandez
3347 Wintercreek Ct
Eugene OR 97405

Call Sign: W6SKI
Kenneth A Check
3084 Wintercreek Dr
Eugene OR 97405

Call Sign: K7ZL
Thomas S Trent
2248 Wisconsin St
Eugene OR 97402

Call Sign: WN7K
Curtis G Chezem
3378 Wisteria St
Eugene OR 974045930

Call Sign: KA7OWW
Mark A Nasholm
2650 York St
Eugene OR 97404

Call Sign: N6VNU
James A Black
3374 Zane Ln
Eugene OR 97404

Call Sign: KE7CWL
Richard S Mason Jr
3388 Zane Ln
Eugene OR 97404

Call Sign: N7BXO
Chris J Heck
3191 Zinnia St
Eugene OR 97404

Call Sign: KA4TKL
Gerry C Mc Kinley
Eugene OR 97401

Call Sign: N7SOJ
James I Elliott
Eugene OR 97402

Call Sign: KB7VIU
Joseph E St Sauver
Eugene OR 97403

Call Sign: KA7MAX
Jervey V Crosby
Eugene OR 97440

Call Sign: KC7ANL
Peter W Nagel
Eugene OR 97440

Call Sign: KG7HO
Stanley L Ulkowski
Eugene OR 97440

Call Sign: N7FIM
Kyle M Anderson
Eugene OR 97440

Call Sign: N7KKN
David S Whitehill
Eugene OR 97440

Call Sign: N7MMO
Philip G Osgood
Eugene OR 97440

Call Sign: N7POT
Joan M Willman
Eugene OR 97440

Call Sign: N7XBU
James N Stowe
Eugene OR 97440

Call Sign: W7JYJ
Laurence H Laitinen
Eugene OR 974030487

Call Sign: K6TOQ
Walter Allen Jr
Eugene OR 97401

Call Sign: KD7SXK
Lane County ARES
Eugene OR 97401

Call Sign: N7EUG
Lane County ARES
Eugene OR 97401

Call Sign: KD7ABO
Ira M Towell
Eugene OR 97401

Call Sign: KD7BMM

Kmtr ARC
Eugene OR 97401

Call Sign: KD7CHL
Colin D Hill
Eugene OR 97401

Call Sign: N7FGF
Johnnie S Bergman
Eugene OR 97401

Call Sign: N7ZWS
Milton E Campbell
Eugene OR 97401

Call Sign: N7JEF
Jeff D Klupenger
Eugene OR 97401

Call Sign: KD7RXB
Bruce L Pedersen
Eugene OR 97401

Call Sign: KD7WSL
Adele O Grimes
Eugene OR 97401

Call Sign: KF7LDD
Brandon D Wheeler
Eugene OR 97401

Call Sign: KD7SQJ
Daniel G Grimes
Eugene OR 97401

Call Sign: KF7SNX
James N Hukill Jr
Eugene OR 97401

Call Sign: K7NEO
James N Hukill Jr
Eugene OR 97401

Call Sign: N7EZG
Linda F Bergman

Eugene OR 97401

Call Sign: KD7SQK
Matthew A Grimes
Eugene OR 97401

Call Sign: KD7TPR
Sheryl T Grimes
Eugene OR 97401

Call Sign: WB7NJO
Gary L Christiance
Eugene OR 97402

Call Sign: KC7DMF
Mark A Johnston
Eugene OR 97402

Call Sign: KC7GTS
Jeffrey L Carns
Eugene OR 97402

Call Sign: KC7OTY
John M Hegg
Eugene OR 97402

Call Sign: KJ7AO
Wendy H Hartman
Eugene OR 97402

Call Sign: N7PLA
Michael D Phillippe
Eugene OR 97402

Call Sign: N7QIE
James F Pelley
Eugene OR 97402

Call Sign: AC7KI
Wendy H Hartman
Eugene OR 97402

Call Sign: KF7SNY
Brian J Jensen
Eugene OR 97402

Call Sign: N7DUK
Brian J Jensen
Eugene OR 97402

Call Sign: KE7LDM
Chris M Cahill
Eugene OR 97402

Call Sign: K7CMC
Chris M Cahill
Eugene OR 97402

Call Sign: KF7IME
Michael E Bastian
Eugene OR 97402

Call Sign: KE7GBO
Thomas R Cleveland
Eugene OR 97402

Call Sign: KF7LQB
Mark I Cameron
Eugene OR 97402

Call Sign: N7NZ
Earl S Gosnell III
Eugene OR 97403

Call Sign: N6ZWU
Pamela K Stewart
Eugene OR 97403

Call Sign: KD7KOH
Karen A Bishop
Eugene OR 97403

Call Sign: KL0BC
Hazel L Shelley
Eugene OR 97404

Call Sign: KD6HTJ
Cathryn L Hunt
Eugene OR 97404

Call Sign: W7RRC
River RC
Eugene OR 97404

Call Sign: KD7RXA
Michael R Fling
Eugene OR 97404

Call Sign: AD7AO
Bruce L Pedersen
Eugene OR 97404

Call Sign: KD7WSJ
Donald E Jacobson Sr
Eugene OR 97404

Call Sign: KD7UJT
J Dezra Johnson Jacobson
Eugene OR 97404

Call Sign: KE7CWF
Michael F Riley
Eugene OR 97404

Call Sign: KA7AOB
Robert Q Burley
Eugene OR 97405

Call Sign: KA7KXL
Mary Y Burley
Eugene OR 97405

Call Sign: KA7OMA
David M Rider
Eugene OR 97405

Call Sign: KA7SDV
Marsha M Walters
Eugene OR 97405

Call Sign: KA7SDW
Robert L Walters Jr
Eugene OR 97405

Call Sign: W6YWI

Marshall S Geller
Eugene OR 97405

Call Sign: KF7MRF
Albert N Capehart
Eugene OR 97405

Call Sign: KE7VLI
Brian L Holmes
Eugene OR 97405

Call Sign: W7BRI
Brian L Holmes
Eugene OR 97405

Call Sign: KC7OJC
Jerry A Daniels
Eugene OR 97440

Call Sign: N7XBW
Doloras Y Stowe
Eugene OR 97440

Call Sign: KB6ZCM
Dennis A Bohlmann
Eugene OR 97440

Call Sign: KD6DFA
George W Nutter
Eugene OR 97440

Call Sign: N6JCE
Michael E Carlson
Eugene OR 97440

Call Sign: N7DOU
David E Heisler
Eugene OR 97440

Call Sign: N7YVA
James B Powell
Eugene OR 97440

Call Sign: WB7QLE
Delbert A Zander

Eugene OR 97440

Call Sign: KD7IKM
Patricia W Sterrett
Eugene OR 97440

Call Sign: KD7NQJ
William Wendell Bateman
Eugene OR 97440

Call Sign: KD7PMI
George W Nutter
Eugene OR 97440

Call Sign: KD7VRT
Barry Stephens
Eugene OR 97440

Call Sign: K7QMB
David E Heisler
Eugene OR 97440

Call Sign: KE7CSS
Michael E Carlson
Eugene OR 97440

Call Sign: K7WWB
William Wendell Bateman
Eugene OR 97440

Call Sign: N5ZR
Thomas S Jakubec
Eugene OR 974020343

Call Sign: WA7NBS
Paul E Compton
Eugene OR 974030537

Call Sign: KK1A
Karl M Fraser
Eugene OR 974040326

Call Sign: KD7IQE
River RC
Eugene OR 974040326

Call Sign: WA2MPG
Sam Jakubec
Eugene OR 974040600

Call Sign: N7IST
Ellwood H Cushman Jr
Eugene OR 974400017

Call Sign: KF6BYO
Christopher B Allen
Eugene OR 974400063

Call Sign: KB7ABA
Clif N Cox
Eugene OR 974401221

Call Sign: KA8TTI
Laura K Williams
Eugene OR 974402006

Call Sign: NI8H
Kevin H Williams
Eugene OR 974402006

Call Sign: KG6UAZ
Robin A Williams
Eugene OR 974402006

Call Sign: KE6SQQ
Robert C Chambers
Eugene OR 974402121

Call Sign: KC7LBK
Donald M Gardner
Eugene OR 974402121

FCC Amateur Radio Licenses in Fall Creek

Call Sign: W7VH
Jonathan A Neher
2683 Kincaid Rd
Fall Creek OR 97438

Call Sign: KF7EOO
Chris M Simmonds
319 Manzanita Dr
Fall Creek OR 97438

Call Sign: W7POW
Chris M Simmonds
1070 Maple Dr
Fall Creek OR 97438

Call Sign: N7LUU
Linda D Mc Cuen
1070 Maple Dr
Fall Creek OR 97438

Call Sign: WG7N
Michael I Mc Cuen
1070 Maple Dr
Fall Creek OR 97438

Call Sign: KB7PSS
Larry M Meyer
7403 Maple Ln
Fall Creek OR 97438

Call Sign: N7UXG
Kenneth B Martwick
38954 Proctor Blvd
Fall Creek OR 97438

Call Sign: KC7EMA
Rene Gruzensky
40306 Winberry Creek Rd
Fall Creek OR 97438

Call Sign: KC7RGP
Michael P Gruzensky
40306 Winberry Creek Rd
Fall Creek OR 97438

Call Sign: N7WNX
Jonathan A Neher
Fall Creek OR 97438

Call Sign: N7HCD

Hilary Dearborn
Fall Creek OR 97438

Call Sign: KE7UOA
Hilary C Dearborn
Fall Creek OR 97438

Call Sign: KF7RSG
John R Baumann
Fall Creek OR 97438

Call Sign: AE7PM
John R Baumann
Fall Creek OR 97438

Call Sign: KD7HAD
Melroy L Urban
Fall Creek OR 974380072

FCC Amateur Radio Licenses in Fields

Call Sign: N6WCT
David M Herman
57735 Whitehorse Ranch Ln
Fields OR 97710

FCC Amateur Radio Licenses in Finn Rock

Call Sign: KB7QDB
Patrick G Campbell
434 Flint St
Finn Rock OR 97488

FCC Amateur Radio Licenses in Florence

Call Sign: KG7YI
Roland M Roesch Jr
1300 2nd Ave 12
Florence OR 97439

Call Sign: KD6TWI

Chris M Mc Donald
1300 2nd Ave 12
Florence OR 97439

Call Sign: W6HVR
Eugene R Koenig
1300 2nd Ave 12
Florence OR 974397700

Call Sign: KF7SXF
Frank T Nulty
9886 33 St
Florence OR 97439

Call Sign: KA7HZB
Phillip A Maggs
31118 4th St
Florence OR 974399714

Call Sign: W7ISO
Laurence L Grimshaw
1855 5th St
Florence OR 97439

Call Sign: WE7J
Merrill L Tibbetts
949 68th St
Florence OR 974399662

Call Sign: KK7OX
Richard F Smith
999 7th Pl
Florence OR 974399022

Call Sign: W7RFS
Richard F Smith
882 7th St
Florence OR 974399022

Call Sign: AD7CE
Richard F Smith
1306 7th St
Florence OR 974399022

Call Sign: KF7SAM

Duane C Mccallister
470 8th Ave
Florence OR 97439

Call Sign: AE7QO
Duane C Mccallister
1698 8th Ave
Florence OR 97439

Call Sign: KM6RE
Dean S Hirst
834 8th St
Florence OR 974398946

Call Sign: KC7FHW
Marjorie A Hirst
2209 8th St
Florence OR 974398946

Call Sign: W6FJP
Richard A Mc Ghee
364 9th St C
Florence OR 97439

Call Sign: KC7BWE
Richard N Whitmore
94483 A St
Florence OR 97439

Call Sign: KC7PFV
Barbara J Whitmore
340 A St 112
Florence OR 974399444

Call Sign: KA6UTC
Lawrence B Bloomfield
808 Adams Ave
Florence OR 974399717

Call Sign: KD7MOP
Christine L Hendrick
2310 Adams Ave
Florence OR 974399717

Call Sign: NN7O

Michael L Hendrick
2675 Adams Ave
Florence OR 974399717

Call Sign: KD7PJN
Kevin M Leasure
5345 Addison Dr S
Florence OR 974399536

Call Sign: KD7OMH
Maureen E Becker
779 Airport Way
Florence OR 974398221

Call Sign: KA7RAM
William A Mason
92085 Akerstedt Rd
Florence OR 97439

Call Sign: K7FR
Gary A Nieborsky
2817 Alameda St
Florence OR 97439

Call Sign: W6ROM
Henry Nieborsky
3115 Alameda St 4
Florence OR 97439

Call Sign: K7FAR
Kathleen J Nieborsky
3062 Alberta Ave NE
Florence OR 97439

Call Sign: KD7LJL
Norman W Creager
22899 Alfalfa Market Rd
Florence OR 974399282

Call Sign: KE7GZV
Charles A Knorr
13856 Alika Dr
Florence OR 97439

Call Sign: K7GZV

Charles A Knorr
13856 Alika Dr NW Makai
Florence OR 97439

Call Sign: N6FSV
George B Land III
1585 Aloha Ct S
Florence OR 974398828

Call Sign: N6FM
Benjamin C Hatheway
25375 Arnold Ln
Florence OR 97439

Call Sign: KE6MEX
Gene R Ross
222 Bain Dr
Florence OR 974398343

Call Sign: KG7KL
Roger D Carlson
633 Bain St SE
Florence OR 974398431

Call Sign: AC7CB
Roger D Carlson
1145 Bair Rd NE
Florence OR 974398431

Call Sign: WA6ASB
James R Wells
1464 Bair Rd NE
Florence OR 97439

Call Sign: N7BCK
Jack L Stalker
19219 Bakerd Rd
Florence OR 97439

Call Sign: KE7GZU
Michael L Myers
Rt 1 Box 126A
Florence OR 97439

Call Sign: KD7LJM

Peter B Walker
215 Boyer Rd
Florence OR 974398634

Call Sign: W0LTN
Raymond H Erickson
1660 Butte Falls Hwy
Florence OR 974398770

Call Sign: N7AHQ
Henry M Rentschler
3030 Crest St
Florence OR 97439

Call Sign: N7NFD
Pat M Rentschler
3214 Crest St
Florence OR 974398304

Call Sign: KC7YON
Kurt C Helphinstine
124 Crest St NE
Florence OR 97439

Call Sign: KF7OPD
James K Garvey
124 Crest St NE
Florence OR 97439

Call Sign: KB6YJR
Arthur F Wales
2630 Cresta De Ruta
Florence OR 974398409

Call Sign: AA7MG
Robert E Kutsch
2630 Cresta De Ruta
Florence OR 974398414

Call Sign: NF6Z
James N Welty
61000 Crown Villa Sp 363
Florence OR 97439

Call Sign: WK7Z

James N Welty
17345 Crownview Dr
Florence OR 97439

Call Sign: KE7OIL
Norma L Welty
672 Crowson Rd
Florence OR 97439

Call Sign: K7RDJ
Shirley G Mazziotti
4080 Cunningham Mhp
Florence OR 97439

Call Sign: K7RDK
Robert L Mazziotti
37181 Cunningham Rd
Florence OR 97439

Call Sign: KF7IYH
Andrew R Dewberry
550 E Jones Creek Rd
Florence OR 97439

Call Sign: KF7IYG
Dylan C Dewberry
54967 E Kirkwood Dr
Florence OR 97439

Call Sign: KF7IYI
Thomas C Dewberry
2623 E Konie Ln S
Florence OR 97439

Call Sign: K6GDO
Alfred C Prien
968 E Yates Rd
Florence OR 974398768

Call Sign: N7VJT
Raymond L Pitts
2074 Goldfinch Ave
Florence OR 97439

Call Sign: KC7BWL

Percy Bernstein
30111 Goldfinch Dr
Florence OR 97439

Call Sign: KC7RC
Roman C Smith
2727 Hartley Ln
Florence OR 97439

Call Sign: KC7DVX
Helen A Swenson
512 Havencrest Ct
Florence OR 97439

Call Sign: WA7SMZ
George W De Stafeno
6017 Homedale Rd
Florence OR 97439

Call Sign: W6EZB
James E Smith
512 Humberd Ln
Florence OR 974399102

Call Sign: KD7PJM
Kevin C Barron
24048 Hwy 20
Florence OR 974398622

Call Sign: W7FZG
Walter C Bugher
820 Jackson Ct
Florence OR 97439

Call Sign: N5HMG
Richard L Stocking II
150 Jackson St
Florence OR 97439

Call Sign: AD7T
Wilbert L Lane
406 Jackson St
Florence OR 97439

Call Sign: KC7INX

Dorothea J Grimshaw
1610 Jackson St SE
Florence OR 97439

Call Sign: N6IDT
William J Collins
4311 Kampstra SE
Florence OR 97439

Call Sign: KF7SXE
Pamela J Franklin
86 Kingsgate Rd A102
Florence OR 97439

Call Sign: KE7MYL
Richard C Franklin
26605 Kingsley Rd
Florence OR 97439

Call Sign: N7RCF
Richard C Franklin
26605 Kingsley Rd
Florence OR 97439

Call Sign: K7JQB
Darrel L Riechel
543 Kingwood Dr NW
Florence OR 97439

Call Sign: KF7BIW
Norman G Mendonca
66865 Lance Rd
Florence OR 97439

Call Sign: K1WZ
Walter W Zandi
3612 Landis St
Florence OR 97439

Call Sign: AA7GJ
Dennis L Ellexson
18926 Landmark St
Florence OR 97439

Call Sign: W6QJU

Robert F Martin
145574 Lanewood Dr
Florence OR 97439

Call Sign: KA7IHL
Melvyn D Tompkins
91028 Leashore Dr
Florence OR 97439

Call Sign: KA7IMT
Edna M Tompkins
520 Leasure St
Florence OR 97439

Call Sign: K7NNK
Robert A Mead
2370 Lee St SE
Florence OR 974399414

Call Sign: N7TYC
Gwen N Meyers
1400 Lewis
Florence OR 97439

Call Sign: W7KHE
Cy Meyers
975 Lewis 4
Florence OR 974398726

Call Sign: KF7SXG
Gregory M Freeze
1602 Linden Ave
Florence OR 97439

Call Sign: WD6ART
Oscar W Larson
7966 Little Falls Ct
Florence OR 974398446

Call Sign: K6VYE
Harry C Goodwater
261 Loto St Apt 11
Florence OR 974399415

Call Sign: AA6H

Augustine H Gray Jr
51405 Mac Ct
Florence OR 97439

Call Sign: KD7ACZ
Clarence A Martell
1948 Madison St
Florence OR 97408

Call Sign: KD7VDB
Jimmy J Scott
373 Majestic Dr
Florence OR 974398937

Call Sign: WW7CC
Farm Animal Contest Club
92074 Maki Rd
Florence OR 97439

Call Sign: KA0CLN
Henry R Caudle
2509 Malarkey Dr
Florence OR 97439

Call Sign: N7SUF
Donald G Strech
33097 Malarkey Ln
Florence OR 97439

Call Sign: WD6ATZ
James R Glab
155 Melvin Ave
Florence OR 97439

Call Sign: KB6WUP
Wolfgang F Merting
4405 Memorie Ln
Florence OR 974399274

Call Sign: KB7PQX
James P Welborn
3434 Meryvale Rd
Florence OR 97439

Call Sign: KB7AGF

Marvin E Tipler
17769 Mt Angel Scotts
Mills Rd NE
Florence OR 97439

Call Sign: W7BNT
Alfred E Owens
512 N 32nd St
Florence OR 97439

Call Sign: N7TOF
James P Mattes
2726 N Davis Ct Unit D
Florence OR 97439

Call Sign: N7ZHK
Sandra L Mattes
1670 N Davis St
Florence OR 97439

Call Sign: N8ZHI
Russell J Petersen
1844 N Davis St
Florence OR 97439

Call Sign: KC7FWL
Bob J Lerman Sr
1170 N Dean St
Florence OR 974399278

Call Sign: KC7OEJ
Audrey G Lerman
7629 N Decator
Florence OR 974399278

Call Sign: K7BIP
Gary W Seidel
353 N Deerlane Dr
Florence OR 974399294

Call Sign: W7HKB
Claud A Eldridge
6210 N Delaware
Florence OR 97439

Call Sign: KC7BWM
Harold J Adams
7155 N Delaware Ave
Florence OR 97439

Call Sign: WA7ZOJ
Leonard E Harris
7945 N Dwight
Florence OR 97439

Call Sign: KC7AGJ
Joan R Palmer
7225 N Fowler Ave
Florence OR 974399759

Call Sign: K6UAV
William G Weathers
141B N State St Ste 115
Florence OR 97439

Call Sign: KA7YQV
Donald B Large
7420 N Stockton
Florence OR 97439

Call Sign: KF7WV
Verne P Broome
5933 N Superior St
Florence OR 97439

Call Sign: KA6LXO
Susan C Weathers
7427 N Syracuse St
Florence OR 97439

Call Sign: N7DQH
Vernon T Woods
935 NE 11th St
Florence OR 97439

Call Sign: W7KUU
Elmer W Lyttle
935 NE 11th St
Florence OR 97439

Call Sign: KB7PBM
Marguerite H Woods
1098 NE 11th St
Florence OR 97439

Call Sign: NA7N
Andrew T Nordahl
1515 NW 137th Av
Florence OR 97439

Call Sign: W7RMD
Renee M Dickerson
2256 Orchard Ave
Florence OR 97439

Call Sign: KC7YOM
William F Githens
3171 NE 11th Way
Florence OR 97439

Call Sign: KD7QOC
Sean R Hermany
364 NW 16th St
Florence OR 97439

Call Sign: KJ7ZZ
David M Lynch
558 Phoenix Ave SE
Florence OR 97439

Call Sign: KE7GZQ
C Jon Kiiskinen
1608 NE 120
Florence OR 97439

Call Sign: KE7LKV
Richard H Holcombe
659 NW 170th Dr
Florence OR 97439

Call Sign: K6ZBA
Warren P Grant
14581 Pine Creek Ln
Florence OR 97439

Call Sign: K8OLS
C Jon Kiiskinen
3404 NE 120th
Florence OR 97439

Call Sign: WB7EZY
Richard H Holcombe
659 NW 170th Dr
Florence OR 97439

Call Sign: KC7INY
Nolan W Korando
3 Pinecrest Dr Blk Lot 2
Florence OR 974399415

Call Sign: N7FMJ
Taylor Young
1608 NE 120th Ave
Florence OR 974399376

Call Sign: K7BHB
Bruce H Bjerke
1735 NW 173rd Ave
Florence OR 97439

Call Sign: N7SBE
Kenneth A Henson
15617 Pkwy Dr
Florence OR 97439

Call Sign: KB7JJO
Gilbert G De Guerre
2009 NE 121st Ave
Florence OR 974397350

Call Sign: W7DJE
David R Crawford
3987 Orcchard Hills Rd
Florence OR 97439

Call Sign: N7TXJ
Holger Theobalt
190 Polaris Cir
Florence OR 97439

Call Sign: KC7BWF
Lorraine H Valentine
1433 NE 12th Ave
Florence OR 97439

Call Sign: KB7RND
Wayne L Lambeth
1678 Orchard
Florence OR 97439

Call Sign: KC7UFD
Ray A Marsh
4100 Post Canyon Dr
Florence OR 974398932

Call Sign: KC7EAC
Vera L Broome
3141 NE 148th Av Apt 215
Florence OR 974398907

Call Sign: KF7SXH
Marcus J Fletcher
1952 Orchard Ave
Florence OR 97439

Call Sign: KD6YNB
Jules A Bilodeau
3060 Powell
Florence OR 974399234

Call Sign: AC7KG
Edgar D De Remer
1101 NE 19th Ct
Florence OR 97439

Call Sign: KF7BIU
Renee M Dickerson
2220 Orchard Ave
Florence OR 97439

Call Sign: AC7ZU
John D Tucker
2330 Ranch Rd
Florence OR 97439

Call Sign: WB6FAK
John D Tucker
18671 Ranch Rd
Florence OR 97439

Call Sign: KB7SLL
Andrew J Dorchester
4343 Rivercrest Dr N
Florence OR 97439

Call Sign: WA7YAE
William G Sadler
4343 Rivercrest Dr N
Florence OR 97439

Call Sign: W1EST
Cliff H West
4156 Riverdale Rd
Florence OR 97439

Call Sign: KB7VOU
Robert L Githens
3939 Riverdale Rd S
Florence OR 97439

Call Sign: KH6WE
Lloyd F Gebhart
4220 Riverdale Rd S
Florence OR 97439

Call Sign: K6WU
John S Sutton
5628 Riverdale Rd S
Florence OR 97439

Call Sign: WM0K
John L Hunt
16614 Riveredge Rd
Florence OR 97439

Call Sign: WA6HIL
Lawrence F Rains
51355 Riverland Ave
Florence OR 97439

Call Sign: KF7OPA
Ronald E Mccrary
15042 Riverloop Dr
Florence OR 97439

Call Sign: KF7IYE
Kevin L Herbig
15042 Riverloop Dr
Florence OR 97439

Call Sign: KD7KJX
John D Rector
3270 Riverplace Dr
Florence OR 974397349

Call Sign: WA6BVG
Charles D Mc Atee
356 Rivershore Dr
Florence OR 97439

Call Sign: N7JRG
James R Gregg
204 Riverside Ave
Florence OR 97439

Call Sign: N7JKN
Rosemary A Young
125 Riverside Dr
Florence OR 97439

Call Sign: N6ZKV
Darrell A Goularte
710 Riverside Dr
Florence OR 94089

Call Sign: KE7GZS
Dayna M Devlin
710 Riverside Dr
Florence OR 97439

Call Sign: N7OOR
Darrell A Goularte
710 Riverside Dr
Florence OR 97439

Call Sign: KG7ZZ
Henry J Chateau
1105 Riverside Dr
Florence OR 97439

Call Sign: KD7LJN
Jeff D Klupenger
2683 S 11th St
Florence OR 974399723

Call Sign: W7LCG
Charles R Campbell
406 S 26th Ave
Florence OR 97439

Call Sign: K7DOE
Philip R Ensminger
545 S 41st Pl
Florence OR 974398934

Call Sign: N7VRU
Curtis M Suckow
1065 S Pacific Hwy Sp 14
Florence OR 974398531

Call Sign: AC7CC
Curtis M Suckow
1184 S Palmetto Way
Florence OR 974398531

Call Sign: KD7KJR
Yvonne D Suckow
16601 S Pam Dr
Florence OR 974398531

Call Sign: WA6UBJ
Richard E Kibitt
325 S R St
Florence OR 97549

Call Sign: K7KVI
William J Collins
768 S R St
Florence OR 97439

Call Sign: K7TI
Bertram D Smart
753 Scenic Hts Dr SE
Florence OR 97439

Call Sign: KB7QOL
Clara N Snider
92545 Silver Butle Rd
Florence OR 97439

Call Sign: KC7ZQU
Jack L Specht Sr
27645 Snyder Rd 37
Florence OR 97439

Call Sign: KB7VOR
Kenneth V Henderson
39601 Scenic St
Florence OR 97439

Call Sign: N5PWL
Richard C Snider
661 Silver Cr Dr
Florence OR 97439

Call Sign: AB6DA
Rick A Olson
1190 Spruce St NE
Florence OR 97439

Call Sign: W7AKN
Forrest R Huntley
41155 School House Rd
Florence OR 97439

Call Sign: KE7SJI
William J Herbner
661 Silver Creek
Florence OR 97439

Call Sign: N7ZIH
Violet O Huntley
3421 Stark St
Florence OR 97439

Call Sign: KI6NRY
John D Edwards
2375 Scoville Rd
Florence OR 97439

Call Sign: K7BBH
William J Herbner
661 Silver Creek Dr
Florence OR 97439

Call Sign: N7SJG
La Verna M Andrews
3492 Stark St
Florence OR 974399679

Call Sign: KE7JND
Anthony D Zuber
13069 Setera Cir
Florence OR 97439

Call Sign: KD7QOB
John W Compton Jr
661 Silver Creek Dr
Florence OR 974398890

Call Sign: W7RQO
John A Andrews
3492 Stark St
Florence OR 974399679

Call Sign: AD7TJ
Anthony D Zuber
3703 Seutter Pl
Florence OR 97439

Call Sign: KD7UCS
Ellen P Shoun
4830 Silversands St W
Florence OR 974398604

Call Sign: KE7OMX
James B Parsons
3405 SW 106th Ave
Florence OR 97439

Call Sign: KC7CMC
Mario M De Piero
3959 Sheridan 308
Florence OR 97439

Call Sign: KF7OPC
Michael L Gottschalk
6685 Simeon Ct
Florence OR 97439

Call Sign: KE7GZR
Lewis R Leonard
3211 SW 10th Ave Apt 405
Florence OR 97439

Call Sign: KE6PLF
Donald R Hogg
16333 Siletz Hwy
Florence OR 97439

Call Sign: K7KDN
Gary E Thompson
2449 Simpson St SE
Florence OR 97439

Call Sign: KD7PJL
Paul Christensen
323 Upham
Florence OR 974399606

Call Sign: KC7SRS
Wallace A Greth
22011 Siletz Hwy 451
Florence OR 97439

Call Sign: KD7PNZ
Jack L Specht Sr
27645 Snyder Rd
Florence OR 97439

Call Sign: KB7NCK
John T Schaffer
3904 Viewcrest Rd S
Florence OR 97439

Call Sign: KJ7H
Michael L Hendrick
1750 W 43rd St 2
Florence OR 97439

Call Sign: KF7OPB
Albert E Schniepp
873 Western Way
Florence OR 97439

Call Sign: WA7MOE
David L Davis
878 Western Way
Florence OR 97439

Call Sign: KD7KJS
Rochelle E Davis
878 Western Way
Florence OR 974399295

Call Sign: KF7OOZ
John G Martinez
2110 Willow Loop
Florence OR 97439

Call Sign: KE7GZT
Ben W Groesbeck
2329 Willow Loop E
Florence OR 97439

Call Sign: K7BWG
Ben W Groesbeck
2329 Willow Loop E
Florence OR 97439

Call Sign: KF7BIV
Blake E Dornbusch
1250 Yew St
Florence OR 97439

Call Sign: K7KIT
Lester D Brush
1501 Yew St
Florence OR 97439

Call Sign: KA7YWX
Fred A Bower III
Florence OR 97439

Call Sign: KB7FYG
Susan Adamyk
Florence OR 97439

Call Sign: KB7JJP
Patrick J Kirby
Florence OR 97439

Call Sign: KB7YZT
Warren H Scherich
Florence OR 97439

Call Sign: KC4GMO
Jan A Maxwell
Florence OR 97439

Call Sign: KC7BWG
Philip T Smith
Florence OR 97439

Call Sign: KC7BWH
David J Robinson
Florence OR 97439

Call Sign: KI7RX
Joyce M Birkenheier
Florence OR 97439

Call Sign: KI7RY
Walter J Birkenheier II
Florence OR 97439

Call Sign: N7QWL
Jeffrey D Taylor Sr
Florence OR 97439

Call Sign: W7DVU
Stephen F Swan
Florence OR 97439

Call Sign: W7KJO

Charles F Wilcox
Florence OR 97439

Call Sign: WA7VME
Elwin A Moore
Florence OR 97439

Call Sign: W7VWW
Rob T Worley Jr
Florence OR 974390033

Call Sign: W7WPS
William P Sherwood
Florence OR 974390167

Call Sign: K7AAA
Fred A Bower
Florence OR 97439

Call Sign: KA6WAG
Robert M Dorsey
Florence OR 97439

Call Sign: KA7YTC
Bradley J Kneaper
Florence OR 97439

Call Sign: KC7BPA
Cheri A Clark
Florence OR 97439

Call Sign: KC7BWI
Elsie M Moore
Florence OR 97439

Call Sign: KC7JBO
William R Craig
Florence OR 97439

Call Sign: KC7JBP
Paul A Pearson
Florence OR 97439

Call Sign: KC7MFX
Walter E Hodgkins

Florence OR 97439

Call Sign: KC7PFU
Romalee F Sherwood
Florence OR 97439

Call Sign: KN6VH
James R Martin
Florence OR 97439

Call Sign: W7FLO
Oregon Coast Emergency
Repeater Inc
Florence OR 97439

Call Sign: WA6QIN
John W Polese
Florence OR 97439

Call Sign: WB4OJI
Harold D Warrington
Florence OR 97439

Call Sign: W7DXZ
Siuslaw Amateur Radio
Communicators
Florence OR 97439

Call Sign: K6JDZ
Jimmie D Zinn
Florence OR 97439

Call Sign: KD7OMG
Richard L Maury III
Florence OR 97439

Call Sign: W7GAL
Cheryl L Gallup
Florence OR 97439

Call Sign: K7AAT
Edward L Gallup Jr
Florence OR 97439

Call Sign: KE7SJJ

Frank M Miles
Florence OR 97439

Call Sign: K7FMM
Frank M Miles
Florence OR 97439

Call Sign: KE7SJH
Henderikus Rijks Van
Oosten
Florence OR 97439

Call Sign: K7QN
James R Martin
Florence OR 97439

Call Sign: AE7FY
Randy M Scott
Florence OR 97439

Call Sign: W7RVO
Rijks Van Oosten
Florence OR 97439

Call Sign: KE7SJK
Steven R Davis
Florence OR 97439

Call Sign: KF7BIT
Susan M Kneaper
Florence OR 97439

Call Sign: KF7OPI
Tracy W King
Florence OR 97439

Call Sign: W7ZZZ
William J Horn
Florence OR 97439

Call Sign: KE7SJG
Louise Van Oosten
Florence OR 97639

Call Sign: KB6YJQ

Judith L Wales
Florence OR 974390001

Call Sign: KD7CHU
Bradley M Stone
Florence OR 974390001

Call Sign: W7NW
Cushman ARC
Florence OR 974390002

Call Sign: AK7CL
Christine D Larkin
Florence OR 974390008

Call Sign: AK7ML
Michael E Larkin
Florence OR 974390008

Call Sign: KB7HJU
Calvin J Crowe Jr
Florence OR 974390037

Call Sign: KC7BWK
John M Brejska
Florence OR 974390047

Call Sign: KC7FIQ
Sean P Barrett
Florence OR 974390071

Call Sign: KD7OBO
Christina D Barrett
Florence OR 974390071

Call Sign: KD7IER
Shawn Condley
Florence OR 974390101

Call Sign: KD7VCZ
Alysha K Atkinson
Florence OR 974390105

Call Sign: KD7VDA
Terri L Atkinson

Florence OR 974390105

Call Sign: KD7LJK
John A Carnahan
Florence OR 974390140

Call Sign: KD7KJU
Carol Rm Foster
Florence OR 974390149

Call Sign: KC7PFT
Matthew A Knoke
Florence OR 974390155

Call Sign: KD7KJV
Bruce R Jarvis
Florence OR 974390164

Call Sign: W7VCL
Eugene V Norris
Florence OR 974390168

Call Sign: KD7PJP
Gabriel S Adel
Florence OR 974390168

Call Sign: KD7KJT
Wendy J Barnes
Florence OR 974390176

Call Sign: N7XBH
Bruce H Bjerke
Florence OR 974390178

Call Sign: KE7GZX
Charles L Darrin
Florence OR 974390243

Call Sign: K7CCL
Charles L Darrin
Florence OR 974390243

**FCC Amateur Radio
Licenses in Fort Klamath**

Call Sign: KC7ODF
Brian K Brown
Fort Klamath OR 97626

Call Sign: WB6JKB
Steven K Bailey
Fort Klamath OR 97626

Call Sign: KE7NGU
Dale A Brown
Fort Klamath OR 97626

**FCC Amateur Radio
Licenses in Fort Rock**

Call Sign: KC7CWP
Margaret E Burroughs
624 S 10th St
Fort Rock OR 97735

Call Sign: KB7CVX
Robert C Reed
Fort Rock OR 97735

**FCC Amateur Radio
Licenses in Fossil**

Call Sign: W7EKO
Leonard H Cibulka
18693 Andy Hill Rd
Fossil OR 978300044

Call Sign: WB7OEB
Jon L Fessler
359 Meadow Dr
Fossil OR 97830

Call Sign: KA7GJQ
Harry F Turner
Fossil OR 97830

Call Sign: KC7ZWX
Travis P Ward
Fossil OR 97830

Call Sign: KC7ZYN
Prescilla D Cibulka
Fossil OR 97830

Call Sign: KD7LIV
Valery S Shean
Fossil OR 97830

Call Sign: KF7RGF
David J Horn
Fossil OR 97830

Call Sign: NL7RS
Ed D Pool
Fossil OR 978300523

**FCC Amateur Radio
Licenses in French Lick**

Call Sign: KF7UFT
Carl E Castle
1670 Spruce Dr B
French Lick OR 97432

**FCC Amateur Radio
Licenses in Gilchrist**

Call Sign: WA7JNQ
Beth A Soukup
297 Camp 12 Loop
Gilchrist OR 97737

Call Sign: WA7FTN
Aloysious H Soukup
297 Camp 12 Loop
Gilchrist OR 97737

Call Sign: N7FJD
Steven M Schroll
1490 Grand Ridge Dr
Gilchrist OR 977379705

Call Sign: KA7KUM
Darlene A Dalebout
24920 Grand Ronde Rd

Gilchrist OR 97737

Call Sign: KA7KUO
Stan R Dalebout
712 Grentle Ct
Gilchrist OR 97737

Call Sign: WB7VQM
Le Roy N Dalebout
91 Gresham St
Gilchrist OR 97737

Call Sign: WA7ZRL
Guy D Holmes
Gilchrist OR 97737

**FCC Amateur Radio
Licenses in Glendale**

Call Sign: K6PQM
Michael D Gallagher
88639 Bill Creek Ln
Glendale OR 974420885

Call Sign: W7KO
Kenneth A Broyles
55520 Gross Dr
Glendale OR 974420065

Call Sign: N6GMW
Marcia A Fasy
160 Iron Mountain Blvd
Glendale OR 97442

Call Sign: KB7VWT
Walter P Annack
38135 Marcy St
Glendale OR 97442

Call Sign: KB7YYI
Carole A Dowdy
Glendale OR 97442

Call Sign: KC7GAE
Ronnie D Dowdy

Glendale OR 97442

Call Sign: KD7BDL
Howard J Ramsey
Glendale OR 97442

Call Sign: KE7WVJ
Alan G Day
Glendale OR 97442

Call Sign: KA6OUQ
Harold J Davasher
Glendale OR 974420787

**FCC Amateur Radio
Licenses in Glide**

Call Sign: KD7DPO
Mary Jo Levins
3380 Balsam Dr S
Glide OR 97443

Call Sign: KE7OVN
Hugh M Harbin
78555 Cedar Park Rd
Glide OR 97443

Call Sign: W7OVN
Hugh M Harbin
78555 Cedar Park Rd
Glide OR 97443

Call Sign: KC6CWP
Doris M Rucker
1418 Hemlock St NE
Glide OR 97443

Call Sign: WA6KHG
Jim R Rucker
70772 Hendergart Ln
Glide OR 97443

Call Sign: KF7MHI
Mark Fowler
82317 Maple Rd

Glide OR 97443

Call Sign: KF7MRH
Mark Fowler
733 Maple St
Glide OR 97443

Call Sign: WA7BWT
Bruce W Engelbrecht
3760 Market St NE Pmb420
Glide OR 97443

Call Sign: WB7SKN
Ralph E Harris
4026 N Massachusetts Ave
Glide OR 974439754

Call Sign: N7LOE
Robert E Kohlhoff
2009 NE 148th Pl
Glide OR 97443

Call Sign: WB7NHU
Rudolph W Engelbrecht
4964 Peyton St N
Glide OR 97443

Call Sign: KB3SBP
Ji Y Park
763 SE 130th
Glide OR 97443

Call Sign: KD6DTR
Charles W Herrington
11285 State St NE
Glide OR 97443

Call Sign: KC7HYZ
Kyle J Hill
Glide OR 97443

Call Sign: KC7NVZ
Roy A Goodpasture
Glide OR 97443

Call Sign: KC7YFF
Bill J Miller
Glide OR 97443

Call Sign: KG6EFH
Robert L Kinney
Glide OR 97443

Call Sign: KF7PTI
Kim Blodgett
Glide OR 97443

Call Sign: KC7LBA
David A Lockwood
Glide OR 97443

Call Sign: K7UNB
Harold J Thompson
Glide OR 974430117

FCC Amateur Radio Licenses in Gold Beach

Call Sign: KC7YCP
Franz A Shindler
909 Millview St
Gold Beach OR 97444

Call Sign: KA7AFH
John E Reinke
266 Aldridge Dr N
Gold Beach OR 97444

Call Sign: KC7DEG
Kim R Olin
2410 Arthur Dr
Gold Beach OR 97444

Call Sign: N6VKW
Donald D Kendall
1215 Auburn Ave
Gold Beach OR 97444

Call Sign: KB7BBY
Scott E Brewer

1465 B St NE
Gold Beach OR 97444

Call Sign: KB7JIU
John N Lampos
2274 Brentwood Dr
Gold Beach OR 97444

Call Sign: KD6DHM
Paul D Hollen
3325 Davidson St SE
Gold Beach OR 974440302

Call Sign: KD6DHO
Millicent J Guinn
3760 Davis Dr
Gold Beach OR 974440302

Call Sign: N7UBQ
Rickie B Streeter
32917 Diamond Hill Dr Sp A
Gold Beach OR 97444

Call Sign: KE7MSA
Louis A Hook
195 E A St
Gold Beach OR 97444

Call Sign: AA7NT
Robert T Van Sickler
2140 Hammerle St
Gold Beach OR 97444

Call Sign: N6FPK
Donald D Sleever
937 Helen Ln
Gold Beach OR 974440683

Call Sign: KF7KMV
Haig Kinosian Jr
2317 High St
Gold Beach OR 97444

Call Sign: KB7JGG

Henrietta De Vore
22906 Hwy 36
Gold Beach OR 97444

Call Sign: KJ7H
Albert D De Vore
22939 Hwy 36
Gold Beach OR 97444

Call Sign: K6UKZ
Kent N Graham
23501 Hwy 36
Gold Beach OR 97444

Call Sign: KD7IRX
Michael D Mathis
24753 Hwy 36
Gold Beach OR 97444

Call Sign: KB6PQE
Warren A Kaften
1150 Idlewood Dr
Gold Beach OR 97444

Call Sign: KB6PSU
Joan D Kaften
1150 Idlewood Dr
Gold Beach OR 97444

Call Sign: KF6TXG
James R Powers
1700 Ivy St
Gold Beach OR 97444

Call Sign: W7OPA
Richard W Ossinger
1700 Ivy St Sp 1
Gold Beach OR 97444

Call Sign: KE6QHI
James S Goodison
3350 Kinsrow Ave 202
Gold Beach OR 97444

Call Sign: KB7TMY

Norm D Johnson
3169 Kinsrow Ave Apt 205
Gold Beach OR 97444

Call Sign: KC7AEO
James R Wilson
3169 Kinsrow Ave Apt 205
Gold Beach OR 97444

Call Sign: KD6BJZ
Joan A Goodison
19212 Kiowa Rd
Gold Beach OR 97444

Call Sign: KF7MWX
Robert P Andrew
7732 Macleay Rd SE
Gold Beach OR 97444

Call Sign: KE7PEJ
Ewald Hopfenzitz
1080 N 10 14
Gold Beach OR 97444

Call Sign: KD7DJY
Carole A Hopfenzitz
1960 N 10 St
Gold Beach OR 974449554

Call Sign: N1PEP
Henry G Lustig
622 N 10th
Gold Beach OR 97444

Call Sign: KE7FVP
George Y Tice
1092 N Douglas Ave
Gold Beach OR 97444

Call Sign: KC7YCN
Robert L Mead
1943 NE Derek Dr
Gold Beach OR 97444

Call Sign: K6EMS

Verdery M Chester
455 NE Quimby Ave 301
Gold Beach OR 97444

Call Sign: K7GF
Douglas E Yoes
184 NW 10th Ave
Gold Beach OR 97444

Call Sign: KD7SYP
Paul Kenis
625 NW 167th Ave
Gold Beach OR 97444

Call Sign: KB7PNP
Jerilyn L Allemand
1315 Oregon St
Gold Beach OR 97444

Call Sign: KE7BDR
Greg A Hood
1840 Paradise Ridge Rd
Gold Beach OR 97444

Call Sign: W7PXX
Alfred A Allworth
1008 Parallel
Gold Beach OR 974449541

Call Sign: KC6SYX
Joyce L Mathis
1325 Perrydale Rd
Gold Beach OR 97444

Call Sign: KD7IZH
Richard A Mathis
8570 Perrydale Rd
Gold Beach OR 97444

Call Sign: N6XMN
Richard A Mathis
15088 Persimmon Way
Gold Beach OR 97444

Call Sign: KC7JJK

Robert B Pinkel
4826 SE 113th
Gold Beach OR 97444

Call Sign: KE7NUP
Bobbi Jones
4826 SE 113th
Gold Beach OR 97444

Call Sign: KF7NTJ
Douglas E Yoes
780 Sheraton Dr
Gold Beach OR 97444

Call Sign: K7ALX
John F Campbell
702 Stark St A
Gold Beach OR 97444

Call Sign: KC7DEI
Alvin G Hyde
5181 Starlit Ct
Gold Beach OR 97444

Call Sign: K6EFT
Frederick E Hempt
3150 SW 108th St
Gold Beach OR 97444

Call Sign: KB6UPC
Brian J Morley
1864 Thomas 4
Gold Beach OR 97444

Call Sign: N6NPA
Glen D Bales
893 Timber Pine Pl
Gold Beach OR 97444

Call Sign: KB7JEZ
Stone M Snider
57401 Timber Rd
Gold Beach OR 97444

Call Sign: N7NBF

Jill C Peters
113 Tom Wayne Ln
Gold Beach OR 97444

Call Sign: KB7JGH
Larry J Olsen
1265 Tutuilla Rd
Gold Beach OR 97444

Call Sign: KA6UNC
Richard P Belz
1265 Tutuilla Rd
Gold Beach OR 97444

Call Sign: N7JQP
Alvin D Ferry
1536 Vera Dr
Gold Beach OR 97444

Call Sign: K7YJL
Robert L Brownell
300 Walker Ct
Gold Beach OR 97444

Call Sign: KB7JGI
Joel M Kuper
Gold Beach OR 97444

Call Sign: KB7YPJ
John J Theis Jr
Gold Beach OR 97444

Call Sign: K7WIC
Don E Brewer
Gold Beach OR 97444

Call Sign: N7BMD
Berna G Oliver
Gold Beach OR 97444

Call Sign: K7SEG
Wally K Blackburn
Gold Beach OR 97444

Call Sign: K7QCN

Mary Louise Knottingham
Gold Beach OR 97444

Call Sign: KA7GNK
Darwin L Rasmussen
Gold Beach OR 97444

Call Sign: KC7QOY
Betty J Gibson
Gold Beach OR 97444

Call Sign: KC7QOZ
Pandora B Gibson
Gold Beach OR 97444

Call Sign: KC7QZY
Robert L Gibson
Gold Beach OR 97444

Call Sign: KC7RAC
Silviu Nedea
Gold Beach OR 97444

Call Sign: KC7ULP
Larry D Adcock
Gold Beach OR 97444

Call Sign: KF6DBK
George M Mc Bride
Gold Beach OR 97444

Call Sign: WA6PKM
William P Henry
Gold Beach OR 97444

Call Sign: KD7YNN
Alan P Mc Guiness
Gold Beach OR 97444

Call Sign: W1NDY
Alan P Mc Guiness
Gold Beach OR 97444

Call Sign: KF7AXV
Frederick P Wright

Gold Beach OR 97444

Call Sign: KE7KEB
John S Truesdell II
Gold Beach OR 97444

Call Sign: K5EN
Richard D Mallery Jr
Gold Beach OR 974440416

Call Sign: KE7UX
Michael L Sinclair
Gold Beach OR 974440690

Call Sign: W6TSL
John D Bailes
Gold Beach OR 974440865

FCC Amateur Radio Licenses in Gold Hill

Call Sign: KA6JMI
Patricia E Claeys
1775 Adkins St 3
Gold Hill OR 97525

Call Sign: N6CPV
Kenneth J Claeys
34124 Adler Ln
Gold Hill OR 97525

Call Sign: K7HVC
Bernardine E Mc Connell
3248 Admiral St
Gold Hill OR 97525

Call Sign: KF7VZ
Richard J Arens
60033 Agate Rd
Gold Hill OR 97525

Call Sign: KB7COZ
Jerry S Parker
4352 Altamont Dr
Gold Hill OR 97525

Call Sign: W7RGN
Gearald L Way
3100 H St
Gold Hill OR 97525

Call Sign: KB7WRQ
Fred M Pierce
16571 Hwy 62
Gold Hill OR 97525

Call Sign: K7DQL
Richard R Zediker
4456 Janice Ave NE
Gold Hill OR 97525

Call Sign: KK7NC
Virgil L Crawford
4456 Janice Ave NE
Gold Hill OR 97525

Call Sign: KA7HTO
Earlene M Schlosser
4596 Janice Ave NE
Gold Hill OR 97525

Call Sign: KE7NCR
Grace E Adams
436 Jerome Ave
Gold Hill OR 97525

Call Sign: KB7WRH
Michael R Moore
5435 Lockford Dr
Gold Hill OR 97525

Call Sign: KC7WAT
Marilyn M Moore
377 Locust Ave
Gold Hill OR 97525

Call Sign: KB2EVN
Ludwell A Sibley
40401 Mohawk River Rd
Gold Hill OR 975259626

Call Sign: WA7NVL
Thomas M May
350 Mona Way
Gold Hill OR 97525

Call Sign: K6SSA
Stanley G Clark
845 Pittview Ave
Gold Hill OR 97525

Call Sign: KB7TXI
Claudia L Clark
904 Pittview Ct
Gold Hill OR 97525

Call Sign: N7DJJ
Richard L Ross
1742 S 22 St
Gold Hill OR 97575

Call Sign: KD7BJL
Rickert J Foster
2451 S 2nd Apt 5
Gold Hill OR 97525

Call Sign: KF7HDQ
Anthony L Douglas
27 S 2nd St
Gold Hill OR 97525

Call Sign: KD7DJX
Ida M Foster
2041 S 2nd St Apt A
Gold Hill OR 97525

Call Sign: KE6FDY
John L Felsch
424 S 40th St
Gold Hill OR 97525

Call Sign: KD7TTQ
Karen M Valdes
4720 SE 111th
Gold Hill OR 97525

Call Sign: KD7TTP
Rylan Valdes
237 SE 111th Ave
Gold Hill OR 97525

Call Sign: KA7YZK
David I V Bake
3306 SE 111th Ave
Gold Hill OR 97525

Call Sign: KA7ZFG
Kevin C Bake
1912 SE 112
Gold Hill OR 97525

Call Sign: KA7BPL
John R Ritter
18244 Shady Hollow Way
Gold Hill OR 97525

Call Sign: WB7CEB
Keith W Endsley
Gold Hill OR 97525

Call Sign: K7ALJ
Amy C Messinger
Gold Hill OR 97525

Call Sign: KA7QYY
Jack D Hendrickson
Gold Hill OR 97525

Call Sign: KC7IJR
Edward L Stilwell
Gold Hill OR 97525

Call Sign: W6BIL
William A Wiest
Gold Hill OR 97525

Call Sign: KF7PPZ
Thomas D Roberts
Gold Hill OR 97525

Call Sign: K6CLU
Robert E Leak
1116 27th Ave SE
Grants Pass OR 97527

Call Sign: KK7FW
Mervin L A Scott
2829 B St
Grants Pass OR 97526

Call Sign: KD7HJF
Clive H Boone
39579 Baptist Church Dr
Grants Pass OR 97527

Call Sign: WA6VQP
James R Hendershot
5046 Barger Dr
Grants Pass OR 97527

Call Sign: WA7OKR
Alfred L Surran
5185 Barger Dr
Grants Pass OR 97527

Call Sign: KD7OBS
Radio Design Group ARC
4800 Barger Dr 76
Grants Pass OR 97527

Call Sign: KC7GLW
Jeffrey S Wilcken
615 Beacon Dr
Grants Pass OR 97527

Call Sign: KB6WOT
Wayne W Judd
2106 Beal Rd
Grants Pass OR 97527

Call Sign: W6QWJ
Douglas W Stowe

2106 Beal Rd
Grants Pass OR 975276003

Call Sign: WA6GEM
Judy E Stowe
855 Beall Ln
Grants Pass OR 975276003

Call Sign: WY7K
Mildred D Thompson
479 Berrydale Ave
Grants Pass OR 97526

Call Sign: WA6KTG
William F Reinert
25905 Bixby Rd
Grants Pass OR 97527

Call Sign: KB7POB
Glendolynn H Harmon
25905 Bixby Rd
Grants Pass OR 97527

Call Sign: N7WQ
Thomas D Miller
858 Blackberry Ln
Grants Pass OR 975268291

Call Sign: N6DQP
Simeon T Wright
2276 Blackburn St
Grants Pass OR 97526

Call Sign: W6ASO
Charles L Smith
2331 Blackburn St
Grants Pass OR 97526

Call Sign: W6PDS
Deirdre M Smith
16184 Blackfeather Ln
Grants Pass OR 97526

Call Sign: KC7ADN
Len L Heriman

35960 Bryant Dr
Grants Pass OR 97527

Call Sign: KE7WVD
Shelly D Binkley
7528 Buckhorn Rd
Grants Pass OR 97527

Call Sign: KD7TME
Donald R Schaeffer
4731 Burlwood Lp
Grants Pass OR 97527

Call Sign: N6DFV
Dorothy C Grajeda
20745 Canterbury Ct
Grants Pass OR 97526

Call Sign: KD7HIZ
Laura D Shaffer
2503 Canterbury St
Grants Pass OR 97526

Call Sign: WB6YQP
Steve R Grajeda
2535 Canterbury St
Grants Pass OR 97526

Call Sign: WA7TXO
Warren G Overpack
2693 Canterbury St
Grants Pass OR 97526

Call Sign: KC7BUM
Robert L Williams Jr
775 Canyon Three Rd
Grants Pass OR 97526

Call Sign: N7XNH
Fred W Schotte
90156 Cape Arago Hwy
Grants Pass OR 97527

Call Sign: KF7AQW
Nancy G Miller

1560 Capitol St NE
Grants Pass OR 97527

Call Sign: KE7ATV
Kenneth W Miller
135 Capitola Ct
Grants Pass OR 97527

Call Sign: KC7GNT
Robert A Martin
16029 Carson Ln
Grants Pass OR 97526

Call Sign: KB7TWP
Patrick R Malloy
1318 Cattle Dr
Grants Pass OR 97527

Call Sign: KE6CJW
John L Taylor
8545 Chance Rd
Grants Pass OR 97527

Call Sign: K7RDP
John R Taft
8965 Chance Rd
Grants Pass OR 97527

Call Sign: KD7WIA
Richard J Huttenga
8965 Chance Rd
Grants Pass OR 97527

Call Sign: KF7UKE
James T Santa Maria
1568 Chemeketa St NE
Grants Pass OR 97527

Call Sign: KB7NFY
Sheilah L Mc Crackin
16500 Christmas Valley
Hwy E
Grants Pass OR 97526

Call Sign: WB6LMA

Francis A Mc Crackin
4710 Christopher Ave SE
Grants Pass OR 97526

Call Sign: KB6PVT
Ernest C Branch
1743 Chukar Ct NW
Grants Pass OR 975269394

Call Sign: K6PS
Edward E Austin
2560 Chula Vista
Grants Pass OR 97526

Call Sign: W7BXB
Madeline M Howard
960 Claggett NE
Grants Pass OR 97526

Call Sign: W7JHC
Joseph H Howard
623 Clairmont Ave
Grants Pass OR 97526

Call Sign: N7GCZ
Donald A Hurd
1955 Cleveland
Grants Pass OR 97526

Call Sign: WA7BAG
Robert L Heisler
6519 Climax Ave
Grants Pass OR 97527

Call Sign: KC6ZPY
Alice B Maxwell
6520 Climax Ave
Grants Pass OR 97527

Call Sign: WO7MX
Merle T Maxwell
65175 Cline Falls Rd
Grants Pass OR 97527

Call Sign: KF7UKI

William D Schultz
675 Conrad Ct
Grants Pass OR 97526

Call Sign: K7MNR
William A Townes
2559 Cubit St
Grants Pass OR 97527

Call Sign: KF7OER
Eldon M Coats
2586 Cubit St
Grants Pass OR 97527

Call Sign: KD6IBF
Gladys H Smith
2586 Cubit St
Grants Pass OR 975277900

Call Sign: KB7RNM
Jeffrey J Elseth
555 Danebo 146
Grants Pass OR 97527

Call Sign: KB7TLW
Janet L Elseth
1606 Danebo Ave
Grants Pass OR 97527

Call Sign: WA6HWW
Robert B Billington
96673 De Moss Rd
Grants Pass OR 97526

Call Sign: KD7IUN
James T Mears
2521 Delores Ln
Grants Pass OR 97526

Call Sign: KA7DJC
Edward M Elmer
2268 Donovan Dr
Grants Pass OR 97526

Call Sign: KB7KNC

Nellie M Elmer
673 Donruss Dr
Grants Pass OR 97527

John A Hudick
38650 E Hst Col Rvr Hwy
Grants Pass OR 975279539

Tera L Harley
61255 Ferguson Rd
Grants Pass OR 97527

Call Sign: KD7CCQ
John R Fryer
272 Douglas Rd
Grants Pass OR 95727

Call Sign: WA6WAL
Thomas J Wiley
1530 E Punkin Center Rd
Grants Pass OR 97526

Call Sign: N6FRA
Joseph Reaves
27958 Fern Ridge Rd
Grants Pass OR 97527

Call Sign: KE7EFY
Joshua T Fryer
2044 Dougles
Grants Pass OR 97527

Call Sign: KF6HRF
Mary A Raftery
25222 45 E Welches Rd
Grants Pass OR 97527

Call Sign: W7JOE
Joseph Reaves
27958 Fern Ridge Rd
Grants Pass OR 97527

Call Sign: K6TAQ
George A Kennedy
8333 Duncan Island Rd
Grants Pass OR 975279609

Call Sign: NK6G
Jay L Raftery
25222 45 E Welches Rd
Grants Pass OR 97527

Call Sign: KC7BH
John Ledwidge
17029 Ferrycreek
Grants Pass OR 97526

Call Sign: KC7DNG
Ryan M Jensen
1350 E 1st Ave 26
Grants Pass OR 97527

Call Sign: W7ITZ
Ruth E Booth
25297 E Welches Rd 58
Grants Pass OR 97526

Call Sign: KA7BRN
Juanita A Ledwidge
17029 Ferrycreek
Grants Pass OR 975267728

Call Sign: KD6MV
Curt Henius
1167 E 22nd Ave
Grants Pass OR 97527

Call Sign: KE7WVH
Edward J Diehl
2064 Elmwood Dr S
Grants Pass OR 97526

Call Sign: KE6ZU
Arthur C Smith
1921 Fir Rd Apt 9
Grants Pass OR 97526

Call Sign: KE6EME
Michael V Hepburn
66642 E Bay Rd 50
Grants Pass OR 97527

Call Sign: KA7TNV
Sue James
88628 Ermi Bee Rd
Grants Pass OR 97527

Call Sign: KF6NAX
Christie L M Anderson
420 Floral
Grants Pass OR 97527

Call Sign: KE7NPM
James A Jurney
1375 E Evans Creek Rd
Grants Pass OR 97527

Call Sign: WN7X
Lucy C Bennett
440 Ervin St
Grants Pass OR 975274921

Call Sign: KF6NAY
Roger D Anderson
450 Floral
Grants Pass OR 97527

Call Sign: KF7UMQ
Grant C Mccarty
231 E Grant St
Grants Pass OR 97527

Call Sign: KD7HJB
William J Hoppe
488 Fairway Ct
Grants Pass OR 97527

Call Sign: KD6JJP
John E Shelton
450 Floral
Grants Pass OR 97527

Call Sign: W6XZ

Call Sign: KE7ATT

Call Sign: K7CMV

Lloyd A Stewart
450 Floral Ave
Grants Pass OR 97527

Call Sign: KB7NFX
Matthew P Olson
671 Florence Ave
Grants Pass OR 97527

Call Sign: WB6ODW
George H Baldwin
4531 Franklin Blvd Sp 92
Grants Pass OR 97526

Call Sign: KD7MN
Derald M Lehman
505 Frankton Rd
Grants Pass OR 97527

Call Sign: N7GZY
Suzanne Lehman
66807 Franson Rd
Grants Pass OR 97527

Call Sign: KC7SRN
David P Pierce
1366 Fruitdale Dr Apt B
Grants Pass OR 97526

Call Sign: KD7WHX
Gregory M Wolf
6202 Fruitland Rd NE
Grants Pass OR 97526

Call Sign: KE7ATS
Susan L Wolf
6434 Fruitland Rd NE
Grants Pass OR 97526

Call Sign: N7EEC
Edwin R Heffleger
4204 Ginkgo St
Grants Pass OR 97527

Call Sign: K7PMB

Ralph E Dean
2669 Gloria Dr
Grants Pass OR 97526

Call Sign: AG7Y
Dr Amore
6615 Glyneagle Dr SE
Grants Pass OR 97526

Call Sign: KA7CZG
Franklin R Randall
34830 Goltra Rd SE
Grants Pass OR 97527

Call Sign: KB7TGO
Anna L Randall
4300 Goodpasture Loop 73
Grants Pass OR 97527

Call Sign: W7QZ
Roger L Collins
45434 Goodpasture Rd
Grants Pass OR 97526

Call Sign: N7TSR
Joseph A Tennyson
45945 Goodpasture Rd
Grants Pass OR 97526

Call Sign: AL7HS
Jerry R Swanson
46833 Goodpasture Rd
Grants Pass OR 975264236

Call Sign: KD7KKL
Randy R Panfil
3204 Grand Ave
Grants Pass OR 97527

Call Sign: KD7RUD
Ellen Panfil
1929 Grand Prairie NE
Cottage 3
Grants Pass OR 97527

Call Sign: KC7IBD
James M Latham
506 Granite St
Grants Pass OR 97527

Call Sign: N7XEO
Daniel Lawrence
1665 Grant
Grants Pass OR 97527

Call Sign: WB7BBV
David G Mc Ginnis
305 Grant St
Grants Pass OR 97527

Call Sign: KD7WHY
Brandon G Michaels
770 Greg Way
Grants Pass OR 97528

Call Sign: AD7X
Richard C Malisch
78520 Grouse Creek Ln
Grants Pass OR 97527

Call Sign: W9KNI
Robert C Locher Jr
9362 Hallelujah Dr NE
Grants Pass OR 97526

Call Sign: KE7NPQ
Andrew J Carpenter
2045 Haviland Dr
Grants Pass OR 97527

Call Sign: KD7QZC
Jessica I Reding
1732 Hayes St
Grants Pass OR 97527

Call Sign: KD7QZD
Joe A Reding
1732 Hayes St
Grants Pass OR 97527

Call Sign: KB7CRG
Elizabeth Hubbard
57120 Hazen Rd
Grants Pass OR 97527

Call Sign: KI7MQ
James R Bowles
31908 Henkle Way
Grants Pass OR 97527

Call Sign: KC7MGG
Daniel G Calvert
6017 Homedale Rd
Grants Pass OR 97527

Call Sign: KB7PRG
Sarah M Sampson
57120 Hazen Rd
Grants Pass OR 97527

Call Sign: WD4PWR
James C Pinckard
6757 Henley Rd
Grants Pass OR 97527

Call Sign: N7DG
Donald R Greenwood
573 Homewood Rd
Grants Pass OR 97527

Call Sign: KD7UIJ
Ron E Wright
961 Helen Ln
Grants Pass OR 97526

Call Sign: KD7HJA
Cary D Cound
439 Heywood Ave
Grants Pass OR 97527

Call Sign: W6JLC
John L Cuha
23400 Hopewell Rd NW
Grants Pass OR 97527

Call Sign: KD7NFJ
Justin T Wright
14586 Helen St SE
Grants Pass OR 97526

Call Sign: N7EEP
Jimmie U Grant
1320 Hiatt St
Grants Pass OR 975274422

Call Sign: KA6LQM
Clement L Maitrejean
95295 Horizon Dr
Grants Pass OR 97527

Call Sign: KD7NBO
Leeann Wright
14586 Helen St SE
Grants Pass OR 975267893

Call Sign: AE7DC
Robert L Short
1534 Hilary St SW
Grants Pass OR 97526

Call Sign: KA6LQY
Betty L Maitrejean
95295 Horizon Dr
Grants Pass OR 97527

Call Sign: KC7WEU
Ernest W Sanford
35394 Helligso Ln
Grants Pass OR 97526

Call Sign: KD7OI
Bruce G Godwin
52 Hillshire Dr
Grants Pass OR 97527

Call Sign: KC6NHM
John F Maitrejean
114 Horizon Ln
Grants Pass OR 97527

Call Sign: KD7FCX
Michael L Pierce
8530 Helmick Rd
Grants Pass OR 97526

Call Sign: ND7Y
Perry H Woodward
159 Hillside Ave
Grants Pass OR 97527

Call Sign: WA6EPL
Wayne A Maitrejean
1250 Horizon Ridge Ct NE
Grants Pass OR 97527

Call Sign: KD7IAB
Dently E Wagner
1625 Henderson Ave Sp C 1
Grants Pass OR 97527

Call Sign: KB7SZB
Steven M Lawrence
4441 Homedale Rd
Grants Pass OR 97527

Call Sign: KD7RUC
Andrea D Maitrejean
100 Hornet Ln
Grants Pass OR 975275116

Call Sign: KD7OBW
Margaret M Wagner
3375 Henderson Way
Grants Pass OR 97527

Call Sign: KB7YNB
Fran W Lawrence
6017 Homedale Rd
Grants Pass OR 97527

Call Sign: KA6KID
Andrea D Maitrejean
100 Hornet Ln
Grants Pass OR 975275116

Call Sign: KA6KRM
Martin E Maitrejean
64629 Horseman Ln
Grants Pass OR 97527

Call Sign: KB7CDA
Jason C Yilek
822 Hwy 395 S Pmb 131
Grants Pass OR 97527

Call Sign: K6ZSX
Dail A De Villeneuve
295 Idaho
Grants Pass OR 97526

Call Sign: W7GIW
Gedney Webb
209 Hoyt Ave
Grants Pass OR 97526

Call Sign: K7KO
Stephen W Andrews
93126 Hwy 42 S
Grants Pass OR 97526

Call Sign: KD6NCM
Nancy A Goss
4689 Idaho Ave NE
Grants Pass OR 975279009

Call Sign: KB7TSX
Leonard M Coleman
209 Hoyt Ave
Grants Pass OR 97526

Call Sign: KF7GEI
Lindsey N Short
11013 Hwy 66
Grants Pass OR 97526

Call Sign: WB6KET
Kenneth C Goss
295 Idaho St
Grants Pass OR 975279009

Call Sign: KE7GMV
Laurita G Smith
4534 Hwy 101 N
Grants Pass OR 97527

Call Sign: KB7EGT
Marsha G Randall
12915 Hwy 66
Grants Pass OR 97526

Call Sign: WX7U
William A Tyner
62116 Igo Ln
Grants Pass OR 97527

Call Sign: N7NBE
Carolee F Kime
5580 Hwy 101 N
Grants Pass OR 97527

Call Sign: KC7KYR
Robert L Short
68625 Hwy 82
Grants Pass OR 97526

Call Sign: KD7IYL
Sandra J Tyner
62116 Igo Ln
Grants Pass OR 97527

Call Sign: WB7VMS
Gerald R Kime
7483 Hwy 101 N
Grants Pass OR 97526

Call Sign: KF7ELZ
Robert L Short
68625 Hwy 82
Grants Pass OR 97526

Call Sign: W7LZS
Raymond T Dickerson
1987 Iler St S
Grants Pass OR 97526

Call Sign: KL7FMH
Delavan S Thomas
12309 Hwy 126
Grants Pass OR 97526

Call Sign: KB7RNN
Inger M Baker
4064 Ibex St NE
Grants Pass OR 97527

Call Sign: W7RDG
Radio Design Group ARC
18610 Indian Creek Dr
Grants Pass OR 97527

Call Sign: KA7MUD
Thomas R Bristol
76750 Hwy 37
Grants Pass OR 97526

Call Sign: WB7VEI
Edward L Baker
3833 Ibis St NE
Grants Pass OR 97527

Call Sign: WA6WNB
Arthur R Schmidt
409 Innsbrook Ct SE
Grants Pass OR 97526

Call Sign: WB6CSG
John D Crabtree
18525 Hwy 395
Grants Pass OR 97527

Call Sign: KE7VPO
John B Allen
1725 Icabod Ct NE
Grants Pass OR 97527

Call Sign: KD7HAX
John E Lawler
6184 Insignia Ave
Grants Pass OR 97526

Call Sign: KM6WA
Eric D Griesheimer
1790 Inverness Dr
Grants Pass OR 975269711

Call Sign: KC7FDL
Barclay B Henry
2180 Irene Ct S
Grants Pass OR 97527

Call Sign: KA6NIJ
Janice S Chapek
25381 Irene St
Grants Pass OR 97527

Call Sign: KC7EPI
Victor C Henry
35532 Iris Way
Grants Pass OR 97527

Call Sign: KC7FDK
Sheila L Henry
5875 Irish Ave Tierra Del
Mar
Grants Pass OR 97527

Call Sign: KC7NCP
Benjamin V Henry
6801 Irish Ln
Grants Pass OR 97527

Call Sign: KC7TYS
Janice L Leiken
1309 Jerome Ave
Grants Pass OR 97527

Call Sign: KC7IXX
William I Leiken
2334 Jerry Rd
Grants Pass OR 97527

Call Sign: KF7IBN
Ronald W Wilson
790 Johnson Ave
Grants Pass OR 97527

Call Sign: WA7SPI
Rodney E George
553 Joseph St SE
Grants Pass OR 97527

Call Sign: WB6TVE
Martin A Robb
553 Joseph St SE
Grants Pass OR 97527

Call Sign: WC7AAD
Josephine County Races
Josephine Cty Ch Dept Of
Emg Svc
Grants Pass OR 97526

Call Sign: KF7LVP
Travis L Smith
3050 Kincaid St
Grants Pass OR 97527

Call Sign: N6ZM
Donald H Artru
6120 Lake Labish Rd NE
Grants Pass OR 97526

Call Sign: KB7EKD
Bruce L Casey
1241 Lakeshore Dr
Grants Pass OR 97526

Call Sign: KE7NPL
Julie K Kanta
7947 Lakeside Dr
Grants Pass OR 99526

Call Sign: KA6WYX
Gerald E Fredrickson
25204 Lamb Rd
Grants Pass OR 97527

Call Sign: KD7GBL
Kelly E Schmidt
5182 Lambert Ln SE

Grants Pass OR 97527

Call Sign: AB7DF
John J Berrier Jr
92087 Lampa Ln
Grants Pass OR 975274256

Call Sign: W7MQL
Cyril J Potts
2422 Lampman Rd
Grants Pass OR 97527

Call Sign: W6KVL
John S Ridley
4882 Lancaster Dr NE Unit
123
Grants Pass OR 97527

Call Sign: KL7FLS
Bessie Anna Fillmore
8315 Lardon Rd NE
Grants Pass OR 97527

Call Sign: N7XEP
Barry Dalton
30428 Lassen Ln
Grants Pass OR 97526

Call Sign: KA7PQV
Anthony L Razzolini
2208 Laurel
Grants Pass OR 97526

Call Sign: KD7KFL
Carol L Hendrix
92041 Lewis And Clark Rd
Grants Pass OR 97527

Call Sign: KB7PQZ
Serena M Smith
1005 Lewis Ave 1
Grants Pass OR 97527

Call Sign: N3NYO
David S Trump

155 Lexington Pl
Grants Pass OR 97527

Call Sign: N3NZO
Elaine O Trump
90889 Libby Ln
Grants Pass OR 97527

Call Sign: WB6VJY
Paul J Miller
39893 Little Fall Creek Rd
Grants Pass OR 97526

Call Sign: KD6WWO
Peter P Rist
5328 Lone Fir Ave SE
Grants Pass OR 97526

Call Sign: KG6IA
Edward V Mc Gough
2380 Long St
Grants Pass OR 975275649

Call Sign: KD7QS
Joan B Davis
85898 Lorane Hwy
Grants Pass OR 97526

Call Sign: AE7AS
Paul J Evan
1723 Lytle St
Grants Pass OR 97527

Call Sign: WA7YJD
Carl L Ventrella
1948 Madison St
Grants Pass OR 97527

Call Sign: KB6KIA
Nancy G Hultman
34050 Mallard Ave
Grants Pass OR 97527

Call Sign: N6BJF
Gary W Hultman

664 Mallard Dr
Grants Pass OR 97527

Call Sign: WA7WMH
Charles E Thomas
10109 Marquam Cir
Grants Pass OR 97527

Call Sign: WB6SOH
William D Mc Grath
21004 McCormick Hill Rd
Grants Pass OR 97526

Call Sign: KD6EIR
Wesley W Molsberry
21004 McCormick Hill Rd
Grants Pass OR 97526

Call Sign: KD6ZKB
Christine M Molsberry
21004 McCormick Hill Rd
Grants Pass OR 97526

Call Sign: KE7FH
Don E Jago
21550 McCormick Hill Rd
Grants Pass OR 97526

Call Sign: KE7WVG
Johnny J Campbell
21795 McCormick Hill Rd
Grants Pass OR 97526

Call Sign: KE7MTO
Dale Yellin
1231 Meadowlawn Pl
Grants Pass OR 975278101

Call Sign: K7MSY
Dale Yellin
1231 Meadowlawn Pl
Grants Pass OR 975278101

Call Sign: W7BGN
Bertrand P Hynum

405 Minthorne Rd
Grants Pass OR 97527

Call Sign: K7TMU
William E Butler
405 Minthorne Rd
Grants Pass OR 975275126

Call Sign: AA7ED
Paul Kelly
1750 Morgan Ln
Grants Pass OR 97527

Call Sign: N7LQB
Ingrid M Moller
3750 Morgan Ln
Grants Pass OR 97527

Call Sign: WA6YYC
Eva Moller
2479 Morning Dove NW
Grants Pass OR 97527

Call Sign: KE7WVF
Thomas R Gilliland
2479 Morning Dove NW
Grants Pass OR 97527

Call Sign: W6IKD
John L Shaw
14129 Morning Sun
Grants Pass OR 97526

Call Sign: AB7EJ
Ronald F Pendergrass
431 Mtn Paradise Dr
Grants Pass OR 97526

Call Sign: KC7NCO
Robert L Hummel III
2330 Mule Deer Ct NW
Grants Pass OR 97526

Call Sign: KA7DFO
William S Benton

626 Murphy Cr Rd
Grants Pass OR 97527

Call Sign: K7DFO
William S Benton
340 Murphy Creek Rd
Grants Pass OR 97527

Call Sign: KF7KLJ
Daniel Gillen
1902 Myers Ln
Grants Pass OR 97527

Call Sign: K7UAQ
George D Farrar
270 Myers St S
Grants Pass OR 97527

Call Sign: KE7TFZ
Brian L O'Connor
912 N 4th 14
Grants Pass OR 97526

Call Sign: KK7PPK
Brian L O'Connor
111 N 4th St
Grants Pass OR 97526

Call Sign: KE7RUC
Katherine W O'Connor
114 N 4th St
Grants Pass OR 97526

Call Sign: K7KOC
Katherine W O'Connor
2510 N 4th St
Grants Pass OR 97526

Call Sign: KE7AIZ
Michael F Laughman
204 5 N 8th St
Grants Pass OR 97526

Call Sign: N7PSM
Merlin D Pendray

6845 N A St
Grants Pass OR 97526

Call Sign: N7XTQ
Ethel B Pendray
240 N Adams 2
Grants Pass OR 97526

Call Sign: KD7OBV
Susan M Gino
290 N Adams St
Grants Pass OR 97526

Call Sign: KB7SKC
Brian T Case
2109 N Adams St
Grants Pass OR 97526

Call Sign: AA7WC
Clyde Little Jr
174 N Adeline Way
Grants Pass OR 97526

Call Sign: KA7YZJ
Linda M Hartzell
503 N Alameda
Grants Pass OR 97526

Call Sign: WB6LNU
Carl F Hartzell
3840 N Alaska St
Grants Pass OR 97526

Call Sign: W7KOX
Charles R Cook
3840 N Alaska St
Grants Pass OR 97526

Call Sign: KD7BAI
Michael H Kortmann
3840 N Alaska St
Grants Pass OR 975280142

Call Sign: KI6BWX
Gary L Valentine

2925 N Boones Ferry Rd
Grants Pass OR 97527

Call Sign: K6ZST
Arthur E Godson
9328 N Buchanan Ave
Grants Pass OR 97527

Call Sign: KE6RTP
Carol A Godson
9533 N Buchanan Ave
Grants Pass OR 97527

Call Sign: W7AEG
Arthur E Godson
5602 N Burrage
Grants Pass OR 97527

Call Sign: KA7NCB
William A Meyer
7155 N Delaware Ave
Grants Pass OR 97526

Call Sign: W7FDU
Howard W Shafer
3355 N Delta Hwy 2
Grants Pass OR 97526

Call Sign: KD7RUE
Robert J Langhorn
63588 N Jade Rd
Grants Pass OR 97527

Call Sign: WA7TGA
Roger W Runge
1156 N Jantzen
Grants Pass OR 97527

Call Sign: KA7UWR
Margaret A Sorensen
1893 N Jantzen
Grants Pass OR 97527

Call Sign: N7GYL
Chris E Sorensen

1521 N Jantzen 364
Grants Pass OR 97527

882 NE Baldwin Dr
Grants Pass OR 97526

2495 NE Cleveland Ave
Grants Pass OR 97526

Call Sign: KD7TMD
Jack E Luce
1521 N Jantzen 364
Grants Pass OR 97527

Call Sign: KO6AB
Gerald L Miller Jr
1120 NE Beacon Dr
Grants Pass OR 97526

Call Sign: KD7TTS
John G Chandler
4423 NE Division
Grants Pass OR 97526

Call Sign: KA7QPS
Hugh Boone
11919 N Jantzen 383
Grants Pass OR 97527

Call Sign: N6CEM
Carol E Miller
1891 NE Beacon Dr
Grants Pass OR 97526

Call Sign: KE7DNE
Elizabeth A Larkin
2980 NE Division Sp 9
Grants Pass OR 97526

Call Sign: KB7TSW
Chris K Youngblood
11919 N Jantzen Ave 383
Grants Pass OR 97527

Call Sign: KE7BSO
GpARC
2442 NE Cafe Way
Grants Pass OR 97526

Call Sign: KA7CJI
Marc E Keating
10730 NE Eugene St
Grants Pass OR 97526

Call Sign: KC5CSU
Derald L Stafford
40 NE 199th Ave
Grants Pass OR 97526

Call Sign: N7LFX
Larry J Robinson
939 NE Cedar Ln
Grants Pass OR 97526

Call Sign: KA7PQS
William O Gibson
4402 NE Failing
Grants Pass OR 975262155

Call Sign: KF6BOW
Ned R Goss
1125 NE 201st Ave
Grants Pass OR 97526

Call Sign: KF7FO
Chris A Maitrejean
2209 NE Clackamas St
Grants Pass OR 97526

Call Sign: KF7QDS
Thomas Harris
12925 NE Faircrest Dr
Grants Pass OR 97526

Call Sign: W7IAL
Kurt P Herzog
1500 NE 27th St 74
Grants Pass OR 97526

Call Sign: KK7BF
Brian I Fritsen
2433 NE Clackamas St
Grants Pass OR 975261321

Call Sign: WY7DOT
Thomas Harris
18035 NE Fairview Dr
Grants Pass OR 97526

Call Sign: KB6JZT
Robert G Holcomb
1400 NE 2nd Ave 1704
Grants Pass OR 97526

Call Sign: WA6LQT
James J Dwyer
8720 NE Clackamas St
Grants Pass OR 97526

Call Sign: N7ZWV
Marvin A Johnson
9529 NE Gertz
Grants Pass OR 97526

Call Sign: W7RGH
Robert G Holcomb
1400 NE 2nd Ave Apt 1711
Grants Pass OR 97526

Call Sign: W7CPV
Betty E Hartzig
1115 NE Clark Dr
Grants Pass OR 975262296

Call Sign: KG6IIP
Randel E Livingood
2023 NE Gibbs Cir
Grants Pass OR 975262227

Call Sign: WA6YSM
Steven R Porter

Call Sign: K6BQ
Franklin Kral Sr

Call Sign: KD7JQP
Einar K Devore

224 NE Holiday Ave
Grants Pass OR 97526

Call Sign: KE7CJB
Michael Eagle
3700 NE Hwy 101
Grants Pass OR 97526

Call Sign: KD7PCL
David D Reeves
1801 NE Lotus Dr
Grants Pass OR 97526

Call Sign: K6LU
Southern Oregon Dx Club
4145 NE Multnomah St
Grants Pass OR 97526

Call Sign: K7XU
M Ben Skinner
12412 NE Multnomah St
Grants Pass OR 97526

Call Sign: KD7RUB
Patrick D Mctamany
2010 NE Steele Ave
Grants Pass OR 97526

Call Sign: KE7YLH
Jay M Jones
1941 NE Stephens
Grants Pass OR 97526

Call Sign: N6KCM
John M Knack
2071 NE Stephens L9
Grants Pass OR 97526

Call Sign: KC7CSI
John J Mafrici Jr
9610 NE Wygant St
Grants Pass OR 97526

Call Sign: KC7LVZ
Victor L Phillips

17494 Noakes Rd
Grants Pass OR 97526

Call Sign: KE7KBU
William H Childs
1780 Northview Blvd 112
Grants Pass OR 97526

Call Sign: KG6CPZ
Scott A Hicks
245 NW 11th St C3
Grants Pass OR 97527

Call Sign: KE7IKP
Terry W Mewhinney
2495 NW 121st Pl
Grants Pass OR 97527

Call Sign: KD6HZR
Neal O Appleton
1080 NW 123rd Ave Apt 28
Grants Pass OR 97527

Call Sign: KE7YZU
Josephine County
Emergency
Communications
32849 NW Bella Vista
Grants Pass OR 97526

Call Sign: KD7VOO
Josephine County ARES
1434 NW Benfield Dr
Grants Pass OR 97526

Call Sign: W1LMA
Josephine County ARES
1434 NW Benfield Dr
Grants Pass OR 97526

Call Sign: KD7ZGM
Joco Sar ARES
4888 NW Bethany Blvd 360
Grants Pass OR 97526

Call Sign: KE7AJA
P W ARES
4888 NW Bethany Blvd Ste
K5 156
Grants Pass OR 97526

Call Sign: KE7GVG
Jo Ko ARES
12000 NW Big Fir Cir
Grants Pass OR 97526

Call Sign: KE7AJB
P H ARES
12205 NW Big Fir Cir
Grants Pass OR 97526

Call Sign: KE7AUF
Jcec ARES 1
12305 NW Big Fir Ct
Grants Pass OR 97526

Call Sign: KE7AUG
Jcec ARES 2
12305 NW Big Fir Ct
Grants Pass OR 97526

Call Sign: KE7BYR
Southern Oregon Amateur
Packet Radio Assn
4525 NW Big Oak Pl 6
Grants Pass OR 97526

Call Sign: KE7BYT
Southern Oregon Amateur
Packet Radio Assn
5611 NW Biggs St
Grants Pass OR 97526

Call Sign: KE7BYS
Southern Oregon Amateur
Packet Radio Assn
5718 NW Biggs St
Grants Pass OR 97526

Call Sign: KE7BYU

Southern Oregon Amateur
Packet Radio Assn
5775 NW Birch Ave
Grants Pass OR 97526

Call Sign: KE7BYV
Southern Oregon Amateur
Packet Radio Assn
2834 NW Birkendene St
Grants Pass OR 97526

Call Sign: KE7CEQ
Jcec ARES
17172 NW Blacktail Dr
Grants Pass OR 97526

Call Sign: W7SHC
Jcec ARES
15067 NW Blakely Ln
Grants Pass OR 97526

Call Sign: KD7BMK
Southern Oregon Amateur
Packet Radio Assn
16160 NW Blueridge Dr
Grants Pass OR 97526

Call Sign: KC7WIS
Josephine County ARES
1649 NW Bonney Dr
Grants Pass OR 97526

Call Sign: KE7OQN
Josephine County ARES
1649 NW Bonney Dr
Grants Pass OR 97526

Call Sign: KE7YLE
Bruce J Mcfarland
2999 NW Cassia Pl
Grants Pass OR 97526

Call Sign: WB6CYK
Burton R Griffin
21280 NW Clearcut Dr

Grants Pass OR 97526

Call Sign: KC7MGF
James L Calvert
17880 NW Deercreek Ct
Grants Pass OR 97526

Call Sign: KF7ELN
Robert A Rupert
665 NW Denton Ave
Grants Pass OR 97526

Call Sign: K6JID
Paul E Melcher
1631 NW Everett St Apt
301
Grants Pass OR 97526

Call Sign: KE7YLD
David F Bullock
17911 NW Evergreen Pkwy
Grants Pass OR 97526

Call Sign: WL7ARM
Duane E Miller
19000 NW Evergreen Pkwy
165
Grants Pass OR 97526

Call Sign: KF7IT
Doyle T Cable
19000 NW Evergreen Pkwy
165
Grants Pass OR 975266350

Call Sign: N7KTU
Nada J Cable
19000 NW Evergreen Pkwy
193
Grants Pass OR 975266350

Call Sign: KD7HJC
Stephen E Wells
4850 NW Fir Pl
Grants Pass OR 97526

Call Sign: W7ELL
Stephen E Wells
4850 NW Fir Pl
Grants Pass OR 97526

Call Sign: W7PUP
James N Woods
2065 NW Flanders 206
Grants Pass OR 97526

Call Sign: N7PCT
Dorian J Blasdell
847 NW Freeman Ct
Grants Pass OR 97526

Call Sign: WB7UZZ
Ronald E Smith
16898 NW Greyhawk Dr
Grants Pass OR 97526

Call Sign: KF7OES
David Brumbach
1152 NW Highland St
Grants Pass OR 97526

Call Sign: KC7YKT
George T Francisco
19880 NW Nestucca Dr
Grants Pass OR 97526

Call Sign: WA7BYD
Robert J Hambly
19935 NW Nestucca Dr
Grants Pass OR 97526

Call Sign: W7CQS
Robert G Howe
20130 NW Nestucca Dr
Grants Pass OR 97526

Call Sign: KD7PHT
Dennis J Ruga
20376 NW Pihl Rd
Grants Pass OR 97526

Call Sign: K4DBV
Herbert C Parker
4160 NW Pinecone Way 6
Grants Pass OR 975263364

Call Sign: WA6YTV
Charles S Hakes
14695 NW Satelite Dr
Grants Pass OR 975261091

Call Sign: W7LMN
Billy G Blakely
930 NW Stockton
Grants Pass OR 97526

Call Sign: N7ZWW
Michael F Maffett
124 NW Utica Ave
Grants Pass OR 97526

Call Sign: N7GER
Thomas E Plater
19335 NW Walker Rd
Grants Pass OR 97526

Call Sign: N7NBG
Anne L Plater
1293 NW Wall Box 18
Grants Pass OR 97526

Call Sign: KD6UUY
Charles H Petty Sr
50055 NW Wilson River
Hwy
Grants Pass OR 97526

Call Sign: KB6PGE
Paul F Chierichetti
15662 Oakdale Rd
Grants Pass OR 97526

Call Sign: WL7L
Charles H Fortier

88779 Old Weigh Station
Rd
Grants Pass OR 97526

Call Sign: KG6KAV
Andreas E Juon
9303 Parrish Gap Rd SE
Grants Pass OR 97526

Call Sign: KI7RU
Bradley E Fritsen
9305 Parrish Gap Rd SE
Grants Pass OR 97526

Call Sign: KC6PJR
Avron Al D Gershen
2170 Patrick Ct
Grants Pass OR 97527

Call Sign: N7REQ
Robert M Scott
15629 Pedrioli Dr
Grants Pass OR 97526

Call Sign: KD4VM
James E Sanford
15690 Pedrioli Dr
Grants Pass OR 97526

Call Sign: N7RGI
Laurena F Scott
17525 Peerless Loop
Grants Pass OR 97526

Call Sign: KD7DPP
Ben W Grubb
5845 Perrin St
Grants Pass OR 97527

Call Sign: KB7WS
Archie Cameron
324 Phoenix St
Grants Pass OR 97527

Call Sign: W7IPQ

Greydon W Gilmer
3252 Phyllis Ct
Grants Pass OR 97527

Call Sign: KG7EK
Edward G Scholz
801 Pinehurst
Grants Pass OR 97526

Call Sign: N6ANY
Marjorie D Rembold
7345 Pineview St
Grants Pass OR 97526

Call Sign: WA7KCL
W Duaine Rembold
217 Pinewood Way
Grants Pass OR 97526

Call Sign: KD7WHU
John D Rousseau
31215 Pipeline Rd
Grants Pass OR 97527

Call Sign: KC7YGP
Flo Toch
15757 Pkwy Dr
Grants Pass OR 97526

Call Sign: WA6YHD
Barry W Burnsides
16913 Ponderosa Cascade
Grants Pass OR 97527

Call Sign: KE7LKX
William K Shryock
1730 Powell Creek Rd
Grants Pass OR 97526

Call Sign: N7JV
Jim Vickonoff
2249 Ptarmigan St NW
Grants Pass OR 97526

Call Sign: W7HZL

Alfred B Cornwall
2570 Ptarmigan St NW
Grants Pass OR 97526

Call Sign: KD7WID
Michael M Gibbs
2577 Ptarmigan St NW
Grants Pass OR 97526

Call Sign: WA7ADW
Donald L Todd
400 Quail Dr
Grants Pass OR 97527

Call Sign: KB7HCN
Jonathan E Heath
618 Quail Ln
Grants Pass OR 97527

Call Sign: KF7QDR
Trenwith L Acton
6970 Rainbow Dr SE
Grants Pass OR 97527

Call Sign: KB5CLX
Ruth A Marsh
20165 Red Sky Ln
Grants Pass OR 975269348

Call Sign: KF7KLK
William P Colisch
1710 Redwood Ct
Grants Pass OR 97527

Call Sign: KD7JQO
Brecken H Uhl
8485 Redwood Dr SE
Grants Pass OR 97527

Call Sign: KC7KT
Kenneth E Koestler
30563 Ridge St
Grants Pass OR 97526

Call Sign: N7DJO

Edith L Koestler
30563 Ridge St
Grants Pass OR 97526

Call Sign: KA7SWI
John Baker
1810 Rifle Range Rd
Grants Pass OR 97526

Call Sign: WD6GAQ
Albert C Nowlin
1810 Rifle Range Rd
Grants Pass OR 97527

Call Sign: W6AFV
Howard H Hands
3620 Rio Vista Way
Grants Pass OR 97527

Call Sign: KF7OEQ
Bruce S Benton
3620 Rio Vista Way
Grants Pass OR 97527

Call Sign: K7TMA
James F Holt
3881 Rio Vista Way
Grants Pass OR 97527

Call Sign: AI7A
Stephen A Shepp
3897 Rio Vista Way
Grants Pass OR 97527

Call Sign: KD7NPZ
Michael E Coleman
3897 Rio Vista Way
Grants Pass OR 97527

Call Sign: KD7EVK
Rogue Community College
ARC
60625 River Bend Dr
Grants Pass OR 97527

Call Sign: W7NLW
Jesse R Calvert Jr
18602 Riverwoods Dr
Grants Pass OR 97527

Call Sign: KE7ATU
Joe E Neiderheiser
38 Riviera 5076 Leonard Rd
Grants Pass OR 97527

Call Sign: KI7UK
Donald K Barkemeyer
2120 Robins Ln SE 187
Grants Pass OR 97526

Call Sign: W1LMA
Wilma M Barkemeyer
2000 Robins Ln SE 78
Grants Pass OR 97526

Call Sign: N7BQD
Timothy S Bruton
4500 Rogue Valley Hwy
Grants Pass OR 97527

Call Sign: KA7NCH
Eldon E Bottoms
240 S 1st Ave
Grants Pass OR 97526

Call Sign: AA7E
Peter J Finch
240 S 1st Ave
Grants Pass OR 97526

Call Sign: KW6O
Dan E Willis
1742 S 22 St
Grants Pass OR 97527

Call Sign: KB7PRH
Rodger B Hoyt
1760 S 22nd
Grants Pass OR 97527

Call Sign: W7BJO
Albert W Whipple
405 S 2nd St Apt 309
Grants Pass OR 97526

Call Sign: KF7NAQ
Adam O Stallsworth
844 S 32nd St
Grants Pass OR 97527

Call Sign: N7XPG
Daniel M Dawson
675 S 37th St
Grants Pass OR 97527

Call Sign: K7KGV
Francis E Huchendorf
934 S 38th St
Grants Pass OR 97526

Call Sign: K7YQM
Forest G White
946 S 3rd Ct
Grants Pass OR 975274559

Call Sign: KE6AH
Richard T Edwards
896 S 44th
Grants Pass OR 97527

Call Sign: KF7RMO
Michael D O'Brien
813 S 44th St
Grants Pass OR 97527

Call Sign: KB7NFW
David J Hockett
288 S 4th Pl
Grants Pass OR 97527

Call Sign: KO6UP
Reta M Lombardi
513 S 4th St
Grants Pass OR 97527

Call Sign: KC7KOT
Danny L Smith
694 S 51st Pl
Grants Pass OR 975275477

Call Sign: KD7UII
Rebecca A Thomas
562 S 53rd St
Grants Pass OR 97527

Call Sign: KF6WJA
David Stephens Sr
658 S 57th Sp 91
Grants Pass OR 97527

Call Sign: KC7FEZ
Perry T Gewecke
251 S 67th St
Grants Pass OR 97526

Call Sign: NI7I
Lee A Staley
6800 S 6th St 47
Grants Pass OR 97527

Call Sign: KF7QKN
Keith A Shaw
575 S 72nd St
Grants Pass OR 97526

Call Sign: WB4UYR
Salvatore F Bannister
6895 S Arndt Rd
Grants Pass OR 97527

Call Sign: W7JUU
Herbert A Swift
301 S Baker St Apt 2
Grants Pass OR 97527

Call Sign: KD7PHR
John W Stubbe
99342 S Bank Chetco Rd
Grants Pass OR 975277213

Call Sign: K7VSU
John W Stubbe
99342 S Bank Chetco Rd
Grants Pass OR 975277213

Call Sign: WA5KTC
Dennis Recla
1355 S Bay Rd
Grants Pass OR 97527

Call Sign: KF6AR
William O Hooper
13685 S Carus Rd
Grants Pass OR 97526

Call Sign: KE7DND
Bruce A Albert
15391 S Maple Ln
Grants Pass OR 97527

Call Sign: KE7DNC
Stephen B Albert
27863 S Meridian Rd
Grants Pass OR 97527

Call Sign: KB7ODZ
Raymond H Berg
18004 S Wesley Ln
Grants Pass OR 97527

Call Sign: N6OEZ
Robert H Lampshire
205 Scorpia Dr
Grants Pass OR 97526

Call Sign: W6LC
Eddy E Pollock
1917 SE 112th Ave
Grants Pass OR 97527

Call Sign: KD7COA
Matthew D Williams
6724 SE 114
Grants Pass OR 97527

Call Sign: KB7RNR
Roger E Kimmel
1336 SE 114th Ave
Grants Pass OR 97527

Call Sign: KD7WIG
Danny Concha
12 SE Kirk Ave
Grants Pass OR 97526

Call Sign: W7HHW
Vernon J Kloepfer
2461 SE Willow Dr
Grants Pass OR 97527

Call Sign: W7RUT
David L Jackson
4431 SE 114th Ave
Grants Pass OR 97527

Call Sign: WB7BYS
Russell A Totman
2608 SE Marigold Ct
Grants Pass OR 97526

Call Sign: N6XMN
Richard A Mathis
6708 SE Woodward
Grants Pass OR 97526

Call Sign: KE7UGU
William S Drummond
12001 SE 122
Grants Pass OR 97526

Call Sign: KC7CSJ
James S Leutwyler
6217 SE Mariner Way
Grants Pass OR 97526

Call Sign: KF7QDQ
Brad W Morris
1429 Sequoia Ave
Grants Pass OR 97527

Call Sign: K7WSD
William S Drummond
15120 SE 122 Ave
Grants Pass OR 97526

Call Sign: K2PSE
Jon L Wacker
1040 SE Marion
Grants Pass OR 97526

Call Sign: KC7VKQ
Franklin Kral Jr
8643 Shaw Sq Rd
Grants Pass OR 97526

Call Sign: KB7EAF
Jennifer D Cornoni
40 SE 129th
Grants Pass OR 97527

Call Sign: KF7IBM
Richard P Woodard
1680 SE Rex St Apt 10
Grants Pass OR 975263944

Call Sign: N7SVG
Peter D Allen
23483 Shepard Rd
Grants Pass OR 97526

Call Sign: N7KOF
Robert N Stinsman
4218 SE 132nd Ave
Grants Pass OR 97526

Call Sign: W7MKA
Robert H Goff II
16916 SE Rhine
Grants Pass OR 97526

Call Sign: N6BDQ
George J Owens Sr
6740 Shepherd Ct
Grants Pass OR 97526

Call Sign: KC7MWC
David C Mc Keen
2238 SE 147th Ave
Grants Pass OR 97526

Call Sign: N7VOV
Clarence M Baker
5605 SE Salmon St
Grants Pass OR 97526

Call Sign: WA6OTP
James A Mc Nutt
7928 Sherman Rd SE
Grants Pass OR 97527

Call Sign: KD7BCR
Glade T Tannehill
1013 SE Anchor Ave
Grants Pass OR 97526

Call Sign: KE7NPI
Brian R Christensen
9316 SE Salmon St
Grants Pass OR 97526

Call Sign: WA6OWE
Karen E Mc Nutt
2443 Sherman SE
Grants Pass OR 97527

Call Sign: KD7WHV
Eddie N Edelen
5205 SE Golden Rd
Grants Pass OR 97526

Call Sign: KA5VPL
Dewey A Miller
24355 SE Strawberry Dr
Grants Pass OR 97527

Call Sign: KC7JPT
Gary V Lynes
1664 Sherman St SE
Grants Pass OR 97527

Call Sign: KG7HZ
Robert P Cann
1430 Silver Falls Dr NE
Grants Pass OR 97526

Call Sign: KE7RZQ
Scott A Fields
1257 Siskiyou Blvd 150
Grants Pass OR 97527

Call Sign: KD7FEG
Randall E Shelman
62273 Ski Run Rd
Grants Pass OR 97526

Call Sign: N6EJK
Gary D Houston
3555 Spicer Dr SE
Grants Pass OR 97527

Call Sign: KB7KNF
Rebecca D Mathiasen
3555 Spicer Dr SE
Grants Pass OR 97527

Call Sign: N7WRW
Luke S Mathiasen
3545 Spicer Rd
Grants Pass OR 97527

Call Sign: KE7VPQ
Oswald Tiefenbach
43924 Spring Creek Loop
Grants Pass OR 97527

Call Sign: N6BIC
Robert L Edwards
25633 Spring Hill Dr
Grants Pass OR 97527

Call Sign: WA7CGW
David R Clearwaters
4471 Spring Meadow
Grants Pass OR 97527

Call Sign: N7JSM
Rex L Mathiasen
718 Spring St
Grants Pass OR 97527

Call Sign: N7JSN
Susan D Mathiasen
2232 Spring St
Grants Pass OR 97527

Call Sign: KC7JPV
Ardel J Herndon
2232 Spring St
Grants Pass OR 97527

Call Sign: K7ZV
Richard Chatelain
42647 Stringtown Ln
Grants Pass OR 975269658

Call Sign: KC7LV
R Paul Glantz
4340 Summit Rd
Grants Pass OR 97527

Call Sign: KA7FTJ
Roger H Soper
3829 Summit Ridge
Grants Pass OR 97527

Call Sign: KA7OGL
Luella K Soper
3829 Summit Ridge
Grants Pass OR 97527

Call Sign: W6UHA
Maxine E Willis
5200 Summit St
Grants Pass OR 97527

Call Sign: KC7BTR
Ronald D Clisby
4995 Sunnyside Rd SE 14
Grants Pass OR 97527

Call Sign: KC7SDU
Jim H Grow
4995 Sunnyside Rd SE 14
Grants Pass OR 97527

Call Sign: KC7DFW
Richard N Headley
641 Sunrise Ave
Grants Pass OR 975278984

Call Sign: KE7VPM
Darrell W Potter
612 Sunset
Grants Pass OR 97527

Call Sign: KF7DZN
Easy Valley Wireless
Society
17500 SW 105th Ave
Grants Pass OR 97527

Call Sign: AA7DA
Easy Valley Wireless
Society
17997 SW 105th Ct
Grants Pass OR 97527

Call Sign: AA7DA
Thomas M Fulmer
14625 SW 106th
Grants Pass OR 97527

Call Sign: KC7NCM
Colleen M Fulmer
22294 SW 106th Ave
Grants Pass OR 97527

Call Sign: N7LFO
Glen J Chinn
17960 SW 109
Grants Pass OR 97526

Call Sign: KE7WVE
Helen Rhoades
17960 SW 109th

Grants Pass OR 97526

Grants Pass OR 97526

Grants Pass OR 97526

Call Sign: KF7OEN
Calvin L Gilbert
1717 SW 10th Ave
Grants Pass OR 97526

Call Sign: KF7RMN
Anthony R Hickey
4365 SW Fraser Ave
Grants Pass OR 97526

Call Sign: AB2ES
William J Potter
21512 SW Kristin Ct
Grants Pass OR 97526

Call Sign: KC6LDG
David L Maltz
8185 SW 71st Ave
Grants Pass OR 97526

Call Sign: N7SER
Wayne L Gillespie
15025 SW Gull Dr
Grants Pass OR 97526

Call Sign: KB7KNH
Morris S Shimanoff
104 SW Lane St
Grants Pass OR 97527

Call Sign: KA7IBV
Jeff A Geddings
6645 SW Alfred St
Grants Pass OR 97526

Call Sign: WB6WHM
John E Brown Jr
49645 SW Hebo Rd
Grants Pass OR 97526

Call Sign: KD6MKO
Robert W Roby
3081 SW Lillyben Ave
Grants Pass OR 97526

Call Sign: KB5WBT
Bart A Benthul
8855 SW Bridletrail Ave
Grants Pass OR 97526

Call Sign: K7WHM
John E Brown Jr
49645 SW Hebo Rd
Grants Pass OR 975265830

Call Sign: KC7EPK
Robert H Goff II
16018 SW Parker Rd
Grants Pass OR 975275440

Call Sign: ND7Z
Clifford C Ostermeier
29840 SW Buckhaven Rd
Grants Pass OR 97526

Call Sign: KF6NFW
Chris A Robinson
5315 SW Idaho St
Grants Pass OR 97526

Call Sign: KJ7CS
Michael P Hughes
3570 SW River Paky 1507
Grants Pass OR 97526

Call Sign: KE7NQK
Jim S Pinder
86 SW Century Dr 371
Grants Pass OR 97526

Call Sign: KD7KFN
Elizabeth S Robinson
6029 SW Idaho St
Grants Pass OR 97526

Call Sign: KD7NBQ
Tom A Brownell
3300 SW River Rd
Grants Pass OR 97526

Call Sign: K7NQK
Jim S Pinder
15910 SW Century Oak Cir
Grants Pass OR 97526

Call Sign: WA7SCQ
Gladys Hegler
10430 SW Kable St
Grants Pass OR 97526

Call Sign: KE7ATP
David M Polen
1103 SW Rouge River Ave
Grants Pass OR 97526

Call Sign: KD7ZTL
Ryan B Fritsen
10480 SW Eastridge St 91
Grants Pass OR 97526

Call Sign: KD7PHU
Kathy L Yellow Eagle
10430 SW Kable St
Grants Pass OR 97526

Call Sign: KE7ATO
Janel A Polen
6426 SW Roundtree Ct
Grants Pass OR 97526

Call Sign: KZ7A
Robert T Fuller
8385 SW Ernst Rd

Call Sign: KA7FCN
James B Pemberton
12658 SW Karen St 18

Call Sign: KE7ATN
Michael J Polen
2030 SW Roxbury Ave

Grants Pass OR 97526

Call Sign: N6ZWZ
Jimmy J Oliver
995 SW Tropicana
Grants Pass OR 97527

Call Sign: N6ZXB
Peggy A Oliver
995 SW Tropicana Ave
Grants Pass OR 97527

Call Sign: W6ODC
Winslow W Lewand
7150 SW Westgate Way
Grants Pass OR 97526

Call Sign: KC6QXQ
Paul A Walker
21190 Swedetown Rd
Grants Pass OR 97527

Call Sign: KD6WHG
Linda M Walker
21190 Swedetown Rd
Grants Pass OR 975275051

Call Sign: KB6AMU
Helen J Mc Nutt
2685 Sykes Creek Rd
Grants Pass OR 97526

Call Sign: N7HGP
Marvin J Mc Nutt
1480 Sykes Creek Rd
Grants Pass OR 97526

Call Sign: N7EZY
Jcec ARES
250 Tech Way
Grants Pass OR 97526

Call Sign: WA7ODN
Jcec ARES
250 Tech Way

Grants Pass OR 97526

Call Sign: KF7CGP
Josephine County
Emergency
Communications
250 Tech Way
Grants Pass OR 97526

Call Sign: K7ICP
Jcec ARES
250 Tech Way
Grants Pass OR 97526

Call Sign: K7GPO
Jcec ARES
250 Tech Way
Grants Pass OR 97526

Call Sign: N7GPO
Josephine County
Emergency
Communications
250 Tech Way
Grants Pass OR 97526

Call Sign: KF7FTE
Josephine County
Emergency
Communications
250 Tech Way
Grants Pass OR 97526

Call Sign: K3GNG
Josephine County
Emergency
Communications
250 Tech Way
Grants Pass OR 97526

Call Sign: KF7HDU
Jcec
250 Tech Way
Grants Pass OR 97526

Call Sign: KF7HDV
Jcec
250 Tech Way
Grants Pass OR 97526

Call Sign: K1GNG
Jcec
250 Tech Way
Grants Pass OR 97526

Call Sign: K2GNG
Jcec
250 Tech Way
Grants Pass OR 97526

Call Sign: KF7IRA
Josephine County
Emergency
Communications
250 Tech Way
Grants Pass OR 97526

Call Sign: WB6YQP
Josephine County
Emergency
Communications
250 Tech Way
Grants Pass OR 97526

Call Sign: WM7K
Jcec ARES Repeater
520 Tech Way
Grants Pass OR 97526

Call Sign: KD7QCT
Jcec ARES
164 Teel Ln
Grants Pass OR 97526

Call Sign: KF7BMM
Jcec Sar
47537 Teller Rd 18
Grants Pass OR 97526

Call Sign: KF7OEP

Jim R Brumbach
3868 Tempest Dr
Grants Pass OR 97527

Denell M GARCeau
140 Tiffany Way
Grants Pass OR 97526

Bonnie J Patterson
216 Troll View Rd
Grants Pass OR 97527

Call Sign: W6RPN
Robert S Hughes
1427 Ten Oaks Ln
Grants Pass OR 975267702

Call Sign: KF6ESC
Sarah M GARCeau
181 Tiffany Way
Grants Pass OR 97526

Call Sign: WA6QPS
Robert J Wisniewski
600 Trollview Rd
Grants Pass OR 975274872

Call Sign: KA9HYD
Anthony R Thorne
415 Thornberry Dr
Grants Pass OR 97526

Call Sign: WA6NDW
De Nise N GARCeau
88052 Tiki Ln
Grants Pass OR 97526

Call Sign: KD7WIH
Harold E Newman
5650 Trout Creek Ridge Rd
Grants Pass OR 97527

Call Sign: WA6LBS
Ted D Taylor
545 Thornbrook Dr
Grants Pass OR 97526

Call Sign: W6OCK
Robert E Ratliff
88108 Tiki Ln
Grants Pass OR 97526

Call Sign: WA6RBQ
Frank W Fisher
6670 Trout Creek Ridge Rd
Grants Pass OR 97527

Call Sign: WB6PRX
Carol A Taylor
2120 Thorne St
Grants Pass OR 97526

Call Sign: WA7JQK
Donald R Hendrickson
890 Tipton Rd
Grants Pass OR 97526

Call Sign: KF7DMX
Gerry D Harmon
32520 Turlay Ln
Grants Pass OR 97526

Call Sign: KB7PJT
Timothy B Miille
670 Three Pines Rd
Grants Pass OR 97526

Call Sign: N6FYI
Leroy R Rice
510 Triller Ln
Grants Pass OR 97527

Call Sign: KA7PQR
Linda E Anderson
3110 Upper River Rd
Grants Pass OR 97526

Call Sign: KE7ATR
Erin S Smith
670 Three Pines Rd
Grants Pass OR 97526

Call Sign: N6GIM
Phyllis C Rice
39058 Trillium Ln
Grants Pass OR 97527

Call Sign: WA7ADT
Ronald G Anderson
3110 Upper River Rd
Grants Pass OR 97527

Call Sign: KE7ATQ
Peggy S Smith
4155 Threemile Ln 139
Grants Pass OR 97526

Call Sign: N6YX
Robert H Bell Sr
2689 Trinity Way
Grants Pass OR 97527

Call Sign: KD7WIE
Annette E Cooper
3675 Upper River Rd
Grants Pass OR 97526

Call Sign: KE7NPN
Skyler D Smith
12936 Thunderhead Way
Grants Pass OR 97526

Call Sign: KE7VPP
Bonnie J Patterson
1384 Tripp St SE
Grants Pass OR 97527

Call Sign: KD7WIF
Donald A Cooper
2175 Val Halla St
Grants Pass OR 97526

Call Sign: KE6MMW

Call Sign: KC7MGH

Call Sign: K4ZLK

Wayne J Foster
5455 Val View Dr SE
Grants Pass OR 97526

Jonathan D Sailer
2199 W Jones Creek Rd
Grants Pass OR 97526

Lawrence L Lewis
509 Wen Dover Cir
Grants Pass OR 975265950

Call Sign: KE7QMA
William B Bartow
700 Veterans Dr
Grants Pass OR 97527

Call Sign: KE7UOK
Travis J Knoll
1486 W Jones Crk
Grants Pass OR 97526

Call Sign: KB7RNO
Betty A Hummel
1718 Wetherbee Dr
Grants Pass OR 97527

Call Sign: KB7IKY
Ian D Goff
878 W Harbeck Rd
Grants Pass OR 97527

Call Sign: KC7GLY
Orla F Goff
392 W Park
Grants Pass OR 97527

Call Sign: KB7TLV
Robert L Hummel Jr
1718 Wetherbee Dr
Grants Pass OR 97527

Call Sign: KD7KKH
George R Triller
1048 W Harbeck Rd
Grants Pass OR 97527

Call Sign: KD7IBJ
Jessica R Darby
391 W Savage Creek Rd
Grants Pass OR 97527

Call Sign: KL0NM
William M Mitchell
149 Whispering Dr
Grants Pass OR 97527

Call Sign: KD7SPG
Billy R Bunton
1240 W Jones Ck Rd
Grants Pass OR 97526

Call Sign: WA6DLL
Delores J George
3150 Walnut Ave
Grants Pass OR 975279678

Call Sign: KC7OBN
Neil G Moody
220 Whispering Willow Dr
Grants Pass OR 97527

Call Sign: WB6JGW
Michael K Gee
464 W Jones Creek Rd
Grants Pass OR 97526

Call Sign: W7TLK
Robert A Farrand
1328 Washington Blvd
Grants Pass OR 97526

Call Sign: KE7FML
Michael C Jones
587 Whitestone Dr
Grants Pass OR 97527

Call Sign: KE7NPK
Dianne J Gee
464 W Jones Creek Rd
Grants Pass OR 97526

Call Sign: KW7S
James D Mc Kenty
124 Waverly Dr
Grants Pass OR 97526

Call Sign: WA7ILA
Francis A Krouse
2221 Williams Hwy
Grants Pass OR 975275687

Call Sign: KF7MYJ
Marco A Pursell
619 W Jones Creek Rd
Grants Pass OR 97526

Call Sign: WA6IYQ
Richard R Pierson
183 Waverly Dr
Grants Pass OR 97526

Call Sign: WB7TVB
Vernon L Ruthart
2657 Williams Hwy
Grants Pass OR 97527

Call Sign: WA6SSO
Kenneth A Fiske
634 W Jones Creek Rd
Grants Pass OR 97526

Call Sign: KG4HEZ
Michael S Haynes
1906 Weatherbee Dr
Grants Pass OR 97527

Call Sign: KB7ZQJ
John J Kightlinger
2798 Williams Hwy
Grants Pass OR 97526

Call Sign: KC7OBO

Call Sign: W7YSM

Call Sign: KD7QFU

James A Johnson
3146 Williams Hwy
Grants Pass OR 975277705

Call Sign: KC7ARU
Elizabeth A Hummel
4052 Williams Hwy
Grants Pass OR 97527

Call Sign: KE7TGA
Michael W Schwartz
5060 Williams Hwy
Grants Pass OR 97527

Call Sign: KA7ZHS
Connie E Young
12061 Williams Hwy
Grants Pass OR 97527

Call Sign: KC7NCN
Jade L Hummel
2778 B Williams Hwy
Grants Pass OR 97527

Call Sign: KE7TGC
Janice K Santrizos
1630 Williams Hwy Pmb 33
Grants Pass OR 97527

Call Sign: KA6EJR
Larry L Evans
517 Williamson Loop
Grants Pass OR 97526

Call Sign: W6MPD
Harry L De Biddle
1374 Willow Ct
Grants Pass OR 97527

Call Sign: KC7IJO
Rodney G Swanson
2535 Winona Rd
Grants Pass OR 97526

Call Sign: WA6ABS

Roy T Hicks
3121 Winona Rd
Grants Pass OR 97526

Call Sign: WB7VKK
Harry P Kuhlman
3172 Woodland Park Rd
Grants Pass OR 97526

Call Sign: KB7POE
Russell A Kruger
1102 Wylie Ln
Grants Pass OR 97527

Call Sign: KF7OEO
Dana M Cound
2015 Yale Ct
Grants Pass OR 97527

Call Sign: KB7EKF
Warren B Olney
Grants Pass OR 97526

Call Sign: KB7YHM
Meghan E Olson
Grants Pass OR 97527

Call Sign: N6BFQ
Robert J Bush
Grants Pass OR 97527

Call Sign: N6DLR
Shirley J Bush
Grants Pass OR 97527

Call Sign: N7SUM
Carol R Olson
Grants Pass OR 97527

Call Sign: N7XEM
Michael E Olson
Grants Pass OR 97527

Call Sign: KA7GVV
William E Campbell

Grants Pass OR 97526

Call Sign: N6KAV
Louis S Grand III
Grants Pass OR 97526

Call Sign: WA6SBC
Albert H Olson
Grants Pass OR 97526

Call Sign: KC0AGW
Mark B Savage
Grants Pass OR 97527

Call Sign: N6OJF
Jo Anne A Seutter
Grants Pass OR 97527

Call Sign: W6IGK
Elmer P Seutter
Grants Pass OR 97527

Call Sign: WA6IKO
John M Olson
Grants Pass OR 97527

Call Sign: KD7NQA
Patricia M Coleman
Grants Pass OR 97527

Call Sign: AC7OG
Michael E Coleman
Grants Pass OR 97527

Call Sign: KF7UKJ
Frank A Schneider
Grants Pass OR 97527

Call Sign: KF7ARI
John T Salinas
Grants Pass OR 97527

Call Sign: KF7LTO
Southern Oregon ARC
Grants Pass OR 97528

Call Sign: KE7LKX
Southern Oregon ARC
Grants Pass OR 97528

Call Sign: K7LIX
Southern Oregon ARC
Grants Pass OR 97528

Call Sign: KB7RLM
L Ruth Highbarger
Grants Pass OR 97528

Call Sign: KB7YD
Patrick G Murray
Grants Pass OR 97528

Call Sign: K6HTA
Timothy A Holmes
Grants Pass OR 97528

Call Sign: KF7IBL
Daniel G Stuelke
Grants Pass OR 97528

Call Sign: KF7KSB
Horace R Stodola
Grants Pass OR 97528

Call Sign: KF7LTM
Horace R Stodola
Grants Pass OR 97528

Call Sign: AA7JS
Horace R Stodola
Grants Pass OR 97528

Call Sign: KE7WVB
Raymond L Rosa
Grants Pass OR 97528

Call Sign: N7ZWU
Sean M Smithers
Grants Pass OR 975280114

Call Sign: KD7BAH
Daniel G Kohler
Grants Pass OR 975280142

Call Sign: N7KS
William B Calvert
Grants Pass OR 975280315

FCC Amateur Radio Licenses in Grass Valley

Call Sign: WB7PPK
David S Earl
121 Bonnie Ln
Grass Valley OR 97029

Call Sign: KB7BJH
Terri R Earl
922 Fairway Dr
Grass Valley OR 97029

Call Sign: KF7HTT
Matthew J Earl
2160 Fairway Loop
Grass Valley OR 97029

Call Sign: KF7HTU
Steven D Earl
928 Fairway Pl
Grass Valley OR 97029

Call Sign: KB7CPC
Daniel S Earl
10656 James Way Dr SE
Grass Valley OR 97029

Call Sign: WB7PPJ
Donald D Earl
10935 James Way Dr SE
Grass Valley OR 97029

Call Sign: WB7PTS
D Stanton Earl
10935 James Way Dr SE
Grass Valley OR 97029

FCC Amateur Radio Licenses in Greenleaf

Call Sign: KF7SOC
Alicia Elkins
1080 NW 107th Ave
Greenleaf OR 97430

FCC Amateur Radio Licenses in Haines

Call Sign: N7VWO
Dennis R Spence
81752 Christmas Tree Rd
Haines OR 97833

Call Sign: KB7SRS
Lewis E Aldrich Jr
1433 NE 12th Ave
Haines OR 97833

Call Sign: KB7VFY
Greg G Specht
Haines OR 97833

Call Sign: KC7JXD
Brandi Parker
Haines OR 97833

Call Sign: KD7RVG
Lionel L Shurtleff
Haines OR 97833

Call Sign: KE7DUR
Brandon C Daniels
Haines OR 97833

FCC Amateur Radio Licenses in Halfway

Call Sign: W7JSY
George W Johnson
Halfway OR 97834

Call Sign: KD7PJD
James D Reed
Halfway OR 97834

FCC Amateur Radio Licenses in Harbor

Call Sign: AA7FP
Carl A Bailey
510 36th Ave NW
Harbor OR 97415

Call Sign: N7SJI
Edna B Jeffrey
265 Holde Rln
Harbor OR 97415

Call Sign: AE7MA
Marion L Ayer
2006 Hwy 101 342
Harbor OR 97415

Call Sign: N7QET
Gary H Wise
7546 S Prairie Rd
Harbor OR 97415

Call Sign: KB7JGJ
William J Goergen
Harbor OR 97415

Call Sign: KC7BTA
Shannon C Musser
Harbor OR 97415

Call Sign: WB6HAK
Herman O Wakeman
Harbor OR 97415

Call Sign: WB7OSN
Stanley H Jeffrey
Harbor OR 97415

Call Sign: KC7PSD
Ernest C Turner Jr

Harbor OR 92415

Call Sign: N7HVW
Lawrence P Hartwell
Harbor OR 97415

Call Sign: AL7FB
Rodney W Giddings Sr
Harbor OR 97415

Call Sign: KA7THK
David R Goodgame
Harbor OR 97415

Call Sign: KC6OJT
John H Stockwell Jr
Harbor OR 97415

Call Sign: KC7SHV
Maxine M Brey
Harbor OR 97415

FCC Amateur Radio Licenses in Helix

Call Sign: W7TAK
Howard L Muller
Helix OR 978350306

FCC Amateur Radio Licenses in Heppner

Call Sign: KC7GST
Martha J Doherty
2828 Calla St
Heppner OR 97836

Call Sign: KD7KSW
Dennis M Wall
88494 Ellmaker
Heppner OR 978360683

Call Sign: AF6ID
Jonathan W Day
63333 Hwy 20

Heppner OR 97836

Call Sign: AE7CP
Jonathan W Day
65024 Hwy 20
Heppner OR 97836

Call Sign: KD7LXR
Dale W Holland
1199 N Terry St Sp 130
Heppner OR 97836

Call Sign: KD7LXS
Karen L Holland
1199 N Terry St Sp 177
Heppner OR 97836

Call Sign: K7CJC
Earl J Blake
Box 394 Willow Creek
Heppner OR 97836

Call Sign: WA7DWI
Robert H Jepsen
Heppner OR 97836

Call Sign: KC7GSQ
Darcy M Bergstrom
Heppner OR 97836

Call Sign: KC7SOY
Morrow County ARES
Heppner OR 97836

Call Sign: N7NUH
Ray E Greenlaw
Heppner OR 97836

Call Sign: WA7DWK
William R Jepsen
Heppner OR 97836

Call Sign: KD7LJI
Frances C Greenlaw
Heppner OR 978360988

Call Sign: KC7URA
Caryn M Sjoren
3354 12th St SE
Hermiston OR 97838

Call Sign: KB7RVS
Kevin C Kamlin
2470 14th Pl
Hermiston OR 97838

Call Sign: KC7FOQ
Walt D Shipley
619 38th Pl
Hermiston OR 97838

Call Sign: KC7FOR
Sandra J Shipley
1146 38th St NE
Hermiston OR 97838

Call Sign: K7SUW
Wesley P Brooks
672 B St
Hermiston OR 978386134

Call Sign: KA7JRM
Susan L Brooks
2114 B St
Hermiston OR 97838

Call Sign: KG6HGA
Barbara J Rincon
2114 B St
Hermiston OR 97838

Call Sign: N7RKA
Warren N Shurtleff
6093 B St SE
Hermiston OR 97838

Call Sign: WB7OQN

Louis M Byrd
34241 Bachelor Flat
Hermiston OR 978389432

Call Sign: WU8L
John O Eiden
Rt 1 Box 10A
Hermiston OR 97838

Call Sign: KE7IZI
John O Eiden
Rt 1 Box 11
Hermiston OR 97838

Call Sign: KB7LBF
Steven A Vermillion
Hc 61 Box 1208
Hermiston OR 97838

Call Sign: KB7LQT
Helen M Vermillion
Hc 61 Box 1208
Hermiston OR 97838

Call Sign: W7SAV
Steven A Vermillion
Rt 6 Box 122
Hermiston OR 97838

Call Sign: KA7EBL
Jewell D Mull
4771 Bramblewood Ln NW
Hermiston OR 97838

Call Sign: W7IDZ
Howard R Patrick
4114 Calaroga Cir
Hermiston OR 97838

Call Sign: KC7BWB
Carmine L Walker
2828 Calla St
Hermiston OR 97838

Call Sign: KC7BWC

Stephen R Walker
2871 Calla St
Hermiston OR 97838

Call Sign: KC7MSP
Ammon J Young
500 Cambridge Dr
Hermiston OR 97838

Call Sign: KB7SPK
Robert E Harness
1725 Camellia Ave
Hermiston OR 97838

Call Sign: KB7PUU
Melvin L Lambert
4245 Campbell Dr
Hermiston OR 97838

Call Sign: KA7VLP
Joan M Gray
4427 Campbell Dr SE
Hermiston OR 97838

Call Sign: N7FCW
Ellen M Minardi
1825 Campus Way
Hermiston OR 97838

Call Sign: K6BNY
Harold M Winters
19208 Carpenterville Rd
Hermiston OR 97838

Call Sign: NB7O
Kevin L Hedgepeth
4802 Carriage Ct NE
Hermiston OR 97838

Call Sign: K7MGO
Michelle A Hedgepeth
4802 Carriage Ct NE
Hermiston OR 97838

Call Sign: KC7JIZ

Gerry Lloyd
1272 College Green Dr
Hermiston OR 97838

Carlene L Benscoter
4368 Essex St SE
Hermiston OR 97838

Umatilla Radio Group
74427 Larson Rd
Hermiston OR 97838

Call Sign: KC7NMD
Leonard D Orman
4125 Devonshire Ct NE
Hermiston OR 97838

Call Sign: AE7JM
James S Morrison
4486 Evergreen SE
Hermiston OR 97838

Call Sign: W7URG
Umatilla Radio Group
695 Larson Way
Hermiston OR 97838

Call Sign: KD7WVB
Lloyd R Hochhalter
51335 Dianne Rd
Hermiston OR 97838

Call Sign: KF7GIT
Rocio Marlene Leon Torres
412 Evergreen St
Hermiston OR 97838

Call Sign: N7OII
Kyonghui C Cross
40705 Larwood Dr
Hermiston OR 97838

Call Sign: K7AVR
Dwain F Mc Mahon
33421 E Hwy 224 12
Hermiston OR 97838

Call Sign: N7LA
Larry E Ross
4213 Evergreen St SE
Hermiston OR 97838

Call Sign: N7ERT
Jody T Cross
18782 Lassen Ct
Hermiston OR 97838

Call Sign: N6XXI
Ples N Parker
2846 El Toro
Hermiston OR 97838

Call Sign: AA7AZ
James M Davis
6585 Failing St
Hermiston OR 97838

Call Sign: K7CNY
Wayne C Harris
104 Marie Cir
Hermiston OR 97838

Call Sign: KD6LUQ
Cheryl L Williams
2064 Elmwood Dr S
Hermiston OR 97838

Call Sign: N7OOV
Nikki R Davis
1071 Fairfield Ave Apt 57
Hermiston OR 97838

Call Sign: KD7LXH
Rochelle L Meyers
860 N 28th Ave
Hermiston OR 97838

Call Sign: KF7WQ
Kenneth M Berry
1987 Esplanade Ave
Hermiston OR 97838

Call Sign: K3EM
Kevin P Kruba Sr
2081 Fairmont Blvd
Hermiston OR 97838

Call Sign: KD7NDL
George H Meyers
1800 N 28th Ct
Hermiston OR 97838

Call Sign: KA7TUR
Leonard L Young Jr
6 Essex Ct
Hermiston OR 97838

Call Sign: KC7LJZ
Craig A Dircksen
34134 Hankey Rd
Hermiston OR 97838

Call Sign: WB7DQL
Lawrence A Barboe
5844 N Fork Rd
Hermiston OR 97838

Call Sign: KA0VVK
Randall K Benscoter
1525 Essex St
Hermiston OR 97838

Call Sign: KA7PDO
Frank E Lockwood Sr
217 La Creole Dr 42
Hermiston OR 97838

Call Sign: KC7BVI
Alan S Vandeman
1833 NE 10th St
Hermiston OR 97838

Call Sign: N7SMF

Call Sign: KD7ZAR

Call Sign: W7DKI

Alan S Vandeman
4720 NE 110th Ave 7
Hermiston OR 97838

Call Sign: KD7CEN
William R Gollyhorn
246 NE 111th Ave
Hermiston OR 97838

Call Sign: KD7JCD
Kaylene A Dickmeier
525 NE 151 Ave
Hermiston OR 97838

Call Sign: KA7TRM
Dale T Mc Creary
673 NE 21st Pl
Hermiston OR 97838

Call Sign: AC7WN
James J Lorenz
3345 NE 25th Ave
Hermiston OR 97838

Call Sign: KD7HXP
Joanne G Lieuallen
6600 NE 78th Ct A3 12613
Hermiston OR 97838

Call Sign: KC7ZKS
Douglas S Lieuallen
6600 NE 78th Ct Ste A3
1803
Hermiston OR 97838

Call Sign: KE7OJR
Nicklas J Goit
1371 NE Barberry
Hermiston OR 97838

Call Sign: KA0UTA
Sharon L Fletcher
1190 NE Rosewood St
Hermiston OR 97838

Call Sign: KL7IXI
Michael Fletcher
547 NE Royal Ct
Hermiston OR 97838

Call Sign: KA7TBH
Richard D Gollyhorn
708 NW 21st St
Hermiston OR 97838

Call Sign: KE7NJX
William Saltiel Gracian
2501 NW 229th Ave
Hermiston OR 978380121

Call Sign: KA7TEU
Letha J Roberts
1321 NW 30th
Hermiston OR 97838

Call Sign: N7FNJ
Todd N Roberts Jr
1331 NW 30th
Hermiston OR 97838

Call Sign: KC7JFH
James M Lloyd
1441 NW B St
Hermiston OR 97838

Call Sign: KD7VX
Whitley H Smith
10901 NW Brentano Ln
Hermiston OR 97838

Call Sign: KE7RSL
Laura L Skeen Cruz
1049 NW Briarcreek Way
Apt 1327
Hermiston OR 97838

Call Sign: KB7FMV
Evalena M Griffin
2102 NW Despain Av
Hermiston OR 97838

Call Sign: KK7CG
William R Griffin Jr
212 NW Despain Ave
Hermiston OR 97838

Call Sign: KD7HWW
Scott P Harrell
10678 NW Helvetia Rd
Hermiston OR 97838

Call Sign: KA7MMQ
Christopher J Early
11263 NW Helvetia Rd
Hermiston OR 97838

Call Sign: KF6EV
Thomas F Martin
18201 NW Heritage Pkwy
33
Hermiston OR 978381085

Call Sign: WB7TEB
Howard E Smith
874 NW Oak Ave
Hermiston OR 97838

Call Sign: KD7HPA
James H Neufeld
11276 NW Skyline Blvd
Hermiston OR 97838

Call Sign: KD7HPB
Ruby J Neufeld
11276 NW Skyline Blvd
Hermiston OR 97838

Call Sign: KB7AOP
Rhonda J Randall
5642 NW Wintercreek Dr
Hermiston OR 97838

Call Sign: N7GBZ
Randy D Randall
2760 NW Wintergreen Pl

Hermiston OR 97838

Call Sign: KB7VGE
Edward O Higginbotham
447 NW Witham
Hermiston OR 97838

Call Sign: K7VGE
Edward O Higginbotham
3930 NW Witham Hill Dr
207
Hermiston OR 97838

Call Sign: N7ZHG
Gary A Cooper
263 S Jw Rd
Hermiston OR 97838

Call Sign: KF7FSR
Morrow County ARES
Races
22085 S Kamrath Rd
Hermiston OR 97838

Call Sign: K7ODN
Oregon Digital Network
14546 S Kelmsley Dr
Hermiston OR 97838

Call Sign: KC7RWC
Umatilla County ARES
567 S Knight St
Hermiston OR 97838

Call Sign: KD7CPP
John E Haff
1487 S Oakdale Ave
Hermiston OR 97838

Call Sign: KE7FBP
Leif N Sjoren
25170 S Oberlander Ln
Hermiston OR 97838

Call Sign: KE7FBQ

Leighton J Sjoren
20891 S Olson Rd
Hermiston OR 97838

Call Sign: KC7AWG
Joseph V Ritchie
20891 S Olson Rd
Hermiston OR 97838

Call Sign: N7ZH
Richard H Misener
4737 San Carlos Ct NE
Hermiston OR 97838

Call Sign: N7GFE
Beverly A Hernandez
585 Sater Ct
Hermiston OR 97838

Call Sign: N7XWG
Karl G Molander
33115 Savage Rd
Hermiston OR 97838

Call Sign: KA7PRZ
Burton H Paine
578 Scotts Glenn Dr
Hermiston OR 97838

Call Sign: KB7WAF
Douglas W Drew
7322 SE 112th Ave
Hermiston OR 97838

Call Sign: KB7KUC
Kerry J Harn
241 SE 154
Hermiston OR 97838

Call Sign: KA7KZG
Georgia M Byrd
4444 SE 30th Ave
Hermiston OR 97838

Call Sign: KB7TLZ

Ollie L Thomason
1642 SE 58th Ct
Hermiston OR 97838

Call Sign: KA7OKJ
M Jean Waits
795 SE 59th Ave
Hermiston OR 97838

Call Sign: N7BZD
David D Waits
640 SE 5th
Hermiston OR 97838

Call Sign: KC7FCQ
Gary W Guggenmos
1970 SE 72nd Ct
Hermiston OR 97838

Call Sign: N7LJY
Bruce C Schofield Jr
4890 SE Ardew
Hermiston OR 97838

Call Sign: KC7IJJ
Kenneth G Sjoren
910 5 SW 10th St
Hermiston OR 97838

Call Sign: KB7EFI
Eugene M Smith
387 SW 25th Cir
Hermiston OR 978386114

Call Sign: KD7GAC
Betty J Smith
1330 SW 25th Ct
Hermiston OR 97838

Call Sign: KE7MCS
Roy D Olson
5721 SW 53rd Ave
Hermiston OR 97838

Call Sign: KA7AHG

Douglas B Paine
368 SW K St
Hermiston OR 97838

Call Sign: KA7IKC
Tia J Paine
378 SW K St
Hermiston OR 97838

Call Sign: KE7RSR
Cherie Dawn N Robins
14155 SW Martingale Ct
Hermiston OR 97838

Call Sign: KB7GGF
Mescal Paine
16893 SW Sarala St
Hermiston OR 97838

Call Sign: KC7THL
Kirk H Mc Loren
655 Three Pines
Hermiston OR 97838

Call Sign: KF7GTJ
David S Elder
2042 Vine
Hermiston OR 97838

Call Sign: WA7FJT
David C Mull
30186 W Bensel Rd
Hermiston OR 97838

Call Sign: KA7PLM
Spencer S Compton
1580 W Brock Ave
Hermiston OR 97838

Call Sign: AC7KA
Dennis F Coykendall
795 W Division Ave
Hermiston OR 97838

Call Sign: KA7GXG

James D Lanphear
960 W Gettman Rd
Hermiston OR 97838

Call Sign: KA7TIQ
Lois I Lanphear
960 W Gettman Rd
Hermiston OR 97838

Call Sign: KE7DWI
Daniel W Smith
540 W Hartley
Hermiston OR 97838

Call Sign: N7FBA
Dennis E Burke
1195 W Hartley
Hermiston OR 97838

Call Sign: KC7JFI
Gerry S Lloyd
710 W Highland
Hermiston OR 97838

Call Sign: KD7SLW
John C Baldwin
611 W Johns Ave
Hermiston OR 97838

Call Sign: KB7WGE
David M Clark
670 W Johns Ave
Hermiston OR 97838

Call Sign: KG7AM
Tim J Heihn
699 W Johns Ave
Hermiston OR 97838

Call Sign: KC7UF
Fred A Morrell
990 W Juniper Ave Apt 66
Hermiston OR 97838

Call Sign: W7XXX

Samuel F Champie
105 W Mc Kenzie
Hermiston OR 97838

Call Sign: N0SCA
Elizabeth A Ballard
180 W Moore Ave
Hermiston OR 97838

Call Sign: KA7ISC
Chester R Bledsoe
880 W Pine Ave
Hermiston OR 97838

Call Sign: KD7NOQ
Ivan E Barzallo
890 W Pine Ave
Hermiston OR 97838

Call Sign: N7YPX
Harold H Manny
489 W Ridgeway
Hermiston OR 97838

Call Sign: KB7HSN
Kevin J Eliason
855 W Ridgeway
Hermiston OR 97838

Call Sign: KB7HTU
Michael E Eliason
855 W Ridgeway
Hermiston OR 97838

Call Sign: KC7VU
Richard D Forsythe
865 W Ridgeway
Hermiston OR 97838

Call Sign: KC7WXE
Gary C Mc Gowan
182 W Ridgeway Ave
Hermiston OR 97838

Call Sign: K7DI

Charles L Stewart
Hermiston OR 97838

Call Sign: KB7CKJ
Charles R Barnes
Hermiston OR 97838

Call Sign: KB7NFU
Colton J Kenshol
Hermiston OR 97838

Call Sign: KC7FFB
Elaine N Schroeder
Hermiston OR 97838

Call Sign: KC7KUG
Hermiston ARC Inc
Hermiston OR 97838

Call Sign: N7ONR
Kathy J Anderson
Hermiston OR 97838

Call Sign: KD7NUD
Mona L Thomas
Hermiston OR 97838

Call Sign: KF7GTK
Daniel C Elder
Hermiston OR 97838

Call Sign: KF7GTL
Jacob S Elder
Hermiston OR 97838

Call Sign: KC7AJS
Candace A Stewart
Hermiston OR 978380394

Call Sign: N7YPW
Ronald R Ridder
Hermiston OR 978383404

**FCC Amateur Radio
Licenses in Hines**

Call Sign: WA7VGR
Walter A Cooper
2261 37th Pl NW
Hines OR 97738

Call Sign: KC7UDW
Scott C Clelland
1414 NE 109th
Hines OR 97738

Call Sign: K7HWZ
Gerald E Mason
4404 NE 129th Pl
Hines OR 97738

Call Sign: K7RPW
Duane D Mason
546 NE 12th Ave
Hines OR 97738

Call Sign: KC0NMP
Vernon L Estes
3705 NE 18th
Hines OR 97738

Call Sign: KF7CRP
Harney County ARES
611 Tennyson Ave 112
Hines OR 97738

Call Sign: KF7CRJ
Harney County ARES
611 Tennyson Ave 112
Hines OR 97738

Call Sign: KF7CRK
Harney County ARES
611 Tennyson Ave 112
Hines OR 97738

Call Sign: KF7CRL
Harney County ARES
611 Tennyson Ave 112
Hines OR 97738

Call Sign: KF7CRM
Harney County ARES
611 Tennyson Ave 112
Hines OR 97738

Call Sign: W7VLE
Vernon L Estes
611 Tennyson Ave 112
Hines OR 977389448

Call Sign: KF7CRN
Harney County ARES
SW 4302 Terlyn Ct
Hines OR 97738

Call Sign: KF7CRO
Harney County ARES
725 Terra Ave 34A
Hines OR 97738

Call Sign: KA7ITJ
Randall T Whitaker
420 W Pettibone Ave
Hines OR 97738

Call Sign: KB7UHW
Michael E Torrey
Hines OR 97738

Call Sign: KB7SIH
Julia L Milleson
Hines OR 97738

Call Sign: KE7YLA
Harney County ARES
Hines OR 97738

Call Sign: KE7YLC
Harney County Radio
Association
Hines OR 97738

Call Sign: KA7RIY
Laurie J Whitaker

Hines OR 97738

Call Sign: KB7TIA
Shirley R Torrey
Hines OR 97738

Call Sign: WA7WKH
Stephen W Ryder
Hines OR 97738

Call Sign: KD7PGM
Jack Trotter
Hines OR 97738

Call Sign: AC7SJ
Jack Trotter
Hines OR 97738

Call Sign: KE7IZH
Alfred J Foulke
Hines OR 97738

Call Sign: KF7GOY
Brandon R Klawitter
Hines OR 97738

Call Sign: KF7JDQ
Brett S Bingham
Hines OR 97738

Call Sign: KF7CIQ
Christopher M Howes
Hines OR 97738

Call Sign: KF7CIP
Eric Haakenson
Hines OR 97738

Call Sign: KF7CIL
Robert N Sharp
Hines OR 97738

Call Sign: KD7ZWX
Dale R Weeks
Hines OR 977380753

FCC Amateur Radio Licenses in Hood River

Call Sign: KF7QA
John A Durkan
16869 65th Ave 305
Hood River OR 97031

Call Sign: WA7BKC
G Peter Geist
5105 A St
Hood River OR 97031

Call Sign: KD7AYG
Douglas A Miller
2225 Arctic Cr
Hood River OR 97031

Call Sign: KC7EKD
Gary F Gilardi
1019 Ash Grove Loop
Hood River OR 97031

Call Sign: W7ETS
John E Foley
1145 Ash St
Hood River OR 97031

Call Sign: WA7GOE
James R Stolhand
1840 Ash St
Hood River OR 97031

Call Sign: KF7ELQ
Steven M Reynolds
1003 B Ave
Hood River OR 97031

Call Sign: WB7VZR
Roy A Dalby
2883 Bailey Ln
Hood River OR 97031

Call Sign: KE7BJD

Mack D Lamb
60865 Billadeau Rd
Hood River OR 97031

Call Sign: KC7CJA
Keith A Clarke
34885 Bond Rd
Hood River OR 97031

Call Sign: KE7ZXJ
Tony K Clark
Rt 2 Box 323
Hood River OR 97031

Call Sign: KC7TJV
Caleb Kaspar
1126 Boyer Ct
Hood River OR 97031

Call Sign: KB7SEW
James Melville
3392 Bursell Rd
Hood River OR 97031

Call Sign: KB7DUA
Alan R Taylor
4732 Cloudcrest Dr
Hood River OR 97031

Call Sign: WP3HN
Homero A Cersosimo
4893 Cloudcroft Ln
Hood River OR 97031

Call Sign: KB7DRT
Anna M Perry
5470 Cloverlawn Dr
Hood River OR 97031

Call Sign: KB7DUB
Paula G Perry
62905 Clyde Ln
Hood River OR 97031

Call Sign: KU7M

Ralph D Perry
55 Coachman Dr
Hood River OR 97031

Call Sign: KC7KHX
David Kalousdian
220 Coachman Dr
Hood River OR 97031

Call Sign: KD6PGI
Kenneth W Jacobs
4625 Coopers Hawk Rd
Hood River OR 97031

Call Sign: KE7AQF
Roy G Fleming
1856 Cottonwood Ave
Hood River OR 97031

Call Sign: KA7ZHW
Dorothy C Collins
2512 Daisy Ln NW
Hood River OR 97031

Call Sign: N7DNV
Jack R Collins Sr
1211 Dakota
Hood River OR 97031

Call Sign: KE7PTI
Nancy J Steele
63163 Dakota Dr
Hood River OR 97031

Call Sign: N7SJE
Nancy J Steele
4703 Dakota Rd SE
Hood River OR 97031

Call Sign: KE7RNY
Gary W Steele
4703 Dakota Rd SE
Hood River OR 97031

Call Sign: KE7RNW

Roy Gaylord
72 Danita Ln
Hood River OR 97031

Call Sign: KD7KOQ
Thomas Keffer
2312 Delta Waters Rd
Hood River OR 97031

Call Sign: WA7RXV
Wilfred Miller
1750 Delta Waters Ste 102
Pmb 312
Hood River OR 97031

Call Sign: KE7AQE
Frederick Kinoshita
89653 Demming Rd
Hood River OR 97031

Call Sign: K1OSH
Frederick Kinoshita
89653 Demming Rd
Hood River OR 97031

Call Sign: KE7RNU
Heather M Kinoshita
24717 Demming Ridge Rd
Hood River OR 97031

Call Sign: KD7OFU
Robin F Hoeye
4491 Doyle St
Hood River OR 97031

Call Sign: WL7AOQ
Mary L Ward
1501 E 14th St
Hood River OR 97031

Call Sign: AL7V
Maynard P Ward
2500 E 16th
Hood River OR 97031

Call Sign: WA7KME
Donald L Moore Jr
760 E Fairview Way
Hood River OR 97031

Call Sign: KG7WY
Ulla Fischer
4701 Fir Mountain Rd
Hood River OR 97031

Call Sign: N7LMS
Christian Fischer Sr
17464 Fir Rd
Hood River OR 970319439

Call Sign: KD7MPT
Eldon V Bailey
88460 Fisher Rd
Hood River OR 97031

Call Sign: W7NCK
Eldon V Bailey
2760 Fisher Rd NE
Hood River OR 97031

Call Sign: W7RAG
Radio Amateurs Of The
Gorge
4970 Galew St
Hood River OR 97031

Call Sign: KA7JNU
Eugene A Mielke Jr
3530 Game Farm Rd 48
Hood River OR 970319785

Call Sign: KC7KLB
Radio Amateurs Of The
Gorge
6792 Ganon St SE
Hood River OR 97031

Call Sign: KA7WVC
Karen L Mielke
21215 Garcia Rd

Hood River OR 97031   Hood River OR 97031   Hood River OR 97031

Call Sign: W7DRG   Call Sign: KE7KIR   Call Sign: KE7RNX
Douglas E Davee   Tracy Willett   Melody Shellman
6721 Glacier Dr   1315 Joplin St S   724 N 9th St
Hood River OR 970319483   Hood River OR 97031   Hood River OR 97031

Call Sign: KB7WFJ   Call Sign: KC7ZGV   Call Sign: KC7EI
Dawn A Lynch   Norman R Gray   Alfred S Guignard
330 Granite Hill Rd   598 Milburn Ct   7056 N Concord Ave
Hood River OR 97031   Hood River OR 97031   Hood River OR 97031

Call Sign: KD7AXM   Call Sign: KB7QP   Call Sign: WK7E
Joshua C Rutledge   Herbert C Morse   Alfred S Guignard
27832 Green Oaks Dr   1837 Minnesota St   6040 N Cutter Cir 303
Hood River OR 97031   Hood River OR 97031   Hood River OR 97031

Call Sign: KD7FEV   Call Sign: KA4NOF   Call Sign: KA7NGA
Gordon D Brennan   Phillip C Hargrave   Charles A Leveque Jr
18995 Hwy 126   2232 Minnesota St   1659 N Danebo Ave
Hood River OR 97031   Hood River OR 97031   Hood River OR 97031

Call Sign: KD7FET   Call Sign: KE7EQE   Call Sign: KD7PNN
David R Brennan   Charles A Dannen   Kenneth P Maddox
Box 17980 Hwy 126   60787 Murphy Rd   2648 NW 13th St
Hood River OR 97031   Hood River OR 97031   Hood River OR 97031

Call Sign: KE7QBJ   Call Sign: KE7DZS   Call Sign: WA7EXI
John F Brennan   Kim D Dannen   Anthony C Corrado
36036 Hwy 140   1124 Murray Ave   2137 Orindale Rd
Hood River OR 97031   Hood River OR 97031   Hood River OR 97031

Call Sign: WD8AMR   Call Sign: K7JUV   Call Sign: WB7QFG
Hubert P Pilkenton   Craig E Terry   Patrick A Moore
295 Idaho St   1012 Murray Dr   13586 Parrish Gap Rd SE
Hood River OR 97031   Hood River OR 97031   Hood River OR 97031

Call Sign: K7PLH   Call Sign: KE7SYR   Call Sign: KB7ASC
Bert B Cates   William I Carroll   Norman H Frisbie
2090 Jasmine Ave   850 N 8th St   190 Polaris Cir
Hood River OR 97031   Hood River OR 97031   Hood River OR 97031

Call Sign: KE7KIQ   Call Sign: N7TDA   Call Sign: KB7POO
Steve L Wrye   Kenneth W Mc Carty   Jon C Thomsen
1395 Jonmart Ave SE   2366 N 8th St   4733 Portland Rd NE 31

Hood River OR 97031

Hood River OR 97031

Hood River OR 97031

Call Sign: W7EQI
Paul E Walden
1337 R St
Hood River OR 97031

Call Sign: KE7NXR
Rebecca A Van Hee
716 S 10th St
Hood River OR 97031

Call Sign: K7XI
Robert A Mac Donald
4446 Sycamore
Hood River OR 97031

Call Sign: KQ7Z
Jonathan R Rose
2649 Rabun Way
Hood River OR 97031

Call Sign: KE7NXQ
Sarah A Van Hee
716 S 10th St
Hood River OR 97031

Call Sign: K7KLC
Xander L Cannon
68015 Taylor Ln
Hood River OR 97031

Call Sign: KE7DZT
Stan E Harryman
52035 Read Loop
Hood River OR 97031

Call Sign: KE7EQF
Mylene A Walden
36869 Shorview Dr
Hood River OR 97031

Call Sign: KB7QMC
James Cannon
1844 Taylor St
Hood River OR 97031

Call Sign: KF7MGI
Edward H Ganley
4820 Rebecca St NE
Hood River OR 97031

Call Sign: K7TS
Thomas R Senior
79336 Stewart Creek Rd
Hood River OR 97031

Call Sign: N7SOG
George H Kirby
2504 Taylor St
Hood River OR 97031

Call Sign: KF7MGJ
Kora J Treiman
4820 Rebecca St NE
Hood River OR 97031

Call Sign: AB7A
Lyle G Nicholson Dvm
2405 Stortz Ave NE
Hood River OR 97031

Call Sign: KB7YKQ
Dorothy L Cannon
842 Taylor St 7
Hood River OR 97031

Call Sign: N7PJS
David L White
4788 Redwing Way
Hood River OR 97031

Call Sign: KE7RNR
Richard W Frank
6212 Sunnyview Rd NE
Hood River OR 97031

Call Sign: KI6VQ
Thomas H Schaefer
300 Thornberry Dr
Hood River OR 970318477

Call Sign: KB7GIK
Gary L Fleck
1325 Ridge Way
Hood River OR 97031

Call Sign: KE7HTA
Mount Hood Radio Group
2619 Swyers Dr
Hood River OR 970319424

Call Sign: KE7RNT
Mark F Brennan
1740 Tucker Rd
Hood River OR 97031

Call Sign: KE7RNP
Leroy S Webster
793 River Bend Rd
Hood River OR 97031

Call Sign: K7MHR
Mount Hood Radio Group
2619 Swyers Dr
Hood River OR 970319424

Call Sign: K4MFB
Mark F Brennan
220 Tucson Ct
Hood River OR 97031

Call Sign: W2OOO
Leroy S Webster
100 River Bend Rd Sp 47

Call Sign: KE7CYK
Cindy E Snapp
4446 Sycamore

Call Sign: KB7ITH
Mathew L Taylor
341 Tudor St

Hood River OR 97051

Call Sign: KB7DRR
Dale M Johnston
3723 Union St
Hood River OR 97031

Call Sign: N8FFS
Albert L Hanson
2149 W Cascade Ste 106A
143
Hood River OR 97031

Call Sign: KE7RNS
Terri G Tyler
2034 W Eugene
Hood River OR 97031

Call Sign: WB7OCE
Gregory P Walden
1504 W Sherman St
Hood River OR 97031

Call Sign: W7EQI
Gregory P Walden
1504 W Sherman St
Hood River OR 97031

Call Sign: KC7EKF
Richard W Dodd
1301 Wasco St
Hood River OR 97031

Call Sign: KC7KIA
Charles V Moon
1532 Wasco St
Hood River OR 97031

Call Sign: N7PHW
Walter A Baumann
1801 Wasco St
Hood River OR 97031

Call Sign: KE7ZXI
Dennis L Berg

2699 Webster Rd
Hood River OR 97031

Call Sign: KE7RNV
Tim Holyoak
3460 Whitten Rd
Hood River OR 97031

Call Sign: K7PJT
Thomas S Rousseau
4179 Willow Flat Rd
Hood River OR 97031

Call Sign: WB7NED
Sandra K Rousseau
4179 Willow Flat Rd
Hood River OR 97031

Call Sign: WA7AR
Columbia River Contest
Club
5270 York Hill Dr
Hood River OR 97031

Call Sign: W7FP
Charles L Clayton
5270 York Hill Dr
Hood River OR 970319611

Call Sign: WA7KMC
Roberta L Clayton
5270 York Hill Dr
Hood River OR 970319611

Call Sign: AD7J
Columbia River Contest
Club
5270 York Hill Dr
Hood River OR 970319642

Call Sign: KA7VAG
Gerald E Larsen
Hood River OR 97031

Call Sign: KB7LDT

Joseph R Reeves
Hood River OR 97031

Call Sign: KC7EKB
Carl H Coolidge
Hood River OR 97031

Call Sign: W2FV
John E Pieszcynski
Hood River OR 97031

Call Sign: KD7RCW
Lisa D Hauge
Hood River OR 97031

Call Sign: KE7ZXB
James C Lombardo Jr
Hood River OR 97031

FCC Amateur Radio Licenses in Huntington

Call Sign: WB7WLA
Ray E Griffin
225 W Jefferson St
Huntington OR 97907

FCC Amateur Radio Licenses in Idleyld

Call Sign: KE7KDY
Ronald J Williams
970 E 43rd Ave
Idleyld OR 97447

Call Sign: KA7RJW
Ronald J Williams
760 E 44th Ave
Idleyld OR 97447

FCC Amateur Radio Licenses in Idleyld Park

Call Sign: WA7LMC
Markell M Mc Crosky

1353 Jones Rd
Idleyld Park OR 97447

Call Sign: KI7UN
Demetro U Tokaruk
5055 NW 180th Ter
Idleyld Park OR 97447

Call Sign: KE7UOJ
Marc C Garst
Idleyld Park OR 97447

**FCC Amateur Radio
Licenses in Imbler**

Call Sign: K7WWV
Delbert W Harper
188 49th Ave SE
Imbler OR 97841

Call Sign: KE7EQR
Roger K Beckner
32242 Cater Rd
Imbler OR 97841

Call Sign: KD7TUG
Bradley J Beckner
943 Caves Hwy
Imbler OR 97841

Call Sign: WA6ZCW
Mary Jane Harper
83541 Jensen Ln
Imbler OR 97841

Call Sign: K7ZCW
Mary Jane Harper
2124 Jeppesen Acres Rd
Imbler OR 97841

Call Sign: WA6WWV
Delbert W Harper
4951 Netarts Hwy W
Imbler OR 97841

Call Sign: KD7CEM
Donald R Magee
1685 NW 130th
Imbler OR 978419705

**FCC Amateur Radio
Licenses in Imnaha**

Call Sign: KD7OOO
Roy G Mc Kinney
2845 Rockydale Rd
Imnaha OR 978428106

**FCC Amateur Radio
Licenses in Ione**

Call Sign: K7ADO
William A Wolfsen
855 Carmel Crest Ct SE
Ione OR 97843

Call Sign: KC7JFE
Jeremy T Tullis
2081 Fairmont Blvd
Ione OR 97843

Call Sign: KK7RF
Rebecca L Doherty
560 Fairmont Dr NE
Ione OR 97843

Call Sign: WA7DWJ
John W Jepsen
Ione OR 97843

**FCC Amateur Radio
Licenses in Irrigon**

Call Sign: KA7LUS
Alfred J Hansen
97046 Agness Rd
Irrigon OR 97844

Call Sign: KA7OTM
Betty J Martin

445 Candalaria Blvd S
Irrigon OR 97844

Call Sign: KD7MQU
Tammi L Van Fossen
467 Denver St SE
Irrigon OR 97844

Call Sign: KA7OTL
Clarence A Martin Sr
555 Freeman Rd 75
Irrigon OR 97844

Call Sign: WB7DKF
Robert A Edwards
1101 Oak St
Irrigon OR 97844

Call Sign: KC7DQM
Edward L Wink
8395 SW Secretariet Ter
Irrigon OR 97844

Call Sign: KD7LXQ
Jesse L Branson
80856 Wagon Wheel Loop
Irrigon OR 978447150

Call Sign: KD7LXU
Marsha C Pratt
80861 Wagon Wheel Loop
Irrigon OR 978447150

Call Sign: KB7TLX
Scott C Green
Irrigon OR 97844

Call Sign: KB7WBS
Sarah M Brooks
Irrigon OR 97844

Call Sign: KB7WBT
Floyd E Brooks
Irrigon OR 97844

Call Sign: KD7MQS
Michele R Ball
Irrigon OR 97844

**FCC Amateur Radio
Licenses in Jacksonville**

Call Sign: KB7VES
Brenda S Thomas
4045 Beck Ave SE
Jacksonville OR 97530

Call Sign: KF7OCO
Cody R Nault
1811 Bennett Creek Rd
Jacksonville OR 97530

Call Sign: WB6QIS
Jeffrey G Borchers
Rt 3 Box 3642
Jacksonville OR 975308947

Call Sign: KA7FGK
David A Uhreen
1708 Bridge St
Jacksonville OR 97530

Call Sign: KB7VFQ
Thomas S Lewis
5005 Cumberland Ct SE
Jacksonville OR 97530

Call Sign: KD7OUD
David R Hangartner
13291 E Borne Dr
Jacksonville OR 97530

Call Sign: KD7IBI
Sherri J Gray
4646 Janice Ave NE
Jacksonville OR 97530

Call Sign: KF7LVU
Monica E Mcfadden
4646 Janice Ave NE

Jacksonville OR 97530

Call Sign: K9MCF
Monica E Mcfadden
305 Janice Way
Jacksonville OR 97530

Call Sign: K6ZNM
Elmer H Metzger
2185 Janna Ct
Jacksonville OR 97530

Call Sign: KB7VQW
John W Roeloffs
1507 Jansen Way
Jacksonville OR 97530

Call Sign: KE7BJH
Dean H Gradwell
1222 La Loma Dr
Jacksonville OR 97530

Call Sign: KC7CHA
Nancy L Brown
16340 Lower Harbor Rd
230
Jacksonville OR 97530

Call Sign: KD7DFK
Richard L Brown Jr
16340 Lower Harbor Rd
A103
Jacksonville OR 97530

Call Sign: KE7IKE
Emmett J Armstrong
22987 Manzanita Ct
Jacksonville OR 97530

Call Sign: KE7IKF
Sarah G Armstrong
22987 Manzanita Ct
Jacksonville OR 97530

Call Sign: KD7DAS

Matthew Epstein
311 Manzanita Dr
Jacksonville OR 97530

Call Sign: AB7CJ
Craig L Faulkner
728 Marino Dr N
Jacksonville OR 97530

Call Sign: KF7UMW
Christopher L Arnold
52417 Miller Rd
Jacksonville OR 975309706

Call Sign: N7XPF
Darin J Rembert
1651 N 16th St
Jacksonville OR 97530

Call Sign: KC7TE
Daurel L Carhart
972 N Bellwood St
Jacksonville OR 975309761

Call Sign: KF6LWG
Adam D Bylund
8926 N Berkeley Ave
Jacksonville OR 97530

Call Sign: N7FMD
Renwick M Ells
1503 N Hayden Island Dr
Sp 236
Jacksonville OR 97530

Call Sign: N7URL
Donald W Wahle
1503 N Hayden Island Dr
Sp 236
Jacksonville OR 97530

Call Sign: WB7USJ
Thomas S Knackstedt
12660 Rachella Ct
Jacksonville OR 97530

Call Sign: WB7SAC
John M Allen
22490 S Springwater Rd
Jacksonville OR 97530

Call Sign: W7IJF
Le Land I Harter
1504 Sherman Ave
Jacksonville OR 97530

Call Sign: N7TGK
Roger L Cornett
2272 Sherman Ave
Jacksonville OR 97530

Call Sign: W7RAA
Richard B Ulrich
2095 Stortz Ave NE
Jacksonville OR 975309302

Call Sign: N7LRT
Thomas K Werner
13620 Tyee Rd
Jacksonville OR 97530

Call Sign: KE7SBA
Allan W Hassett
1805 Upper Applegate Rd
Jacksonville OR 97530

Call Sign: KA6FUB
Dennis L Matzen
1805 Upper Applegate Rd
Jacksonville OR 975300148

Call Sign: KF7ICH
Phil F Dollison
6500 Upper Applegate Rd
Jacksonville OR 97530

Call Sign: KF7QNH
James O Backes
6621 Upper Applegate Rd
Jacksonville OR 97530

Call Sign: KW7JIM
James O Backes
6621 Upper Applegate Rd
Jacksonville OR 97530

Call Sign: WA6LNE
Christopher J Beekman
9885 Upper Applegate Rd
Jacksonville OR 97530

Call Sign: KB6KRC
Ann M Dollison
11831 Upper Applegate Rd
Jacksonville OR 97530

Call Sign: KD7FZR
John C Hart
38446 Upper Camp Creek
Rd
Jacksonville OR 97530

Call Sign: WB7TEM
John M Gomperts
38446 Upper Camp Creek
Rd
Jacksonville OR 975308991

Call Sign: KD7HAU
Harry R Gates
1685 Wagon Trl Dr
Jacksonville OR 97530

Call Sign: KD7HRG
Harry R Gates
1685 Wagon Trl Dr
Jacksonville OR 97530

Call Sign: AB7BY
Mara B Jackson
Jacksonville OR 97530

Call Sign: KB7KBF
Wade T Parker Jr
Jacksonville OR 97530

Call Sign: KB7PPD
Ray L Driskell
Jacksonville OR 97530

Call Sign: KC7BIW
Jared C Jackson
Jacksonville OR 97530

Call Sign: KC7BIX
Paul C Jackson
Jacksonville OR 97530

Call Sign: N7AKF
John L Connolly
Jacksonville OR 97530

Call Sign: N7FGP
Fred S Page
Jacksonville OR 97530

Call Sign: N7PMF
Daid D Thompson
Jacksonville OR 97530

Call Sign: KC0FVV
Richard Hager
Jacksonville OR 97530

Call Sign: KC7NQA
Joe A Stagg
Jacksonville OR 97530

Call Sign: KG7HJ
David L Aikins
Jacksonville OR 97530

Call Sign: WA6QWN
William L Protzek Jr
Jacksonville OR 97530

Call Sign: W9PCI
Arlen F Hatlestad
Jacksonville OR 97530

Call Sign: KD7OUF
Patricia B Arnold
Jacksonville OR 97530

Call Sign: KF7JVV
Owen D Jurling
Jacksonville OR 97530

Call Sign: K7QWN
William L Protzek Jr
Jacksonville OR 97530

Call Sign: KF7UMK
John P Armstrong
Jacksonville OR 975300116

Call Sign: KD6UIH
Robert C Earl
Jacksonville OR 975301752

Call Sign: AD6WD
Barry Kilpatrick
Jacksonville OR 975301771

FCC Amateur Radio Licenses in Jasper

Call Sign: K7CIS
Kenneth E Syfert
Jasper OR 97438

Call Sign: KC7BHH
Charles R Keech
Jasper OR 97438

Call Sign: KD7QOD
Scott A Mattie
Jasper OR 974380299

FCC Amateur Radio Licenses in John Day

Call Sign: KC7WRD
Edward A Petersen
3201 Campus Dr Oit

John Day OR 97845

Call Sign: K7QQQ
Robert W Willey
940 NW Dale Ave
John Day OR 97845

Call Sign: KC7USO
Christine M Rowe
16367 S Hiram Ave
John Day OR 97845

Call Sign: KC7USN
Charles F Rowe
12497 SE Imperial Crest St
John Day OR 97845

Call Sign: N7VUV
Gary A Misbach
5930 SW 207th Ave
John Day OR 97845

Call Sign: KC7EGV
James M Earl
W Bench Rd
John Day OR 97845

Call Sign: KC1MC
Robert D Reimiller
John Day OR 97845

Call Sign: K7JUC
Lorene Allen
John Day OR 97845

Call Sign: KA6GKB
Carl Chadwick
John Day OR 97845

Call Sign: KC7WSW
Edward R Carwithen
John Day OR 97845

Call Sign: KD6UED
Barbara L Settlemyre Kirk

John Day OR 97845

Call Sign: KD7BRG
Ronald M Smith
John Day OR 97845

FCC Amateur Radio Licenses in Jordan Valley

Call Sign: K7JVO
Jordan Valley Oregon Radio
Society
206 E 10th St
Jordan Valley OR 97910

Call Sign: KC7GLR
Kenneth F Matteri
609 E 10th St
Jordan Valley OR 97910

Call Sign: KD7SDZ
Jordan Valley Oregon Radio
Society
2437 E 10th St
Jordan Valley OR 97910

Call Sign: N0CFF
Philip A Bourk Jr
Jordan Valley OR 97910

FCC Amateur Radio Licenses in Joseph

Call Sign: KD7TLS
Donald L Davis
330 E Main
Joseph OR 97846

Call Sign: KD7SYN
Patricia D Davis
511 E Main
Joseph OR 97846

Call Sign: KC7ESX
Kay C Cutler

35256 Edna Ln
Joseph OR 97846

Call Sign: WB7EUX
Tom S Bingham
692 Ewald Ave S
Joseph OR 97846

Call Sign: KC7JPR
Philip R Stonebrook
690 Franklin Ave
Joseph OR 97846

Call Sign: KD7ZQS
Zachary J White
255 Kruse 11
Joseph OR 97846

Call Sign: KG6PXR
Frank J Miller
48750 Little Nestucca River
Rd
Joseph OR 97846

Call Sign: KE7ZSJ
James R Hayes
900 Main Ave
Joseph OR 97846

Call Sign: KA7QPD
Jack W Burris
Ski Run Rd
Joseph OR 97846

Call Sign: KB7CGT
Steven D Kangas
55853 Snow Goose Rd
Joseph OR 97846

Call Sign: KB7VFW
Kristy J Kangas
3376 Snow Peak Pl
Joseph OR 97846

Call Sign: KF7HNJ

Wallowa County ARES
Joseph OR 97846

Call Sign: WA7LLO
Wallowa County ARES
Joseph OR 97846

Call Sign: KB7DZR
Scott M Hampton
Joseph OR 97846

Call Sign: KF6MS
John B Thompson
Joseph OR 97846

Call Sign: N7WVX
Shirley M Burns
Joseph OR 97846

Call Sign: NG7X
Ronald L Burns
Joseph OR 97846

Call Sign: KD7RMK
John L Anderson
Joseph OR 97846

Call Sign: KD7RMQ
Earl D Loree
Joseph OR 97846

Call Sign: W2TDZ
Daniel T O Connell
Joseph OR 97846

Call Sign: W7TDZ
Daniel T O Connell
Joseph OR 97846

Call Sign: KF7MS
John B Thompson
Joseph OR 97846

Call Sign: KF7JVT
Keith R Stebbings

Joseph OR 97846

Call Sign: KE1THR
Keith R Stebbings
Joseph OR 97846

Call Sign: KE7KAJ
Paul R Kent
Joseph OR 97846

Call Sign: KE7GI
David E Gilbert
Joseph OR 978460036

FCC Amateur Radio Licenses in Junction City

Call Sign: KE7QOJ
James A Stephens
1112 26th Ave
Junction City OR 97448

Call Sign: W7OQ
Vardell Nelson
264 9th St
Junction City OR 97448

Call Sign: K7CCP
Don A Lohff
1855 9th St
Junction City OR
974489590

Call Sign: KD7MHX
Dean E Edwards
1129 Applegate St
Junction City OR 97448

Call Sign: KD7MHY
John K Edwards
21 Becket
Junction City OR 97448

Call Sign: KD7UYH
Mathew N Lillie

22 Becket
Junction City OR 97448

Call Sign: KC7HZB
Dennis E Marra
22 Becket
Junction City OR 97448

Call Sign: KD7IVC
Susie R Sturman
241 Blue Ridge Dr
Junction City OR 97448

Call Sign: K7HY
James J Sturman
12275 Blue Ridge Dr
Junction City OR 97448

Call Sign: KE7YYG
Levi M Mosley
26050 Bud Ln
Junction City OR 97448

Call Sign: KE7YYF
Rachel R Mosley
1721 Buelah
Junction City OR 97448

Call Sign: KD7RLD
Richard G Lewin
1312 Cherry
Junction City OR 97448

Call Sign: KF7RU
Jerold A Goetsch
540 Colonial Ct
Junction City OR
974481531

Call Sign: AA6BB
Gerald D Branson
6672 E St
Junction City OR 97448

Call Sign: AB7UR

Naokatsu Nagasaki
6672 E St
Junction City OR 97448

Call Sign: KA7DPJ
Michael J Skinner
330 Edwards
Junction City OR
974481567

Call Sign: KA1CES
Arthur L Stoddard
2157 Ferguson Ln
Junction City OR
974482807

Call Sign: N7CEJ
Michael A Ray
2934 Forest Gale Dr
Junction City OR 97448

Call Sign: W6BGA
Raymond L Wilson
36 Heritage Ave
Junction City OR 97448

Call Sign: KD7DWT
John L Tatum
1378 Hillendale Dr SE
Junction City OR 97448

Call Sign: KA7KTK
Louise Campbell
2006 Hwy 101 Pmb 162
Junction City OR 97448

Call Sign: KD7YN
Dale O Kite
36036 Hwy 140
Junction City OR 97448

Call Sign: KA7VCQ
George I Nielsen
39040 Jerger St
Junction City OR 97448

Call Sign: KD7PJV
Melissa A Sturman
657 Karic Way
Junction City OR 97448

Call Sign: KD7LDC
Steven S Sturman
33215 Karis Ln
Junction City OR 97448

Call Sign: AA7PO
Tim C Cogswell
1506 Lorane Hwy
Junction City OR 97448

Call Sign: KJ7BW
Edward E Cooper
7684 Lost River Rd
Junction City OR 97448

Call Sign: N7QPK
John E Twedt
7725 Lost River Rd
Junction City OR 97448

Call Sign: K7TBV
Robert L Nelson
405 Menthorne Rd
Junction City OR 97448

Call Sign: KC7IMT
William R Phillips
726 Mooney St
Junction City OR 97448

Call Sign: KA7RON
Michael J Mc Feron
2875 NW 154th
Junction City OR 97448

Call Sign: KC7BIU
Sandra L Jenness
10211 Old Fort Rd
Junction City OR 97448

Call Sign: N7BFT
Charles E Berg Sr
8100 Old Stage Rd N
Junction City OR 97448

Call Sign: KA6NWP
William A Ahlquist
3007 Periwinkle St
Junction City OR 97448

Call Sign: KD6MMZ
Brandon T Skirvin
26553 Priceview Dr
Junction City OR 97448

Call Sign: KA7BCV
Raymond F Trefren Jr
490 Prim St
Junction City OR 97448

Call Sign: KA7ZZR
Dahlia M Trefren
2220 Primrose Ln
Junction City OR 97448

Call Sign: KC7MHR
Alma J Sapienza
3569 Pringle Rd SE
Junction City OR 97448

Call Sign: KC7MHS
Tom J Sapienza
3230 Pringle Rd SE 40
Junction City OR 97448

Call Sign: KC7IND
Ronald G Van Devender
257 Rainier Dr SE
Junction City OR
974489475

Call Sign: W7FZO
Nels H Andersen
20390 Rogers Rd

Junction City OR 97448

Call Sign: KD5IGX
Frances M Keaton
233 Rogue River Hwy
Junction City OR 97448

Call Sign: KD5IGY
Alan L Keaton
1679 Rogue River Hwy 20
Junction City OR 97448

Call Sign: KA7VCX
Terrence J Flaherty
83425 S Cove Dr
Junction City OR 97448

Call Sign: KA7VCY
Betty May O Flaherty
249 S E St
Junction City OR 97448

Call Sign: KB7TXD
Dean C Kilgore
4146 S E St
Junction City OR 97448

Call Sign: KB7SXZ
Wilma L Schultz
94915 Shelley Ln
Junction City OR 97448

Call Sign: WA7GVE
Francis R Schultz
94915 Shelley Ln
Junction City OR 97448

Call Sign: KE7AKO
Angelo L Bazzi
1657 Sun Glo Dr
Junction City OR 97448

Call Sign: KA7HFW
Carol L Christensen
1208 SW K St

Junction City OR 97448

Call Sign: KB7SXY
Daniel L Michelson
959 Terry St
Junction City OR 97448

Call Sign: W6HCS
Carl P Chapman
25117 Turner Rd
Junction City OR 97448

Call Sign: W6MZR
Robert G Biswell
1750 W 1st Ave
Junction City OR 97448

Call Sign: W7MZR
Robert G Biswell
1750 W 1st Ave
Junction City OR 97448

Call Sign: KD7ZHQ
Danny R Beer
1085 W 1st Ave Unit Q
Junction City OR 97478

Call Sign: WL7ZL
Fritz W Hunter
665 W 4th Ave
Junction City OR 97448

Call Sign: KB7VIV
Kevin R Lynde
Junction City OR 97448

Call Sign: W7ADW
Ken E Henderson
Junction City OR
974480172

Call Sign: WB7NAM
Dan R Stoe
Junction City OR 97448

Call Sign: KG6AYY
Karen D Crisp
Junction City OR 97448

**FCC Amateur Radio
Licenses in Keno**

Call Sign: AH2CS
Edward A Hadley
341 Aspen Dr
Keno OR 97627

Call Sign: KF7MGG
Wes Steiner
22875 Jennie Rd
Keno OR 97627

Call Sign: KF7MMF
Wes Steiner
22875 Jennie Rd
Keno OR 97627

Call Sign: KA6ARR
Robert P Swift
5430 N Depauw St
Keno OR 976270992

Call Sign: N6YSG
La Verne Swift
6334 N Depauw St
Keno OR 976270992

Call Sign: W7ARR
Robert P Swift
6323 N Detroit
Keno OR 976270992

Call Sign: WB6DFH
M Jack Coy
19207 Rose Rd
Keno OR 97627

Call Sign: KA7TXE
Clarence N Lewis
16122 Timberline Ln

Keno OR 976270949

Call Sign: KA7YTM
Sharon S Lewis
7760 Timothy Ln NE
Keno OR 976270949

Call Sign: KB7JEK
Ian L Ericson
Keno OR 97627

Call Sign: KB7REM
Lynnea A Perry
Keno OR 97627

Call Sign: KB7TMN
Edwin J Meyer
Keno OR 97627

Call Sign: N7SOW
Nancy A Frazier
Keno OR 97627

Call Sign: N7YIY
Meredyth J Hurt
Keno OR 97627

Call Sign: WB6SZD
Melvin H Miller
Keno OR 97627

Call Sign: N7SOV
Lois M Kiger
Keno OR 97627

Call Sign: W7UFM
Hollis C Kiger
Keno OR 97627

Call Sign: WD6AGX
Ichiro Komatsuzawa
Keno OR 97627

Call Sign: K7ENO

Keno Amateur Repeater
Association
Keno OR 97627

Call Sign: KA7ZRP
Kenneth I Kiger
Keno OR 97627

Call Sign: KB7WVB
John A Johnson
Keno OR 97627

Call Sign: KB7YEZ
Nettie Lou Johnson
Keno OR 97627

Call Sign: KC7OCZ
Timothy I Mc Guire
Keno OR 97627

Call Sign: KE6HKU
Albert L Pion
Keno OR 97627

Call Sign: N6RYK
Michael S Poole
Keno OR 97627

Call Sign: N7IPG
Warren Morehead
Keno OR 97627

Call Sign: N7LAW
Beverly M Hamilton
Keno OR 97627

Call Sign: N7LAY
Merrill K Frink
Keno OR 97627

Call Sign: N7SOU
Brent D Frazier
Keno OR 97627

Call Sign: N7YIX

Dennis D Hurt
Keno OR 97627

Call Sign: WD6EAW
Thomas A Hamilton III
Keno OR 97627

Call Sign: KD7JEC
Albert L Pion
Keno OR 97627

Call Sign: KD7MGW
Courtney A Patterson
Keno OR 97627

Call Sign: KF7KBW
Barbara L Michielsen
Keno OR 97627

Call Sign: KE7IDT
Christina M Ingram
Keno OR 97627

Call Sign: KE7OTB
Krichele Johnson
Keno OR 97627

Call Sign: AD7TW
Michael S Poole
Keno OR 97627

Call Sign: KE7DDN
Randy W Ingram
Keno OR 97627

Call Sign: KE7GML
Sandi L Morehead
Keno OR 97627

Call Sign: KE7GMN
Richard C Hone
Keno OR 976260764

Call Sign: KB7AGB
John R Martin

Keno OR 976270307

Call Sign: KB7OGA
John C Perry
Keno OR 976270493

Call Sign: KE7GMM
Michael E Hormann
Keno OR 976270883

Call Sign: KC7VKR
Robert S Better
130 River Ave 21
Kerby OR 97531

Call Sign: W7TCT
Lester G Basham
130 River Ave 21
Kerby OR 97531

Call Sign: W7TYQ
Gary G Williams
60769 River Bend Dr
Kerby OR 97531

Call Sign: KD7EJL
Michael F Krska
Kerby OR 97531

Call Sign: KL7BXP
Thomas E Acord
Kerby OR 97531

Call Sign: KD7HMP
Darlene K Varney
Kerby OR 97531

Call Sign: KC7ZKO
Ron L Varney
Kerby OR 975310302

Call Sign: KE7LTZ
Clarence O Harvey
1674 Jean Ct
Kimberly OR 97848

Call Sign: KE7LOE
Andrew I Ricker
1809 26th St Unit 56
Klamath Falls OR 97605

Call Sign: KC7WXC
Paul M Harmon
1300 2nd Ave 31
Klamath Falls OR 97601

Call Sign: N7YNB
Sadie Schultz
420 Ave I
Klamath Falls OR 97601

Call Sign: KA7RGS
Ted E Suiter
146 Bamboo Ln
Klamath Falls OR 97601

Call Sign: WA7YXO
James R L Mueller
300 Bandon Ave SW
Klamath Falls OR 97601

Call Sign: KD7EVE
Michael R Howard
4800 Barger Dr 63
Klamath Falls OR 97603

Call Sign: KB7LDJ
Jeremy D Sale
3833 Barry Ave
Klamath Falls OR 97603

Call Sign: KE7PNV
Glenn W Vest
801 Bartlett St
Klamath Falls OR 97603

Call Sign: KB6QFY
Grace E Peterschick
598 Barton Rd
Klamath Falls OR 97603

Call Sign: KF7FQL
Sylvia E Pinney
7304 Baseline Rd
Klamath Falls OR 97603

Call Sign: KB6QFZ
Harley V Peterschick
7900 Baseline Rd
Klamath Falls OR 97603

Call Sign: KB7RBY
Don E Crownover
5738 Basin View Dr
Klamath Falls OR 97603

Call Sign: KD7QZF
William C Havlina
62809 Baskin Ct
Klamath Falls OR 97603

Call Sign: K6QIE
William C Havlina
2782 Bastille Ave SE
Klamath Falls OR 97603

Call Sign: KE7PNT
Dwight B Bickmore
2863 Bastille Ave SE
Klamath Falls OR 97603

Call Sign: KF6BME
Ryan W Glover
32255 Baxter Rd
Klamath Falls OR 97603

Call Sign: KF6BME
Ryan W Glover
32614 Baxter Rd
Klamath Falls OR 97603

Call Sign: KF2FUN
Ryan W Glover
1588 Baxter Rd SE
Klamath Falls OR 97603

Call Sign: N7SFB
Gregory L Banes
3640 Bayonne Dr SE
Klamath Falls OR 97603

Call Sign: W7HOO
Daniel G Reid
506 Beachwood Ave
Klamath Falls OR 97601

Call Sign: KD7AD
Scott F Teeples
2423 Benson Ln
Klamath Falls OR 97601

Call Sign: K7TRB
Gordon E Ward
1122 Bentley St E
Klamath Falls OR 97603

Call Sign: N7FHV
Bonnie D Teeples
26825 Berg Dr
Klamath Falls OR 97601

Call Sign: K7YFW
Dennis L Henderson
26825 Berg Dr
Klamath Falls OR 97603

Call Sign: KE7P
Charles R Gasaway
36400 Big Trout Rd
Klamath Falls OR 97603

Call Sign: N7RBK
Edward D Dolan Jr
721 Bills Rd
Klamath Falls OR 97603

Call Sign: N7SEM
Joycelyn S Dolan
2005 Birch
Klamath Falls OR 97603

Call Sign: W7FJQ
Joycelyn S Dolan
7655 Birch Ave
Klamath Falls OR 97603

Call Sign: WB7RBZ
Hugh T Brown
1237 Birch Ct
Klamath Falls OR 97601

Call Sign: KA7BIA
Dorothy M Silani
190 Boone Rd SE 56
Klamath Falls OR 97603

Call Sign: KG6GHZ
Johnathan C Wu
205 Boone Rd SE Unit 28
Klamath Falls OR 97603

Call Sign: AA7UK
Michael F Peterson
32771 Boones Bend Rd
Klamath Falls OR
976037911

Call Sign: KB7RHY
Mary J Peterson
22791 Boones Ferry Rd NE
Klamath Falls OR
976037911

Call Sign: N7MWE
William L Bramble

75746 Booth Kelly Camp
Rd
Klamath Falls OR 97603

Call Sign: KB7JRK
Becky A Soubie
75859 Booth Kelly Camp
Rd
Klamath Falls OR 97603

Call Sign: K7MDX
Leo Smothers
4855 Boquist Rd
Klamath Falls OR 97603

Call Sign: K7DXV
Edward C Ewell
Rt 1 Box 458
Klamath Falls OR
976034192

Call Sign: KC7RTP
Bobby J Vincent
Rt 2 Box 468 Bald Peak Rd
Klamath Falls OR 97603

Call Sign: KF6ZTN
Brian W Varney
Rt 1 Box 960 12
Klamath Falls OR 97603

Call Sign: N7CEG
Haldane Harris
1009 Brandon Way
Klamath Falls OR 97601

Call Sign: W6IIF
Robert L Boring
20222 Bridge Creek SE
Klamath Falls OR 97601

Call Sign: K6YGI
Robert L Boring
14215 Bridge Ct
Klamath Falls OR 97601

Call Sign: K7JNG
Bruce A Froemke
1708 Bridge St W
Klamath Falls OR 97601

Call Sign: KD7AQM
David J Willis
2095 Broadview Ave
Klamath Falls OR 97601

Call Sign: WB7ECQ
Terry A Smith
1859 Broadway St
Klamath Falls OR 97603

Call Sign: WB7ECP
Geraldine M Smith
2327 Broadway St NW
Klamath Falls OR 97603

Call Sign: N7BSS
Donald B Kelley
1011 Brookdale
Klamath Falls OR 97603

Call Sign: K7UOB
Robert G Leeling
3770 Brush College Rd NW
Klamath Falls OR 97603

Call Sign: K7TFD
Glenn R Sanborn Sr
7528 Buckhorn Rd
Klamath Falls OR 97603

Call Sign: KC7LMM
Clinton E Woodhams Jr
7528 Buckhorn Rd
Klamath Falls OR 97603

Call Sign: KJ7AB
Ronald L Griffith
52446 Cascade Ct
Klamath Falls OR 97603

Call Sign: KE7DD
Richard O Fischer
315 Cascade Dr
Klamath Falls OR 97603

Call Sign: N7ZMQ
Charles K Phillips
2360 Chambers St 530
Klamath Falls OR 97601

Call Sign: N7YBQ
Brenda F Phillips
23897 Chambreau Rd
Klamath Falls OR 97601

Call Sign: KF7OFU
Nathaniel L Lawson
33470 Chinook Plz
Klamath Falls OR 97601

Call Sign: KE7LEE
Oit ARC
8100 Churchill Ct
Klamath Falls OR 97601

Call Sign: W7MHS
Oit ARC
30 Churchill Downs Dr
Klamath Falls OR 97601

Call Sign: KF7CQW
Klamath County ARES Eoc
38 Churchill Downs Dr
Klamath Falls OR 97601

Call Sign: KF7KLA
Klamath County ARES Eoc
6125 Churchill Downs Dr
Klamath Falls OR 97601

Call Sign: KF7HTG
Robert A Roach Jr
6125 Churchill Downs Dr
Klamath Falls OR 97601

Call Sign: N7QZG
Leon A Buzzard
6108 Churchill Downs Dr
Klamath Falls OR 97601

Call Sign: N7QZH
Susan E Buzzard
251 Churchill Downs St SE
Klamath Falls OR 97601

Call Sign: KD7TNG
Sky Lakes Hospital ARES
1885 Churchill St
Klamath Falls OR 97601

Call Sign: KB7GVC
Harold K Schorr Jr
853 Clark
Klamath Falls OR 97603

Call Sign: KB7WRR
Randy J Scheeler
4627 Clark Ave NE
Klamath Falls OR 97603

Call Sign: N7FHJ
Dolly S Wenstrom
4707 Cloudcrest Dr
Klamath Falls OR 97601

Call Sign: KC7COB
David B Sweeney
4707 Cloudcrest Dr
Klamath Falls OR 97603

Call Sign: KC7PMJ
Johnathan A Fullman
4676 Commercial St SE 227
Klamath Falls OR 97601

Call Sign: KC7LML
James L Smith
4544 Croisan Scenic Way S
Klamath Falls OR 97603

Call Sign: NL7NZ
Jacqueline V Grandbois
5233 Crooked Finger Rd
NE
Klamath Falls OR 97603

Call Sign: W5YHY
Robert N Frizzell
69400 Crooked Rd
Klamath Falls OR 97603

Call Sign: KD7STU
Brandon R Cortner
107 Cross Pl
Klamath Falls OR
976037431

Call Sign: N7LAZ
Susan B Mc Laughlin
576 Crystal Dr
Klamath Falls OR 97601

Call Sign: N7LBA
Patrick M Mc Laughlin
730 Crystal Dr
Klamath Falls OR 97601

Call Sign: KI7AF
Victor L Creed
714 J David St SE
Klamath Falls OR 97603

Call Sign: KE7OSE
Ray A Kinney
141 Debernardi Ln
Klamath Falls OR 97601

Call Sign: N7RQE
Ray A Kinney
2517 Debok Rd
Klamath Falls OR 97601

Call Sign: KE7LOJ
Paul D Stuevens

606 Deerwood Ct
Klamath Falls OR 97603

Call Sign: WB7OHR
John Kalayjian
34123 Del Monte Ave
Klamath Falls OR 97603

Call Sign: KD7EVF
Brandon M Purkhiser
89580 Dick Way
Klamath Falls OR 97601

Call Sign: KF7UDZ
Jerry P Hardy
61825 Dobbin Rd
Klamath Falls OR 97601

Call Sign: KB7LDN
Shawn A Jeanes Jackson
1675 Dogwood St
Klamath Falls OR 97603

Call Sign: KB7LDL
Angela J Moore
86864 Dokhobor Rd
Klamath Falls OR 97603

Call Sign: KF7OFT
Rose M Beardsley
4083 Donald St Apt G
Klamath Falls OR 97603

Call Sign: N7RDO
Scott B Ekstrom
620 Dovetail Ln
Klamath Falls OR 97603

Call Sign: AC7WE
Terry L Jones
31130 Dowd Rd
Klamath Falls OR 97603

Call Sign: KB7ISJ
James S Mc Fadden

1708 E 13th
Klamath Falls OR 97601

Call Sign: KA6AKE
Milton F Hains
1955 E 2nd Ave
Klamath Falls OR 97603

Call Sign: KF7CAX
Phillip C Van Buren
22055 E Beaver Creek Rd
Klamath Falls OR 97603

Call Sign: N7RBS
Paul M Novak
107 E Burnett St
Klamath Falls OR
976011806

Call Sign: N7YBR
Jean A Ellis
15105 E Burnside St
Klamath Falls OR 97603

Call Sign: W7STV
Robert W Baker
68980 E Cedar Hill Lp
Klamath Falls OR
976036645

Call Sign: K7WME
John B Lundberg
34579 E Columbia Ave
Klamath Falls OR 97601

Call Sign: K1KWH
Kenneth W Hunt
8172 E Evans Ck Rd
Klamath Falls OR 97603

Call Sign: KB7EAO
David J O Brien II
9463 E Evans Creek Rd
Klamath Falls OR 97603

Call Sign: KA7YWL
Robert M Sayler
13645 E Evans Creek Rd
Klamath Falls OR 97603

Call Sign: KC7TSJ
Michael E Anderson
8961 E Evans Creek Rd Sp
19
Klamath Falls OR 97603

Call Sign: KB7ECL
Barbara L Thompson
27437 E Marion Rd
Klamath Falls OR 97603

Call Sign: KE7BTH
Stefan J Lever
838 E Powell St
Klamath Falls OR 97601

Call Sign: N7RBI
Bennett W Robertson
855 E Quince
Klamath Falls OR 97603

Call Sign: KC7BYR
Paula S Brown
5128 E St
Klamath Falls OR 97601

Call Sign: KA7FCL
Roger D Brown
940 E St NE
Klamath Falls OR 97601

Call Sign: KA7RVQ
Dale G Johnson
91009 E Summit Prairie Rd
Klamath Falls OR 97601

Call Sign: KE7TPX
Andrew D Abbott Jr
500 E Wheeler St
Klamath Falls OR 97601

Call Sign: K7ADA
Andrew D Abbott Jr
2299 E Whiteaker Ave
Klamath Falls OR 97601

Call Sign: KB7TJX
Donald E Vradenburg
2335 Emmett
Klamath Falls OR 97601

Call Sign: KB7GYU
Christopher P Tipton
2340 Emmett Dr NW
Klamath Falls OR 97601

Call Sign: KG4QYL
Jonathan C Ledbetter Jr
6736 Fenwick Ct N
Klamath Falls OR 97601

Call Sign: KI7SE
Charles E Thurston Sr
15016 Fern Ridge Rd SE
Klamath Falls OR 97603

Call Sign: KC7HEY
Lee D Miller
14930 Ferns Corner Rd
Klamath Falls OR 97601

Call Sign: KB7MVC
Tsunenori Kogawa
1655 Fernwood
Klamath Falls OR 97601

Call Sign: N6VDC
John N Wallner
3270 Fir Ridge Rd
Klamath Falls OR 97601

Call Sign: KC7IAE
Helen B Mc Cracken
5176 Firwood Dr

Klamath Falls OR
976016410

2719 Greentree Rd
Klamath Falls OR 97603

3450 Hathaway Ave
Klamath Falls OR 97603

Call Sign: WA7OYC
Edward O Mc Cracken
5176 Firwood Pl
Klamath Falls OR 97601

Call Sign: KA7BTV
Darrell B Hagan
2719 Greentree Rd
Klamath Falls OR 97603

Call Sign: KB7TMP
Carolyn M Clarke
37555 Hauger Mountain Ln
Klamath Falls OR 97603

Call Sign: WD6AXO
Arthur B Martin
66806 Franson Rd
Klamath Falls OR 97601

Call Sign: N7XBK
Richard D Coffman Sr
2016 Hamilton Ln
Klamath Falls OR 97603

Call Sign: N7KF
Gordon D Clarke
37555 Hauger Mt Ln
Klamath Falls OR 97603

Call Sign: WD4NED
Phillip A Harbin Jr
711 Freadman Ln
Klamath Falls OR 97601

Call Sign: KK7KK
Thomas E Parnell
775 Hammel Rd
Klamath Falls OR 97603

Call Sign: N7RBF
Gary E Griffith
14405 Hightor Dr
Klamath Falls OR 97603

Call Sign: WB7WDZ
Claude T Tomera
301 Freeman Rd 1
Klamath Falls OR 97603

Call Sign: AB7VP
Robert D Hunsucker
3484 Hampton Way
Klamath Falls OR 97601

Call Sign: W7IX
Ron J Spears
340 Hillhouse Ave
Klamath Falls OR 97601

Call Sign: N7RBE
Scott D Mahaffey
810 Fremont Ave
Klamath Falls OR 97601

Call Sign: KB7JEJ
Andrew S Wonser
5640 Harlan Dr
Klamath Falls OR 97603

Call Sign: KC7QNF
Henry L Lucht
8405 Holden Rd
Klamath Falls OR 97603

Call Sign: KA7YTJ
Douglas C Ewing
92548 Ft Clatsop Rd
Klamath Falls OR 97603

Call Sign: KB7LDO
Andrew C Lakey
6318 Harlan Dr
Klamath Falls OR 97603

Call Sign: KF7HWU
Henry L Lucht
163 Holder Ln SE
Klamath Falls OR 97603

Call Sign: KB7LUF
Katharine L Kenyon
424 Garnet Ln
Klamath Falls OR 97601

Call Sign: KB7YQZ
Donald A Coffman
9602 Harlan Rd
Klamath Falls OR 97603

Call Sign: WA7AAC
Sidney L Parnell
53500 Holiday Dr
Klamath Falls OR 97603

Call Sign: KA7FUL
Joseph L Revoir
7670 Garrison Ave
Klamath Falls OR 97601

Call Sign: KE7LOH
Kevin Mccullough
1631 Harvey St SE
Klamath Falls OR 97603

Call Sign: KD7HSB
Raymond R Risley
2690 Holiday Dr S
Klamath Falls OR 97603

Call Sign: KC7ODB
Charles L Paulsen

Call Sign: KB7EDF
David R Harrington

Call Sign: KA7QKS
Bobby G Thompson

2690 Holiday Dr S
Klamath Falls OR
976037535

Call Sign: KC5X
Albert E Robertson Jr
2433 Hope St
Klamath Falls OR 97603

Call Sign: KB7KAT
Douglas W Meksch
28788 Hunter Creek Loop
97
Klamath Falls OR 97603

Call Sign: KD7LSF
Matthew R Vinson
62896 Hwy 101
Klamath Falls OR 97603

Call Sign: KF7HTF
Ryan D Russel
615 Hwy 101 Alt
Klamath Falls OR 97601

Call Sign: KE7LOF
Jeff H Dougherty
4805 Hwy 101 S
Klamath Falls OR 97601

Call Sign: K4XAM
John H Skudstad
90971 Hwy 101 Sp 15
Klamath Falls OR
976012921

Call Sign: KC7PFL
Toshiko Foster
87292 Hwy 202
Klamath Falls OR 97501

Call Sign: N7QJF
Ben L Cornelius
87292 Hwy 202
Klamath Falls OR 97601

Call Sign: KF7AHV
Michael J Mattingly
88771 Hwy 202
Klamath Falls OR 97601

Call Sign: N0FQN
Daniel J Mattingly
89869 Hwy 202
Klamath Falls OR 97601

Call Sign: AD7W
Marcia E Dobry
57405 Hwy 204
Klamath Falls OR 97603

Call Sign: KF7J
Len A Dobry
26102 Hwy 211 S
Klamath Falls OR 97603

Call Sign: KB7YRE
Alonzo F Monroe Jr
7529 Hwy 214
Klamath Falls OR 97603

Call Sign: KC7LGJ
Joe M Lopez Jr
60906 Hwy 216
Klamath Falls OR 97603

Call Sign: KC6YLZ
Justin J Dowling
9444 Hwy 234
Klamath Falls OR 97603

Call Sign: KE7LOB
Jonathan M Mcnamara
34628 Hwy 26
Klamath Falls OR 97601

Call Sign: KC7LMO
William A Deutschman
34628 Hwy 26

Klamath Falls OR
976012337

Call Sign: KD7OUE
Elaine M Deutschman
34662 Hwy 26
Klamath Falls OR 97601

Call Sign: N6TBS
Ruth D Lyras
34662 Hwy 26
Klamath Falls OR 97601

Call Sign: KF0USA
John H Hodges Sr
34662 Hwy 26
Klamath Falls OR 97601

Call Sign: KK7RN
Mineyuki Hanano
5740 Hwy 30 W 12
Klamath Falls OR 97601

Call Sign: KF7CAY
Brent F Asay
7551 Hwy 42
Klamath Falls OR 97603

Call Sign: KB7JSY
Jeremy F Rippe
20479 Hwy 42
Klamath Falls OR 97603

Call Sign: N7BDQ
Daniel M Whitlatch
20479 Hwy 42
Klamath Falls OR 97603

Call Sign: N7PXR
Keith L Leistikow
93126 Hwy 42 S
Klamath Falls OR 97603

Call Sign: W0NJQ
Neil P Turner

22710 Hwy 62
Klamath Falls OR 97603

Call Sign: N7OHO
Oletta C Spears
6499 Hwy 66
Klamath Falls OR 97601

Call Sign: KB7MMC
Karen E Kunz
15797 Hwy 66
Klamath Falls OR 97603

Call Sign: KB7ECN
Fred D Hall
15797 Hwy 66
Klamath Falls OR 97603

Call Sign: N7ZMN
Robert T Thorpe
19047 Hwy 99E NE
Klamath Falls OR 97601

Call Sign: KG7DR
Vernor C Buckley Sr
1661 Hwy 99N 10
Klamath Falls OR 97603

Call Sign: W7PIH
Gordon C Meade
515 Hyde Park
Klamath Falls OR 97601

Call Sign: KC7VKP
Walter R Jones
515 Hyde Park Rd
Klamath Falls OR
976039391

Call Sign: KE7GMQ
Genevieve Jones
1 Hyten Ct
Klamath Falls OR 97603

Call Sign: W7GEB

Genevieve Jones
1 Hyten Ct
Klamath Falls OR 97603

Call Sign: KC7WJ
Walter R Jones
1 Hyten Ct
Klamath Falls OR
976039391

Call Sign: W7MJM
Andrew L Schorr Sr
4600 Idaville Rd 13
Klamath Falls OR 97603

Call Sign: K7RFO
Ruth A Schorr
4600 Idaville Rd Sp C1
Klamath Falls OR 97603

Call Sign: KB7MQU
Jeremy W Martin
4600 Idaville Rd Unit 28
Klamath Falls OR 97603

Call Sign: KD7AA
Carson S Kendall
2649 J St
Klamath Falls OR 97601

Call Sign: WA6MJF
James E Reisinger Jr
63589 Jd Estates Dr
Klamath Falls OR 97603

Call Sign: WB6MMM
Ralph F Cornelius
401 Jefferson Scio Dr 65
Klamath Falls OR 97601

Call Sign: KB7QBU
Lester D Tillson
610 Jefferson St
Klamath Falls OR 97601

Call Sign: KC7JJD
Wendell T Parrick
2430 Jefferson St
Klamath Falls OR 97601

Call Sign: KK7HZ
David L Foster
2430 Jefferson St
Klamath Falls OR 97601

Call Sign: N7RBG
Delayne M Hollis
2430 Jefferson St
Klamath Falls OR 97601

Call Sign: N7RBT
Ruth O Hollis
2465 Jefferson St SE
Klamath Falls OR 97601

Call Sign: N7RBO
Karen L Lilly
88323 Jenica Way
Klamath Falls OR 97601

Call Sign: W7BXD
John K Lilly
88323 Jenica Way
Klamath Falls OR 97601

Call Sign: KG6KBN
John W Roper Jr
507 Kenwood Ave
Klamath Falls OR 97603

Call Sign: KF7FQJ
Benjamin W Seput
4350 Kings Valley Hwy
Klamath Falls OR 97601

Call Sign: KD7ORE
Micheal C Bailey
291 Knapp Ln
Klamath Falls OR 97603

Call Sign: KE7BFT
Sam S Bailey
291 Knapp Ln
Klamath Falls OR 97603

Call Sign: KD7UEL
Shirleen F Bailey
93024 Knappa Dock Rd
Klamath Falls OR 97603

Call Sign: N7RBH
Connie M Bechdoldt
5322 Knoll Way
Klamath Falls OR 97601

Call Sign: ND7V
Frederick D Bechdoldt
35516 Knox Butte Rd E
Klamath Falls OR 97601

Call Sign: KA7ZIS
Robert M Jackson
1119 Lafayette Ave
Klamath Falls OR 97603

Call Sign: KB7AQH
Eric J Jackson
11175 Lafayette Hwy
Klamath Falls OR 97603

Call Sign: KA6RDV
William V Mattingly
2422 Lampman Rd
Klamath Falls OR 97601

Call Sign: N7WVO
Donna J Gibson
1328 Larch Dr
Klamath Falls OR 97601

Call Sign: WB7OKX
Raymond I Gibson
6502 Larch Dr
Klamath Falls OR 97601

Call Sign: KB7KVA
Edward M Kotz
970 Laurel
Klamath Falls OR 97603

Call Sign: KE7GMR
Ann L Brakora
1027 Laurel
Klamath Falls OR 97603

Call Sign: KE7Q
Harold F Freeman
114 Lewis
Klamath Falls OR
976038527

Call Sign: K7WVT
Phyllis J Weir
2620 Lewis St
Klamath Falls OR 97603

Call Sign: W6UCF
Roland L Weir
1755 Lewisburg Rd
Klamath Falls OR 97603

Call Sign: KB7YHL
Keith A Wells
767 Lexington Ave
Klamath Falls OR 97603

Call Sign: KA7QQS
Kenn R Stump
6707 Lipscomb St SE
Klamath Falls OR 97601

Call Sign: KC7MJW
James C Marsden
6947 Lipscomb St SE
Klamath Falls OR 97601

Call Sign: KI7TR
Gary D Phillips
815 Lisa Pl
Klamath Falls OR 97601

Call Sign: K7WMM
Clyde E Freed
1170 Lorella Ave
Klamath Falls OR 97601

Call Sign: KA7BGQ
John W Paxton
830 Lori St
Klamath Falls OR 97601

Call Sign: KB6OHH
Marvin D Sommerville
670 Loring Dr NW
Klamath Falls OR 97601

Call Sign: WA7MS
Marvin D Sommerville
670 Loring Dr NW
Klamath Falls OR 97601

Call Sign: KB7REJ
Betsy M Smith
1246 Lottie Ln NW
Klamath Falls OR 97601

Call Sign: KI7GX
Stephen E Tillson
16494 Lovell Ln
Klamath Falls OR 97601

Call Sign: N7GWS
Dan A Soule
16340 Lower Harbor Rd Ste
1 337
Klamath Falls OR 97603

Call Sign: KD6GVR
Stanley D Speegle
300 Luman Rd 15
Klamath Falls OR 97601

Call Sign: KD6GVS
Carol R Speegle
300 Luman Rd 16

Klamath Falls OR 97601

Call Sign: KC7ODD
Marguerite D Dorsey
3181 Macy Ct NE
Klamath Falls OR 97603

Call Sign: KC7ODE
Robert M Dorsey
39961 Mad Creek Rd
Klamath Falls OR 97603

Call Sign: KB7PTT
Eddie P Mundall
1948 Madison St
Klamath Falls OR 97601

Call Sign: KC7OTQ
Jeffrey M Lord
1948 Madison St
Klamath Falls OR 97601

Call Sign: W7SBU
Roy H Felix
1115 Madison St NE Pmb
835
Klamath Falls OR 97601

Call Sign: KA7KEB
Duane L Fitzsimmons
2507 Mangan St
Klamath Falls OR 97601

Call Sign: K7IX
Michael W Hudson
89860 Manion Dr
Klamath Falls OR 97601

Call Sign: N7EHG
Dorothy M Hudson
89860 Manion Dr
Klamath Falls OR 97601

Call Sign: KA7LEC
Dorothy M Hudson

41241 Manitau Rd
Klamath Falls OR 97601

Call Sign: KD7GVG
Ryan P Niemi
1001 Marie Ave
Klamath Falls OR 97603

Call Sign: KA7PKY
Gene Cannon
781 Marilyn Dr
Klamath Falls OR 97603

Call Sign: W7GQJ
Dale M Mueller
12691 Marion Rd SE
Klamath Falls OR 97601

Call Sign: KC7FFA
Bert L Morgan
2331 Marion SE
Klamath Falls OR
976038130

Call Sign: KD7POK
Steve L Vick
403 May St
Klamath Falls OR 97603

Call Sign: N7PXF
Bill O Clark
2790 May St
Klamath Falls OR 97603

Call Sign: KF7Z
John G Pierce
21004 McCormick Hill Rd
Klamath Falls OR 97603

Call Sign: KD7AQN
Clinton D John
31225 McCraven Ln
Klamath Falls OR 97603

Call Sign: K7JIX

Robert C Purkhiser
53189 McKenzie Hwy
Klamath Falls OR 97601

Call Sign: KE7PNR
Margaret A John
53189 McKenzie Hwy
Klamath Falls OR 97603

Call Sign: K7JIY
Rose M Purkhiser
44221 McKenzie Hwy Sp
34
Klamath Falls OR 97603

Call Sign: N7RBR
Robert L Purkhiser
3818 McKenzie Passway
NE Apt 104
Klamath Falls OR 97603

Call Sign: N7SFA
Shirley A Shown
16950 McKimmens Rd
Klamath Falls OR 97603

Call Sign: KB7REL
John A Meeker
6261 McLaughlin Dr
Klamath Falls OR 97601

Call Sign: KD7FWK
Patricia Bailey
47600 Meadow Ln
Klamath Falls OR 97601

Call Sign: KD7FWL
John L Bailey
47600 Meadow Ln
Klamath Falls OR 97601

Call Sign: KD7KDP
Thomas A Rylander
20328 Medical Springs
Hwy

Klamath Falls OR 97603

Call Sign: W7ACN
Thomas A Rylander
59805 Medicine Hat Ln
Klamath Falls OR 97603

Call Sign: KB7KUJ
Donald E Jamison
37150 Meredith Dr
Klamath Falls OR 97603

Call Sign: WA7VNS
John Klein Jr
29365 Miller View Ln
Klamath Falls OR 97601

Call Sign: KA7QAA
William R Finnell
1200 Mira Mar Ave 1136
Klamath Falls OR 97601

Call Sign: KB7EVN
Ian J Wery
480 Monroe Ave
Klamath Falls OR 97601

Call Sign: N7LAL
James L Wery
1430 Monroe Ave
Klamath Falls OR 97601

Call Sign: KB7OMN
Barbra D Dahl
2020 Monroe St
Klamath Falls OR 97601

Call Sign: KB7MNW
Scott T Miller
8608 Mt Angel Hwy
Klamath Falls OR 97603

Call Sign: KE7DDJ
David S Geigle
33219 Mt Lakes Dr

Klamath Falls OR 97601

Call Sign: KA7NKG
George A Allen
49425 Mtn View Rd
Klamath Falls OR 97603

Call Sign: KB7MQT
Steven D Miller
49425 Mtn View Rd
Klamath Falls OR 97603

Call Sign: N7LLT
Keith E Penman
218 Munsel Creek Loop
Klamath Falls OR 97603

Call Sign: KD7MGU
Zachary P Johnson
820 Munsel Creek Loop
Klamath Falls OR
976019306

Call Sign: KD7MGV
James A Johnson
5617 Munsel Ln
Klamath Falls OR
976019306

Call Sign: K7GFF
Averil L Burrell
94924 Mystery Ln
Klamath Falls OR 97603

Call Sign: AD7LI
Christopher C Sigsbee
2690 N 3rd St
Klamath Falls OR 97601

Call Sign: KB7UO
Kenny N Kranenburg
2652 N 5th St
Klamath Falls OR 97603

Call Sign: WB7DSH

Susan M Lawrie
348 N 7th St
Klamath Falls OR 97603

Call Sign: KB7ECM
Jason A Snook
84 N 8th Ave
Klamath Falls OR 97603

Call Sign: K7HMI
William J Jones
850 N 8th St
Klamath Falls OR 97601

Call Sign: KD7GBI
Neil S Moffatt
98373 N Bank Rd
Klamath Falls OR 97601

Call Sign: KF7CAW
Jacob P Nelson
153 N Baxter St
Klamath Falls OR 97601

Call Sign: N7WVQ
Samuel J Dunlap
531 N Bridgeton Rd Slip 6
Klamath Falls OR 97601

Call Sign: KB7TMQ
Lisa L Stilwell
5601 N Campbell Ave
Klamath Falls OR
976011567

Call Sign: KB7TMR
Steven M Stilwell
612 N Cascade Dr 93
Klamath Falls OR
976011567

Call Sign: KD7LDL
Daniel J Kuenzi
7743 N Coast Hwy
Klamath Falls OR 97601

Call Sign: KF7OFV
Ronald L Brumble
714 N Columbia Blvd
Klamath Falls OR 97601

Call Sign: N7RBM
John K James
1501 N Hayden Island Dr
17B
Klamath Falls OR 97601

Call Sign: KB7VKW
Delos B Parks Jr
406 N Holladay
Klamath Falls OR 97601

Call Sign: KE7LOA
Wilton J Burke
63760 N Hwy 97
Klamath Falls OR 97601

Call Sign: KA7VPM
Thomas C Turner
704 N River St
Klamath Falls OR 97601

Call Sign: KD7ZKU
Justus F Brammeier
722 N Riverside Ave Rm
107
Klamath Falls OR 97601

Call Sign: WA6GRL
Thomas P Dudy
802 NE 183rd Ave Sp 14
Klamath Falls OR 97601

Call Sign: KA5EZM
Richard I Walker Jr
4064 NE 18th Ave
Klamath Falls OR
976012968

Call Sign: KA7DZI

Johnny A Wolford
1420 NE 18th Pl
Klamath Falls OR 97601

Call Sign: KD7GRV
James M Alig
1640 NE 238th Dr
Klamath Falls OR
976037037

Call Sign: WA7JZT
James M Alig
1105 NE 239th Pl
Klamath Falls OR
976037037

Call Sign: KB7EAL
Devon W Schrader
3835 NE Skidmore St
Klamath Falls OR 97603

Call Sign: KE7DDK
Delbert T Bell
646 NW 12th Ave
Klamath Falls OR 97601

Call Sign: N7EQP
Glenn Chamberlin
930 NW 12th Ave 303
Klamath Falls OR 97601

Call Sign: KC7FEX
Thomas L Miller
4779 NW 138th Pl
Klamath Falls OR 97603

Call Sign: K7BOQ
C L Price
322 NW 18th St
Klamath Falls OR 97601

Call Sign: KB7RRO
Nina E Price
663 NW 18th St
Klamath Falls OR 97601

Call Sign: KE7ZOU
William T Vaughn III
4035 NW 192
Klamath Falls OR 97601

Call Sign: KA7TBG
Andrew L Schorr Jr
1929 Oregon Ave
Klamath Falls OR 97603

Call Sign: KC7QXQ
Dennis W Drake
61592 Orion Dr
Klamath Falls OR 97601

Call Sign: KB7ARZ
Tracey L Ferguson
4405 Panther Ct NE
Klamath Falls OR 97603

Call Sign: W7IEO
Don S Nichols
4405 Panther Ct NE
Klamath Falls OR
976036739

Call Sign: KB7BDA
Gary W Morris
4405 Panther Ct NE
Klamath Falls OR
976036740

Call Sign: N4LYP
Christopher C Sigsbee
2628 Park Ct
Klamath Falls OR 97601

Call Sign: KD7WAT
Kenneth J Harroun
3220 Park Dr
Klamath Falls OR 97601

Call Sign: KB7YQX
Lyle W Ahrens

29381 Park St
Klamath Falls OR 97601

Call Sign: KC7RHZ
Richard E Barnum
607 Park St No 8
Klamath Falls OR 97601

Call Sign: KC7HFC
John E Taylor
3560 Parker Rd
Klamath Falls OR 97601

Call Sign: KE7PNY
Sarah L Taylor
3560 Parker Rd
Klamath Falls OR 97601

Call Sign: KD7NGJ
Kai J Fiegi
3560 Parker Rd
Klamath Falls OR 97601

Call Sign: KB6UBP
Robert L Beattie
1364 Parnell Dr
Klamath Falls OR 97601

Call Sign: KB7MEF
Alfred T Beattie
138 Paroz Ln
Klamath Falls OR 97601

Call Sign: KB7YQW
Randy S Bailey
101795 Paulina Hwy
Klamath Falls OR 97601

Call Sign: N7HIQ
Keith E Bailey
829 Pavilion Pl
Klamath Falls OR 97601

Call Sign: N7SAT
Jon S Wayland

493 Pavillion Dr
Klamath Falls OR 97601

Call Sign: KC7BVK
Kristin A Bienz
1135 Pawnee Cir SE
Klamath Falls OR 97601

Call Sign: KB7ALO
James R Uerlings
287 Pawnee St
Klamath Falls OR 97601

Call Sign: KE7BQM
Jamie W Zipay
31010 Peach Cove Rd
Klamath Falls OR 97601

Call Sign: KA7AZV
Irene M Currin
855 Peacock St
Klamath Falls OR 97601

Call Sign: WA6JNM
Donald D Younker Sr
5845 Perrin St
Klamath Falls OR 97603

Call Sign: KD6GIY
Allen L White
4497 Pinecrest Dr
Klamath Falls OR 97603

Call Sign: W7KHD
Allen L White
4497 Pinecrest Dr
Klamath Falls OR 97603

Call Sign: W7KFA
Lester A Craft Jr
6601 Pioneer Rd
Klamath Falls OR 97603

Call Sign: KD7AQL
Ralph I Warner

39700 Pleasant Ave
Klamath Falls OR 97603

Call Sign: KZ7H
Peter P Rodriguez Sr
19759 Poplar St
Klamath Falls OR 97603

Call Sign: N7HWA
Lois Rodriguez
19958 Porcupine Dr
Klamath Falls OR 97603

Call Sign: KA6CEV
Paul Zuest IV
20073 Porter Pl 2
Klamath Falls OR 97603

Call Sign: N7MWO
Richard D Wylie
1919 Quinton St
Klamath Falls OR
976012262

Call Sign: N7WVK
Carol L Wylie
1314 R St 3
Klamath Falls OR 97601

Call Sign: WB5OUS
Patrick M Shann
340 Raintree Dr
Klamath Falls OR 97603

Call Sign: KA7SUL
Jessee G Barker
1020 Rand Rd
Klamath Falls OR 97601

Call Sign: KB7MRI
Donald F Gifford
87239 Reynolds Dr
Klamath Falls OR 97601

Call Sign: W7FNE

Benjamin P Lane
6330 Rhododendron Dr
Klamath Falls OR 97601

Call Sign: N6RTO
Kenneth G Mickelson
6820 Ridgeway Rd
Klamath Falls OR 97601

Call Sign: KD7MGY
Richard A Sinclair
244 Riessen Rd
Klamath Falls OR 97601

Call Sign: W7BW
Phillip A Rand
929 Rilance Ln
Klamath Falls OR 97603

Call Sign: KF7UEA
Kenneth E Banes
38652 River Dr
Klamath Falls OR 97603

Call Sign: KC7VWW
Klamath County Schools
ARC
39055 River Dr
Klamath Falls OR 97603

Call Sign: KB7DWX
William R Switzer
41980 River Dr
Klamath Falls OR 97603

Call Sign: KD7CUI
Max H Denning
4010 Robin Pl Apt 15
Klamath Falls OR 97603

Call Sign: KE7NH
Ronald L Grant
1277 Rock Creek Dr S
Klamath Falls OR 97601

Call Sign: N7CPE
Ronald L Grant
1762 Rock Creek Dr S
Klamath Falls OR 97601

Call Sign: N3AAV
Charles G Lomas
1762 Rock Creek Dr S
Klamath Falls OR 97603

Call Sign: AB7ET
Carolyn M Brooks
17445 Rock Creek Rd
Klamath Falls OR
976037777

Call Sign: NV7N
Erwin T Brooks
36265 Rock Hill Dr
Klamath Falls OR
976037777

Call Sign: KF7TKP
Mark L Sargent
1633 Roseburg Rd
Klamath Falls OR 97601

Call Sign: KB7LRX
Craig A Lane
3941 Ross Inlet Rd
Klamath Falls OR 97601

Call Sign: KE6IJA
Troy A King
4055 Royal Ave 137
Klamath Falls OR 97603

Call Sign: KD6JLF
Eddy Voskanian
33996 S Ball Rd
Klamath Falls OR 97601

Call Sign: KF7FQN
Michael A Vail
18966 S End Rd

Klamath Falls OR 97603

Call Sign: N7ABL
Robert G Parker
1000 S Hwy 395 A 137
Klamath Falls OR 97601

Call Sign: N7UIT
Joseph E Shook
69370 Sabrina Ln
Klamath Falls OR 97601

Call Sign: KE7IDR
William F Fleckner
3232 SE 115th
Klamath Falls OR 97603

Call Sign: KE7PNX
Benjamin Quen
1509 SE 12th Ave
Klamath Falls OR 97603

Call Sign: KE7ZKF
Roy Anderson
4208 SE 130th
Klamath Falls OR 97601

Call Sign: KF7CBA
Mike Anderson
131 SE 130th Dr
Klamath Falls OR 97601

Call Sign: WF7C
Mike Anderson
131 SE 130th Dr
Klamath Falls OR 97601

Call Sign: KD7NGI
Steven S Schultz
80661 Shanemah Rd
Klamath Falls OR 97603

Call Sign: KE7EJ
Danford A Laurance
9254 Shaw Square Rd

Klamath Falls OR 97603

Call Sign: KA7BAH
Carl D Dodson
446 Sherwood Loop
Klamath Falls OR
976034437

Call Sign: KE7TPY
Steven R Shirts Md
3830 Silver Falls Dr NE
Klamath Falls OR 97603

Call Sign: W7SRS
Steven R Shirts Md
3830 Silver Falls Dr NE
Klamath Falls OR 97603

Call Sign: WB7OUQ
Morris G Ayers
37453 Solso Dr
Klamath Falls OR 97603

Call Sign: KB7JRJ
Hans Christ Bang
3820 Spring Blvd
Klamath Falls OR 97603

Call Sign: KE7ZKG
William M Wood
2467 Spring Brook
Klamath Falls OR 97603

Call Sign: KD7YBS
Dusty C Collier
3503 Stark
Klamath Falls OR 97603

Call Sign: KB7MER
Jeremy W Yahn
1550 Sterling Creek Rd
Klamath Falls OR 97603

Call Sign: N7OSE
Kevin T Milani

3763 Sterling Woods Dr
Klamath Falls OR 97603

Call Sign: K7ONR
Earl D Bedord
1763 Sunburst Terr NW
Klamath Falls OR 97603

Call Sign: KA7ARC
William L Larimore
19001 Suncrest Ave
Klamath Falls OR 97601

Call Sign: N7RPU
Darlene K Larimore
433 Suncrest Ave NW
Klamath Falls OR 97603

Call Sign: KB7EAK
William L Seibt II
512 Suncrest Ave NW
Klamath Falls OR 97603

Call Sign: KD7TNF
Klamath County ARES
19820 Suncrest Dr
Klamath Falls OR 97603

Call Sign: KE7CSD
Klamath Basin Repeater
Association
1268 Suncrest Rd
Klamath Falls OR 97603

Call Sign: WA7YPR
Dennie L Dunkeson Jr
2279 Suncrest Rd
Klamath Falls OR 97603

Call Sign: WB7EIG
Marie R Dunkeson
814 Sundance St
Klamath Falls OR 97603

Call Sign: KA7ZIR

Dale A Cross
814 Sundance St
Klamath Falls OR 97603

Call Sign: KB7LDM
Hyrum K Hunt
990 Sundance St
Klamath Falls OR 97603

Call Sign: KB7MWC
Joseph A Hunt
17897 Sundown Ct
Klamath Falls OR 97603

Call Sign: KE7LRA
Daniel L Longstreet
1670 Sundown Dr
Klamath Falls OR 97603

Call Sign: KI7XR
James M Mac Allister
3820 Sundown Rd
Klamath Falls OR 97603

Call Sign: KF7PFV
Scott E Stewart
4578 Sunflower Way NE
Klamath Falls OR 97603

Call Sign: KB7MQV
Joshua C Andrade
633 Sunlake Dr
Klamath Falls OR 97603

Call Sign: KB7GTQ
Margaret A Meyer
960 Sunmist Ct SE
Klamath Falls OR 97603

Call Sign: KF7KBS
Jerry A Shearer Sr
1145 Sunny Ln
Klamath Falls OR 97603

Call Sign: WA7PZW

Mazama High School ARC
1176 Sunny Ln
Klamath Falls OR 97603

Call Sign: KB6NZP
Peter A Mc Caffrey
20819 Sunny Vista Ct
Klamath Falls OR 97603

Call Sign: KE7PNS
James L Shelton
24065 Sunnycrest Rd
Klamath Falls OR 97603

Call Sign: K7SBA
Louise R Williams
946 Sunnyhill Dr
Klamath Falls OR 97603

Call Sign: N7FVG
Norman L Grey
615 Sunnyside Dr
Klamath Falls OR 97601

Call Sign: KB7LDK
William L Gibbs
4280 SW 107th Ave
Klamath Falls OR 97603

Call Sign: KU7K
Joseph L Rogers
22480 SW 107th Ave
Klamath Falls OR 97603

Call Sign: N7YBT
Karen B Rogers
22480 SW 107th Ave
Klamath Falls OR 97603

Call Sign: N7IXR
Erin R Banks
16326 SW 107th Ct
Klamath Falls OR 97603

Call Sign: W6KSX

Kenneth C Banks
15088 SW 107th Ter
Klamath Falls OR 97603

Call Sign: KB6EEP
David B Oxley
6915 SW 8th Ave
Klamath Falls OR 97603

Call Sign: KB6EEQ
Marganne Oxley
8658 SW 90th
Klamath Falls OR 97603

Call Sign: KG6WOI
Kimberly L Halverson
6107 SW Murray Blvd Apt
317
Klamath Falls OR 97601

Call Sign: AF6BZ
Mark D Halverson
15725 SW Oak Hill Ln
Klamath Falls OR 97601

Call Sign: N7IWV
Victor S Versteeg
273 Sycamore Ave
Klamath Falls OR 97603

Call Sign: W7PPJ
Victor S Versteeg
273 Sycamore Ave
Klamath Falls OR 97603

Call Sign: KG7UL
Scott D Mc Mahon Sr
390 Tan Bark
Klamath Falls OR 97603

Call Sign: KA7VZB
David J Phelan
2811 Tandy Turn
Klamath Falls OR
976034181

Call Sign: KF7GQX
Sherry G Bowlby
95800 Timber Hill
Klamath Falls OR 97601

Call Sign: KC7BVR
Robert F Lander
570 Tina Way
Klamath Falls OR 97601

Call Sign: KF7QET
Curt M Christian
2006 Unity St
Klamath Falls OR 97601

Call Sign: WB7DHW
John W Claybaugh
17485 University Ave
Klamath Falls OR 97601

Call Sign: K7DDI
Richard E Suber
87845 Upland St
Klamath Falls OR 97601

Call Sign: KB7EKB
Ivy D Suber
7936 Upper Applegate Rd
Klamath Falls OR
976012482

Call Sign: N7GOU
Alice J Trump
2929 Vale Rd
Klamath Falls OR 97603

Call Sign: N7PEL
Quentin M Trump
64935 Valeview Dr
Klamath Falls OR 97603

Call Sign: KC7FBZ
Robert H Stier
64935 Valeview Dr

Klamath Falls OR 97603

Klamath Falls OR 97603

Klamath Falls OR 97601

Call Sign: W6IIF
Emery C Boring
2460 Valley Ave
Klamath Falls OR 97603

Call Sign: KC7XW
Frances Hausherr
1838 Vine Ct
Klamath Falls OR 97601

Call Sign: N7LOY
Robert J Krusmark
2312 Western St
Klamath Falls OR 97603

Call Sign: KF7CAZ
Gene S Bruner
2460 Valley Ave
Klamath Falls OR 97603

Call Sign: KZ7X
Maurice R Hausherr
836 Vine Maple Dr
Klamath Falls OR 97601

Call Sign: KA7NTC
Wayne I Smith
4511 Weyerhaeuser Rd
Klamath Falls OR 97601

Call Sign: KD7LSH
Gunder F Coaty
217 Vashti Way
Klamath Falls OR 97601

Call Sign: KC7FEU
Shirley A Tipton
2244 Wantland Ave
Klamath Falls OR 97601

Call Sign: WA7TDU
Samuel L Hawley
2419 Wiard St
Klamath Falls OR 97601

Call Sign: KF7QNF
James P Mclaren
610 Vaughn Ln 79
Klamath Falls OR 97601

Call Sign: KC7FEV
Alice A Tipton
2244 Wantland Ave
Klamath Falls OR 97601

Call Sign: KD7AIO
Charles W Fastenau Jr
2635 Wiard St
Klamath Falls OR 97603

Call Sign: KD7KLV
Lee W Matchett
6908 Verda Vista Pl
Klamath Falls OR 97603

Call Sign: WA7RTD
James F Gansberg
1776 Washburn Way
Klamath Falls OR 97601

Call Sign: KE7RNO
Paul B Clark
2835 Wiard St
Klamath Falls OR 97603

Call Sign: K6TFG
Barbara D Krizo
6910 Verda Vista Pl
Klamath Falls OR 97603

Call Sign: KC7ODA
Rocio Swartz
10460 Washburn Way
Klamath Falls OR 97603

Call Sign: K7TDX
Donald E Quick
1523 Wilford Ave
Klamath Falls OR 97601

Call Sign: W6ZOF
Philip Krizo
117 Verna Ln
Klamath Falls OR 97603

Call Sign: KI7PS
Terry L Swartz
10460 Washburn Way
Klamath Falls OR 97603

Call Sign: KA7EXF
Steve E Quick
1523 Wilford Ave
Klamath Falls OR 97601

Call Sign: K7XG
Wallace L Kelly
32127 Vernonia Hwy
Klamath Falls OR 97603

Call Sign: KB7TMS
Mark T Bienz
19619 Webber Rd
Klamath Falls OR 97603

Call Sign: KB7JSZ
Paul J Duncan Jr
4322 5 Winter Ave
Klamath Falls OR 97603

Call Sign: KA7KLG
Judy A Baldwin
2042 Vine

Call Sign: N7RBJ
Wilma J Krusmark
2312 Western St

Call Sign: KA7BAI
Delbert V Ellis
4647 Winter Ave Sp 42

Klamath Falls OR 97603

Call Sign: KB2VTA
Rachel A Chevalier
5473 Wocus Rd
Klamath Falls OR 97601

Call Sign: KL7GMQ
Neil A Savidge
5889 Wocus Rd
Klamath Falls OR 97601

Call Sign: N7PXQ
David W Robbins
Klamath Falls OR 97601

Call Sign: N7RBQ
Martha F Russell
Klamath Falls OR 97601

Call Sign: K7SNX
Donald M Boyle
Klamath Falls OR 97602

Call Sign: KA7QDZ
Helen J Fleming
Klamath Falls OR 97602

Call Sign: KE7GMO
Joseph L Loser
Klamath Falls OR 97601

Call Sign: KC7KDU
Sal F Ardizzone
Klamath Falls OR 97601

Call Sign: KC7WLX
Sandra Soho
Klamath Falls OR 97601

Call Sign: KC7WLY
Sandra A Falk
Klamath Falls OR 97601

Call Sign: KE6ZGO

Stephen L Cross
Klamath Falls OR 97601

Call Sign: N7NFH
Dixie J Wonser
Klamath Falls OR 97601

Call Sign: N7WVM
Robert D Taylor
Klamath Falls OR 97601

Call Sign: WA6DMM
John T Bradley II
Klamath Falls OR 97601

Call Sign: WB7ROX
Mark R Wonser
Klamath Falls OR 97601

Call Sign: WL7AZL
William L Hawkins
Klamath Falls OR 97601

Call Sign: KD7NGK
Robert J Allen
Klamath Falls OR 97601

Call Sign: KE7GMP
Carl J Swendsen
Klamath Falls OR 97601

Call Sign: KE7BFS
Claude I Kansaku
Klamath Falls OR 97601

Call Sign: KD7VMN
Dana A Nelson III
Klamath Falls OR 97601

Call Sign: KF7KBT
Dean L Rice
Klamath Falls OR 97601

Call Sign: KF7KUO
Martin Sliwak

Klamath Falls OR 97601

Call Sign: KF7FQK
Sean K Callaghan
Klamath Falls OR 97601

Call Sign: KE7GMK
Timothy M Evinger
Klamath Falls OR 97601

Call Sign: KA7WEZ
Donald D Ohlde
Klamath Falls OR 97602

Call Sign: KC7YET
Jessica R Asbill Case
Klamath Falls OR 97602

Call Sign: KI7AE
Donald E Lewis
Klamath Falls OR 97602

Call Sign: N7LPH
Colleen L Rambo
Klamath Falls OR 97602

Call Sign: W7VW
Klamath Basin Amateur
Radio Association
Klamath Falls OR 97602

Call Sign: W7FJG
Frank J Gipe
Klamath Falls OR 97602

Call Sign: KE7WTH
David M Ramirez
Klamath Falls OR 97602

Call Sign: N7NFJ
Bruce U Gosnell Sr
Klamath Falls OR
976010036

Call Sign: KE7LOD

Aaron C Miller
Klamath Falls OR
976018801

Call Sign: N2RSI
Terry S Bell
Klamath Falls OR
976020825

Call Sign: N2RSN
David L Bell
Klamath Falls OR
976020825

**FCC Amateur Radio
Licenses in La Grande**

Call Sign: W7IDW
Arthur D Pelphrey Sr
887 6th St
La Grande OR 97850

Call Sign: WB7PKX
Robert N Zweifel
2306 6th St
La Grande OR 97850

Call Sign: WB7PMG
Matthew W Sirrine
355 7th St
La Grande OR 97850

Call Sign: K5MVS
Jerry H Winkle
5835 82nd Ave SE
La Grande OR 97850

Call Sign: KE7ZSI
Landon B Wright
1714 9th St
La Grande OR 97850

Call Sign: KC7YAC
Jean W Cate
529 A St

La Grande OR 97850

Call Sign: KE7ZSH
Johnes Z Wynn
2824 Adams Ln SE
La Grande OR 97850

Call Sign: KE7ZRW
Stuart M Croghan
57902 Adams Rd
La Grande OR 97850

Call Sign: KC7WZY
Pier G Jones
57902 Adams Rd
La Grande OR 97850

Call Sign: KC7FI
George C Gooder
57902 Adams Rd
La Grande OR 978509432

Call Sign: KF7IFQ
Union County Oregon
ARES
552 Agate St
La Grande OR 97850

Call Sign: K7UNI
Union County Oregon
ARES
1128 Agate St
La Grande OR 97850

Call Sign: WB7PME
Royal R Denning
210 Ave D
La Grande OR 97850

Call Sign: KE7QYU
Jeffrey L Crews
3185 Ave G
La Grande OR 97850

Call Sign: KF7NHW

Gary F Anger
19135 Bedford Dr
La Grande OR 97850

Call Sign: KF7OWI
Gary F Anger
1345 Beebe Ln
La Grande OR 97850

Call Sign: W7GFA
Gary F Anger
511 Beebe Rd
La Grande OR 97850

Call Sign: KF7AYB
Richard R Mason
38798 Beech St
La Grande OR 97850

Call Sign: KF7OWG
Mark W Larson
3074 Bellinger Ln
La Grande OR 97850

Call Sign: K7OWG
Mark W Larson
3700 Bellinger Ln 6
La Grande OR 97850

Call Sign: W7KVV
James W Simmons
1606 Best Ln 4
La Grande OR 97850

Call Sign: AB7WE
Eric S Dickson
468 Blackstone St
La Grande OR 97850

Call Sign: KB7DUH
William S Ficken
468 Blackstone St
La Grande OR 97850

Call Sign: W7PPQ

W Kirk Braun
943 Cahill Way
La Grande OR 97850

Call Sign: KF7HHI
Christopher S Rickert
1232 Centennial Blvd
La Grande OR 97850

Call Sign: KE7ZSE
Robert L Bork
52655 Center Dr
La Grande OR 97850

Call Sign: N7JPO
Richard H Misener
52655 Center Dr
La Grande OR 97850

Call Sign: KB7HNG
Mendi R Carroll
440 College Ave
La Grande OR 97850

Call Sign: KA7GQB
M Marian Mustoe
1753 Combs Flat Rd
La Grande OR 97850

Call Sign: KC7IZF
Andrew E Anderson
63333 Deschutes Mkt Rd
La Grande OR 978503923

Call Sign: KC7NXX
Marc D Shaffer
3710 Dethman Ridge Rd
La Grande OR 97850

Call Sign: KB7SIB
Shea J Hawes
733 E Main St
La Grande OR 97850

Call Sign: K7VHN

Marlene R Leitch
2993 Elysium
La Grande OR 97850

Call Sign: KD7WBN
Fred S Hawkins
805 Foxley Rd
La Grande OR 97850

Call Sign: KC7YAD
Shelley Page
4163 Fuller Ave
La Grande OR 97850

Call Sign: KB7QER
Carlos E Easley
315 Fulton SE
La Grande OR 97850

Call Sign: WB7PNP
Clark E Hiatt
515 Fulton St
La Grande OR 97850

Call Sign: WB7PNQ
Shirley E Hiatt
1301 Fulton St 419
La Grande OR 97850

Call Sign: KD7VY
Irwin H Smutz
21575 Gooseneck Ck Rd
La Grande OR 97850

Call Sign: KC7URG
Carl C Bond
18723 Griffin Gulch Ln
La Grande OR 97850

Call Sign: KC7WZT
Douglas A Toland
5207 Griffin Ln
La Grande OR 97850

Call Sign: WB7FBG

Stephen A Campbell
450 Hansen Ave S
La Grande OR 97850

Call Sign: KE7SZJ
Grande Ronde Radio
Amateur Association
63510 Johnson Ranch Rd
La Grande OR 97850

Call Sign: W7GRA
Grande Ronde Radio
Amateur Association
1628 Johnson St
La Grande OR 97850

Call Sign: W7YVT
James R Ince
1895 Lake Cove Ave
La Grande OR 97850

Call Sign: W5LUJ
James R Ince
400 Lake Creek Loop Rd
La Grande OR 97850

Call Sign: KE4KR
Le Roy W Berreth
3935 Liberty Rd S
La Grande OR 97850

Call Sign: KF7OWH
Arthur J Trice
295 McClure Ave
La Grande OR 97850

Call Sign: N7TQH
Frank N Lang
56640 McKenzie Hwy M3
La Grande OR 97850

Call Sign: KB8CXQ
Stephen B Tanner
3806 McKenzie Pass Wy
NE Apt 107

La Grande OR 97850

La Grande OR 97850

La Grande OR 97850

Call Sign: KB7DRI
Barbara B Hicks
1855 Meadow Glen
La Grande OR 97850

Call Sign: KF7SGA
Linda K Sweet
501 N Morrison
La Grande OR 97850

Call Sign: KC7URB
Walter L Shelman Jr
12043 S Butte Creek Rd
La Grande OR 97850

Call Sign: W4PJS
Graham H Hicks Jr
2111 Meadow Glen
La Grande OR 97850

Call Sign: KC7YAA
Deward D Hext
411 Old Hwy 995
La Grande OR 97850

Call Sign: KE7ZSB
Molly K Burke
10794 SE 129th Ave
La Grande OR 97850

Call Sign: N7GFU
Walters D Stuart
522 5 N 5th St
La Grande OR 97850

Call Sign: W7ZTC
Victor G Shinsel
2792 Old Stage Rd
La Grande OR 97850

Call Sign: KE7OVS
Donald J Tusten
10794 SE 129th Ave
La Grande OR 97850

Call Sign: AB7CA
Terry L Neustel
6949 N Greenwich
La Grande OR 97850

Call Sign: K7ZPL
William A De Lashmutt
3157 Paramont St
La Grande OR 97850

Call Sign: KE7ZSC
Norm E Burke Jr
210 SE 12th Ave
La Grande OR 97850

Call Sign: W7GQE
John P Britschgi
5521 N Harvard St
La Grande OR 97850

Call Sign: KE7ZSL
Boyd M Burton
780 Pebble Beach Ct
La Grande OR 97850

Call Sign: N7WYU
Frances F Hicks
3265 SW 100th Avwe
La Grande OR 97850

Call Sign: N7NSL
Edward A Ivester
9242 N Kellogg St
La Grande OR 97850

Call Sign: K7KRP
James F Leitch
91409 Place Ln
La Grande OR 97850

Call Sign: WB7VHY
James A Nelson
3916 Terrace Dr
La Grande OR 97850

Call Sign: N7OMK
Margaret E Ivester
9242 N Kellogg St
La Grande OR 97850

Call Sign: KC7IYZ
Milo G Walker
901 J Q Adams St
La Grande OR 97850

Call Sign: KA7OAR
Patricia L Muncy
50410 Umapine Rd
La Grande OR 97850

Call Sign: K7AQT
Levonia Y Burkhead
3136 N Kilpatrick St
La Grande OR 97850

Call Sign: KC7AWL
Robert D Lynch
14307 Ravenwood Dr
La Grande OR 97850

Call Sign: KA7BBE
Lois E Rogers
1421 W Ave
La Grande OR 978500171

Call Sign: N7WZD
Charles H Gillis
1300 N Klimeh Ln

Call Sign: KE7ZSF
Clifton A Tarpy
24 Royal Oaks Dr

Call Sign: KB7NAU
Robert A Clark
2312 Willow St

La Grande OR 97850

Call Sign: W7LYO
Donald L Eggebrecht
1213 X Ave
La Grande OR 97850

Call Sign: KB7WDI
Joseph W Nolan
1603 X Ave
La Grande OR 978503730

Call Sign: K7RBE
Velda Klein
1201 Y Ave
La Grande OR 97850

Call Sign: KD7MED
Jack A Cassity
2110 Y Ave
La Grande OR 97850

Call Sign: KC7IGC
Larry O Witten
1401 Z Ave
La Grande OR 978503643

Call Sign: KA7EPS
Pamala G Thompson
La Grande OR 97850

Call Sign: KA7GNG
Joe R Easley
La Grande OR 97850

Call Sign: KB7DAC
Perry D Gooder
La Grande OR 97850

Call Sign: KC7ALS
Cherie C Austin
La Grande OR 97850

Call Sign: KA7TWQ
Philip L Gray

La Grande OR 97850

Call Sign: KA7EJS
Maurice H Rogers
La Grande OR 97850

Call Sign: KC7LUD
Mark D Rhodes
La Grande OR 97850

Call Sign: WB7PMF
Patrick L Pridgen
La Grande OR 97850

Call Sign: KF7GOR
Diane M Lunsford
La Grande OR 97850

Call Sign: KE7ZRZ
Donna R Fuhrman
La Grande OR 97850

Call Sign: KE7ZRV
Greg K Walker
La Grande OR 97850

Call Sign: KE7ZSA
Harold G Paul
La Grande OR 97850

Call Sign: KK7JX
Julian N Pridmore Brown
La Grande OR 97850

Call Sign: KF7HHJ
William J Rautenstrauch
La Grande OR 97850

Call Sign: N7JMM
Alan D Eberstein
La Grande OR 97850

Call Sign: N7RRC
Leonardo R Sancoy
La Grande OR 97850

Call Sign: KE7MBO
Rocky R Mink
La Grande OR 97850

Call Sign: NE7SE
Courtney Loomis
La Grande OR 978507755

FCC Amateur Radio Licenses in La Pine

Call Sign: KU6O
Sandy E Porter
4319 Arthur St
La Pine OR 97739

Call Sign: WB7NUM
Darrell L Stiers
8520 Bay Front Ln
La Pine OR 97739

Call Sign: KD7LHY
Terry W Gilmore
35395 Bayside Gardens Rd
La Pine OR 97739

Call Sign: KD8KFK
Paul M Stenzel
5200 Brooklake Rd
La Pine OR 97739

Call Sign: KA7AUX
Edeltraud Hoffman
5360 Brooklake Rd NE
La Pine OR 97739

Call Sign: W6IOF
Earl L Burmeister
4879 C St
La Pine OR 97739

Call Sign: W6IOG
Loretta M Burmeister
6342 C St

La Pine OR 97739

La Pine OR 97739

La Pine OR 97739

Call Sign: KD6EPE
Gordon T Irwin
4610 Chambers Ln
La Pine OR 977392622

Call Sign: KC6KTX
Jerry L Page
835 D St
La Pine OR 97739

Call Sign: N7VYF
David N Kirkman
54120 E Marmot Rd
La Pine OR 97739

Call Sign: KC7OYA
Newberry Crater ARSs
2875 Champagne Ln
La Pine OR 97739

Call Sign: AA6SN
Stephen R Page
3301 D St NE 37
La Pine OR 97739

Call Sign: KF7FKL
James L Kinyon
6545 E St
La Pine OR 97739

Call Sign: W7WED
Edward W Sekor
1001 Charles St
La Pine OR 97739

Call Sign: KA7ABF
Harold M Wynne
315 Dellwood Dr
La Pine OR 97339

Call Sign: KC7YHA
Rick B Noble
6545 E St
La Pine OR 97739

Call Sign: KL7IUR
Forrest R Baker
27171 Clear Lake Rd 15
La Pine OR 97739

Call Sign: KD7OIG
Roger Allen
1617 Dragon Tail Pl
La Pine OR 97739

Call Sign: W6VIP
Clifford F La Greide Sr
35027 Fremont Ave
La Pine OR 97739

Call Sign: N7CHA
Lawrence W Smith
4893 Cloudcroft Ln
La Pine OR 97739

Call Sign: KA7VGK
Hanno H Wigand
645 E 11th
La Pine OR 97739

Call Sign: WB7ALR
Jack W Rothweiler
555 Henley Way
La Pine OR 97739

Call Sign: KD7FCM
Dora D Cox
18525 Columbia Ave
La Pine OR 97739

Call Sign: KD7ACL
Mary J Mohr
420 E 2nd St
La Pine OR 977393157

Call Sign: KC0UMR
Suresh Annachi
5597 Hwy 66
La Pine OR 97739

Call Sign: KD7FCN
James L Cox Sr
33151 Columbia Beach Ln
La Pine OR 97739

Call Sign: WA6EMS
Ryan J Aviano
633 E Archwood 98
La Pine OR 97739

Call Sign: N6KWX
Herbert J Crowther
39040 Jerger St
La Pine OR 97739

Call Sign: WA7SPL
Earl W Collins
837 Columbine Way
La Pine OR 97739

Call Sign: KC7HIT
Merl S Wilson
1200 E Central Ave 25
La Pine OR 97739

Call Sign: KE7JEF
Curtis R Owens
442 Loma Linda Ln
La Pine OR 97739

Call Sign: KC7LPT
Wanda L Collins
837 Columbine Wy

Call Sign: KF7NZ
Paul S Richmond
2301 E Irwin Way

Call Sign: KY7OR
Curtis R Owens
590 Lomas Rd

La Pine OR 97739

Call Sign: WA7PFJ
Glenn E Plance
5074 Lone Oak Rd SE
La Pine OR 97739

Call Sign: N7VCJ
Alfred G Beesley
20951 Marsh Orchid Ct
La Pine OR 97739

Call Sign: KQ7D
James E Sampson
23083 Maverick Ln
La Pine OR 97739

Call Sign: N7GFF
Linda M Sampson
204 May St
La Pine OR 97739

Call Sign: N7RFL
Willard E Daughtry
2324 May St
La Pine OR 97739

Call Sign: K9QAM
Ronald J Smith
425 McKinley St SE
La Pine OR 977397802

Call Sign: N7RPE
Nancy A Smith
8512 McLaughlin Ln
La Pine OR 97739

Call Sign: K7ZM
William J Sawders
8512 McLaughlin Ln
La Pine OR 977397802

Call Sign: K7VKI
Vicki D Sawders
9205 McLaughlin Ln

La Pine OR 97739

Call Sign: K7ZZZ
Central Oregon Contest
Club
3361 McNaught St
La Pine OR 97739

Call Sign: K7SSS
Central Oregon Contest
Club
12921 McNeil Creek Rd
La Pine OR 97739

Call Sign: N7YVK
Roger S Hogue
9302 N Allegheny Ave
La Pine OR 977391937

Call Sign: WB6SYB
Robert H Buddell
360 N Alvord
La Pine OR 977393253

Call Sign: KA6SOC
Susan Ludemann
18977 Pacific Crest Dr
La Pine OR 97739

Call Sign: KE7CQX
Kerri J Raymond
3782 Pine Canyon Dr
La Pine OR 97739

Call Sign: K7TEC
Kerri J Raymond
14581 Pine Creek Ln
La Pine OR 97739

Call Sign: KF7AJ
David F Royer
4497 Pinecrest Dr
La Pine OR 97739

Call Sign: KE7RJM

Crater Lake Amateur Radio
Klub
3553 Poplar
La Pine OR 97739

Call Sign: KK7IP
James C Henderson
2180 Poplar Dr 120
La Pine OR 97739

Call Sign: KK6FU
Ronnie D Burnett
1395 Poplar Dr 213
La Pine OR 97739

Call Sign: W7KNP
Charles L Holdiman
2215 Poplar Dr 4
La Pine OR 97739

Call Sign: NR7ON
Crater Lake Amateur Radio
Klub
1497 Poplar Dr Apt 6
La Pine OR 97739

Call Sign: KA7OOV
James S Mura
7955 Portland Rd NE
La Pine OR 97739

Call Sign: KA7WXL
Russell N Laycock
5422 Portland Rd NE 126
La Pine OR 97739

Call Sign: KA7UNX
Le Roy W Steece
4264 Post Canyon Dr
La Pine OR 977390606

Call Sign: KA7WEK
Sharon K Kaehler
3039 Pringle Rd SE
La Pine OR 97739

Call Sign: KF7LCT
Mark E Rose
7610 Ridgewood Dr
La Pine OR 97739

Call Sign: KG7NJ
Larry E Crye
570 Rose St NE
La Pine OR 97739

Call Sign: KK7YC
Ronnie D Burnett
240 S 1st Ave
La Pine OR 97739

Call Sign: KA7BGH
Louis L Henson
953 Spring Way
La Pine OR 97739

Call Sign: KA7QAV
Creagh P Williams
569 Springbrook Rd
La Pine OR 97739

Call Sign: W7KVQ
Charles W Stewart
1312 Stonehaven Dr
La Pine OR 97739

Call Sign: KV7N
Roland W O Brien
92127 Svensen Mkt Rd
La Pine OR 97739

Call Sign: KE6WEH
Pal Ham
17110 W Dr
La Pine OR 97739

Call Sign: N6WZR
Paul J Bowman
17110 W Dr
La Pine OR 977399712

Call Sign: N6WZQ
Justun M Bowman
17110 W Dr
La Pine OR 977399712

Call Sign: N6XAC
Charlene P Bowman
17110 W Dr
La Pine OR 977399712

Call Sign: KD7RZB
Travis M Irvin
53317 Woodstock
La Pine OR 97739

Call Sign: W6RRP
Virginia E Charlton
15920 Wright Ave
La Pine OR 97739

Call Sign: N7VIZ
Larry R Charlton
15920 Wright Ave
La Pine OR 97739

Call Sign: KC7BTV
Alan N Mac Fadyen
La Pine OR 97739

Call Sign: KC7BTW
Ian R Smith
La Pine OR 97739

Call Sign: KD7XV
Stephen W O Brien
La Pine OR 97739

Call Sign: KM6KM
Richard W Werner
La Pine OR 97739

Call Sign: W7MT
Russell R Spalding
La Pine OR 97739

Call Sign: W7SVQ
Robert N Hoaglin
La Pine OR 97739

Call Sign: KC7AMT
Jenny R Jardine
La Pine OR 97739

Call Sign: WA7KPX
Rodney G Wright
La Pine OR 97739

Call Sign: N6FWF
Norma A Porter
La Pine OR 97739

Call Sign: KB7BDC
William J Horn
La Pine OR 97739

Call Sign: KB7ORH
Monte H Harmon
La Pine OR 97739

Call Sign: KB7WUN
Virginia E Charlton
La Pine OR 97739

Call Sign: KC7RIA
Richard B Gurwell
La Pine OR 97739

Call Sign: KC7UZD
Cecil Ott
La Pine OR 97739

Call Sign: KC7WPI
Norma P Tate
La Pine OR 97739

Call Sign: KE6YYX
James D Sprott
La Pine OR 97739

Call Sign: KL7HMC
Larry W Simpson
La Pine OR 97739

Call Sign: N7PWK
Robert M Smith
La Pine OR 97739

Call Sign: N7RGA
James W Hankins Jr
La Pine OR 97739

Call Sign: N7TYN
Luana K Lewis
La Pine OR 97739

Call Sign: W6IBL
John R Strand
La Pine OR 97739

Call Sign: W7XYZ
George E Stevenson
La Pine OR 97739

Call Sign: WA7TYD
James A Williams
La Pine OR 97739

Call Sign: WB7UMO
Michael J Finazzi
La Pine OR 97739

Call Sign: WB7WSM
Ellen L Finazzi
La Pine OR 97739

Call Sign: N6DFW
Beverly J Irwin
La Pine OR 97739

Call Sign: KE7EWW
James D Sprott
La Pine OR 97739

Call Sign: W7CFL

James D Sprott
La Pine OR 97739

Call Sign: KE7BHN
Orman F Waddle
La Pine OR 97739

Call Sign: WD6ECC
Patricia J Cook
La Pine OR 97739

Call Sign: KD7SKP
Robert A Fischer
La Pine OR 97739

Call Sign: KD7SQD
Sherrie L Fischer
La Pine OR 97739

Call Sign: K7DLT
David L Tucker
La Pine OR 97739

Call Sign: KA7EED
Craig S Farrier
La Pine OR 97739

Call Sign: KC7TVD
John E Tate
La Pine OR 97739

Call Sign: KC7OTN
Robert E Pittaway
La Pine OR 977392187

Call Sign: WA7RYD
Norman D Ribail
La Pine OR 977392592

Call Sign: KD7HJD
Beverly J Irwin
La Pine OR 977392622

Call Sign: WA7JZV
James M Dreiling

La Pine OR 977393088

Call Sign: KD7ACK
Cyrus C Mohr
La Pine OR 977393157

FCC Amateur Radio Licenses in Lakeside

Call Sign: KL7JCZ
Robert W Kurtti
16646 Butteville Rd
Lakeside OR 97449

Call Sign: KD7EZL
Phillip D Drehmer
4780 Gardner Rd SE
Lakeside OR 97449

Call Sign: N7NCH
George E Luff
1260 Jackson Ave SW
Lakeside OR 97449

Call Sign: W7XG
Melvin W Topliss
1651 Lexington Ave Rm
C102
Lakeside OR 97449

Call Sign: KE7QVZ
Mary Urso
2411 Lindley Way
Lakeside OR 97449

Call Sign: KC7SDT
William H Collien
3363 N Farragut St
Lakeside OR 97449

Call Sign: KD7MWY
Gene E Corso
930 N Holladay Dr
Lakeside OR 97449

Call Sign: K6RGC
Gene E Corso
1901 N Holladay Dr
Lakeside OR 97449

Call Sign: N7VRR
Vicky J Warthen
425 N Holly St
Lakeside OR 97449

Call Sign: K6TC
Thomas H Corso
2161 NW 15th Ct
Lakeside OR 97449

Call Sign: AA1IO
Betsy A Carlson
716 NW 15th St
Lakeside OR 97449

Call Sign: N7FHE
Richard A Johnson
10627 NW 195th Ave
Lakeside OR 97449

Call Sign: N7HVU
James R Russell
925 Royalty Dr NE
Lakeside OR 97449

Call Sign: KD6KUX
Brigitte M Gastreich
23575 Sandlake Rd
Lakeside OR 97449

Call Sign: KE6CGW
James J Gastreich
24420 Sandlake Rd
Lakeside OR 97449

Call Sign: W7DIF
Corinne L Keyser
6901 SE 110th
Lakeside OR 97449

Call Sign: KB6QWE
Marvin T Rogers Sr
661 Silver Creek Dr
Lakeside OR 97449

Call Sign: K9PSW
Richard J De Witt
32874 Sunset Rd
Lakeside OR 97449

Call Sign: KD7EZN
Ray A Morgan
676 Sunset Way
Lakeside OR 97449

Call Sign: KB7YFV
Tris J Norton
Lakeside OR 97449

Call Sign: W7IF
Brian A Boyd
Lakeside OR 97449

Call Sign: WB6DYA
Vaughn Z Rains III
Lakeside OR 97449

Call Sign: KD7VCQ
Andrew S Hoyle
Lakeside OR 97449

Call Sign: KD7VDC
Devon G Phillips
Lakeside OR 97449

**FCC Amateur Radio
Licenses in Lakeview**

Call Sign: KF7GSZ
Lakeview ARC
809 Beach Dr
Lakeview OR 97630

Call Sign: K7LKV
Lakeview ARC

1231 Beach Dr
Lakeview OR 97630

Call Sign: KE7DDM
Steven W Yates
1231 Beach Dr
Lakeview OR 97630

Call Sign: W7EGL
Steven W Yates
3956 Beach Loop Dr
Lakeview OR 97630

Call Sign: KF7IO
Brian A Conger
1782 Cal Young Rd
Lakeview OR 97630

Call Sign: KB7CYL
Brian J Clark
69705 Camp Polk Rd
Lakeview OR 97630

Call Sign: KF7TKO
Cory L Thornton
68922 E Cedar Hill Loop
Lakeview OR 97630

Call Sign: N6QLL
John F Aldrich
6545 E St
Lakeview OR 97630

Call Sign: N6TJS
Debra M Aldrich
6575 E St
Lakeview OR 97630

Call Sign: KE7QP
Robert L Thornton
3659 Hwy 234
Lakeview OR 97630

Call Sign: KF7GSY
Lake Co ARC

4000 Hwy 234
Lakeview OR 97630

Call Sign: K7LDH
Lake Co ARC
4586 Hwy 234
Lakeview OR 97630

Call Sign: KA7FOP
Ronald C Collier
4752 Jean Ct NE
Lakeview OR 97630

Call Sign: W5TFS
Robert G Howard
504 N 14th St
Lakeview OR 976301152

Call Sign: KE7DMX
Robert G Howard
1918 N 14th St
Lakeview OR 976301152

Call Sign: KB7PTV
Robert G Howard
2300 N 14th St
Lakeview OR 976301152

Call Sign: K7TMR
Albert W Clark
229 N Gun Club Rd
Lakeview OR 97630

Call Sign: K6DSI
John R Clough
9530 N Van Houten Ave
Lakeview OR 97630

Call Sign: KB6UWY
Ralph U Hyde Jr
3065 NW 159th Ter
Lakeview OR 97630

Call Sign: KF7TKR
Kenneth A Chartier

716 NW 15th St
Lakeview OR 97630

Call Sign: KB7CUE
Ben L Alexander
3835 NW 172nd Pl
Lakeview OR 97630

Call Sign: KG6HOT
Mark Webber
5192 NW 172nd Pl
Lakeview OR 97630

Call Sign: W7MLJ
Byron H Warburton
1765 NW 173rd Ave 716
Lakeview OR 976301239

Call Sign: N6KMS
Josephine E Caley
340 NW 17th St
Lakeview OR 97630

Call Sign: KC7ZED
Jules I Gilpatrick
2350 Paasch Dr
Lakeview OR 976300590

Call Sign: K7SXW
Harry B Morris
240 S 1st Ave
Lakeview OR 97630

Call Sign: KE7USS
Dennis H Kniskern
8169 S Myrtle Rd
Lakeview OR 97630

Call Sign: W7DHK
Dennis H Kniskern
3555 S Pacific Hwy Unit
132
Lakeview OR 97630

Call Sign: KF7TKQ

Kenneth D Turkle
1453 Southwood Ct SE
Lakeview OR 97630

Call Sign: KF7FQM
Patrick L Roach
3201 Southwood Dr
Lakeview OR 97630

Call Sign: KF7PAT
Patrick L Roach
4527 Souza Ct
Lakeview OR 97630

Call Sign: N6WRC
John E Blacet III
3827 Sturdivant Ave
Lakeview OR 97630

Call Sign: KE7DJW
Courtney A Woodward
21012 Thomas Dr
Lakeview OR 97630

Call Sign: AD7OU
Courtney A Woodward
1404 Thomas Rd
Lakeview OR 97630

Call Sign: KD7DL
William P Cogburn
Lakeview OR 97630

Call Sign: KF7QMX
John R Hodges
Lakeview OR 97630

**FCC Amateur Radio
Licenses in Langlois**

Call Sign: WD8DQK
Merle A Smith Jr
1260 Jackson Ave SW
Langlois OR 97450

Call Sign: WB5VFZ
Frank W Kattein Jr
975 Juanita Ave
Langlois OR 97450

Call Sign: KE7CYQ
Ginger M Snaps
4232 Lombard Dr
Langlois OR 97450

Call Sign: KB7DNN
Michael D Murphy
1005 Meadowlawn Dr SE
Langlois OR 974500145

Call Sign: W3VG
Donald J Crane
2062 Morning View Dr
Langlois OR 974501045

Call Sign: W7BC
Donald J Crane
2062 Morning View Dr
Langlois OR 974501045

Call Sign: KI7HL
Patricia E Reed
Langlois OR 97450

Call Sign: W6PWQ
Frank A Reed Jr
Langlois OR 97450

Call Sign: KC7FHX
Beverly A King
Langlois OR 97450

Call Sign: N7LND
Julian C King
Langlois OR 97450

Call Sign: W7BCD
Beverly A King
Langlois OR 97450

Call Sign: KE7JSJ
Michael S Rosellini
Langlois OR 97450

Call Sign: KF7UFU
Sandra R Randolph
Langlois OR 97450

Call Sign: KF7GTU
Jason P Randolph
Langlois OR 97450

Call Sign: KB6NZV
Phillip F Barker
Langlois OR 974501027

FCC Amateur Radio Licenses in Leaburg

Call Sign: KA7KXA
Lewis L Jones
364 Monica Dr
Leaburg OR 97489

Call Sign: KB7PAQ
Philip D Johnson
225 Monteflora Terr
Leaburg OR 97489

Call Sign: KB7QNP
Daniel P Johnson
2809 Montelius St
Leaburg OR 97489

Call Sign: K6YIS
Gene T Knight
135 Montello Ave 3
Leaburg OR 97489

Call Sign: W7AD
Edwin H Staar
Leaburg OR 97489

Call Sign: N7GFN
Frank I Moore

Leaburg OR 97489

FCC Amateur Radio Licenses in Lexington

Call Sign: KD7LXT
Charles W Mc Connell
1060 N Knott
Lexington OR 97839

Call Sign: KA7KVP
Thomas C Mc Connell
Lexington OR 97839

FCC Amateur Radio Licenses in Long Creek

Call Sign: KD7LVO
Norman L Smotony
Long Creek OR 97856

FCC Amateur Radio Licenses in Lorane

Call Sign: N7MSX
Bruce C Atkins
Lorane OR 97451

FCC Amateur Radio Licenses in Lostine

Call Sign: WD6BFT
George J Floyd
711 Jenny Ln
Lostine OR 97857

Call Sign: KD7PIB
Matthew J Calhoun
Lostine OR 97857

Call Sign: KD7RML
Brian C Buck
Lostine OR 97857

Call Sign: KC6UHI
Eugene K Bell
4826 Eaststar Ct NE
Lowell OR 974529727

Call Sign: KF7HQ
Cecil P De Lange
1286 Kimberly Ct NE
Lowell OR 97452

Call Sign: KC7JVP
Mary E Pruitt
1286 Kimberly Ct NE
Lowell OR 97542

Call Sign: KC7MHT
Gregory T Davlin
1754 Kimberly Dr
Lowell OR 97452

Call Sign: KC7MVU
Patrick L Byrne
3720 N Roxy Dr
Lowell OR 97452

Call Sign: KB6TYG
Theresa M Plata
Lowell OR 97452

Call Sign: KD7BKY
Kimberly A Kagelaris
Lowell OR 97452

Call Sign: N6QPW
Daniel M Plata
Lowell OR 97452

Call Sign: KB0WVU
Jerry E Miller

1809 26th St 55
Madras OR 97741

Call Sign: KB0YIW
Monica R Miller
1809 26th St Sp 83
Madras OR 97741

Call Sign: N7RGG
Troy M Phifer
209 Alder St
Madras OR 97741

Call Sign: KE7SZK
Jefferson County Amateur
Emergency
Communications
88 Lewis St
Madras OR 97741

Call Sign: KZ2E
Kermit R Kumle
1318 Lewis St
Madras OR 97741

Call Sign: WT7K
Kermit R Kumle
1318 Lewis St
Madras OR 97741

Call Sign: KB7JDC
Frances E Hoffman
42550 Mill Rd
Madras OR 97741

Call Sign: WA7OTZ
Arthur G Statt
205 Morton Rd
Madras OR 97741

Call Sign: N7RFS
Daniel P Comingore
7043 N Borthwick Ave
Madras OR 97741

Call Sign: K7FIL
Phil Comingore
489 N Broadway
Madras OR 97741

Call Sign: N7RFT
Herman E Hansen
4423 NE Division St
Madras OR 97741

Call Sign: KA7CPZ
Verne S Campbell
1999 NE Division St Apt 23
Madras OR 97741

Call Sign: KC7WHX
Merle D Collins
934 NE Foothills Dr
Madras OR 97741

Call Sign: KB7SIA
Fabian Roth
934 NE Foothills Dr
Madras OR 97741

Call Sign: KB7ORX
John P Curnutt
52 NE Fremont St
Madras OR 97741

Call Sign: N7VLZ
Merlin Moon
62424 NE Frontage Rd
Madras OR 97741

Call Sign: N7RFV
Roger I Powers
10355 NW Engleman St
Madras OR 97741

Call Sign: N7RFW
Dorothy B Powers
2045 NW Eucalyptus Dr
Madras OR 97741

Call Sign: KB7GDC
Vaughn M Skinner
1961 NW Grant 4
Madras OR 97741

Call Sign: KB7GDD
Marie E Skinner
2240 NW Grant Ave
Madras OR 97741

Call Sign: KB7IUU
Caleb Skinner
3510 NW Grant Ave
Madras OR 97741

Call Sign: KB7JJK
Ginger S Skinner
1425 NW Green Pl
Madras OR 97741

Call Sign: KD7TMW
Steven J Waldorf
3120 NW John Olsen Ave
15 102
Madras OR 97741

Call Sign: KE7BEL
Timothy A Birky
10572 NW La Cassel Crest
Ln
Madras OR 97741

Call Sign: KD7LVN
Darrell Y Miller
495 S Hwy
Madras OR 97741

Call Sign: KA7FHB
Dan H Skeels
705 SE 8th
Madras OR 97741

Call Sign: KC7NBB
Darlene J Skeels
3937 SE 91st

Madras OR 97741

Call Sign: KD7MPD
David H Hassler
2765 SE Cleveland Dr
Madras OR 97741

Call Sign: KE7SEO
Rosella J Miller
28110 SE Fern Dr
Madras OR 97741

Call Sign: KB7SIF
Bobbie C Easlon
43085 SE Kiesecker Rd
Madras OR 97741

Call Sign: N7VME
Paul A Easlon Jr
5096 SE King
Madras OR 97741

Call Sign: N7YBJ
Paul A Easlon
20874 SE King Hezekiah
Madras OR 97741

Call Sign: N7YBM
Lucille E Gregg
15227 SE La Crescenta
Way
Madras OR 97741

Call Sign: KB7QCE
Bill K Randolph
8116 SE Taylor Ct
Madras OR 97741

Call Sign: KB7HCS
Nelda R Mc Cool
12665 SW Barlow Rd
Madras OR 97741

Call Sign: WA7IKD
Roberta A Mc Conkey

12700 SW Barlow Rd
Madras OR 97741

Call Sign: N7RYR
Stephen W Rogers
6774 SW Becket Ct
Madras OR 97741

Call Sign: KD7FWS
William H Nill
6170 SW Cross Creek Dr
Madras OR 97741

Call Sign: KB7HCR
Gerald W Mc Cool
17645 SW Elder View Dr
Madras OR 97741

Call Sign: KB7FOJ
Michael W Mc Cool Sr
17031 SW Eldorado Dr
Madras OR 97741

Call Sign: KB7HCQ
Dorothy M Mc Cool
17240 SW Eldorado Dr
Madras OR 97741

Call Sign: N7RFU
Corina G Mc Cool
17240 SW Eldorado Dr
Madras OR 97741

Call Sign: N7RFX
Michael W Mc Cool Jr
13795 SW Electric 38
Madras OR 97741

Call Sign: KD7OJH
Holly E Kumle
3979 SW Halcyon Rd
Madras OR 97741

Call Sign: KA7FHD
Delvin L Hoffman

3755 SW Marshall Pl
Madras OR 97741

Call Sign: KC7OUH
Daniel E Comingore
Madras OR 97741

Call Sign: N7UBT
Theron L Hicks Jr
Madras OR 97741

Call Sign: W7AAV
Robert S Smith
Madras OR 97741

Call Sign: KD7LDM
Josh J Wisely
Madras OR 97741

Call Sign: KF7OUH
Jillian M Mcintosh
Madras OR 97741

Call Sign: KF7CIB
Norman C Mcintosh
Madras OR 97741

Call Sign: K1GER
Norman C Mcintosh
Madras OR 97741

FCC Amateur Radio Licenses in Malin

Call Sign: KC7IEW
Nancy Ann Thorne
Malin OR 97632

Call Sign: KE7CGU
Daniel J Johnson Sr
Malin OR 97632

Call Sign: K7POW
Daniel J Johnson Sr
Malin OR 97632

Call Sign: KE7DFJ
Drew A Kalina
Malin OR 97632

FCC Amateur Radio Licenses in Mapleton

Call Sign: N6KWG
Theodore L Naylor Jr
1415 E 7th Ave
Mapleton OR 97453

Call Sign: N6KWH
Jeanette S Naylor
125 E 8th Ave
Mapleton OR 97453

Call Sign: KC7YMZ
Brian R Mc Allister
594 Empress Ave
Mapleton OR 974539630

Call Sign: KE7SJF
Ralph A Gamache
1290 Fenwick St
Mapleton OR 97453

Call Sign: KC2EUC
Robert R Emerson
2578 Jacksonville Hwy
Mapleton OR 97453

Call Sign: KF7BIS
Elyssa J Emerson
126 Jacob Hale Way
Mapleton OR 97453

Call Sign: KF7BIR
Hahnna N Emerson
310 Jacob Hale Way
Mapleton OR 97453

Call Sign: KF7BIQ
Josiah R Emerspm

1220 Jacobs Dr Apt 6
Mapleton OR 97453

Call Sign: KD7PJO
David P Lynch
29700 Park Dr
Mapleton OR 974539619

Call Sign: K6DRO
James S Welman
215 Sweetbriar Dr
Mapleton OR 974539636

Call Sign: KA7FJQ
Walter L Brooks
Mapleton OR 97453

Call Sign: KB7VOS
Ralph E Garrison
Mapleton OR 97453

Call Sign: KF7RGD
Ada M Mcclory
Mapleton OR 97453

Call Sign: KF7OPG
Michael J Mcclory
Mapleton OR 97453

Call Sign: KD7QOA
Trevor J Lynch
Mapleton OR 974530262

FCC Amateur Radio Licenses in Marcola

Call Sign: KA7BPS
Robin S O Kelly
611 Immonen Rd
Marcola OR 97454

Call Sign: KF7NAI
Amy K Ganieany
4063 Imperial Dr
Marcola OR 97454

Call Sign: KF6LST
Anne Rock
722 Morgan Ln
Marcola OR 97454

Call Sign: KB7PCB
Daymen C Kessler
424 N 3rd St
Marcola OR 97454

Call Sign: KD7BNG
Kody T Kessler
424 N 3rd St
Marcola OR 97454

Call Sign: W7PCB
Daymen C Kessler
638 N 3rd St
Marcola OR 97454

Call Sign: KD7BKW
Sandie K Kessler
21320 N Coburg Rd
Marcola OR 97454

Call Sign: KG7PC
Charles G Fuller Jr
783 Savage Creek Rd
Marcola OR 97454

Call Sign: KD7LYA
Lloyd N Anderson
38816 Wendling Rd
Marcola OR 97454

Call Sign: AA7FL
Steven C Milewski
Marcola OR 97454

Call Sign: KB7NNG
Hilda B Fuller
Marcola OR 97454

Call Sign: WA7TSF

Samuel A Mc Ghehey
Marcola OR 97454

FCC Amateur Radio Licenses in Maupin

Call Sign: WA4RPY
Douglas D Fowley
34933 Hwy 20
Maupin OR 97037

Call Sign: WA7IEK
Wayne A Odom
2746 Ladarrah St
Maupin OR 97037

FCC Amateur Radio Licenses in Mc Kenzie Bridge

Call Sign: KD7ABJ
Robert M Wert
364 Monica Dr
McKenzie Bridge OR
97413

Call Sign: KD7LYL
Vim Toutenhoofd
5112 NW 167 Pl
McKenzie Bridge OR
974139614

Call Sign: KD6URR
Joseph C Lippold
92121 Yale Ln
McKenzie Bridge OR
97413

Call Sign: KD6WWZ
Angelique A Laskowski
McKenzie Bridge OR
97413

Call Sign: KC6NAX
Irene H Maxwell

McKenzie Bridge OR
97413

FCC Amateur Radio Licenses in Meacham

Call Sign: K7SHG
Ronald E Eves
Meacham OR 97859

Call Sign: KA7UGW
Howard R Naegeli
Meacham OR 97859

Call Sign: KB7CCG
Margaret E Herd
Meacham OR 97859

Call Sign: KC7BVZ
Judy A Kleng
Meacham OR 97859

Call Sign: KC7PJE
Walter A Davis
Meacham OR 97859

Call Sign: KD7FYR
Kenneth J Elliston
Meacham OR 97859

Call Sign: KD7GVT
Lorna C Elliston
Meacham OR 97859

Call Sign: W7ALT
Walter A Davis
Meacham OR 97859

Call Sign: KF7AZW
Charles R Dickson
Meacham OR 97859

Call Sign: KC7BWA
Nicholas G Kleng
Meacham OR 98759

Call Sign: KC7RQF
Charlene E Davis
Meacham OR 978590044

**FCC Amateur Radio
Licenses in Medford**

Call Sign: KB7MM
James O Dukes
2710 33rd St
Medford OR 97504

Call Sign: KF7AU
Robert W Hunt
310 6th St
Medford OR 97504

Call Sign: AL7LF
Herbert D Brazil
4242 Avalon Pl
Medford OR 97504

Call Sign: N7ZYH
David J Catalano
503 B Ave
Medford OR 97504

Call Sign: K6BUN
Richard D Fraser
2829 B St
Medford OR 975014464

Call Sign: WA7TEG
Kenneth F Kugler
287 Bailey Dr
Medford OR 97504

Call Sign: KD7EHC
Larry G Wright
2883 Bailey Ln
Medford OR 97504

Call Sign: KA7ZEW
Henrietta W Kugler

2883 Bailey Ln
Medford OR 97504

Call Sign: KE7LAC
L Byron Patton
2952 Bailey Ln
Medford OR 97504

Call Sign: KF7QNI
Raymond P Ackerman
3381 Bailey Ln
Medford OR 97501

Call Sign: W7BND
John H Beinhauer
15975 Baldy Ck Rd
Medford OR 975045017

Call Sign: KF7SIS
Todd F Carney
1360 Barker Rd
Medford OR 97504

Call Sign: N7RBP
Robert R Ross
5319 Baxter Ct SE
Medford OR 97504

Call Sign: WA6MSE
Nigel B Lemaire
3128 Bayview Ter
Medford OR 97501

Call Sign: KG6QE
Margaret L Van Tuyl
809 Beach Dr
Medford OR 97501

Call Sign: KB7ZMG
Harvey D Myers II
600 Beach St
Medford OR 97504

Call Sign: NE3L
Harvey D Myers II

600 Beach St
Medford OR 97504

Call Sign: KC7AEF
Jenny A Myers
506 Beachwood Ave
Medford OR 97504

Call Sign: KB7WIT
Carl G Palinkas
3146 Beacon St NE
Medford OR 97504

Call Sign: N7RAQ
Mark A Lewis
114 Bellevue Ave
Medford OR 975014441

Call Sign: N7RAR
Perry K Lewis
211 Bellevue Dr
Medford OR 975014441

Call Sign: KB7REK
Hazel K Frodsham
24743 Bellfountain Rd
Medford OR 97504

Call Sign: N7HWW
Eric S Kees
25097 Bellfountain Rd
Medford OR 97504

Call Sign: KD7OUC
Edward F Mccumsey
1441 Bilger Creek Rd
Medford OR 97501

Call Sign: KB7LHT
Steve A Cave
84400 Boods Rd
Medford OR 97504

Call Sign: W7LLG
Clifford J La Brie

Hcr 87 Box 530
Medford OR 97501

221 Bridge St
Medford OR 97501

28511 Cascade Loop
Medford OR 97501

Call Sign: W4EIN
Julian W Smith
Rt 1 Box 54L
Medford OR 97504

Call Sign: N7GSN
Diane C Chamberlain
88890 Bridge St
Medford OR 97504

Call Sign: WA7NEQ
Lloyd M Miles
911 Cascade St
Medford OR 97501

Call Sign: KE7PMN
Paul D Moser
Hc 52 Box 562
Medford OR 97504

Call Sign: N7GSP
Stephen P Chamberlain
88890 Bridge St
Medford OR 97504

Call Sign: N7LTR
Frieda A Lorton
911 Cascade St
Medford OR 975014116

Call Sign: WA7UVU
Joseph E Heideman
Rt 1 Box 898
Medford OR 97501

Call Sign: AD6BS
Clifford G Simonsen
805 Bronco Ave
Medford OR 97504

Call Sign: KC7ZCD
Maria K Mc Neely
32242 Cater Rd
Medford OR 97504

Call Sign: K7LVS
William J C Clifford
Hc 86 Box 91
Medford OR 97501

Call Sign: N7GFL
James D Rittenbach
1325 Buck St
Medford OR 97504

Call Sign: K7BOT
A Howard Arant
18811 Cathy Adams Dr
Medford OR 97504

Call Sign: KC7REL
Katherine A Ford
3999 Brae Burn Dr
Medford OR 97501

Call Sign: KB7APD
Robert W Wolcott
16073 Burgess Rd
Medford OR 97504

Call Sign: KA6HHM
Timothy E Fredericy
18811 Cathy Adams Dr
Medford OR 97504

Call Sign: N7SC
Steven C Chastain
2999 Brett Loop
Medford OR 97501

Call Sign: KC7NEX
Karl D Sargent
3800 Carmen Dr A214
Medford OR 97504

Call Sign: KE7KZX
Von H Taylor
3550 Cedar
Medford OR 97504

Call Sign: WB7CBM
Patricia A Chastain
2999 Brett Loop
Medford OR 97501

Call Sign: KE7SZN
Patricia A Andries
407 Carthage Ave
Medford OR 97504

Call Sign: KD7EQA
Robert E Perry
3595 Cedaroak 10
Medford OR 975045806

Call Sign: KB6LNF
Victor J Pribyl Jr
2999 Brett Loop
Medford OR 97504

Call Sign: K6ELU
George S Clark
591 Cascade Dr
Medford OR 975045194

Call Sign: W6MZX
Herbert V Ellingson Sr
11718 Cedarwood Dr
Medford OR 97504

Call Sign: W7EFZ
Jack F Wheeler

Call Sign: KC7WO
Bill J Lorton

Call Sign: KF7JVY
Robert O Wolcott

11718 Cedarwood Dr
Medford OR 97504

1063 Cinnamon Ave
Medford OR 97501

405 Crouse Way
Medford OR 97504

Call Sign: W7ROW
Robert O Wolcott
78364 Ceder Parks Rd
Medford OR 97504

Call Sign: WB7VSN
David R Phillips
1740 Clearlake
Medford OR 97501

Call Sign: W6NIB
Kenneth W Taylor
26074 Crow Rd
Medford OR 975049278

Call Sign: W7TJJ
Wayne W Mc Elroy
3403 Cheuron Dr
Medford OR 97504

Call Sign: N7ZYH
David J Catalano
87749 Collins Ln
Medford OR 97504

Call Sign: W7NIB
Kenneth W Taylor
27482 Crow Rd
Medford OR 975049278

Call Sign: KC6WWY
Marlene L Cash
3510 Chow Mein Ln 11
Medford OR 975049785

Call Sign: KD7ZYX
Christopher L Bay
5050 Columbus 42
Medford OR 975017943

Call Sign: W6NIB
Kenneth W Taylor
28119 Crow Rd
Medford OR 975049278

Call Sign: WB6OSD
Edward J Cash
3510 Chow Mein Ln 16
Medford OR 97504

Call Sign: W7FYF
Wallace B Brill
4325 Commerce St 111
Medford OR 97504

Call Sign: K7NIB
Kenneth W Taylor
33382 Crown Point Dr
Medford OR 975049278

Call Sign: WF7G
Terry A Schultz
6363 Christie Ave
Medford OR 97504

Call Sign: WA6LCR
Dennis T Matheny
2288 Corona Ave
Medford OR 97504

Call Sign: KC7VKT
Kai V Aiello
63237 Crown Point Rd
Medford OR 97504

Call Sign: KD7EYA
Karl Hargrave
30060 Church Dr
Medford OR 97504

Call Sign: W7DGU
Charles R Williams
1973 Cottontail Ct NE
Medford OR 97501

Call Sign: N7KOE
Daniel S Jones
1786 Curtis Ave
Medford OR 97504

Call Sign: W7NFU
Marvin E Reed
32221 Church Rd
Medford OR 97504

Call Sign: WC7B
Mark V Kounz
607 Cottonwood
Medford OR 97501

Call Sign: KE7ANN
David G Sherbourne
193 Cypress Ct
Medford OR 97504

Call Sign: KD7GVI
Joshua J Mathis
843 Church St E
Medford OR 97501

Call Sign: KC7WG
Michael D Langston
76387 Crestview
Medford OR 97501

Call Sign: N7YIG
Richard L Croly
1913 D St
Medford OR 975019661

Call Sign: W7KZU
David W Putman

Call Sign: KE7BZG
David J Catalano

Call Sign: K7MKG
John T Amsden

1928 D St
Medford OR 97501

Call Sign: KA7SQG
Robert R Stewart
115 D St 1
Medford OR 97501

Call Sign: KF7ELL
Laurance E Masten
54208 Dahlgren Rd
Medford OR 97504

Call Sign: K6UHM
Raymond P Kimmel
3159 Days Creek Rd
Medford OR 97504

Call Sign: N7NZK
John E Mc Cormack
69331 Deer Ridge Ln
Medford OR 97504

Call Sign: K7UIO
Victor D Goll
915 Deer Run Ln
Medford OR 97504

Call Sign: N7PJG
Edward A Goll
3131 Deer Trl Ln
Medford OR 97504

Call Sign: N7CHK
John F Berry
4261 Devonshire Ct
Medford OR 97504

Call Sign: KD7UVX
Brian M Bowie
89580 Dick Way
Medford OR 97504

Call Sign: N0FGR
Sharon A Ireland

89580 Dick Way
Medford OR 97504

Call Sign: KF7JWG
Elmer L Coffman
1305 Division St
Medford OR 97504

Call Sign: KC7TCR
Curtis C Hodnefield
5050 Donald St
Medford OR 97504

Call Sign: WA7JWY
B C Knauber
12002 Duggan Rd
Medford OR 97501

Call Sign: KD7KPB
Michael J Barlow
36981 Dusty Ln
Medford OR 97501

Call Sign: K7NND
Lawrence E Mc Tevia
645 E 11th
Medford OR 97501

Call Sign: N6PLY
Edward A Ullrich
1100 E 11th
Medford OR 97501

Call Sign: N6PNG
Catherine P Ullrich
1301 E 11th
Medford OR 97501

Call Sign: N7LZR
Robert E Ransmeier
546 E 11th Pl
Medford OR 97501

Call Sign: N7JES
Otto E Mc Clung

615 E 11th St
Medford OR 97501

Call Sign: KF7EPA
Daniel S Bell
655 E 32nd Ave
Medford OR 97501

Call Sign: WA7IHU
Jacob O Schock
615 E Ball Ave
Medford OR 97501

Call Sign: KA6ZSJ
Barbara J Stober
12110 E Burnside St Apt
203
Medford OR 97504

Call Sign: KA6TIX
M David Stober
5316 E Burnside St Apt 6
Medford OR 97504

Call Sign: KB7CLZ
Steven W Deitemeyer
3672 E Chinook
Medford OR 97504

Call Sign: KG7DT
Henry C Gates
3672 E Chinook
Medford OR 97504

Call Sign: KC7RYQ
Gary L Morrell
633 E Columbia River Hwy
104
Medford OR 975045869

Call Sign: KF7JVZ
Fred A Robinson
309 E Columbia St
Medford OR 97504

Call Sign: N7XEN
Nery R Alcantara Jr
2301 E Irwin Way
Medford OR 97501

Call Sign: KF6VY
Osborne Becklund
125 E Rail Rd
Medford OR 97504

Call Sign: W7FVY
Osborne Becklund
329 E Rose St
Medford OR 975048812

Call Sign: KF6VY
Osborne Becklund
64633 E Sandy River Ln
Medford OR 975048812

Call Sign: KE6UD
Henry Dettmann
62582 Eagle Rd
Medford OR 97504

Call Sign: N7UYI
Steven G Arnold
62860 Eagle Rd
Medford OR 97504

Call Sign: KB7FHI
William W Riffe
130 Elm St
Medford OR 97504

Call Sign: NC7Y
Robert G Gresham Sr
33985 Elm St
Medford OR 97504

Call Sign: KE7EAF
Larry D Kendrick
705 Elma SE
Medford OR 97504

Call Sign: N7CGC
Albert G Edwards III
3791 Elmira Rd
Medford OR 97504

Call Sign: W7SBT
John D Patton
4008 Elmwood
Medford OR 975046013

Call Sign: N7WIU
Joyce L Clymer
2340 Emmett Dr NW
Medford OR 97504

Call Sign: W7TAH
Wayne S Clymer
2340 Emmett Dr NW
Medford OR 97504

Call Sign: N7DLF
David B Arrasmith
1200 Engleside
Medford OR 97504

Call Sign: AB6QX
Stephen A Weldon
707 F Ave
Medford OR 97504

Call Sign: KA0YEQ
John B Wasson
96121 Fairview Sumner Ln
Medford OR 97504

Call Sign: KA6WEA
Henry H Jenkins
6885 Fairway Ave SE
Medford OR 97504

Call Sign: KD6DVR
Edward D Crews
8905 Fiddle Cr Rd
Medford OR 97504

Call Sign: WB6OFO
Robert Goldberg
440 Fielder Crk Rd
Medford OR 975048490

Call Sign: WB7FJP
Wendell K Sale
1364 Filbert St
Medford OR 97501

Call Sign: N7IGN
John T Park
3270 Fir Ridge Rd
Medford OR 97504

Call Sign: N4UBU
Terry L Mitchell
3270 Fir Ridge Rd
Medford OR 97504

Call Sign: N7MWN
Lisa A Park
1045 Fir St S Apt 114
Medford OR 97504

Call Sign: W0JDD
Gerald D Allen
1938 Fircrest Dr
Medford OR 97501

Call Sign: KB7PEF
Stephen R Watkins
5295 Firwood Rd
Medford OR 97504

Call Sign: KB7RHZ
John W Berry
5648 Foothill Blvd Sp 12
Medford OR 97501

Call Sign: KF6BFU
Linda S Mc Farlin Lawson
756 Garfield St
Medford OR 97501

Call Sign: N7AEC
Dale L Casey
756 Garfield St
Medford OR 97501

Call Sign: KC7TCS
Richard C Isabell
24465 Gellatly Way
Medford OR 97504

Call Sign: N6KOB
Bruce A Fiero
24465 Gellatly Way
Medford OR 975049408

Call Sign: KE7SZR
Michael L Wells
4300 Goodpasture Lp Apt
116
Medford OR 97504

Call Sign: KG7PX
Richard E Dumont
23246 Gooseneck Rd
Medford OR 975044964

Call Sign: KE7KIM
Sean R Kilpatrick
2465 Gould Ave
Medford OR 97504

Call Sign: N7DXN
Paul L Andrews
248 Gunnell Rd
Medford OR 97504

Call Sign: KF7MM
Ron L Forsyth
4312 Hager St SE
Medford OR 97504

Call Sign: KB7TXE
Scot V Mc Queen
3700 Hagers Grove Rd
Medford OR 97504

Call Sign: KD7ZUS
Bud F Kilbury II
23309 Hall Rd
Medford OR 97501

Call Sign: KD7ZTI
Teresa E Kilbury
24171 Hall Rd
Medford OR 97501

Call Sign: K7LVO
Lewis V Osborn
825 Harrison Ave
Medford OR 97504

Call Sign: W7FSO
James D Mac Kenzie Sr
1875 Harvard Dr
Medford OR 97501

Call Sign: AA6MW
Yvon O Johnson
2508 Hawkins Ln
Medford OR 975049657

Call Sign: KA6JDD
Ronald W David
3874 Hayesville Dr NE
Medford OR 97504

Call Sign: N7TIF
Steven P Mitchell
3874 Hayesville Dr NE
Medford OR 97504

Call Sign: KF7JVU
Richard A Bourne
14884 Heather Glen Dr
Medford OR 97504

Call Sign: KE7VPL
Gregory D Fischer
610 Hidden Valley Rd
Medford OR 97504

Call Sign: KF7ISH
Gregory D Fischer
2068 Hidden Valley Rd
Medford OR 97504

Call Sign: KC7EWM
Keith O Johnson
1377 Highland Ave
Medford OR 97501

Call Sign: N6WN
Daniel B Curtis
1424 Highland Ave
Medford OR 97501

Call Sign: KI6SSQ
Rita Derbas
5941 Highland Ave
Medford OR 94560

Call Sign: KF7UMY
Eugene N Bruce
747 Highland Dr 11
Medford OR 97501

Call Sign: N7OLL
Jonathan M Vote
747 Highland Dr Apt 11
Medford OR 97501

Call Sign: KF6TSR
John P Ivey
630 Highline Rd
Medford OR 97501

Call Sign: KB7SKD
Brian J Kufner
24080 Highpass Rd
Medford OR 97501

Call Sign: KD5BVM
Lorrin M Jacobs
2091 Hilyard
Medford OR 97501

Medford OR 97504

Medford OR 975012325

Call Sign: KC7JPS
Doyle C Powell
8792 Holmquist Rd
Medford OR 97504

Call Sign: N7PFM
Philip J Meunier
2823 Homedale Rd
Medford OR 97501

Call Sign: KC7SKR
Amateur Radio Support
Organization
2288 Hubbard Creek Rd
Medford OR 97504

Call Sign: AF7F
Melvin L Maas Sr
512 Humberd Ln
Medford OR 97501

Call Sign: N6ZZL
Paul J Carasi
2700 Humbug Crk Rd
Medford OR 975011725

Call Sign: W6GNX
Willard D Tiffany
1443 Hunter Ave N
Medford OR 975049795

Call Sign: KB7ZKK
Joseph Sem
63557 Hunters Cir
Medford OR 97504

Call Sign: KA7IYG
Hugh A Dodge
2750 Hwy 101 N Box 50
Medford OR 97504

Call Sign: KB7FPG
Vel Saddington
12309 Hwy 126

Call Sign: KB7GNP
Donald M Pinnock
12309 Hwy 126
Medford OR 97504

Call Sign: N7DKK
David J Healy
40316 Hwy 228
Medford OR 97504

Call Sign: N6SYD
Robert V Viale
33766 Hwy 26
Medford OR 97504

Call Sign: K7OPR
Philip K Henning
16870 Hwy 66 17
Medford OR 97501

Call Sign: WA6TBK
Eugene C Goodson
1979 Icabod St NE
Medford OR 97504

Call Sign: K7ISH
Donald W Denson
295 Idaho St
Medford OR 975048624

Call Sign: KD7OUA
Joshua J York
1046 Judson St SE
Medford OR 97501

Call Sign: KB7KBG
Robert E Wille
1130 Juniper St
Medford OR 97504

Call Sign: KD7DAR
Wayne A Meeds
1525 Juniper St

Call Sign: KB5EUO
Michael D Nuss
41134 Kampy Ln
Medford OR 97504

Call Sign: KB5EUP
Kelly M Nuss
5559 Kane Creek Rd
Medford OR 97504

Call Sign: KD7AOT
Robin R Porter
1700 Kellenbeck Ave Apt
306
Medford OR 975012116

Call Sign: KL7IN
Donald E Ritter Sr
196 Kilborn Dr
Medford OR 97501

Call Sign: KF7LAC
Richard A Stitt
9570 Kilchis Rv Rd
Medford OR 97501

Call Sign: KC7AWB
Anthony M La Ford
7550 Killam Creek Rd
Medford OR 97501

Call Sign: KA7OFM
Judith E Shrader
906 Killingsworth Ave
Medford OR 97501

Call Sign: W7QMU
William R Shrader
906 Killingsworth Ave
Medford OR 97501

Call Sign: KG6ATQ
Arthur L Borland

1286 Kimberly Ct NE
Medford OR 97501

Call Sign: K7SGQ
Harry T Litts
5600 Kimmels Riverside Ln
Medford OR 97501

Call Sign: KD7NG
Gene W Merrigan
7 Kincaid Rd
Medford OR 97504

Call Sign: KC7HPP
David M Chesmore
2041 King Ln
Medford OR 97501

Call Sign: KG7BP
Donald C Bennett
2041 King Ln
Medford OR 975013232

Call Sign: KB7FMF
Norbert M Omann
1216 King Mountain Trl
Medford OR 97501

Call Sign: KN6WW
Charles W Mahler
3855 Kirsten St
Medford OR 975048614

Call Sign: N6PQX
Stanley W Rugh
300 La Creole Dr 276
Medford OR 97504

Call Sign: W7SDX
William W Brawn
12641 Larchwood Dr
Medford OR 97501

Call Sign: KF6WIS
Susan L Bohn

60731 Liberty Rd
Medford OR 97501

Call Sign: KA7VBL
Thomas T Beers
9823 Liberty Rd S
Medford OR 97504

Call Sign: WB6ZOC
Eugene P Brummett
4074 Liberty Rd S 90
Medford OR 97504

Call Sign: K7AOK
William C Messer
1380 Loredo Dr
Medford OR 97501

Call Sign: KB7MML
Shawn C Weatherford
300 Luman Rd Unit 170
Medford OR 97504

Call Sign: KE7PMO
Patrick K Sullivan
1805 Madison St
Medford OR 97504

Call Sign: KD7HMQ
Donald E Blancke
92074 Maki Rd
Medford OR 97501

Call Sign: KD7YVL
Ryon M Kershner
1890 Manihi Dr
Medford OR 97504

Call Sign: KB7VFS
Willard H Patterson Jr
40011 McDowell Creek Dr
Medford OR 97504

Call Sign: KC7TCP
Stacie L Austin

6626 McLeod Ln
Medford OR 97501

Call Sign: N7NKW
Richard D Pflugrad
6745 McLeod Ln NE
Medford OR 975019532

Call Sign: KE7NOB
Nicholas E Jones
33408 Medlik Dr
Medford OR 97501

Call Sign: KF7ICM
Ellis Feinstein
36233 Meyer St
Medford OR 97504

Call Sign: K7MFR
Ellis Feinstein
19385 Meyers Rd
Medford OR 97504

Call Sign: KF7DMU
Richard D Cano
33890 Miller Ln
Medford OR 97501

Call Sign: KW7SMA
Richard D Cano
66946 Miller Ln
Medford OR 97501

Call Sign: AC7EZ
Karl D Sargent
66946 Miller Ln
Medford OR 975018137

Call Sign: K7KDS
Karl D Sargent
66946 Miller Ln
Medford OR 975018137

Call Sign: NE7RD
Stephen R Watkins

1235 More St 30
Medford OR 97504

Call Sign: WA7JBW
John B Wasson
1441 Morrow Rd 114
Medford OR 97504

Call Sign: KF7EF
George E Cox
6801 Moses Pass
Medford OR 97501

Call Sign: KF6LDP
Wayne M Harris
6801 Moses Pass
Medford OR 97504

Call Sign: KE7CIM
Deltha J Harris
1325 Mosier Rd
Medford OR 97504

Call Sign: KZ6P
Don L Carmean
1863 Moss St
Medford OR 97504

Call Sign: N0DMC
William D Cook Jr
193 Mossflower Ln
Medford OR 97504

Call Sign: K7MUK
Jerry S Lausmann
3000 Mossy Ln
Medford OR 97504

Call Sign: KF7UMX
Robert D Hart
4130 Munsel Creek Dr
Medford OR 97501

Call Sign: KD7EHB
Scott M Cummings

4130 Munsel Creek Dr
Medford OR 975011264

Call Sign: KK6OS
Kerry V Provancha
15151 Mustang Rd
Medford OR 97504

Call Sign: K7WGF
William G Fullenwider IV
94465 Myrtle Acres
Medford OR 97501

Call Sign: KC7WWJ
Leona J Wobbe
51082 Myrtle Creek Rd
Medford OR 97504

Call Sign: KC7CFA
Ernest G Gaulden
507 N 19th Ave Sp 82
Medford OR 97504

Call Sign: WD6ANB
Robert J Donaghy
507 N 19th St
Medford OR 97504

Call Sign: WA7MW
Maurice H Whitlock
425 N 1st 42
Medford OR 97504

Call Sign: K6GPF
Blair W Beckett Sr
1287 N 1st Ave
Medford OR 97504

Call Sign: WD6ESU
Robert N Tangel
357 N 1st Ave 23
Medford OR 975048576

Call Sign: KD7AUE
Arthur V Sochor

900 N 2 St 3
Medford OR 975048555

Call Sign: KI7XW
Ray E Hill
97666 N Bank Chetco River
Rd Pmb 128
Medford OR 97504

Call Sign: WB7ABU
Lawrence H Mitchelmore
6743 N Bank Rd
Medford OR 97504

Call Sign: N7AEG
Albert J Good
6743 N Bank Rd
Medford OR 97504

Call Sign: WA3USA
Masataka Shimamoto
7035 N Catlin Ave
Medford OR 97504

Call Sign: K7MTP
Bruce D Braaten
2905 N College St
Medford OR 975047500

Call Sign: KD7RQ
Ryan T Le Page
3355 N Delta Hwy Sp 140
Medford OR 97501

Call Sign: N7AED
Curtis M Kline
13225 N Lombard
Medford OR 97504

Call Sign: K7TKC
Curtis M Kline
8316 N Lombard 364
Medford OR 97504

Call Sign: KF7UMP

Caryn I Steward
7248 N Macrum
Medford OR 97504

Call Sign: N7NS
Peter A Bateman
26 N Wahanna Rd N 4
Medford OR 97501

Call Sign: W6JBC
Robert F Jenks
1920 N Winchell
Medford OR 97504

Call Sign: N7WIT
Ann M Kingman
1920 N Winchell
Medford OR 97504

Call Sign: KB7PPE
Noreen L Arrell
3941 NE 10th Ave
Medford OR 97501

Call Sign: KB7NNR
Jack D Arrell
308 NE 10th Ct
Medford OR 97501

Call Sign: KD7FZS
Kenneth J Maloney
1916 NE 113th Ave
Medford OR 97501

Call Sign: N7EET
Michael E Kenney
4044 NE 129th Pl
Medford OR 97501

Call Sign: N7VTK
Shirley A Trautman
2007 NE 12th Ave
Medford OR 97501

Call Sign: WX7MFR

Jefferson Amateur Weather
Service
3321 NE 12th Ave
Medford OR 97501

Call Sign: KC7PJX
Jefferson Amateur Weather
System
3331 NE 12th Ave
Medford OR 97501

Call Sign: N7IXS
Dale D Trautman
4822 NE 12th Ave
Medford OR 97501

Call Sign: WA7SZU
Thomas R May
4911 NE 12th Ave
Medford OR 97504

Call Sign: KB7RNQ
Kami L Gettling
1155 NE 190th Pl
Medford OR 97501

Call Sign: N7VTL
William W Gettling
211 NE 202nd Ave
Medford OR 97501

Call Sign: N7YID
Scott W Gettling
4336 NE 20th Ave
Medford OR 97501

Call Sign: KA6BFO
Ferdinand H Laun
1823 NE 226
Medford OR 97504

Call Sign: WK7Z
Ferdinand H Laun
810 NE 22nd
Medford OR 97504

Call Sign: KA7ONA
Joseph R Neville
5138 NW 167th Pl
Medford OR 97501

Call Sign: W7VSE
Victor B Seeberger
5722 NW 179th Ave
Medford OR 975011831

Call Sign: KE7IKG
Kyler C Taft
2603 Old Military Rd
Medford OR 97501

Call Sign: KE7IKH
William C Taft
2603 Old Military Rd
Medford OR 97501

Call Sign: N7XBJ
Michael R Fowler
2603 Old Military Rd
Medford OR 97501

Call Sign: KB7RIA
Sylvia M Long
3961 Pam St
Medford OR 97501

Call Sign: N7ZZH
Maham Long Jr
407 Panda Loop
Medford OR 97501

Call Sign: KD7QZE
David W Wilson
2478 Panorama Dr
Medford OR 97501

Call Sign: N6OAB
Robert L Smith
175 Pardee Ln Apt 1A
Medford OR 97504

Medford OR 97504

Call Sign: KA7CUW
James A Albright
798 Park Ave
Medford OR 97501

Call Sign: WB7TBZ
Teri L Wingard
607 Park St Apt 15
Medford OR 97501

Call Sign: WA6PWR
Don G Nelson
7500 Peavy Arboretum
Medford OR 97501

Call Sign: KD7JQM
Robert G Biegert
19349 Pinehurst Rd
Medford OR 97501

Call Sign: KF7ICN
John R Page
38776 Place Rd
Medford OR 97501

Call Sign: N7MWR
Lawrence W Chastain
128 Pleasant Creek Rd
Medford OR 97501

Call Sign: WB2FYW
Harry J Ekelund
93041 Powerline Rd
Medford OR 97504

Call Sign: N9VCF
James P Mc Conville
860 Prefontaine Way
Medford OR 97501

Call Sign: KS4SM
Brian H Nicholson
715 Prescott Ln
Medford OR 97501

Call Sign: AF6Y
David R Basden
945 Prescott Ln
Medford OR 975019317

Call Sign: W7OQ
David R Basden
951 Prescott Ln
Medford OR 975019317

Call Sign: AE7NY
Harry J Ekelund
2479 Queen Ave SE Apt 34
Medford OR 97504

Call Sign: WA7IRB
Milon A Wall
2479 Queen Ave SE Apt 34
Medford OR 97504

Call Sign: WB4GIA
Floyd W Sherwood
2479 Queen Ave SE Apt 34
Medford OR 97504

Call Sign: KA7CNZ
William L Carter
2030 Queen Ave SE Apt B
202
Medford OR 975044661

Call Sign: W7NCO
George H Durand
16635 Queen Mary
Medford OR 97504

Call Sign: KE7OGB
Kristopher J Mortensen
1665 Queen Mary Ave
Medford OR 97504

Call Sign: K7PTI
Alvin G Edwards
2517 Queen St

Call Sign: KD7PHV
Dennis C Poncia
980 Ratcliff Dr SE
Medford OR 97504

Call Sign: WB7OGP
Jeff S Statchwick
82984 Rattlesnake Rd
Medford OR 97504

Call Sign: W7KNX
Jeff S Statchwick
26377 Ravens Rise Ln
Medford OR 97504

Call Sign: K7RVM
Rogue Valley Manor ARC
28573 Redwood Hwy
Medford OR 97504

Call Sign: KU6Y
Albert W Anderson Jr
28573 Redwood Hwy
Medford OR 975044523

Call Sign: KB7LCJ
Jeffrey R Dovci
242 Ridgecrest Dr N
Medford OR 97504

Call Sign: W7OVO
Kenneth D Knackstedt
12705 River Rd Apt 402A
Medford OR 97501

Call Sign: K7PTK
Carroll E Brown
1523 River Rock Dr
Medford OR 97504

Call Sign: W7DTA
Rogue Valley ARC
4165 Riverview Dr

Medford OR 97504 | Medford OR 975047745 | Medford OR 97501

Call Sign: W7LNG
Robert L Larson
1372 Riverwood Ct N
Medford OR 975046515

Call Sign: W7OLZ
Samuel S Evans
15049 S Macksburg Rd
Medford OR 97501

Call Sign: KC6WIZ
Robert L Starcher
18980 S Springwater Rd
Medford OR 97501

Call Sign: W7OEK
Rogue Valley ARC
11713 Riverwood Dr SE
Medford OR 97504

Call Sign: WD0ECB
Harold P Graber
4601 21 S Pacific Hwy
Medford OR 97501

Call Sign: KB7TXG
John C Ramsey
800 S State St
Medford OR 97501

Call Sign: KB7LHU
Betty J Bullock
11713 Riverwood Dr SE
Medford OR 97504

Call Sign: KC7KER
David H Pollock
3431 S Pacific Hwy 112
Medford OR 97501

Call Sign: KC7TBS
Ben F Greaser
800 S State St Lot 25
Medford OR 975018829

Call Sign: KB7NOA
Wallace D Raker
4055 Royal Ave 95
Medford OR 97504

Call Sign: KB7FMC
Justin M Bates
4069 S Pacific Hwy 141
Medford OR 97501

Call Sign: WB6YPS
Nolen J Miller
19613 S Suncrest
Medford OR 97501

Call Sign: KD6EL
James S Heaton
325 S 5th St 7
Medford OR 975044512

Call Sign: KA7EFN
Glenn A Mc Kinney
3431 S Pacific Hwy 39
Medford OR 97501

Call Sign: K7PDV
Richard H Young
16045 S Swansea Ln
Medford OR 97501

Call Sign: KC7JXL
Sharon D Ely
18087 S Boone Ct
Medford OR 97504

Call Sign: KB7HE
Dale N Hodges
3966 S Pacific Hwy 47
Medford OR 97501

Call Sign: KB7QVW
Joyce M Jones
20744 S Sweetbriar Rd
Medford OR 97501

Call Sign: KF7FPN
Robert C Santee
15092 S Bradley Rd
Medford OR 97504

Call Sign: KF7ICI
Kenneth W Baker
3966 S Pacific Hwy 47
Medford OR 97501

Call Sign: WA6RHK
Johnny M Jones
21116 S Sweetbriar Rd
Medford OR 97501

Call Sign: KD7OUB
Wayne L Mcanally
15132 S Forsythe Rd
Medford OR 97501

Call Sign: KE7PMQ
Albert L Dickerson
16380 S Springwater Rd
Medford OR 97501

Call Sign: KD7PMU
William G Fullenwider IV
18610 S Upper Highland Rd
Medford OR 97501

Call Sign: W7MMI
Herbert J Grey
15897 S Lammer Rd

Call Sign: N6JTY
Kip S Grant
16461 S Springwater Rd

Call Sign: WA6PJG
William G Fullenwider IV
22282 S Upper Highland Rd

Medford OR 97501

Medford OR 97504

Medford OR 97504

Call Sign: N7ITS
Cecile M Morse
22284 S Upperhighland Rd
Medford OR 97501

Call Sign: KA6HDE
David C Wyatt
421 Sherwood Loop
Medford OR 97504

Call Sign: KD6VEV
Robin E Williamson
37873 Soap Creek Rd
Medford OR 97504

Call Sign: WB7SZM
John W Morse
22284 S Upperhighland Rd
Medford OR 97501

Call Sign: KE7HFD
David C Wyatt
428 Sherwood Loop
Medford OR 97504

Call Sign: KE7UST
Patrick C Claflin
4527 Souza Ct
Medford OR 97501

Call Sign: KJ7FI
Cyril E Jones
939 S Valley View Rd 32
Medford OR 97501

Call Sign: KC7WQ
James E Wanamaker
436 Sherwood Loop
Medford OR 97504

Call Sign: KF7UYZ
Songpon Saisamuth
30686 Sparta Ln
Medford OR 97501

Call Sign: AB0TN
John F TavARES
3102 Salishan Ct
Medford OR 97501

Call Sign: KG6MZU
Walter E Deutsch
436 Sherwood Loop
Medford OR 97504

Call Sign: N5EG
Thomas C Mc Dermott
4346 Spring St
Medford OR 97504

Call Sign: AD4RR
D Ray East
8100 Sawtell Rd
Medford OR 97501

Call Sign: W6GGM
Walter R Keller
233 Shirley St
Medford OR 97504

Call Sign: KB6GXJ
Delores Pinto
5996 St Helena St
Medford OR 97504

Call Sign: KD7DAT
Keith A Biddulph
4775 Scenic Dr
Medford OR 97504

Call Sign: N7OLM
Darrel V Mansveld
62273 Ski Run Rd
Medford OR 97501

Call Sign: KB7VFN
Jack L De Bus
63428 Stacy Ln
Medford OR 97504

Call Sign: KD7LP
William S Ault
180 Schofield Dr
Medford OR 97504

Call Sign: KF6STM
James A Macmillan
1 Skyline Dr Apt 3312
Medford OR 97504

Call Sign: KB7YTZ
Eve A De Bus
297 Stadiium Dr W 2
Medford OR 97504

Call Sign: N7JKQ
Everett C Mc Shane
90406 Shadows Dr
Medford OR 97504

Call Sign: KD7NTZ
Scott D Rowan
17 Smith Dr
Medford OR 975048118

Call Sign: KB7VQY
Jimmy H Andrews Jr
75254 Stage Gulch Rd
Medford OR 97504

Call Sign: KA5BXG
Robert T Wohosky
6203 Shaw Ln SE

Call Sign: KE7CIL
Priscilla A Peak
37873 Soap Creek Rd

Call Sign: K7JQS
Barbara R Svensen
3139 Stage Rd S

Medford OR 97504

Call Sign: K7JQO
Norman Svensen
3955 Stage Rd So 8
Medford OR 97504

Call Sign: WB7NXJ
Merlin D Farnsworth
215 Stanley
Medford OR 97501

Call Sign: WA6PCH
Jack F Buckley
317 Stanley Ave
Medford OR 97504

Call Sign: KC7ANN
Derek G Melbourne
2630 Stanton
Medford OR 97504

Call Sign: W7ISP
Delmer L Wright
2630 Stanton
Medford OR 97504

Call Sign: KF7UKG
Stephan L Barott
1064 State Ave
Medford OR 97504

Call Sign: KA7JOC
Mary M Lekey
4154 State St 4 SE
Medford OR 97501

Call Sign: WA7YTA
Thomas F Coleman
900 State St B174
Medford OR 97501

Call Sign: WB7RQG
Robert L Butler
53196 Stateline Rd

Medford OR 97504

Call Sign: KD7FNC
Lewis R Constable
28749 Strebin
Medford OR 97501

Call Sign: KO7S
C Gordon Morris
28749 Strebin
Medford OR 975046753

Call Sign: N7IMS
Don R Koegler
2012 Stringer Gap Rd
Medford OR 97501

Call Sign: WB6FUI
Philip V Pastere
4225 Sturdivant Ave
Medford OR 97504

Call Sign: KD7EXZ
Charles J Thomas
4412 Sturdivant St
Medford OR 975042145

Call Sign: KC7MND
Kenneth C Shaw
19488 Sugar Mill Loop
Medford OR 97504

Call Sign: KQ7Q
James R Howe
1115 Sunnyside Dr
Medford OR 97504

Call Sign: WA7NWA
Thomas E Coesens
4785 Sunnyside Rd SE
Medford OR 975012648

Call Sign: KC7BTS
Joel H Ehrlich
46836 Sunset Ave

Medford OR 97504

Call Sign: K7VS
Arnold D Sias
92127 Svensen Mkt Rd
Medford OR 97504

Call Sign: KC7TCL
Richard L Veghte
14783 SW 109th 9
Medford OR 97501

Call Sign: KA7LWK
Clayton M Dempton
1802 SW 10th 201
Medford OR 97501

Call Sign: KA7QFY
John W Newman
575 Sweetgum Ln
Medford OR 97501

Call Sign: N7YII
Leo C Cook
2252 Table Rock Rd 203
Medford OR 97501

Call Sign: N7CCX
Arthur E Friesen
2252 Table Rock Rd 215
Medford OR 97501

Call Sign: K7RTY
Arthur E Friesen
2252 Table Rock Rd 215
Medford OR 97501

Call Sign: K6ZVB
Richard E Jones
5792 Tablerock Rd
Medford OR 97501

Call Sign: KD7PHS
Barbara J Jones
2669 Tahitian Ave

Medford OR 97501

Call Sign: KC7NVV
David M Beskow
12330 Takilma Rd
Medford OR 97504

Call Sign: KD7AXI
Nathan J Beskow
727 Talbot Rd SE Sp 7
Medford OR 97504

Call Sign: WH6MC
Ted R Krempa
370 Tamarack
Medford OR 97504

Call Sign: K7TRK
Ted Krempa
1316 Tamarack Ct SW
Medford OR 97504

Call Sign: K7DD
Wendell R Bastow
33947 Tarbell Rd
Medford OR 97504

Call Sign: KE7KZW
Jackson Baures
60987 Targee Dr
Medford OR 97504

Call Sign: KD7WWP
Devin M Eskridge
460 Taz Ln
Medford OR 97504

Call Sign: KB7OAH
Kenneth M Toohey
1595 Ten Oaks Ln
Medford OR 97504

Call Sign: WA7MRG
Christopher W Defty
2128 Terrel Dr

Medford OR 975047557

Call Sign: AC7ZM
John F TavARES
24472 Territorial Hwy
Medford OR 975018139

Call Sign: KC7LZZ
Douglas R Turman
475 Thomas Rd
Medford OR 97501

Call Sign: WA6ULA
Lowell G Tobin
140 Tiffany Way
Medford OR 97504

Call Sign: KG7UG
George A Sendelbach
93701 Upper Loop Ln
Medford OR 97504

Call Sign: WA6KBB
Richard W Pence
26355 Valley View Dr
Medford OR 97504

Call Sign: KF6DZJ
Patrick D Mc Donald
1330 Vanderbeck Ln
Medford OR 97504

Call Sign: WS7Q
James W Stewart
1021 Vawter Rd
Medford OR 97501

Call Sign: WB7DVH
William A Chicano Jr
308 Ventura Ave
Medford OR 97501

Call Sign: KF6CAZ
Wilfred D Thorne
30066 Vicki Ln

Medford OR 97501

Call Sign: KF7ZV
Geoffrey C Nankervis
93057A Vida Prince Ln
Medford OR 975013850

Call Sign: N7OMH
Evelyn J Nankervis
3410 Videra Dr
Medford OR 97501

Call Sign: KB7RHX
Paul G Schurman
1420 Village Center Dr
Medford OR 975044501

Call Sign: KB6QR
John M Prosser
1429 Village Center Dr
Medford OR 97504

Call Sign: K7GF
Robert L Brouwer
1429 Village Center Dr
Medford OR 97504

Call Sign: KE6JCS
Ann P Barger
109 Village Dr
Medford OR 97504

Call Sign: KE6JCT
H Ford Barger Jr
119 Village Dr
Medford OR 97504

Call Sign: KE7EAE
Richard A Backes
1175 W 11th
Medford OR 97501

Call Sign: KD7RYK
Dean R Skaw
1875 W 12th Apt A

Medford OR 97501

Call Sign: WB6KBB
Arlen F Hatlestad
5142 W Griffin Ck Rd
Medford OR 97501

Call Sign: KF7UMM
Richard J Dumanowski
2602 W Mc Andrews Rd
Medford OR 975012242

Call Sign: KF7HU
Gerald R Robertson
28 Washington St
Medford OR 97501

Call Sign: WA7RZB
Robert F Sterritt
3051 Waterford
Medford OR 97504

Call Sign: K7FH
Vernon L Ward
3051 Waterford Ct
Medford OR 97504

Call Sign: WA7LLG
Lavila J Ward
3051 Waterford Ct
Medford OR 97504

Call Sign: W6IUI
Winston R Mc Call
3073 Westminster Dr
Medford OR 97504

Call Sign: KD7VZU
Andreas A Blaurock
1722 Westwood Dr
Medford OR 97501

Call Sign: WB7QPZ
Barbara M Borgman
1802 Whitman Ave

Medford OR 97501

Call Sign: KC7CJK
Rona Gillette
1902 Wildflower Cir
Medford OR 97504

Call Sign: K7EAW
Mary Van De Kamp
125 Willamette Ave
Medford OR 97504

Call Sign: KI6OZN
Laurie M Hopkins
516 Willamette Ave
Medford OR 97504

Call Sign: AA6IC
Geral Dean De Vore
62 Winema Way
Medford OR 97501

Call Sign: N7DAB
David A Baleria
Medford OR 97501

Call Sign: N7WCN
Emery E Mc Capes
Medford OR 97501

Call Sign: N7XCW
Lester N Garwood
Medford OR 97501

Call Sign: WD6CYG
Andy J Roy
Medford OR 97501

Call Sign: KB7COV
Neal A Kovalyak
Medford OR 97501

Call Sign: N7VGM
Richard E Cusic
Medford OR 97501

Call Sign: WB7BJP
John W Keener
Medford OR 97501

Call Sign: KC7QZZ
Wayne A Frostad
Medford OR 97504

Call Sign: KE7VPR
Benjamin C Sober
Medford OR 97504

Call Sign: KF7ARG
Steven W Evans
Medford OR 97504

Call Sign: KE6IQY
Colin D Fagan
Medford OR 975010011

Call Sign: W7TMF
Elmore D Spencer
Medford OR 975010074

FCC Amateur Radio Licenses in Merlin

Call Sign: N7GMP
Larry J Murphy
3108 B St
Merlin OR 975320207

Call Sign: KG6LIE
Michael R Van Polanen
Petel
17029 Ferry Creek
Merlin OR 97532

Call Sign: K7MO
William G Jago
3650 Inland Ct Unit 3
Merlin OR 97532

Call Sign: N7CNG

Shirlee M Jago
3650 Inland Ct Unit 3
Merlin OR 97532

Call Sign: KF6MH
Alvin E Maynard
3272 Inland Dr S
Merlin OR 97532

Call Sign: KC7IB
Jack S Stafford
3596 Kiarn Ave S
Merlin OR 97532

Call Sign: KD6LKW
Anthony W Freitas
190 Kirk Ave
Merlin OR 97532

Call Sign: K7AWF
Anthony W Freitas
836 Kirk Ave
Merlin OR 97532

Call Sign: K7VX
Robert W Lahde
7190 N Hwy 97
Merlin OR 97532

Call Sign: KB7GEX
Paul P Peck
5410 NW 196th Pl
Merlin OR 97532

Call Sign: KA7USW
Vance R Todd
180 Pruden Dr
Merlin OR 97532

Call Sign: N7KAX
Helen F Bell
41144 Pumpkinseed Rd
Merlin OR 97532

Call Sign: N7KDM

Harold W Bell
4650 Punchbowl Rd
Merlin OR 97532

Call Sign: KL7CDG
Jimmie J Tvrdy
73224 Purchase Ln
Merlin OR 97532

Call Sign: KC7JJG
George E Malmstrom
400 Robinhood Ave
Merlin OR 97532

Call Sign: KC7MGH
Anita L Malmstrom
2120 Robins Ln SE 66A
Merlin OR 97532

Call Sign: N7IJL
Ralph R Orton
410 S Cammann St
Merlin OR 97532

Call Sign: K6PY
Paul A Cooper
2120 Thorne St
Merlin OR 97532

Call Sign: KB7PNV
Richard L Mc Millen
1261 Wildflower Dr
Merlin OR 97532

Call Sign: K6ZX
Douglas K Beck
Merlin OR 97532

Call Sign: KB7ZFA
Bernadette M Beck
Merlin OR 97532

Call Sign: W7MQY
Merlin Hill Uhf Society
Merlin OR 97532

Call Sign: KF6ETP
Bryan E Hawkins
Merlin OR 90713

Call Sign: KD7WVD
Merlin ARS
Merlin OR 97532

Call Sign: AA6CC
Gary R Harwell
Merlin OR 97532

Call Sign: KA7YZI
Phyllis Fox Krupp
Merlin OR 97532

Call Sign: KB6DJ
Jim T Smith
Merlin OR 97532

Call Sign: KB7FCI
Gary V Ingram Sr
Merlin OR 97532

Call Sign: KC7MSL
Tina Zima
Merlin OR 97532

Call Sign: KD7DAU
Albert K Noda
Merlin OR 97532

Call Sign: KF6ETQ
Laura C Hawkins
Merlin OR 97532

Call Sign: KI7SD
Gary K Stookey
Merlin OR 97532

Call Sign: N7EZY
Carl E Krupp
Merlin OR 97532

Call Sign: N7UGC
Robert H Huerta
Merlin OR 97532

Call Sign: WA7TZG
Douglas G Crick
Merlin OR 97532

Call Sign: WM7K
Paul C Johnston
Merlin OR 97532

Call Sign: N7EB
John E Lawler
Merlin OR 97532

Call Sign: KE7TFY
Bob J Bach
Merlin OR 97532

Call Sign: KD7WIB
Jon A Crissup
Merlin OR 97532

Call Sign: N2SFQ
Linda M Miller
Merlin OR 97532

Call Sign: KD7KKJ
Cindy L Thomas
Merlin OR 97532

Call Sign: KE7EAG
Robert C Locher III
Merlin OR 975320680

Call Sign: W7GH
Robert C Locher III
Merlin OR 975320680

Call Sign: KD7HJE
Richard F Marino
Merlin OR 975320974

FCC Amateur Radio Licenses in Merrill

Call Sign: K7TDY
Lynn R Pope
24200 Queen Anne
Merrill OR 97633

Call Sign: W6RTC
Thomas J Coit Jr
1513 Taylor St
Merrill OR 97633

Call Sign: W7WLV
Kermit J Farnsworth
Merrill OR 97633

Call Sign: WB7RMH
George A Carleton
Merrill OR 97633

Call Sign: KA7YBS
Frank Spaits
Merrill OR 97633

Call Sign: WB7DEX
Richmond J Carleton
Merrill OR 97633

Call Sign: WA7SZO
Kenneth A Barnett
Merrill OR 976330177

FCC Amateur Radio Licenses in Metolius

Call Sign: KE7HJY
Terri L Jones
3600 Ave G Sp 24
Metolius OR 97741

Call Sign: KD7QHP
Kermit R Kumle
295 Idaho St
Metolius OR 97741

Call Sign: KE7LRS
Kermit R Kumle
295 Idaho St
Metolius OR 97741

Call Sign: KE7HJZ
Justin P Jones
3791 Ave G
Metoluis OR 97741

FCC Amateur Radio Licenses in Midland

Call Sign: WB7DQG
Jim R Underwood Sr
910 Osprey Dr
Midland OR 976340415

Call Sign: WB7TOZ
Patrick M Walsh
Midland OR 97634

Call Sign: KE7TPW
Gregory L Widner
Midland OR 97634

FCC Amateur Radio Licenses in Milton Freewater

Call Sign: N7IGS
Joseph A Kizlauskas
53880 Beach Loop Rd
Milton Freewater OR 97862

Call Sign: KB7FMR
Norma H Chea
6719 Beckton Ave
Milton Freewater OR 97862

Call Sign: KB7ZP
James A Ralph
710 Broccoli St
Milton Freewater OR 97862

Call Sign: AC7NE
James A Ralph
710 Broccoli St
Milton Freewater OR 97862

Call Sign: KD7NPB
James G Ralph
77583 Brock Rd
Milton Freewater OR 97862

Call Sign: KD7FQR
Heath R Wells
1050 Butler Mkt Rd NE 6
Milton Freewater OR 97862

Call Sign: KA7YLB
Leonard L Taylor
5650 Buttonwood Ct SE
Milton Freewater OR 97862

Call Sign: KA7YMR
Harold L Birdwell
2925 Buxton Ct
Milton Freewater OR 97862

Call Sign: KA7EAI
Edwin C Werhan
16765 Bw Paddington Dr
Milton Freewater OR 97862

Call Sign: WB7RCL
Douglas L Humphrey
61135 Cabin Ln
Milton Freewater OR 97862

Call Sign: KA7JQR
Richard B Jenkins
1945 Cal Young Rd
Milton Freewater OR 97862

Call Sign: K7EL
Eugene F Frank
1796 Cal Young Rd Apt 17
Milton Freewater OR 97862

Call Sign: N7TSD
Darrell A Wilson
1197 Calvin St
Milton Freewater OR 97862

Call Sign: W7OUC
James A Reese
299 Cambridge Dr
Milton Freewater OR 97862

Call Sign: KA7JLW
Jerry W Schroeder
2575 Campus Dr 275
Milton Freewater OR 97862

Call Sign: N7IFS
Harold G Steen
17104 Canal Cir
Milton Freewater OR 97862

Call Sign: KB7KVG
Laura R Hall
6560 Canary Rd
Milton Freewater OR 97862

Call Sign: K7BAC
Steele A Bacus
16465 Devonshire Dr
Milton Freewater OR 97862

Call Sign: K7PCT
Donald A Mohr
2509 E L Ave
Milton Freewater OR
978627953

Call Sign: KF6BNW
David C Van Gundy I
9000 Eighth St
Milton Freewater OR 97862

Call Sign: KA7YHE
Rolland W Potter
4910 Fern Valley Rd

Milton Freewater OR 97862

Call Sign: KE7MSP
Aimee C Linde
67580 Hwy 20
Milton Freewater OR 97862

Call Sign: KD7SQE
Jessica C Hansen
84599 Hwy 339
Milton Freewater OR 97862

Call Sign: KI7FY
Robert L Moon
37894 Kelly Rd
Milton Freewater OR 97862

Call Sign: N7DWE
Raymond E Ralph
51405 Mac Ct
Milton Freewater OR 97862

Call Sign: KF7RDR
Randall R Pierce
2635 Montana St
Milton Freewater OR 97862

Call Sign: KB7MHA
Ty A Walker
3995 Munker St SE
Milton Freewater OR 97862

Call Sign: KE7NUM
Brennan E Springer
6133 NE 36 Ave
Milton Freewater OR 97862

Call Sign: KE7NUL
Jeremy A Springer
1021 NE 365th
Milton Freewater OR 97862

Call Sign: KD7RFR
Keith D Jenkins
3636 NE 42nd Ave

Milton Freewater OR 97862

Call Sign: W7KDJ
Keith D Jenkins
548 NE 43rd Ave
Milton Freewater OR 97862

Call Sign: KD7TSM
Tamara L Jenkins
2215 NE 43rd Ave
Milton Freewater OR 97862

Call Sign: W7TLJ
Tamara L Jenkins
3546 NE 43rd Ave
Milton Freewater OR 97862

Call Sign: KA7JFK
Barbara G Jensen
3144 NE Cesar E Chavez
Blvd
Milton Freewater OR 97862

Call Sign: N7KVL
Peter H Jensen
2455 NE Chalmers Way
Milton Freewater OR 97862

Call Sign: KB7ESS
Frank M Turner
26400 NW Bacon Rd
Milton Freewater OR 97862

Call Sign: KC7JK
Bill J Woolard
3285 NW Bauer Woods Dr
Milton Freewater OR 97862

Call Sign: KD7OCV
David W Saager
2010 NW Bayshore Dr
Milton Freewater OR 97862

Call Sign: WB7FAB
Oscar L Gilliam

4551 NW Bramblewood Ln
Milton Freewater OR 97862

Call Sign: N7UNG
Paul M Webb
3364 NW Brandt Pl
Milton Freewater OR 97862

Call Sign: KC7IEA
Raymond L Sowell
340 NW Brentwood Apt
202
Milton Freewater OR 97862

Call Sign: KB7QYT
Donald J Rudy
259 NW Brier Pl
Milton Freewater OR 97862

Call Sign: K7WTA
Jesse E Blanchard
63339 NW Britta St 4
Milton Freewater OR 97862

Call Sign: K7NUL
Larry L Odoms
47525 Perkins St
Milton Freewater OR 97862

Call Sign: W7FMJ
Newton W Brumbach
16886 Ponderosa Cascade
Dr
Milton Freewater OR 97862

Call Sign: KA4RHU
Robert P Kaye
19821 Ponderosa St
Milton Freewater OR 97862

Call Sign: KC7USG
Davena M Burton
1936 Rainier Rd
Milton Freewater OR 97862

Call Sign: KA7DKP
Connie A Dirks
11871 S Riggs Damm Rd
Milton Freewater OR 97862

Call Sign: W7IDB
David D Dirks
3490 S River Rd
Milton Freewater OR 97862

Call Sign: KB7CDM
Richard L Worden
791 S Shasta
Milton Freewater OR 97862

Call Sign: KE7BAZ
Clinton L Mc Munn
368 SE 16th Ave
Milton Freewater OR 97862

Call Sign: KB7BGL
Dennis J Jones
61445 SE 27th Sp 43
Milton Freewater OR 97862

Call Sign: KC7WFH
Norman A Wallace
23035 Shepard Rd
Milton Freewater OR 97862

Call Sign: KB7IED
Larry A Hall
3205 Steven St
Milton Freewater OR 97862

Call Sign: N7JPX
Gordon D Hall
5664 Stockton Ave S
Milton Freewater OR 97862

Call Sign: KF7AJL
Robert H Tinker
2440 Stoltz Hill Rd
Milton Freewater OR 97862

Call Sign: KA7ZDB
Tyler S Schroeder
1312 Stonehaven Dr
Milton Freewater OR 97862

Call Sign: KD7ZQR
Larry J Skyler
5705 SW 206th Ave
Milton Freewater OR 97862

Call Sign: KE7ALX
Iris A Crossman
2435 SW 206th Pl
Milton Freewater OR 97862

Call Sign: KE7IKV
Kathie A Yeager
8923 Umatilla St NE
Milton Freewater OR 97862

Call Sign: KE7BJK
Don M Marlatt
16615 Umbenhower Ln
Milton Freewater OR 97862

Call Sign: KB7ESR
Mark F Turner
121 W Broadway
Milton Freewater OR 97862

Call Sign: KB7EST
Erica T Turner
121 W Broadway
Milton Freewater OR 97862

Call Sign: KB7HFJ
George K Walker
312 W Broadway
Milton Freewater OR 97862

Call Sign: WA7JCS
Stanley D Christensen
55207 Walla Walla River
Rd
Milton Freewater OR 97862

Call Sign: KB7JIO
Stewart A Hammill
53873 Willow Ln
Milton Freewater OR 97862

Call Sign: N7CSE
Lowell J Swift
403 Willow St
Milton Freewater OR 97862

Call Sign: KB7ESW
Aaron M Wildman
Milton Freewater OR 97862

Call Sign: KB7EWD
Heather S Wildman
Milton Freewater OR 97862

Call Sign: KB7FAC
Brenda B Wildman
Milton Freewater OR 97862

Call Sign: KB7YMW
John A Hoffman Sr
Milton Freewater OR 97862

Call Sign: K6QEF
Arthur F Barnaby
Milton Freewater OR
978620703

Call Sign: KA7MEB
Rebecca A Hendricks
Milton Freewater OR 97862

Call Sign: KB7SAG
Raymond G Haddon II
Milton Freewater OR 97862

Call Sign: KC7KLM
Flora J Goforth
Milton Freewater OR 97862

Call Sign: KD7BEK

Paul M Pengelly
Milton Freewater OR 97862

Call Sign: WA7IPM
Scott A Hendricks
Milton Freewater OR 97862

Call Sign: KD7JKN
Avis M Barnaby
Milton Freewater OR
978620703

Call Sign: AC7GT
Arthur F Barnaby
Milton Freewater OR
978620703

**FCC Amateur Radio
Licenses in Mitchell**

Call Sign: N7BK
Richard D Mc Ginley
1945 Cal Young Rd
Mitchell OR 97750

Call Sign: W7QZO
Richard E Dixon
12314 Mascher Rd NE
Mitchell OR 97750

Call Sign: KF7CVD
Stephanie L Drynan
Mitchell OR 97750

**FCC Amateur Radio
Licenses in Moro**

Call Sign: WA7COD
Mac N Hall
4637 Hubbard Creek Rd
Moro OR 97039

Call Sign: K7WXW
Donald R Markham
Moro OR 97039

FCC Amateur Radio Licenses in Mosier

Call Sign: W4EYT
Victoria J Smith
4816 Climax Ave
Mosier OR 97040

Call Sign: N7GVO
Mike D Tingey
9308 E Burnside St
Mosier OR 97040

Call Sign: KC7TYP
Holly K Wells
1200 E Central Ave 125
Mosier OR 97040

Call Sign: KC7TBJ
Nat Wells III
1200 E Central Ave 94
Mosier OR 97040

Call Sign: KD7FES
Joshua J Despain
45678 Eagle Creek Rd
Mosier OR 97040

Call Sign: KE7RNQ
Dennis M Berg
2035 N Blandena
Mosier OR 97040

Call Sign: N7SOH
Debra L Dobbs
33607 Perkins Ln
Mosier OR 97040

Call Sign: N7VMQ
James E Mac Millan Jr
1940 Stevens Rd
Mosier OR 97040

Call Sign: KF7JFX

Wasco ARSs Inc
421 Stevens Rd 14
Mosier OR 97040

Call Sign: WC7EC
Wasco ARSs Inc
421 Stevens Rd Sp 21
Mosier OR 97040

Call Sign: KF7RFI
Wasco ARSs Inc
737 Stevens St Apt 104
Mosier OR 97040

Call Sign: KF7LN
Howard H Flint
2595 Stewart
Mosier OR 97040

Call Sign: KC7UNO
Emilio D GARCiaruiz
Mosier OR 97040

Call Sign: KC7ZKT
Tammy L GARCiaruiz
Mosier OR 97040

Call Sign: KC7VPF
Richard E Frost
Mosier OR 970400325

Call Sign: KI7RL
Daniel M Rasmussen
Mosier OR 970400565

FCC Amateur Radio Licenses in Mount Hood Parkdale

Call Sign: KA7ZQU
David V Taylor
1913 Breakwood Cir SE
Mount Hood Parkdale OR
97041

Call Sign: N7IVQ
Shawn S Summersett
570 N 10th Ave 8
Mount Hood Parkdale OR
97041

Call Sign: WB7UYX
William B Chase Jr
88528 Trout Pond Ln
Mount Hood Parkdale OR
97041

Call Sign: K6TNV
Sandra M Whittaker
4345 Woodworth Dr
Mount Hood Parkdale OR
97041

FCC Amateur Radio Licenses in Mount Vernon

Call Sign: KF7PMX
Kevin C Kyriss
13355 SW Violet Ct
Mount Vernon OR 97865

Call Sign: W7ZQB
Jack C Mc Kenna
Mount Vernon OR 97865

Call Sign: KD7SLY
Floyd E Rasmussen
Mount Vernon OR 97865

FCC Amateur Radio Licenses in Murphy

Call Sign: N7SUJ
Larry H Berg
Murphy OR 97533

Call Sign: N7YLB
Charles L Smale
Murphy OR 97533

Call Sign: N7QFC
Veronica S Evensen
Murphy OR 97533

Call Sign: K7TLP
Thomas L Pomes
Murphy OR 97533

Call Sign: KD7LCK
Dean W Anderson
Murphy OR 97533

Call Sign: KD7LTM
Pamela Calvert
Murphy OR 97533

Call Sign: KF7UKD
Marcy M Young
Murphy OR 97533

Call Sign: KC7IXY
Jesse R Calvert III
Murphy OR 975330338

Call Sign: KC7LBD
Todd G Calvert
Murphy OR 975330338

**FCC Amateur Radio
Licenses in Myrtle Creek**

Call Sign: KC7ASF
Richard T Mc Kinnis
1811 Bennett Creek Rd
Myrtle Creek OR 97457

Call Sign: KC7NFU
Theodore K Steensland
916 Brighton Ave
Myrtle Creek OR 97457

Call Sign: KC7GZU
Gerald F Portnell
4880 Bristol Ave
Myrtle Creek OR 97457

Call Sign: AD7FK
Francis J Kekacs
10045 Cape Arago Hwy
Myrtle Creek OR 97457

Call Sign: KK7QR
Francis J Kekacs
90156 Cape Arago Hwy
Myrtle Creek OR 97457

Call Sign: KC7SPW
Leland F Nelson
8495 Crater Lake Hwy
Section 1
Myrtle Creek OR 97457

Call Sign: KD7AOU
Beulah P Neel
50229 Deer Ln
Myrtle Creek OR 97457

Call Sign: W0QOT
Norman L Neel
25445 Deer Ln
Myrtle Creek OR 97457

Call Sign: WA6IMS
David F Baker
6703 Dogwood St
Myrtle Creek OR 97457

Call Sign: N7JFN
Thomas O Brown
555 Freeman Rd 238
Myrtle Creek OR 97457

Call Sign: KD7AOQ
Orval H Haigh
69219 Harness
Myrtle Creek OR
934579769

Call Sign: KE7KEC
Grant H Patitz

302 Idlewood SE
Myrtle Creek OR 97457

Call Sign: KD7DPR
Autumn M Slater
170 Kermanshah
Myrtle Creek OR 97487

Call Sign: WB0VEQ
Roger D Lustri
519 Kingwood Dr NW
Myrtle Creek OR 97457

Call Sign: AI7RR
Roger D Lustri
543 Kingwood Dr NW
Myrtle Creek OR 97457

Call Sign: KC7AUH
Yvonne N Laursen
4742 Liberty Rd S 123
Myrtle Creek OR 97457

Call Sign: KB7QMS
Helen D Lucas
20747 Livengood Way
Myrtle Creek OR 97457

Call Sign: KC7VPP
Janice Mueller
250 Mac Arthur St
Myrtle Creek OR 97457

Call Sign: KE7DQL
Charles M Dieckman
3812 NE 102 Ave
Myrtle Creek OR 97457

Call Sign: KC7NWC
Griffith T Davies
3812 NE 102 Ave
Myrtle Creek OR 97457

Call Sign: KE7KEA
Rolando Gonzalez

2716 NE 102nd
Myrtle Creek OR 97457

Call Sign: KE7AMF
Jacob A Migliore
1940 NE 21st Ave
Myrtle Creek OR 97457

Call Sign: KE7TFF
Lawrence W Jackson
665 NE Clover Ave
Myrtle Creek OR 97457

Call Sign: KC7IXU
Wayne E Johnson
1263 NE Grant St Apt A
Myrtle Creek OR 97457

Call Sign: KD7AXP
Clemens Schotborgh
392 Pine Gravel Rd
Myrtle Creek OR
974578706

Call Sign: KD7AOV
Dortha M Myers
85172 S Slough Rd
Myrtle Creek OR
974579572

Call Sign: KD7AOW
Ray C Myers
85668 S Slough Rd
Myrtle Creek OR
974579572

Call Sign: KB7WDP
Steven G Burke
30686 Sparta Ln
Myrtle Creek OR 97457

Call Sign: KD7IAE
William C Redmond
320 Standley Rd
Myrtle Creek OR 97457

Call Sign: AA9KU
Howard D Lash
14733 SW 109th Ave Apt 1
Myrtle Creek OR 97457

Call Sign: KB7ZQL
Curtis J Costlow
2254 Torrey Pines
Myrtle Creek OR 97457

Call Sign: W7OHK
Charles A Reinhart
1541 Valley View Dr
Myrtle Creek OR
974579767

Call Sign: KD7AXQ
Charles M Buckler
306 Vine St
Myrtle Creek OR 97457

Call Sign: KI7WU
Robert C Jones
Myrtle Creek OR 97457

Call Sign: KA7WXH
Raymond L Lucas
Myrtle Creek OR 97457

Call Sign: KA6APV
Gary E Marquard
Myrtle Creek OR 97457

Call Sign: KC7DRB
Richard A Harvey
Myrtle Creek OR 97457

Call Sign: KC7NLQ
Judy M Steensland
Myrtle Creek OR 97457

Call Sign: KC7NOT
Darin J Mc Michael
Myrtle Creek OR 97457

Call Sign: KD7AOX
John L Craig Jr
Myrtle Creek OR 97457

Call Sign: N7KLC
Lloyd E Sherwin
Myrtle Creek OR 97457

Call Sign: WB7PJG
Chancy C Kirsch
Myrtle Creek OR 97457

Call Sign: KD7PMN
Bob E Marson
Myrtle Creek OR 97457

Call Sign: KD7QPL
Nellie J Eggiman
Myrtle Creek OR 97457

Call Sign: KD7QPM
Ora A Eggiman
Myrtle Creek OR 97457

Call Sign: KF7RHT
Gregory J Churchill
Myrtle Creek OR 97457

Call Sign: KE7ORK
Jack M Steen
Myrtle Creek OR 97457

Call Sign: KJ7ELL
Jack M Steen
Myrtle Creek OR 97457

Call Sign: KE7LDY
Ryan D Marson
Myrtle Creek OR 97457

Call Sign: KE7CVR
Zachariah A Amela
Myrtle Creek OR 97457

Call Sign: N7JCZ
George N Radovich
Myrtle Creek OR
974570106

Call Sign: KE7FNC
Ronald J Parazoo
540 8th St
Myrtle Point OR 97458

Call Sign: KE7SAA
Nancy L Humphrey
2415 9th Ave SE
Myrtle Point OR 97458

Call Sign: KF7BXQ
Tyler A Greene
775 Arcadia Dr
Myrtle Point OR 97458

Call Sign: K0JAK
Charles A Lindsey
4885 Aster St Apt 103
Myrtle Point OR 974581307

Call Sign: KL7JKT
Charles M Roesel
1394 Beekman Ave
Myrtle Point OR 97458

Call Sign: W6NOF
Charles R Short
380 Bushnell Ln E
Myrtle Point OR 974581464

Call Sign: KC7JJL
L Monte Lund
850 Cacade St
Myrtle Point OR 97458

Call Sign: KC7JJH
Waldo J Carlson

947 California Ave
Myrtle Point OR 97458

Call Sign: W7VMU
Clarence M Ralph
2197 Camellia Way
Myrtle Point OR 97458

Call Sign: KE7CL
Olive M Gorst
3201 Campus Dr Oit
Myrtle Point OR 97458

Call Sign: KB7GPI
Huie D Knight Jr
6560 Canary Rd
Myrtle Point OR 97458

Call Sign: K6TAD
Wilbur E Hutchinson
410 Candy Ln
Myrtle Point OR 97458

Call Sign: WA7NZO
Coquille Hs ARC
4500 Cannon Ave 89
Myrtle Point OR 97458

Call Sign: KA6UQT
Daniel P Martin
415 Gibson Rd
Myrtle Point OR 974581115

Call Sign: KE7RZW
George R Smidt
2555 Greenwood Rd 5
Myrtle Point OR 97458

Call Sign: W7WTC
George R Smidt
2485 Greenwood Rd S
Myrtle Point OR 97458

Call Sign: KE7EGA
Dalton D Caudle

4752 Jean Ct NE
Myrtle Point OR 97458

Call Sign: K7EGA
Dalton D Caudle
4877 Jean St NE
Myrtle Point OR 97458

Call Sign: KE7IPX
Rosella M Caudle
4877 Jean St NE
Myrtle Point OR 97458

Call Sign: K7IPX
Rosella M Caudle
12070 Jeane S Pl
Myrtle Point OR 97458

Call Sign: N6UZQ
Carol L Oliver
243 Laurel St
Myrtle Point OR 974581749

Call Sign: KE7OMT
Q C W A Chapter 220
409 Laurel St
Myrtle Point OR 97458

Call Sign: W7VU
Ronald J Oliver
409 Laurel St
Myrtle Point OR 974581749

Call Sign: W7QCA
Q C W A Chapter 220
777 Laurel St
Myrtle Point OR 97458

Call Sign: KE7DG
Garry N Gorst
676 Lochaven
Myrtle Point OR 97458

Call Sign: N7FQQ
Beatrice I Wilson

17167 Merced Rd
Myrtle Point OR 974581444

Call Sign: KE7DFW
Coos County ARES
2710 NE Division
Myrtle Point OR 97458

Call Sign: KD7ZDQ
Janet L Jinkner
3325 NE Douglas St
Myrtle Point OR 97458

Call Sign: KE7CKN
Janet L Jinkner
827 NE Garden Valley Blvd
3
Myrtle Point OR 97458

Call Sign: KD7UNN
John A Ireland
23572 NE Hagey Rd
Myrtle Point OR 97458

Call Sign: AD7EV
John A Ireland
488 NE Mariposa Ave
Myrtle Point OR 97458

Call Sign: KC7NSC
Kathleen A Howard
322 S 8th St
Myrtle Point OR 97458

Call Sign: W7MLT
Brian P Howard
344 S 8th St
Myrtle Point OR 97458

Call Sign: KC7BGZ
Jeffrey A Bramblet
384 S 8th St
Myrtle Point OR 97548

Call Sign: N7DCD

Coos County ARES
65230 Smokey Ridge Rd
Myrtle Point OR 97458

Call Sign: KE7EIB
Dell M Mansker
65230 Smokey Ridge Rd
Myrtle Point OR 97458

Call Sign: KE7OAM
Marilyn D Mansker
1209 Snapdragon Ln
Myrtle Point OR 97458

Call Sign: KJ7OQ
David R Autrey
2937 Stark St
Myrtle Point OR 97458

Call Sign: KD7ZD
Phil Logan Kelly
14785 SW 104th Ave
Myrtle Point OR 97458

Call Sign: W7HYT
Heather A Logan Kelly
14785 SW 104th Ave
Myrtle Point OR 97458

Call Sign: KF7JN
Paul W Chase
3904 Viewcrest Rd S
Myrtle Point OR 97458

Call Sign: W7VOR
David E Pinkerton
1606 Willow
Myrtle Point OR 97458

Call Sign: KC6ZUD
Carrie L Kritcher
Myrtle Point OR 97458

Call Sign: N6ZAA
Robert P Kritcher

Myrtle Point OR 97458

Call Sign: N6ZRV
Linda M Kritcher
Myrtle Point OR 97458

Call Sign: KE7USF
Cameron J Scott
Myrtle Point OR 97458

Call Sign: KE7VXM
Linda M Kritcher
Myrtle Point OR 97458

Call Sign: N6ZRV
Linda M Kritcher
Myrtle Point OR 97458

Call Sign: K7ZRV
Linda M Kritcher
Myrtle Point OR 97458

Call Sign: KE7VXL
Robert P Kritcher
Myrtle Point OR 97458

Call Sign: N6ZAA
Robert P Kritcher
Myrtle Point OR 97458

Call Sign: K7ZAA
Robert P Kritcher
Myrtle Point OR 97458

Call Sign: K6AXT
John E Dolan
Myrtle Point OR 974589803

**FCC Amateur Radio
Licenses in New Pine
Creek**

Call Sign: KC7NPZ
Michael S Lindberg
Hwy 395

New Pine Creek OR 97635

Call Sign: WA6ZBO
Virginia A Stribling
New Pine Creek OR 97635

Call Sign: WB6ZJQ
Edward P Stribling
New Pine Creek OR 97635

Call Sign: KG6GBY
James J Waldburger
New Pine Creek OR 97635

Call Sign: KE7YTI
Gregory T Hall
New Pine Creek OR 97635

Call Sign: W7GTH
Gregory T Hall
New Pine Creek OR 97635

FCC Amateur Radio Licenses in North Bend

Call Sign: KA7TJO
Ronald J Burns
65418 73rd St
North Bend OR 97459

Call Sign: K7QEO
Clarence E Pierce
5547 7th Ave SE
North Bend OR 97459

Call Sign: KC7FRO
Judith A Burns
355 7th St
North Bend OR 97459

Call Sign: WA2NDJ
Syd R Samuels
4795 Auburn Rd NE
North Bend OR 974592503

Call Sign: WB6GXR
Willert L Mc Bride
4344 Badger Ave
North Bend OR 974599590

Call Sign: KD7TY
Albert D Muse
1122 Bentley St E
North Bend OR 97459

Call Sign: W6OFF
Lyle A Nelson
2619 Berkeley St
North Bend OR 97459

Call Sign: N7SBV
Jonathan R Saxton
5850 Berry Dr
North Bend OR 97459

Call Sign: KC7CQQ
Thomas E Ayres
2087 Bonnie Ln
North Bend OR 97459

Call Sign: KF7JXN
Linda L Bufton
Rt 1 Box 1274 A
North Bend OR 97459

Call Sign: KG7DK
Everett V Richardson
911 Cascade St
North Bend OR 97459

Call Sign: KB7UDC
William D Alvey
2022 Cedar St
North Bend OR 974592409

Call Sign: KF7GTV
Patricia L Sanden
3595 Cederoak Dr 10
North Bend OR 97459

Call Sign: KD7YUL
Christopher J Humphrey
2110 Cemetery Rd
North Bend OR 97459

Call Sign: KF7FJV
Steven C Sanden
611 Centennial Blvd
North Bend OR 97459

Call Sign: KE7MI
Charles R Sawyer
4865 Crater Ave N
North Bend OR 97459

Call Sign: KC7FLM
Kerry W Case
4544 Croisan Scenic Way S
North Bend OR 97459

Call Sign: KA7A
Steven L Humphrey
10141 E Burnside St
North Bend OR 97459

Call Sign: W7OC
Southwestern Oregon
Repeater Association
17316 E Burnside St Apt 12
North Bend OR 97459

Call Sign: AC7IR
Bruce W Beauchamp
19121 E Clubhouse Rd
North Bend OR 97459

Call Sign: KE7CAN
Ellis B Berliner
1346 El Dorado Ave
North Bend OR 97459

Call Sign: N7PBZ
Jeanne R Hincke
7560 Fawcett Cr Rd
North Bend OR 97459

Call Sign: W7LDC
J Lee Byer
4023 Fawn Ave
North Bend OR 97459

Call Sign: WA6LFJ
Buddy R Hincke
4042 Fawn Ave
North Bend OR 97459

Call Sign: KE7CNA
Sandra K Garner
89241 Fields Rd
North Bend OR 97459

Call Sign: KE7CMX
William C Garner
89246 Fields Rd
North Bend OR 97459

Call Sign: KC7JMR
James F Ferris
89246 Fields Rd
North Bend OR 97459

Call Sign: KE7CND
Gregory D Dalton
10124 Friendly Acres Rd
North Bend OR 97459

Call Sign: KE7JSK
Dennis A Dalton
170 Friendship Ave SE
North Bend OR 97459

Call Sign: KC7AGV
Arthur E Hoffschneider
18770 Frost Rd
North Bend OR 97459

Call Sign: KC7NLX
David C Grimes
2798 Goldfinch Loop SE
North Bend OR 97459

Call Sign: KD7VMQ
Brandi M Grimes
2798 Goldfinch Loop SE
North Bend OR 97459

Call Sign: W7AMA
Marc D Rohlfes
1267 Green Park Dr
North Bend OR 97459

Call Sign: KA7GNL
James N Howard
42955 Green River Dr
North Bend OR 97459

Call Sign: W7LXW
J R Nathan Olson
9505 Helmick Rd
North Bend OR 97459

Call Sign: KL7DF
Edward J Harwood
3780 Hemlock Pl SE
North Bend OR 97459

Call Sign: N7BOW
Peter R Liverca Jr
37422 Hills Creek Rd
North Bend OR 97459

Call Sign: KD7HOW
Kevin L Hedgepeth
1699 Huckleberry Dr
North Bend OR 974591930

Call Sign: KD7IEP
Michelle A Hedgepeth
1840 Huckleberry Dr
North Bend OR 974591930

Call Sign: NQ7F
Cecil M Brown
1992 Huckleberry Dr
North Bend OR 97459

Call Sign: AE7MS
Michael E Stoll
31873 Huckleberry Ln
North Bend OR 97459

Call Sign: W6UOR
E King Frey
570 Hughes St
North Bend OR 97459

Call Sign: KD7EEV
Dennis G Leverenz
690 Hughes St
North Bend OR 97459

Call Sign: KB6ALN
Arthur D Cordell
25117 Hunter Rd
North Bend OR 97459

Call Sign: KF7CIR
Jeffrey W Howes
2178 Juliet Ct S
North Bend OR 97459

Call Sign: KF6QON
Thomas A Cloutier
2178 Juliet Ct S
North Bend OR 97459

Call Sign: KE7WVU
Thomas A Cloutier
1888 Juneau St S
North Bend OR 97459

Call Sign: KF7DFN
Jaclyn A Rosenberg
2800 Juniper Canyon Rd
North Bend OR 97459

Call Sign: KC2LPD
Jacob Z Rosenberg
4863 Juniper Ct N
North Bend OR 97459

Call Sign: KB7VOQ
Floyd B Talley III
91956 Koppisch
North Bend OR 97459

Call Sign: KF5PO
John W Cossey
1118 Lancaster Dr NE 383
North Bend OR 97458

Call Sign: N7ASC
Euwel L Pearson
11 Lani Way
North Bend OR 97459

Call Sign: WB7CUS
Roger N Morrell
964 Little Valley Rd
North Bend OR 97459

Call Sign: KF7DLL
Mark R De Brito
2124 Lonnon Rd
North Bend OR 97459

Call Sign: W7OLH
John H Brelage
53030 Loop Dr
North Bend OR 97459

Call Sign: N7TYD
Joseph L Frischman
8250 Magnolia Dr
North Bend OR 97459

Call Sign: WA7MGM
Richard E Reynolds
899 Main St
North Bend OR 97459

Call Sign: KE6RSZ
Patrick K Elliott
2420 Main St SE
North Bend OR 97459

Call Sign: KE7FXJ
Gail D Holmes
2420 Main St SE
North Bend OR 97459

Call Sign: K7NUK
Clifford E Lang
14351 Marion Rd NE
North Bend OR 974591450

Call Sign: KC7PQT
Bay Area Hospital ARC
850 Marion St
North Bend OR 97459

Call Sign: K7CME
Carol M Emery
6626 McLeod Ln NE
North Bend OR 97459

Call Sign: KE7FXP
Larry F Fisher
6626 McLeod Ln NE
North Bend OR 97459

Call Sign: KE7VBU
Sarah A Shewell
34419 Meyer Rd
North Bend OR 97459

Call Sign: KC7LMI
Timothy C Wakeling
1093 Montgomery Ave
North Bend OR 97459

Call Sign: KD7IIB
Bradley J Kohn
1022 N 2nd St
North Bend OR 97459

Call Sign: KB6EMM
Delayne D Gehman
1055 N 5th St 80
North Bend OR 97459

Call Sign: KD6TDE
Rebecca L Talas
687 N 64
North Bend OR 97459

Call Sign: WD6BPK
David P Granicy
667 N 65th St
North Bend OR 97459

Call Sign: KE7CYP
Daniel E Tapia
185 N 6th St
North Bend OR 97459

Call Sign: W7DET
Daniel E Tapia
321 N 6th St
North Bend OR 97459

Call Sign: KE7LHW
Celeste A Granicy
455 N 6th St
North Bend OR 97459

Call Sign: K7CAG
Celeste A Granicy
850 N 6th St
North Bend OR 97459

Call Sign: KE7CMW
Christina M Sanchez
1041 N 6th St
North Bend OR 97459

Call Sign: K7NBO
David P Granicy
115 N 72nd St
North Bend OR 97459

Call Sign: KE7CMV
Carl A Talas
1226 N 7th Ct
North Bend OR 97459

Call Sign: KB7JVS
Max R Staton
4788 N Lombard 7
North Bend OR 97459

Call Sign: KB7PXO
John R Thomas
1430 Patterson St
North Bend OR 97459

Call Sign: KC7FZH
Minka K Guenther
383 S 6th St
North Bend OR 97459

Call Sign: KA7MLK
Jon E Sumpter
8316 N Lombard St 438
North Bend OR 97459

Call Sign: N7WRY
Joe J Thomas
1430 Patterson St
North Bend OR 97459

Call Sign: KB7PXL
Maria E Jones
1509 SE 12th Ave
North Bend OR 97459

Call Sign: N6FAK
Jack G Silveira
8316 N Lombard St 438
North Bend OR 97459

Call Sign: KA7DRN
Edward A Meyer
1937 Portland St
North Bend OR 97459

Call Sign: KA7YZR
Donald W Smith
8819 SE 12th Ave
North Bend OR 97459

Call Sign: W7CSD
Robert E Baird
1657 Old Garden Valley Rd
North Bend OR 97459

Call Sign: KF7KYR
Shane O Gill
1937 Portland St
North Bend OR 97459

Call Sign: KI7SK
John Pingree
1014 SE 130 Ave
North Bend OR 97459

Call Sign: WB7PFA
Stephen H Wright
26914 Old Holley Rd
North Bend OR 97459

Call Sign: W7SOG
Shane O Gill
2633 Portland St Apt 1
North Bend OR 97459

Call Sign: KE7SAH
Claude O Coffman
100 Short St
North Bend OR 97459

Call Sign: KA7GNM
Michael J Burdick
40698 Old Hwy 30 Unit 20
North Bend OR 97459

Call Sign: KF7QPD
Michael J Dees
3463 Quail Ridge Ln
North Bend OR 97459

Call Sign: W7GNV
Lucile W Peck
367 Short St
North Bend OR 97459

Call Sign: KC7CCF
Josef E Dieckman
8401 Old Stage Rd 70
North Bend OR 97459

Call Sign: W7ARF
Michael J Dees
115 Quail Run
North Bend OR 97459

Call Sign: KE6DZA
William T Blume
3657 Short St SE
North Bend OR 97459

Call Sign: KD6KZB
John R Soper
333 Old Stage Rd S
North Bend OR 97459

Call Sign: KE7LHV
Robert F Wassam
3500 Redwood Rd
North Bend OR 97459

Call Sign: N7IWC
Edward E Thomas Jr
3781 Shropshire
North Bend OR 97459

Call Sign: KE7FNB
John L Doubek
11773 Orchard Ave
North Bend OR 97459

Call Sign: KE7TMZ
Philip C Lagesse
11992 Royalty Ct 9
North Bend OR 97459

Call Sign: KB7CTD
Harry J Foster
8 Sibelius Ct
North Bend OR 97459

Call Sign: WB7ELK
William F Belk
2978 Sienna Ct
North Bend OR 97459

Call Sign: WB7QIF
Merril A Borgman
2450 Sierra Vista Ln
North Bend OR 97459

Call Sign: KF6AKW
Robert C Freeman
2462 Siskiyou Blvd
North Bend OR 97459

Call Sign: KD7MWX
Richard N Vigue
17450 Skyliners Rd
North Bend OR 97459

Call Sign: KB7UDE
Mark J Thimm
55478 Stateline Rd
North Bend OR 97459

Call Sign: KC7NSB
Audrey M Duke
39450 Staton Scio Rd
North Bend OR 97459

Call Sign: KD7EZM
Teresa L Faulkner
300 Stewart Ave
North Bend OR 97459

Call Sign: N7OSL
Jim E Morrison
87356 Stewart Ln
North Bend OR 97459

Call Sign: KD7IQT
Eric R Kohler
67274 W Westview Rd
North Bend OR 97458

Call Sign: KE7ADI
Lee C Mullins
821 Wall St
North Bend OR 97459

Call Sign: KD7ABD
Michael L Beyer
890 Wall St
North Bend OR 97459

Call Sign: KE7FXH
Rosemary S Bertha
2217 Wall St
North Bend OR 97459

Call Sign: KE7RSB
Rosemary S Bertha
2217 Wall St
North Bend OR 97459

Call Sign: KE7FXN
John A Bertha
2217 Wall St
North Bend OR 974591466

Call Sign: NB7JB
John A Bertha
2217 Wall St
North Bend OR 974591466

Call Sign: WB7VIK
Robert L Mason
2395 Wall St
North Bend OR 97459

Call Sign: W7JCN
James M Shumake
94898 Willanch Ln
North Bend OR 97459

Call Sign: KA7QHB
Lu H Noggle
1440 Willanch Way
North Bend OR 97459

Call Sign: WD6AGM
Robert L Jensen
95257 Windsong Ln
North Bend OR 97459

Call Sign: KA7QHU
Michael L Anderson
410 Zara Dr
North Bend OR 97459

Call Sign: K7CCH
Coos County RC
68645 Zara Rd
North Bend OR 97459

Call Sign: WA7PHI
Michael K Anderson
68645 Zara Rd
North Bend OR 97459

Call Sign: KA7ZIQ
William J Guenther
North Bend OR 97459

Call Sign: KC7AGU
John Celentano
North Bend OR 97459

Call Sign: K7NG
David G Borcher
North Bend OR 97459

Call Sign: KC7DVZ
Eugene A Teal
North Bend OR 97459

Call Sign: KD7IFS
Leonard C Hall Jr
North Bend OR 97459

Call Sign: W7WLW
Daniel D De Salvo
North Bend OR 97459

Call Sign: W7YOU
Leonard C Hall Jr
North Bend OR 97459

Call Sign: KE7SAG
Sam A Terzo
North Bend OR 97459

Call Sign: N7MSH
Neal A Chamberlain
North Powder OR 97867

Call Sign: K7CIG
Orville C Moore
2703 Quartz St
Noti OR 97461

Call Sign: KA0NTV
Melody E Fair
Noti OR 97461

Call Sign: N0EMD
Roy E Fair
Noti OR 97461

Call Sign: KB7RSA
Birk R Lowrie
Noti OR 974610311

Call Sign: KE7EWL
Mark A Mason
Noti OR 974610371

Call Sign: KB7IHY
Samuel L Widmer
2145 N 31st St Sp 53

Nyssa OR 97913

Call Sign: K7WSV
Richard L Labby
717 N Elm St
Nyssa OR 979133200

Call Sign: KD7QLO
Edward M Marsh
905 N Harbour Dr Unit 6
Nyssa OR 97913

Call Sign: K7VMU
William P Simpson
34641 N Harney Ln
Nyssa OR 97913

Call Sign: KD4COZ
Gaylen G Spear
1503 N Hayden Island Dr
Sp 59
Nyssa OR 97913

Call Sign: KD4EXX
Jeanne J Spear
3316 NE 18th Ave
Nyssa OR 97913

Call Sign: W7RFG
Frank T Morgan
61092 River Bluff Tr
Nyssa OR 97913

Call Sign: KD7FPG
Ralph R Page
1529 Summitt Loop
Nyssa OR 97913

Call Sign: W7PAG
Ralph R Page
519 Summitt Ridge Dr
Nyssa OR 97913

Call Sign: KE7IDM
Richard B Runnels

1330 Wilson Ln
Nyssa OR 97913

Call Sign: KE6SFP
Craig J Hinkel
1242 Lees Creek Rd
O Brien OR 97534

Call Sign: KF6QAW
Judy L Hinkel
88039 Leeward Dr
O Brien OR 975340147

Call Sign: K6MLR
John L Parris
224 Mariposa Ter
O Brien OR 975349716

Call Sign: KB6FK
Eric C Lundgren
275 NE 23rd St
O Brien OR 97534

Call Sign: KB7FK
Eric C Lundgren
3050 NE 23rd St Apt 11
O Brien OR 97534

Call Sign: AB7GI
David R Thelander
O Brien OR 97534

Call Sign: KC7HDA
Barbara L Thelander
O Brien OR 97534

Call Sign: KE7ATX
Michael J Thelander
O Brien OR 97534

Call Sign: N7NSC
Philip M Waste
33678 Canaan Rd
Oakland OR 97462

Call Sign: KA7PSQ
Richard L Jethro
445 Candalaria Blvd S
Oakland OR 97462

Call Sign: N7LMU
Daniel R Parker
1528 Clearview Way NE
Oakland OR 97462

Call Sign: KE7OVI
Paul A Reeves
2557 Fontaine Cir
Oakland OR 97462

Call Sign: KE7ORN
Ronald W Patston
4635 Foothill
Oakland OR 97462

Call Sign: KD7DRX
Wilbur G Friend
60 Hawthorne St
Oakland OR 97462

Call Sign: KC7NHP
Timothy M Baimbridge
4343 Herman
Oakland OR 97462

Call Sign: AC4ZI
Henry E Sill
19866 Melody Ln
Oakland OR 97462

Call Sign: W9AE
Wayne A Estes
10048 NE Campaign St
Oakland OR 97462

Call Sign: KB7ZDK
John E Caig
5021 NE Cully Blvd
Oakland OR 97462

Call Sign: KB7HHT
James S Young
10762 SE Melita Dr
Oakland OR 97462

Call Sign: KC7LZX
Franklin H Rankin
500 Whitehackle Ln
Oakland OR 974629652

Call Sign: KD7CZU
Chantele L Bangs
1339 Wildflower Ln
Oakland OR 97462

Call Sign: KC7BVL
Myron J Dabich
Oakland OR 97462

Call Sign: N6AXP
Gene M Stager
Oakland OR 97462

Call Sign: W7QNB
John S Sandige
Oakland OR 97462

Call Sign: KF7FHX
Tiana L Patitz
Oakland OR 97462

**FCC Amateur Radio
Licenses in Oakridge**

Call Sign: N8FJU
John J Herscher
42162 Bagley Ln
Oakridge OR 97463

Call Sign: WA7OMC
John J Herscher
42162 Bagley Ln
Oakridge OR 97463

Call Sign: KF7ANG
Jason A Hale
7545 Cason Cir
Oakridge OR 97463

Call Sign: K7TIV
Jack L Curtis
7555 Cason Ln
Oakridge OR 97463

Call Sign: W7ALX
Charles W Weiss
7706 Donegal Ave
Oakridge OR 97463

Call Sign: W7MJJ
Michael J Jenson
624 Hwy 101 S
Oakridge OR 97463

Call Sign: W7ULA
Don A Skaife
1290 Morrow Rd Apt 8
Oakridge OR 97463

Call Sign: KA6PRW
Darrell M Jones
7324 N Chase Ave
Oakridge OR 97463

Call Sign: W7SVP
Richard R Howard
7324 N Chase Ave
Oakridge OR 97463

Call Sign: NK3B
Richard R Howard
8019 N Chautauqua Blvd
Oakridge OR 97463

Call Sign: W7XJ
Richard R Howard
1403 N Cherry St
Oakridge OR 97463

Call Sign: W7EU
Richard R Howard
8958 N Clarendon Ave
Oakridge OR 97463

Call Sign: W7BC
Richard R Howard
1601 N Clark
Oakridge OR 97463

Call Sign: KF6CYZ
Robert P Samuelson
2040 Pleasant Creek Rd
Oakridge OR 97463

Call Sign: KD7DXO
Rebecca L Mc Murrick
975 S 1st St
Oakridge OR 97463

Call Sign: KC7FFV
David A Mc Murrick
975 S 1st St
Oakridge OR 97463

Call Sign: WB7DLL
William A Maggs
15083 SE 124th Ave
Oakridge OR 97463

Call Sign: KD7SDD
Jason S Smith
2359 Temple Ct
Oakridge OR 97463

Call Sign: KA7WJV
David B Murdough
47765 W 2nd St
Oakridge OR 97463

Call Sign: KA7QBD
Leland M Holst
Oakridge OR 97463

Call Sign: KC4VQV
Carol L Reed
Oakridge OR 97436

Call Sign: K7SAZ
Kenneth D Boyce
Oakridge OR 97463

Call Sign: KA7NOW
James E Rowan
Oakridge OR 97463

Call Sign: W7YGB
Marion P Hays
Oakridge OR 97463

Call Sign: KF7JGE
Elmer C Taylor
Oakridge OR 97463

Call Sign: K7ECT
Elmer C Taylor
Oakridge OR 97463

Call Sign: KD7WYU
Richard L Veatch
Oakridge OR 97463

Call Sign: KK7FY
Earl D Omvig
Oakridge OR 974630244

FCC Amateur Radio Licenses in Odell

Call Sign: KF7GGO
Clyde R O'Bannon
Odell OR 97044

FCC Amateur Radio Licenses in Ontario

Call Sign: W7NOM
Raymond L Westcott
648 49th Ave SE
Ontario OR 97914

Call Sign: KC7TRO
Lawrence G Ogden Sr
86568 Bailey Hill Loop
Ontario OR 97914

Call Sign: W7SNW
Sherman N Weisgerber
2811 Bailey Ln 62
Ontario OR 97914

Call Sign: KF7PQE
Linda M Williams
463 Clarmar Dr NE
Ontario OR 97914

Call Sign: KC7ERB
Ronald E Manley
700 Crater Lake Ave 75
Ontario OR 97914

Call Sign: N7XGI
Alvin A Gafford
8495 Crater Lake Hwy
Ontario OR 97914

Call Sign: W7OWL
Alvin A Gafford
8495 Crater Lake Hwy 1
Ontario OR 97914

Call Sign: KF7DPU
Martin F Creson
6353 D St
Ontario OR 97914

Call Sign: KC7MLC
Emanuel G Gonzales
7010 D St
Ontario OR 97914

Call Sign: KB7HZZ
Thomas V Belknap
111 Daffney Ct
Ontario OR 97914

Call Sign: KC7AVN
Edward L Renk
406 E 3rd St
Ontario OR 97914

Call Sign: KC7DAZ
Norma L Steele
70521 E Terrace Dr
Ontario OR 97914

Call Sign: KC7DBA
Stephanie Steele
70521 E Terrace Dr
Ontario OR 97914

Call Sign: K7JWR
Jeremy W Rule
46161 Goodpasture Rd
Ontario OR 97914

Call Sign: KE7KQB
Jeremy W Rule
47227 Goodpasture Rd
Ontario OR 97914

Call Sign: WA7DHD
Ross H Kinney
426 Greenacre Dr NW
Ontario OR 97914

Call Sign: KE7CJC
John L Switzer
430 Holly Ave
Ontario OR 97914

Call Sign: W7JLS
John L Switzer
430 Holly Ave
Ontario OR 97914

Ontario OR 97914

Call Sign: KB7IBA
Kenneth E Smith
20328 Medical Springs
Hwy
Ontario OR 97914

Call Sign: WA7IVU
Loretta M Williamson
10912 N Applegate Rd
Ontario OR 97914

Call Sign: KE7FT
Carl L Peterson
115 N Arney Rd 141
Ontario OR 97914

Call Sign: KD7NPQ
Leonard L Ryals
9225 N Tyler Ave
Ontario OR 97914

Call Sign: KY4DWD
Dennis W Delvin
640 NE 10th St
Ontario OR 97914

Call Sign: KB7FXD
Darren D Lee
2105 NW 14th St
Ontario OR 97914

Call Sign: KA7V
Barry K Wright
225 NW 6th St 38
Ontario OR 97914

Call Sign: KC7RFO
Jackie F Sams
1616 NW Angeline Ct
Ontario OR 97914

Call Sign: KD7ZVI
Brad L Cleaver
4615 NW B Ave

Call Sign: W7MGL
Kathie C Cook
764 NW Beaver Pl
Ontario OR 97914

Call Sign: W7MHR
Ben B Cook
1045 NW Beca Ave
Ontario OR 97914

Call Sign: KB7ZMR
Michael A Pratt
470 Old Hwy 62 12
Ontario OR 97914

Call Sign: AD7AZ
Michael A Pratt
8520 Old Hwy 99 S
Ontario OR 97914

Call Sign: KF7RDF
Tach J Lehman
86364 Panorama Rd
Ontario OR 97914

Call Sign: KE7CSK
Brule J Lehman
86364 Panorama Rd
Ontario OR 979148811

Call Sign: W7MUD
Paul W Hughes
133 Plumtree Ln
Ontario OR 97914

Call Sign: KB7YRB
Silvie M Smith
5355 River Rd N Sp 17
Ontario OR 97914

Call Sign: W7GBP
Charles J Smith
5355 River Rd N Sp 59

Ontario OR 97914

Call Sign: KA7U
Ronald J Morell
66925 Rock Island Ln
Ontario OR 97914

Call Sign: K7RVS
Robert H Batcheller
21735 S Lower Highland
Rd
Ontario OR 97914

Call Sign: KC7EIN
Conrad R Anderson
1955 S Ott Rd
Ontario OR 97914

Call Sign: K7RHB
Robert H Batcheller
390 S Wasson
Ontario OR 97914

Call Sign: WB7REQ
Edwin M Carter Jr
8118 SE 39th Ave
Ontario OR 979140135

Call Sign: KC9CNK
Robert A Hogan
37845 Soap Creek Rd
Ontario OR 97914

Call Sign: KB7USR
Naadene M Petersen
8668 Stayton Rd SE
Ontario OR 97914

Call Sign: KC7IQQ
Harry C Petersen
40000 Stayton Scio Loop 7
Ontario OR 97914

Call Sign: KB7JAZ
Edna L Kilpatrick

40000 Stayton Scio Loop 7
Ontario OR 97914

Call Sign: WB6FUV
James E Hetle
40040 Stayton Scio Lp
Ontario OR 97914

Call Sign: KD7LSB
Lee N Killkenny
3592 SW 103rd Ave
Ontario OR 97914

Call Sign: KE7HBR
Mary K Mitchael
4777 SW 11th St
Ontario OR 97914

Call Sign: N7UUX
Rodney J Wood
12200 SW 12th St
Ontario OR 97914

Call Sign: KC7QDU
Cipriano C Lujan
8932 SW 149th Pl
Ontario OR 97914

Call Sign: N7ZOH
James H Mc Culley
27845 SW 207th
Ontario OR 97914

Call Sign: KC7RFM
Kenneth S Soule
1520 SW 208 Ave
Ontario OR 97914

Call Sign: K7MAN
Robert L Stewart
5235 SW 208 Ct
Ontario OR 97914

Call Sign: WA7JPE
Fredrick A Leaders

2425 SW 27th St
Ontario OR 97914

Call Sign: KA7EPV
Edith P Woodward
7511 SW 31st
Ontario OR 97914

Call Sign: W7NO
Charles E Harland
7036 SW 31st Ave
Ontario OR 97914

Call Sign: W7WX
Reese D Jenkins
11627 SW 31st Ct
Ontario OR 979141867

Call Sign: N7HPQ
Daniel L Mc Gowan
1483 W Idaho Ave
Ontario OR 97914

Call Sign: N7KIF
Frances M Mc Gowan
1483 W Idaho Ave
Ontario OR 97914

Call Sign: KA7ALI
Ruth E Sears
251 W Idaho Ave 13
Ontario OR 97914

Call Sign: KC7JT
Paul R Sears
251 W Idaho Ave 13
Ontario OR 97914

Call Sign: KB7PAA
Michael D Jones
Ontario OR 97914

Call Sign: KC7RT
Sherman N Weisgerber
Ontario OR 97914

Call Sign: W7SNW
Sherman N Weisgerber
Ontario OR 97914

Call Sign: KF7CEN
David F French
Ontario OR 97914

Call Sign: KE7ZUB
William L Storms
Ontario OR 97914

FCC Amateur Radio Licenses in Ophir

Call Sign: AC7NS
Melbourne R Githens
Ophir OR 97464

Call Sign: N7PQ
Melbourne R Githens
Ophir OR 97464

FCC Amateur Radio Licenses in Paisley

Call Sign: KF6QKN
Roric J Padgett
Paisley OR 97636

Call Sign: KF6WHO
William E Earlywine
Paisley OR 97636

FCC Amateur Radio Licenses in Parkdale

Call Sign: NA2Y
William D Stenson
230 Bluebird Ln
Parkdale OR 97041

Call Sign: KB7GIJ
Christine L Taylor

3423 Breezewood Ave
Parkdale OR 97041

Call Sign: KC7OOB
Jonathan G Taylor
53000 Breitenbush Rd
Parkdale OR 97041

Call Sign: KD7JWA
Brenda L Brandt
4394 Bren Loop NE
Parkdale OR 97041

Call Sign: KD7JWB
Cory J Brandt
3150 Brenna St NE
Parkdale OR 97041

Call Sign: KC7PHV
Kristi M Taylor
63712 Brenner Cyn Rd
Parkdale OR 97041

Call Sign: KB7DTZ
Harold W Bruggeman
204 Crescent Dr
Parkdale OR 97041

Call Sign: KD7ZZT
John W Robbins
25370 Crescent Hill Rd
Parkdale OR 97041

Call Sign: KC7UVL
Stephen D Darling
8 Crescent St
Parkdale OR 97041

Call Sign: KA7THD
Leslie M Ritchey
932 Dearborn Ave N
Parkdale OR 97041

Call Sign: KB7DRS
Robert D Parrott

255 Douglas Rd
Parkdale OR 97041

Call Sign: KB7SIM
Terry C Stratton
13550 Jason Lee Dr
Parkdale OR 97041

Call Sign: KE7SDZ
Lyle S Mcalexander
309 Truman Ln
Parkdale OR 97041

Call Sign: K6DAD
William F Van Overmeer
4345 Woodworth Dr
Parkdale OR 97041

Call Sign: KB7OMY
Lori A White
Parkdale OR 97041

Call Sign: KB7UPM
Lester K White Jr
Parkdale OR 970410406

FCC Amateur Radio Licenses in Pendleton

Call Sign: WA7ZCL
Steven R Stewart
2414 1st St NW
Pendleton OR 97801

Call Sign: N7REH
Doug M Doyle
1302 3rd St
Pendleton OR 97801

Call Sign: N7UAQ
Brandi L Zeckman
42537 Bagley
Pendleton OR 97801

Call Sign: KB7DRJ

Earl L Shepard
465 Calico St NW
Pendleton OR 97801

Call Sign: W7WXB
William R Allison
180 Calvert Dr
Pendleton OR 97801

Call Sign: KA7GMZ
Paul J Wachter
69805 Camp Polk Rd
Pendleton OR 97801

Call Sign: KC7PIZ
Dennis L Papineau
80298 Hamlet Rd
Pendleton OR 97801

Call Sign: KC7TKJ
Tanya F Papineau
80298 Hamlet Rd
Pendleton OR 97801

Call Sign: KD7BDB
Rocky B Correa
649 Jaynes Dr
Pendleton OR 97801

Call Sign: KA7KTE
Kay R Weston
2300 Meadow Ln NE
Pendleton OR 97801

Call Sign: N7GFD
Pamela M Weston
3639 Meadow Park Loop
NE
Pendleton OR 97801

Call Sign: W7ZKH
Paul E Weston
3651 Meadow Park Loop
NE
Pendleton OR 97801

Call Sign: WA7V
Brett E Mueller
205 Morton Rd
Pendleton OR 97801

Call Sign: K7ROO
Charlyn R Mueller
205 Morton Rd
Pendleton OR 97801

Call Sign: WB7CYS
John A Wilson
222 NE 197 Ave
Pendleton OR 97801

Call Sign: KB7AOR
Melvin F Poole
6600 NE 78th Ct Ste A3
A4224
Pendleton OR 97801

Call Sign: KC7PZD
Mindi S Hymas
1036 NW 25th St Apt B
Pendleton OR 97801

Call Sign: WB7PTK
Curtis D Reynolds
1560 NW Avery
Pendleton OR 97801

Call Sign: WX7PDT
Blue Mountains Skywarn
Association
12433 NW Barnes Rd 110
Pendleton OR 97801

Call Sign: KC7ZNF
Blue Mountains Skywarn
Association
12410 NW Barnes Rd 368
Pendleton OR 97801

Call Sign: KB7ZNS

Randy T Burnett
849 NW Bridge St
Pendleton OR 97801

Call Sign: WB7RDO
Norman T Burnett
1674 NW Bridgeway Ln
Pendleton OR 97801

Call Sign: KA7OPN
Kevin J Michel
3901 NW Clarence Cir
Pendleton OR 97801

Call Sign: N7UAS
Lonnie L Michel
15665 NW Clay Horse Dr
Pendleton OR 97801

Call Sign: KB7ZNO
Loren E Frost
3146 NW Colonial Dr
Pendleton OR 97801

Call Sign: KC7TAW
Diane B Gregg
20358 NW Colonnade
Pendleton OR 97801

Call Sign: N7OVH
Ronald N Taft
3465 NW Dimple Hill Rd
Pendleton OR 97801

Call Sign: KD7RVF
Bob J Tobin
3465 NW Dimple Hill Rd
Pendleton OR 97801

Call Sign: KB0NYC
Dennis D Hull
2880 NW Gibson Hill Rd
Pendleton OR 97801

Call Sign: KE7DXT

Becky G Marks
17754 NW Gilbert Ln
Pendleton OR 97801

Call Sign: KE6HUA
John Gratton
430 NW Hartmann Ave
Pendleton OR 978011639

Call Sign: KE6SKI
Linda V Hill
13835 NW Hartung Ct
Pendleton OR 978011639

Call Sign: KB5MOO
John M Carrington
12035 NW Lovejoy
Pendleton OR 97801

Call Sign: WB5CW
John M Carrington
1829 NW Lovejoy St Apt
206
Pendleton OR 97801

Call Sign: N7GZZ
Keith L Hallmark
9840 NW Maring Dr
Pendleton OR 97801

Call Sign: KD7YOS
Rod K Townsend
4860 Redwood Ave
Pendleton OR 97801

Call Sign: WN7RKT
Rod K Townsend
5057 Redwood Ave
Pendleton OR 97801

Call Sign: N7DSW
Rod K Townsend
87 2395 Redwood Ave
Pendleton OR 97801

Call Sign: KD7HUN
Bill D Gailey
29891 S Hawthorne Ln
Pendleton OR 97801

Call Sign: KD7HUO
Justin A Hubbard
9141 S Heinz Rd
Pendleton OR 97801

Call Sign: KD7HUM
Jeremy B Crowder
16367 S Hiram Ave
Pendleton OR 97801

Call Sign: KC7LTH
Karen J Wilson
552 SE 13th
Pendleton OR 97801

Call Sign: KA7RSR
Janlyn G Hood
13741 SE 242nd
Pendleton OR 97801

Call Sign: KA7RWV
John L Hood
13741 SE 242nd Ave
Pendleton OR 97801

Call Sign: KB7DJR
Susan D Hood
2425 SE 24th
Pendleton OR 97801

Call Sign: KC7YGJ
Crystal A Severe
9550 SE 302nd Ln
Pendleton OR 97801

Call Sign: KC7WBY
Monty Z Severe
11225 SE 31 Ave
Pendleton OR 97801

Call Sign: WZ0K
Mark O Torgerson
918 SE 50th St
Pendleton OR 97801

Call Sign: AA0CU
Leann B Thompson
1905 SE 51st Ave
Pendleton OR 97801

Call Sign: KC7PJC
Linda K Heintz
18303 SE Anusugger Rd
Pendleton OR 97801

Call Sign: KE7YX
Emery J Heintz
1110 SE April Ct
Pendleton OR 97801

Call Sign: KB7VFV
Bert Jager
1808 SE Arborwood Ave
Pendleton OR 97801

Call Sign: N7ZUB
Marten C Jager
1932 SE Arborwood Ave
Pendleton OR 97801

Call Sign: KD6HRJ
John R Mathis
11415 SE Ash Ct
Pendleton OR 97801

Call Sign: W7TUC
Frank Henrikson
37661 SE Bearcreek Ln
Pendleton OR 97801

Call Sign: W7DSG
Archie J Bowman
13639 SE Clay St
Pendleton OR 978012476

Call Sign: KD7QYQ
Micah J Thompson
17848 SE Clay St
Pendleton OR 97801

Call Sign: KM7EMT
Keri M Clark
4970 SW 141st Ave
Pendleton OR 97801

Call Sign: KA7QGT
Linda L Ruud
7305 SW 34th Ave
Pendleton OR 97801

Call Sign: KE7DWF
Walter S Westover
5200 SE Drake Rd
Pendleton OR 97801

Call Sign: W7PL
Pendleton ARC
6565 SW 155th St
Pendleton OR 97801

Call Sign: KA7UKM
Don M Meengs
4923 SW 35th Pl
Pendleton OR 97801

Call Sign: KD7BCZ
Ann M Adams
6356 SE Drake St
Pendleton OR 97801

Call Sign: WB7TDG
Denton E Sprague Jr
13209 SW 157th Ave
Pendleton OR 97801

Call Sign: KB7WRS
Andrew P Emert
8004 SW 45th
Pendleton OR 97801

Call Sign: N7GZX
Jeffrey C Burnett
41400 SE George Rd
Pendleton OR 97801

Call Sign: KE7DWJ
Vivian C Sprague
9750 SW 158th Ave
Pendleton OR 97801

Call Sign: WJ7D
Thomas E Laird
5102 SW 45th Ave Apt 7
Pendleton OR 97801

Call Sign: N7FIV
Kenneth H Long
5048A SE Hawthorne Blvd
Pendleton OR 97801

Call Sign: KC7URE
Douglas R Garlets
14335 SW 161 Ave
Pendleton OR 97801

Call Sign: W7JOG
Theodore A Smith
6805 SW 49th Ave
Pendleton OR 97801

Call Sign: KD7HKO
Gary S Crowder
15253 SE Laurie
Pendleton OR 97801

Call Sign: KB7AZZ
Phillip A Coffman
1241 SW 2nd Ave
Pendleton OR 97801

Call Sign: KK7RO
Dwayne E Patton
821 SW 4th
Pendleton OR 97801

Call Sign: KD7HUL
Cristopher S Crowder
14885 SE Laurie Ave
Pendleton OR 97801

Call Sign: KA7TXP
Bill I Tapley
815 SW 30th
Pendleton OR 97801

Call Sign: N7FQI
Claude W Eley
18230 SW Broad Oak Ct
Pendleton OR 97801

Call Sign: K7PXO
Henry C Lorenzen
900 State St H231
Pendleton OR 97801

Call Sign: KA7QJG
Steele A Bacus
1040 SW 33rd Ave
Pendleton OR 97801

Call Sign: KF6PZZ
David N Wayne
8460 SW Crater Loop
Pendleton OR 978012160

Call Sign: KD7IVL
Aaron J Perry
13870 SW 114th Ave
Pendleton OR 97801

Call Sign: KA7MOU
Philip M Ruud
400 SW 345th
Pendleton OR 97801

Call Sign: KF6RCX
Susan C Woellert
51934 SW Creekview Pl
Pendleton OR 978012160

Call Sign: KA7PFH
Paul E Zummach
71116 SW Douglas Dr
Pendleton OR 97801

Call Sign: N7FRO
Audrey A Zummach
10943 SW Dover Ct
Pendleton OR 97801

Call Sign: KC7N
Rudy R Rittenbach
5220 SW Dover Ln
Pendleton OR 978019449

Call Sign: N7DGX
Patricia K Rittenbach
5482 SW Dover Ln
Pendleton OR 978019449

Call Sign: N7XYU
Wendy R Harris
9455 SW Downing Dr Apt 3
Pendleton OR 978019449

Call Sign: N7ZUA
Rory V Rittenbach
9455 SW Downing Dr Apt 4
Pendleton OR 978019449

Call Sign: W7FPT
James W Bostwick
159 SW Florence 57
Pendleton OR 97801

Call Sign: KD7EPZ
Robert L Perry
12045 SW Fulmar Ter
Pendleton OR 97801

Call Sign: N7PIH
Thomas W James
1060 SW Goucher St

Pendleton OR 97801

Call Sign: KY6E
William I Tapley Jr
1679 SW Goucher St
Pendleton OR 97801

Call Sign: KA7LXE
Dale W Bacus
8820 SW Grabhorn Rd
Pendleton OR 97801

Call Sign: KC7SN
Bryce F Newell
3110 SW Grace Ln
Pendleton OR 97801

Call Sign: KD7HXQ
Andrew M Crowder
3110 SW Grace Ln
Pendleton OR 97801

Call Sign: KD7IPD
Seth T Keele
13778 SW Halcyon Ter
Pendleton OR 97801

Call Sign: KB7VFX
Gary R Porter
13778 SW Halcyon Ter
Pendleton OR 97801

Call Sign: N7JDH
Leland R Quinn
9625 SW Jacktown Rd
Pendleton OR 978012953

Call Sign: KD7RVE
Jon C Mittelstadt
3752 SW Lake Dr
Pendleton OR 97801

Call Sign: WA7SWB
David L Senter
32153 SW Lake Dr

Pendleton OR 978019577

Call Sign: N7KMK
Jeffrey W Wood
71581 SW Lake Dr
Pendleton OR 97801

Call Sign: W7NO
David L Senter
32550 SW Lake Point Ct
Pendleton OR 97801

Call Sign: W7SWB
David L Senter
32660 SW Lake Point Ct
Pendleton OR 97801

Call Sign: KL7DI
Daniel I Mahlum
4618 SW Martha
Pendleton OR 97801

Call Sign: AB7OC
Michael E Califf Sr
4618 SW Martha
Pendleton OR 978014153

Call Sign: N7UAR
Zach R Zeckman
5211 SW Martha St
Pendleton OR 97801

Call Sign: N7ZPE
Chuck F Heath
365 SW Meadow Dr
Pendleton OR 97801

Call Sign: N7IHW
Kreg N Hawkins
39225 SW Oak Ln
Pendleton OR 97801

Call Sign: KD7KFB
Richard D Wilson
428 SW Oak St

Pendleton OR 97801

Call Sign: KE4TRR
Alan L Polan
1343 SW Orchard Ave
Pendleton OR 978014422

Call Sign: KE7LOI
Mark J Adelman
4518 SW Perkins Ave
Pendleton OR 97801

Call Sign: KB4EN
James E Murry III
4518 SW Perkins Ave
Pendleton OR 97801

Call Sign: W0OX
James E Murry III
6357 SW Peston Rd
Pendleton OR 97801

Call Sign: W7BX
James E Murry III
6356 SW Peyton Rd
Pendleton OR 97801

Call Sign: KD7BDA
Gary S Birch
3195 SW Raleighview Dr
Pendleton OR 97801

Call Sign: KB7ZNR
Winifred L Burnett
752 SW Riverview Pl
Pendleton OR 97801

Call Sign: WB7RDO
Randy T Burnett
10318 SW Riverwood Ln
Pendleton OR 97801

Call Sign: KA7QBR
Thomas A Bostwick

28008 SW Vanderschuere
Rd
Pendleton OR 97801

Call Sign: KD7MUR
Cheryl L Davis
45346 Trail Dr
Pendleton OR 97801

Call Sign: KC7URF
Jack L Davis
45346 Trail Dr
Pendleton OR 97801

Call Sign: KE7DWG
Keenan Davis
10140 Trask River Rd
Pendleton OR 97801

Call Sign: KE7DWH
Kyra J Davis
27650 Trask River Rd
Pendleton OR 97801

Call Sign: N7FPU
La Vonna R Griffin
42184 Tweedle Ln
Pendleton OR 97801

Call Sign: N7FPV
Delbert V Griffin
42223 Tweedle Ln
Pendleton OR 97801

Call Sign: KB7VFT
Otto B Broker
Pendleton OR 97801

Call Sign: KB7TLY
Clinton E Thompson
Pendleton OR 97801

Call Sign: N7YQJ
Donald I Morris
Pendleton OR 97801

Call Sign: KB7SSP
Robert W Bonner
Pendleton OR 97801

Call Sign: W7RK
Harris Jr Academy ARC
Pendleton OR 97801

Call Sign: KA7TXG
Mel S Zinberg
Pendleton OR 97801

Call Sign: KB7AOQ
Michael C Critchlow
Pendleton OR 97801

Call Sign: KB7HDL
Kathy R Zeckman
Pendleton OR 97801

Call Sign: KC7FYU
James J Clark
Pendleton OR 97801

Call Sign: KC7WZX
David L Messer
Pendleton OR 97801

Call Sign: N7XZB
Dave F Worden
Pendleton OR 97801

Call Sign: WA7HJV
Jack R Zeckman Jr
Pendleton OR 97801

Call Sign: WB7OJC
Harris Jr Academy ARC
Pendleton OR 97801

Call Sign: WB7WEQ
Normand E Marks
Pendleton OR 97801

Call Sign: KF7LPN
Andrew T Hendrickson
Pendleton OR 97801

Call Sign: KF7LPO
Clifford D Hendrickson
Pendleton OR 97801

Call Sign: KD5ZEA
Johnny L Blagg
Pendleton OR 97801

Call Sign: KE7VNS
Joy L Kelley
Pendleton OR 97801

Call Sign: KD7ZCL
Tony R Marshall
Pendleton OR 97801

Call Sign: KF7GGC
Vincent P Papol
Pendleton OR 97801

Call Sign: KI7AK
Frank E Lassen
Pendleton OR 97801

Call Sign: AA7ER
Russell A Kelley
Pendleton OR 978010084

**FCC Amateur Radio
Licenses in Phoenix**

Call Sign: KA7OKN
Edward R Beeson
2749 Altemont Dr
Phoenix OR 97535

Call Sign: KF7UMR
Alan D Mitchell
31811 Belgium Ct
Phoenix OR 97535

Call Sign: WB7VUF
Lyle E Hood
1700 Bunker Hill Rd S
Phoenix OR 97535

Call Sign: KD7BCS
Chris K Novara
2600 Cape Meares Loop
NW
Phoenix OR 97535

Call Sign: KD7RYL
Susie A Novara
841 Capital Ln
Phoenix OR 97535

Call Sign: KD7SDA
John G Novara
841 Capital Ln
Phoenix OR 97535

Call Sign: W6VA
Walter A Lund Sr
63438 Capitol Dr
Phoenix OR 97535

Call Sign: KA6ZSX
Steve L Hay Jr
2801 Davidson St SE
Phoenix OR 97535

Call Sign: KF7UMI
Gene R Griffith
24465 Gellatly Way
Phoenix OR 97535

Call Sign: KC5IY
Mario F Signorelli
2526 Greentree Dr NE
Phoenix OR 97535

Call Sign: K7BBS
David A Katz
24824 Hwy 395 S
Phoenix OR 97535

Call Sign: KE7BBS
David A Katz
45468 Hwy 402
Phoenix OR 97535

Call Sign: KE7INS
Jackson County ARES
80542 Kik Rd
Phoenix OR 97535

Call Sign: K7GE
Randy P Miltier
80542 Kik Rd
Phoenix OR 97535

Call Sign: K7RPM
Randy P Miltier
80542 Kik Rd
Phoenix OR 97535

Call Sign: KB7COW
L Daniel Bulkley
85510 McCumber Rd
Phoenix OR 97535

Call Sign: KF6CXM
Susanne K Manley
85510 McCumber Rd
Phoenix OR 97535

Call Sign: KA0DFN
Calvin J Burt
85510 McCumber Rd
Phoenix OR 97535

Call Sign: KB7NHV
Raymond Battey Jr
64595 McDermott Rd
Phoenix OR 97535

Call Sign: KE7ORL
Christopher P Cahill
54092 Morrison Rd
Phoenix OR 97535

Call Sign: KA7PKA
Ruth F Wade
35242 S Ferwood Ln
Phoenix OR 97535

Call Sign: N7ZCF
Robert F Wade
11625 S Finnegans Way
Phoenix OR 97535

Call Sign: N7DIR
William V Kidson
333 S State St 299
Phoenix OR 97535

Call Sign: N6NY
Earl P Olsen
800 S State St 36
Phoenix OR 975359622

Call Sign: KD7JQQ
John J Daly
2841 Schafer Ln SE
Phoenix OR 97535

Call Sign: AA2XL
David A Tinney
17757 Schalit Way
Phoenix OR 97535

Call Sign: WA7NY
David A Tinney
17757 Schalit Way
Phoenix OR 97535

Call Sign: KD6NSN
David L Blackman
307 W 2nd St
Phoenix OR 975357733

Call Sign: KB7PPF
Connie L Statchwick
Phoenix OR 97535

Call Sign: KB7VQX
David E L Goodnature
Phoenix OR 97535

Call Sign: N7SLM
Donald L Rendahl
Phoenix OR 97535

Call Sign: WB7QVG
Leander F Wade
Phoenix OR 97535

Call Sign: KB7VFO
Catherine L Fipps
Phoenix OR 97535

Call Sign: KB7VFP
Ronald G Fipps
Phoenix OR 97535

Call Sign: KE7WTJ
Micah T Maeda
Phoenix OR 97535

FCC Amateur Radio Licenses in Pilot Rock

Call Sign: KD7FAU
Jon F Mitchell
135 NE 8th St
Pilot Rock OR 97868

Call Sign: KD7KMI
Jack R Mann
3746 NE Holman St
Pilot Rock OR 97868

Call Sign: KD7YOR
Sheila R Holman
275 SW Central Ave
Pilot Rock OR 97868

Call Sign: KB5CDX
Brett E Mueller
Pilot Rock OR 97868

Call Sign: KB7DNH
Glen A Engen
Pilot Rock OR 97868

Call Sign: KB7DPS
Trudi M Engen
Pilot Rock OR 97868

Call Sign: KD7FJB
David L Baird
Pilot Rock OR 97868

Call Sign: N0XVK
Charlyn R Mueller
Pilot Rock OR 97868

Call Sign: KD7NDM
Troy Holman
Pilot Rock OR 97868

Call Sign: KE7LZK
James A Smith
Pilot Rock OR 97868

FCC Amateur Radio Licenses in Pistol River

Call Sign: KD7EXB
Joseph M Martin
Pistol River OR 97444

FCC Amateur Radio Licenses in Pleasant Hill

Call Sign: W7GIL
Charles L Deeming
1468 Fetters Loop
Pleasant Hill OR 97455

Call Sign: KD7RG
James R Green
26916 Hwy 36 16
Pleasant Hill OR 97455

Call Sign: N7WME
Richard F Ries
19542 Jack Ln SE
Pleasant Hill OR 97455

Call Sign: N7HVL
Claudia S Hardwick
25821 Jeans Rd
Pleasant Hill OR 97455

Call Sign: WB7SMF
Lyle J Payne
2116 Kimberly Dr
Pleasant Hill OR 97455

Call Sign: N8FGS
Mary C Ford
107 Kimberly Way
Pleasant Hill OR 97455

Call Sign: W8QR
James A Ford
115 Kimeron St SE
Pleasant Hill OR 97455

Call Sign: W7TWC
Thomas W Christian
1780 Periwinkle Cir
Pleasant Hill OR 97455

Call Sign: KB7DHI
James H Holman
594 Stanton Blvd
Pleasant Hill OR 97455

Call Sign: KD6KZM
Kathy L Ratiu Kelley
35886 Willama Vista St
Pleasant Hill OR 97455

Call Sign: N6ZOC
Michael S Kelley
35886 Willama Vista St
Pleasant Hill OR 97455

Call Sign: W7CN
Michael S Kelley
35886 Willama Vista St
Pleasant Hill OR 97455

Call Sign: KE7AIY
Raina A Kelley
35886 Willama Vista St
Pleasant Hill OR 97455

Call Sign: N7RVX
Leo M Hall
Pleasant Hill OR 97455

Call Sign: KA7FXX
James E Patterson Sr
Pleasant Hill OR 97455

Call Sign: KD7MTM
Jeremy B Stahl
Pleasant Hill OR 97455

FCC Amateur Radio Licenses in Port Orford

Call Sign: N6OYR
Gerald L Steinhorst
33570 Bellinger Scale Rd
Port Orford OR 97465

Call Sign: N7YBI
Levi E Easlon
33570 Bellinger Scale Rd
Port Orford OR 97465

Call Sign: N7YBJ
Levi E Easlon
4751 Bellm Dr 111
Port Orford OR 97465

Call Sign: KB6UFU
John E Cervini
1012 Bellview Ave
Port Orford OR 97465

Call Sign: N6UCA
Louise E Langenbach
33470 Chinook Plz 335
Port Orford OR 974650429

Call Sign: N6UCD
Jack Langenbach
806 Chinook St
Port Orford OR 974650429

Call Sign: N7PYJ
Robert E Dailey
Elk River Rd
Port Orford OR 97465

Call Sign: KC7HVM
Harry R Bryant Jr
35136 Kings Valley Hwy
Port Orford OR 97465

Call Sign: KD7KAY
Gayanne C Bryant
36418 Kings Valley Hwy
Port Orford OR 97465

Call Sign: KD7KKN
Carron N Bryant
309 Kingsbury Ave
Port Orford OR 97465

Call Sign: KD7MSL
Lavaughn A Merryman
1920 Myrtle St
Port Orford OR 97465

Call Sign: AC7AD
Eddy L Mc Kinnis
135 Park Village Loop
Port Orford OR 97465

Call Sign: KA7TAW
Dale E Lee
35350 Skogan Rd
Port Orford OR 97465

Call Sign: KB7HNK
Daniel A Ells
Port Orford OR 97465

Call Sign: KF7JNC
Port Orford ARC
Port Orford OR 97465

Call Sign: K7POH
Port Orford ARC
Port Orford OR 97465

Call Sign: AA7FB
Valerie J Kramer
Port Orford OR 97465

Call Sign: K6QQS
Mary Lou Hill
Port Orford OR 97465

Call Sign: KC6UMK
Reggie B Wills
Port Orford OR 97465

Call Sign: WA7FGR
David G Mosses
Port Orford OR 97465

Call Sign: KF7OBD
Beverly A Hawk
Port Orford OR 97465

Call Sign: KZ7HWK
Beverly A Hawk
Port Orford OR 97465

Call Sign: KF7LSQ
Denise K Anderson
Port Orford OR 97465

Call Sign: KF7MWY
Jeffery L Glemser
Port Orford OR 97465

Call Sign: KE7FXM

Jim D Wills Jr
Port Orford OR 97465

Call Sign: KF7KWQ
Katherine R Kelly
Port Orford OR 97465

Call Sign: KF7OOB
Nancy K Glemser
Port Orford OR 97465

Call Sign: KF7LSP
Robert L Mielenz
Port Orford OR 97465

Call Sign: W7FML
Berkeley Brandt Jr
Port Orford OR 97465

Call Sign: N7BBQ
Rachel P Brandt
Port Orford OR 97465

Call Sign: KC6VLD
Duane E Byers
Port Orford OR 97465

Call Sign: KJ7CW
Dorman H Jacobsen
Port Orford OR 974651054

Call Sign: WW7CAT
Dorman H Jacobsen
Port Orford OR 974651054

Call Sign: KF7KWP
Chane L Fullmer
Port Orford OR 974651349

FCC Amateur Radio Licenses in Powell Butte

Call Sign: N7VMJ
Patricia B Burrell
1794 Cal Young Rd 226

Powell Butte OR 97753

Call Sign: KD6XD
Raffi G Simon
396 Calice St NW
Powell Butte OR 97753

Call Sign: KB7RFL
Dennis R Duff
3201 Campus Dr Oit
Powell Butte OR 97753

Call Sign: K7LOB
Donald L Hanna
2420 S Tudor Way
Powell Butte OR
977531563

Call Sign: KA7OZD
William A Marshall
1138 S Water
Powell Butte OR 97753

Call Sign: KC7LPN
Donald R Dunbar
6864 SW Alden St
Powell Butte OR 97753

Call Sign: WB6WEQ
Thomas H Barnes
2470 SW Binford Pl
Powell Butte OR 97753

Call Sign: KE7BHQ
Thomas E Weeks
21294 SW Makan Ct
Powell Butte OR 97753

Call Sign: KF7MUH
Joel W Camicia
2665 SW Mt Baker St
Powell Butte OR 97753

Call Sign: KF7OUD
H Curtiss Burrell

62 SW Parvenu Pl
Powell Butte OR 97753

Call Sign: WD6BQV
Arthur N Henke Jr
19425 SW Pomona Dr
Powell Butte OR 97753

Call Sign: W7BQV
Arthur N Henke Jr
19425 SW Ponoma Dr
Powell Butte OR 97753

Call Sign: KC7MZG
Scott C Granger
31990 SW Unger Rd
Powell Butte OR 97753

Call Sign: KL7NH
Ellwood T Hackman
Powell Butte OR 97753

Call Sign: KC7GQR
Melinda S Eder
Powell Butte OR 97753

FCC Amateur Radio Licenses in Powers

Call Sign: KF6PKF
Lawrence A Northup
691 Anderson Ln
Powers OR 97466

Call Sign: KF7PPM
Lajuana J Baldwin
Powers OR 97466

Call Sign: KD7TAH
Ronald E Allen
Powers OR 97466

FCC Amateur Radio Licenses in Prairie City

Call Sign: AL7LL
Samuel W Kyriss
407 Carthage Ave
Prairie City OR 978690863

Call Sign: KC7PAX
Gary J Reigel
3115 Hillcrest Rd N
Prairie City OR 97869

Call Sign: N7HTN
Gary J Reigel
3305 Hillcrest Way
Prairie City OR 97869

Call Sign: N9RKZ
Juan T Vargas
Prairie City OR 97869

FCC Amateur Radio Licenses in Princeton

Call Sign: KV7L
Lynn D Apperson
6575 E St
Princeton OR 97721

Call Sign: WB7QKV
Thurston D Inglis
4545 Lower Klamath Lake
Rd
Princeton OR 97721

Call Sign: KF7JDS
Erna E Watts
240 S 1st Ave
Princeton OR 97721

Call Sign: KF7CIK
David P Watts
240 S 1st Ave
Princeton OR 97721

FCC Amateur Radio Licenses in Prineville

Call Sign: KC7PYC
Kenneth H Kuehn
1410 34th Ave SE
Prineville OR 97754

Call Sign: KD7VPC
David S Dethlefsen
17061 Crestview Dr
Prineville OR 97754

Call Sign: KB7SHS
James R Allison III
2196 Davis Rd S
Prineville OR 97754

Call Sign: N6URT
Robert L Howell
35227 E Lacomb Rd
Prineville OR 97754

Call Sign: K7EJY
Alvin G Jones
1605 Johnson Dr
Prineville OR 97754

Call Sign: KD7AKK
Elsie S Jones
63560 Johnson Ranch
Prineville OR 97754

Call Sign: KB7MRP
Walter L Matthews
39580 Lacomb Dr
Prineville OR 97754

Call Sign: N7AMS
Thomas L Wilson
830 N Main St Sp 43
Prineville OR 97754

Call Sign: N7OOF
Patricia A Petrusse
41980 N River Dr
Prineville OR 977549118

Call Sign: KA7HAM
Gene A Kimzey
525 N Santiam Hwy
Prineville OR 977540235

Call Sign: KA7LMC
Elvira E Kimzey
525 N Santiam Hwy
Prineville OR 977540235

Call Sign: KE7CXR
Gerry A Beard
6600 NE 78th Ct A3 10407
Prineville OR 97754

Call Sign: KF7AQA
Brandi L Lange
757 NE Baldwin Dr
Prineville OR 97754

Call Sign: KE7ZLR
John G Ayala
498 NE Fircrest Pl
Prineville OR 97754

Call Sign: KF7ELY
Carroll R Tracy
251 NE Ginseng Dr
Prineville OR 97754

Call Sign: KE7CXP
Elizabeth M Hamlin
2870 NE Hogan Rd E 150
Prineville OR 97754

Call Sign: KE7BLO
Betty L Welch
3102 NE Rocky Butte Rd
Prineville OR 97754

Call Sign: KE7BLP
Robert A Welch
3111 NE Rocky Butte Rd
Prineville OR 97754

Call Sign: AD7ML
Robert A Welch
1543 NE Rocky Ridge Dr
Prineville OR 97754

Call Sign: KB7CBS
Donald R Petrusse
1733 NE Rosewood Dr
Prineville OR 97754

Call Sign: KF7OUG
Chrissie M Wise
8716 NE Russell St
Prineville OR 97754

Call Sign: KF7OUI
David A Wise
12031 NE Russell St
Prineville OR 97754

Call Sign: KF7CVF
William R Gowen
2990 NE Saber Dr
Prineville OR 97754

Call Sign: K7WRG
William R Gowen
5727 NE Sacramento St
Prineville OR 977549100

Call Sign: KL7JKV
Dr David D Anderson
108 NE Sherman St
Prineville OR 97754

Call Sign: WA6CBV
Michael D Milliron
15846 NE Thompson Ct
Prineville OR 97754

Call Sign: KE7OQT
Darrell R Antram
23886 NE Treehill Dr
Prineville OR 97754

Call Sign: KF7APX
Benita Y Fall
2669 NE Twinknolls Dr 109
Prineville OR 97754

Call Sign: KF7APW
Carter L Fall
845 NE Victoria St 20
Prineville OR 97754

Call Sign: KE7CPL
Volker A Baensch
Pmb 1224 NE Walnut St
337
Prineville OR 97754

Call Sign: KE7EML
Michael C Redhead
2643 NE Wintergreen Dr
Prineville OR 97754

Call Sign: WE7EZ
Michael C Redhead
2643 NE Wintergreen Dr
Prineville OR 97754

Call Sign: KE7EMM
Edna C Redhead
5140 NE Wistaria Dr
Prineville OR 97754

Call Sign: N7GW
Glen P Winkler
4935 Netarts Hwy W
Prineville OR 977549211

Call Sign: W7KFO
David B Freitag
20566 New Bedford Cir
Prineville OR 97754

Call Sign: WB7EOC
Gary L Spencer
2577 New Hope Rd

Prineville OR 97754

Call Sign: KF7CVH
Mark E Grimes
1260 NW Kline Pl
Prineville OR 97754

Call Sign: KC7EFX
Julie A Garner
496 NW Lava B
Prineville OR 97754

Call Sign: W7HBA
Everett G Mc Bee
3235 NW Metke Pl
Prineville OR 97754

Call Sign: KF7BFK
Terry L Moore
6385 NW Oelrich Rd
Prineville OR 97754

Call Sign: KF7APZ
Brandon L Smith
2329 NW Pettygrove St
Prineville OR 97754

Call Sign: WA7RGS
Lee D Romine
2250 NW Phillips Rd
Prineville OR 97754

Call Sign: KF7APY
Mike A Owen
19766 NW Phillips Rd
Prineville OR 97754

Call Sign: N7NXP
Philip A Rapp
25490 NW Pumpkin Ridge
Rd
Prineville OR 97754

Call Sign: KD7EQS
Bennie L Hayes

1600 NW Putnam Rd
Prineville OR 97754

Call Sign: WA7BTW
Arnold L Stegner
8010 NW Siskin Dr
Prineville OR 97754

Call Sign: WA7JNS
Arlene G Stegner
5421 NW Skycrest Pkwy
Prineville OR 97754

Call Sign: KC7IHO
Melvin A Berthold
1575 NW Skyline Dr
Prineville OR 97754

Call Sign: KE7HKB
John C Jackson
8275 NW Starview Dr
Prineville OR 97754

Call Sign: KD7MJZ
Larry S Stowell
17674 NW Sue Ct
Prineville OR 977547716

Call Sign: KF7APR
Beckie L Griffith
3930 NW Witham Hill Dr
Apt 207
Prineville OR 97754

Call Sign: KF7APS
Jeff G Griffith
3930 NW Witham Hill Dr
J87
Prineville OR 97754

Call Sign: KA7HHG
Arthur Bigelow
4749 NW Woodside Terr
Prineville OR 97754

Call Sign: K7LUV
Lois D Barth
889 Oakdale Ave 138
Prineville OR 97754

Call Sign: W7GG
Dennis R Barth
263 Oakdale Dr
Prineville OR 97754

Call Sign: KB7SHT
Jim M Burge
15662 Oakdale Rd
Prineville OR 97754

Call Sign: KF7AQF
David G Pepper
17234 Oakdale Rd
Prineville OR 97754

Call Sign: N6EAL
Lonnie G Neal
21655 Obsidian Ave
Prineville OR 97754

Call Sign: N7OTJ
William R Clemens
4110 Pearl St
Prineville OR 97754

Call Sign: KB7QNN
Donald E Barber
805 Pinecrest Terr
Prineville OR 97754

Call Sign: NP4GQ
Daniel Gonzalez
1525 S Ivy St
Prineville OR 97754

Call Sign: N7CVE
Carmen A Fones
22208 S Parrot Crk
Prineville OR 97754

Call Sign: KF7RQD
Ronald R Ward
1617 SE 51 Ave
Prineville OR 97754

Call Sign: N7VMF
Robert L Ueland Sr
6640 SE Austin Dr
Prineville OR 97754

Call Sign: W7GLG
Hector R Guevara
14465 SE Bevington Ct
Prineville OR 97754

Call Sign: KE7ZNS
Dennis J Hedden
18850 SE Caruthers St
Prineville OR 97754

Call Sign: W7DJH
Dennis J Hedden
2114 SE Caruthers St Apt
11
Prineville OR 97754

Call Sign: WA7CVC
Eldon D Nimmo
3612 SE Conrad Ct
Prineville OR 97754

Call Sign: KF7GUP
Jimmy L Spegel Jr
1112 SE Emigrant
Prineville OR 97754

Call Sign: KF7AQE
Louis E Haehnlen
43737 SE Erin Ln
Prineville OR 97754

Call Sign: WB7DWD
Robert V Andrews
2209 SE Evans Ave
Prineville OR 97754

Call Sign: KB7TUZ
Charles E Rhodes
2223 SE Evans Ave
Prineville OR 97754

Call Sign: KF7AQD
Raymond C Lee
2645 SE Evans Ave
Prineville OR 97754

Call Sign: KF7AQC
Kim G Kichenmaster
502 SE Evans Ln
Prineville OR 97754

Call Sign: KF7AQB
Tj Kichenmaster
1282 SE Evans Loop
Prineville OR 97754

Call Sign: W7TAM
Theodore A Macarthur
5408 SE Harold St
Prineville OR 97754

Call Sign: KF7APV
Jo Mullis
86 SE Jones St
Prineville OR 97754

Call Sign: KE7BLN
Mark E Stevenson
61394 SE King Jehu Way
Prineville OR 97754

Call Sign: KF7TEZ
John A Thurman
7455 SE King Rd 17
Prineville OR 97754

Call Sign: N5IME
Steven L Bates
15254 SE La Marquita Way
Prineville OR 97754

Call Sign: KD7NYQ
Andrew R Jackman
15111 SE Lee Ave
Prineville OR 97754

Call Sign: N7LTP
Rose M Carlson
6206 SE Lincoln
Prineville OR 97754

Call Sign: KF7OMP
Bryon L Wilcox
15100 SE Monner Rd
Prineville OR 97754

Call Sign: KD7QWS
Donald R Chaffee
9648 SE Ramona St
Prineville OR 97754

Call Sign: KF7APT
Lynda M Massingham
9648 SE Ramona St
Prineville OR 97754

Call Sign: KF7APU
Thomas C Massingham
5769 SE Rancho St
Prineville OR 97754

Call Sign: KC7EXX
Pat D Mc Lain
15021 SE Robinette Ct
Prineville OR 97754

Call Sign: KC7PYH
Arthur L Rowe
14647 SE Sterling Ct
Prineville OR 97754

Call Sign: WA7VLM
Ricky L Wright
11341 SE Stevens Rd
Prineville OR 97754

Call Sign: KF7CVG
Sherry M Bouris
10858 SE Valley Way
Prineville OR 97754

Call Sign: K7JZZ
Sherry M Bouris
23163 SE Van Curen Rd
Prineville OR 97754

Call Sign: KF7BFO
Devan L Koehn
9105 SE Velma Ct
Prineville OR 97754

Call Sign: N7VC
Dennis R Barth
15967 SE Webster Rd
Prineville OR 97754

Call Sign: WB7AYE
James W Scott
31375 SE Wildcat Mtn Dr
Prineville OR 97754

Call Sign: KF7CVE
Karen L Yeargain
11193 SW Gilbert Creek Rd
Prineville OR 97754

Call Sign: NR7Y
Clinton C Carlson
7256 SW Nevada Ter
Prineville OR 97754

Call Sign: KD7YPE
William F Selfe
3001 Walnut Ln SE
Prineville OR 97754

Call Sign: N7OBL
Joseph P Azenara
Prineville OR 97754

Call Sign: N7ZUM
Mark E Berry
Prineville OR 97754

Call Sign: WB7CPO
Robert R Goodrich
Prineville OR 97754

Call Sign: KA7KPL
Mark V Loiler
Prineville OR 97754

Call Sign: KD7NVM
James A Wilson
Prineville OR 97754

Call Sign: KD7QWR
Gerald J Dennis
Prineville OR 97754

Call Sign: KF7RQC
Craig A Brookhart
Prineville OR 97754

Call Sign: KE7UCF
James G Mcpherren
Prineville OR 97754

Call Sign: W7MVV
Joseph P Azenara
Prineville OR 97754

Call Sign: KE7CXT
Karen L Nielsen
Prineville OR 97754

Call Sign: KD7UNP
Robert F Orlando
Prineville OR 97754

Call Sign: KF7SMZ
Ron G Cholin
Prineville OR 97754

Call Sign: KD7UNQ

Ronnell S Kurth
Prineville OR 97754

FCC Amateur Radio Licenses in Prospect

Call Sign: KC7PYD
Robert N Mc Laughlin
29501 Myrtle Ln
Prospect OR 97536

Call Sign: WB7EHU
Russell C Albee
960 Riessen Rd
Prospect OR 975369719

Call Sign: WA6WGD
Garrison D Wilson
Prospect OR 97536

Call Sign: WA6WNT
Carol L Wilson
Prospect OR 97536

Call Sign: KD7LEL
Nathan J Overbey
Prospect OR 97536

FCC Amateur Radio Licenses in Redmond

Call Sign: KC7HJC
Ezekiel W Currier
1536 45th Ave NE
Redmond OR 97756

Call Sign: KD7EQW
Nora L Currier
4382 45th Ave NE
Redmond OR 97756

Call Sign: KD7EQX
Leslie T Currier
564 45th Pl SE
Redmond OR 97756

Call Sign: N7BWI
Jean W Reed
255 46th Ave SE
Redmond OR 97756

Call Sign: KD7ILO
Gregory T Bone
473 48th St
Redmond OR 97756

Call Sign: NT7N
Donald L Hendrix
545 4th Ave
Redmond OR 97756

Call Sign: KC7JOW
William G Lareau
1107 4th St
Redmond OR 97756

Call Sign: KC7HJD
Allan W Hilgers
73960 Blok Ln
Redmond OR 97756

Call Sign: KC7PYM
Jason R Roley
221 Glenwood Dr
Redmond OR 97756

Call Sign: KC7LPO
Raymond C Roley
221 Glenwood Dr
Redmond OR 97756

Call Sign: WA7ZCB
John C Blunt
2208 Laurel St
Redmond OR 97756

Call Sign: KD6PPG
Barbara J Collins
71868 London Wey Rd
Redmond OR 977569277

Call Sign: K7WTZ
Frank H Kline
2015 Manorview Cir NW
Redmond OR 977567302

Call Sign: N6DQX
Michael A Byrum
7403 Maple Ln
Redmond OR 97756

Call Sign: K7PMW
Roger L Hebert
773 N Egan Ave
Redmond OR 97756

Call Sign: N7VMA
Joshua D Barnet
232 N T St
Redmond OR 97756

Call Sign: KA7SUG
Marilyn L Fullman
818 NE 153rd Ave
Redmond OR 97756

Call Sign: N7HSJ
Harold E Fullman
818 NE 153rd Ave
Redmond OR 97756

Call Sign: K7PEK
Wayne E Linschied
1625 NE 153rd Pl
Redmond OR 977560521

Call Sign: N7VOK
Earl Thompson
1724 NE 2nd Ave
Redmond OR 97756

Call Sign: KC7PYP
Todd C Lafontaine
607 NE 35th St
Redmond OR 97756

Call Sign: KB7SHR
Nick V Kezele
1700 NE 60th
Redmond OR 97756

Call Sign: KE7TMP
Susan Ferns
1324 NE Barnes Ct
Redmond OR 97756

Call Sign: KE7WDE
Tim Gorman
5710 NE Ochoco Hwy
Redmond OR 97756

Call Sign: KQ7R
Richard E Lovin
1292 NE Setting Sun Dr
Redmond OR 97756

Call Sign: KE7BHP
Dan D Swearingen
10334 NE Shaver St
Redmond OR 97704

Call Sign: W7ICY
Dan D Swearingen
13171 NE Shaver St
Redmond OR 97704

Call Sign: KD7ILT
Lyle W Linschied
1725 NE Shepard Rd
Redmond OR 97756

Call Sign: KO6EP
Everett V Johnson
876 Niagara Falls Dr
Redmond OR 97756

Call Sign: W7BLA
Steve C Holmes
505 NW 185th Ave
Redmond OR 97756

Call Sign: KA7YCQ
Richard J Fassett
739 NW 20 Th St
Redmond OR 97756

Call Sign: KL0YE
Travis J Garnick
1285 NW 20th Ave
Redmond OR 97756

Call Sign: KB7OOQ
Brian L Fassett
1420 NW 20th Ave 501
Redmond OR 97756

Call Sign: KD7EQK
Matthew S Simmons
2178 NW 25th Pl
Redmond OR 977561113

Call Sign: W7GER
Andrew Holmes Jr
729 NW 2nd St
Redmond OR 97756

Call Sign: K7KCC
Kathy E Swensen
835 NW 2nd St
Redmond OR 97756

Call Sign: KC7MRL
Daniel J Drayton
65151 NW 78th St
Redmond OR 97756

Call Sign: KE7CQV
Jeffrey C Anderson
1186 NW 8th St
Redmond OR 97756

Call Sign: W7CCV
Jeffrey C Anderson
1805 NW 8th St
Redmond OR 97756

Call Sign: W7ZSL
Wallace D Young
375 NW 95th
Redmond OR 97756

Call Sign: WA7LEG
Elizabeth A Young
205 NW 95th Ave
Redmond OR 97756

Call Sign: KE7CQW
Kent A Johnson
333 NW 9th Ave Apt 913
Redmond OR 97756

Call Sign: WB6AGE
Robert L Cosentino
1670 NW Arthur Cir
Redmond OR 97756

Call Sign: KB7WCY
Jerry L Johnson
2421 NW Ava Ave
Redmond OR 97756

Call Sign: N7QOA
Meridith A Johnson
17965 NW Avalon Dr
Redmond OR 97756

Call Sign: KD7ERJ
Mary C Williams
10308 NW Barclay Ter
Redmond OR 97756

Call Sign: KC7CWQ
Loren C Rasmussen
1597 NW Bella Vista Ct
Redmond OR 97756

Call Sign: K7CWQ
Loren C Rasmussen
510 NW Bella Vista Dr
Redmond OR 97756

Call Sign: WA7UHC
William M Day
41744 NW Bellingham Ct
Redmond OR 97756

Call Sign: KE7TPP
Jeffery W Cannon
18205 NW Bronson Apt M4
Redmond OR 97756

Call Sign: KE7TPO
Zach A Cannon
2180 NW Brownly Heights
Dr
Redmond OR 97756

Call Sign: WB7AUS
Charles E Kenshol
41745 NW Buckshire St
Redmond OR 97756

Call Sign: KC7MIC
Jan P Anderson
31380 NW Buxton Lookout
Rd
Redmond OR 977568220

Call Sign: KC7PDK
Betty G Warrington
787 NW Canal Blvd Apt
106
Redmond OR 97756

Call Sign: KF7CCX
Jim E Erickson
1530 NW Canyon Dr
Redmond OR 97756

Call Sign: KA0RCE
Janet M Lakin
18317 NW Chemeketa Ln
Apt D
Redmond OR 97756

Call Sign: KA0RCF
Kristy A Lakin
1462 NW Cherry Dr
Redmond OR 97756

Call Sign: KD6B
Kenneth M Lakin
22855 NW Chestnut St
Redmond OR 97756

Call Sign: KE7EJX
Kristyn L Dodge
22855 NW Chestnut St
Redmond OR 97756

Call Sign: KE6GKC
Bruce J Burgess
17565 NW Country Dr
Redmond OR 97756

Call Sign: KE7BE
Wendell A Elspas
9033 NW Dick Rd
Redmond OR 97756

Call Sign: KF7SXI
Connie D Gentis
9033 NW Dick Rd
Redmond OR 97756

Call Sign: KB7KLU
Nancy E Williams
9033 NW Dick Rd
Redmond OR 97756

Call Sign: KE7TMW
Judith D Godfrey
24200 NW Dierdorff Rd
Redmond OR 97756

Call Sign: KF7BFN
Michael H Bouvia
2266 NW Dogwood Ln
Redmond OR 97756

Call Sign: K7YRU
George W Murphy
5757N NW Galloway Ln
Redmond OR 97756

Call Sign: N7HNH
James R Speakman
14855 NW Hunters Dr
Redmond OR 97756

Call Sign: N7YSG
Harold R Diehl
2188 NW Maser Pl
Redmond OR 97756

Call Sign: KD7TRI
Steven J Schenck
9911 NW Murlea Dr
Redmond OR 97756

Call Sign: K6ANN
Harry R Collins
822 NW Murray Blvd 127
Redmond OR 977569277

Call Sign: KC7VGW
Michael P Schuch
822 NW Murray Blvd 155
Redmond OR 97756

Call Sign: KC7OTM
Edwin J Long
1445 NW Porland Ave
Redmond OR 977569392

Call Sign: AK7W
Edwin J Long
1247 NW Portland Ave
Redmond OR 977569392

Call Sign: WA7SNY
Richard A Perkins
2845 NW Post
Redmond OR 97756

Call Sign: AA7IJ
Phyllis A Long
3008 NW Povey Ave
Redmond OR 97756

Call Sign: AK7W
John E Long
4207 NW Powers Ave
Redmond OR 97756

Call Sign: WA7YDH
Harold E Majxner
10820 NW Rainmont Rd
Redmond OR 97756

Call Sign: KB7FAH
William J Kelley
2810 NW Savier
Redmond OR 97756

Call Sign: KD7SKQ
Wayne A Bessett
2351 NW Westover Rd
1105
Redmond OR 97756

Call Sign: KJ6CPL
John M Sand
2221 Oak 334
Redmond OR 97756

Call Sign: KD7ZIR
Darin R Hollingsworth
65 Oak Ct
Redmond OR 97756

Call Sign: KD7BRE
Roger N Cross
60885 Oasis Pl
Redmond OR 97756

Call Sign: KE7RLF
Frank B Miller
15505 Oceanview Dr 32
Redmond OR 97756

Call Sign: KD7ILR
Cory A Davis
490 S Oregon St
Redmond OR 97756

Call Sign: KF6EJF
James A Reed
42882 SE Phelps Rd
Redmond OR 97756

Call Sign: KE6SLQ
Marcia L Williams
10220 SW 130th Ave
Redmond OR 97756

Call Sign: WB7RQF
Terry M Shrader
14250 SW 22nd St
Redmond OR 97756

Call Sign: K7IFY
Vale W Lantz
13650 SW 24th St
Redmond OR 97756

Call Sign: KD7CAH
Gerry J Glunz
54 SW 25th St
Redmond OR 977561433

Call Sign: KB7SIC
Carol A Elek
13000 SW 2nd St
Redmond OR 97756

Call Sign: N7BJE
William C Claridge
818 SW 3rd Ave 1224
Redmond OR 97756

Call Sign: KE7BHH
Gregg G Webb
9312 SW 40th
Redmond OR 97756

Call Sign: KD7QHN
James D Taylor
4535 SW 78th Ave
Redmond OR 97756

Call Sign: K9TKR
James D Taylor
15540 SW 79th
Redmond OR 97756

Call Sign: KE7CSN
Barb J Williams
15480 SW 79th Ave
Redmond OR 97756

Call Sign: KB7HAK
Jeannette L Muise
11555 SW 88th Ave 23
Redmond OR 97756

Call Sign: N7PZS
Alan L Muise
7630 SW 89th Ave
Redmond OR 97756

Call Sign: W7MX
Alan L Muise
7705 SW 89th Ave
Redmond OR 97756

Call Sign: WA7JTU
Steven G Jeffery
10831 SW Cascade Ave
Redmond OR 97756

Call Sign: KC7YRK
Bryan M Ivie
11555 SW Diane Pl
Redmond OR 97756

Call Sign: KB7ORG
Janice M Liddell
8911 SW Hillsboro Hwy
Redmond OR 977568328

Call Sign: KB7OVF
Richard W Liddell
16540 SW Hillsboro Hwy
Redmond OR 977568328

Call Sign: KE7BSW
George P Lanning
19928 SW Inglis Dr
Redmond OR 97756

Call Sign: KB1SA
Kenneth J Nurmi
4800 SW Macadam 207 43
Redmond OR 977569413

Call Sign: KC7CKE
Mark R Corbet
43466 SW Mckay Dr
Redmond OR 97756

Call Sign: KN7J
James R Gibson
3211 SW Odsidian Ave
Redmond OR 97756

Call Sign: KA7KQI
Wesley R Peavy
24880 SW Old Hwy 99 W
Redmond OR 97756

Call Sign: KE7KSB
Saeed J Saadeddin
10160 SW Old Orchard Ln
Redmond OR 97756

Call Sign: KD7EQI
Michael L Rogers Sr
4518 SW Perkins Ave
Redmond OR 97756

Call Sign: KC7PYL
Richard A Wickham
2852 SW Quartz Ave
Redmond OR 97756

Call Sign: KD7QWQ
Joseph P Jones
3025 SW Quartz Ave
Redmond OR 97756

Call Sign: KC7YSA
Timothy J Wallis
16755 SW Queen Anne Ave
Redmond OR 977568033

Call Sign: KB7OLG
James M Fenton
6280 SW Quietcreek Dr
Redmond OR 97756

Call Sign: KD7VKI
Donald K Webber
2939 SW Reindeer Ave
Redmond OR 97756

Call Sign: K7DKW
Donald K Webber
20775 SW Ribera Ln
Redmond OR 97756

Call Sign: N7YLW
Ronald J Marshall
21775 SW Ribera Ln
Redmond OR 97756

Call Sign: KE7KSA
Mike J Beaudin
17223 SW Rivendell Dr
Redmond OR 97756

Call Sign: KE7JXG
David R Trass
121 SW Salmon St
3Wtc0407
Redmond OR 97756

Call Sign: KE7JXF
Tessa J Trass

121 SW Salmon St
3Wtc0407
Redmond OR 97756

Call Sign: KB7WWA
George D Rainwater
11725 SW Timberline Ct
Redmond OR 97756

Call Sign: KC7DAE
Scott L Davis
2767 SW Titleist Cir
Redmond OR 97756

Call Sign: K7DFM
Charles E Albright
2267 SW Tower Ln
Redmond OR 97756

Call Sign: KL7ZW
Thomas J Wilde
13310 SW Wacker Rd
Redmond OR 97756

Call Sign: KA7VBR
Don L Grace
923 W Antler
Redmond OR 97756

Call Sign: W0WI
Willis C Jenson
123 W Antler 2
Redmond OR 97756

Call Sign: N7JZI
Richard M Copeland
4211 W Hwy 126
Redmond OR 97756

Call Sign: KB7USD
Dale A Gilbert
Redmond OR 97756

Call Sign: W7HCW
Fred S Winkleman

Redmond OR 97756

Call Sign: KA7PWX
Robert A Mc Wayne
Redmond OR 97786

Call Sign: KB5KNV
Ethan A Walker III
Redmond OR 97756

Call Sign: KB7KLS
Jennifer N Williams
Redmond OR 97756

Call Sign: KC7FIE
Pamela M Gilbert
Redmond OR 97756

Call Sign: KC7LPP
Troy L Price
Redmond OR 97756

Call Sign: KC7LPQ
Julie A Price
Redmond OR 97756

Call Sign: KE7TMQ
Beverly A Schmidt
Redmond OR 97756

Call Sign: KF7LPM
Ethan A Walker III
Redmond OR 97756

Call Sign: KE7CXS
Joshua L Richesin
Redmond OR 97756

Call Sign: KD7UCP
Ashley J Nykiel
Redmond OR 97756

Call Sign: KD7UCO
Linda M Voci
Redmond OR 97756

Call Sign: KB7KLT
Michael A Williams
Redmond OR 97756

Call Sign: KD7PGN
David S Lane
Redmond OR 977560202

Call Sign: KH6JUC
Wayne E Linschied
Redmond OR 977560521

**FCC Amateur Radio
Licenses in Reedsport**

Call Sign: KC7ICO
Norman E Powell
2423 Benson Ln
Reedsport OR 97467

Call Sign: WA7ANU
Herschel E Nickels
Rt 1 Box 148B2
Reedsport OR 97467

Call Sign: KC7C
Martin E Lane
19566 Butteville Rd NE
Reedsport OR 97467

Call Sign: KC7FZK
David C Orr
6405 Colonial Way
Reedsport OR 97467

Call Sign: WB7PGQ
James H Eckersley Jr
55410 Delta Rd
Reedsport OR 97467

Call Sign: K7BL
Carlin R Williams
2768 Donnalee Dr
Reedsport OR 97467

Call Sign: KA6QNL
Gail E Jensen
910 E 2nd Ave
Reedsport OR 97467

Call Sign: KF7KYS
James R Zimmer
88664 Ellmaker Rd
Reedsport OR 97467

Call Sign: AE7KF
James R Zimmer
7702 Ellsworth Cir
Reedsport OR 97467

Call Sign: KE7HLH
Barry L Nelson
3315 Ford Dr
Reedsport OR 97467

Call Sign: KE7YZM
John E Steininger
16880 Ford Rd
Reedsport OR 97467

Call Sign: KE7SAD
Robert V Traina
2855 Front St Apt 9A
Reedsport OR 97467

Call Sign: KE7SAE
Sheila A Traina
2855 Front St NE Apt 9A
Reedsport OR 97467

Call Sign: N6YQX
Charles W Prather Sr
510 Gilles St
Reedsport OR 974674400

Call Sign: KB7PXK
William I Moldt
77750 Gillispie Rd
Reedsport OR 97467

Call Sign: KE6DBS
Terry L Bilbrey
8260 Hale Way
Reedsport OR 97467

Call Sign: W7DAN
Arlie M Thomason
3418 Hidden Valley Rd NW
Reedsport OR 974671050

Call Sign: KC7FLL
Linda I Pierson
47445 Hwy 101 S
Reedsport OR 97467

Call Sign: KJ7FN
Luther R Pierson
24610 Hwy 101 S Sp 15
Reedsport OR 97467

Call Sign: WA7DUC
Kent A Abendroth
4064 NE 18th Ave
Reedsport OR 97467

Call Sign: KC7CEF
Dale L Allen Sr
885 Perrydale Rd
Reedsport OR 97467

Call Sign: KB7UDD
Merlyn J Hafen Sr
1068 River Rd
Reedsport OR 97467

Call Sign: KD7MWU
Loretta K Hafen
1210 5 River Rd
Reedsport OR 97467

Call Sign: W6UWP
Robert B Finch Sr
20439 Rocky Top Ct
Reedsport OR 97467

Call Sign: KC6WTZ
Earl S Burke
1436 Rockydale Rd
Reedsport OR 974671385

Call Sign: W7BK
David G Morgan
6651 SE 122nd Ave
Reedsport OR 97467

Call Sign: N7VRO
V Bonita Morgan
4620 SE 122nd Ave 301
Reedsport OR 97467

Call Sign: KC7YWX
Mhaire Merryman
1016 SE 123rd
Reedsport OR 97467

Call Sign: KD7MWZ
Tina I Dean
115 Westwood Ct
Reedsport OR 97467

FCC Amateur Radio Licenses in Richland

Call Sign: KB7MLF
Karen L Riener
880 Fairview Ave SE 4
Richland OR 97870

Call Sign: AL7FZ
Pete A Martin
375 Fairview Ave SE Apt 215
Richland OR 97870

Call Sign: KD7CZW
Allen J Chapin
2502 Jeppesen Acres Rd
Richland OR 978706676

Call Sign: KA6GVA
William V Andrade
11285 State St NE
Richland OR 97870

Call Sign: KE7RMX
Curtis J Aman
35647 Whitman Ln
Richland OR 97870

Call Sign: K7RMX
Curtis J Aman
35647 Whitman Ln
Richland OR 97870

FCC Amateur Radio Licenses in Riddle

Call Sign: WB7TIR
Gale R Burk
2727 Hartley Ln
Riddle OR 97469

Call Sign: KD7EIY
Kenneth D Redinger
336 S 30th St
Riddle OR 97469

FCC Amateur Radio Licenses in Rogue River

Call Sign: KA7QQU
Dennis W Classick
5591 Alder Ln
Rogue River OR 97537

Call Sign: KF7DMW
Jonathan D Chester
963 Cascade Way
Rogue River OR 97537

Call Sign: N7FNY
David L Sepich
61713 Catching Sl Rd
Rogue River OR 97537

Call Sign: W7VOT
Delmer W Wagner
22200 E Lolo Pass Rd
Rogue River OR 97537

Call Sign: KB7CTT
Charles R Matejka Jr
148 Elkay Dr
Rogue River OR 97537

Call Sign: W6KGU
William P Dart
1753 Elkay Dr
Rogue River OR 97537

Call Sign: N7ZMR
Tyson E Schultz
1753 Elkay Dr
Rogue River OR 97537

Call Sign: KC7GZX
Fredrick R Burns
6446 Elkhead Rd
Rogue River OR 97537

Call Sign: N7ZHD
Maybel B Simon
8641 Elkhead Rd
Rogue River OR 97537

Call Sign: KF7ELM
Michael A Pare
8641 Elkhead Rd
Rogue River OR 97537

Call Sign: W6LWO
Creighton T Cosner
13854 Elkhead Rd
Rogue River OR 97537

Call Sign: KE7CDV
Joel W Kolstad
13854 Elkhead Rd
Rogue River OR 97537

Call Sign: KF7CXM
Tyler W Kovachy
4812 Elkhorn Dr SE
Rogue River OR 97537

Call Sign: KC6QCA
Allan R Hornung
670 Ellen Ave
Rogue River OR 975379727

Call Sign: K6KWZ
John F Bell
560 Fairmont Dr NE
Rogue River OR 97537

Call Sign: KF7KLI
Lynn A Wardle
3684 Felton S
Rogue River OR 97537

Call Sign: WA7AFU
Carl R Simon
580 Fenster St
Rogue River OR 97537

Call Sign: N6LYP
Patricia A Payne
491 Gerth Ave
Rogue River OR 97537

Call Sign: WA7MGE
Ronald E Lopes
15240 Gopher Valley Rd
Rogue River OR 97537

Call Sign: KF4JXS
Robert E Dorman
2006 Hwy 101 741
Rogue River OR 97537

Call Sign: KC7YKS
Gerald G Lyon
4205 Hwy 101 N
Rogue River OR 97537

Call Sign: N6SIQ
Scott A Christopherson
3760 Hwy 101 N 32
Rogue River OR 97537

Call Sign: KC7JPW
Daisy J Alcantara
8096 Meridian Rd NE
Rogue River OR 97537

Call Sign: KD7BOI
Rick L Mead
16500 Mt Angel Scotts
Mills Rd NE
Rogue River OR 97537

Call Sign: KD7ATZ
Rebecca L Mead
507 N 19th Ave Sp 82
Rogue River OR 97537

Call Sign: KC7CNW
William D Parks
507 N 19th Ave Sp 92
Rogue River OR 97537

Call Sign: KB7SMK
Lester H Gertz
31162 Peterson Rd
Rogue River OR 97537

Call Sign: KG7VU
Charles W Kanavle
19759 Poplar St
Rogue River OR 97537

Call Sign: KD7LTL
Sean C Laws
1201 Progress 39
Rogue River OR 97537

Call Sign: KF7ELJ
Glenn D Crane
1201 Progress Dr Apt 12

Rogue River OR 97537

Call Sign: KD6IRF
Joan D Mac Kenzie
1201 Progress Dr Apt 12
Rogue River OR 97537

Call Sign: KD6IRH
James E Mac Kenzie
1440 Progress Loop
Rogue River OR 97537

Call Sign: KE7WVI
Kathleen E Olney
2 Progress Way
Rogue River OR 97537

Call Sign: KE7YLF
William C Olney
818 Promontory Ave
Rogue River OR 97537

Call Sign: KI7XC
Roland N Henderson
1183 Prospect
Rogue River OR 97537

Call Sign: N7VGN
Sandra L Fiese
2930 Prospect
Rogue River OR 97537

Call Sign: KB7YTX
William G Sabados
1721 Prospect Ave
Rogue River OR 97537

Call Sign: K7ML
Craig D Warren
1721 Prospect Ave
Rogue River OR 97537

Call Sign: WA6ZJU
John H Danskin
2401 Reimer Rd

Rogue River OR 97537

Call Sign: KD7EHD
Wayne A Van Delden
2401 Reimer Rd
Rogue River OR 97537

Call Sign: KF6SOP
Bradley J Fry
430 Reiten Dr
Rogue River OR 97537

Call Sign: WB7AYY
Garland R Sewell Jr
807 Reiten Dr
Rogue River OR 97537

Call Sign: W6HKA
Garland R Sewell Jr
375 Reiter Dr
Rogue River OR 975379614

Call Sign: N6YBK
Galen J Kelm
15020 Remuda Rd
Rogue River OR 97527

Call Sign: KE7LM
Galen J Kelm
2640 Renaissance Ct
Rogue River OR 97527

Call Sign: KF7DMV
Kevin M Malone
3150 Siskiyou Blvd
Rogue River OR 97537

Call Sign: KB7OCM
David T Christensen
34037 Sykes Rd
Rogue River OR 97537

Call Sign: N6QP
William D Edwards
64688 Sylvan

Rogue River OR 97537

Call Sign: K7BBD
Charles W Jaeger
4932 W Evans Creek Rd
Rogue River OR 97537

Call Sign: KD7WHZ
Mariann Kynsi
4957 W Evans Creek Rd
Rogue River OR 97537

Call Sign: W7ISN
Richard R Trautwein
5865 W Evans Creek Rd
Rogue River OR 97537

Call Sign: W7ISQ
Evelyn M Trautwein
5865 W Evans Creek Rd
Rogue River OR 975374632

Call Sign: KI6US
Blakeney Kilburn
7325 W Evans Creek Rd
Rogue River OR 97537

Call Sign: KI6RJT
Roger G Carter
7390 W Evans Creek Rd
Rogue River OR 97537

Call Sign: KE7EI
Robert G Prell
9975 W Evans Creek Rd
Rogue River OR 97537

Call Sign: KD7QFT
Robert A Hoffman
2701 W Evans Crk Rd
Rogue River OR 97537

Call Sign: KB7NGA
Edward I Fiese Sr
Rogue River OR 97537

Call Sign: N7ZHC
Greg H Doty
Rogue River OR 97537

Call Sign: W7ICH
Donavon C Rumbaugh
Rogue River OR 97537

Call Sign: KA7TRL
Michael Stephen
Rogue River OR 97537

Call Sign: KB7CVY
Karl R Prefontaine
Rogue River OR 97537

Call Sign: KC7PMT
John T Considine
Rogue River OR 97537

Call Sign: KF6CTJ
Donald D Coons
Rogue River OR 97537

Call Sign: N7IZL
La Verne M Swartz
Rogue River OR 97537

Call Sign: W6RKH
William C Daly
Rogue River OR 97537

Call Sign: WA7Z
Juel F Swartz Jr
Rogue River OR 97537

Call Sign: KE7TGB
Larry G Hamblin
Rogue River OR 97537

Call Sign: KE7TGD
Micki F Hamblin
Rogue River OR 97537

Call Sign: KF7NNL
Pat Brady
Rogue River OR 97537

Call Sign: KF6FGD
Judith A Coons
Rogue River OR 975371164

FCC Amateur Radio Licenses in Roseburg

Call Sign: KD7GJT
Christina M Mills
1840 39th Ave SE
Roseburg OR 97470

Call Sign: KE7EGI
Christina M Mills
2806 3rd St
Roseburg OR 97470

Call Sign: KD6LWA
Carl E Foti
875 57th St
Roseburg OR 97470

Call Sign: KD7VKK
Shelley L Johnson
336 9th St
Roseburg OR 97470

Call Sign: WA7IXX
James D Medford
2890B Beach Loop Dr
Roseburg OR 97470

Call Sign: KC7GNC
Gayle A Stout
439 Belle Ct
Roseburg OR 97470

Call Sign: KE7BBT
Lorie R Blodgett
114 Bellevue Ave
Roseburg OR 97470

Call Sign: KC7EEK
Theodore S Benice Jr
114 Bellevue Ave
Roseburg OR 97470

Call Sign: KE7WMR
Richard W Barrett
541 Blue Moon Dr
Roseburg OR 97471

Call Sign: WB3DRF
Charles S Jekofsky
541 Blue Moon Dr
Roseburg OR 974718975

Call Sign: K7AZW
Leighton W Stumpe
1711 Blue Moon Ln
Roseburg OR 974718975

Call Sign: K6AZW
Leighton W Stumpe
230 Bluebird Ln
Roseburg OR 97470

Call Sign: KE7KDW
Michael J Gunville
5855 Bly Mountain Cutoff Rd
Roseburg OR 97470

Call Sign: KE7MVX
George R Roth
2037 Boes Ave
Roseburg OR 97470

Call Sign: KB7FZQ
Joseph R Harper
Rt 2 Box 2567
Roseburg OR 97470

Call Sign: KC7ENX
Frank W Slater
229 Bridge St

Roseburg OR 97470

Call Sign: KE7BZE
Christopher J Galbick
1960 Broadway St NE
Roseburg OR 97470

Call Sign: KF7QKK
Melvin N Stewart
5030 Caplinger Rd SE
Roseburg OR 97471

Call Sign: KF7UBP
Patricia A Stewart
39369 Card St
Roseburg OR 97471

Call Sign: KC7BIY
Gary J Albertson
17571 Cardinal Dr
Roseburg OR 97470

Call Sign: WB7RFG
Pearl A Mulder
19118 Case Rd NE
Roseburg OR 97470

Call Sign: KA7AXN
Donald K Mulder
5760 Casey Ln SE
Roseburg OR 97470

Call Sign: WB6MFV
Harold D Hanson
66933 Central St
Roseburg OR 97470

Call Sign: W7IRJ
Harold F Hanson
67006 Central St
Roseburg OR 97470

Call Sign: K7RBG
Douglas County Amateur
Radio Emerg Service

67168 Central St
Roseburg OR 97470

Call Sign: KF7MGD
Western Douglas County
ARES Operation Center
3976 Century Dr
Roseburg OR 97470

Call Sign: K7RPO
Western Douglas County
ARES Operation Center
2406 Century Loop
Roseburg OR 97470

Call Sign: KB7WDR
Gerald H Eifert
3196 Century Way
Roseburg OR 97470

Call Sign: KD7SLT
Marilyn F Eifert
633 Cessna St
Roseburg OR 97470

Call Sign: K7TJB
Timothy J Ballard
633 Cessna St
Roseburg OR 97470

Call Sign: KC7NFY
Douglas County Amateur
Radio Emerg Service
653 Cessna St
Roseburg OR 97470

Call Sign: AE7ER
Gerald H Eifert
724 Cessna St
Roseburg OR 97470

Call Sign: KC7PJK
Mark M Lawler
763 Cessna St
Roseburg OR 97470

Call Sign: KC7FQV
Albert D Hash
3414 Cherry Ave Ste 150
Roseburg OR 97470

Call Sign: KC7FQW
Jean A Hash
20470 Cherry Blossom Ln
Roseburg OR 97470

Call Sign: AD7HP
Malcom S Dayton
27619 Clear Lake Rd
Roseburg OR 97471

Call Sign: K7BZ
Malcom S Dayton
27619 Clear Lake Rd
Roseburg OR 97471

Call Sign: KD7IVR
James E Sundahl
83200 Clear Lake Rd
Roseburg OR 97470

Call Sign: KE7KED
Beverly L Patitz
1498 Clearsprings Dr
Roseburg OR 97470

Call Sign: KE7KEE
Roger E Patitz
1195 Clearview Ave NE 91
Roseburg OR 974704554

Call Sign: KE7YZJ
Paul D Apple
521 Clearview Dr
Roseburg OR 97471

Call Sign: AD7ZL
Paul D Apple
541 Clearview Dr
Roseburg OR 97471

Call Sign: N7UHU
Jason E Stone
2845 Coker Butte Rd
Roseburg OR 97470

Call Sign: NK7G
Eric B Gustafson
866 Crestview Dr
Roseburg OR 97471

Call Sign: KD7RCE
Marilyn J Gustafson
1403 Crestview Dr
Roseburg OR 97471

Call Sign: KD7MTS
Paul J Sackinger
63770 Cricketwood Rd
Roseburg OR 97470

Call Sign: W2VJN
George A Cutsogeorge
695 Crimson Way
Roseburg OR 97471

Call Sign: KD6TEO
Daniel R Smith
2155 Dalton Dr
Roseburg OR 97470

Call Sign: KF7FID
Robert L Williams
4881 Dark Hollow Rd
Roseburg OR 97471

Call Sign: KI6HHW
David S Haskins
714 J David St SE
Roseburg OR 97470

Call Sign: KL7HJD
Harold C Steves
3405 Deer Park Dr SE
Roseburg OR 97470

Call Sign: KF7KTN
Kyle D PeARCe
130 Deerbrook Dr
Roseburg OR 97470

Call Sign: KE7LDZ
John C Donner
591 E 2nd St 1
Roseburg OR 97470

Call Sign: KE7LDW
Eugene W Regan
610 E Sunset Dr
Roseburg OR 97470

Call Sign: KB7WTA
Donald C Fulton
310 Divison Ave
Roseburg OR 97470

Call Sign: KF7LJC
Jane S Birchard
2229 E Burnside 26
Roseburg OR 97471

Call Sign: KB7ONK
David W Byrd
25093 E Tiger Lilly
Roseburg OR 97470

Call Sign: KE7KDX
Barbara L Fulton
1018 Dixie Dr
Roseburg OR 97470

Call Sign: KF7AHZ
Craig Pierce
11751 E Burnside Apt 59
Roseburg OR 97470

Call Sign: KC7GID
Lindy S Gomez
2305 Fernwood Cir
Roseburg OR 97470

Call Sign: N7WIJ
William Gauer
4870 Dogwood Dr
Roseburg OR 97470

Call Sign: KF7AHY
Larissa R Pierce
5316 E Burnside Apt 7
Roseburg OR 97471

Call Sign: KC7GIF
David J Lampert
1668 Ferry 2
Roseburg OR 97470

Call Sign: KA7ELK
Rosalie M Gauer
117 Dogwood Dr
Roseburg OR 97470

Call Sign: KF7AIA
Media L Pierce
4735 E Burnside St
Roseburg OR 97471

Call Sign: KF7KTO
Albert J Mcjunkin
41871 Fish Hatchery Dr
Roseburg OR 97471

Call Sign: WA7FEC
Orville H Cornett
83072 Dufur Valley Rd
Roseburg OR 97470

Call Sign: W7DUR
Russel O Nelson
8911 E Burnside St
Roseburg OR 97470

Call Sign: KF7TEY
Lesa G Mcjunkin
41871 Fish Hatchery Dr
Roseburg OR 97471

Call Sign: K7RKP
Carl A Anfora
2320 E 10th St
Roseburg OR 974701053

Call Sign: WB7OTM
Jim H Zurcher
665 E Exeter St
Roseburg OR 97470

Call Sign: N7UHW
Elmer B Estelle
28882 Fish Hatchery Rd
Roseburg OR 97470

Call Sign: KA7AID
Theodore C Conwell
2830 E 10th St
Roseburg OR 97470

Call Sign: WB6HUY
David R Whited
1707 E Main St
Roseburg OR 97470

Call Sign: KF7LJB
Dean K Allison
3872 Friar Ct SE
Roseburg OR 97471

Call Sign: KB7LWT
Frank C Aiken
504 E 13th St
Roseburg OR 97470

Call Sign: KE7TFD
Dale E Williams
729 E Scenic Dr
Roseburg OR 97470

Call Sign: W6VDF
Larry L Prestwood
3892 Friar Ct SE
Roseburg OR 97470

Call Sign: KA7KLM
Winfried H Seidel
4439 Frieda
Roseburg OR 97470

Call Sign: KJ6FXQ
Michael W Gross
2444 Gardener Rd
Roseburg OR 97471

Call Sign: KF7LVR
Robert A Reneman Jr
9584 Golf Club Rd SE
Roseburg OR 97471

Call Sign: N7RRQ
Larry W Gauer
66146 Golf Course Rd
Roseburg OR 97471

Call Sign: KC6NSK
Raymond G Grout
822 Golf View Dr Apt 205
Roseburg OR 97470

Call Sign: WA7NWV
Earl L Adams
1546 Harbor Dr
Roseburg OR 97470

Call Sign: AC7SP
Tim D Clauson
97869 Harbor View Cir
Roseburg OR 97470

Call Sign: KE7PWU
Caitlin F Clauson
97867 Harbor View Cir Box
3170
Roseburg OR 97470

Call Sign: AC7XM
Charlotte A Clauson
4697 Harcourt Ave NE

Roseburg OR 97470

Call Sign: KD7TYN
Mattie C Clauson
133 Harding Blvd
Roseburg OR 97470

Call Sign: AD7BL
Mattie C Clauson
133 Harding Blvd
Roseburg OR 97470

Call Sign: AE7MC
Mattie C Clauson
184 Harding Blvd
Roseburg OR 97470

Call Sign: KD7NZF
Christopher S Coble
4962 Harvard Ct
Roseburg OR 97470

Call Sign: KF7JFZ
Robert A Rapp
937 Helen Ln
Roseburg OR 97471

Call Sign: KC7QXT
Robert W Flynn
945 Helen Ln
Roseburg OR 97470

Call Sign: KA7HOP
Johnathan D Lenker
4816 Herrin Rd NE
Roseburg OR 97470

Call Sign: KE7LDV
Vicki L Weaver
6200 Hilyard Ave
Roseburg OR 97470

Call Sign: KE7LDU
Walter D Weaver
6225 Hilyard Ave

Roseburg OR 97470

Call Sign: KF7AHX
Alan D Paulson
6924 Hilyard Ct
Roseburg OR 97471

Call Sign: KC5PXZ
Leroy P Hanson
777 Hixson Dr
Roseburg OR 97470

Call Sign: KA7MIG
Cameron L Litvin
580 Homewood Rd
Roseburg OR 97471

Call Sign: KE7NXU
Theodore D Lalande
295 Idaho St
Roseburg OR 97470

Call Sign: N6WNE
Roger D Loiler
1700 Kellenbeck Ave Apt
318
Roseburg OR 97470

Call Sign: W6JBO
Manfred R Stever Jr
7002 Keller Ct
Roseburg OR 97471

Call Sign: K8DZO
Ronald J Karlosky
296 Klaskanine Ave
Roseburg OR 97470

Call Sign: KF6FSF
Aurora R Fryer
7607 Kress Dr
Roseburg OR 97471

Call Sign: NT6E
Gary N Fryer

| 7607 Kress Dr | 2112 Martin Dr | 275 N Alder |
| Roseburg OR 97471 | Roseburg OR 97471 | Roseburg OR 97471 |

Call Sign: N7WJK
Michael L Wooden
5291 Larden Rd NE
Roseburg OR 97470

Call Sign: KC7CNQ
Knute J Takle
52366 Miller Rd
Roseburg OR 974705264

Call Sign: KC7SRI
Kory K Parsons
57023 N Bank Rd
Roseburg OR 97470

Call Sign: KB7ZNY
Stephen P Sproule
890 Leigh St
Roseburg OR 97470

Call Sign: KC7QNH
Pablo E Arronte
902 Mtn View Dr
Roseburg OR 97470

Call Sign: N7UHZ
Lyle G Cochran Jr
1283 N Broadway Ave
Roseburg OR 97470

Call Sign: KC7WQN
Laural Kay Sproule
1031 Leigh St
Roseburg OR 97470

Call Sign: KC7HYY
Douglas J Buier
5003 Mtn View Dr
Roseburg OR 97470

Call Sign: KF7LJA
Craig M Kinney
391 N Dawn
Roseburg OR 97470

Call Sign: N7AYA
Francis L Glass
1404 Lexington Ave
Roseburg OR 974709868

Call Sign: N7ZIN
Bradley E Keitzman
600 Mtn View Rd
Roseburg OR 97470

Call Sign: KC7QNI
Glenna J Erickson
7153 N Lancaster
Roseburg OR 97470

Call Sign: KF7AIB
Toby T Gibbons
7054 Liberty Rd S
Roseburg OR 97470

Call Sign: KE7LNJ
Merry A Dawson
1003 N 54th St
Roseburg OR 97470

Call Sign: KC7QXR
Melanie J Erickson
10102 N Leonard St
Roseburg OR 97470

Call Sign: KC7TTO
James A Barr
1410 Maple St
Roseburg OR 97470

Call Sign: KD7LIJ
George F Brannon
1003 N 54th St
Roseburg OR 97470

Call Sign: KC7RPI
Lisa J Erickson
651 N Lincoln St
Roseburg OR 97470

Call Sign: KA6GSD
Arthur G Zacharias
2025 Maple St
Roseburg OR 97470

Call Sign: N7WBZ
Christopher M Mangus
1051 N 56th St
Roseburg OR 97470

Call Sign: KC7OLL
Gary L Moothart
41980 N River Dr
Roseburg OR 97470

Call Sign: WA7FZN
Irena P Buckle
20951 Marsh Orchid Ct
Roseburg OR 97470

Call Sign: KE7GHU
Eric J Dawson
830 N 6th St
Roseburg OR 97470

Call Sign: N7OLS
William C Stiles
911 NE 122 Ave Apt 12
Roseburg OR 97470

Call Sign: KD7KLZ
Eric D Cornelius

Call Sign: KF7BSJ
Dirk E Brinkman

Call Sign: KC7UGA
Peter W Hengel

365 NE 15th Ct
Roseburg OR 97470

522 NE Geraldine Dr
Roseburg OR 97470

3132 NE Oregon St
Roseburg OR 97470

Call Sign: AA7OP
Robert C Phillips
270 NE 20th Pl
Roseburg OR 97470

Call Sign: KF7KTK
Kelly S Applegarth
2728 NE Harvey Ln
Roseburg OR 97470

Call Sign: KC7YFE
Dale E Wilson
7985 NE Park Ln Dr
Roseburg OR 97470

Call Sign: N7OSI
Frances J Phillips
535 NE 20th Pl
Roseburg OR 97470

Call Sign: KE7ZIH
Fred S Birch
4352 NE Hassalo St
Roseburg OR 97470

Call Sign: KC6UOO
Brad E Johnson
4536 NE Prescott St
Roseburg OR 97470

Call Sign: KB7CMB
Daniel A Lee
3613 NE 22nd Ave
Roseburg OR 97470

Call Sign: AE7MQ
Fred S Birch
5219 NE Hassalo St
Roseburg OR 97470

Call Sign: KD7AOP
Edward B Havicus
711 NE Rocky Top Rd
Roseburg OR 97470

Call Sign: KB7ODY
Helen E Lee
5730 NE 22nd Ave
Roseburg OR 97470

Call Sign: KE7FB
Fred S Birch
12506 NE Hassalo St
Roseburg OR 97470

Call Sign: KF7LIZ
Gerald V Applegarth
13625 NE Rose Pkwy
Roseburg OR 97470

Call Sign: AC7ED
Daniel R Smith
223 NE 22nd Ave Apt A
Roseburg OR 97470

Call Sign: KF7KTP
Chris T Boice
17435 NE Hillside Dr
Roseburg OR 97470

Call Sign: W7APP
Gerald V Applegarth
15145 NE Rose Pkwy
Roseburg OR 97470

Call Sign: KF7FHY
Patrick P Parson
1970 NE Conifer Blvd
Roseburg OR 97470

Call Sign: N7VEZ
Bradley G Crenshaw
2665 NE Jill Ct
Roseburg OR 97470

Call Sign: KG6YC
Billy R Smith
1281 NE Setting Sun Dr
Roseburg OR 97470

Call Sign: WB7RGJ
Donald E Koch
18835 NE Flanders
Roseburg OR 97470

Call Sign: N8OKI
Dick G Wamser
1218 NE John Dr
Roseburg OR 97470

Call Sign: KB7TVA
Barbara J Booher
4224 NE Shaver St
Roseburg OR 97470

Call Sign: KC7FLJ
Helenl Diess
2768 NE Forum Dr
Roseburg OR 97470

Call Sign: KC7LBB
Curtis L Moothart
1280 NE Kane Rd
Roseburg OR 97470

Call Sign: KC7VPB
Robert A Jensen
4440 NE Shaver St
Roseburg OR 97470

Call Sign: KD7BJY
Jason C Willett

Call Sign: KE6QCJ
James P Sparks

Call Sign: WB7QFT
Rick H Kluver

1000 NE Snowberry St
Roseburg OR 97470

Call Sign: W7DFV
Rick H Kluver
14700 NE Spring Creek Ln
Roseburg OR 97470

Call Sign: W7RNG
Bruce E Rein
1370 NE Tucson Way
Roseburg OR 97470

Call Sign: KF7AHW
Samuel D Tolleson
1225 Netherlands Rd
Roseburg OR 97470

Call Sign: KC7KPB
Alice A Johnson
1172 Netzel St
Roseburg OR 974701449

Call Sign: N7XRR
Douglas A Cahill
20566 New Bedford Cir
Roseburg OR 97470

Call Sign: N7ORU
Arthur H Litka
1011 Newcastle
Roseburg OR 97470

Call Sign: KE7YZO
Terry M Thomas
1016 Newcastle Ave
Roseburg OR 97470

Call Sign: K6CHB
Einar N Lee
2611 Newcastle St
Roseburg OR 97470

Call Sign: KE7PHV
Lynn C Patterson

1065 Noble St
Roseburg OR 974701539

Call Sign: W7HDU
Lynn C Patterson
4945 Noren Ave
Roseburg OR 974701539

Call Sign: W7EEY
Marvin E Carroll
922 NW Circle Blvd Ste
160 Pmb 218
Roseburg OR 97470

Call Sign: KF7QKP
Samuel J Shell
922 NW Circle Ste 160 Pmb
337
Roseburg OR 97470

Call Sign: N7JNJ
Robert M Harper
155 NW Cornelius Pass Rd
34
Roseburg OR 97470

Call Sign: W6EG
Frank Hatanaka
9033 NW Dick Rd
Roseburg OR 97470

Call Sign: KA7IJC
Joe L Meyer
477 NW Douglas St
Roseburg OR 97470

Call Sign: KA7IJD
Floyd J Meyer
1325 NW Draper Pl
Roseburg OR 97470

Call Sign: WA6CHD
Edward E Huson
1333 NW Eastman Pkwy
Roseburg OR 97470

Call Sign: KC7IKQ
Keith C Olsen
7045 NW Grandview Dr
Roseburg OR 97470

Call Sign: KF7KTM
James T Mcelhatton
1544 NW Ithaca
Roseburg OR 97471

Call Sign: AE7QK
James T Mcelhatton
2007 NW Ivy Pl
Roseburg OR 97471

Call Sign: KG7JH
Walter S Wallen
13880 NW Logie Trl
Roseburg OR 97470

Call Sign: KF7FIB
James N Stuntz
7670 NW Mc Donald Cir
Roseburg OR 97471

Call Sign: KF7LIY
Christopher A Noel
7670 NW Mc Donald Cir
Roseburg OR 97471

Call Sign: N7UHT
Thomas E Pitcairn
1420 NW Menlo Dr
Roseburg OR 97470

Call Sign: KC7MGU
James S Popham
1905 NW Menlo Dr
Roseburg OR 97470

Call Sign: KF7UJA
David B Owen
2436 NW Mill Pond Rd
Roseburg OR 97471

Call Sign: K7DSS
David B Owen
5070 NW Millstone Way
Roseburg OR 97471

Call Sign: KC7RPH
Amy T Baker
525 NW Monroe 202
Roseburg OR 97470

Call Sign: K7NBW
Bertram H Fiddy Sr
4160 NW Pineconeway 6
Roseburg OR 97470

Call Sign: KB7NUN
Eugene M Landers
16567 NW Sheltered Nook
Rd
Roseburg OR 97470

Call Sign: W7DFV
Charles Kluver Jr
1217 NW Sherwood Pl
Roseburg OR 97470

Call Sign: W5LXK
Harold L Sunderland
32480 NW Shipley Rd
Roseburg OR 97470

Call Sign: N7TPK
Steven L Sunderland
3210 NW Shooting Star Dr
Roseburg OR 97471

Call Sign: KC7PZE
Jeffrey E Plummer
11276 NW Skyline Blvd
Roseburg OR 97470

Call Sign: WB7WSO
Dewey A Johnston

15848 NW West Union Rd
145
Roseburg OR 97470

Call Sign: KF7QKR
Jack Reilly
514 NW Wide Ave
Roseburg OR 97471

Call Sign: KE7WMT
Drew J Coughlin
20972 NW Windstone Ct
Roseburg OR 97471

Call Sign: KB7SUJ
Stanley M Guido
1825 NW Woodland Dr
Roseburg OR 97470

Call Sign: KC7NCJ
Jerry L Foster
32070 Oak Plain Dr
Roseburg OR 97470

Call Sign: W6PHP
Robert W Kindig
704 Oak St
Roseburg OR 97470

Call Sign: W6BWO
Dale S Bose
1067 Oak St
Roseburg OR 97470

Call Sign: WB7NHT
Beatrice P Engelbrecht
436 Oceanview Dr
Roseburg OR 97470

Call Sign: WB7VSP
Patricia A Zurcher
1809 Oregon Ave
Roseburg OR 97470

Call Sign: KA7IAX

Leland W Svarverud Jr
2250 Orr Ln
Roseburg OR 97470

Call Sign: KI7SO
Clarence A Mills
173 Oscar Dr
Roseburg OR 97470

Call Sign: KA7LYQ
Douglas S Pritchett
17140 Osprey Ct
Roseburg OR 97470

Call Sign: N7INP
Alvin A Trumble
1067 Pali Dr NW
Roseburg OR 97470

Call Sign: KD7IUO
Tim D Clauson
1067 Pali Dr NW
Roseburg OR 97470

Call Sign: KD7QZB
Charlotte A Clauson
695 Palisades Dr SE
Roseburg OR 97470

Call Sign: KD7SDF
Mattie C Clauson
1896 Palisades Lake Ct
Roseburg OR 97470

Call Sign: KA7YDS
Howard H Burks
16941 Parkview Dr
Roseburg OR 974701056

Call Sign: KB7PFA
Vernan C Zimmerman
3011 Pine St
Roseburg OR 97470

Call Sign: KF7HXG

Wayne E Cook
3345 Redwood Hwy Bld Y
Roseburg OR 97471

Call Sign: KC7IKR
Susan A Singer
1161 River St
Roseburg OR 97470

Call Sign: WB7QNA
Ray J Weaver
5626 River St
Roseburg OR 97470

Call Sign: KA7RNJ
Lenora M Weaver
5655 River St
Roseburg OR 97470

Call Sign: KB7FWS
Raymond C Leland
4005 Robin Pl Apt 6
Roseburg OR 97470

Call Sign: AB7DC
Melvin R Trammell
2120 Robins Ln SE 131
Roseburg OR 97470

Call Sign: KC7BVM
Trelene D Trammell
2120 Robins Ln SE 57
Roseburg OR 97470

Call Sign: KC7GND
Verna Dean E Trammell
2120 Robins Ln SE Unit187
Roseburg OR 97470

Call Sign: WD6DNV
James C Kyle
6931 Rock View Dr SE
Roseburg OR 97470

Call Sign: W7JXT

Robert H Hiltunen
2175 Rocky Ln
Roseburg OR 97470

Call Sign: K7QPB
Roland I Jones
7505 Rocky Rd
Roseburg OR 97470

Call Sign: WA7WNX
Ruth S Jones
20439 Rocky Top Ct
Roseburg OR 97470

Call Sign: W6OV
Richard P Kemp
20439 Rocky Top Ct
Roseburg OR 97470

Call Sign: KC7GNI
John M Proctor
1107 Roseburg Rd
Roseburg OR 97470

Call Sign: KD7TYM
Tommy A Thompson
4900 Royal Ave 14
Roseburg OR 97470

Call Sign: KC7IKP
Joseph A Thomas
4900 Royal Ave 35
Roseburg OR 97470

Call Sign: KB7TUY
Frederick A Rhodes
726 Royal Ave 40
Roseburg OR 97470

Call Sign: KD7EOO
Patricia L Fouts
17205 S Abiqua Rd
Roseburg OR 97470

Call Sign: KG6BYC

Norman P Anderson
15360 S Bradley Rd
Roseburg OR 97470

Call Sign: KE7IHO
Howard W Newport Jr
22909 S Central Pt Rd
Roseburg OR 97470

Call Sign: WA7TNE
Jack C Smith
4191 S Shore Blvd
Roseburg OR 97470

Call Sign: KE7RTZ
Tonya A Spears
1307 S Water St Unit 85
Roseburg OR 97470

Call Sign: KE7YZL
Saundra L Romero
95691 Saunders Ck Rd Sp
1A
Roseburg OR 97470

Call Sign: KE7YZK
Gene M Hale
180 Schofield Dr
Roseburg OR 97471

Call Sign: KE7IKO
David J Tucker
21035 Scottsdale Dr
Roseburg OR 97470

Call Sign: N7XFF
Frank W Dittmer
3971 SE Boise
Roseburg OR 97470

Call Sign: KE7YZS
Gerri L Smith
5051 SE David Way
Roseburg OR 97470

Call Sign: KE7YZT
Tommy W Smith
5350 SE David Way
Roseburg OR 97470

Call Sign: KC7TSV
Jim R Miller
6052 SE David Way
Roseburg OR 97470

Call Sign: W7JRM
Jim R Miller
5096 SE Davis Loop
Roseburg OR 97470

Call Sign: KE7WMU
Brian D Neely
6882 SE Drake St
Roseburg OR 97470

Call Sign: AA7BN
Brian D Neely
5996 SE Drake St 18
Roseburg OR 97470

Call Sign: KB7ONJ
Pamela S Byrd
1222 SE Flavel St
Roseburg OR 97470

Call Sign: KC7SIA
Milton W Bernheisel
620 SE Juniper Ct E
Roseburg OR 97470

Call Sign: W7TUI
Robert F Reece
2307 SE Lindenbrook Ct
Roseburg OR 97470

Call Sign: W7LNE
John I Nicholas
29300 SE Loriat Ln
Roseburg OR 97470

Call Sign: N7PJW
Lila K Armstrong
1404 SE Malden St
Roseburg OR 97470

Call Sign: W7GUE
La Ray G Armstrong
5724 SE Mall
Roseburg OR 974709713

Call Sign: KB7ZDL
Dale L Allred
5724 SE Mall St
Roseburg OR 97470

Call Sign: KE7YZR
Charles N Martin
1136 SE Maple Apt 111
Roseburg OR 97470

Call Sign: KD7MX
Don H Tate
469 SE Marlin Ave
Roseburg OR 97470

Call Sign: KA3HRE
Deborah E Harding
15702 SE Martins St
Roseburg OR 97470

Call Sign: KF7RBN
Jim D Hunt
6708 SE May St
Roseburg OR 97470

Call Sign: W5TFE
Walter I Barry
9035 SE Morrison St
Roseburg OR 974703408

Call Sign: KC7UFZ
Edward V Stinson
1718 SE Orient Dr Apt
2129
Roseburg OR 97470

Call Sign: KD7ZBH
Gary R Winchell
6336 SE Plum Dr
Roseburg OR 97470

Call Sign: WO7A
Ned W Landis
12429 SE Stephens
Roseburg OR 97470

Call Sign: KC7GZV
Christopher A Hutton
1176 SE Tamora Ave
Roseburg OR 97470

Call Sign: KC7EZZ
John H Eiseman II
269 SE Tee Ct
Roseburg OR 974704820

Call Sign: KD7DFW
Robert E Feigel
1371 Stonehedge Ct NE
Roseburg OR 974719314

Call Sign: KF7SHH
Mercy Medical Center Ham
Club
450 Stringer Rd
Roseburg OR 97471

Call Sign: W6LXC
Richard L Brock
4311 Sturdivant
Roseburg OR 97470

Call Sign: KE7TFA
Joanne C Welker
16190 SW 108 Ave
Roseburg OR 97470

Call Sign: KE7KDZ
Jeanne E Hutcheson
13620 SW Beef Bend Rd 95

Roseburg OR 97470

Call Sign: KE7JFQ
Kerry A Hutcheson
13620 SW Beef Bend Rd 95
Roseburg OR 974704605

Call Sign: WA7KKR
Jimmy A Collins
11900 SW Burlcrest Dr
Roseburg OR 97470

Call Sign: KB7MXA
David L Hord
23425 SW Casavant Dr
Roseburg OR 97470

Call Sign: KB7ONH
Aaron J Fuchs
8675 SW Cecilia Ter
Roseburg OR 97470

Call Sign: KB7FWG
Veronica H Peterson
1057 SW Fairview Ave
Roseburg OR 97470

Call Sign: WB7RKR
Keith A Peterson
13785 SW Fairview Ct
Roseburg OR 97470

Call Sign: AI7I
Terry D Norcott
13615 SW Harness Ln
Roseburg OR 97470

Call Sign: KA7CGJ
Sandra M Norcott
111 SW Harrison Apt 15C
Roseburg OR 97470

Call Sign: KB7ONI
Gary D Damron

222 SW Harrison St Apt
24B
Roseburg OR 97470

Call Sign: N7IBT
Todd M Beal
14155 SW High Tor Dr
Roseburg OR 97470

Call Sign: W7HKE
Reuben A Stoltenberg
12255 SW Jaeger Ter
Roseburg OR 97470

Call Sign: K7QNP
Thomas C Scott
21199 SW Kenneth Ct
Roseburg OR 97470

Call Sign: KD7EHH
Charles E Lathrop Sr
7800 SW Landau St
Roseburg OR 97470

Call Sign: N7AVN
J O Richards
5575 SW Menlo Dr
Roseburg OR 97470

Call Sign: KF7QKQ
Robert A Sechler
55659 Swan Rd
Roseburg OR 97471

Call Sign: KC7PZH
Matthew P Grigsby
1930 Todd St
Roseburg OR 97471

Call Sign: KF7KTL
Sam J Russo
1655 Tudor Way SE
Roseburg OR 97471

Call Sign: W7EBH

Edward B Havicus
2358 Upper Cow Creek Rd
Roseburg OR 97470

Call Sign: KD7ERD
Devin R Scott
775 W Amanda
Roseburg OR 97471

Call Sign: KD7ERE
Brenda K Scott
775 W Amanda Ave
Roseburg OR 97471

Call Sign: KD7ERF
Michael R Scott
775 W Amanda Ave
Roseburg OR 97471

Call Sign: N6WOJ
Avon A Hodge
177 W Angela Ct
Roseburg OR 97471

Call Sign: K7ZKY
Erwin R Post
413 W Berdine
Roseburg OR 97470

Call Sign: N7XRP
William S Cantwell
1932 W Bertha Ave
Roseburg OR 97471

Call Sign: KB7YYH
Helen R Brink
326 W Bradford
Roseburg OR 97470

Call Sign: KC7TKW
Joseph L Darneille
532 W Broccoli
Roseburg OR 97470

Call Sign: N7PJY

Doris J Wharton
385 W Center St
Roseburg OR 97470

Call Sign: KC7NGK
Roseburg Senior High
School Technology Club
547 W Chapman
Roseburg OR 97470

Call Sign: KA7VFI
Ercell J Gifford
935 W Fromdahl
Roseburg OR 97470

Call Sign: N7PSY
Sandra L Gifford
935 W Fromdahl
Roseburg OR 97470

Call Sign: KA5RKZ
Susan P Benson
504 W Harrison
Roseburg OR 97470

Call Sign: W7BWO
Robert A Ellenwood
513 W Harrison St
Roseburg OR 97470

Call Sign: KF7SAJ
William W Metzler
1970 W Harvard 232
Roseburg OR 97471

Call Sign: KC7IXT
Judi D Kiepert
Pmb 5204 1030 W Harvard
Ave
Roseburg OR 97470

Call Sign: AC7EC
Steven R Kiepert
Pmb 5204 1030 W Harvard
Ave

Roseburg OR 97470

Call Sign: W7ARH
Ray R Rosenholm
1970 W Harvard Ave Apt
306
Roseburg OR 974702776

Call Sign: N6SSM
Robert D Board
313 W Hickory St
Roseburg OR 97471

Call Sign: N7XFS
Finn E Flood
2741 W Lorraine
Roseburg OR 97470

Call Sign: KF7FHZ
John W Jasper
3077 W Lorraine Ave
Roseburg OR 97471

Call Sign: W7SHA
Donald L Bell
928 W Nebo St
Roseburg OR 97470

Call Sign: N7PZV
Curtis J Rittenour
3114 W Normandy
Roseburg OR 97470

Call Sign: N7YRO
Steve H Thompson
3247 W Normandy Ave
Roseburg OR 97470

Call Sign: WB6ZEL
Emily C Neves
757 W Pilger
Roseburg OR 97470

Call Sign: K7ETU
Jerry L Hathaway

2840 W Sprague Ct
Roseburg OR 974716818

Call Sign: KE7IHP
John W Knox
1114 W Winter Ridge
Roseburg OR 97470

Call Sign: WB7TQZ
Jared C Gibbs
1740 Westview Dr
Roseburg OR 97471

Call Sign: W6DSW
Robert A Minto
1296 Whipple St
Roseburg OR 97470

Call Sign: KC7CNP
Pauline Woodward
247 Whisperine Pine
Roseburg OR 97470

Call Sign: KB7UMO
Joseph H Woodward Sr
247 Whispering Pine
Roseburg OR 97470

Call Sign: KE7YZQ
Susan E Augustine
291 Whispering Pines Way
Roseburg OR 97471

Call Sign: KD7NRL
Morrie A Chappel
621 Whistlers Park Rd
Roseburg OR 97470

Call Sign: KE6LBK
Esther I Schan
2665 Whistlers Park Rd
Roseburg OR 97470

Call Sign: KF6TLT
Dean V Schan

2665 Whistlers Park Rd
Roseburg OR 97470

Call Sign: K6PBE
Boyd B Brown Jr
180 Whitetail Ln
Roseburg OR 97470

Call Sign: N7XCK
Jane Brown
180 Whitetail Ln
Roseburg OR 97471

Call Sign: N7PJX
Nancy A Pahl
1440 Wild Iris Ln
Roseburg OR 97470

Call Sign: W5PII
Edward O Pahl Jr
1440 Wild Iris Ln
Roseburg OR 97470

Call Sign: KC7ZWA
Ron C Hackley
1942 Wild River Dr
Roseburg OR 97470

Call Sign: KD7JQV
Ruth M Hackley
1942 Wild River Dr
Roseburg OR 97470

Call Sign: N7HC
Milton W Mc Clung
2823 Wild River Dr
Roseburg OR 97470

Call Sign: KE7IHN
Jerry L Kingore
1918 Wildriver Dr
Roseburg OR 97470

Call Sign: KF7FIA
Eldon N Hopkins

130 Zachary Dr
Roseburg OR 97470

Call Sign: WB7RAM
Lloyd E Dewing
110 Zeus Ln
Roseburg OR 97470

Call Sign: KC6HIF
Idamarie L Heiner
Roseburg OR 97470

Call Sign: KB7IIQ
Gary E Hall
Roseburg OR 97470

Call Sign: KB7YLY
Thomas C Hyers Jr
Roseburg OR 97470

Call Sign: N6PWS
J Leath Padgett
Roseburg OR 97470

Call Sign: N7VNN
Gary F Galbick
Roseburg OR 97470

Call Sign: W7SCL
Jack H Chandler
Roseburg OR 97470

Call Sign: WA7NBN
Phillip J Goodman
Roseburg OR 97470

Call Sign: WB7NVE
Fred Schroeder
Roseburg OR 97470

Call Sign: WB7UCX
Jana L Chandler
Roseburg OR 97470

Call Sign: KC6YKG

Holly A Waddell
Roseburg OR 97470

Call Sign: KC7CDL
Kirk A Butler
Roseburg OR 97470

Call Sign: KC7HYX
Steven R Kiepert
Roseburg OR 97470

Call Sign: KC7LBC
Linda S Hyers
Roseburg OR 97470

Call Sign: KC7TLY
Umpqua Valley ARC
Roseburg OR 97470

Call Sign: KC7UAV
Umpqua Valley ARC
Roseburg OR 97470

Call Sign: KD7ABC
Robert L Parsons
Roseburg OR 97470

Call Sign: KF6BGJ
Jeff S Akers
Roseburg OR 97470

Call Sign: KF6BUP
Judy A Akers
Roseburg OR 97470

Call Sign: N7VOW
Ricky D Hall
Roseburg OR 97470

Call Sign: W7TCH
Thomas C Hyers Jr
Roseburg OR 97470

Call Sign: W7LSH
Linda S Hyers

Roseburg OR 97470

Call Sign: KE7BTJ
Bobby D Girdley
Roseburg OR 97470

Call Sign: KE7TFC
Clinton Waddell
Roseburg OR 97470

Call Sign: KE7TFE
Dorothy G Woodward
Roseburg OR 97470

Call Sign: KF7KTQ
Jeffrey D Hughes
Roseburg OR 97470

Call Sign: KF7KTR
Jeffrey M Orr
Roseburg OR 97470

Call Sign: N6MOK
Richard C Wharton
Roseburg OR 974700449

FCC Amateur Radio Licenses in Rufus

Call Sign: KB7OZV
Loretta M Meyer
Rufus OR 97050

FCC Amateur Radio Licenses in Scottsburg

Call Sign: AE7EP
John E Carroll
5247 Chapman St S
Scottsburg OR 97473

Call Sign: WB6SZL
Walter J Butkus
1875 State Rd
Scottsburg OR 974739710

Call Sign: N7MUC
Bernice E Peterson
Scottsburg OR 974730535

Call Sign: N7MUI
Edward A Peterson
Scottsburg OR 974730535

FCC Amateur Radio Licenses in Selma

Call Sign: KA5ZJP
Jose C GARCia
112 E 5th St
Selma OR 97538

Call Sign: KD7BJX
Aaron C Weber
825 E 5th St
Selma OR 97538

Call Sign: KD7HMO
David D Weber
825 E 5th St
Selma OR 97538

Call Sign: KD7HMR
Norma D Spurgin
500 E 6th Apt 300
Selma OR 97538

Call Sign: WG7H
Donne P Rathburn
234 E 6th Ave
Selma OR 97538

Call Sign: WA6PHO
Donna Straight
723 Jq Adams St
Selma OR 97538

Call Sign: KI6GUO
Terrell M Stevens
1256 Linden Ct

Selma OR 97538

Call Sign: N7NYK
Glen E Cochran
423 Lindley Ln
Selma OR 975380892

Call Sign: N7OPJ
Keith A Mc Niel
5184 Linn Ln
Selma OR 97538

Call Sign: N7PNX
Lonna I Mc Niel
2345 Linnet Ln
Selma OR 97538

Call Sign: KC6UJP
Robert W Rosenberg
815 Lisa Pl
Selma OR 97538

Call Sign: AD7LB
Robert W Rosenberg
4677 Lisa St NE
Selma OR 97538

Call Sign: KD6JFJ
Larae E Rosenberg
4677 Lisa St NE
Selma OR 97538

Call Sign: KC7SRL
Kurt F Prentner
600 River Loop 1
Selma OR 975389725

Call Sign: KE7ATW
Nancy A Wilson
1552 River Loop 1
Selma OR 97538

Call Sign: KB7TGN
Doloris M Lloyd
Selma OR 97538

Call Sign: KC7COA
David M Stafford
Selma OR 97538

Call Sign: KB7TGM
Glen A Lloyd
Selma OR 97538

Call Sign: N0JJZ
Dale Reams
Selma OR 97538

Call Sign: WB7WNP
Ernest P Bezanson
Selma OR 97538

Call Sign: KF7KLL
Robin L Binkley
Selma OR 97538

FCC Amateur Radio Licenses in Seneca

Call Sign: WB7WSF
Thomas R Bessler
2191 Birchwood Ave
Seneca OR 978730217

FCC Amateur Radio Licenses in Shady Cove

Call Sign: K6UGS
W V Hajek
2599 Brookside Dr
Shady Cove OR 97539

Call Sign: NZ6W
Jerry A Vettrus
2251 Dick George Rd
Shady Cove OR 97539

Call Sign: KB7NOC
Kenneth A Hoff

12831 Jefferson Hwy 99E
SE
Shady Cove OR 97539

Call Sign: KC6YRM
Albert B Carter
4233 Jefferson Marion Rd
SE
Shady Cove OR 97539

Call Sign: KC7HFA
Ronald R Asbill
2 Jefferson Pkwy Apt A4
Shady Cove OR 97603

Call Sign: KC7WXA
Sharon L Asbill
1309 Jerome Ave
Shady Cove OR 97539

Call Sign: KF6PMT
James W Seavey
32744 Kend Springs Rd
Shady Cove OR 97539

Call Sign: KF6PMU
Verna L Norris
164 Kendall Estates Ln
Shady Cove OR 97539

Call Sign: N6TDO
Robert L Temple
38927 Morning Star NE
Shady Cove OR 97539

Call Sign: KD7UVW
Jennifer L Johnson
61478 Orion Dr
Shady Cove OR 97539

Call Sign: KD7TTU
Mike W Johnson
61478 Orion Dr
Shady Cove OR 97539

Call Sign: KD7WZE
Cheryl L Chang
61573 Orion Dr
Shady Cove OR 97539

Call Sign: WA7ZUT
David E Westerfield
3006 SE 112
Shady Cove OR 97539

Call Sign: KD7IBG
Jeremy A Mathis
5124 SE 115th
Shady Cove OR 97539

Call Sign: K7VO
Paul L Miller
Shady Cove OR 97539

Call Sign: KE7MVI
Rogue Valley D Star
Shady Cove OR 97539

Call Sign: K6VWP
Donald R Biggs
Shady Cove OR 97539

Call Sign: KC7VFF
Ervin L Rodgers
Shady Cove OR 97539

Call Sign: WA6WBB
Mervin N Whitney
Shady Cove OR 97539

Call Sign: KD7KKG
Timothy N Mathis
Shady Cove OR 97539

Call Sign: KD7KKI
Connie A Mathis
Shady Cove OR 97539

Call Sign: KD7MLN
Jeff L Staten

Shady Cove OR 97539

Call Sign: KD7QDD
Juliana M Mathis
Shady Cove OR 97539

Call Sign: K7GVI
Joshua J Mathis
Shady Cove OR 97539

Call Sign: W7BRO
Carl S Van Orden
Shady Cove OR 97539

Call Sign: NS7R
Jeremy A Mathis
Shady Cove OR 97539

Call Sign: KD7ZTK
Orlinda M Mathis
Shady Cove OR 97539

FCC Amateur Radio Licenses in Silver Lake

Call Sign: KE7KJU
Alan B Ashby
34895 S Ellis Rd
Silver Lake OR 97638

FCC Amateur Radio Licenses in Sisters

Call Sign: W7YJ
Jack B Peterson
526 5th St
Sisters OR 97759

Call Sign: KB7GAC
Marjorie S Turner
104 Brolin Ct
Sisters OR 97759

Call Sign: KE7CQS
Warren C Rice

1388 Buck St
Sisters OR 97759

Call Sign: KE7NRO
David F Liddell
1340 Church St NE
Sisters OR 97759

Call Sign: KE7NRL
Peter W Liddell
1815 Church St SE
Sisters OR 97759

Call Sign: AL7AN
David A Hagstrom
40007 Cole School Rd
Sisters OR 97759

Call Sign: W7JSJ
William D Richins
40007 Cole School Rd
Sisters OR 97759

Call Sign: N6KCS
Zeke Duge
93787 Dorsey Ln
Sisters OR 92869

Call Sign: KC7SPL
Irene A Smith
737 Doty
Sisters OR 97759

Call Sign: W7FGT
Gustav E Wendland
140 E Ashland Ln
Sisters OR 977593201

Call Sign: KE7TMR
Mark W Miller
60450 Elkai Woods Dr
Sisters OR 97759

Call Sign: KC7PYZ
Kirk J Jacobsen

2695 Everett Ave
Sisters OR 97759

Call Sign: WB5LAN
Joe B Gustafson
3926 Fairview Ave
Sisters OR 97759

Call Sign: N7YBP
Stan G Torry
510 Gilles St
Sisters OR 97759

Call Sign: KE7ULY
Evan Hjelmstad
5365 Goodrich Hwy
Sisters OR 97759

Call Sign: KE7CQT
Anita L Maze
3398 Goose Cross Ln
Sisters OR 977599839

Call Sign: KC7VGU
Kent R Achterhof
439 Heywood Ave
Sisters OR 977599716

Call Sign: KD6AVV
Russell L Weir
28450 Hillaire
Sisters OR 97759

Call Sign: K6AVV
Russell L Weir
28450 Hillaire
Sisters OR 97759

Call Sign: KE7AQG
Beverly J Tucker
4608 Holly St
Sisters OR 97759

Call Sign: W7BUG
Beverly J Tucker

463 Hollyhock Pl N
Sisters OR 97759

Call Sign: KD7YUV
Danny J Tucker
14359 Hollyview Ln
Sisters OR 97759

Call Sign: W7DUX
Danny J Tucker
3355 Hollywood Ave
Sisters OR 97759

Call Sign: KE7CQR
Sue Morgan
77380 Hwy 99
Sisters OR 97759

Call Sign: KE7BYW
Steven F Johnson
93390 Hwy 99
Sisters OR 97759

Call Sign: KC7SNY
Cascade Emergency Service
ARC
300 Limpy Creek Rd
Sisters OR 97759

Call Sign: KD7AKI
Nancy R Miller
300 Limpy Creek Rd
Sisters OR 97759

Call Sign: KJ7GQ
William N Miller
190 Lincoln 2
Sisters OR 97759

Call Sign: KF7FGM
Dylan T Hicks
923 Lone Rock Rd
Sisters OR 97759

Call Sign: WA6IKJ

Dean R Billing
54825 Lonesome Pine Rd
Sisters OR 97759

Call Sign: KB7ORK
Gordon D Halsten
2358 Long Branch Rd
Sisters OR 97759

Call Sign: N4TTR
Walter F Bailey
2075 McCormick Lp
Sisters OR 97759

Call Sign: W7WRK
Joseph E Wright
1565 N Main St
Sisters OR 97759

Call Sign: KB7YPH
John D Culver
7197 NE 1st
Sisters OR 97759

Call Sign: N7TYO
David R Culver
3039 NE 1st Ct
Sisters OR 97759

Call Sign: KD7AKG
Mary K Golden
835 Oregon Way
Sisters OR 97759

Call Sign: N7ZTM
Gordon N Golden
2137 Orindale Rd
Sisters OR 97759

Call Sign: KE6DYM
Eva E Eagle
1474 Poplar Dr 3
Sisters OR 97759

Call Sign: WB7SAD

Bruce D Bowen
2190 Poplar Dr 65
Sisters OR 97759

Call Sign: KD7KAA
Christopher S Peterson
73224 Purchase Ln
Sisters OR 97759

Call Sign: N7SQ
Darren W Ferwalt
19575 River Rd Sp A1
Sisters OR 97759

Call Sign: KC7TPF
Kristin E Lush
Sandvik
Sisters OR 97759

Call Sign: KF6GTJ
Susan P Antifaoff
1322 Saunders Ln SE
Sisters OR 97759

Call Sign: KD7VZ
Robert L Stephenson
3605 SE 115th
Sisters OR 97759

Call Sign: N7VLY
Neal B Wineman
25633 Springhill Dr
Sisters OR 97759

Call Sign: N6EIA
William H Le Sage
5217 Starlit Ct
Sisters OR 97759

Call Sign: KD7RIQ
Levi L Johnson
900 State St C195
Sisters OR 97759

Call Sign: KB7UDT

Janet C Culver
1831 Tamarack Ct
Sisters OR 97759

Call Sign: KD7FNY
Thomas L Ross
57401 Timber Rd
Sisters OR 97759

Call Sign: KA7RPL
Carolyn A Nielsen Smith
32520 Turlay Ln
Sisters OR 97759

Call Sign: K7BYH
Ben L Gifford
Sisters OR 97759

Call Sign: N7RGF
John A Pagano
Sisters OR 97759

Call Sign: KB7HNS
John R Crabtree II
Sisters OR 97759

Call Sign: KC7AYC
John T Turner
Sisters OR 97759

Call Sign: KC7JLY
Christopher M Gillan
Sisters OR 97759

Call Sign: KC7LGA
Raymond F Derize
Sisters OR 97759

Call Sign: KC7LPJ
Sandra L Veeck
Sisters OR 97759

Call Sign: KC7OAP
David W Gillan
Sisters OR 97759

Call Sign: KC7PZA
Stephen R Fisher
Sisters OR 97759

Call Sign: KC7ZNU
James D Dekorte
Sisters OR 97759

Call Sign: KJ7DA
Alwyn F Stockley
Sisters OR 97759

Call Sign: N7NNN
Cheresse N Howard
Sisters OR 97759

Call Sign: W7YAQ
Robert S Norin
Sisters OR 97759

Call Sign: KD7JZY
Joe W Green
Sisters OR 97759

Call Sign: KD7KLT
Nickalaus A Newport
Sisters OR 97759

Call Sign: KD7LNS
Barbara G Jack
Sisters OR 97759

Call Sign: KD7TCC
Andrew Holmes Jr
Sisters OR 97759

Call Sign: KD7TCA
Bill E Stevens
Sisters OR 97759

Call Sign: KE7TMT
David K Moyer
Sisters OR 97759

Call Sign: KE7CQQ
Debby L Miller
Sisters OR 97759

Call Sign: KD7TCB
Dona G Smith
Sisters OR 97759

Call Sign: KD7TBZ
Jane W Stevens
Sisters OR 97759

Call Sign: KD7TCE
Joan V Jacobsen
Sisters OR 97759

Call Sign: K7JVJ
Joan V Jacobsen
Sisters OR 97759

Call Sign: KD7TCD
Kathryn A Cooper
Sisters OR 97759

Call Sign: KD7VZO
Kathy E Swensen
Sisters OR 97759

Call Sign: KE7CQU
Phillip A Gale
Sisters OR 97759

Call Sign: KE7CQP
Roy W Miller
Sisters OR 97759

Call Sign: KD7WSA
Timothy N Bell
Sisters OR 97759

Call Sign: W7TDP
Robert A Mc Clanathan
Sisters OR 977591810

Call Sign: KD6EB

Mosby L Simmons III
Sisters OR 977591949

Call Sign: KD7EB
Mosby L Simmons III
Sisters OR 977591949

Call Sign: AB7LV
John B Mc Gilvary
Sisters OR 977593500

FCC Amateur Radio Licenses in Sixes

Call Sign: KW7USA
Janet L Scanlon
42126 Bachman Ln
Sixes OR 97476

Call Sign: NN7DX
Roy F Scanlon
42126 Bachman Ln
Sixes OR 97476

Call Sign: KA6UZN
Glenn E Hewitt
21365 Back Alley
Sixes OR 97476

Call Sign: KF7OYU
Thomas E Whitehead
1100 Clayton Way
Sixes OR 97476

Call Sign: KA7ZNU
Janet R IIda
Sixes OR 97476

Call Sign: K2KF
Allen L Vail
Sixes OR 97476

Call Sign: K7KJO
Kelly M Perkins
Sixes OR 97476

Call Sign: KA7TXI
Ray B IIda
Sixes OR 97476

FCC Amateur Radio Licenses in Sprague River

Call Sign: KD6LFU
Michael G Hodges
69749 Squawback Rd
Sprague River OR 97639

Call Sign: N7NCA
Michael G Hodges
90306 Squire Dr
Sprague River OR 97639

Call Sign: KF6OBU
Dennis H Worden
1446 St Andrew Way
Sprague River OR 97639

Call Sign: KF7QMY
Douglas J Youngberg
Sprague River OR 97639

FCC Amateur Radio Licenses in Spray

Call Sign: KL7ISE
Keith B Brant
Spray OR 97874

FCC Amateur Radio Licenses in Springfield

Call Sign: KF7NXY
Aaron L Danner
515 1st St
Springfield OR 97477

Call Sign: N7RLL
Ralph B Richardson
2730 1st St

Springfield OR 97478

Call Sign: KA7ABR
Edward L Mc Gillvrey Jr
4513 46th Ave NE
Springfield OR 97478

Call Sign: KD7KDV
Robert W Younger
1814 48th Ave SE
Springfield OR 97478

Call Sign: KD7OBT
Ted L Weiss
1303 4th St
Springfield OR 97478

Call Sign: KE7MEX
Ronald C Alley
320 7th Ave
Springfield OR 97477

Call Sign: KC7UQH
David L Mc Coy
718 9th St
Springfield OR 974773702

Call Sign: KE6FXZ
Jack Burgess
2833 A St
Springfield OR 97477

Call Sign: KE6OYQ
Olga M Burgess
5105 A St
Springfield OR 97477

Call Sign: W7JAC
Jack Burgess
5105 A St
Springfield OR 97477

Call Sign: W7OMB
Olga M Burgess
5105 A St

Springfield OR 97477

Call Sign: KF7QMW
Mark H Cross
999 Abernethy Rd
Springfield OR 97477

Call Sign: KD7UYG
Dennis D Shew
21830 Abiqua Rd NE
Springfield OR 97477

Call Sign: KC8BRY
Dean P Walton
79096 Agnew Rd
Springfield OR 97478

Call Sign: KC7ART
Scott A Farley
59140 Airport Rd
Springfield OR 97478

Call Sign: N7DSC
Jeffrey D Bantz
23115 Airport Rd NE Box
11
Springfield OR 97477

Call Sign: KA7I
Bruce C Fingerhood
4095 Alameda Ave NE
Springfield OR 97477

Call Sign: KD7SDC
Michael J Sheetz
4095 Alameda Ave NE
Springfield OR 97478

Call Sign: W7SOT
Scott O Thayer
2153 Alex Ave SE
Springfield OR 97478

Call Sign: KF7DGA
Matthew J Peterson

25489 Alsea Deadwood
Hwy
Springfield OR 97478

Call Sign: W3UGV
Matthew J Peterson
3911 Alsea Hwy
Springfield OR 97478

Call Sign: KF7JGF
John A Cahill
3911 Alsea Hwy
Springfield OR 97478

Call Sign: KD7KDW
Carl A Robertson
5672 American Ave
Springfield OR 97478

Call Sign: KC7VWM
Keelan J Kindt
5672 American Ave
Springfield OR 97478

Call Sign: KE7ISV
David A Gonzalez
61575 American Ln
Springfield OR 97478

Call Sign: KE7FCL
William M Thornton
39242 Amherst St
Springfield OR 97478

Call Sign: K7THO
William M Thornton
92982 Amie Loop
Springfield OR 97478

Call Sign: WA7ZQR
Robert D Dorr Jr
32801 Amity Ln
Springfield OR 97478

Call Sign: N7GEQ

Ralph A Bonnell III
1271 Annabelle Ln
Springfield OR 97478

Call Sign: W7PDL
Kermit W Wright
4587 Antelope Rd
Springfield OR 97478

Call Sign: N7NFS
Thomas R Germaine
4587 Antelope Rd
Springfield OR 97478

Call Sign: KD7ZBF
Jeremy S Henricks
537 Antelope Way 2
Springfield OR 97478

Call Sign: K7HKS
Jeremy S Henricks
1580 Anthony Ave
Springfield OR 97478

Call Sign: KE7UXZ
Joseph P Prenevost III
1580 Anthony Ave
Springfield OR 97478

Call Sign: W7JPP
Joseph P Prenevost III
14280 Antioch Rd
Springfield OR 97478

Call Sign: KF7ULW
Peak Radio Association
19273 Apache Rd
Springfield OR 97477

Call Sign: W7PRA
Peak Radio Association
72154 Apiary Rd
Springfield OR 97477

Call Sign: K7TVL

Chris K Novara
6677 Apollo Rd
Springfield OR 97477

Call Sign: KF7DGC
C Wade Richardson
13444 Applegate Ter
Springfield OR 97478

Call Sign: KF7AHT
Jacob L Richardson Jr
92109 Applegate Trl
Springfield OR 97478

Call Sign: KB7VIS
Kirk H Johnson
53752 Appleton Rd 59
Springfield OR 97478

Call Sign: KF7BUC
Samantha R Corbin
460 Arnos St 98
Springfield OR 97477

Call Sign: W7SNK
James A Corbin
436 Ash St
Springfield OR 97477

Call Sign: K7MES
Marie E Schmidt
1149 Ash St
Springfield OR 97477

Call Sign: W7JS
John F Schmidt
1435 Ash St
Springfield OR 97477

Call Sign: KE7LDJ
Eric P Montbriand
625 Atwater Rd
Springfield OR 97478

Call Sign: KD7MXN

Kenneth E Townsend
4686 Auburn Rd
Springfield OR 97478

Call Sign: W7MBG
Michael B Gregory
4730 Auburn Rd NE 52
Springfield OR 97478

Call Sign: KE7IYJ
Rebecca L Gregory
4730 Auburn Rd NE 52
Springfield OR 97478

Call Sign: W7BKI
Rebecca L Gregory
4730 Auburn Rd NE Sp 120
Springfield OR 97478

Call Sign: KC7SVO
Joseph Z Johnson
33 Auburn St
Springfield OR 97478

Call Sign: KD7SWZ
Michael B Gregory
620 Audel Ave
Springfield OR 97478

Call Sign: KD7ILU
Michael A Guidero
3381 Bailey Ln
Springfield OR 97478

Call Sign: K7WDL
W David Larson
4425 Battlecreek Rd SE
Springfield OR 97477

Call Sign: KE7VLK
W David Larson
5855 Battlecreek Rd SE
Springfield OR 97477

Call Sign: KD7MTN

Benjamin D Stores
202 Bayberry Ct
Springfield OR 97477

Call Sign: WD6EGE
Wayne R Doster
620 Best View Dr
Springfield OR 97478

Call Sign: WB7DLA
Burley W Duncan
6656 Blackwell Rd
Springfield OR 97477

Call Sign: KB7MB
Doyle G Wright
221 Bridge St
Springfield OR 97477

Call Sign: KB7MW
Norma E Wright
1708 Bridge St
Springfield OR 97477

Call Sign: KE7CRA
Randy A Huntoon
66724 Brooks Rd
Springfield OR 97477

Call Sign: W7SFD
Emerald ARS
3835 Brooks St
Springfield OR 97477

Call Sign: WA7FQD
Emerald ARS
752 Brookside Dr
Springfield OR 97477

Call Sign: WA7TUV
Richard S Jenkins
1143 Brookside Dr
Springfield OR 974771460

Call Sign: KE7DFR

Dennis H Rech
62886 Buchanan Ln
Springfield OR 97478

Call Sign: KB7AHA
Edward L Mc Gillvrey III
63358 Buchanan Ln
Springfield OR 97478

Call Sign: KE7JFL
James W Phillips
4380 Burlington Loop NE
Springfield OR 974776508

Call Sign: KB7RAG
Michael L Barker
27973 Bush Ln
Springfield OR 97478

Call Sign: KB7HST
Jason R Heimann
352 Bush St S 75
Springfield OR 97478

Call Sign: KF7DGB
Jeffrey L Stover
88580 Carter Creek Rd
Springfield OR 97478

Call Sign: W7STO
Jeffrey L Stover
1639 Carter Ln
Springfield OR 97478

Call Sign: KD7AHR
James R Peterson
2791 Chester Ave NE
Springfield OR 97478

Call Sign: KB7HCK
Robert D Manning
2812 Chester Ave NE
Springfield OR 97478

Call Sign: KG7FU

James S Kaplan
505 Chester St
Springfield OR 97477

Call Sign: WA7JIC
Donald G Baity
1434 Church St
Springfield OR 97478

Call Sign: KF7GPI
Nate W Beckett
4143 Cloud Dr S
Springfield OR 97477

Call Sign: KF7AHS
Gavin S Thorpe
4501 Cloudcrest Dr
Springfield OR 97477

Call Sign: W7FXJ
Flora C Nichols
4381 Cloudview Dr S
Springfield OR 97478

Call Sign: N7KKU
Arlo C Joranger
289 Columbia Loop
Springfield OR 97477

Call Sign: KA7TWX
Paul J Kleman
24426 Columbine Dr
Springfield OR 974773254

Call Sign: KE7VXJ
Robert S Case Jr
80660 Craig Rd
Springfield OR 97477

Call Sign: KE7CWN
Jeff H Collins
1710 Dairy Loop Rd
Springfield OR 97478

Call Sign: K7FMJ

Jeff H Collins
5335 Daisey 91
Springfield OR 97478

Call Sign: KF7IMH
Charles E Sullivan
134 Driftwood Dr
Springfield OR 97477

Call Sign: WB7PQT
Roger R Haxby
19103 Driftwood Dr
Springfield OR 97477

Call Sign: KD7EFN
Mickey C Mc Kinney
2944 Dry Creek Rd
Springfield OR 97477

Call Sign: KD7JBF
William A Martin
4138 Dry Creek Rd
Springfield OR 97478

Call Sign: K7JBF
William A Martin
1001 Dry Creek Rd
Springfield OR 97478

Call Sign: K9CKP
Curtis K Porter
4336 Duane Dr S
Springfield OR 97478

Call Sign: KC7OEN
Marvin R Curl
11340 Duggan Rd
Springfield OR 97478

Call Sign: KD7QCG
Rick A Iverson
823 E 4th St
Springfield OR 97477

Call Sign: W7RAI

Rick A Iverson
925 E 4th St
Springfield OR 97477

Call Sign: KB7NMK
Lucas S P Carlson
21955 E Beaver Creek Rd
Springfield OR 97478

Call Sign: KD7IET
Ronald N Snow
914 E Main St
Springfield OR 974789505

Call Sign: KD7LYK
Charles A Bill
2610 E Nob Hill St SE
Springfield OR 97478

Call Sign: KD7ZU
Ransom R Southerland
855 E Quince
Springfield OR 97478

Call Sign: N7VTD
Simon L Skiles
39380 Evans St
Springfield OR 97477

Call Sign: KD7PAY
Jack W Peters
51449 Evans Way
Springfield OR 97478

Call Sign: KC7EGC
Sheri Anne M Andersen
267 Evelyn Ave NE
Springfield OR 97478

Call Sign: KD7VYQ
Johnathan W Anderson
444 Evelyn St
Springfield OR 97478

Call Sign: K7EGC

Sheri Anne M Andersen
575 Evelyn St
Springfield OR 97478

Call Sign: KD7QYZ
Maynard D Williamson
577 Evelyn St
Springfield OR 97478

Call Sign: W7MDW
Maynard D Williamson
63276 Everest Rd
Springfield OR 97478

Call Sign: KD7YVP
Danny J Daves
42424 Evergreen Acres Ln
Springfield OR 97478

Call Sign: KC7ANE
Eric J Andersen
42424 Evergreen Acres Ln
Springfield OR 97478

Call Sign: KD7KDU
David W Blomquist
526 Evergreen Dr
Springfield OR 97478

Call Sign: W7DWB
David W Blomquist
526 Evergreen Dr
Springfield OR 97478

Call Sign: KD7DIF
Garner S Warren II
3032 Evergreen Dr
Springfield OR 97477

Call Sign: KD7KLM
Robert L Stuart
61255 Ferguson Rd
Springfield OR 97478

Call Sign: KA7AYP

Donald O Hibbetts
6149 Fernhillloop
Springfield OR 97478

Call Sign: KC7FEW
Thomas J Woginrich Jr
8905 Fiddle Cr Rd
Springfield OR 97477

Call Sign: KE7PWV
Albert P Gauche
29665 Fir St
Springfield OR 97477

Call Sign: N7NIM
Donald D Grigsby Sr
5026 G Foothills Rd
Springfield OR 974774039

Call Sign: W7DAB
Douglas A Blount
1509 Franklin St
Springfield OR 97478

Call Sign: WB7FCN
Tony R Newman
2625 Fulton St SE
Springfield OR 974774158

Call Sign: KB7CUV
David C Pettit
701 G Ave
Springfield OR 97477

Call Sign: WE1DUX
Robert S Case Jr
769 Gardendale Ave
Springfield OR 974778105

Call Sign: KA7MLU
Donna M Mc Cown
411 Griffith Ln
Springfield OR 97478

Call Sign: N7BKV

Frankie J Mc Cown
630 Griffith Ln
Springfield OR 97478

Call Sign: KB7BVV
Terry H Neeley
3040 Grove St
Springfield OR 97477

Call Sign: KC7OUB
Lillian B Lehmkuhl
18011 Hamaker Ln
Springfield OR 97478

Call Sign: KC7HIX
Ronald M Lehmkuhl
1700 Hamilton Ct Apt 316
Springfield OR 97477

Call Sign: W7RML
Ronald M Lehmkuhl
1980 Hamilton Ln
Springfield OR 974774326

Call Sign: KB7SYA
Gene Spores
575 Hamlin Dr
Springfield OR 97477

Call Sign: W7AWL
Andrew W Landen
624 Harrison Ave
Springfield OR 97478

Call Sign: KB2SRQ
Andrew W Landen
2840 Harrison Ave
Springfield OR 97478

Call Sign: KC7TSU
Lynn D Turley
3308 Hill Crest Hwy
Springfield OR 97477

Call Sign: N7WZB

James C Hamaker
17115 Hofer Ct
Springfield OR 97477

Call Sign: N7FKB
Lola M Ollar
590 Hoffman A101
Springfield OR 97477

Call Sign: W7FKS
Mildred D Wildman
2015 Hoffman Rd NE
Springfield OR 97477

Call Sign: WD6AER
Frederick L Guiol
963 Hogan Rd
Springfield OR 97477

Call Sign: KC7VWN
Michael R Arens
30311 Holiday Rd
Springfield OR 97477

Call Sign: KE7MDY
Bob L Kindrick
4699 Hubbard Creek Rd
Springfield OR 97477

Call Sign: AB7IE
Bernard P Michlanski
4779 Hubbard Creek Rd
Springfield OR 97477

Call Sign: KF7LVI
Jesus Rivas
6480 Hubbard Creek Rd
Springfield OR 97477

Call Sign: KD7WYT
Laurie A Monico
6480 Hubbard Creek Rd
Springfield OR 97477

Call Sign: KG6DAI

Alicia M Ramos
9064 Hubbard Creek Rd
Springfield OR 97477

Call Sign: KA7HAQ
Rex E Heide
1829 Hubbard Ln
Springfield OR 97477

Call Sign: KE7TEH
John J Garland
29009 Huber Rd
Springfield OR 97477

Call Sign: N7JQT
William D Page
33766 Hwy 26
Springfield OR 97478

Call Sign: KF7TUD
David G Spiro
20551 Hwy 62
Springfield OR 97478

Call Sign: W7DGS
David G Spiro
22090 Hwy 62
Springfield OR 97478

Call Sign: KF7OMY
Gil I Lewis
22710 Hwy 62
Springfield OR 97478

Call Sign: K2BTF
Gil I Lewis
37009 Hwy 62
Springfield OR 97478

Call Sign: KD7RLB
David J Casarez
14946 Hwy 66
Springfield OR 97478

Call Sign: WA7BFE

Leslie W Lessard
14946 Hwy 66
Springfield OR 974787581

Call Sign: KF7GPJ
Joseph J Hazelton
95531 Jerrys Flat Rd
Springfield OR 97477

Call Sign: KD7IVD
Mary Anne Mobley
58605 Kavanaugh St
Springfield OR 97477

Call Sign: K7CRR
William L Spalding
58605 Kavanaugh St
Springfield OR 97477

Call Sign: KD7FNX
David J Germaine
2074 Kayleigh Way
Springfield OR 974774345

Call Sign: KD7SWX
Mickey D Snook
535 Kbel Yliniemi Ln
Springfield OR 97477

Call Sign: KE7FLB
Terry J Oberfoell
384 Kearney St
Springfield OR 97477

Call Sign: KF7SNW
Peter R Racette
5600 Kimmels Riverside Ln
Springfield OR 97478

Call Sign: KB7SXV
Ronald C Chase
91292 Kirwen Dr
Springfield OR 97478

Call Sign: KB7FNK

Tammy L Bolt
1492 Lakeshore Dr
Springfield OR 97478

Call Sign: KF7FGC
Daniel D Basaraba
647 Larch Rd
Springfield OR 97477

Call Sign: KD6GQ
John A Wellcome
96515 Larson Ln
Springfield OR 97478

Call Sign: WA7JW
John A Wellcome
75503 Larson Rd
Springfield OR 97478

Call Sign: KI4OJ
John H Mc Coy Sr
4720 Liberty Rd S
Springfield OR 97477

Call Sign: N5ADI
Ronnie L Little
35630 Little Walluski Ln
Springfield OR 97478

Call Sign: KD7WSO
Earl W Cavin
310 Littlebrook Ln
Springfield OR 97478

Call Sign: KD7HAE
Marta B Gee
86621 Lorane Hwy
Springfield OR 974772183

Call Sign: KD7HAF
Kenney M Gee
86621 Lorane Hwy
Springfield OR 974772183

Call Sign: KF7PY

Lloyd A Lovaasen
7185 Los Verdes Dr
Springfield OR 97478

Call Sign: W7BPA
Robert P Veness
2475 Mangan St
Springfield OR 97477

Call Sign: KB7YTN
Robert E Crossler
2507 Mangan St
Springfield OR 97477

Call Sign: WA7VLK
Robert J Latimer Sr
645 Mardon Ct
Springfield OR 97477

Call Sign: N7CVC
Phill E Root
54841 McKenzie River Dr
Springfield OR 97477

Call Sign: WB6SXW
David F Nelson
1006 Meadow Ave
Springfield OR 97477

Call Sign: W7FPY
Robert W Shelby
2167 Meadow Pl SE
Springfield OR 974785426

Call Sign: KE7ACZ
Duncan C Patterson
35088 Meadow Rd SW
Springfield OR 97478

Call Sign: KE7CNK
Emerald ARS
1008 Meadow Ridge St NE
Springfield OR 97478

Call Sign: KC7OHH

Cindy L Mc Kinney
1614 Meadow View Dr
Springfield OR 97477

Call Sign: AA0BY
Larry G Mahlberg
3835 Meadow View Dr
Springfield OR 97477

Call Sign: KA7CRB
James E Greathouse
45686 Meadowlark Ln
Springfield OR 97478

Call Sign: WA7MOK
Eunice E Brown
1030 Meadowlark Ln NE
Springfield OR 97478

Call Sign: KA7UGL
Lee J Delorme
766 Meadowlawn Dr
Springfield OR 97478

Call Sign: N7YUL
Garry A Meyer
12160 Meadowlawn Dr
Springfield OR 97478

Call Sign: KF7UJF
David P Heaton
2480 Melrose Loop
Springfield OR 97477

Call Sign: K8THH
David P Heaton
2480 Melrose Loop
Springfield OR 97477

Call Sign: WD8KDG
Craig C Heaton
2512 Melrose Loop
Springfield OR 97477

Call Sign: KE7ERS

Eileen E Parrack
2038 Mockingbird Dr S
Springfield OR 97478

Call Sign: KE7ERR
Paul Sandland
5635 Modesto Ct S
Springfield OR 97478

Call Sign: AD7HA
Paul Sandland
86435 Modesto Dr N
Springfield OR 97478

Call Sign: KA7LLC
Lorena M Reid
986 Moneda Ave N
Springfield OR 97477

Call Sign: KA7LLD
Alan D Reid
1145 Moneda Ave N
Springfield OR 97477

Call Sign: KB7YJC
Frederick A Hugi
364 Monica Dr
Springfield OR 97478

Call Sign: KE7HEU
Veronica R Stirnitzke
4220 Myrtle Wood
Springfield OR 97477

Call Sign: K0AEY
Larry L Ravlin
1918 N 14th Box 1050
Springfield OR 974788816

Call Sign: AA7LR
Larry L Ravlin
501 N 14th St
Springfield OR 97478

Call Sign: N7XRQ

Timothy F Mc Cutcheon
2356 N 22nd Ct
Springfield OR 97478

Call Sign: KE7OMY
Duane R Jacobson
947 N Birch
Springfield OR 97478

Call Sign: K7DRJ
Duane R Jacobson
966 N Birch
Springfield OR 97478

Call Sign: KB0EBO
Thomas H Jones
7575 N Edgewater St
Springfield OR 97477

Call Sign: K7AHT
Darwin W Mc Carroll
116 N Elm St
Springfield OR 97477

Call Sign: K7SNV
Richard S Maulding
7655 N Emerald Ave
Springfield OR 97477

Call Sign: KD7WSN
Kathleen A Shaw
1040 N Fir
Springfield OR 97477

Call Sign: WA7SWY
Dolores M Welty
170 N Fir Villa Rd
Springfield OR 97477

Call Sign: KC7RYG
Randal E Dornon
33435 N Fork Rd SE
Springfield OR 97477

Call Sign: N7NOT

Joseph L Bovee
8228 N Foss
Springfield OR 97477

Call Sign: N7GFO
Greg W Hendrickson
335 N Gale
Springfield OR 97477

Call Sign: W7JCM
John C Montgomery
335 N Gale
Springfield OR 97478

Call Sign: W7ADL
Robert N Faught
150 N Garfield St
Springfield OR 97478

Call Sign: KD7FZI
Derik Z Smith
150 N Garfield St 301
Springfield OR 974771820

Call Sign: WA7YVU
Keith A Lowe
120 N Garfield St Sp 1
Springfield OR 97477

Call Sign: WA7ZLY
Virginia R Lowe
5133 N Gay Ave
Springfield OR 97478

Call Sign: N6MYD
Randall K Rounds
1711 N Going St Lower
Level
Springfield OR 97478

Call Sign: KA7QNZ
Leon G Mc Ginnis
736 N Gould St
Springfield OR 97478

Call Sign: KA7APR
Clarence A Ludwig
1265 N Grant St
Springfield OR 97477

Call Sign: KB7SXX
Delilah R Ludwig
6935 N Greenwich
Springfield OR 97477

Call Sign: KC7NHS
James F Bates
641 N H St
Springfield OR 97477

Call Sign: KB7KLV
Christopher S Williams
75 N Hayden Bay Dr
Springfield OR 97478

Call Sign: KD7WSM
Linda D Baughman
322 N Hayden Bay Dr
Springfield OR 97478

Call Sign: N7NSF
Phillip R Carey
468 N Hayden Bay Dr
Springfield OR 97478

Call Sign: KC7PFJ
Michael P Mullarkey
1503 N Hayden Island Dr
Springfield OR 97478

Call Sign: W7KNE
Theodore G Suomela
1501 N Hayden Island Dr
64
Springfield OR 97477

Call Sign: N7XRN
Gary L Lutman
1503 N Hayden Island Dr
Sp 236

Springfield OR 97478

Call Sign: KD7ZHP
Adam R Egan
910 N Henry St
Springfield OR 97477

Call Sign: KB7HGC
Oscar F Oberman
1040 N Henry St
Springfield OR 97477

Call Sign: WA7ZMG
Dorothy A Van Cleef
1840 N Hwy 101
Springfield OR 97478

Call Sign: KE7BJI
Michael O Kirschenman
3700 N Hwy 101
Springfield OR 97478

Call Sign: KA7DEC
Cheryl C De Moss
3196 NW 157th Pl
Springfield OR 97477

Call Sign: WB7WVK
Charles P De Moss Jr
985 NW 158th Ave
Springfield OR 97477

Call Sign: WA7ZMA
Clinton L Van Cleef
1107 NW 15th St Apt D 137
Springfield OR 97478

Call Sign: KA7POJ
Lorretta J Duncan
2336 NW 161st Ave
Springfield OR 97478

Call Sign: KD7ZLN
Cristin M Zulaski

88779 Old Weigh Station
Rd
Springfield OR 97477

Call Sign: KA7FDG
Robert J Beaver
6552 Palomino Way
Springfield OR 97477

Call Sign: KA7FDH
E Joyce Beaver
6589 Palomino Way
Springfield OR 974773222

Call Sign: KB7PEK
Jerry D Leedy
24610 Paradise Dr
Springfield OR 97478

Call Sign: KB7QDF
Chris W Jones
5665 Peninsula Rd
Springfield OR 97478

Call Sign: KD7CHK
Shirley A Keech
201 Penn Ave
Springfield OR 97478

Call Sign: N6IU
Kirk H Taylor
466 Phyllis Dr
Springfield OR 97477

Call Sign: WB7ARV
Douglas F Keene Sr
3710 Portland Rd NE
Springfield OR 97477

Call Sign: K7RRS
Joyce M Schiro
40272 Providence Dr
Springfield OR 97477

Call Sign: KK7IQ

Byron E Vanderpool
795 Ralston Dr
Springfield OR 97477

Call Sign: KE7CWJ
C Annette Gilmer
7811 Rambler Dr NE
Springfield OR 97477

Call Sign: KX7H
Dale G Erickson
3096 Ramblewood Ln
Springfield OR 97477

Call Sign: KB7JHV
Christopher J Urhausen
2532 Ranch Ct NW
Springfield OR 97477

Call Sign: KF7TMF
Robin A Huntoon
8510 Redwood Hwy
Springfield OR 97477

Call Sign: KF7NXW
Ron K Craig
8510 Redwood Hwy
Springfield OR 97477

Call Sign: AE7QN
Ron K Craig
10141 Redwood Hwy
Springfield OR 97477

Call Sign: KE7CWG
Bradley J Prophet
834 Reece
Springfield OR 97477

Call Sign: KD7UJU
Steven C Gorsuch
2642 Reston Rd
Springfield OR 97477

Call Sign: N3PMW

Jaya P Nelapudi
3483 Reston Rd
Springfield OR 97477

Call Sign: KD7BHP
Christopher M Shomler
3483 Reston Rd
Springfield OR 97477

Call Sign: KE7CQZ
Jesse M Applegate
7380 Rickreall Rd
Springfield OR 97477

Call Sign: K7EX
John D Hultgren
7610 Ridgewood Dr
Springfield OR 97477

Call Sign: N7LSF
Daniel P Smith
16768 S Copley Ct
Springfield OR 97478

Call Sign: W7JJS
Jack J Shields
127 S Cornell Ct
Springfield OR 97478

Call Sign: WA7ELP
Edward H Lillie
127 S Cornell Ct
Springfield OR 97478

Call Sign: KB7EHZ
Jerry L Abell
21480 S Crestview Dr
Springfield OR 97478

Call Sign: W7AXN
Jerry W Nichols
21480 S Crestview Dr
Springfield OR 97478

Call Sign: KE7UOB

Brian D Crow
599 S D St
Springfield OR 97478

Call Sign: KE7HZM
Nick D Wedmore
12712 S Dart Rd
Springfield OR 97477

Call Sign: KC7MHW
John L Hubbard
23693 S Day Hill Rd
Springfield OR 97478

Call Sign: KF7TMG
Bobby N Ross
30465 S Deardorff Dr
Springfield OR 97478

Call Sign: KB7QOO
Chester R Webb
30465 S Deardorff Dr
Springfield OR 97478

Call Sign: KI7UJ
Nancy J Ives
17927 S Dick Dr
Springfield OR 97478

Call Sign: KD7JXS
Eric M Barker
36125 S Dickey Prairie Rd
Springfield OR 97478

Call Sign: W7NB
Rick A Iverson
36125 S Dickey Prairie Rd
Springfield OR 97478

Call Sign: N0GZU
Burton D Cox Sr
3132 6 S Dryland Rd
Springfield OR 97478

Call Sign: KE7SLV

Dwayne A Keely
555 S Empire Blvd Sp 18
Springfield OR 97478

Call Sign: KC5YGH
Billy G Hayles
551 S H St
Springfield OR 97477

Call Sign: KB6LEN
Sheldon E Perry
1242 S I St
Springfield OR 97478

Call Sign: KA7LAF
Dolores B Mc Gillvrey
1990 S Little Butte Rd
Springfield OR 97478

Call Sign: KD7BQS
Marie A Grinstead
16675 S Pam Dr
Springfield OR 97478

Call Sign: N7KDZ
Roger L Grinstead
72 S Pl Way
Springfield OR 97478

Call Sign: WA7SKY
Doug L Simpson
5565 S Santiam Hwy
Springfield OR 97477

Call Sign: KD7CHV
Daryl A Swan
4191 S Shore Blvd
Springfield OR 97478

Call Sign: KQ4QO
James R Marlin
2601 Salem Ave
Springfield OR 97478

Call Sign: N0GZV

Clara B Cox
4915 SE 113th
Springfield OR 97478

Call Sign: W7ZJT
Kenneth M Krey
3312 SE 115th Ave
Springfield OR 974787451

Call Sign: W7EPC
Arthur F Brinkman
1720 SE 130th Ave
Springfield OR 97477

Call Sign: WA7CIT
John E Otterstedt
1818 SE 130th Ave
Springfield OR 97478

Call Sign: KD7MIF
Michael W Ferguson
14958 SE 130th Dr
Springfield OR 97477

Call Sign: KB7PBS
Christie A Gilbert
1201 Shannon Dr
Springfield OR 97477

Call Sign: KD7EIJ
Sequoia Vhf Society
1091 Shannon Dr
Springfield OR 97477

Call Sign: WI6Z
Kirk K Gilbert
92067 Sharewater Ln
Springfield OR 97477

Call Sign: KI7RK
Sequoia Vhf Society
1090 Sharon Lp SE
Springfield OR 97477

Call Sign: KE7NB

Jesse N Whitfield
18900 Shenandoah Dr
Springfield OR 97477

Call Sign: K7NSC
William C Cheesman
780 Sheraton Dr
Springfield OR 97477

Call Sign: KD7ZBG
Christopher M Underwood
5215 Skyline Rd S
Springfield OR 97478

Call Sign: K7UND
Christopher M Underwood
6454 Skyline Rd S
Springfield OR 97478

Call Sign: KD7TYF
David B Smith
196 SW Cervantas
Springfield OR 97478

Call Sign: W7JWB
Jeffrey W Blomquist
439 T St
Springfield OR 97477

Call Sign: AJ7V
Jeffrey W Blomquist
2385 Table Rock Rd 126
Springfield OR 97477

Call Sign: KD7CUH
Duane F Eckley
2252 Table Rock Rd 203
Springfield OR 97477

Call Sign: W7KTQ
Frank M Wakeland
6945 Thurston Rd
Springfield OR 97478

Call Sign: N6WKL

Krista A Johnson
8944 Thurston Rd
Springfield OR 97478

Call Sign: W7NQE
Robert J Watt Sr
9032 Thurston Rd
Springfield OR 97478

Call Sign: W7WWK
Lee Hart
1660 Thurston St SE
Springfield OR 97478

Call Sign: W7QLA
Marven J Hart
1008 Tiara St
Springfield OR 97478

Call Sign: KD7M
William A Dunn Jr
15084 Tiller Trl Hwy
Springfield OR 97477

Call Sign: KD7QLE
Reis R Kash
41729 Timber Cir
Springfield OR 97478

Call Sign: KC7UJH
Gerald F Lahart
112 Twin Oaks Loop
Springfield OR 97478

Call Sign: KC7UJI
Geraldine E Lahart
190 Twin Oaks Loop
Springfield OR 97478

Call Sign: KD7LYM
Anthony M Sabbato
131 Upper Applegate Rd
Springfield OR 97478

Call Sign: KB7VIW

Loree D Darrough
38446 Upper Camp Creek
Rd
Springfield OR 97478

Call Sign: KI7AY
James E Darrough
38446 Upper Camp Creek
Rd
Springfield OR 97478

Call Sign: KD7TPS
Corey E Darrough
820 Upper Cleveland
Rapids Rd
Springfield OR 97478

Call Sign: KE7EIO
Heather A Darrough
3191 Upper Cow Creek Rd
Springfield OR 97478

Call Sign: KD7VKL
Beverley L Thomas
3545 Verbena Dr
Springfield OR 974771633

Call Sign: K7ZX
Gregory R Combs
6412 Verda Vista Ct
Springfield OR 974771634

Call Sign: N7THR
Bill R Cole
1713 Villa Rd
Springfield OR 97477

Call Sign: KE7PGO
Richard A Parnell
3420 Virginia St
Springfield OR 97478

Call Sign: KB7ICD
Barry R Swanson
428 Vista Ave SE

Springfield OR 97478

Call Sign: KA7SRI
Ruth A Schneider
2406 W 10th 35
Springfield OR 97477

Call Sign: W7GPC
Jackie E Shepherd
350 W D St
Springfield OR 97477

Call Sign: W7DAT
Sandra V Shepherd
350 W D St
Springfield OR 97477

Call Sign: KA7VFL
Joyce V Shepherd
350 W D St
Springfield OR 97477

Call Sign: KD7PHL
Eunice J Friend
531 W D St
Springfield OR 97477

Call Sign: KD7WSP
Kenneth E Brown
1583 W Fairview Dr
Springfield OR 97477

Call Sign: W7BDO
Maxwell E Coombs
839 W M St
Springfield OR 97477

Call Sign: KF6EHV
Robert A Jones
608 W N St
Springfield OR 97477

Call Sign: KE7SO
David B Gibson
761 W N St

Springfield OR 97477

Call Sign: KB7EOY
Fibes Ruby T Gibson
761 W N St
Springfield OR 97477

Call Sign: KC7CJD
William H Brown
790 W N St
Springfield OR 97477

Call Sign: KD6YOA
Matthew J Struthers
687 W Quinalt St
Springfield OR 97477

Call Sign: KB7TNG
Michael J Paris
2850 Wayside Ln
Springfield OR 97477

Call Sign: KC7RYE
Donald Bennett
2885 Wayside Loop
Springfield OR 974771329

Call Sign: AA7XP
Herbert E Leyson
670 Woodcrest Dr
Springfield OR 97477

Call Sign: KC7BHI
Linda M Hunt
3044 Yolanda Ave
Springfield OR 97477

Call Sign: W7CQZ
Dennis R Hunt
3044 Yolanda Ave
Springfield OR 97477

Call Sign: KC7BIC
Nellie M Olaen
3060 Yolanda Ave

Springfield OR 97477

Call Sign: KF7KTW
Nicholas M Edwards
3401 Yolanda Ave
Springfield OR 97477

Call Sign: KE4PGV
Dale G Ormsbee
Springfield OR 97477

Call Sign: KK7WC
Wayne A Cayton
Springfield OR 97477

Call Sign: KD7IEQ
David R Mobley
Springfield OR 974770101

FCC Amateur Radio Licenses in Stanfield

Call Sign: KC7WBX
Marilyn G Atwood
3579 Ehrck Hill Dr
Stanfield OR 97875

Call Sign: KD7HES
Dennis F Coykendall
375 Elm St
Stanfield OR 97875

Call Sign: KB7HTS
Melvin A Salverson
2351 Fissure Loop N
Stanfield OR 97875

Call Sign: KC7LZS
Stephen E Dircksen
2351 Fissure Lp N
Stanfield OR 97875

Call Sign: KC7PJD
Roberta S Dircksen
3625 Five Mile Rd

Stanfield OR 97875

Call Sign: N7KML
Gerald L Enders
4977 Harvard Ct
Stanfield OR 97875

Call Sign: KF7GCG
Steven D Mccoy
370 N Tamarack St
Stanfield OR 97875

Call Sign: K7SDM
Steven D Mccoy
370 N Tamarack St
Stanfield OR 97875

Call Sign: N7NKT
Michael S Gemelke
27988 Thimbleberry
Stanfield OR 97875

Call Sign: W3CP
James M Headrick
Stanfield OR 97875

Call Sign: W7IFK
Ralph L Krause
Stanfield OR 97875

FCC Amateur Radio Licenses in Summer Lake

Call Sign: KE7CXQ
Jackalynn C Hill
5875 Little River Rd
Summer Lake OR 97640

FCC Amateur Radio Licenses in Summerville

Call Sign: KB7DTQ
Richard A Anderson
98651 Camellia Dr
Summerville OR 97876

Call Sign: KA7QJP
Gail E Hinshaw
1009 Meadow Ave
Summerville OR 97876

Call Sign: KD7JG
Joel D Hinshaw
38937 Meadow Creek Ln
Summerville OR 97876

Call Sign: N7XIK
Adam M Messinger
901 J Q Adams St
Summerville OR 97876

FCC Amateur Radio Licenses in Sunny Valley

Call Sign: KB7FLP
Mary Jo Chierichetti
1207 Cascade Ave
Sunny Valley OR 97497

Call Sign: KD7UIK
Joseph R Swallow
2835 E Mc Andrews Rd
Sunny Valley OR 97497

Call Sign: KD7WHT
Sharon K Swallow
465 E Mississippi Ave
Sunny Valley OR 97497

Call Sign: KB7VWW
Apolinar P Arechiga
38954 Proctor Blvd 334
Sunny Valley OR 97497

FCC Amateur Radio Licenses in Sunriver

Call Sign: WA6JJR
Robert M Emery
3930 Brush College Rd NW

Sunriver OR 977072326

Call Sign: WA5CAW
Austin Smith
2177 Del Vista Dr
Sunriver OR 977079317

Call Sign: KC7PYB
Anthony G Anusich
807 Delaware
Sunriver OR 977079317

Call Sign: KE7JWZ
Percy M Lewis
5922 Delaware
Sunriver OR 97707

Call Sign: KB7SGZ
Elgeon L Johnson
807 Delaware Ave
Sunriver OR 97707

Call Sign: KD7QVR
Alan R Hornish
4014 Delaware Ave
Sunriver OR 97707

Call Sign: KD7WRZ
Edward E Coman
875 Delaware Ave SE
Sunriver OR 97707

Call Sign: KD7OID
Walter F Cundiff
77778 Delena Mayger Rd
Sunriver OR 97707

Call Sign: KD7IYD
Joesph J Mcguckin
79061 Delena Mayger Rd
Sunriver OR 97707

Call Sign: W7JMC
Joesph J Mcguckin
2177 Dell Vista Dr

Sunriver OR 97707

Call Sign: W7LWS
Leland W Schaefer
2177 Dell Vista Dr
Sunriver OR 97707

Call Sign: W7VCQ
Frederick J Baker
1180 Dellmoor Way
Sunriver OR 97707

Call Sign: WA7YIF
Rodney L Le Roy
59540 E Sleepy Hollow Dr
Sunriver OR 97707

Call Sign: W7ITT
Bruce P Bischof
30225 E Springhill Rd
Sunriver OR 97707

Call Sign: W7WAW
William A Wheeler
2703 J St
Sunriver OR 97707

Call Sign: KE7BHI
Matthew M Lawler
61280 Parrell Rd 5
Sunriver OR 97707

Call Sign: KD6ENJ
Lohrman A Nelson
Wu 900 State St B214
Sunriver OR 977072223

Call Sign: KF7RXC
Carrie Ann Husband
16314 White Tail Ln
Sunriver OR 97707

Call Sign: KC7BUA
Clarence C Langvein
16942 Whittier Dr

Sunriver OR 97707

Call Sign: W7CJT
Cheryl J Thorne
Sunriver OR 97707

Call Sign: KA7NUU
Michael J Finazzi III
Sunriver OR 97707

Call Sign: KB7OCV
Nikki K Finazzi
Sunriver OR 97707

Call Sign: KB7QCB
John P Decker
Sunriver OR 97707

Call Sign: N7EEK
Marla E Finazzi
Sunriver OR 97707

Call Sign: W7VHM
David P Friedley
Sunriver OR 97707

Call Sign: KB7HJY
Roger O Peterson
Sunriver OR 97707

Call Sign: KC7LGH
Martin W Lundstrom
Sunriver OR 97707

Call Sign: KC7LGI
Blake M Lundstrom
Sunriver OR 97707

Call Sign: KD7EQP
William M Wood III
Sunriver OR 97707

Call Sign: NH6KF
R Richard Conners IV
Sunriver OR 97707

Call Sign: W7LEP
Glenn B Coughlan
Sunriver OR 97707

Call Sign: W7SJC
Shay J Collins
Sunriver OR 97707

Call Sign: KE7SEP
Stephen M Russell
Sunriver OR 97707

FCC Amateur Radio Licenses in Sutherlin

Call Sign: KD7JAB
Terry M Walker
2237 B St
Sutherlin OR 97479

Call Sign: KM6UW
Elmer A Tidmarsh Jr
2829 B St
Sutherlin OR 97479

Call Sign: KE7LEA
Joseph M Henderson
4077 Colonial Rd
Sutherlin OR 97479

Call Sign: KB0KKA
Mark R Defrees
2140 E 34th Ave
Sutherlin OR 97479

Call Sign: AC7SQ
Mark R Defrees
715 E 36 St 6
Sutherlin OR 97479

Call Sign: AJ7S
Scott A Warren
444 E Vine St
Sutherlin OR 97479

Call Sign: KF6OTZ
Sean F Mac Knight
30909 Eben Ray Ln
Sutherlin OR 974799667

Call Sign: N6LP
John W Olsen
4243 Faber Ave
Sutherlin OR 97479

Call Sign: AD7EJ
Lorie R Stout
28288 Redwood Hwy
Sutherlin OR 97479

Call Sign: KB7NYB
Millard L Cluck
2016 Eberlein
Sutherlin OR 97479

Call Sign: N0CPE
Ronald G James
4067 Fehrenbacher
Sutherlin OR 97479

Call Sign: AB7D
Loyd C Stout
1337 Redwood St
Sutherlin OR 97479

Call Sign: KF7SAL
Mark C Mclain
665 Edwards Dr
Sutherlin OR 97479

Call Sign: KD7YDK
Jack A Miller
200 Ferndale Dr
Sutherlin OR 97479

Call Sign: KE7EFZ
Roger D Hazzard
1714 Russell Ave
Sutherlin OR 97479

Call Sign: W6CKF
Frank C Trumble
3080 Eliot Dr
Sutherlin OR 97479

Call Sign: KC7CMB
Jean R Miller
607 High St
Sutherlin OR 97479

Call Sign: KC6DXI
Louis Strauss
22269 S Bristlin Rd
Sutherlin OR 97479

Call Sign: WA7QZN
Larry F Dowd
824 Elizabeth Ave
Sutherlin OR 974799625

Call Sign: KC7EAE
Willard W Miller
1169 High St
Sutherlin OR 97479

Call Sign: N7SRV
Walter L Woody
24251 S Central Point Rd
Sutherlin OR 97479

Call Sign: KG6AFZ
Charles Hensley Jr
165 Elizabeth Dr
Sutherlin OR 97479

Call Sign: KB7TVS
Donna A Mc Daniel
5033 Kelsie Ct
Sutherlin OR 97479

Call Sign: N7ZFR
Walter W MARChbank
401 S Central Valley Dr
Sutherlin OR 97479

Call Sign: WB7BIV
Robert P Joiner Sr
185 Elizabeth Dr
Sutherlin OR 974799625

Call Sign: KB7TVT
Jerry L Mc Daniel
87950 Kelsie Way
Sutherlin OR 97479

Call Sign: N7ZFS
Ben G Hugel
1895 S Church St
Sutherlin OR 97479

Call Sign: KC7UWC
Ralph E Woodring
88367 Ellmaker Rd
Sutherlin OR 97479

Call Sign: KF7QKO
Richard F Shorey
1318 M St
Sutherlin OR 97479

Call Sign: KB7YLX
Vada J MARChbank
21521 S Clearview Ct
Sutherlin OR 97479

Call Sign: N7POX
Dora L Sensabaugh
21623 Ettlin Loop NE
Sutherlin OR 97479

Call Sign: KC7LWC
Thomas H Kerry
662 NW 170th Dr
Sutherlin OR 97479

Call Sign: WJ7E
Steven P Maxwell
2124 S Franklin Apt 7
Sutherlin OR 97479

Call Sign: KE7BZF
Aaron R Dunbar
210 SE 129th Ave
Sutherlin OR 97479

Call Sign: K7ARD
Aaron R Dunbar
210 SE 129th Ave
Sutherlin OR 97479

Call Sign: KA6YYB
Grover E Zierle
3134 SE Hathaway Dr
Sutherlin OR 97479

Call Sign: KD7JXT
Billy R Wilkinson
3860 SE Naef Rd
Sutherlin OR 97479

Call Sign: KB7QMR
Carl M Ashley
1928 Spicer Wayside SE
Sutherlin OR 97479

Call Sign: KB6RFT
Willa J Mc Manigal
115 Thomason St
Sutherlin OR 974799761

Call Sign: N6OVW
Wayne C Mc Manigal
537 Thompson Creek Rd 22
Sutherlin OR 97479

Call Sign: KB7CTU
Clyde L Anderson
687 W 6th St
Sutherlin OR 97479

Call Sign: KA7RAL
Peggy S Davis
667 W Central
Sutherlin OR 97479

Call Sign: N7FMQ
Rollen L Davis
667 W Central
Sutherlin OR 97479

Call Sign: WB7BOH
Benjamin J Burks
810 W Comstock Rd
Sutherlin OR 974799050

Call Sign: KD7WMI
Jay A Crum
1776 W Duke Rd
Sutherlin OR 97479

Call Sign: KD6UPK
Gary J Lund
Sutherlin OR 97479

Call Sign: WB7AHN
Wayne B Hoobler
Sutherlin OR 97479

Call Sign: KA7DCL
D Keith Mc Farland
Sutherlin OR 97479

Call Sign: KA7VFG
Vernon C Ludwick
Sutherlin OR 97479

Call Sign: KB6SMK
John P Gates
Sutherlin OR 97479

Call Sign: KB6YIO
Brenda F Gates
Sutherlin OR 97479

Call Sign: KL7FK
Fred C Graham
Sutherlin OR 97479

Call Sign: KD7LII

Monte K Waller
Sutherlin OR 97479

Call Sign: KD7SDG
Francis F Keavy
Sutherlin OR 97479

Call Sign: KD7SDJ
Brenda I Howard
Sutherlin OR 97479

Call Sign: KF7QKS
Dan R Mccormick
Sutherlin OR 97497

FCC Amateur Radio Licenses in Swisshome

Call Sign: AL7FN
Robert W Leuband
525 Village Pines Cir
Swisshome OR 974800067

Call Sign: KC7CRU
James L Wingate
Swisshome OR 97480

Call Sign: KC7NDP
Mark L Palmer
Swisshome OR 97480

Call Sign: KD7AJE
Jared S Anderson
Swisshome OR 974800145

FCC Amateur Radio Licenses in Talent

Call Sign: KE7GTL
Kenneth L Gosling
120 3rd St
Talent OR 97540

Call Sign: N6LTN
Roland W Kretschmann

41541 Baptist Church Dr
Talent OR 97540

Call Sign: K7WTP
Carl M Benward
1555 Bar M Dr
Talent OR 97540

Call Sign: W7YEY
Gene A Stringer
82324 Bay Rd
Talent OR 97540

Call Sign: N6WVV
Patricia Pascoe
2310 Bennett Creek Rd
Talent OR 97540

Call Sign: KD6PZX
Ronald H Caffin
3044 Elk Ln
Talent OR 97540

Call Sign: KD6RON
Ronald H Caffin
135 Elk Mountain Ln
Talent OR 97540

Call Sign: KE7USR
Cleve Mosley
6499 Hwy 66
Talent OR 97540

Call Sign: KE7LAD
Donna M Hernandez
2250 Lombard St
Talent OR 97540

Call Sign: WB6KVC
Stanley E Mc Intosh
10199 N Applegate Rd
Talent OR 97540

Call Sign: K6AQA
Stanley E Mc Intosh

10199 N Applegate Rd
Talent OR 97540

Call Sign: N7NFW
Vernon L Cordier
1050 N Cedar Point Rd Sp
B14
Talent OR 97540

Call Sign: W7KIU
Walter R Lochmiller
6717 N Concord Ave
Talent OR 97540

Call Sign: WB6PMB
Thomas C Todd
279 Ridgefield Rd
Talent OR 97540

Call Sign: WB7NSZ
Thomas M Cleveland
7085 Ridgegate Dr
Talent OR 97540

Call Sign: KC7CFB
Mallory B Lynch
2110 Sunset Dr
Talent OR 97540

Call Sign: KC7TYR
John S Casad
63869 Sunset Dr
Talent OR 97540

Call Sign: KD7VZT
Antone T Hernandez Jr
3485 Sweetwater Ave
Talent OR 97540

Call Sign: KK7OI
Walter L Marmont
232 Talent Ave 36
Talent OR 97540

Call Sign: KD7MQZ

Table Rock ARC
1154 Tall Oaks Ct
Talent OR 97540

Call Sign: W7TRR
Table Rock Arg
1254 Tall Oaks Dr
Talent OR 97540

Call Sign: KE7ZHF
Karen C Horn
60275 Tumalo Cir
Talent OR 97540

Call Sign: KE7FMA
Charles W Brown
8548 Wagner Creek Rd
Talent OR 97540

Call Sign: NP2CM
Keith R Rogers
9601 Wagner Creek Rd
Talent OR 97540

Call Sign: K7DNA
Steven R Sutfin
110 West St
Talent OR 97540

Call Sign: K7LCN
John L Hall
Talent OR 97540

Call Sign: N7FPF
Paul I Miller
Talent OR 97540

Call Sign: KA7GNN
Robert O York
Talent OR 97540

Call Sign: KC7JJE
James C Gleaves
Talent OR 97540

Call Sign: W7GUF
Milo S Lacy
Talent OR 97540

Call Sign: KF7QNG
Anthony P Bounds
Talent OR 97540

Call Sign: KF7LVJ
John Dollison
Talent OR 97540

Call Sign: AE7PK
John Dollison
Talent OR 97540

Call Sign: KF7ELO
Troy N Mcguire
Talent OR 97540

FCC Amateur Radio Licenses in Tenmile

Call Sign: KB7LSE
Douglas T Steidl
1688 Jean Ct
Tenmile OR 97481

Call Sign: KF6RAV
Kevin P Reed
611 Tennyson Ave 112
Tenmile OR 97481

Call Sign: KA7VSG
Marie E Brock
Tenmile OR 97481

Call Sign: KB7RXS
Tim R Draper
Tenmile OR 97481

Call Sign: KD7QZA
Martin D Struss
Tenmile OR 97481

Call Sign: KE7OES
John E Hannan
Tenmile OR 97481

Call Sign: KE7PQT
Tim R Draper
Tenmile OR 97481

FCC Amateur Radio Licenses in Terrebonne

Call Sign: N7ZKH
Darrell L Muzingo
1074 4th Ave
Terrebonne OR 97760

Call Sign: KD6VXC
Mark L Ford
4578 Cambon St
Terrebonne OR 97760

Call Sign: KD7UCA
Mark L Ford
1500 Cambria Pl
Terrebonne OR 97760

Call Sign: KB7DKG
Russell E Geidl
2162 Camp Baker Rd
Terrebonne OR 97760

Call Sign: KE7FXC
Janette G Corson
79924 Cannon Rd
Terrebonne OR 97760

Call Sign: N7JRN
Janette G Corson
1315 Cannon St SE
Terrebonne OR 97760

Call Sign: N7RFZ
Tami R Applegate
5050 Columbus St SE Sp 17
Terrebonne OR 97760

Call Sign: KB7QZU
Kefton S Black
1629 Harbor Dr
Terrebonne OR 97760

Call Sign: KJ7WB
Michael A Knoke
2041 King Ln
Terrebonne OR 97760

Call Sign: N7VMK
Jeremy Groesz
801 N Central Ave 9
Terrebonne OR 97760

Call Sign: N7VML
Jason M Risch
1015 N Watts St
Terrebonne OR 97760

Call Sign: W9NAX
Douglas R Magill
12604 NE Halsey
Terrebonne OR 97760

Call Sign: K7SGC
Roy S Grey Cloud
4353 NE Halsey 5
Terrebonne OR 97760

Call Sign: K7IHP
Roger C Anderson
131 NW 20th D Al114
Terrebonne OR 97760

Call Sign: KD7ILQ
Mindi M Miller
1410 NW City Heights Dr
Terrebonne OR 97760

Call Sign: N7WMN
David E Mc Neill
9015 NW Skyline Blvd
Terrebonne OR 97760

Call Sign: WB7AAO
William A Day
330 Riverside Dr
Terrebonne OR 97760

Call Sign: KC7ZTC
William L Spalding
1831 SW Park 110
Terrebonne OR 97760

Call Sign: KD7TCG
Dennis R Fehling
6500 SW Perch
Terrebonne OR 97760

Call Sign: KL1QL
Billie B Willson
6500 SW Perch
Terrebonne OR 97760

Call Sign: K7DNS
Dennis R Fehling
3200 SW Peridot Ave
Terrebonne OR 97760

Call Sign: KD7TCF
Pamela E Bigoni
4416 SW Perkins
Terrebonne OR 97760

Call Sign: KD7OIL
Ralph Mathis
9185 SW Sattler St
Terrebonne OR 97760

Call Sign: KC7FHZ
Ralph B Reaume
18138 SW Shady Meadow
Ct
Terrebonne OR 97760

Call Sign: KE7HKA
Michael W Folkestad
10740 SW Sunny Hill Ln

Terrebonne OR 97760

Call Sign: WA0LZQ
James H Platz Jr
3710 SW US Veterans Hosp
Rd
Terrebonne OR 97760

Call Sign: KB7WTT
Scot Stovall
Terrebonne OR 97760

Call Sign: N7RFO
Herbert N Morrow
Terrebonne OR 97760

Call Sign: KD7TCH
Roy S Grey Cloud
Terrebonne OR 97760

Call Sign: KE7BTN
High Desert Amateur Radio
Group
Terrebonne OR 97760

Call Sign: WB7NGN
Anthony H Ellis
Terrebonne OR 97760

Call Sign: WB7VZB
Norman W Mc Clung
Terrebonne OR 97760

Call Sign: KF7TFY
Arman B Kluehe
Terrebonne OR 97760

Call Sign: KD7TKF
Carolyn J Johnson
Terrebonne OR 97760

Call Sign: W3AWT
Carolyn J Johnson
Terrebonne OR 97760

Call Sign: KE7NRM
Darwin D Mckibbon
Terrebonne OR 97760

Call Sign: W7RGP
Roger G Peters
Terrebonne OR 97760

Call Sign: KE7ECB
Stewart W Taylor
Terrebonne OR 97760

Call Sign: KD7RTE
David A Stangland
Terrebonne OR 977609318

**FCC Amateur Radio
Licenses in The Dalles**

Call Sign: W7CCV
Leonard E Gates
134 2nd St
The Dalles OR 97058

Call Sign: K7UKW
Craig A Crichton
144 42nd Way
The Dalles OR 97058

Call Sign: KD7KOX
Clinton S Ewing
1107 4th St
The Dalles OR 97058

Call Sign: W7HRG
Charles L Phillips
247 Carrollwood Dr
The Dalles OR 970581668

Call Sign: KE7ZXK
Roberta A Anderson
527 Carrollwood Dr
The Dalles OR 97058

Call Sign: W7JDU

Hazel A Phillips
527 Carrollwood Dr
The Dalles OR 970581668

Call Sign: KA7CCK
Anthony C Anderson
1955 Carter Ln
The Dalles OR 97058

Call Sign: KF7TJP
Donald D Arbon
78555 Cedar Park Rd
The Dalles OR 97058

Call Sign: KF7TZK
Katherine L Arbon
5535 Cedar Pl
The Dalles OR 97058

Call Sign: KF7MYQ
Thomas R Oaks
151 Chetco Ct
The Dalles OR 97058

Call Sign: W7RLW
Hobart W Lynch
75 Cormorant At
The Dalles OR 97058

Call Sign: KF7MYT
Steven M Conover
4483 Corn Creek Rd
The Dalles OR 97058

Call Sign: KE7BJF
Brian E Fix
2272 Corona Ave
The Dalles OR 97058

Call Sign: KE7FOU
Dara E Doty
2180 Country Dr S
The Dalles OR 97058

Call Sign: KB7WEB

Gerald R Adams
9155 E Evans Creek
The Dalles OR 97058

Call Sign: N7SJF
Raymond A Meengs
1375 E Evans Creek Rd
The Dalles OR 97058

Call Sign: KA7NTT
Stephen H Lehmann
108 E Hillcrest Dr
The Dalles OR 97058

Call Sign: KC7TV
Lincoln J Shadley
25223 E Hunter Rd
The Dalles OR 97058

Call Sign: W7HJD
Jay B Whitwell
207 E Main St
The Dalles OR 97058

Call Sign: N7OHX
Cynthia A Graham
500 E Oak St
The Dalles OR 97058

Call Sign: KA7MPI
Sidney M Johnson
309 E Park St
The Dalles OR 97058

Call Sign: W7TRH
Malvin C Ball
63186 E Port Rd
The Dalles OR 97058

Call Sign: KF7EL
Jim C Wahlstrom
33838 E River Dr 119
The Dalles OR 970583912

Call Sign: KC7I

Michael D Julian Lewis
64775 E Sandy River Ln
The Dalles OR 97058

Call Sign: N7MYZ
William E Baumeister
70100 E Skookum Ln
The Dalles OR 97058

Call Sign: W7CKF
Haydn E Waddington
550 E Trail Creek Rd
The Dalles OR 97058

Call Sign: KE7YLX
Bill A Seymour
1252 E View Pl
The Dalles OR 97058

Call Sign: KF7TZM
Donald E Knowland
1252 E View Pl
The Dalles OR 97058

Call Sign: N7QEQ
David O Mitchell
444 E Vine
The Dalles OR 97058

Call Sign: W7AEL
Bruce N Witzel
1910 East St
The Dalles OR 97058

Call Sign: KB7YCZ
Haydn E Waddington
1910 East St
The Dalles OR 97058

Call Sign: KF7TZL
Carla D Randall
231 East St
The Dalles OR 97058

Call Sign: KC7NGV

Hugh G Holte
21730 Eastmont Dr 15
The Dalles OR 97058

Jerry R Wahlstrom
178 Esther Ct
The Dalles OR 97058

Timothy D Robertson
38696 Griggs Dr
The Dalles OR 97058

Call Sign: KE7CYJ
Camden J Lindsay
2836 Eastmount St
The Dalles OR 97058

Call Sign: KA7CDK
Robert J Robertson
105 Fairway Village Ln
The Dalles OR 97058

Call Sign: KE7FBR
Terry N Teeters
1234 Hillendale Dr SE
The Dalles OR 97058

Call Sign: KB7WNX
Jo Ann S Lewis
2648 Edgewood Dr Unit 1
The Dalles OR 97058

Call Sign: KB7LFH
Gary L Swift
804 G Ave
The Dalles OR 97058

Call Sign: W7DWZ
Robert L Wheeler
164 Jersey Ave
The Dalles OR 97058

Call Sign: KA7FXW
Robert A Puerner
665 Edwards Dr
The Dalles OR 97058

Call Sign: KB7YKT
Marlene F Thompson
4780 Gardner Rd SE
The Dalles OR 97058

Call Sign: WB7EKA
Charles D Wallen
80542 Kik Rd
The Dalles OR 97058

Call Sign: KB7NXS
Shaun D Jonilionis
665 Edwards Dr
The Dalles OR 97058

Call Sign: N7VVI
Patrick E Thompson
866 Garfield
The Dalles OR 97058

Call Sign: N7SOZ
Walter H Kleefkens
2644 Kristin Ct NE
The Dalles OR 97058

Call Sign: KC7DWU
Ivan R Bork
665 Edwards Dr
The Dalles OR 97058

Call Sign: KP2K
George I Ruddell
1154 Gibbon Rd
The Dalles OR 97058

Call Sign: W7EKD
Ralph A Buckles
2168 Madison St SE
The Dalles OR 97058

Call Sign: KC7WNR
Leola E Bork
665 Edwards Dr
The Dalles OR 97058

Call Sign: WT4D
Kenneth L Ruddell
27640 Gibraltar Loop
The Dalles OR 97058

Call Sign: W7ACC
Robert H Howell
55500 Madrone Dr
The Dalles OR 97058

Call Sign: KE7EEM
Gorge East Amateur Radio
5860 Estate Dr
The Dalles OR 97058

Call Sign: KG6MEO
Michael D Mccallum
221 Glenwood Dr
The Dalles OR 97058

Call Sign: W7EYL
Betty J Howell
1549 Magnolia Ave
The Dalles OR 97058

Call Sign: KF7FOW
Jerry R Wahlstrom
2330 Estes St
The Dalles OR 97058

Call Sign: KE7OHE
Michael D Mccallum
4801 Glenwood Dr
The Dalles OR 97058

Call Sign: KB7KTG
Patricia A Sexton
40401 Mohawk River Rd
The Dalles OR 97058

Call Sign: AE7KD

Call Sign: KC7QOM

Call Sign: N7BAV

Edward L Goodman
1719 N 17th St 5
The Dalles OR 97058

Call Sign: KF7MYO
Michael C Pritchett
1055 N 5th St 20
The Dalles OR 97058

Call Sign: WB7TSI
Linford R Fitch
4104 N Colonial Ave
The Dalles OR 97058

Call Sign: KA5IMS
Louis Monkiewicz
3355 N Delta Hwy Sp 26
The Dalles OR 97058

Call Sign: KB7VGA
Anna L Monkiewicz
499 N Delta Rd
The Dalles OR 97058

Call Sign: KE7ICV
Robert H Kirby
5333 N Denver Ave
The Dalles OR 97058

Call Sign: WA7H
Robert H Kirby
6717 N Denver Ave
The Dalles OR 97058

Call Sign: N7WEW
Gunter H Schmidt
3738 Orindale Rd
The Dalles OR 97058

Call Sign: KD7ID
William D Weimar
45 Oriole Ln
The Dalles OR 97058

Call Sign: KF7TJQ

Amber L Perry
7298 Park Ter Dr NE
The Dalles OR 97058

Call Sign: KD7GKB
Jack V Thornton
291 Pyle Dr
The Dalles OR 97058

Call Sign: AD7GE
Jack V Thornton
720 Pyle Dr
The Dalles OR 97058

Call Sign: AA7KH
Jim R Wideman
1280 Q St
The Dalles OR 97058

Call Sign: WB7UNJ
Peter L Wasser
1280 Q St
The Dalles OR 970584462

Call Sign: KF7MYS
Michael L Davidson
37360 Resort Dr
The Dalles OR 97058

Call Sign: AA7TY
James H Thurston
90036 Sheffler Rd
The Dalles OR 97058

Call Sign: KF7VCX
Jedidiah J Van Den Bosch
15972 Sunrise Blvd
The Dalles OR 97058

Call Sign: KD7LTV
Daniel N Williams
670 Three Pines Rd
The Dalles OR 97058

Call Sign: K7UVZ

Ronald W Elton
939 Valley View Rd 20
The Dalles OR 97058

Call Sign: KE7DCD
Hamvets
700 Veterans Dr
The Dalles OR 97058

Call Sign: W7OVH
Hamvets
700 Vetrans Dr
The Dalles OR 97058

Call Sign: KA7WOL
James J Knoll Sr
3024 Via Verde Cir
The Dalles OR 97058

Call Sign: KI7KV
Lee J Bateman
428 Vick Ln
The Dalles OR 97058

Call Sign: WB7EUL
Robert W Avery
222 View Ln
The Dalles OR 97058

Call Sign: N7RHB
Christopher C Witthaus
2912 W 10th St
The Dalles OR 97058

Call Sign: KA7IDO
Ernest L Stillwell
719 W 11th St
The Dalles OR 97058

Call Sign: KD7K
Sam L Sparks
917 W 11th St
The Dalles OR 97058

Call Sign: K7CUO

Benjamin L Roth
803 W 11th St 4
The Dalles OR 97058

Call Sign: KB7LAR
Shirley C Roth
202 W 12th
The Dalles OR 97058

Call Sign: W7NUF
George A Moore
690 W 13th St
The Dalles OR 97058

Call Sign: N7ZUL
Colin B Malcolm
3361 W 14th
The Dalles OR 97058

Call Sign: WA7HVL
Leo D Whitman
2040 W 17th Ave
The Dalles OR 970581664

Call Sign: KE7FIC
Carl B Lovitt
1215 W 1st St
The Dalles OR 97058

Call Sign: KA7CDL
Marvin M Rickett
907 W 23rd
The Dalles OR 97058

Call Sign: KB7QMI
Mark E Telep
210 W 4th St
The Dalles OR 97058

Call Sign: W7XXZ
Jeffrey C Nyman
3800 W 6th St Sp 4
The Dalles OR 97058

Call Sign: KK7CW

Marshall D Johnson Sr
3120 W 7th St
The Dalles OR 97058

Call Sign: N7SPA
Connie Ebdon
720 W 9th
The Dalles OR 97058

Call Sign: KD7FEU
Kent P Arbon Jr
404 W 9th St
The Dalles OR 97058

Call Sign: WA4TOM
Paul F Ebdon
720 W 9th St
The Dalles OR 97058

Call Sign: KE7FID
Aleta P Girard
2811 W 9th St
The Dalles OR 97058

Call Sign: KA7YIJ
Harry R Ketchum
The Dalles OR 97058

Call Sign: KB7SKA
Gerald C Sexton
The Dalles OR 97058

Call Sign: W7HVN
Harry H Walters
The Dalles OR 97058

Call Sign: KA7DOM
Reginald W Seden Jr
The Dalles OR 97058

Call Sign: KC7LVF
Le Roy J Booth
The Dalles OR 97058

Call Sign: N7XSL

Michael D Thompson
The Dalles OR 97058

Call Sign: W7HVQ
James F Roth
The Dalles OR 97058

Call Sign: W7RHS
Jerry R Skaugset
The Dalles OR 97058

Call Sign: WB7QXU
Michael J Finn
The Dalles OR 97058

Call Sign: KE7AQD
Bryan Dean
The Dalles OR 97058

Call Sign: KE7FIF
Erin N Wisbey
The Dalles OR 97058

Call Sign: KF7MYR
Leo J Fritz
The Dalles OR 97058

Call Sign: KE7FHY
Rueben K Hall Jr
The Dalles OR 97058

Call Sign: K7RKH
Rueben K Hall Jr
The Dalles OR 97058

Call Sign: KE7KLD
Sally A Hall
The Dalles OR 97058

Call Sign: KC7WUK
Sue R Sterling
The Dalles OR 97058

**FCC Amateur Radio
Licenses in Tiller**

Call Sign: KA6HDZ
Terry F Zdun
709 E Franklin
Tiller OR 97484

Call Sign: K7PMG
Larry R Anderson
20949 S Harris Rd
Tiller OR 974849723

Call Sign: WA7DAF
David W Ronk
4015 S Hemlock
Tiller OR 97484

Call Sign: KG7FR
Murrell G Lancaster
Tiller OR 97484

Call Sign: KF7AID
Judy A Canada Coultas
Tiller OR 97484

Call Sign: KF7AIC
Thomas E Coultas
Tiller OR 97484

Call Sign: KI6JUH
Robert M Mccrackin
Tiller OR 97484

FCC Amateur Radio Licenses in Trail

Call Sign: KF6KHH
Joshua B Goldsmith
17142 Fern Ridge Rd
Trail OR 97541

Call Sign: KC7NVY
Martin F Jackson
636 Flaming
Trail OR 97541

Call Sign: KE6MOS
Anton A Boogaard
65290 Hwy 20 W
Trail OR 97541

Call Sign: KF7OCN
William G Washington
1593 Marigold St NE
Trail OR 97541

Call Sign: N7VFX
George T Fuller
1900 Montana St
Trail OR 975419636

Call Sign: KF6HVW
Allan P Holm
1310 NW 119th Pl
Trail OR 97541

Call Sign: KB7RHS
Larry L Baldridge
Trail OR 97541

Call Sign: KD7CYC
Johnathan F Ohlund
Trail OR 97541

FCC Amateur Radio Licenses in Tygh Valley

Call Sign: KD7KOY
James F Sprouse
2114 B St
Tygh Valley OR 97063

Call Sign: KE7EFC
John E Goleman
28243 Old Rainier Rd
Tygh Valley OR 97063

Call Sign: AC6OZ
Ronald A Du Pree
528 Tyler St Apt 1
Tygh Valley OR 97063

Call Sign: K7NUT
Geoffrey S Mcallister
Tygh Valley OR 97063

FCC Amateur Radio Licenses in Ukiah

Call Sign: WA7SZP
James D Stroud Sr
210 W Despain St
Ukiah OR 97880

Call Sign: KB7OPX
Dewey G Cunningham
Ukiah OR 97880

Call Sign: KC7PJA
Michael W Mcveigh
Ukiah OR 97880

Call Sign: N7GIY
Donna M Meengs
Ukiah OR 97880

Call Sign: W7CCJ
Raymond S Meengs
Ukiah OR 97880

Call Sign: K7LKY
Dewey G Cunningham
Ukiah OR 97880

Call Sign: KD7ZCM
Kenneth L Hogeland
Ukiah OR 97880

Call Sign: KE7JKI
Mark S Kirschenman
Ukiah OR 97880

Call Sign: KR7N
Mark S Kirschenman
Ukiah OR 97880

Call Sign: KE7TAM
Tennie M Hogeland
Ukiah OR 97880

Call Sign: KD7MVP
Michelle L Randleman
256 Arrow Way
Umatilla OR 97882

Call Sign: KT7R
Michael P Randleman
176 Arrowhead Pass
Umatilla OR 97882

Call Sign: K7UXK
Jay W Gamble
2768 Chad Dr
Umatilla OR 97882

Call Sign: KE7PUP
Robert O Striker
225 E 39th Ave
Umatilla OR 97882

Call Sign: KQ6QX
Hiram J Webb
610 Holmes Ln
Umatilla OR 97882

Call Sign: WA7BVG
Eugene F White
22875 Jennie Rd
Umatilla OR 97882

Call Sign: KC7BVY
Deric E Casey
3145 Kings Valley Hwy
Umatilla OR 97882

Call Sign: KB7IVD
Nolan T Wetterling
93263 Knappa Platt Rd

Umatilla OR 97882

Call Sign: AB7HB
Bernard J Fineberg
18760 Rock Creek Cir 122
Umatilla OR 97882

Call Sign: KB7IVE
Cory J Hart
215 Walla Walla St
Umatilla OR 97882

Call Sign: KC7QYU
Carrol L Sheraden
82280 Wildwood Ln 1
Umatilla OR 97882

Call Sign: KA7EEF
Michael W Merryman
Umatilla OR 97882

Call Sign: KB7ZJH
Jeff D Dickerson
Umatilla OR 97882

Call Sign: KC7IMR
Douglas R Mcfadden
Umatilla OR 97882

Call Sign: KD7MUQ
Brent H Baker
Umatilla OR 97882

Call Sign: W6NMR
Douglas R Mcfadden
Umatilla OR 97882

Call Sign: N7QJQ
Amos A Case
2975 Independence Hwy
Umpqua OR 97486

Call Sign: KB7VGG
John P De Angeles
4279 Independence Hwy
Umpqua OR 97486

Call Sign: KF7BX
G William Gibson
3175 Independence Hwy
NW
Umpqua OR 97486

Call Sign: N7HZL
Carl M Fullen
205 Independence Way
Umpqua OR 97486

Call Sign: KC7GZW
Rodolfo Mayorga Jr
205 Independence Way
Umpqua OR 97486

Call Sign: KC7JNP
Rodolfo Mayorga III
259 Indian Bend Rd
Umpqua OR 97486

Call Sign: KD7GTW
Alan D Weldon
1025 Indian Bend Rd
Umpqua OR 97486

Call Sign: WC6J
Thomas H Orlando
17435 Joshua Ct
Umpqua OR 97486

Call Sign: KA6TAJ
James G Britton
17435 Joshua Ct
Umpqua OR 97486

Call Sign: WB6NEE
David M Thomas
93206 Knappa Dock Rd
Umpqua OR 97486

Call Sign: W7PHR
Paul H Rossiter
15757 Pkwy Dr
Umpqua OR 97486

Call Sign: KE7COO
Hendrarto Nuradi
14486 Tyee Rd
Umpqua OR 97486

Call Sign: KU2B
Hendrarto Nuradi
14486 Tyee Rd
Umpqua OR 97486

Call Sign: KE7HLI
Elizabeth Johnson
14598 Tyee Rd
Umpqua OR 97486

Call Sign: KE7HLJ
Leleand R Johnson
15957 Tyee Rd
Umpqua OR 97486

Call Sign: K6IVY
Dennis W Killeby
57294 Tygh Valley Rd 11
Umpqua OR 97486

Call Sign: KA0ZOU
Don L Adams
827 Tyler Creek Rd
Umpqua OR 97486

Call Sign: KF7LIX
Cynthia D Pakros
Umpqua OR 974864596

Call Sign: K6IVY
Cynthia D Pakros Ms
Umpqua OR 974864596

FCC Amateur Radio Licenses in Union

Call Sign: N5PLG
Robert E Sanders
27 James Pl
Union OR 97883

Call Sign: KC7JFG
Mabelle M Murphy
570 N 10th Ave 3
Union OR 97883

Call Sign: KC7JFD
Ronald A Murphy Jr
570 N 10th Ave 5
Union OR 97883

Call Sign: KC7IZB
Ronald A Murphy Sr
570 N 10th Ave 5
Union OR 978839132

Call Sign: KE7ZSD
Jean N Allamand
2630 N Hayden Island Dr
Union OR 97883

Call Sign: W7NZX
James A Brady
79002 N Loop Rd
Union OR 97883

Call Sign: WA6ZHQ
James D Russell Sr
272 S Columbia Dr
Union OR 97883

Call Sign: W7ZHQ
James D Russell Sr
309 S Columbia Dr
Union OR 97883

Call Sign: K7KKM
Ervin J Reed

30602 S Roaring Bull Ln
Union OR 97883

Call Sign: WA7YPJ
Ronald C Kiesel
1145 SW 85
Union OR 978830584

Call Sign: KA7BAK
William M Delepierre
467 W Bryan
Union OR 97883

Call Sign: N7ETN
George N Mc Donald Jr
Union OR 97883

Call Sign: W7LWM
Marvin G Gilkison
Union OR 97883

Call Sign: KC7WZU
Sandra F Terry
Union OR 97883

Call Sign: KD7NYH
Charles D Wyllie
Union OR 97883

Call Sign: K7CDW
Charles D Wyllie
Union OR 97883

Call Sign: KF7RYC
David J Selinsky
Union OR 97883

Call Sign: KF7QGT
Kristina Selinsky
Union OR 97883

Call Sign: KF7STP
Michael C Orcutt
Union OR 97883

Call Sign: KD7WEN
Tracy D Wyllie
Union OR 97883

Call Sign: K7TDW
Tracy D Wyllie
Union OR 97883

FCC Amateur Radio Licenses in Unity

Call Sign: KB7RCF
Michael G Cummings
1602 Riverside Dr 11
Unity OR 978840006

FCC Amateur Radio Licenses in Vale

Call Sign: N6GRU
Ray H Hamilton
4633 Hayesville Dr NE
Vale OR 97918

FCC Amateur Radio Licenses in Veneta

Call Sign: KC7SVP
James E Waggoner Sr
3836 Anita Dr NE
Veneta OR 97487

Call Sign: WB7DUB
Raymond A Chase
1307 Aspen Dr
Veneta OR 97487

Call Sign: KC7SVR
James E Waggoner Jr
653 Cessna St
Veneta OR 97487

Call Sign: KC7SVS
Diana L Waggoner
653 Cessna St

Veneta OR 97487

Call Sign: W7WYV
Calvin E Deonier
2261 Corinthian Ct
Veneta OR 97487

Call Sign: KO7N
Richard W Ewing
195 Country Aire Dr
Veneta OR 97487

Call Sign: W7AJP
James W Phillips
2850 Country Club Ct
Veneta OR 974879511

Call Sign: KE7ATH
Christopher S Glenzer
220 Creekside Ter
Veneta OR 97487

Call Sign: NO7T
James P Humphrey
4569 Cregan Ave
Veneta OR 97487

Call Sign: WB6VMI
John R Burger
155 Dubois Ln
Veneta OR 97487

Call Sign: KB7TXO
Raymond A Bales
1493 Elaine Way
Veneta OR 97487

Call Sign: KD7NBX
Scott L Nelson Jr
162 Fenton St Apt C
Veneta OR 97487

Call Sign: KB7RBH
David B Lancaster
16171 Foothill Lp S

Veneta OR 97487

Call Sign: KC7RPK
Joseph T Smelser
59074 Foothill Rd
Veneta OR 97487

Call Sign: K7WWL
Joseph T Smelser
5001 A Foothills Rd
Veneta OR 97487

Call Sign: KB7YDY
George P Roberts Jr
5022 Foothills Rd Apt B
Veneta OR 97487

Call Sign: KC7DDZ
Patricia M Roberts
5043 Foothills Rd Apt G
Veneta OR 97487

Call Sign: K6GCK
Anthony B Marr
3713 Geary St SE
Veneta OR 97487

Call Sign: KA7UTA
Donald C Shipp Sr
4893 Gloria Gayle Way
Veneta OR 97487

Call Sign: KZ7S
Robert J Olson
54655 Jack Pine Rd
Veneta OR 97487

Call Sign: KZ7W
Frances G Olson
4255 Jackpine St NE
Veneta OR 97487

Call Sign: W7SHO
Ronald E Kraft
54299 King Rd W

Veneta OR 97487

Call Sign: WB6HKA
Robert A Van Winkle
3636 Marlin Ct SE
Veneta OR 97487

Call Sign: N7GUF
William L Childers
992 Merlot Ave NE
Veneta OR 974879613

Call Sign: W7WLC
William L Childers
121 Merrill St
Veneta OR 974879613

Call Sign: KA7OXT
Daryl R Meekins
1837 NW 156th Ave
Veneta OR 97487

Call Sign: KK7EK
Rodney E Wood
723 J Q Adams St
Veneta OR 974879622

Call Sign: KC7QBB
Robin E Wood
901 J Q Adams St
Veneta OR 974879622

Call Sign: KB7AMB
Judy L Summers
1130 SW 10th Ave
Veneta OR 97487

Call Sign: W7FHD
Charles L Summers
7739 SW 10th Ave
Veneta OR 97487

Call Sign: KB7TNH
Michael D Suarez
91204 Territorial Rd

Veneta OR 97487

Call Sign: KD7AAC
Barry A Reinoehl
33872 Vista Ln
Veneta OR 97487

Call Sign: KE7OA
Earl C Reinoehl
33872 Vista Ln
Veneta OR 97487

Call Sign: KB7VIX
James S Demings
25827 Wiggins Ln
Veneta OR 97487

Call Sign: WN7ODD
Donald F Leaders
25883 Wildwood Rd
Veneta OR 974879608

Call Sign: N7NPA
Scott L Wood
24158 Wolf Ck Rd
Veneta OR 97487

Call Sign: N7NRK
Fred J Warren
23432 Wolf Creek Rd
Veneta OR 97487

Call Sign: N7TTL
Diana L Wood
24158 Wolf Creek Rd
Veneta OR 97487

Call Sign: KC7MHQ
R Lynn Wegand
25370 Wolfcreek Rd
Veneta OR 97487

Call Sign: KC7GTW
Sonny D Ovens
Veneta OR 97487

Call Sign: KC7SJT
Bryan W Barnard
Veneta OR 97487

Call Sign: KF6WAT
Lisa R Gladiola
Veneta OR 97487

Call Sign: KF6WJD
Everlynn Z Gladiola
Veneta OR 97487

Call Sign: W6TRU
Philip L Writer
Veneta OR 97487

Call Sign: KE7TIZ
Robert G Loschiavo
Veneta OR 97487

FCC Amateur Radio Licenses in Vida

Call Sign: WB7SED
Karen L Dobroth
7220 Fairview Rd
Vida OR 97488

Call Sign: WA7DXN
Victor W Dobroth
54672 Fairview Rd
Vida OR 97488

Call Sign: KB7ENT
Dale L Barth
151 Hawksdale Dr
Vida OR 97488

Call Sign: KB7ESX
Larry C Maxwell
2712 Haworth Ave
Vida OR 97488

Call Sign: KF7TFK

Elaine L Bryson
1414 Hawthorne Ave
Vida OR 97488

Call Sign: AA7QU
Russell B Carpenter
3417 Hawthorne Ave
Vida OR 97488

Call Sign: K7WWW
Walter W Wilson
4481 Hawthorne Ave
Vida OR 97488

Call Sign: K9AZZ
John K Stevens
31350 Lynx Hollow Rd
Vida OR 97488

Call Sign: KE7DOC
Brad V Bolton
Vida OR 97488

FCC Amateur Radio Licenses in Wallowa

Call Sign: KE7SMH
James M Healy II
1107 Roseburg Rd
Wallowa OR 97885

Call Sign: KD7RMM
Rebecca J Byers
Wallowa OR 97885

FCC Amateur Radio Licenses in Walterville

Call Sign: W7JWW
John W Wasti
Walterville OR 97478

Call Sign: WA7VUP
Robert E Kalbfell
Walterville OR 97489

Call Sign: KD7WKX
Julia Breninger
Walterville OR 97489

Call Sign: KD7WKY
Barbara L Schibler
Walterville OR 974890399

FCC Amateur Radio Licenses in Walton

Call Sign: WA7UHI
Samuel W North Jr
209 Jacobson Way S
Walton OR 97490

Call Sign: N7IKR
Lois D Montgomery
260 Jacobson Way S
Walton OR 97490

Call Sign: N7UHX
Jon D Zook
2160 NW 107th Pl
Walton OR 97490

Call Sign: KW6M
Stephen L Jackson
Walton OR 97490

Call Sign: KE7UCG
Anthony B Wright Jr
Walton OR 97490

FCC Amateur Radio Licenses in Wamic

Call Sign: N7RYU
Ronald L Rathke
16675 S Pam Dr
Wamic OR 97063

Call Sign: N7NUT
Jennifer E Mcallister

Wamic OR 97063

FCC Amateur Radio Licenses in Warm Springs

Call Sign: W7QPT
Orville P Bailey
Warm Springs OR 97761

FCC Amateur Radio Licenses in Wasco

Call Sign: K7VTF
Gordon W Hilderbrand
92659 Hwy 202
Wasco OR 97065

Call Sign: N6PMS
Robert E Thomas Jr
Wasco OR 97065

FCC Amateur Radio Licenses in Wedderborn

Call Sign: KA7NCJ
Peter E Peters
Wedderburn OR 97491

Call Sign: KC7NOM
Ian W Keusink
Wedderburn OR 97491

Call Sign: KK6IS
Neil M Graham
Wedderburn OR 97491

Call Sign: WB3CCY
Michael D Crane
Wedderburn OR 974910287

FCC Amateur Radio Licenses in Westfir

Call Sign: KD7LYJ

Seth M Okey
7440 SW 102
Westfir OR 97492

Call Sign: KE7PGQ
Leigh A O'Key
7440 SW 102
Westfir OR 97492

Call Sign: KE7NHV
Leslie S Howard
47563 W Oak
Westfir OR 97492

Call Sign: N7PAN
Leslie S Howard
47563 W Oak
Westfir OR 97492

Call Sign: KF7DTS
Karla D Golay
46443 Westfir Rd 19
Westfir OR 97492

**FCC Amateur Radio
Licenses in Westlake**

Call Sign: KD7LB
Glen D Harter
4769 Circuit Rider Ln S
Westlake OR 97493

Call Sign: N7ENR
Barbara A Harter
4769 Circuit Rider Ln S
Westlake OR 97493

Call Sign: KF7OPF
John R Pershing
4769 Circuit Rider Ln S
Westlake OR 974939707

Call Sign: AE7NI
John R Pershing
2803 Citadel St

Westlake OR 974939707

Call Sign: KF7OPE
Marilyn E Pershing
628 Citation Dr NE
Westlake OR 97493

Call Sign: AE7NJ
Marilyn E Pershing
1345 City View
Westlake OR 97493

Call Sign: N7NMT
Roy V Daniels
1263 Clinton Dr
Westlake OR 97493

Call Sign: KB7VOF
John S Moore
Sub 185 George Fox
College
Westlake OR 97493

Call Sign: KB7VOG
Zack F Moore
1629 Georgia SE
Westlake OR 97493

Call Sign: KB7VOH
Sandra A Moore
80260 Gerking Flat Rd
Westlake OR 97493

Call Sign: N6LJN
David E Meintsma
710 Riverside Dr
Westlake OR 97493

Call Sign: KL7IIK
Michael A Brown
85334 S Willamette St
Westlake OR 97493

Call Sign: KA7YQU
David D Rankin

104 S Williams Ave Apt E
Westlake OR 97493

Call Sign: KB7QBT
K Dianne Rankin
15890 S Wilshire Cir
Westlake OR 97493

Call Sign: N6ORH
Leland B Schmidt
Westlake OR 97493

Call Sign: KD7KJQ
Charlie F Uhls
Westlake OR 974930237

**FCC Amateur Radio
Licenses in Weston**

Call Sign: KA7WVO
Roy L Herndon
3627 Calle Vista Dr
Weston OR 97886

Call Sign: KC7DQK
Scott W Spendlove
1315 James St
Weston OR 97886

Call Sign: KB7ESU
Sara B Turner
15800 McDonald Rd
Weston OR 97886

Call Sign: KB7ETX
Rick J Turner
15800 McDonald Rd
Weston OR 97886

Call Sign: WB7UQA
William C Boyd Jr
26801 SE Wally Rd
Weston OR 97886

Call Sign: KB7KVH

Florence J Ruthstrom
Weston OR 97886

Call Sign: KC5URK
Martin W Cunningham
Weston OR 97886

**FCC Amateur Radio
Licenses in White City**

Call Sign: KC7FRP
Shorty Tigre
751 3rd St
White City OR 97503

Call Sign: W7GZL
Eugene L Mahoney
3039 Beall Ln
White City OR 97503

Call Sign: KF7LAD
Christopher Macauley
6572 Beam
White City OR 97503

Call Sign: KF7GEJ
Edwin T Macauley
82724 Bear Creek
White City OR 97503

Call Sign: N8FY
Edwin T Macauley
21349 Bear Creek Rd
White City OR 97503

Call Sign: KB7LHR
Travis H Eubanks
800 Beaver Creek Rd
White City OR 97503

Call Sign: KS7A
Arthur W Coolidge III
29494 Beaver Creek Rd
White City OR 97503

Call Sign: KD7OIM
Leslie C Terrell
2050 Beaver Creek Rd 101
140
White City OR 97503

Call Sign: K7PRN
Leslie C Terrell
2050 Beaver Creek Rd 101
140
White City OR 97503

Call Sign: KF7UML
Robin G Tankersley
2050 Beaver Creek Rd 101
140
White City OR 97503

Call Sign: KB7LHQ
Margaret A Eubanks
2050 Beaver Creek Rd 101
140
White City OR 97503

Call Sign: KF4CRF
Brian W Ganoe
2815 Beaver Ct
White City OR 97503

Call Sign: KE7FMK
Gregory B Acedo
741B Bever Dr NE
White City OR 97503

Call Sign: N7YIF
Terry L Welburn
3729 Beverly Ave 53
White City OR 97503

Call Sign: N7KDA
Orva L Wayman
1623 Birch St
White City OR 97503

Call Sign: WA7K

James E Wayman
1834 Birch St
White City OR 97503

Call Sign: AA7DQ
Russell L Wright
2005 Birch St
White City OR 97503

Call Sign: N7ZYZ
Gerald E Sutherland
2135 Birchwood Ave
White City OR 97503

Call Sign: KB7YTW
Robert J Schriener
484 Birchwood Rd
White City OR 97503

Call Sign: KB7RHR
Loren W Oden
52432 Bird Rd
White City OR 97503

Call Sign: KB7GOS
Christopher C Malott
5865 Bird Song Way
White City OR 97503

Call Sign: KB7ILU
Richard E Pierce
5865 Bird Song Way
White City OR 97503

Call Sign: W7UYS
Atha C Saralecos
3703 Bisbee
White City OR 97503

Call Sign: KE7DNA
Delena F Shaw
53913 Bitney Dr
White City OR 97503

Call Sign: KF6IGQ

Werner Strube
Rt 2 Box 2601
White City OR 97503

Dennis E Wallace
89525 Divide Ln
White City OR 97503

Everett J Steiger
7874 Jani Ct NE
White City OR 975038507

Call Sign: KD6KTR
Joseph F Jones
73344 De Bast Rd
White City OR 97503

Call Sign: KD7NUB
Robert W Berger
7514 Division
White City OR 97503

Call Sign: KF7LVT
Trent R Carpenter
4436 Janice Ave NE
White City OR 97503

Call Sign: KC7JTO
Patrick C Meyer
84778 Didion Ln
White City OR 97503

Call Sign: N7VTJ
Charles E Pedigo
1420 E Main
White City OR 97503

Call Sign: W7FAL
Michael S Wheeler
19610 Poplar St
White City OR 97503

Call Sign: KF6RNF
Donald L Deree
50900C Dike Rd
White City OR 94503

Call Sign: KD7IAC
Jack D Whitehouse
2740 Foothils Dr
White City OR 97503

Call Sign: K7ESJ
Howard B Talmadge
Va Domiciliary Sec 5
White City OR 97503

Call Sign: KB7YTY
Udo K Gegeny
85388 Dillard Access Rd
White City OR 97503

Call Sign: KA7ZHJ
Lester D Chapman
241 Gardenia Dr
White City OR 97503

Call Sign: KB7JYQ
Joseph F Cranford
Va Domiciliary Section 6
White City OR 97503

Call Sign: KD7TTR
Allan D Dawkins
3975 Dillard Rd
White City OR 97503

Call Sign: N7LWJ
Alfred L Salazar Sr
6675 Halliburton Rd
White City OR 975031114

Call Sign: N7OLW
Alex Novak
30066 Vicki Ln
White City OR 97503

Call Sign: N7WIV
Brent E Reasons
85529 Dilley Ln
White City OR 97503

Call Sign: KA7SXG
Robert E Hanson
540 Hillcrest Rd
White City OR 97503

Call Sign: W6TPP
Robert H Bedell
Vocational Rehab Therapy
117H
White City OR 97503

Call Sign: KD7NUA
Robert F Onore
36505 Ditch Ck Rd
White City OR 97503

Call Sign: AC7RJ
Robert E Hanson
540 Hillcrest Rd
White City OR 97503

Call Sign: KB7TXF
Arthur R Kennedy
White City OR 97503

Call Sign: KB7OOC
Ronald A Pugh
89525 Divide Ln
White City OR 97503

Call Sign: KF7UMV
Phil B Porter
7874 Jani Ct NE
White City OR 97503

Call Sign: N7THS
Frank D Marion
White City OR 97503

Call Sign: N7WPG

Call Sign: WA7ABP

Call Sign: KE7ENN
Raymond M Bledsaw II

White City OR 97503

Call Sign: KB7TXL
James E Fiaren
White City OR 97503

FCC Amateur Radio Licenses in Wilbur

Call Sign: KC7SXT
Shane A Mcfarland
Wilbur OR 97494

FCC Amateur Radio Licenses in Wilderville

Call Sign: KE7BAW
Robert E Sweat
490 Ripple Rd
Wilderville OR 97543

Call Sign: W7BAW
Robert E Sweat
1174 Risden Pl
Wilderville OR 97543

Call Sign: K6TJX
Louis S Grand
2547 Risher Rd
Wilderville OR 97543

Call Sign: KD7DPS
Jon L Wacker
6930 Riva Ridge
Wilderville OR 97543

Call Sign: K7YEV
John A Wittich
7230 Sollie Smith Rd
Wilderville OR 97543

Call Sign: N6DCA
Bernard C Conger
1433 Spyglass Ct
Wilderville OR 97543

FCC Amateur Radio Licenses in Williams

Call Sign: WA6OFM
Lowell F Pine
10010 Bruin Way
Williams OR 97544

Call Sign: KM6NH
Craig H Rasmussen
40141 Cole School Rd
Williams OR 97544

Call Sign: N7IPD
Thomas D Downs
265 College St S 8
Williams OR 97544

Call Sign: KE7NPP
Micah T Owens
2103 College Way
Williams OR 97544

Call Sign: KE7UGV
Jason M Bauer
820 E Kennedy Ave
Williams OR 97544

Call Sign: K2JMB
Jason M Bauer
175 E Main
Williams OR 97544

Call Sign: KF7UKK
Ronald G Tate
1950 Laurel Ave NE 4
Williams OR 97544

Call Sign: KE7EFJ
Eric C Johnson
86279 Lorane Hwy
Williams OR 97544

Call Sign: KG6BQS

Eric C Johnson
86621 Lorane Hwy
Williams OR 97544

Call Sign: KB7OCN
James N Rigel
63071 Pennsylvania Rd
Williams OR 97544

Call Sign: KB7POC
Barbara J Rigel
3857 Peppertree Dr
Williams OR 97544

Call Sign: KB7POD
David N Rigel
4714 Pepperwood Ct
Williams OR 97544

Call Sign: KC7YKU
Dale E Rice
690 Radar Rd
Williams OR 97544

Call Sign: N6DHT
Douglas L Stewart
2518 Radcliffe
Williams OR 97544

Call Sign: KC7IXS
Margaret E Stone
2450 Radcliffe Ave
Williams OR 97544

Call Sign: K6UDD
Richard O Worth
1600 Rhododendron Dr
Williams OR 97544

Call Sign: N6GUX
Stephen W Mc Keown
580 Shorepines Way
Williams OR 97544

Call Sign: N6HKZ

Laurie E Mc Keown
67297 Shorewood Dr
Williams OR 97544

Call Sign: KK7XN
Stephen W Mc Keown
89091 Short Rd
Williams OR 97544

Call Sign: WA6VOW
Patrick L Simpson
112 The Trees Dr
Williams OR 97544

Call Sign: K7HMN
Robin L Smith
218 Theo Dr
Williams OR 97544

Call Sign: KA7CWL
Grover C Sherrill
2480 Upper River Rd
Williams OR 97544

Call Sign: AL0Y
Harvey W Davis
16032 Water Gap Rd
Williams OR 97544

Call Sign: W7JZK
Eugene A Armbruster
18251 Williams Hwy
Williams OR 97544

Call Sign: KF6GPA
Rebecca R Smith
Williams OR 92595

Call Sign: KL0KT
Laura J Barlow
Williams OR 97544

Call Sign: N7SVH
Lee L Stone
Williams OR 97544

Call Sign: WA7WAR
Mark V Watkins
Williams OR 97544

Call Sign: KD7WHW
Janet M Gunter
Williams OR 97544

Call Sign: KE7WTG
Thomas A Miller
Williams OR 97544

Call Sign: KF6GPB
Wayne E Smith
Williams OR 97544

Call Sign: AL7CR
Dean J Shutt
Williams OR 975440170

**FCC Amateur Radio
Licenses in Winchester**

Call Sign: KB6NSK
Eileen M Sanders
667 Driftwood Dr
Winchester OR 974958932

Call Sign: KA6BKY
Richard L Sanders
4716 Driftwood Dr
Winchester OR 97495

Call Sign: N7EUT
Marshall L Farrell
Winchester OR 97495

Call Sign: N7YGF
Daniel J Murphy
Winchester OR 97495

Call Sign: KA6IRU
James E Swegles
Winchester OR 97495

Call Sign: KA7RUZ
Floyd F Jennie
Winchester OR 97495

Call Sign: KB7OOB
David J Camky
Winchester OR 97495

Call Sign: KC7PZF
Wesleigh J Stoltz
Winchester OR 97495

Call Sign: KC7QXW
Huston E Dickson
Winchester OR 97495

Call Sign: KD7NFI
Mike H Lee
Winchester OR 97495

Call Sign: KD7SDH
Floyd V Lewis
Winchester OR 97495

Call Sign: KE7TFB
Barbara E Wright
Winchester OR 97495

Call Sign: KE7GMU
Christian D Brages
Winchester OR 97495

Call Sign: KF7SAK
Raymond D Jarvis
Winchester OR 97495

**FCC Amateur Radio
Licenses in Winchester
Bay**

Call Sign: N7OKB
Patrick T Flury
Winchester Bay OR 97467

Call Sign: WB6TQB
John B Lewis
Winchester Bay OR 97467

Call Sign: N7QQT
Peggy A Edson
Winchester Bay OR 97467

Call Sign: AA7TF
Patrick T Flury
Winchester Bay OR 97467

Call Sign: K7QBC
Cloys N Smith
Winchester Bay OR
974670806

FCC Amateur Radio Licenses in Winston

Call Sign: WB7FAI
Ralph D Groover
619 38th Pl
Winston OR 97496

Call Sign: N7FDH
Robert J Cunningham
1545 Capitol St NE
Winston OR 97496

Call Sign: K7RIS
Christina M Mills
7 Cedar Dr
Winston OR 97496

Call Sign: K7CAM
Clarence A Mills
73521 Cedar Dr
Winston OR 97496

Call Sign: KC7FW
James W Aday
184 E 26th Ave
Winston OR 974969609

Call Sign: KD7SDI
Minnie E Aday
1672 E 26th Ave
Winston OR 974969609

Call Sign: K6PID
Frank D May Jr
21955 E Beaver Creek Rd
Winston OR 97496

Call Sign: KD7JAD
Marjorie J Biggers
1277 Green Valley Rd
Winston OR 97496

Call Sign: KC7VWG
Michael A Putman
295 Idaho St
Winston OR 97496

Call Sign: WB6RHW
John M Phillips
3093 Juniper St
Winston OR 97496

Call Sign: KA7MMT
Roy P Vanderhoff
1357 Koyoda St
Winston OR 974961422

Call Sign: KB3XY
Ralph J Benson
1536 Larch St
Winston OR 97496

Call Sign: KD7KRR
John P Woodward
340 Mary Ann Dr
Winston OR 97496

Call Sign: WB0UNC
Jerry L Frisbie
2207 Oregon Ct
Winston OR 97496

Call Sign: WB0UND
Jacqualine S Frisbie
50281 Oregon Hwy 203
Winston OR 97496

Call Sign: KD7DPQ
Randy L Blatter
543 Peterson Rd
Winston OR 97496

Call Sign: KA6GHA
Robert D Link
34632 Riverside Dr
Winston OR 97496

Call Sign: N5KS
Gene D Matheny
9530 SW Brentwood Pl
Winston OR 97496

Call Sign: K7BTX
Eugene E Anderson Sr
8303 SW Tygh Loop
Winston OR 97496

Call Sign: KD5PVJ
Shirley T Anderson
31 Twin Oaks Rd
Winston OR 97496

Call Sign: N1GH
Glen R Haight
13620 Tyee Rd
Winston OR 97496

Call Sign: KF7UBQ
Steven D Randolph
2480 Upper River Rd
Winston OR 97496

Call Sign: KB7WDQ
Timothy A Trunkey
6300 W Willis Cr Rd
Winston OR 97496

Call Sign: KE7YZN
Patricia E Langille
1640 Winston Section Rd
Winston OR 97496

Call Sign: AE7Q
David L Lee
Winston OR 97496

Call Sign: N7QDE
Philip G Curry
Winston OR 97496

Call Sign: N7VNO
Bruce W Lettsome
Winston OR 97496

Call Sign: N7XRS
Steven C Simon
Winston OR 97496

Call Sign: K6GUU
Robert E Smith
Winston OR 97496

Call Sign: KC7NKX
Timothy K Martin
Winston OR 97496

Call Sign: KD7CZT
Dan L Fitzgerald
Winston OR 97496

Call Sign: KI7KQ
Jerry G Burkhart
Winston OR 97496

Call Sign: KI7WS
Jeff A Ellenwood
Winston OR 97496

Call Sign: N7VNM
Prentiss L Jordan
Winston OR 97496

Call Sign: WB7BEF
John P Lazarus
Winston OR 97496

Call Sign: KD7IAD
William R Burkhart
Winston OR 97496

Call Sign: KD7JAC
Marie A Fitzgerald
Winston OR 97496

Call Sign: KD7JAE
Jayson A Broadsword
Winston OR 97496

Call Sign: KD7YNX
Donald W Crowder Jr
Winston OR 97496

Call Sign: KE7BBU
Edward G Frankenstein
Winston OR 97496

Call Sign: KF7OQW
Patrick W Harris
Winston OR 97496

Call Sign: KB7SZT
Chuck D Simon
Winston OR 97496

FCC Amateur Radio Licenses in Wolf Creek

Call Sign: KE7JHE
Wolf Creek Fire Emergency
Communication
16465 Devonshire Dr
Wolf Creek OR 97497

Call Sign: K7WCF
Wolf Creek Fire Emergency
Communication
2120 Devos St

Wolf Creek OR 97497

Call Sign: KD7JLB
Leonard M Coleman
2120 Devos St
Wolf Creek OR 97497

Call Sign: N6JMH
Michael D Mathews
821 Laurel St
Wolf Creek OR 97497

Call Sign: KB7TSV
David J Converse
3610 Osborn Ave NE
Wolf Creek OR 97497

Call Sign: N7SUL
Glenn A Mc Cutchen
5217 Springcrest Dr S
Wolf Creek OR 97497

Call Sign: KD6GN
Carter S Rose
Wolf Creek OR 97497

Call Sign: WV6V
Sharon P Schultz
Wolf Creek OR 97497

FCC Amateur Radio Licenses in Yoncalla

Call Sign: WA7YDA
Fred S Whitford
1384 Flower Ln
Yoncalla OR 974999702

Call Sign: KD7EQV
James M Rufener
169 Foch St
Yoncalla OR 97499

Call Sign: W7SPI
Thomas F Janik

6123 Foley Ln
Yoncalla OR 974999730

Call Sign: N7ZFT
Lois J Sutton
34379 Riverside Dr SW
Yoncalla OR 97499

Call Sign: KC7KOS
Jannelle Wilde
1097 S 69th Pl
Yoncalla OR 97499

Call Sign: KC7KPC
Adam H Falk
822 S 69th St
Yoncalla OR 97499

Call Sign: KA7ABT
Dennis L Brooks
Yoncalla OR 97499

Call Sign: N7WMG
Gordon W Miller
Yoncalla OR 97499

Call Sign: KG7QN
Douglas V Boyer
Yoncalla OR 97499

Call Sign: KF7GPY
Hubert M Rines
Yoncalla OR 97499

Call Sign: N7GPY
Hubert M Rines
Yoncalla OR 97499

Call Sign: KA5EYX
Leonard A Weldon
Yoncalla OR 974993759

www.ingramcontent.com/pod-product-compliance
Lightning Source LLC
Chambersburg PA
CBHW081143270326
41930CB00014B/3021